Birder Interrupted

Birder Interrupted

A Twelve-Month US Journey Beginning in 1962 That Ended in 2005

by
M. RALPH BROWNING

Foreword by Kenn Kaufman

RESOURCE *Publications* · Eugene, Oregon

BIRDER INTERRUPTED
A Twelve-Month US Journey Beginning in 1962 That Ended in 2005

Copyright © 2024 M. Ralph Browning. All rights reserved. Except for brief quotations in critical publications or reviews, no part of this book may be reproduced in any manner without prior written permission from the publisher. Write: Permissions, Wipf and Stock Publishers, 199 W. 8th Ave., Suite 3, Eugene, OR 97401.

Resource Publications
An Imprint of Wipf and Stock Publishers
199 W. 8th Ave., Suite 3
Eugene, OR 97401

www.wipfandstock.com

PAPERBACK ISBN: 979-8-3852-0245-4
HARDCOVER ISBN: 979-8-3852-0246-1
EBOOK ISBN: 979-8-3852-0247-8

VERSION NUMBER 020524

Dedicated to birders and nature enthusiasts, young and old, who help preserve nature and travel to experience it, and to Linda, who was there.

Contents

Forewrod by Kenn Kaufman | ix
Preface | xi
Acknowledgments | xv
Abbreviations | xvii
Illustrations | xix
Introduction | xxi

Chapter 1: Initiation | 1

Chapter 2: Malheur Was Good | 18

Chapter 3: Meandering Snake | 31

Chapter 4: Red Rock | 44

Chapter 5: Yellowstone, the First Days | 55

Chapter 6: More Yellowstone and Big Sky Country | 70

Chapter 7: Mainly the Plains | 85

Chapter 8: Mosquito Coasts | 99

Chapter 9: Warblering | 113

Chapter 10: A Stint in Time on the Way East | 126

Chapter 11: Remembering Maine | 143

Chapter 12: August Assemblage | 155

Chapter 13: Hawk Mountain | 167

Chapter 14: Capital Birding | 182

Chapter 15: Dismal, Hatteras, Mattamuskeet | 195

Chapter 16: Whiskers and Doing Charleston | 211

Chapter 17: Okefenokee on My Mind | 228

Chapter 18: Florida, the Early Miles | 241

Chapter 19: The Florida Keys and Christmas Count Fever | 257

Chapter 20: Everglades and a New Plan | 274

Chapter 21: Going North, Going Home | 293

Chapter 22: Forty-Two Years Later | 312

Chapter 23: Texas Migrants and Chickens | 327

Chapter 24: Austin City Limits and Southward | 344

Chapter 25: Up the River and around the Bend | 361

Chapter 26: Go West . . . Man | 379

Chapter 27: Arizona Byways | 398

Chapter 28: Oh, Those California Birds | 415

Chapter 29: The Last Bird | 432

Foreword

IT WAS THE MOST influential footnote in the history of birding.

In 1953, the renowned American naturalist Roger Tory Peterson took his equally famous British friend, James Fisher, to visit natural habitats around North America—from Newfoundland to Florida to California to Alaska—on a grand tour of more than three months. The book they wrote about their journey, *Wild America*, became an instant classic of nature writing. Peterson and Fisher observed, and wrote about, every aspect of nature, from bears to barracudas to butterflies. But they were primarily birdmen, and they carefully tallied every bird species they saw. Fisher went back to England before the end of summer, but Peterson traveled and birded a bit more, to run up his list of species seen during that calendar year. In a brief footnote near the end of the book, Peterson wrote: "Incidental information: my year's list at the end of 1953 was 572 species."

Keeping a year list was hardly a new idea. As long ago as the 1890s, two friends had competed to see who could find more bird species in a year in Lorain County, Ohio. By the 1930s, affluent birders were making more extensive trips within the U.S. and comparing annual totals above 400. But the idea hadn't reached a wider audience before the appearance of *Wild America*. The wonderful, lyrical writing in that book, combined with that pointed footnote, seemed almost designed to inspire others to hit the road and count birds.

And it worked. One of the first to take up the challenge was an avid teenage birder from Oregon, Ralph Browning. In June 1962, the day after he graduated from high school, Browning set off on a planned one-year journey to hit all the major birding hotspots in the lower 48 states and to locate just as many bird species as he could.

He was among the first (and among the few in the 1960s), but he would not be the last. Increasingly in the 1970s and 1980s, and even more in the years since, keen birders would arrange to take a full year to trek all over North America north of the Mexican border, pushing the record for the number of bird species tallied to ever higher numbers. Such efforts have come to be called "Big Years." They have sparked a whole genre of books, and eventually a 2011 Hollywood film based very loosely on a true story, so that even the general public has a vague (if somewhat misleading) idea of the world of competitive bird-listing.

But when Ralph Browning began his quest in 1962, it was about learning and adventure, not competition, because there was essentially no one else to compete with at the time. His year of birding would turn out to be completely different from anyone else's—because it was interrupted before the year was over, only to be completed more than 40 years later.

In that four-decade gap, Browning had not been idle, nor uninvolved with birds. Quite the opposite: He had become not only an expert birder but also a professional ornithologist. He had a stellar career working in the Division of Birds of the National Museum of Natural History at the Smithsonian Institution in Washington, DC. Working alongside several of the other top ornithologists of the twentieth century, Browning wrote many scientific papers, treating geographic variation, new subspecies, corrected nomenclature, and distributional records of birds. His early passion for learning all he could about birds transformed into a life of solid contributions to science.

And after he took early retirement, he did something that few people would have considered: he went back to his 1962 trip notes and picked up where he had left off, completing the rest of his circuit around the country in 2005. Having begun his one-year journey as a wide-eyed kid, he completed it as a seasoned expert.

When Ralph Browning mentioned, several years ago, that he planned to write an account of his interrupted adventure, I told him I was eager to read it. Now that the book has arrived, it's even better than I'd anticipated. This is not just two adventure tales under one cover. The author uses his traveler's observations from 1962 to illuminate and add depth to those of 2005, and the reverse as well, with a healthy dose of insights gleaned from his intervening years as a scientist. The result is a unique and fascinating travelogue that doubles as a perceptive recent history of birds, conservation, birders, and ornithologists of the United States.

Birder Interrupted is a remarkable tale of a lifetime obsession with birds, and a testament to the ways that nature can continue to inspire us, year after year after year.

Kenn Kaufman

Preface

THE WHIR OF THE air-cooled engine forced my 1955 Volkswagen Beetle up the western slope of the forested Cascade Mountains. It was 2 June 1962. Just the right amount of adrenaline kept my mood poised between nervousness about my next days and months, satisfaction that I was beginning the fulfillment of a dream, and impatience to experience what geography and birds were around the next corner.

Almost three years earlier and barely 16 years old, I unveiled to my parents a plan befitting 2 June 1962. My mood then straddled my apprehension and confidence as a teenager.

"Sorry. Son, would you repeat that?"

"Sure." I was looking across the kitchen table at my dad. It was an early fall day in 1959, just after a Saturday lunch. My dad looked concerned. I knew his anxiousness was not about the season or our Saturday meal. My mom, sitting to my right, looked as if she had heard bad news.

I eased into my repeat. "High school graduation is about two years away. After that, I could either get a job, or I might be drafted." The Vietnam War had been a work in progress for some time then, and even young high schoolers were hearing rumors that a draft might one day kill our futures. Another issue of my immediate time was that my parents and others thought I should go to college, which was an activity I did not embrace.

Before either parent could reply to my comments, I had another option to present. Not missing a beat, I blurted out what I really wanted to say. "After high school graduation, I want to travel the country for a year to look for birds. You know, like Peterson and Fisher's book *Wild America*." I had that book by my side for months. I explained, "I want to do a trip kind of like they did, only longer and just around the country."

Looking a little stern but clearly rattled, my mom said, "Ralph, you have close to two years before graduation and plenty of time to decide what to do after school." What she actually meant was she was not in favor of

PREFACE

me birding across the country. That was clear when she added, "Oh, I don't know, Ralph."

At least she did not call me Marvin Ralph. That would mean she was mad at me for planning to do what she thought would be dangerous and irresponsible. No, neither my mom nor dad were overly upset, though they did not exactly radiate enthusiasm about my idea.

It was good to know I remained just Ralph, but I needed more ammunition to convince my parents that I needed to see our country and its birds. I again evoked the book with that ringing title of *Wild America*, and that the tome had lit a light bulb in my developing brain. Actually, I did not mention my brain or development. I hoped that my parents would think of me as capable, maybe not at that moment, but by the time I would start the trip. After all, it is a jungle out there, but no jungles were on my route circumnavigating the US. I explained that my trip would be a learning experience. My dad nodded. After going over the details of planning the trip, he placed his hand over my mom's closest hand resting on the table and said he thought I should make the trip. My mom nodded in agreement. So, with my parents' support, I was on my way to be on my way. Would I be ready?

At 18 years of age, when I began traveling, I was a lanky 155-pound Danny McSkunk sporting wetness-behind-the-ears who needed experience other than having to participate in the ongoing Vietnam War. I needed to go birding. I believed I could take care of myself, that I would be safe and not fall victim to foul play. How could I since I would be too busy with fowl play?

For weeks and months to come, my supportive parents had little reason for worry. I learned to take care of myself, my only traveling companion, the teeny tiny Volkswagen Beetle, and live to write home about it. During my time on the road, it was not unusual for me not to see anyone for days. From Oregon to Maine, I slept in the same tent that Linda, my future wife, jokingly wondered if it would accommodate the two of us. Eventually, I converted the vehicle to function as a motor home. That kept me dry and prevented feeding mosquitoes. During the trip, I had the privilege to meet and know so many outstanding birders and enjoy the opportunity to experience hundreds of species of great birds, even a few unexpected waifs. Those early years became part of my mold that helped direct my future.

During my travel, my trusty typewriter helped me pound out at least a page per day of single-spaced chronicle covering the trip. The pages were periodically sent home so my parents and Linda could follow my adventure. The trip ended prematurely, which was about 10 months from its beginning, and the collection of notes stayed in a box for years. Thoughts of turning the notes into a manuscript were abandoned as I became busy with school,

PREFACE

military service, and employment in the Division of Birds at Smithsonian's National Museum of Natural History. In 2005 and eight years after an early retirement, Linda, then my wife, and I, completed the interrupted journey that began in 1962.

Notes also chronicled the 2005 leg of the trip. The sum of the notes and rewarding experience at the museum became a project. The skeletal notes were fleshed out and developed into chapters. The chapter material, the places, birds, people, and more was updated, partly to show the wins and losses of habitat. Chapters were written and rewritten. The elusive hunt for a final draft, a nonexistent entity, had a life of its own. Finally, a story with agreed upon versions, iterations and drafts, the story of *Birding Interrupted*, warts and all, can be shared.

In the book, the narrative follows a date of the record. My original journal entries of the early 1960s are mostly edited from my then-teenage lingo. A section break near the end of each chapter separate narratives from more current perspectives on history, conservation, change, and, frequently, my views based on years of birding and a career in the Division of Birds at Smithsonian. I follow the convention of the American Ornithological Society (formerly American Ornithologists' Union) Committee on Classification and Nomenclature by capitalizing all English names of birds, which avoids confusion and recognizes the names are proper nouns just as names of rivers and mountains are capitalized. For example, the Rio Grande, not the rio grande, the Rocky Mountains, not the rocky mountains, Western Bluebird, not western bluebird. Confusion also is avoided since there are several species of fork-tailed storm-petrels, but only one Fork-tailed Storm-Petrel, and more than one curve-billed thrasher, but only one Curve-billed Thrasher. Steller's Jays are blue jays, but they are not Blue Jays. English names in this work are those in current usage, which may differ from those in use in the early 1960s.

M. Ralph Browning

Acknowledgments

NUMEROUS PEOPLE ASSISTED MY travel during *Birder Interrupted*. For their encouragement, I thank my loving parents, Thomas McCamant, and my then future wife who did not go on the sixties leg of the trip but did go on the second leg of the journey. Thanks to National Wildlife Refuge managers, biologists, and staff for offering me a place to sleep and guiding me to great birds. Too many other people making my travels easier are long since passed, but they deserve considerable thanks. Mostly in order that I met them include Gene Kridler, Olin Pettingill, Paul Savage, Howard Axtell, Kenneth Able, Virginia and Harry Chadbourne, Aaron Bagg, George Deisher, Irma and Maurice Broun, Alexander Wetmore, George Watson, Phil Humphrey, Russ Mason, Margaret Hundley, Allan Cruickshank, Howard Langridge, Sandy Sprunt, Bill Robertson, Anne Zuparko, Brandon Crawford, Suzanne Scott, Chuck Sexton, Mark Flippo, Tom Beatty, Debbie and Jim Parker, Jerry Lorenz and Paul Gray of Audubon Florida, Steve Godwin, Norm Barrett, and Jim Livaudais. Jon Dunn offered invaluable information on finding birds in Texas, Arizona, and California. My humble thanks goes to Kenn Kaufman for his words of wisdom. For their encouragement to chronicle birding around the country, I owe gratitude to several friends and colleagues including Richard Banks and Frank Izaguirre. I especially thank members of Wipf and Stock Publishers for their invaluable help and patience. To Linda, who was with me in spirit and later by my side, I thank her for everything.

Abbreviations

ABA—American Birding Association
AOS—American Ornithological Society
AOU—American Ornithologists' Union
BLM—Bureau of Land Management
C and O—Chesapeake and Ohio
CCC—Civilian Conservation Corps
COVID—coronavirus disease
DEET—N,N-Diethyl-meta-toluamide
FWS—Fish and Wildlife Service
NACC—North American Check-List Committee
NF—National Forest
NM—National Monument
NOAA—National Oceanic and Atmospheric Administration
NP—National Park
NWR—National Wildlife Refuge
PCT—Pacific Crest Trail
RV—Recreational Vehicle
SUV—Sport Utility Vehicle
USNM—museum designation for specimens in Smithsonian's National Museum of Natural History
VW—Volkswagen
WPA—Works Progress Administration
YMCA—Young Men's Christian Association

Illustrations

Figure 1. Author and what was packed in the VW

Figure 2. Approximate route

Figure 3. The first morning

Figure 4. The second night

Figure 5. Prairie and pothole country

Figure 6. Appalachian Mountains

Figure 7. Atlantic shore, Maine

Figure 8. Flagler Beach, Florida

Figure 9. Flamingo, Everglades NP

Figure 10. Just one of many Florida herons and egrets

Figure 11. In shock

Figure 12. Entering Sabal Palm, Texas

Figure 13. Rio Grande, Big Bend NP

Figure 14. East side of Chiricahua Mountains

Figure 15. Little house, Madera Canyon

Figure 16. Happy in San Diego

Figure 17. Hoping for a Pacific pelagic

Figure 18. Working mine

Figure 19. Burney Falls

Figure 20. A juvenile Great Gray Owl

Introduction

OTHER THAN A LITTLE backseat birding across the country's midsection and a meandering trip during a family vacation in southern British Columbia, I had hardly birded outside the state of Oregon. I was not old enough to vote but I was approaching fledgling age. Whenever my time to leave the nest might arrive, I knew birds would be at the forefront of adventure. The seed for that adventure sprouted a few years after the book bearing the 1955 title of *Wild America* was published by Houghton Mifflin Company. I devoured *Wild America* from cover to cover. Other tomes fed a building appetite for birding and travel. I vicariously traveled with Edwin Way Teale as he and his wife explored nature up and down, and across America. In the meantime, I was also driving my parents and anyone within earshot crazy by exuberantly talking and breathing birds. Fried chicken at dinner became an anatomy lab. Rereading *Wild America* lit a light bulb in my developing brain. Why couldn't I make a tour around the United States? That's it. I could watch birds from Oregon, my home, to Maine, Florida, Southern California, and back to Oregon.

So, I began a dream, one that should involve seeing lots of birds and travel. As a skinny teenage bird nut and oppressed nomad, I was not sure how to plan a long birding trip. I did have a few ideas and knew I had a lot of work to do before I even saw my first trip bird.

In the beginning stage of planning, I was unable to know when I could begin my year of birding. After graduation, I reasoned, might be ideal, but what about the military? In my copious and verbose notes, I wrote about the dream. "Once I complete high school, I will be required to serve a 6-month hitch in the military reserves. I hope that I will not have to attend the meetings every week and the 2-week training camps, which will allow me more time for the dream about an extended trip birding." Of course, there was little to no guarantee of getting into the reserves and the specter of military duty continued to shadow my plans and occasionally caused me to wonder

INTRODUCTION

if I would have the freedom to take the trip. However, the inspiration from *Wild America*, the travels of naturalist Edwin Way Teale, and others pushed me on. I finally convinced myself that I could travel around the country and see birds and just maybe not in a military uniform. Nonetheless, my worries about the military continued to rain down on my every thought. Would a draft be instituted and, if so, would I be recruited the moment I turned 18? What would be the personal outcome? What were my options? Meeting possible military obligations contributed an overpowering apprehension among my friends and myself. That worry dominated my plans so much that I could not give complete consideration of the season I might start the trip. Would the recruiting office order me to be available next winter or should I make myself available all the time to be snatched up for active duty? Should I abandon the idea of birding around the country? I did not know if or when, and the authorities, if they knew, were not saying. I tried to ignore thoughts of military service. If the trip was to be a reality, I reasoned I should begin my year the day after graduating high school. I would stick to the route circumnavigating the country and hope where I might be at a particular season would maximize birding possibilities.

Believing all was well on the birding front, I grew more serious about planning. Resources for information on finding birds was limited. I discovered the Pettingill's guides to finding birds. Other bird finding resources were rare. There was no American Birding Association bird finding guides. The American Birding Association would not come into existence until 1968. In the early 1960s, *Audubon Magazine*, then much more geared to bird watchers than today, published lists of available regional checklists and short articles on good places to find birds. Its sister journal, *Audubon Field Notes*, provided names and addresses of birdwatchers seemingly anywhere in the United States. I then began a campaign with requests for checklists covering individual wildlife refuges and parks and sent letters to Christmas Count Compilers and anyone else who I thought might be of help along my route. As for the route of the trip, an attempt to duplicate *Wild America* was not in my plans. After considerable thought, I decided to drive east from Oregon to Yellowstone, Michigan, and end up in Maine. From there, I would travel south. For those who already know or are looking at a map, driving south from Maine would put anyone in the Atlantic Ocean. During travel down the East Coast, I would try to avoid the largest cities except Washington, DC. My plans included more time in Florida than other states. After Everglades NP, I would travel west along the Gulf Coast to Texas, and up the Rio Grande to Big Bend for a Colima Warbler. From there, my route would be to Arizona, north in California, and back to southern Oregon. Unlike Peterson and Fisher, I could not go to Mexico or Alaska. Financial

INTRODUCTION

handicaps limited travel to the contiguous 48 states. It was not a perfect route since I would not be in the right place and the right time for numerous species. Snowy Owl, redpolls, and a number of shorebirds, alcids, and others would not be in my line of sight.

What funds I had for the trip came from summer jobs and part time jobs while in school. During summers, work included orchards, a ranch, mowing lawns, whatever I could do to amass what became a spartan budget for my travel. During school months, I worked evening shifts and weekends at a service station (for those younger readers, a service station sold gas, and also cleaned windshields, checked the oil, fixed flats, even performed brake jobs and minor repairs). Could I save enough to fund a year-long trip? Old yellowing notes recorded some of my early thoughts. "I plan to buy a car that gets about 30 miles per gallon. At the going price of $0.30 (average) a gallon, I can get by on about $180.00 for gasoline. I plan to get by on less than $3.00 per day for food by cooking out of doors. I can limit lodging to less than $10.00 per week by sleeping in the car or tenting at roadside parks. It would cost $1,000.00 to 900.00 for a year of birding."

Please, keep in mind that my ideas about expenditures were not from the mind of a crazy person. Those ideas were from the imagination of a teenager, which some might think crazy. Especially perplexing was the thought of spending $10 per week for lodging. Perhaps I was thinking of what it might cost for a night at a YMCA. Of course, fuel, food, lodging, everything cost far less than current prices.

I decided whatever kind of car I should buy should be small, probably with a rear engine. My reasoning for a rear engine probably had something to do with the fear of getting stuck. A heavy engine in the rear might prevent that. Four-wheel or front-wheel drives were not options then. I was not concerned with the outside appearance of my prospective vehicle. I wrote that the car should be reasonably clean inside and that I plan to make it as comfortable as I can by adding a steering knob and extra padding to make the driver's seat as supportive as possible. How a steering knob would contribute to my comfort is beyond my twenty-first-century comprehension. There were more plans for customizing the interior of the car. I hoped to install a folding shelf under the dash that would function as a desk to support a small typewriter for record-keeping. Also, I needed a collapsible platform to allow me to sleep in the car more comfortably.

After reaching 16 years of age, most of my friends in school either had a car or wished they had one. I was no different, except my car had to be a good birding car. Contrary to most who wanted loud exhaust and more horsepower than is really needed, I bought a 1955 VW Sun liner. It was mine for $500, a sum covered by my tiny savings account. The car needed work and repairing the transmission and bodywork cost $265. The interior was in good condition, and the motor ran well. It was hard to start, but that would be repairable. I wrote in my journal about planning to fix one of the seats so that it would recline into a bed, which almost qualified the VW to be a motor home. There were handy side pockets in the doors for a book or two and maps.

About a year before high school graduation, the local military recruiter advised that I should take my trip immediately after graduating and face the consequences of the military once I return home. I wrote in my journal that "I now have the money and then some" and chronicled that "I have the time, that is, if the war does not become worse." Yes, the personal threat of that pesky war was powerful.

I had gradually gathered a few things I would pack in the car. My old notes reported that "all the necessary books to take on the journey will include Sewall Pettingill's two volumes on bird-finding. Along with the books will be a card file I am compiling that covers bird-finding areas found in *Audubon Magazine*, especially information from the column called 'Bird Finding with Sewall Pettingill.' The card file of names of people to contact will be set up in chronological sequence according to the order states are visited." I listed the reference books I will need. "The collection included Peterson's field guides for the west, east, and for Texas, the Pough guides, Sprunt's book on birds of prey, and more."

While planning what else to stuff in my vehicle, I kept busy corresponding with individuals who I thought might offer information on birding at their localities. Part of my trip budget covered the postage of so many outgoing pieces of mail. Postage was only 4 cents for a first-class letter, and my efforts and expense paid great dividends. Most people replied to my inquiries, often writing several pages explaining where and what to see and invitations to stop by for a visit. I am not sure the responses today would be as positive as they were 60 years ago. Sixty years ago and counting.

To continue from my notes, I wrote that "the plans of my exact route as far as upper Michigan are complete," with state road maps from one of the finer oil companies that were obtained from my single request for an entire lot of maps. I did not mention watching birds since birding then was not taken as seriously as it is today. The company sent the maps free of any charges. Roadways of my route were marked on each map and symbols were used to indicate points of interest that included locations of Christmas Bird Counts, Winter Bird Populations Studies, and Breeding Bird Censuses. Filed separately but cross-referenced to the symbols were the correspondence from replies from Christmas Count compilers and others, as well as names and addresses of contributors to various bird counts, and regions

INTRODUCTION

listed in *Audubon Field Notes*. A few places not listed in Pettingill that I considered of birding value were also marked on the maps and cross-referenced in a card file. Page numbers on the maps refer to the appropriate pages in the Pettingill guides. Another symbol, a green circle outlined with red, indicated that there was a checklists or notes in my file. The master file, a metal file box with a hinged lid, contained maps, letters from people volunteering to guide me to find birds, and scores of checklists from about 60 national wildlife refuges, national parks, and a multitude of lists from local chapters of the Audubon Society, states, counties, and individuals. All of the checklists were sent free of charge! I am not making that up.

My notes reported, "Work at the school wood shop continues on a portable bookcase, and I plan to build a wooden box for food. A box for car tools is almost complete. If I have to make any mechanical repairs, I am ready." I had learned to make minor repairs automotive from my father, the part time-work in a garage at a service station, and on the ranch where I once worked and where something was always breaking.

There were also a few chores around my parents' house, shopping for the clothes and other items I thought I would need for my year and planning and more planning. Of course, there was time for working on the VW. With the help of my dad, the engine and transmission were pulled to have the latter overhauled. We put it back together, replaced the spark plugs and battery, and worked on the dented body. We repainted it off-white with two red rally stripes down the middle from end to end and put an extra brake light in the center of the rear of the car. I would, after all, be stopping for birds and did not want to be rear-ended. Reading about birds continued with titles including Hall's *A Gathering of Shore Birds*, Robert Allen's two Audubon Society publications, one on Flamingos and one on Whooping Cranes, Tyler's *Fundamentals of Ornithology*, and Tinbergen's *Herring Gull World*.

Preparations were not limited to birds. My notes continued. "Physical conditioning was important." A recent article in the local newspaper reported a world speed record for hiking in rough terrain. The record was 17 hours of uninterrupted hiking on 54 miles of the rugged Rogue River Trail in southwestern Oregon. After beginning the hike in the darkness of an early morning, my companion tied the record by about 40 minutes. I stumbled to the destination 40 minutes later, too numb to remember if there were birds along the way. Mounting tires at the local service station was exercise during my last school year.

Of course, I made time for birding, even a trip in November to observe migrating ducks and geese at Lower Klamath and Tule NWR. The next three months were busy times. One day I purchased a small pup tent, the same day Linda and I were soliciting ads for our school paper. We both laughingly wondered if the tent could sleep two.

With little over six months before my planned departure, I was even more worried about the military, money, and having what I hoped were the right things to take on the year-long journey. More and more troops were required to feed the war in Vietnam, and I knew I could have easily been a troop member or dismember. Money was my second worry. I wrote on 2 October 1961, "Got a $.15 per hour raise at the service station; 6 Oct. tore inner tube accidentally while changing a customer's tire." That was a disaster because the $3 mistake had to come from my meager pay. On 19 November, I put two new spark plugs in the VW, worked on bird notes and seasonal report to *Audubon Field Notes*, and wrote, "The typewriter still isn't working properly." I wrote on 20 November, "Exchanged typewriter"; 25 November: "Worked in the gas station for 9 hours. Ordered a 2-man rubber life raft for $19.95." "Have trip mapped thru [sic] Florida"; 29 December: "Finally have complete trip mapped."

Just nine days before 1 June 1962, the day I had planned to depart, the reality of the trip started to sink into my teenage brain. I would be spending an entire year birding. The thought of such an adventure almost scared me. I would be leaving my best friend behind. Still, the planning continued. I purchased an extra 35 millimeter camera to take color with one camera and black and white pictures with the other camera. Both cameras were of snapshot quality, which was the best I could do on my budget but would allow me to document the journey. I was also worried about the extra weight of the portable bookcase filled with books and papers and references to help find birds and identify them. I was concerned about the mechanical safety of the car and had nine days to check the brakes, get an oil change, and lube. Getting a lube in the 1960s meant forcing heavy grease into zerks connected to certain moving joints of a vehicle. Those same moving joints are now factory packed. The trans-axle still leaked. Replacing the axle's 90-weight oil with a heavier 140 slowed the rate of leaking. The brake light I placed high and in the center of the rear of the VW may have been a first. Maybe it protected me from all those sudden stops. Actually, the idea of the third brake light was apparently tested in 1974 and became required on cars in 1986.

All the planning was sometimes an ordeal, but overall, it was a learning experience and an enjoyable challenge. I am not the only one who looks forward to planning a trip. When enjoying a two-day pelagic trip out of San Diego in 2012, I bumped into Sandy Komito, a champion big year birder in 1998 and a subject in a book and a movie. He admitted that planning a big year was as much fun if not more fun than the time birding.

INTRODUCTION

The cost of doing business, the amount of money for birding across the US, still worried me, but I did manage to stay close to my budget. I owe much of that to my stubbornness to live on what was occasionally less than comfortable and the kindness of strangers who gave me room and board, for which I am forever grateful. Another concern was the military lurking over life. After the trip, I managed to remain a civilian for a few more years before years of short haircuts and saluting. While at the museum, a destination of another story, I learned that some of my elder colleagues, notably Allan Phillip and Ralph Palmer, shared my concerns about military duty. Both survived World War II, but neither were particularly fond of their experiences. They did manage to see a few interesting birds, and Allan lived to give us his *Known Birds of Middle and North America*[1] and more, and Ralph selflessly gave us five volumes of his handbook on North American birds.[2]

Of course, I was not prepared for the sudden and premature termination of the trip around the country. Aside from the fact my car stopped working, there was one regret during the 1962–63 leg of the trip. Since our fourth-grade meeting, Linda and I had become good friends. During the planning stages of the early trip, we thought briefly that we could make the trip together. Convention of the time was against such a venture. We shelved the idea but kept in touch during the trip with my trip notes and letters. After the premature termination of the sixties trip, we had no idea that we would complete the interrupted bird trip together. That good fortune arrived in 2005 when it became possible to finish what I had started. Planning the 2005 stage of the birding trek was almost done for us. Practically all that was needed to do was to pluck out the salient facts from the now available and excellent bird finding guides. Once the itinerary was completed, I asked friend and legendary birder Jon Dunn to look it over. Birding in 2005 was my first time for birding Texas, Arizona, and Southern California. That was definitely more fun than planning it.

So, why go on a trip around the United States or anywhere just to see birds? Really. Why? I cannot answer that better than to paraphrase what mountain climbers say: "Because they are there." All those birds and so little time to see them. In fact, too many species will not be around to see as time and extinction march onward. Of course, extinction was already going on in the sixties when, for example, I learned of missing likely the last Bachman's Warbler by just months. At the time, I did not realize I would never have a chance meeting of the species. In the planning stages I was even going to try for the Ivory-billed Woodpecker. I also had high hopes of finding

---

1. Two privately published and often cited tomes printed in 1986 and 1991.
2. Yale University Press, published from 1962 to 1988.

INTRODUCTION

an Eskimo Curlew. The last curlew was seen in 1962 at locality on my route. I did hope for a few waifs. I was painfully aware that, because of my route and the seasons, I would miss several species. My trip list would not be competitive with others in the early sixties and would be no match for the current deep-pocket sport we call a Big Year. That is when a person scours the country during a calendar year from Alaska to Florida to find not just the low and medium hanging fruit of my efforts but reach into the rarified air of over 700 species.

During the early part of the trip, I experienced what it was like to be on my own while traveling America. I became acquainted with a heart-stoppingly beautiful country, the splendor of national parks and nature, felt the appalling segregated South, the hustle and traffic of cities, the spectacular birds, and wonderful, generous people. I found disappointment, sometimes lived a comedy of errors, but most of all, I learned. I experienced trouble with southern police thinking I was smuggling cigarettes, and a close call and escape from a wily young and amorous girl offered new lessons to chase away my naivety. To a wet-behind-the-ears and small-town Northwesterner, all this was surprising and occasionally shocking, and very educational. I learned that any species missed just meant the thrill of seeing them some other year. The trip, interrupted for decades and later completed, was a gift that keeps on giving. Admittedly, the first day, 2 June 1962, made me wonder what was I getting into.

Chapter 1

Initiation

1 June 1962

THE PLANNED DEPARTURE DATE of 1 June was not possible because the valve cover on the $19.95 inflatable life raft was missing. No, I had not responded to one of those $19.95 ads on TV. The cost of the raft was the going rate for a cheap two-man raft at the local sporting goods shop. The shop supplied the missing part. In my excitement, I overlooked the need for food, which was another reason to delay my departure. I decided to leave the next day.

2 June 1962

The second day of June was a day of mixed emotions, with gratitude for the support from my parents and knowing I will miss them, my friends, and, most of all, Linda. My anxiety and happiness blended with sadness and regret. Should I have planned more? Should this trip be shared with someone by my side? Will the military draft catch up with me, put me in a war that has robbed so many and that will take more from humankind? Is it permissible for me to enjoy birding around the country? My determination to depart was partly coming from stubbornness and a belief that the trip was something I must do. I was feeling impatient to get on the road, anticipating the adventure, and knowing I would return with a hunger for more and still have unanswered questions. Whatever might happen, life would never be the same. The little engine of my VW whirred to life, and I drove away. The trip began.

It was late spring, the time in southwestern Oregon when the winter rains stopped. It is when the dry season begins, and when temperatures rise close to 100 degrees. A few summer days might be even hotter. Today was cool for a normal early June, and clouds signaled rain was possible. Early wildflowers had bloomed, with a few producing seeds. Summer was about three weeks away. Warblers, tanager, vireos, and others had arrived, and most of those would be great to put on my trip list. Birds such as Oak Titmice, Wrentits, and more would be out of my range just as fast as I could drive from the home turf of the Rogue Valley. I reasoned I would find all the birds unique to the valley when returning next year. Going east was my primary goal.

After a little over an hour and 30 minutes of snaking alongside the Rogue River, I had gained 1,000 feet in elevation and I stopped at Mill Creek Falls. The falls plunges 240 feet into the Rogue River. My 20-minute stop and a short walk to Mill Creek Falls through a forest of mixed conifers ranging from pine to Douglas fir and smooth, gnarly red-barked madrone had promise. However, the gentle slope to the edge of a canyon overlooking the river and the falls where Dippers might forage revealed nothing.

Uncharacteristically, I made no record of the birds I saw at the Mill Creek Falls or, for that matter, anywhere else that first day. I thought something possibly might happen on this first day that would end my plans prematurely causing me to return home. Perhaps there was little reason to keep notes on the first day. The trip might be over before actually getting started. I was one part pessimist and one part optimist and too preoccupied with worry. Birding would get better. It would have been good to get the trip going with a Hermit or Black-throated Gray Warbler, species that breed in the region. There might have been a migrating Townsend's Warbler or a calling Pacific-slope Flycatcher. Any of those species would have been good to start the trip list. Where are interesting species when you need them?

The overloaded little VW rolled over Oregon state highway 62 that took me away from the river deeper into the Cascade Mountains and to my first-night camping. The odometer indicated I traveled about 50 miles. I had hoped that things would look up by then, but a cold pouring rain quieted bird life considerably and tried to silence my spirit. To quote my journal, I wrote that "most vigor is gone, leaving only the dreaded thought of setting up camp in the rain or sleeping in the cramped quarters of the VW where I now sit twisting sideways to pound the typewriter now resting on a box in the jump seat."

INITIATION

The author and what was packed into the VW.

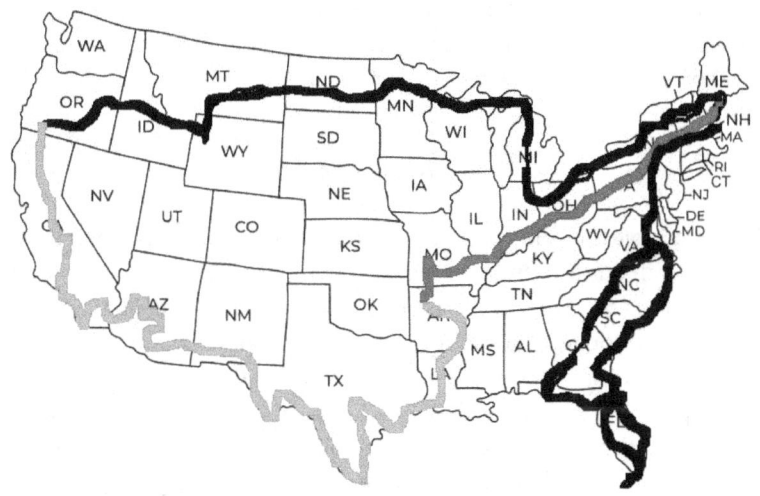

Approximate route. Black is the 1962 and 1963 route, dark gray is 1963 during car trouble, and pale gray is the route in 2005.

My first night was just off a gravel road that led to Huckleberry Mountain, a well-traveled mountain known to Indigenous Americans and later settlers for its cool air and abundant huckleberries. My chosen campsite was a level spot bulldozed from the mountainside at the edge of the Forest Service road a few yards from the paved highway. There were no travelers up either the highway or the gravel road that night. Missing people were fine, but missing spring was not. Sitting in the car on the wet gravel road was time to think about the seasons. Signs of late spring in the Rogue Valley, with its average elevation of about 1,400 feet, was left behind. Wildflowers were barely showing at Mill Creek Falls and my campsite at 4,400 feet was too high for spring. I was beginning to think I had entered winter. A little discouragement filled my mood while the pup tent sat unpacked in the car. There was no lull in the rain, and it would soon be dark. I was running out of time and light, and I pitched the tent. It would be possible to heat food by using the gas stove inside the tent, but the thought of fire and monoxide poisoning made that option too risky. My only alternative was a cold can of corned beef hash moistened with cream corn. The meal created a lump in my stomach, and I began to lose more of my already fading enthusiasm. I unrolled the sleeping bag and crawled in, clothes and all, and then zipped up the bag to the top, all the while shivering in the freezing darkness of the little tent.

Later in the night, I heard snapping twigs, heavy breathing, and grunting just outside the tent. Was this the beginning of the end, that is, my end? What was sniffing around my tent? I let out a loud yell that, in the still of the night, probably startled me more than the visitor.

3 June 1962

Uncomfortable hours later, a new day arrived, with relief of not hearing the patter of rain on the tent. I peeked out only to see snow floating from the early morning sky and that it was beginning to cover the cold hard ground. It was time to snuggle back in my sleeping bag. Within an hour, I began to worry that the snow last night might strand me and crawled out the stiff door flap to find about an inch of frozen rain, and snow blanketed the tent and the gravel road. The snow almost obliterated deer tracks around the tent. The car door lock required heating with a match to insert the key. Feet and hands were almost too cold to function. My stiff boots began to soften, and my feet slowly thawed as I jogged up and down the frozen road near the car. I managed to cook a hasty breakfast of eggs and bacon. Normally, I like my eggs fried enough so that nothing is moving. A little liquid yolk is fine but this morning the eggs, and bacon, were ice-cold before I could get either to my lips. The hot brown coffee saved me.

INITIATION

The first morning. Snow hid the red rally stripes and froze the author.

Wispy clouds, the color of the snow, disappeared with the rising sun, and within 30 minutes, everything melted. Everything but my hands and feet thawed. Two Steller's Jays and a flock of Golden-crowned Kinglets joined in the sound of dripping lodgepole pines.

Even though the tent was finally free from caked-on ice, it was still wet. I hurriedly rolled it up anyway and packed the car. The cold engine barely turned over. I let the car warm, which took about 30 minutes. The extra heavy 140-weight transmission oil, which reduced the slow leak, was now stiff from the frigid temperature. With difficulty shifting gears, I made my way back to the highway that climbed over the ridges radiating south of Mount Mazama, the mountain cradling Crater Lake. The straight trunks of lodgepole pine grew smaller than those surrounding my camp. Good for native lodges as the name suggests, the trees became even smaller and were growing closer together as I ascended the Cascade Divide. The dense growth, locally called a dog hair forest, was full of trees competing for the same space. Several trees had lost their bid for space and sun, their dead trunks fallen to the ground and others leaning against live trees.

The first Pettingill location for bird finding that was on my itinerary was Crater Lake NP. Highway 62 traverses the southern part of the park, and below the caldera was where Clark's Nutcracker would be a sure thing. Recalling Peterson and Fisher finding Gray-crowned Rosy-Finch when they visited the rim at Crater Lake, I wrestled with the idea of driving to the 7,100-foot Rim Village. It was a winter day in the Hudsonian zone, and the rim of Crater Lake would be much too cold, even for a couple of new species. Warmer temperature and not driving on slippery snow persuaded me to head for lower elevations on the east side of the Cascades.

The highway would take me to Fort Klamath, the town. Fort Klamath, the fort, established in 1863, was a few miles away. As I drove onward, I reviewed what little I knew about the history of my route. Amazingly, I could remember a few dates, but otherwise my knowledge was but an outline. Soldiers from the fort opened a military road in 1865, the same year the Civil War ended. Some say the road was built in 1863 and I believe the route was likely already established by natives. The original road, now Highway 62, avoided large trees, rock outcroppings, and other impediments. Traveling west from Fort Klamath to the Cascade Mountains and the Rogue River Valley must have taken days. I knew that driving the route today took only two and a half hours.

Mid-morning cloudy, windy, and wintry weather greeted me at Fort Klamath, Oregon. The region is at the northern end of the Klamath Basin, a huge area of marshes, lakes, or at least former wetlands before agricultural interest took control. The watershed of the lake is larger than Indiana. Here streams flood the alder-conifer forests and flat, lush meadowlands where Great Gray Owls may sit motionless, mounted on a dead snag or tree trunk. Fort Klamath had a reputation of being a good place to find Great Gray Owls, and Ms. Ana Strahan, resident and elementary school teacher of the small town, offered to show me this wonderful bird. However, we never found the owls.

Among 18 species seen during the search were Mountain and Western Bluebirds, Purple Finches but no Cassin's Finches. Spring birds, including Western Wood Pewees, Tree Swallows, and MacGillivray's and Wilson's Warblers were there to breed.

I left the Fort Klamath region with plans to be at Upper Klamath NWR late in the afternoon. The road from Fort Klamath to the refuge and south to Klamath Falls, built in the 1800s, was an essentially level dirt road at the edge of the forested Cascades and the shore of Upper Klamath Lake. It was really a surface more or less scraped clear of vegetation, with rocks protruding upward from the reddish roadbed that would cause any driver to worry. It was necessary to dodge the dangerously large sharp rocks looming out of the surface of the road. Tall scaly barked ponderosa pines dominated the forest. My twentieth-century wagon gave me a rough ride to the refuge that protects a small portion of marshlands along the western shore of vast Upper Klamath Lake. No one would be at the abandoned headquarters as a

INITIATION

letter from the refuge manager informed me earlier. I decided that the best place to sleep was inside the steel refuge observation tower.

The second night was in the now destroyed lookout tower of Upper Klamath NWR.

4 June 1962

Yesterday, after being skunked by the Great Gray Owls at Fort Klamath, I was glad to see new birds when I arrived at Upper Klamath National Wildlife Refuge. Before night, I found Western Grebes [the grebe was split into Western and Clark's Grebes, and birds I saw might have been one or the other or both species] were abundant, and there were gulls and other new species. Last night I was lulled to sleep by the multi-bird chorus 134 feet below the metal tower. However, the periods of sleep were shortened by the wind rocking the tower. Each time I turned over, the tower shook even more.

A cold and damp morning was topped off with a stiff breeze. My view of the forest from the tower was full of multiple shades of green from the dark green of Douglas fir to paler hues of pines and new and shiny deciduous leaves of an occasional maple. The grass was showing spring growth in an opening or two where the conifers let in the sun. Looking east, I saw the marsh reflected a different green, a flatter and softer color that waved with the wind. Beyond was the dark water of Upper Klamath Lake. The big black and white grebes seen yesterday evening were gone.

To tour part of the marsh in my life raft in wind would be foolish. So, I waited for the weather to change. The temperature rose from cold to barely warmer and the wind seemed to subside. I was ready and, after gingerly climbing into the raft, and paddling out from shore about 50 feet, the wind began to blow the raft toward the other shore of the lake, which was miles away. I paddled and paddled harder to reach the safety of the small dock on the shore below the observation tower. Exploring any of the marsh by raft was too risky.

After the near mishap with the raft, I was more than content to look for birds from solid ground. The frigid conditions were great for Canada Jays but must have been bad for the few Olive-sided and Willow flycatchers near the lake's edge. Out on the lake were colorful Eared Grebes, American White Pelicans, and Double-crested Cormorants. The collection of ducks and geese for the trip list began with Canada Goose, Mallard, Canvasback, and Lesser Scaup. There also were rafts of Ruddy Ducks, the males with bills turned blue to help attract the demure females. Three Forester's Terns ventured close enough to be found. Western Tanagers and Bullock's Orioles were singing near the observation tower. Birds not usually found west of the Cascades were common here, including Black-billed Magpies, mostly seen along the roadways while they search for road kills, and a dozen raspy-voiced Yellow-headed Blackbirds. The first towhee for the list was a Spotted Towhee.

Leaving the refuge, I drove 20 miles southward in Klamath Falls where the weather was still miserably cold. My plans for tomorrow with Mr. Warner Kimble were off; he will visit Fort Klamath to photograph a pair of Mountain Bluebirds, the very same pair of birds I had earlier observed nest building. No camping sites existed within miles of Klamath Falls, and the local YMCA did not cater to overnight lodgers. I had to spend the night in a cheap hotel. The hotel room was cheap all right; it was $1.50! The clerk must have felt sorry for me. Not only did I get a cheap room and no trouble during the night, not even with bedbugs, but I had also seen a variety of good birds during the day and, at last, began thawing out.

5 June 1962

I overslept in my dingy but at least warm and dry hotel room. By then, most of the guests had departed when I descended the creaky wooden stairs. I headed for the Link River and Moore Park, a city park of the town of Klamath Falls at the north edge of town and on the southern shore of Upper Klamath Lake. While I was fixing breakfast, the number of ponderosa pines in Moore Park reminded me to look for White-headed Woodpeckers. None were there. That is probably a species I would find in California during the homeward trek.

The Link River flows for a little over three miles from the southern end of Upper Klamath Lake to the Klamath River. Some of the species found on the Link River were surprises. According to local Klamath Falls birders, Caspian Terns are uncommon, but I found two flying overhead and displaying their large bright salmon beaks and slightly forked tails. Two female Common Goldeneyes were also unexpected. Although information from my phone conversation with Warren Kimble did not yield White-headed Woodpeckers, he did point me to locations for finding two species of herons to add to the trip list. Directions took me up the Link River to numerous Black-crowned Herons that silently lumbered out of the low-growing cottonwoods where they were roosting along the edge of the river, and a Green Heron bolted from the shore.

Yellow Warblers and Song Sparrows were singing throughout the day. Unseen Common Yellowthroats scolded with a characteristic *thimk*. After finding 43 species, I headed east to Lakeview, a small town nestled at the foot of the Warner Mountains. Sitting at 4,800 feet in elevation, Lakeview is one of Oregon's highest towns. A local informed me that its two uranium mines closed last year. Since then, its population of 3,260 has been slowly dwindling. Except for topping off the gas tank and enjoying a milkshake, I veered northward to the more arid parts of Lake County where vegetation and birds became sparse. Even the numerous bodies of water, some alkaline, others fresh, were almost birdless. A sparrow would flit across the highway now and then, and it might have been profitable to look them over. However, to travel 15,000 miles and stop at all the better areas still requires a schedule.

I drove until the sun dictated the end of the day. The sky had become blue but it was gradually turning a golden bronze in the west. I turned off the deserted highway near the southern shore of Lake Abert, a huge glacially dug basin of water that might be the resting place for a few late migrants and nesting waterfowl. A narrow dirt track off the highway meandered to a camping location at the top of a bald hill overlooking the highway and lake. The air was crisp at 6,200 feet elevation. Tabletop plateaus rimmed the yellow grassy slopes that would soon become green before the late summer parched their roots and browned their blades. Sagebrush was the next dominant plant. Dark perpendicular basalt rock cliffs up to 2,000 feet, Abert Rim, borders the western side of Lake Abert for 30 miles; the lake is 60 miles long. The rim dwarfed the Western and Eared Grebes dotting the water. The sun was still beaming down, though by no means was it warm. I quickly pitched the tent—making sure to face one wall toward the sun so that the inside would become halfway warm by the time I completed the evening meal. From camp, I searched the shore below me. A Willet that I had seen earlier had disappeared. When I turned in for the night, I heard the frog-like peeping of Eared Grebes. There were no other sounds.

Before sleep, I reviewed the past days. In a ledger of expenses, I recorded my daily expenditures. My strict budget required accounting for every cent. The groceries I almost forgot to buy on 1 June came to a total of $10.58. At Fort Klamath, I treated myself to a 35 cent strawberry milkshake. I also bought a quart of white gas for 15 cents. That was my fuel for the camp stove and lantern.

On the fourth day of the trip, I had a bowl of chili and a candy bar (35 cents) for my evening meal at Klamath Falls and the next day purchased groceries and lunch for less than $3. According to the ledger, I bought gas a couple of times before the night at Lake Abert. I was overly cautious because each of the two times the amount was less than six gallons—the tank held a little over 10 gallons, and the average mileage was about 30 miles per gallon. I bought stamps and a postcard at the Fort Klamath post office (8 cents) and added new ice to the chest upon reaching Klamath Falls (20 cents).

Before leaving Klamath Falls, I replaced the gasket in the gas tank lid. A minuscule amount of gasoline had sloshed against the lid. The gasoline was just enough to dampen the exposed neck of the tank. The problem might not seem too serious, but for those who did not have the pleasure of owning a VW Beetle, access to the gas tank of the early models, such as mine, was inside the front hood. That might not be the correct term. The hinged door covering the rear engine probably should be called the hood. The hinged door on the front part of the car covered the gas tank and a small storage area, the VW's answer to a trunk. Any gasoline in that area, even a trace, quickly permeated everything in the trunk and wafted fumes into the passenger compartment. The passenger compartment was a well-crafted module, and, again, for those who have not experienced a Beetle, there was always a race to see who could close their door first. Because the passenger area was so air-tight, the last door to shut required considerable force to compress the interior air. And, yes, Beetles could float, but I never put my VW to that test.

The route from Lakeview to Lake Abert and beyond to the next stop, Malheur NWR, was almost empty of vehicles. The US highway connects the sparsely populated eastern towns and ranches in Oregon. It is used mainly for hauling livestock and hay and a few wayward tourists. During the fall months, the route is a favorite of hunters traveling from southwestern Oregon to hunt antelope in eastern Oregon or to hunt elk in neighboring Idaho. Birders use the same highway while traveling to the birding oasis of Malheur NWR.

༄

A few years ago, in early June 2018, I decided to hike to Mill Creek Falls for 41 minutes, the same number of minutes consumed while hiking that trail in 1962. It was warmer during the 2018 trek. Every year is warmer than the last, but I will try to focus on what birds I found other than the deadly advancing global climate change. In 2018, I found a handful of Hermit Warblers and a couple of singing Warbling Vireos. Both species are common in the region. Shamefully, I missed Hermit Warbler in 1962. Missing Hermit Warbler on the trip was then considered acceptable since I was in such a hurry to travel eastward and would soon be leaving their narrow breeding range. Although I missed Warbling Vireo that first day, I had ample sighting later. These birds have a vast range, a range I was in for months. Today, I have little trouble identifying both the western and eastern vireos, which sing different songs and differ in several other characters. The two populations surely will someday be realized to represent two separate species that I might count on a future birding journey.

Decades since camping on the Huckleberry Mountain Road among lodgepole pine, I realize the locality is a good birding spot. A couple of miles up the road Norm Barrett, then biologist for Rogue River NF, studied Flammulated Owls. A snow park is now near the intersection of the Highway 62 and Huckleberry Mountain Road and is about a quarter of a mile from where I camped. The snow park is where Black-backed Woodpeckers often nest and where American Three-toed Woodpecker are known. Overlooking the owls and woodpeckers seems reasonable since the habitat in 1962 was not then suitable for the woodpeckers. As for the owls, they were a few miles and higher in elevation than my early camp and inaccessible in early June until the snow melts.

It was so cold that first night that I used the word "vigor" in my notes, a word that surprises my older self. The cold seemed worse because the heaters in vintage VWs ranged from poor to hardly adequate. There was no mechanism to blow the heat except the air-cooled engine itself. Had I ignored the frigid weather and taken the time to drive to the rim of the lake at Crater Lake NP, Cassin's Finch and perhaps other species would have made their way on the trip list. Clark's Nutcrackers were found later. The probability of seeing Gray-crowned Rosy-Finches was low but possible. Maybe I should have tried anyway because there was not a single rosy-finch on the trip list. The road beyond the rim would have been closed because of snow; the park employees considered it good luck if they had the road bare earlier than 4 July. Would the half-day of birding in the upper reaches of Crater Lake NP have been worth missing Anna Strahan, who early on 3 June might be showing me my first Great Gray Owl?

Rosy-finches to this day remain elusive around the rim. Beginning in the twenty-first century, Rim Drive is more frequently opened after 4 July. In the 1960s, the rim would be covered by about 12 feet of snow, but the average annual snowfall is decreasing. That is just one symbol of increasing temperatures and diminishing snow as global climate change began and continues its choke-hold on the planet. Climate change also changed bird distribution and abundance. For example, during my early visits to Crater Lake, Clark's Nutcrackers seemed everywhere around the rim at Crater Lake NP, but today, not so much. Clark's Nutcrackers are considered keystone species since the species cache white-bark pine seeds, ultimately planting a new crop of trees growing from the pine nuts the birds do not eat. The relationship between nutcrackers and white-bark pines is now being interrupted by blister rust that is killing the trees and therefore contributing to fewer seed trees. The rust, a fungus, was introduced from nursery plants from France and inadvertently shipped to Vancouver, BC, in 1910. Since then, the fungus has made its way south and, without abatement, will change the landscape. A 2000 study acknowledged 20 percent of the white-bark pine in Crater Lake is infected with the deadly rust and predicts a 46 percent decline in trees by 2050.[1] The study also stated that planting rust-resistant seeds of the pines supplemented with nutcracker dispersal will

---

1. Michael P. Murray and Mary Rasmussen. "Status of Whitebark Pine in Crater Lake National Park." Unpublished report, US Department of Interior, Park Service, Crater Lake National Park, Resource Management Division. https://www.craterlakeinstitute.com/research-at-crater-lake/botany-research/statue-whitebark-pine-2000/status-01/.

INITIATION

help save the trees and the birds. The more rust-resistant seeds, the more trees, and the more nutcrackers to eat more seeds. The rust is likely only one factor that is contributing to the demise of the boisterous nutcracker.

A couple of years after passing up the chance to find rosy-finches at Crater Lake NP, I ended up working at the park during two summers between sessions of college calisthenics. The unmarried seasonal employees were bivouacked in what once was the ranger's dorm, a sturdy two-story structure that later became a visitor center. Larry Smith was one of my roommates. Larry and his twin brother, Lloyd, are well known at Crater Lake, having spent 23 summers as rangers. In 2009, Larry emailed me that 523 white-bark pine seedlings were planted in the park. There is more to the blister-rust story, but I will stop here and leave room for other stories. For example, while at Crater Lake, I put a couple of bands on Clark's Nutcrackers at Rim Village, a project began by Donald Farner, author of *Birds of Crater Lake National Park*, published in 1952. The monograph is a fine piece of work and today is still an important reference on the birds of the park. Unlike many current publications, Farner did not discuss when and where to find birds in the park. A new publication, based mostly on *Birds of Oregon: A General Reference*, of which I was the taxonomic editor, stated the obvious that Crater Lake is a good place to find Gray-crowned Rosy-Finches and Clark's Nutcrackers. Linda and I have seen rosy-finches in Crater Lake in July. They were foraging a few hundred feet down the steep caldera. Peering nearly straight down through binoculars at the finches flitting from rock to rock, with the blue lake a thousand or more feet below, is a dizzying view.

On 3 June 1962, I drove along the edge of Castle Creek, a major creek of the park. Water roared from the canyon floor about 200 feet below. Three years later, I saw a Cassin's Finch there, another species missed in 1962. More years later, Clark's Nutcrackers foraged along Annie Creek, the creek flowing along Highway 62 toward Fort Klamath.

The little town of Fort Klamath has scarcely changed in the last 40-plus years, although the surrounding cattle pastures have fewer scatterings of trees. The gas station at Fort Klamath where I stopped is gone and the restaurant where I savored the strawberry milkshake burned down around the turn of the century. A visit there in 2018 revealed several singing western Nashville Warblers under the watchful eyes of a soaring Swainson's Hawk. The town, not the actual fort where Charles Bendire, military medical doctor and ornithologist, was stationed, has had a population for years that hovers between 21 to 32 individuals. There are far more bovines grazing south of town on the flats north of Upper Klamath Lake.

In 1962, I had no inkling that Fort Klamath (the fort) was one of Charles Bendire's old stomping grounds. Pioneering Bendire, one of the founding members of the American Ornithologists' Union in 1883, was stationed at Fort Klamath in 1882 and 1883. His legacy there and elsewhere is an altogether different story, a story that on 3 June 1962 was barely background noise. His collections of eggs formed the basis for his publications and his egg collection was the seed for a larger collection that provided A. C. Bent much of the information on eggs he incorporated in his famous life histories of birds. At Smithsonian, I had the privilege and pleasure to curate eggs collected by Bendire. As for naming new birds discovered by Bendire, that fell to Robert Ridgway, probably one of the greatest ornithologists ever. Years later I would author an ornithological paper or two on birds collected by Bendire. Incidentally, the route I took from Medford, Oregon, to Fort Klamath was the same route sometimes taken by Bendire on his way to Jacksonville, the first town in the Rogue Valley.

The history of the Klamath region reveals the Klamath Indians were once prosperous and self-sufficient, in part from owning forests and practicing sustain-yield forestry. Historically, they were the only tribe in the US to pay income taxes that funded the administrative costs of the Bureau of Indian Affairs. Peace existed between Fort Klamath and the Klamath Indians, who sold lumber milled to the fort in 1873. Nonetheless, their forested reservation was taken away in the horribly named Klamath Termination Act of 1954, which is no surprise since breaking treaties is a well-known Anglo-American behavior. Finally, in 1986, sovereignty was reestablished to the Klamath Indians, but the former reservation was not.

The wetlands of the Klamath Basin, likened to the western Everglades, are now only 25 percent of their former size. Agriculture now occupies most of the former marshland. Peterson and Fisher once zipped past the eastern shore of Upper Klamath Lake while on their way to Crater Lake, where they found two Gray-crowned Rosy-Finches in the park in mid-June. The birding duo also wrote about water and waterfowl populations found in Tule and Lower Klamath refuges in California. The three refuges depend on water slowly draining from Upper Klamath Lake. Dependent on that water are also a couple of endangered sucker fish and coho salmon downstream, farmers and ranchers, and Klamath Indians who had dominion over the region in the first place. What water a chronic drought might supply to the refuges is subject to untoward politics, death to wildlife from lack of water, and constant pressure from agriculturists to quench their crops and cattle. And then there is avian botulism, caused by a soil bacterium that often rears its ugly head when water levels become low. That and heat, combined with dead prey that might be ingested by a hungry duck, produces a cocktail of a horrible death to waterfowl. There is more to it than that, but the result is the same, loss of muscle control, starvation, and drowning.

INITIATION

Linda and I drove the 1962 route in the Klamath Basin in 2003. The former rocky scrape on the west side of Upper Klamath Lake where I had bumped along in 1962 now presents an effortless drive on a wide and smooth blacktopped surface constructed in the 1970s. Now, large freight trucks speed down the lanes pushing 60 miles an hour while taking a shortcut to sawmills in Klamath Falls or Medford. Most of the wildlife we saw was road kills. Before straightening and laying down blacktop, the dirt road along the west side of the lake was traveled by troops in the 1800s on their way from Fort Klamath to what is now Lava Beds NM in northern California, a location where I also worked one summer.

The old road and the new one overlap near a location known for Yellow Rails. I did not know about it in 1962 as the species was thought to be extirpated in Oregon until 1982. The observation tower in Klamath NWR was gone by 2018 and no one, including refuge employees, could offer a date when it was removed. In June 2018, I used up a couple of hours to locate the site of the old tower, which now has fewer trees near the tower site and far less open water where I attempted rafting.

At Klamath NWR, I added two species of flycatchers, including Willow Flycatcher, and a third member of the family on my visit to Moore Park. While at Smithsonian I needed to evaluate the different subspecies of Willow Flycatcher and, in 1993, published a revision of the species that was later cited in the Congressional Record because one of the subspecies was considered endangered. In 1962, it never occurred to me that I might have a role in the conservation of the species.

Another flycatcher seen in 1962 has a story. Since then, the late Burt Monroe and I published a 1991 paper with the fancy title "Clarifications and Corrections of the Dates of Issue of Some Publications Containing Descriptions of North American Birds." Burt Monroe was then chairman of the Committee on Classification and Nomenclature of the American Ornithologists' Union. He was chairman extraordinaire, friend, and teacher to multitudes. I was among those who had the pleasure of his wit and enjoyment of the knowledge he shared. He was also a highly competitive and challenging hoopster who frequently would get a game going during lulls at scientific meetings. Burt and I met during sessions of the AOU Check-list Committee and at meetings and talked on the phone, especially ironing out details of our manuscripts. He would always answer the phone with an enthusiastic twang, "Ralph, how in the hell are you?" His voice and the question are still clear in my head.

Our fancy paper's primary function was to establish the dates when scientific names were published, which is important because usually, but not always, the scientific name used for a bird is the first one published. The paper with Burt led to a 1995 publication by Richard C. Banks and me that took into consideration the dates of publication and how they should be applied to current nomenclature. The late Dick Banks, with many claims to fame, including chair of the Check-List Committee, and who is a book himself, is the person who hired me for employment at the museum. We coauthored several publications, which we called the B and B papers. One of the species we discussed in one of those papers was the Olive-sided Flycatcher, a species seen at Klamath NWR in 1962. Then, I had no inkling that I would be writing about its scientific name. I was then barely becoming aware of scientific names. I knew birds had them, but those hard to pronounce and difficult to spell scientific names were Greek and mostly Latin to me.

So, what was the problem concerning the scientific moniker of the Olive-sided Flycatcher? There were two available binomials for the species. That paper Burt and I published determined that Nuttall published the name *cooperi* for the specific name of the Olive-sided Flycatcher before Swainson published the name *borealis* for the same species. Therefore, we concluded that the scientific name for Olive-sided Flycatchers is *cooperi*. That might seem an abrupt change for such a widely known species but, as it turned out, the name *cooperi* was not an obscure name in the literature of the later twentieth century. However, the binomial *borealis* was also in use for the same species. It is not proper to have two or more binomials for the same species. I am trying hard to avoid the technicalities of how names are used in zoological nomenclature because it can get very sticky. There is even a published code and a body of learned people who make final rulings on how names should be used.

Dick Banks and I did present another nomenclatural situation that might have confused more people than using *cooperi* for specific of the Olive-sided Flycatcher. It concerns the potential change of the specific scientific name for the House Wren. Again, because of the publication dates Burt and I corrected, it turns out that Alexander Wilson, in his landmark volumes of *American Ornithology* applied the name *domesticus* for the specific name of our familiar wren before Vieillot dreamed up and published the name *aedon* for the same species. What to do, what to do? Dick and I believed that even though a handful of twentieth-century authors thought the name *domesticus* should be used for the House Wren, the name *aedon* was in such widespread usage that it should be retained for the species. However, because *domesticus* was an earlier name, we had to write the head nomenclatural guys a proposal to retain *aedon* for the House Wren. Our paper had the fancy title "*Bombycilla cedrorum* Vieillot, [1808] and *Troglodytes aedon* Vieillot, [1809] (Aves, Passeriformes): Proposed Conservation of the Specific Names." Two years later, in 1998, our case, actually assigned as Case 2969, was voted on by the head nomenclaltural body and the results of the learned international commission ruled 44 to 1 in favor of *aedon*. Of course, in 1962, the House Wrens I was seeing were just House Wrens.

In addition to changes in scientific names, there may be about the spelling of common names of birds. Name changes, whether Latin, Greek, or English tend to drive birders up the wall at times, but there are reasons for the changes. English names are probably the most troublesome changes and often produce controversy and confusion. We usually get over the name changes, but one that seems hard to take is not recognizing the name of a particular kind of bird as a proper noun. The convention set by the American Ornithologists' Union is to capitalize the proper common names of birds. The wren I saw at Klamath NWR was a House Wren and the dastardly cowbird, a Brown-headed Cowbird, a name to countless species who lay their eggs in nests of other species to be hatched by the unwilling or not understanding host. Unfortunately, if I were to write about Steller's Jays and Brown-headed Cowbirds in the local newspaper, the sophisticated editor might print them as Steller's jay and brown-headed cowbird. A Medford, Oregon, editor once insisted on changing Steller' to stellar.

The nomenclature of birds has, since 1962, changed more than the regions of Lakeview to Burns near Malheur NWR, where I was then heading. In 1996, Linda and I saw less than five vehicles on the long stretch between Lake Abert and Malheur, about the same number that I saw 34 years earlier. Later trips across the region happily have revealed much the same density of vehicles. The terrain surrounding Lake Abert and the alkaline lakes along the way appeared to have not changed. Stopping at a pull-off above Lake Abert not long before the sunset mirrors that 1962 time, an unseen grebe trilled. There were no other sounds.

Chapter 2

Malheur Was Good

6 June 1962

THE NIGHT AT LAKE Abert and the nearly 120-mile drive to Burns, Oregon, were both uneventful, although I did worry through the night that a crazed traveler would attack me. I had heard too many stories, too many warnings about strangers, marauding cougars, quicksand, and of course, almost anything that could poke out an eye. The miles between Lake Abert and Burns seemed long and were barren except for an occasional unidentified bird whisking across the empty highway. The refreshing and familiar smell of Douglas fir and other evergreens was replaced with dry odors of eastern Oregon. I sped on, or as speedy as a seven-year-old used and persevering VW can speed. Arrival at Burns meant short miles to the famous Malheur NWR and potentially great birding.

At Burns, I picked up mail from home. When I arranged to have my first general delivery, I thought Burns was a greater distance from home than it is. The 300 miles is further away than I had usually soloed from home. There was a nice letter from a school buddy wishing me good birding and a mention of my best friend, Linda. As I drove south from town and topped a low hill, the green of Malheur was not far away. The refuge would be my new home, at least for a night or two.

Malheur sits on the arid 4,000-foot plateau of eastern Oregon, much of which is in the rain shadow of the Cascade Mountains. The surrounding territory is unforgiving, with its dry and hot summers, powdery alkaline lake beds, and miles of sagebrush and juniper. Malheur is an oasis. The water source for this parched land is the Steens Mountains to the south and the Blue Mountains to the north that reach up to 9,700 feet to catch the annual snowfall that feeds the streams flowing to the Malheur basin. Harney and Malheur lakes collect the spring runoff helping to create the largest freshwater marsh in the western US. Malheur Lake is about 45,000 acres of lush, deep marsh interspersed with occasional areas of open water. A strip of land, the Narrows, separates Malheur and Harney Lakes. The bed of Harney Lake, the lowest point in the basin, has no outlet, and consequently, the 30,000-acre lake is very saline and devoid of most vegetation.

The region's history is long and exciting, with Native American wars, pioneers, settlement, and cattle. My coveted Gabrielson and Jewett's *Birds of Oregon* had explained that Charles Bendire, who collected and observed birds at Fort Klamath, also had done in the same in 1874–78 at Fort Harney, a historic site north of the refuge. Bendire visited Malheur Lake before trappers, plume hunters, and others slaughtered the region's swans, grebes, egrets. Finally, in 1908, 81,786 acres of the region became the Lake Malheur Reservation. In 1935, the name of the region was changed to the Malheur Migratory Refuge, with an additional 64,717 acres added to the preserve. The present name, Malheur National Wildlife Refuge, went into the annals of officialdom in 1940.

The refuge had a reputation of being a great birding area, and I was anxious to see as many species as possible. Gene Kridler, the refuge biologist, outlined several localities to bird before taking me to the nearby old CCC (Civilian Conservation Corps) barracks where I would spend the next two nights. Gene and I then walked up to the barracks that stood straight but worn by decades of icy winters and hot baking summers, the outside walls of sun- and snow-weathered boards guarding the former mess hall of the CCC crew. We entered an expansive room; the mess tables and benches crowded the floor on a wall away from the creaky door. I looked over the long wooden mess hall where occasional overnight visitors stayed. Looking pleased, Gene excused himself while I took in my new abode. Benches lined the walls, and a couple of these placed side by side should make a perfect place for my sleeping bag. There were electric lights, running water, and an old broken down but serviceable electric range for cooking. What great luck. After unloading bedding, cookware, ice chest, and can goods, I hurried back to refuge headquarters.

It was afternoon. A Veery, a not too common species in this part of Oregon, flew from a cottonwood but not before a good view of its salient field marks. I climbed a nearby observation tower that loomed even higher than the one at the Upper Klamath NWR. The tower sat on a hilltop behind the headquarters, and it seemingly caught every bit of wind that whistled through its steely spindle legs. I eased myself slowly inside the sun-warmed enclosed room at the top of the tower, and narrowly avoided being stung by a big red wasp circling the ceiling. Big Red was not alone. Things really began to buzz when I climbed up into the bright windowed room. There were hundreds of Big Reds, and they were all mad at my bare-armed intrusion. I stayed long enough to take a couple of quick pictures of the scene below. No stings.

Back down on earth, a few birds put on good shows. Brewer's Sparrows were breezing out of almost every bush. Great, a new life bird. A flycatcher perched on an electric line. Unfortunately, the bird never let out a peep. It was an *Empidonax* and was in a habitat that might be suitable for two species, Dusky and Gray flycatchers. The plumage had a faint touch of olive above and an ever so slight yellowish wash below. I was not sure which species was teasing me. Maybe this is one that was going to get away. Just as I was about to give up, I heard a soft *wit* emanating from the mystery bird. Still, I hesitated to call it. One more minute of staring and I heard an almost sad *deehic* followed by a crisp *sillit*. The sound was nothing like the very audible wit or the lively *chi-bit* of a Gray Flycatcher. This was the trip's first Dusky Flycatcher, although I almost wished it had been a Gray Flycatcher because I would soon be leaving its breeding range.

Back at the CCC mess hall, a Poor-will struck up a loud and repeated *poor-will*. My stomach also began to call. Planning a meal would not be easy since the hot daytime temperature had thawed the ice in the ice chest. I had to discard a half-pound of hamburger I had been saving for tonight. Most of the bacon that I had on ice was spoiled. I kept the remaining slices of bacon cool that night and had the surviving hamburger with eggs and fried potatoes for my evening meal. The fried diet was balanced, so I thought, with a can of green beans and a glass of grape juice. Although my hamburger patty had an odd taste, it had no ill effects.

Thirty minutes later, I was ready to spend the rest of the daylight hours birding. Gene had suggested a short drive down Cole Island Dike Road, where I might see Burrowing Owls. Several Long-billed Curlews called loudly, perhaps startled by a Northern Harrier coursing low over the green marsh grass. Savannah Sparrows flew up from the dusty dike road as I drove. I did find a Burrowing Owl, a species I knew well from a colony that lived near home during my early years. The lone Burrowing Owl standing on its long legs outside its nesting burrow was not nearly as exciting as five Short-eared Owls coursing back and forth over the cattails. Their round faces were constantly searching for careless prey. The sun began to set on their flashing wings with reflections of reddish-gold that bathed the west horizon. Soon only black silhouettes revealed them stalking the marsh. On the way back to the barracks, something large flew across the dike road and then back to reveal its identity. Night was falling and the Great Horned Owl owned it.

7 June 1962

Gene could not get away from work on grasshopper control, but he took time to mark a refuge map with my route to the southern boundary at Frenchglen. The small settlement of Frenchglen took its name from Pete French and Dr. Hugh Glenn, Pete French's father-in-law. A ranch, with the moniker "P" Ranch, became the headquarters for the French-Glenn Livestock Company in 1872. Pete French owned 150,000 acres of what is now known as the Frenchglen Valley at the base of the Steens Mountains. My route would take me into part of the best birding regions of the refuge, Gene remarked. He told me that the tall vegetation in the refuge would hinder birding; April, before the vegetation grows, seems to be the best spring month at Malheur. Part of the route was up Donner und Blitzen Valley (I am not making that up) south of refuge headquarters, then past Rattlesnake Butte and Diamond Craters to a small lake near Buena Vista Station.

One of the species I needed for the trip list and my life list was Sandhill Crane. Gene had circled a couple of areas on the map for cranes. The drive to the closest area would conserve time and gasoline; 30 cents a gallon adds up. I reached the spot where a long-necked, stilt-legged bird was striding through a marshy green meadow bordered by an almost gray sagebrush. I will never forget that exciting feeling of my first sight of a Sandhill Crane. Long-billed Curlews whistled a mellow plea in their seeming despair while I inadvertently approached their nest. Not wishing to disturb the curlews, I retreated several yards and soon found Franklin's Gulls, with crisp black hoods sticking to the pure white bodies. They looked quite different from my first Franklin's Gull, an immature straying to my familiar Rogue Valley in southwestern Oregon.

Of course, Red-winged Blackbirds were clacking about in the cattails. A chorus of bright yellow-headed Yellow-headed Blackbirds called raspy territorial "songs." Two males came to territorial arms at a border dispute. Another yellowish bird, the ubiquitous Northern Yellowthroat, stayed out of sight most of the time, but one would almost always dart into the open when I spished. Cliff, Barn, and Violet-green swallows zipped over the dikes and marsh. Fewer Northern Rough-winged Swallows joined the mix, as each species seemed to forage at slightly different elevations. New ducks were added to the trip list, including Blue-winged and Cinnamon teals.

Willets flashed black and white wings across the marsh expanse as I followed the refuge map. At rest, Willets almost faded into the background. Only when one occasionally stretched a wing could they be spotted easily. Of course, their voice also gave them away. I was surprised when I heard a sweet *pill-will-willet* as a bird softly repeated its song on a fence post about 30 feet from me.

The flashy Willets were by no means common in the refuge. In fact, the refuge checklist considered the species uncommon during spring, summer, and fall. Words such as common, uncommon, abundant are confusing. Words denoting abundance mean, as they do to the average person, the number of individuals observed. Granted, the idea of an average person may be debatable; I did see several Avocets, which are listed as common on the refuge checklist. Of course, there are questions here. How average was the day I saw Avocets? And how many Avocets did I see? I admit that I did not record the number. Western Sandpipers are listed as abundant, but I saw none. Willets, listed as uncommon, were, in the course of five hours of birding, found more often than the "common" Avocet. About equal time was spent searching for what is probably favorable habitat for the two species. I appreciate the availability of a checklist when coming to a new region. I like to think of the checklists as informal guides to an area, not statements of actual populations.

As noon arrived, I discovered that I had left the lunch I packed at the CCC mess hall. Only one species remained on the list of what I call needed species. And what could be harder to find at such a season than the Greater Sage Grouse? Gene confirmed my thoughts about the mating dances. The dancing activity had begun to slack off about a month ago. Not only was I too late seasonally, the early morning, the best time to find these birds, was well behind me. Not even a languid waltzing bird would be found. My stomach began to knot as the day passed lunchtime, and the hot sun beamed down to add to the discomfort. About three miles south, I would have a very remote chance of seeing a grouse. After about an hour of searching, I gave up. Frenchglen would have to be another time. I turned back, driving with plummeting blood sugar north past Saddle Butte, then west of Coyote Buttes, and back to headquarters to my waiting sandwich. Disappointed, mostly with myself, I made a mental note to always have something to eat stowed in the car.

Nourished, I drove from the mess hall to the artificial body of water called the Display Pond. The pond hosted various species of ducks, coots, and the newly transplanted Trumpeter Swan, a species I hoped to see in wilder conditions at Red Rock Lakes NWR Refuge in southwestern Montana. A photographers' blind at the edge of Display Pond tempted me even though I lacked a telephoto lens. However, the hot dry air outside the blind had driven all the mosquitoes within a mile radius into the cool and more humid blind. I stayed inside just long enough to peek out a hole facing the water, and long enough to feed several of the mosquito sisters.

After considerable cursing and even more scratching, I carried my bug-bitten body to the headquarters where Gene was examining a caged bird that he captured yesterday using a complex system of mist nets. The bird was sitting on a perch inside a wire cage. The bird was one of several that had snared themselves in mist nets set up at headquarters. Like so many other unsuspecting birds, individuals cannot see the fine fabric entangling nets. Migrants respond to the only tall trees around headquarters and are caught by mist nets. Such birds would otherwise go unnoticed had they not been caught. Gene and I saw the bird for a while and studied plates of different species of thrushes in an open reference book. I knew I had seen this bird earlier. Of course. It looked identical to the Veery that I observed yesterday. We went outside to the nets that Gene explained must be checked regularly to prevent birds from possibly injuring themselves, suffering from exposure, or from being so tangled in the netting that extricating them is next to impossible. All but one of the nets was empty. Snared, and its head dangling down, was another migrant that I saw yesterday, a Western Tanager. The bird's red face fit its apparent mood when he showed his temper by biting the hand that firmly held him. Once weighed, banded, and released, this bird would soon forget its ordeal as it wings its way to a montane coniferous forest nesting ground.

A different wire cage in Gene's office held a bird unfamiliar to me. It was a Flammulated Owl, a migratory species snared in a mist net early today. Gene told me that the last previous record for this small dark-eyed owl was in 1940. The owl's angry eyes flashed when I approached the cage for a better look. I couldn't count this diminutive and rare owl; my self-imposed rule that I could not count captive birds was hard to follow. If I had seen the owl earlier, it would have been a keeper, even a bird snared in a mist net, because by my standards, the bird was not quite captive, yet.

∽

Malheur NWR occupies 187,757 acres, or nearly 4,000 more acres than in 1962. The refuge is in part of the Harney Basin that, 9,600 years ago, give or take a decade or two, contained one large lake—a 225,000-acre lake. Drought began to change the region, leaving expansive marshes and resources to support native occupants, including the Burns Paiute Tribe and wildlife of today. By European explorer standards, the region was not welcoming. Peter Skene Ogden, that gad-about employee of the Hudson Bay Company, visiting Malheur in 1826, found the much sought-after beaver were absent and that the water was either salty or had a bad taste. Ogden marked his map with the word *malheur*, meaning misfortune, and the region was not of interest to setters until 20 years later. That is when a westward-bound wagon train also found "malheur." Various military expeditions were in the Malheur region in the mid-1800s, including one of John Fremont's associates, Colonel James William Abert, who is the namesake for Lake Abert near where I spent the night on the way to Malheur. Abert also has a towhee named in his honor. It is a Southwestern species, but I am getting ahead of myself.

During school days, I paid about average attention while in class listening to a beleaguered instructor attempting to teach a modicum of Oregon history to students who are more interested in making their own immediate history. An occasional word or phrase from the teacher did pique my interest and, as I became more of a quasi-history buff, my curiosity begged for more information. For example, were plume hunters limited to the Everglades and other eastern heron colonies or did they "hunt" in the West? It turns out that plume hunters nearly exterminated Common Egrets around the Malheur region during the late nineteenth century and into the early 1900s. Indiscriminate hunting was not the only factor in decimating birds at Malheur. Another problem was and is elusiveness of shoreline real estate for nesting birds. Lake levels in the refuge are primarily dependent on the amount of winter precipitation, rate of evaporation, and the amount of water diverted for agriculture and other non-wildlife reasons. All those factors translate to the location of shorelines being up or down, even non-existent, depending on the water level or lack thereof. Too much water and a nest could drown. Too little or no water and a nest might fail. The lake was completely dry in 1934. In 1962, Malheur Lake was 11 percent of its normal acreage, which sources say is slightly less than 50,000 acres. During the early 1980s, lakes in the interior West, including the Great Salt Lake, became engorged with unusual amounts of rain. In 1982, Malheur Lake covered 64,000 acres when Harney Lake and the Narrows merged. During the 1980s, Cole Island Dike that I once drove was inundated and was eventually destroyed by water and ice erosion. There are no plans to rebuild the dike because reconstruction was estimated to cost $7 million.

The checklist of birds of the refuge used in 1962 listed 213 species recorded since 1908. A wonderful 1990 monograph, *Birds of Malheur National Wildlife Refuge, Oregon* by Carroll D. Littlefield, listed 312 species recorded in the refuge since 1874 by Bendire and offers far more detail than that four-page available to me in 1962. Littlefield was the biologist of Malheur NWR a few years after Gene Kridler held the helm. The reputation of the refuge as a great birding area has grown since 1962. The CCC mess hall and other adjacent buildings have been used since the 1970s as an educational facility by a consortium of colleges. The field station is replete with 250 beds and has rental trailers and campsites for the general public. In 1962, the only people I recall seeing were refuge staff members; there was not a soul at the CCC area day or night. Reservations may be in order today.

The CCC built far more than the mess hall where I slept. They constructed the Sodhouse (near refuge headquarters), canals and dikes, miles of fences, and the lookout tower. The CCC built the infrastructure of the refuge. Countless, well, maybe some are counted, locations across the US are touched by the labor of the CCC. Huge amounts of their sturdy constructions stand at the beginning of the 2000s, and their excellent work marks a kind of hallowed ground where they toiled and improved the country.

Gene Kridler later became the biologist at Hawaii NWR and was well known as a master bird bander. He and I crossed paths a couple of times during my career at Smithsonian. A friend of Gene's and his predecessor as a biologist at Malheur NWR is David B. Marshall, who, with Gene, contributed considerable information about the birds of the refuge. Earlier, Ray Charles Erickson had been a biologist at Malheur. He comes to the story of this trip a few chapters beyond. Both Gene and Dave sent specimens to the museum, where I, often with Richard C. Banks, verified species identifications and compared them to other specimens to identify the birds to subspecies. Most of the Malheur specimens sent to the museum are now in the Division of Birds collection at Smithsonian's Museum of Natural History.

The broad brushstroke of the history of my old outfit, the Biological Survey, deserves a little more attention, especially since Malheur NWR and Gene Kridler had significant influence over my unresolved brain. Sure, as an even younger Danny McSkunk, I had cajoled my parents into driving me across the Cascades to Tule and Lower Klamath NWRs. I had a taste of the refuge system, but my small nibble had yet to sway any thought of the future. Besides, I could then barely spell the word ornithology and was then leaning away from wanting to be a cowboy or firefighter to becoming a park ranger. Time at Malheur NWR changed that by at least partially screwing in the light bulb. So, what I was getting myself into was an organization founded in the 1800s, with an initial focus on birds controlling agricultural pests. The roots of the survey (and Patuxent Wildlife Research Center) also trace back to a formal agreement with the Smithsonian Institution in 1889. By 1905, my old unit was known as the Bureau of Biological Survey. Just four years before I was born, the Bureau of Biological Survey was replaced with the Fish and Wildlife Service and re-designated in 1956 as the US Fish and Wildlife Service. Beginning in the late 1960s, when Dick Banks and I worked in Smithsonian's Division of Birds, we were employed by the US FWS and specifically by the Biological Survey. The National Wildlife Refuge group was and still is, last I checked, under the US FWS. Just after I retired in the mid-1990s, my old outfit was placed under the US Geological Survey. I thought that the odd coupling of the Biological Survey with geology would mean us bird people would at least have free topographical maps. No, we still had to pay for them out of our pitifully small budget. Any aspect of research by members of the former Biological Survey, such as taxonomic studies at Smithsonian's Division of Birds, became in the purview of the Geological Survey. Dick, myself, and many others continue to regard ourselves as members of the Biological Survey. For those possibly confused by who answered to who, the Smithsonian employees did not answer to the Biological Survey but employees such as me answered to the Geological Survey.

During my work at the museum, I published a review of Carroll D. Littlefield's 1984 *Birds of Malheur National Wildlife Refuge, Oregon*. I was not and never will be an expert on Malheur, but I was interested on Littlefield's taxonomy. My interest went beyond the refuge, and almost immediately at the beginning of my early retirement, I began working the next five years as a taxonomic editor on a book on birds of Oregon. The senior editor was none other than Dave Marshall, who, with Mathew Hunter and long-time friend Alan Contreras, corralled hundreds of species accounts into the book *Birds of Oregon: A General Reference*. Dave was instrumental in awarding a small Fish and Wildlife Service to study birds on offshore islands of Oregon in the late sixties. Carroll Littlefield wrote the species account on Sandhill Crane in *Birds of Oregon*. Although Gene Kridler did not directly contribute to the book, his and Littlefield's information is listed in the literature cited. Gene's active banding and collecting documented new records in the book. So many aspects of life bring old acquaintances full circle for the opportunity to compare stories, discuss how much or little we have learned, and see how bad or how well we have aged.

The *Empidonax* flycatcher I observed at Malheur NWR would have been much easier to identify in the company of Alan R. Phillips or Ned K. Johnson. Of course, that allows imagination to flicker beyond reality. Had that dream team been with me, Gray and Hammond's flycatchers would probably have been on my trip list. Western Flycatcher would be another that their keen ears and eyes would have snapped up faster than a flycatcher catches flies. Years after 1962, Ned would discover that the so-called Western Flycatcher represented two distinct species, the Cordilleran and

Pacific-slope flycatchers. Never mind that Allan held considerable disdain toward Ned, and that, although he was too kind to say so, Ned may have felt the same toward Alan. The reasons were petty, unimportant, and it would be unreasonable that they would be in the field together, especially coaching a wet-behind-the-ears, Danny McSkunk teenager stirring up Malheur dust in his little VW Beetle. Regrettably, I never had the pleasure to be in the field with either of my late lamented friends. ARP, as associates called Allan Phillips, and not always affectionately by all, was a regular correspondent and museum visitor. He was a guest at my home during many of his long visits to the museum. I spent hours poring over his shoulder while he examined specimens. ARP was for me the equivalent of being at a top-notch university run by a highly skilled but a considerably opinionated professor. Ned was more introspective and more deliberate in his research and conversation. The two are missed.

My concern about checklists and the terms used for abundance grew as I traveled in national wildlife refuges. That was when I realized that most of the checklists were using terms that suggest how easy it might be to see a given species. At least that is my interpretation, but should those terms of abundance be subject to different definitions? My idea back in the day was that the terms in the checklists should reflect a semblance of science. In part, they did, but there seemed to be room for improvement. I settled with the idea that the terms of abundance were terms reflecting how easy it is to detect a given species. Perhaps that was what a checklist compiler meant, but those early checklists were misleading. The Willets at Malheur were noticeable because of their repeated flights and flashing black and white wing patterns. According to Littlefield's book on Malheur birds, the status of Willets is common, not uncommon as the 1962 checklist indicated. Avocets were less vocal than Willets and did not fly around a lot. The tall grass probably prevented seeing any Western Sandpipers, but, more than likely, the species is not abundant contrary to the checklist because these migrants are mostly gone by early June. Most checklists of birds from refuges today try to list the status (e.g., common, uncommon) of each species with greater accuracy. The designations lean more towards indicating actual abundance rather than the ease of observing a given species. Littlefield attempted to make status designations less qualitative but omitted actual numbers of birds seen in any one-time period. Because I was especially concerned about avoiding nebulous terms for the status of birds in lists, I followed Arbib's system, which published a list of standards defining the terms common, uncommon, rare, and more. These easy-to-use standards put a number with a term so that it was no longer necessary to guess the numerical status and ease of detecting a given species. Gene's old friend and colleague, Dave Marshall, along with yours truly, used Arbib's standards in the 2003 *Birds of Oregon*.

I enjoyed ticking off 67 species during my two days at Malheur. If I had worked harder or had not forgotten my lunch, maybe gotten up earlier in the morning, I would have observed more species. Maybe that funny-tasting hamburger blurred my vision. Regardless of the number of species, I found meeting Gene Kridler, seeing Sandhill Cranes, and me, not the cranes, sleeping on mess hall benches in the old CCC building were my best times at the famed refuge.

Two species seen in the refuge were not countable on my list of birds. The first, and by far the largest, were Trumpeter Swans. They were introduced to the refuge by Dave Marshall in 1957 when he drove a pickup load of swans back from Red Rock NWR. I did not allow myself to count species considered not yet established. Trumpeter Swans were seen at Red Rock Lakes NWR a few days after leaving Malheur in 1962. The second species, and definitely teeny-tiny, was a Flammulated Owl. Perhaps I should have counted this truly rare species but counting a captive bird did not seem right. The next Flammulated Owl in the refuge appeared in May 1976, 13 years after the one I saw in the cage at headquarters. A wild, free-range Flammulated Owl did not grace me until 2009. It was on the slope of Huckleberry Mountain, less than an hour's drive on a winding and narrow dirt road from my first camp on 2 June 1962. Adding that species to my life list required me to spend several nights during four different summers stumbling in the dark forest while hoping not to encounter a Sasquatch.

Concerning worrying about my safety, it did not take more than two nights before I stopped fretting and found it easy to sleep through the sound of rushing traffic. I was probably in more danger from coming to grips with *E. coli* or some milder or less lethal kind of food poisoning than having trouble with humans. I would like to think that I kept my food clean and fresh and that I slept with one ear open, but who knows how many, if any, close calls I had. Perhaps an iron stomach and that the stuff in my car was not rob-worthy saved me from peril.

Years after my introduction to Malheur NWR, real peril did occur at the refuge in the form of an invasion of armed human thugs on 2 January 2016. The long and sordid story began with armed right-wing extremist men and women occupying refuge headquarters. The group claimed they wanted the US government to turn over federal lands (e.g., Bureau of Land Management, Fish and Wildlife Service) to individual states, apparently thinking the states would change land-use policies. I am just guessing since a journalist embedded with the group of illegal interlopers indicated they were mostly ill-advised. Anyway, local ranchers were not impressed and, in fact, were displeased, as was the nation. The destructive siege of Malheur was over by 11 February. A couple dozen of the hooligans were arrested. Most were found not guilty, though 12 pleaded guilty. The longest jail time any of the terrorists was sentenced was only about three years. Some of the sentences included house arrests, meaning all the ice cream you can eat. Amazingly, two of the principles of the armed invasion of Malheur NWR were acquitted of federal charges. Speaking of charges, the ridiculous and dangerous plundering cost taxpayers an estimated $9 million for security and other federal, state, and local law enforcement issues and cleaning up the mess left from the 41 days of armed occupation. A few examples of cleaning up included sanitizing places despoiled by the occupiers' garbage and raw sewage, repairing land where a road was built and repairing heavy machinery damaged by the gang, revamping water supplies including restoring water supplies to habitats, trying to mend disturbances of tribal archaeological sites, rebuilding files and data scattered about the headquarters, and more than one should have to comprehend. Shamefully, certain politicians thought the ring-leaders ought to be pardoned.

The refuge and staff returned to a new brand of normal, when, finally, by 2017, the office and the visitor center opened for business. That was possible after the offices had been repaired and cleaned of spoiled food, vandalized equipment, and trash. Outside, human feces required burying, and damaged roads and fences needed repairs. Burns, a small hamlet of around 3,500 souls in 1960 and down by about 800 fewer people in 2020, must have suffered economically. Birders were not interested in renting a room or buying a meal because the occupation and its aftermath translated to no access to the refuge. Currently, most everyone in the region is reportedly at peace with the refuge, including almost everyone in Burns. What would Robert Burns, the namesake of the town, have thought about what happened? The refuge staff is weary and on alert to criminal interlopers should they raise their ugly heads. As for Linda and me, our last visit to the refuge was in 2012. Of course, we loved every minute and vowed to return. We need to do that.

Malheur NWR is a major place, a place of safety for birds while migrating or when breeding, and is a great location for birders. My story pales to those by Dave Marshall and those of several others.[1] In 1962, I did not realize all of what the refuge had to offer. Malheur influenced my thinking about a career. Working on a refuge had considerable appeal, but that thought was only the turning point of things to come. Perhaps if I had I not

---

1. There are many great accounts in Alan Contreras, ed. *Edge of Awe: Experiences of the Malheur Steens Country*. (Corvallis: Oregon State University Press, 2019).

already been working at Smithsonian, I would have been discouraged by the idea of working for the refuge system. Four respected authors, including Littlefield, penned a paper on refuges that everyone should read. Cited numerous times and followed by related topics, the learned authors outline the good, bad, and ugly that concerns our national wildlife refuges.[2] Though published in 1978, it could be reprinted with a current date and require few amendments. In the meantime, I should have stayed at Malheur another day or more. There was so much to see, so much to learn, but my Zugunruhe jitters drove me eastward.

2. C. E. Braun et al. "Management of National Wildlife Refuges in the United States: Its Impacts on Birds." *Wilson Bulletin* 90 (1978) 309–21.

Chapter 3

Meandering Snake

8 June 1962

MY LAST GLANCE BACK at Malheur led my eyes high over the dry sagebrush where a dark bird soared. The trusty 7 x 35 binoculars would not bring the bird in close enough for a definite identification, but my 20 x 50 scope mounted on a gun stock was always handy for just such an occasion. I nestled the butt of the stock that I had hand-carved just months earlier into my right shoulder, took careful aim, and there it was, an adult Swainson's Hawk. The drive from Burns was otherwise uneventful as the green oasis of Malheur became a speck in my rearview mirror. Arid sand and sagebrush surrounded me. A stop east of town for a noonish meal put me next to an upset Sagebrush Sparrow. More than likely, it became upset because I parked too close to its nest. This species was 109 for the trip, one species I had searched for, along with Sage Thrashers, at Malheur. The thrasher would have to wait.

Leaving Oregon, my home state, was going to be a watermark, a threshold of sorts, something that I was anxious to cross. I had birded in Malheur, and even found some of the species I was hoping to find there. I felt I had earned my wings to go onward, that this trip was not just a fantasy, but that my plans could make the dream a reality. The road eastward held promise, and soon I would be crossing the magic border into a new state. A steep descent brought me out of the winding Malheur River Canyon and into the Snake River Valley near Nampa, Idaho. The thickets of sagebrush began to thin to make room for cultivated crops irrigated by a myriad of water-choked canals. The hills, now behind to the west, blotted out the sun and shaded the edge of the valley.

Crossing the Snake River today would not be the only crossing during the trip. The Snake River meanders or snakes its way for 1,038 miles from its headwaters near the 10,000-foot Continental Divide at Two Ocean Plateau in Yellowstone Park to Teton National Park, southern Idaho, and north to form part of the border between Oregon and Idaho. Along that border, the river flows through Hells Canyon, the deepest gorge in North America. The mountains at the gorge rise to 9,000 feet or 1.5 miles above the river. The Snake finally bends west in Washington state at 340 feet above sea level where it empties into the Columbia River near Kennewick.

It was late in the day once crossing the Snake River and into Idaho. Naturally, I needed light to set up camp and cook the evening meal, but where in this populated farmland? My only idea was to stop at a farm home to ask if I might pitch my tent in their pasture for the night. Luck was with me when I stopped at a small white house just off the highway west of Nampa where a five-foot white-haired lady answered. After explaining the need for a place to camp, she gazed eastward across the flat and wide expanse of agricultural land marked by the occasional cottonwood groves planted to slow the wind. Motioning down the road, she directed my attention to a smaller house that she said was vacant, and that I was welcome to use the lawn for my campground.

I was grateful to have a place to eat and sleep. Before turning in I wrote Linda a short letter to let her know that I was alive and that I had crossed the border into the next state. I wondered what she was thinking. Tomorrow will mark the first week of being on the road. How could that be? What happened to the time? My mind was full of questions and anticipation as I dozed off for a night of sleep interrupted more often than I cared by freight truck tires wearing away while the diesel engines roared down the highway. Were the trucks full of potatoes?

9 June 1962

Morning came as bright sun warming me as I gathered my things and packed them for a short ride to Deer Flat NWR. The refuge is an important site for waterfowl migrants and winter residents. Refuge manager Gene Crawford told me that Mallards are the most abundant species found during the peak wintering with flocks of about 300,000. Mallards and other species wet their feet in Lake Lowell, a reservoir of about 10,000 acres called Deer Flat. Monthly aerial censuses of 28 miles of the Snake River NWR (part of Deer Flat NWR), with its 35 islands in the Snake River, and 11,000 acres of Deer Flat are conducted by Gene Crawford. One of the reasons for these counts is to decide what private areas might become additions to the refuge.

The caring manager of Deer Flat discussed his negative opinion of hunting clubs and their control of so much waterfowl habitat. He was also concerned about the power hunters had on hunting seasons and how they pressured refuges to open more land for hunting. My host explained that refuges, public lands, once set aside to benefit habitat, are now in danger of being altered or destroyed by special interest groups, such as hunters, agriculture, and waterpower systems wanting to either inundate or drain marshes. Demands for agriculture have taken their toll. I related little I knew about the battle for water rights at Upper Klamath Lake and refuges including Tule and Lower Klamath Lake NWRs in far southern Oregon and northern California. Deer Flat was no exception in the water wars between agriculture and refuges.

The day passed quickly talking to Mr. Crawford. There were questions and answers about working for the refuge system. I was not sure what I wanted to do for the rest of my life but working for the Fish and Wildlife Service as a refuge manager or as a biologist sounded inviting. It was interesting to talk to someone who was doing what I might like as a career. It was a good day. I pitched my tent near a refuge service building and drifted to sleep after thinking of the birds I saw.

10 June 1962

The refuge checklist, updated in 1961, did not include a species seen today. In one of the few marshy areas near Deer Flat, I found two pairs of Virginia Rails. Confirmation of my sight record should require a specimen identified by an expert. Before leaving the refuge, another marsh tempted my curiosity enough for a delay of the 200-mile trek to the next destination. At the edge of the marsh was a lone fence post standing in shallow water. Perched at its top was a Wilson's Snipe that sat quite still for several seconds before suddenly bursting nearly straight up into the air. As suddenly as it took flight, the bird began a steep dive back to its original perch. An eerie hum whistled from its feathers as, with bent wings, the displaying bird plummeted earthward. I walked into the marsh toward the post. Again, the bird sat motionless on the fence post, then exploded high into the sky, and plummeted back on whistling wings. The closer my approach, the louder the winnowing sound.

Other birds added life into the marsh for the early morning chorus. Common Yellowthroats seem to say *thimk* at my intrusion. Yellow-headed Blackbirds were making their grating buzz-saw call in their effort to maintain their territories. Redwings, females mostly, slipped from the thicker vegetation and disappeared when I passed. Their nests were nearby. Several species of ducks exploded from an open pool. One of them was a male Cinnamon Teal and, holding true to its fast-flying reputation, it quickly passed a couple of Mallards that had labored from the same pool. Before my marsh exploration was almost over, I watched a Virginia Rail closely following another, strolling from a tuft of grass from the edge of an adjacent meadow. Both birds disappeared into the cattails. Once I rounded the final corner of my circular path, two more rails sneaked into the protective vegetation.

From Deer Flat, I drove northeast to Mountain Home where I began a shortcut on Idaho Highway 68. At first, the road was a narrow but paved passage. Not far up the road, I entered Boise National Forest where pavement became dirt. For the next 20 or so dusty miles, I wondered about what the shortcut was cutting. The road was rough and full of bumps, not unlike mountain logging roads traveled in southwestern Oregon. This route was a long shortcut, but I did enjoy finding a pair of Mountain Bluebirds. They were nesting in a hole of a wooden directional sign set at a junction. When I stopped to peek in the nesting cavity, a steely blue male was on the nest. The male bolted out when he saw a strange eye peering into the cavity. He left five gaping and hungry mouths. The male flew across the road and chattered disapproving notes until I departed.

Dust, unexpected bumps, more dust, and Mountain Bluebirds were left behind me as the dirt road turned to the pavement at Hill City. Not all shortcuts are short but not all are necessarily bad. Today was a perfect time, watching the passage of seasons, with summer near the Snake River and late spring and nesting bluebirds at high elevations. My nights felt like winter, a situation making me even more anxious to get east of the Rockies. There were still places to see, and there were more western birds on the horizon. After nearly 200 miles, I reached the 4,783 foot elevation of Carey, the last town before Craters of the Moon NM. It was cooler than expected, but the monument is yet higher and should be cooler, with dreaded cold nights. As usual, I was hungry and, not knowing how long I would stay in the monument while eating my own cooking, I decided to splurge at a restaurant in Carey and ordered something that I would not cook on my two-burner gas camp stove. It was nice to vary my diet. Before leaving town, a local grocery had the peanut butter and mustard I needed to add to my provisions.

In less than an hour, the bright afternoon sky lit my arrival at the Craters of the Moon NM where I selected a tent site that overlooked the lunar landscape of dark craters and jagged black lava flows. According to a brochure I picked up when entering the monument, the borders of Craters of the Moon NM hold 53,545 acres. The monument runs essentially from northwest to southeast for 60 miles, with a width ranging from one and a half miles to five miles and embracing a part of the Pioneer Mountain foothills to the north, and a vast region of lava flows and cinder cones to the south at the northern edge of the Snake River Plain. Elevation ranges from 7,700 feet to 5,300 feet. Headquarters and the nearby campground where I slumbered are about 5,900 feet in elevation. The formation of the Craters of the Moon Lava Field was from a rift that was the source of over 60 lava flows, 25 cinder cones of varying sizes, and numerous eruptions. In 1962, 175,278 people visited Craters of the Moon NM.

What the brochure did not say is that the cinder and ashy dust made driving tent stakes almost impossible. I ended up driving the stakes deep and out of sight into the loose ground. The tent finally had to be secured by rocks placed over the buried stakes. Finding rocks was not a problem.

Washing dishes in the twilight has not always been my ideal, but the Rock Wren singing from a nearby lava spire made the chore much easier. The muffled boom of a Common Nighthawk added percussion to the chorus. With the aid of a flashlight, I glanced through the monument's leaflet. Terms such as rifts, spatter cones, lava tubes, pit craters, and other new and intriguing terms filled the pages. Little was mentioned about birds. My eyes became heavier. Tomorrow will wait.

11 June 1962

A morning chorus of Rock Wrens filled the dark desolation of lava. The sun quickly warmed up everything as the campground began to come alive. People staggered and stretched out of their tents, looked around with squinting eyes, and quickly made their way to the closest restroom. Soon breakfast was frying and popping all around. I heard campers grumbling about the "dirty park." It seemed fine to me. My cup of coffee cleared the way to reason, allowing me to realize that the breeze that night had carried dust into the campground. The grit did not get into the sleeping bag, but it did pepper my exposed hair and the tent floor needed sweeping out. My short hair let most of the grit succumb to gravity and fortunately out of my eyes.

Night temperatures in Craters of the Moon NM were for the first time relatively comfortable. The black landscape soaked up the sun by midmorning to what could be called room temperature. I remembered a trip in

1956 (before I began birding) with my parents in late June. Our visit to the monument was brief because the blistering sun pelted the region to a hot, dehydrating, and inhospitable place.

Today, a full day of birding and exploring part of the monument was rewarding geologically and ornithologically. Just 15,000 years ago, a brief time geologically, a rift opened to spew lava and volcanic debris of all kinds. Cinder cones dotting the weird lunarscape churned out cinders forming lava froth called pumice, a rock that is so full of air pockets that it will float on water. The largest of the cinder cones is Big Cinder Butte, rising about 800 feet above its base. Lava flows cover the monument and suggest a peaceful rather than explosive period when the rift slowly oozed molten rock from its openings. I hiked across the most recent of these flows. Called the North Crater Flow, it is the pahoehoe (pah-hoe-ay-hoe-ay) type of lava. Pahoehoe is a smooth, billowing, or ropey conformation. This type of lava flow is relatively easy to walk on, while the aa (ah'-ah) is extremely rough, broken, and irregularly shaped formations of jagged corners and sharp spines. That would tear a good pair of boots to shreds in short order and a fall could range from painful to deadly. I suppose the name "aa" came from someone experiencing the pain of its sharp surfaces. It could have been one of those times when you fall and cannot get up. I managed to stay on my feet, appreciated my heavy boots, and was glad that I came across more pahoehoe, with its smoothish twists, pleats, and folds.

Lava tubes formed by molten steam, some of them collapsed, weaved their way under and to the surface of the expansive solid rock that accented the rough landscape. I did not venture into any of the lava tubes. No birds underground, well, usually. The wind had swirled volcanic ash into holes and cracks in the lava floor. An Indian paintbrush grew in one such crevice giving its orange and silvery-green color to the rough and dark blackish basaltic background. The scanty "soil" was a precarious niche. The plant would need enough water to complete at least its reproductive cycle. An obscure lizard darted on the side of a frozen lava wall. An insect, possibly blown off course or looking for a plant to pollinate, winged by to disappear on the lava. Maybe it would be a meal for the lizard. Without an appreciation for the plants and animals, the lava flows would be lonely and boring. This place was neither.

Few birds were on the North Crater Flow. I reasoned that it was because of the sparse vegetation that consisted of an occasional paintbrush and various species of composites or daisies. Of course, Rock Wrens, apparently the most common species in the monument, were always nearby. The wrens on the flow were less approachable and usually sung from hidden perches when compared to the same species in and around the campground. One had perched on the tent and burst into a full song. After crossing the flow, I found myself surrounded by birds where limber pine was the dominant plant. Hugging the cinder-covered ground were common shrubs, including sage, beermat, and rabbitbrush. The area seemed a mecca for more Green-tailed Towhees than I had ever seen. Two pairs of Mountain Bluebirds flew nearby and, in a shrub, a Warbling Vireo quietly foraged. A yellow-throated Yellow-rumped Warbler flitted from tree to tree in every direction. A male Western Tanager outdid the warblers for most and brightest colors. Chipping Sparrows and even an American Robin found the environment not too disagreeable. Violet-green Swallows glided and circled overhead. A bustling colony must have come somewhere on the face of a distant crater wall. Back at camp, I noticed Violet-green Swallows winging directly toward Big Cinder Butte. Walking five difficult miles brought four new species to the trip list. These include the towhee, nutcracker, vireo, and Mountain Chickadee. I wondered how I could have missed such species these last 10 days.

I phoned my parents to let them know that I was all right. I also wanted them to know that, so far, I was doing what I planned to do and to reminisce that I was calling from a place the family had enjoyed visiting years earlier.

In my first letter to my parents, which was a follow up to the brief phone call, I wrote, "I have worked out a deal so that I can eat as cheaply, but still as well as I had previously planned. I cook my own breakfast. The last two mornings I had potatoes and eggs fried in butter (very good) topped off with a cup of coffee. Then I fix a lunch, which is usually a baloney sandwich and a peanut butter sandwich. Dinner most of my days has been at a café. This I do for the lump sum of about a dollar per day. When I fix all my meals it even costs me less, but it is more trouble. I eat what I like and when I get hungry, and for unknown reasons, I have been hungry all day. Fortunately for the pocketbook, I am too far from any store to buy a snack, and too stubborn to eat more than my allotted sandwiches per day." Further in the letter, I wrote that "my worst enemies have been the absence of camping areas, cold and windy weather, and heat, which caused the spoilage of perishable food earlier at Malheur NWR." I also asked them, and this is embarrassing, "does sausage spoil as easily as hamburger?"

Confidence and fortitude were gaining ground as I became more comfortable with outdoor living and my solo birding. I am not lonely.

12 June 1962

Packed and fired up, the VW was ready for a short trip to civilization at Idaho Falls. After too many days of living without a clean change of clothes,

I was inspired to visit the local laundromat and find a hot shower. Probably anyone that came near me appreciated my inspiration. Thanks to the YMCA, an organization that I joined before leaving Oregon, I enjoyed the hot water and soap. It felt great to be clean again. Detouring to the eastern part of Idaho Falls to get that much-needed shower at the YMCA had meant crossing the Snake River twice since leaving Oregon. I checked my road maps. The second crossing will be the last crossing until later when and if I make it to Yellowstone NP.

An hour north of Idaho Falls and still on the Snake River Plain was my last of major birding stops in Idaho. Today, I am driving almost 40 north of the Snake River to Camas NWR, a watery oasis surrounded by sagebrush. Although the Camas refuge checklist offered little promise in seeing anything new, my visit to Camas was unforgettable. When I arrived in the late afternoon, Robert Twist, the manager, was out in the field so I decided to try my luck alone. The road along a dike was barely high enough to see over the tall willows and marsh vegetation. Only two species of ducks were missing from my trip list that might be at Camas. Both were easy. In no time, I had Mallards, Northern Pintails, Gadwalls, Redheads, and others checked off beside the two I was looking for, Green-winged Teal and American Wigeon.

By the time I reached a section of open grassland, several Long-billed Curlews and Willets were becoming agitated by a dark cloud looming out of the north. The wind had begun to blow through the cattails across the road so strongly a Savannah Sparrow practically bounced on the dusty road before regaining its composure and hiding in the vegetation at the other side. At a culvert, a Black-crowned Night Heron squawked and lumbered out of its protective nook. A twinge of guilt was felt for flushing the heron, even if it was accidental. The wind became stronger as the dark cloud moved closer and towered over the grass bent by the force of the gale. I decided to wait for the storm to pass. Even though I aimed the car into the gale-force wind, it shook and rocked at each blast. Now every bird was out of sight, probably clinging to some plant anchor for dear life. The gales swept across the marsh, creating flowing waves of water in the cattails. Everything pulsated to the command of the unrelenting wind. Still, no birds were in sight, so, with nothing else to do I tallied the trip list. The storm subsided ever so little during the drive back to refuge headquarters to meet Mr. Twist.

As luck would have it, the manager invited me to his home and served a great home-cooked meal, the first since leaving Oregon. By the end of the meal, the storm had moved on to the south. Robert Twist decided to take me for a drive for close-up waterfowling. Jumping into his pickup, he told me that the best way to see ducks was to catch them by surprise. He was correct. The ducks did not flush until they were abreast of the pickup. Sometimes we even passed them; leaving puzzled Northern Shovellers and scaups behind as we roared at speeds only a stunt driver would attempt and still stay on the road. At no time were any birds harmed by the speeding truck, other than being momentarily frightened. We skidded around a muddy turn onto a side road. Part of the road was inundated but we splashed through and flooded the engine. Luckily, the heat from the engine must have turned the unwanted water into steam. The engine came back to life. Our ambush was successful as Mallards, Canvasbacks, and 10 other surprised kinds of ducks shared their field marks as we rocketed past them. On the way back through the flooded road, we rushed through, driving even faster and causing spray to shoot as high as the pickup cab and out in a wide fan of flying water. We crossed six or more culverts. Almost every one was accompanied by a Black-crowned Night Heron, a species that learned that there are easy pickings for prey in the shallow water flowing through the culvert. Robert said that water flows through the culverts according to the inflow of Camas Creek, the source for numerous lakes and ponds in the refuge. When more water flows over the corrugated steel culverts, fish, frogs, and aquatic insects travel through the pipes. Evidently, the water levels of the numerous ponds and lakes remain about the same when only minor flows occur from one body of water to another.

In addition to the two needed ducks, I added American Bittern to the trip list. The only other species in Camas NWR that I looked for but missed were Greater Sage-Grouse. Maybe I should have spent more time in the upland habitat where I saw a frightened pronghorn antelope bolting across my path. The marshes kept me busy. There, I would have missed what was to be an overwhelming density and amount of Marsh Wrens. Perhaps I should have spent less time in the marshes and racing ducks in a pickup. I would also miss the wild evening ride into the marsh and being eye to eye with so many ducks. They were so close I could hear them breathe. I wondered if any other visitors had the treat of waterfowling by a speeding pickup.

Crowds of Marsh Wrens and ducks up close, and a view of the Teton Mountains looming steeply to the east. What more could I need? I knew that on the other side of those grand mountains was a south-flowing Snake River where I planned be in a few days.

Back in the sixties, almost anyone using a telescope mounted on a rifle stock was okay most of the time. Only once was I rousted by someone suspecting my rig was a gun or a rocket launcher. That was when a ranger in

Lassen Volcanic NP about a year before making the trip in 1962 came to a screeching stop at an overlook I was enjoying. He jumped out of his vehicle and walked up, said something sounding like "huh" as he realized my scope was harmless. *Audubon Magazine* advertised stocks especially configured for strapping on a spotting scope. I even used the scope and stock set-up in Washington, DC, without incident. Today, no one should carry or use anything that looks anything like a gun. The authorities might hassle you at best, and, at worst, they might shoot you before you could explain you are only watching birds. Nonetheless, my rig for bringing birds closer was practical and even admired at Malheur and Deer Flat refuges.

In addition to changes in perception concerning weaponry used by birders, changes in actual numbers of wintering Mallards population censused at Deer Flat NWR by Gene Crawford were changing. A count of 300,000 was high, but only 100,000 were tallied in 2004. Data from winters of 2016 and 2017 are even lower, with counts hovering around 25,000. The results are surprising since male Mallards are sexually aggressive and mate or try to mate most females in their sight. Perhaps the ducks were wintering elsewhere.

My concerns about conservation as discussed with Gene in 1962 have not lessened; the water wars continue, wilderness areas, national parks, and refuges are underfunded and are under constant attack for their timber and water and from attempts to privatize the land. Fortunately, conservation organizations have grown in number, membership, and power, but the populations of those people choosing to be ignorant or who just do not care about conservation have likewise grown in number and power. Nothing has changed.

Specific to Deer Flat NWR, the number of acres during my visit was 10,800 acres. The acreage was 11,614 acres by 2020. An increase in acres is good. However, invasive plants are choking out prime forage vegetation. Invasive plants along with introduced species of animals is a worldwide problem that causes habitat loss and declines in native species. Carelessness and deliberate misbehavior of invasive humans continue to be the origin of invasive species.

Checklists and comments on abundance again reared their ugly head. Virginia Rails in Deer Flat refuge went from not being on the checklist to uncommon in spring and common during the summer as of 2004 and more recently in a 2020 checklist. If the relative descriptors of abundance are based on actual numbers, perhaps it is possible to think Virginia Rails are doing well at Deer Flat. Were these secretive birds simply overlooked or was the population assigned a different number? According to the North American Breeding Bird Survey, Virginia Rail populations are trending downward, including in Idaho. A twenty-first-century checklist of birds occurring in Deer Flat NWR now lists Virginia Rail. I thought back in the day that a specimen was required to add the species to the checklist. Certainly, most distributional records were specimen-based, but that convention was slowly evolving, partly at the hands of anti-collectors and technology. As for the former, do not get me started, at least for now. As for technology, cameras were improving until now almost anyone with a little patience and a decent digital camera is capable of documenting a sight record. Was my 1962 sighting of Virginia Rails in Deer Flat NWR the reason the species was on an official checklist? I hope so.

Admittedly, rails are often hard to detect, and population estimates may not be accurate. The population of Virginia Rail is apparently stable in Deer Flat, but as a state, Idaho lost more than 50 percent of its wetlands from 1970 to 1980. According to the US Fish and Wildlife Service, in the last 200 years in the contiguous US, about 60 acres of wetlands are lost per hour! Protection of existing wetlands is imperative, whether for the benefit of Virginia Rails, prevention of coastal flooding, or reservoirs. That Virginia Rail populations are stable in Deer Flat NWR is inconsistent with rapid habit loss. There seem to be possible theories that might explain the inconsistency. One, people's talent for detecting these secretive birds has changed or improved, two, the density of breeding Virginia Rails is greater than formerly believed, and three, I am wrong about one and two. I could rail on about habitat and sneaky rails, but I refrain from doing so.

Better information on the status of birds in Idaho would have been appreciated in 1962, but such a source did not become available until 1972 when Thomas D. Burleigh's book on the birds of Idaho hit the streets. Burleigh, retired from the Biological Survey, was an avid collector and preparator of bird specimens. His specimens were generally well made and useful in taxonomic studies. I will not go into the details of how to prepare a study specimen, but some of Burleigh's specimens had shortcomings. The legs were not anchored into the body as well as possible; the specimens were often too round and tended to roll over. The legs needed to be securely attached to the body to support a specimen label tied to them. The specimens needed to be less round so that they stay either on their backs or on their ventral side. When a bird reaches the stage of a museum specimen, ornithologists should not have to contend with the bird moving. Burleigh described and named several subspecies of birds during his career, several of which I needed to evaluate. The majority of new subspecies Burleigh proposed, as found by my studies and those of others, were usually paler than adjacent populations. The consensus among ornithologists is that Burleigh washed his specimens with something that removed pigments from the feathers. He collected specimens from wherever he lived, and during his retirement, he lived and collected birds from several different localities in the western United States, including Idaho. These specimens of which I had the pleasure to curate into the collection at Smithsonian are a great and priceless contribution.

Although I did not venture into any lava tubes at Craters of the Moon NM, a summer job in the fire control unit of the Park Service during the college years put me into lava tubes at Lava Beds NM in northeastern California. One of our jobs at Lava Beds was to remove any refuse left by the public. Those were the days of Polaroid cameras, the throw-away cover of their film, and the days of glassy flashbulbs. The fire crew found dozens of such items from pretend nature photographers. Over a decade later I learned that lava tubes were wonderful places for Barn Owls to regurgitate the bones of their prey. The deposit of the bones was a mine for any astute paleornithologist such as Storrs Olson, who started working at Smithsonian the year I began there with the Biological Survey.

People visiting Deer Flat NWR have changed. A 1961 leaflet from the refuge stated that 150,000 hunters, anglers, wildlife viewers, and others visit the refuge each year. Even more people visit the refuge today, and if the trend is the same in many regions of the country, there are fewer hunters and likely more birders. Visitation to Craters of the Moon in 1962 was 175,278, up about 50,000 in 1961. About 40,000 fewer people came to the monument in 1963, making me wonder if I left my campsite an unsavory mess. The number of visitors grew from about 100,000 in 1995 to 178,823 in 2003, 250,000 in 2015, and 250,872 in 2020. Surely more throngs have trampled the monument since 2020.

While I visited Craters of the Moon in 1962, I was unaware that there were plans to add 5,360 acres to the monument. The extra acreage, the Carey Kipuka Addition, was first considered in 1956 by F. R. Fosberg from the National Academy of Sciences. Dr. Fosberg occasionally visited my colleague next door to my Smithsonian office. In 2002, the Craters of the Moon Monument and Preserve administered 750,000 acres. A national preserve is a protected area, but where hunting, fishing, mining, and gas and oil extraction are allowed. In addition to the preserve, 485,000 acres became administered in 1993 at the Morley Nelson Snake River Conservation National Conservation Area. It is located not far from Deer Flat NWR and near Boise, home to the Peregrine Fund, a much-discussed organization early in my career in the Biological Survey.

Extra protected acres for the monument and other public lands are a good thing since these areas are under so much pressure from climate change and from more people visiting public lands. During my 1962 visit to the monument, I hiked south from the campground. Too many decades interrupt the possibility of recalling the location of the campground, which has changed from place to place in the monument. The campground was once near the employee residences. If my memory serves me well, the campground was remote and my hike took me into even more remote parts of the monument. There were no trails, although unofficial trails were here and there. Since 1962, the monument has built official trails to protect previously vandalized geological features. Most people visiting public lands are simply curious, looking for panorama and a few pictures to take home. However, parks, monuments, rare or endangered birds, and habitats are too often loved to death. That is why the National Park Service places travel limitations in certain parks; administers of guided tours on buses in Yosemite National Park, for example, are trying to prevent popular parks from being loved to death. A refuge near Austin, Texas, closes part of its habitat to prevent the rare Golden-cheeked Warbler and Black-capped Vireo from being loved to death.

Camas Creek, like so many waterways, now flows through a drought-stricken Idaho. Camas NWR currently reports locations for duck hunting in the refuge are dry.

Chapter 4

Red Rock

13 June 1962

The route the next few days would be in remote regions, and a stop for food and gasoline should be sufficient for me to cross the Rocky Mountains. Dubois, just north of Camas NWR, was my last chance for supplies. I purchased groceries to cover seven days for $4.19. The grub was to last until I left Yellowstone National Park a week away. I also bought lunch for 65 cents, had filled the gas tank in Idaho Falls ($3.35 for 9.1 gallons), and had 40 cents of fluid squirted into the leaky transmission.

After a few miles northward, the VW lumbered over Monida (pronounced muh-NEI-duh) Pass at 6,870 feet. The route over the Centennial Mountains is at the borders of Idaho and Montana and is the Continental Divide. The Continental Divide forms the boundary between much of eastern Idaho and Montana. The Centennial Range runs from Monida Pass for about 60 miles to the east toward Yellowstone National Park. The pass is relatively low for many of the continental passes I had crossed as a teenager on those whirlwind trips to see the Midwestern grandparents.

I would not be keeping a life list of passes, but I ticked off the third state for the trip, Montana, which was a new life state. Below, on the north side of Monida Pass and a few miles to the east, I would be able to tick off a new life bird, wild Trumpeter Swan. Just barely into Montana, I left the main highway and entered a small desolate town called Monida, also pronounced muh-NEI-duh. Its buildings along the main street were old from decades of harsh weather and like something out of a Zane Grey or Louis Lamour novel. Nothing stirred except wisps of dust from the dry ground. The town's small general store, with its high ceiling and the flat front of the adjacent buildings, made me expect to see six-shooters hanging on the men and hear snorting horses tied to a rail just outside. There were no guns and no horses, just old and worn residents, and very used pickup trucks. It was dark inside the store, but I could see shelves that were well-stocked to the point of clutter with everything from food to nails. Over to one side of the four walls and facing the can goods and linens was the town's post office where I would soon be picking up my mail from home. Sadly, there was no mail, so I left a forwarding address for my next general delivery. Home seemed far away and ever farther in a brand-new state at a town where time seemed to stand still. It was a place that was hardly hanging on economically.

Three elderly men huddled around a large wood stove. They looked to have been talking to each other until I came in, being announced by me closing the well-used front door. They were not glaring, just looking me over, the stranger in town. One burly man said hello and asked me if I needed help. I probably appeared as if I did, but I said no. He grinned.

"You know how the town got its name?"

"No," I replied, not thinking about history so much, at least until I entered the town and seemingly stepped back in time.

"Well," he said, on the verge of laughing, "the *Mon* is for Montana, and the *ida* is for Idaho."

One of the men chuckled; the third never blinked. The one laughing stared at me as if waiting for me to join. I worked up a grin, which seemed to satisfy everyone.

"Yep, Monida's named for the two states it is almost in. Actually, we are sittin' in Montana, just barely."

A red spot on the side of the woodstove began to grow during the explanation. That caused the Monida trio to move a foot and a few inches from their source of warmth. They then asked me where I was from and where I was going. I had been asked those same questions many times, but I felt a little like this was an interrogation. I said Oregon and Red Rock NWR. They wondered why and I said to see birds, especially Trumpeter Swans. The trio seemed mildly intrigued. They were more interested when I asked about road conditions east of the refuge. I heard the words "oh, bad," "slippery," and "what you drivin'?"

Before I could answer, one of the men volunteered a question that caused me to doubt my plan to drive east of the refuge. "Wasn't Jim stuck for a couple hours up there?"

"Yeah. What'd you say was your rig?"

Thinking quickly, I eliminated my telescope and gunstock rig, my typewriter rig, and several other possible rigs, and guessed that what I was driving must be my rig. I said I was driving a Volkswagen Beetle, which made all three laugh and warn me that I would never make it over the mountain pass. I nodded, keeping to myself that surely my more or less modern VW would make it over the pass at least as well as the rusty pickups parked outside.

Leaving the store, I looked down the quiet street and the empty, cold dark buildings standing gray in the crisp mountain air. I read somewhere that Monida was established in the 1880s, that the post office in Monida opened in 1891, closed only two years later, and opened again in 1896. A railroad brought tourists to Monida, and residents of Monida shipped out sheep and cattle. The tourists, who were going to and from Yellowstone NP, arrived in town, then took the only "public" access, the Monida-Yellowstone Stage Line east, traveling past the Red Rock Lakes, across Red Rock Pass, and on to Yellowstone. About 100 residents once thrived in Monida. Most of the nearby ranchers left, leaving just the three people huddled around a potbellied stove at the general store.

Leaving behind the weathered wooden boards holding up the buildings of Monida, I drove east on the dirt scrape called Red Rock Pass Road. The drive east took me into the heart of the Centennial Valley and the home of Red Rock Lakes NWR. The region was a surprise. The valley and the refuge offer beauty that is competitive with most national parks. According to a brochure I picked up in Monida, the Centennial Valley averages 15 miles wide and 45 miles long. In all that wide-open space, no one disturbed this quiet beauty.

Today was a day of blue sky, accented by only a few wispy cirrus clouds high over the Centennial Mountains. I drove east, away from Monida, with a cloud of dust boiling from the dirt track. The dust settled, not to be disturbed by another vehicle, possibly for hours. I was going into a wilderness more remote than Lake Abert, Malheur, and most other places I had ever been. In minutes I was entering Red Rock Lakes NWR. At about 6,600 feet, its elevation is barely less than that of Monida Pass where I crossed the Continental Divide. The panorama took my breath. From a hillock on the side of the muddy and potted road, I could see the refuge buildings in the distance. I gathered nearby snow that, packed tightly, would melt slowly and hopefully before a pound each of hamburger and bacon succumbed to my diet or spoilage.

Blue sky and beaming sunlight framed Red Rock NWR. Vesper Sparrows were exploding from every sprig of grass; among the sparrows were Dark-eyed Juncos and Western Meadowlarks. The air smelled of wet ground oozing clear water from snow melting rapidly into the road and on to the Red Rock Lakes. My eyes strained as I panned the horizon and down to Lower Red Rock Lake. No swans were in view. Green marshland surrounded by stately conifers, blue primeval water, and the reddish hues of the snow-capped Centennial Mountains with steep stratified faces was like a painting, a site that few have seen, and a place that I was happy to soak in. Habitats ranged from wetlands to arctic life zones taking in the cliffs and rocky northern slope of the Centennial Mountains, with a foreground full of sagebrush, scrub, aspen, conifers of varying shades of green. The setting for the headquarters looked like a place I might like to work. A cluster of mostly rustic buildings, including two vintage log cabins for residents, even a bunkhouse, a maintenance shop, a laboratory, and other structures looked as if they belonged to the remoteness. The self-contained community of refuge staff kept things going no matter the frequent road closures during winter snow. Most of winter had melted and I was happy it was spring. It was time to enjoy a field of yellow wildflowers and the crisp clean air framing the deep brown buildings, nearby tall conifers, and pale green cottonwood. I should have gotten the names of the flowers; perhaps they were buttercups.

Presently, I wanted to check in with refuge staff to find out where the best place is for viewing Trumpeter Swans. Inside headquarters was humming. A regional inspector was there, and the biologist was planning to take him on a flight over the refuge. Though busy, George Devan, the biologist, spent several minutes helping me plan my stay in the refuge, including where to find the famous swans.

One reason Trumpeter Swans are scarce is because populations are recovering from humans. For example, early settlers wanted to vary their diet, and unlucky birds became swan stew, and in the mid-1800s, still more Trumpeter Swans lost their skins to hunters that ended up in the hands of the Hudson Bay Company. Even cygnets were prized, often being sold to zoos and apiarists. The nesting region shrunk to southwestern Montana, northeastern Idaho, and northwestern Wyoming. Canadian populations survived only in British Columbia and Alberta. Red Rock Lakes NWR, 40,000-acre preserve, was established in 1935, where Trumpeters have continued to breed as they have for countless seasons.

The biologist at the refuge directed me to a road south of Red Rock Pass Road. About two miles down the main road, I turned onto a narrow road that had once served miners, perhaps gold miners. The narrow road, starting at about 6,700 feet in elevation led me to Odell Creek and the northern slope of 9,629-foot Sheep Mountain. The roughly hewn road carried with it a risk of high centering my car, so I parked and began to make my way up the canyon. I had hardly gotten started before both feet were wet after my unsuccessful attempt to cross Odell Creek. Maybe in a half of a mile up the canyon, the going became steeper and muddier. A wind pitched down from the craggy upper slopes; by now I could see stratified rock outcrops poking out of the snowy slopes. At about 7,200 feet, the wind drowned almost any sound with its steady downdraft pushing at and through the trees. I will never know why I made that climb toward Sheep Mountain. What did I expect to find? Was it just to see what was around the corner, what was over the next rise? I do not recall. Nineteen sixty-two and a decade or so beyond was a time when climbing mountains became important, even if the chances of finding birds was low. What was I thinking?

Anyway, the wind made birding impossible. I decided to head up a deer trail to get away from the buffeting. Going into the underbrush was not the preferred solution though in sheltered localities, I found, once again, an abundance of Vesper Sparrows, juncos, and also Western Tanagers, and a few Pine Siskins. I also found mosquitoes, or they found me. That was when my interest in birding became dominated by my interest to keep my blood. Back in the wind and back down the canyon, I saw a bird flying over the road and perch on a dead branch about 30 feet away. A new species, a Townsend's Solitaire, made the trip up the canyon worth the effort. Yellow-rumped and Wilson's warblers and Chipping Sparrows were added to the list of birds seen in the canyon.

Along the aspen-lined upper lake were Yellow Warblers, American Goldfinches, with a mixture of Vesper Sparrows, their white outer tail feathers flicking, and of course, Song Sparrows. A Red-naped Sapsucker and three species of flycatchers were along the road, including Willow Flycatcher, Western Wood-Pewee, and the white-breasted Eastern Kingbird but no Western kingbirds. Mountain Bluebirds and Chipping Sparrows were everywhere. The campground at Upper Red Rock Lake, sitting in a grove of quaking aspen about a mile north of Sheep Mountain and near the road, offered White-crowned Sparrows and Warbling Vireos. More warblers were there, but nothing new. It was a wonder I saw any birds at the campground as I waved and slapped at the hordes of attacking mosquitoes. The birds disregarded my behavior, but I could not ignore the behavior of the mosquitoes.

Trumpeter Swans were feeding about a quarter of a mile from the lake shore campground. I counted at least 30. They were too far away to be startled by my mosquito defense system. Their distant bugle, which is low in frequency, swept across the lake drowning out the sounds of the smaller species of waterfowl on the lake. The distant Redheads, Eared Grebes, Canada Geese, barely identifiable with the scope, were unaware of my frantic gestures. Most of the big swans appeared to be in pairs. They swam slowly and occasionally dipped their long necks deep down into the pristine water. During the night, and easily heard over the pesky buzz of hungry mosquitoes, the Trumpeter Swans broke the quiet with their double-noted bugle.

14 June 1962

The mosquitoes last night were so unbearable that I was afraid to pitch my tent. They were too hungry to be slowed down by zippers or netting and would soon be like flying barracudas in a feeding frenzy. It was a matter of triage, so I left the tent, its stakes half impaled in the red soil. There seemed nothing else to do but to sleep in the car. The car, packed to the gills, means the back of the driver's seat cannot be tilted anywhere near horizontal. "Sleep" will require me to sit upright in a "driving the car" position. The hungry mosquitoes were waiting just outside the protective glass window, expecting me to become a human sacrifice.

Last night's attempt to sleep in the car left my body full of stiff aches, but fewer mosquito bites. However, by the last bite of the eggs I fried, the mosquitoes were again in their feeding frenzy. I hurriedly gulped my breakfast, pulled up the stakes of the unused tent, packed the car, and enjoyed my last view of Trumpeter Swans at Red Rock Lakes NWR. The coffee was still hot as I sat in the car, the windows rolled up to keep out mosquitoes and to keep in the warmth of the morning sun as it began piercing the campground. From my comfortable perch, I was able to enjoy the coffee, the unparalleled panorama, and listened to the bugling swans.

My route east on Red Rock Pass Road was a 30-mile dirt road to the paved highway that would lead to Yellowstone NP. Several refuge staff including the refuge manager doubted I would make it. The warnings were not ill-founded. I had thought the slightly graveled road from Monida to refuge headquarters was bad. However, the dirt road over the pass to the pavement near West Yellowstone, I was about to realize, was dreadful, a term that was worse than bad. The long road was rough and full of holes. Portions of the road were underwater because of fast melting snow. Each time I crossed these lakelets, the large bridgeless water gaps in the road, I wondered if the bottoms of the water bodies would be solid or soft with miring mud. With much relief, the bottom of these waterways was merely slippery; the weight of the rear engine supplied enough traction to reach dry land. Parts of the road were under water that was too deep to negotiate. However, it was a sink or swim situation because I was determined to make it over Red Rock Pass. I remembered that VWs are supposed to float. At one 20-foot-wide inundated spot along the lonely road, the car may have floated. Before fording the waterway, I stopped, looked it over, and gunned the engine. As most owners of vintage VWs have learned, gunning such an underpowered car is mostly an effort of futility. Still, I went fast enough to create a wave that almost rocked the car. Muddy water rushed up the rounded front of the car to the windshield. This could be real trouble. Did I float? At least I reached the far shore during the navigation, the engine did not stall, and not a drop of water made it inside the car.

Gradually I began to climb upward and away from the gloriously beautiful Centennial Valley. On the final ascent to the summit of Red Rock Pass, a little over 7,000 feet, was a climb too steep for giant pools of water and slippery mud. Only first gear, and only after getting a running start, was I able to push the car to climb the lonely ridges and reach the summit.

Availability of gasoline, ice, food, and water were always on my mind. Having enough gas to get from place to place increased my chances of finding birds and helped propel me to ice to cool perishable food and water for my canteen. My vintage VW did not have a gas gauge. Deciding the amount of existing gas was accomplished by keeping track of the miles driven and knowing the approximate miles per gallon, which was 30 miles per gallon for my 1955 VW. Another way to determine how much gas might be available was to look directly into the 10-gallon tank. The tank was in the front under the bonnet or hood depending on your background. A large opening and good lighting allowed for guessing the amount left in the tank. Inserting a clean 18-inch wooden stick into the open tank as one would use a dip-stick to check oil was better than nothing. I always hoped the withdrawn stick would be mostly wet. As a precaution concerning running out of gas, an emergency half-gallon of gas was available by turning a mechanical switch located inside the passenger compartment.

Portions of what I generally ate required refrigeration, which meant ice. Commercial ice was sometimes difficult to find and frequently only available in large sacks containing far more ice than my cooler could hold. The opportunity to gather roadside snow for the cooler was helpful but I knew the ice or snow was only marginally maintaining my perishables and that the snow resource would soon be absent once I crossed the Rockies. A diet change seemed on the horizon.

Most grocery stores so far in 1962 were small to large, though not giant expanses as are available today. Being able to eat safe food was a major concern. Between eating baloney sandwiches and questionably safe sausage and hamburger, it is a wonder I lived to write this today. A diet of lots of bread, ground-up scraps of various body parts and spices called sausage and fat dyed red to hide it among the sparse bits of muscle called hamburger is not a diet for living long. Canned vegetables and fruit helped balance my diet. I have since given up sausage, and any hamburger from the grocery has to be the leanest they sell. As for baloney, I never cared for it, but it was cheap. I have not had a baloney sandwich in decades, although I rarely indulge in a good hot dog, which I realize is mostly baloney reshaped.

Finding water was never a problem. I kept my canteen full, mostly from tap water and occasionally from a rivulet of water from melting snow. I drank rarely from streams that I judged safe, but what did I know? What you cannot see actually can hurt you. Drinking directly from a stream today is asking for it, it being a possibly lengthy line of symptoms.

As the annual piling on of years occurred, my interest in history grew from hardly recognizing the past when I was a young Danny McSkunk, to a real curiosity beginning while approaching adulthood to now, a grayed and wrinkled version of the guy in 1962. Even then, the sight of Monida woke up my curiosity more than ever. Monida was then on the cusp of becoming a ghost town. How did it get from a prosperous community to what I saw, and what has happened to Monida since 1962 when the population was about 45 souls? The post office closed in 1964. Mail of residents near Monida now goes to Lima, Montana, a small town about 20 miles up the local interstate highway. Yes, Monida is accessed presently via an interstate highway by turning on exit zero. By 2004, about a baker's dozen lived in Monida. Some of the people are descendants of generations past, while others moved there for a slower pace. A few of the residents escape the harsh winters by heading south or at least to lower elevations. The privately owned historic buildings are still standing; the old stage barn was being remodeled into a house in 2004, although I understand the outside was to remain unchanged. The water system, built for the town by the railroad, was turned over to the extant families. The population continued to dwindle, which according to most recent sources, states the total population of Monida is a resounding two. Recent photographs of the general store and post office reveal abandoned buildings. And, for that 1962 meeting with the three men at the hot woodstove in Monida, the conversation was as remembered. At least, that is my story, and I am sticking to it.

Birding in Red Rock Lakes NWR allowed me to add native Trumpeter Swans to my trip list. Visiting the refuge was a dream since early high school when I read Winston Banko's detailed publication on the plight of the species.[1] He reported that, in 1932, there were fewer than 70 individual Trumpeter Swans from the entire range of the species. Half of those, only 35, were found at Red Rock Lakes and in Yellowstone NP. About 16,000 now live in North America.

The road from Monida that meanders through Red Rock Lakes NWR, closely following the old stage route, connects to the paved highway leading to Yellowstone. The road through Centennial Valley was dirt in 1962. It is now labeled on maps as a gravel road as far as the refuge, and the part east of the refuge is designated as "improved" dirt. The refuge does not have an entrance gate that might provide a count of visitors. Based on the names in their sign-in log, only 35 people enjoyed the refuge in 1962. Most of the 35 were representing other agencies working in the refuge. Numerous fishing and hunting folks were mentioned but not counted in the 1962 refuge report. In 2003, not counting the unknown multitudes that came for the hunting and fishing, at least 8,000 people converged on the refuge. The estimate for the present century is 15,000. The increase in traffic is so much that the remaining ranchers, who love the solitude and beauty of the Centennial Valley, are, along with conservationists, concerned about adverse impacts on wildlife.

The refuge, with 40,000 acres in 1962, is now 51,386 acres. Conservation easements add almost 24,000 more acres of protection. Two campgrounds now host visitors. Only one campground near Upper Red Rock Lake was available in 1962. Waking to the sounds of morning in a wetland is a special treat, but most national wildlife refuges prohibit overnight visitations. My journey so far has included nights spent in refuges, which were charitable bending of the rules by kind refuge managers. Red Rock NWR policy allows camping has come with a price. The grove of aspen at the Upper Lake campground is now fenced. I am not sure why, but grazing is allowed in the refuge, and grazing has an impact on seedling aspen, which are either eaten or trampled. In the late 1980s, pathogens were discovered in the campground grove. Were they introduced by human campers or grazing bovines? Whatever the answer, I sure hope I did not leave a plant-hating germ back in 1962.

Centennial Valley has changed little though visitation is high; in 1962, the only people I saw were at Monida and employees at the refuge. By 1991 a biological survey ranked the valley important because of its expansive wetland, native biodiversity, and an important zone for linking ungulates and predators in the Greater Yellowstone ecosystem. The Centennial Valley

---

1. Winston E. Banko. *The Trumpeter Swan: Its History, Habits, and Population in the United States.* North American Fauna 63. (U.S. Fish and Wildlife Service, 1960).

has some of the oldest forests in southwestern Montana and is home to the Arctic grayling, one of the state's rarest fish. Record population densities of Peregrine Falcons in the valley are reported by The Nature Conservancy. The valley also has the highest nesting density of breeding Trumpeter Swans in western North America. Thanks to The Nature Conservancy, the few remaining local landowners, and the Fish and Wildlife Service, most of the Centennial Valley will be saved from us.

The Centennial Mountains, a subrange of the Bitterroot Mountains, trend from east to west, and are found south of the Centennial Valley. The mountains are dominated by Douglas fir and have been heavily logged on the gentler slopes in Idaho. The more rugged Montana side has had a reprieve. The Bureau of Land Management manages part of the mountains as a "primitive area." The Gravelly Mountains, the range on the north side of Centennial Valley, are "protected" in portions of the range but even the wilderness areas are subject to wavering governmental policies. Naturally, the mere designation of primitive attracts people that might not have otherwise tramped such land. There are thousands, no millions, of individuals attracted by official designations such as national park and monument, recreation, and wilderness areas, and, as I was in 1962, national wildlife refuges. More people are entering regions designated for their beauty by ugly means such as motor vehicles, be they sedans, SUVs, off-road vehicles and other wheeled transports, snowmobiles, you name it. If the region is drop-dead gorgeous and on a snow-covered mountain, people want to create vertical clear-cuts or what recreators fondly call ski runs. Once the snow melts, we share tent pegs all the while pretending the mountain air is unpolluted by multitudes of cars. In 1962, we were just beginning to love our wilderness to death with a proliferation of snowmobiles, off-road vehicles, and four-wheel-drive SUVs. As of early 2021, skiing in the Centennial Mountains, aided by helicopter, called heli-skiing, was being debated and more and more people drove into wildlands, hikers pulverized the trails, and they filled nature with human love that is eroding away the wildness we seek.

To this day, I remember feeling sad as I drove east and out of the Centennial Valley. Time, or so it seemed, had stood still in Monida, but would it in the valley? Once the word gets out, your favorite picnic spot or fishing hole might not be a secret, but a place overrun not by Trumpeter Swans but by people. Not a soul was seen on my route out of the valley in 1962. Today, the estimated 15,000 people who travel the slightly improved route are creating a different world. Thankfully, the road is not paved or more would travel the route between Yellowstone NP and Monida. As for myself and probably including the three men at the store in Monida, the bumps, holes, and emptiness of the road decades ago are fond memories.

Chapter 5

Yellowstone, the First Days

14 June 1962, the Remainder of the Day

THE JUNCTION FROM DIRT to pavement was a welcome reprieve. The blacktop seemed to offer the smoothest ride I had experienced after the jarring travel since Monida, Montana. I must admit a fraction of relief was that if I had gotten in trouble, I was not where fellow humans might come to my aid. My wait for a rescue could have been days. Still, I was happy I made the journey over the mountains. Eight miles west of Yellowstone National Park would be yet another crossing of the Continental Divide. My earlier crossing of Monida Pass placed me in the eastern watershed where the streams would make their final destination into the Gulf of Mexico. The crossing at Red Rock Pass put me back on the Pacific slope, and the traversing of 7,072-foot Targhee Pass placed me once again on the eastern watershed.

In minutes, I was in West Yellowstone, one of five entrances to the Yellowstone NP. I planned to enter the park on the west side, use the south entrance to travel to and from Grand Teton NP, and exit the north entrance at Mammoth. The different entrances connect to interior roads that form a figure eight, and I will drive most of the lower part of the eight and the eastern half of the upper part of the eight. During this time, I plan to see the sights and birds for about five days.

West Yellowstone and the western entrance seemed busy. The small and bustling resort town is at 6,667 feet elevation and just outside the west entrance of Yellowstone NP. Today was the time for the flocking behavior of tourists. It was the thronging season, and the cars backed up for miles from the entrance station of one of the most visited national parks. Four rangers in dark green uniforms and round flat-brimmed hats worked from their busy 12-by-12-foot entrance building. They leaned out their booth to hand drivers a detailed map and leaflet about the park in exchange for a $3 entrance fee.

Visitors were from every state and country and probably had as many reasons as possible to come to Yellowstone. There are reasons to visit: history, all kinds of botanical and zoological reasons, camping, fishing, hiking, photography, and more. Besides birds and geology, I was enjoying watching the various behaviors of people in the park.

My first night in Yellowstone was appropriately at the campground at Madison near the location, according to the literature handed out at the entrance station, where a group of men talked about the region they were exploring, a place Native Americans called Rock Yellow River. It was in 1870 when General Henry Washburn, the surveyor-general of Montana, the Honorable Nathaniel P. Langford, and Lieutenant Gustavus C. Duane made a momentous decision. After experiencing the unique geology and beauty of the region, the group decided "to set apart" what they saw for the use and enjoyment of the people. A couple of years later, in 1872, Ulysses S. Grant signed the documents protecting what we now know as Yellowstone NP. Almost every president since has set aside public land though more acres are welcome.

15 June 1962

My first public campground a few days ago at Craters of the Moon NM was a relatively peaceful experience. The campground at Madison was my second experience camping in a large public facility, and campers at Madison seemed almost anxious, not the relaxed group back in Idaho. After the jostle through the busy west entrance, Madison was perhaps their first campground in Yellowstone. The campground was crowded, which was enough to fray most visitors' nerves, and it was cold. There were fewer tents here compared to Craters of the Moon. People were sleeping in their station wagons, tall and top-heavy pickup campers, and fancy tents as big as houses. My pup tent occupied one of the 16 campsites. A few people were dragging behind them trailers of varying sizes. After almost too many cold and sleepless nights, the result of weather and bugs, a trailer did not seem like a bad idea.

Of course, tent camping lets one experience the elements. Besides the elements of nature, I met my next "door" neighbors, who were friendly though eager to head out to the next campground before the noonday sun. After finishing breakfast cooked over the camp stove, I realized the sun might not shine through the clouds until noon. That is when tiny hailstones began to fall. Darkening clouds swirled overhead, and the hailstones coming down were gradually becoming larger and larger. The pelting ice was too much for my head and shoulders. It was not weather for outdoor cooking. I turned off the gas burners and stuffed the hot stove under a picnic table and escaped the prickly hail from the inside of my car. Because the area was moist from melted snow, worrying about starting a forest fire from the hot stove was low on my list of safety priorities. I gathered the partially cooked food and myself into the protective shell of my car. The white round balls of ice continued to fall, and the clouds darkened to a blackish gray-blue.

The trailer campers were probably enjoying their breakfast now. They probably were not hungry, nor were their ears stinging from the bombardment of icy pellets. I would be fine and this was a good time to acquaint myself with the park, but the bold letters on a separate leaflet first drew my attention. At the top of the paper was a picture of a bear, its mouth open and teeth exposed, and front paws stretched wide from its body as if ready to attack. Underneath the picture was the warning that bears are dangerous. Instructions below the impressive picture stated that stored food needs to be in airtight containers and that any unwashed or greasy utensils should not be in the open.

About the time of reading the last word of the leaflet, I glanced up at my camp stove. My view of the stove also included an adjacent black bear. The hungry-looking black bear was sniffing my stove. I wondered what I should do. The most sensible tact would be to remain a respectful spectator and hope the camp stove survived in one piece. The stove did not appeal to the bruin. It looked toward me before ambling to the back of the car. Perhaps it thought food was there instead of the rear engine. It was time for me to remain quiet and still. The hailstones had continued to fall and were by now about a quarter of an inch in diameter. The noise of the hailstones striking the car, or the size of the stones, sent the bear loping into the nearby trees. Something besides the pounding of my heart sent it scurrying. I am not sure what it was, but I was grateful. That I had given the stove a thorough cleaning just before today's meal may explain why the bear did not tear it to pieces.

The size of the hailstones reached one-half inch diameter before the storm abated. After clearing camp, which meant leaving the campsite absent of any signs that I had been there, I drove north for 14 miles to Norris. I had never been to Norris. My only visit to Yellowstone was in 1955 when my parents veered off the beaten path to my grandparents' house. I do not recall much about our visit except that it was less than two hours, part of which was milling around with hundreds of other visitors waiting for Old Faithful to erupt. In 1955, I had vowed to revisit Yellowstone to see more of the park.

The hailstorm, with its penetrating cold, apparently passed the Norris Geyser Basin. The hot springs and cold air produced a fog of steam. I missed seeing the eruption of the world's tallest active geyser, Steamboat. It can erupt to more than 300 feet and shower unsuspecting viewers with its mineral-rich waters. Steamboat thunders with powerful jets of steam for hours following a major eruption. The literature handed to me days ago reported that full eruptions are entirely unpredictable and may not occur for months or years. I had only time for part of the Norris Geyser Basin and hurried down the boardwalks and paths, stopping only for taking pictures. There were no birds seen or heard. Where were the Steamboat's eruption and montane birds when I needed them? Time passed rapidly, and five o'clock soon rolled to the present. I was hungry most of the time and became even hungrier at my usual mealtimes. The sulfurous fumes that floated all around in an airborne cloak did not deter my appetite.

Back in the car and out of the fumes, I drove north a few miles, stopped several times, and still could not find any birds. I turned around and stopped to look over the trailhead at the Norris Geyser Basin. A big black limousine pulled up beside the little VW, then two men jumped out, one in a top hat, and began making movies. Apparently satisfied, they jumped into their chauffeured car and lurched northward. I became interested and followed them. For the next few miles, the limo stopped, the same two men would leap hurriedly out of their car, expose a few feet of film, and jump back in the limo. They then were chauffeured to the next site where they repeated, top hat and all, their earlier documentation of their trip to Yellowstone. Finally, tiring of my game of people watching, I again turned south to a new campground at Old Faithful Village.

My arrival to possibly one of the most famous locations on earth was not too late to see the big eruption. The area around the mouth of Old Faithful teemed with people waiting for the next eruption. Old Faithful symbolizes the park, and erupts about every 65 minutes, with durations between eruptions ranging from 33 minutes to 95 minutes. Today the timing was average, but the sight and sound of Old Faithful were far from average. Just before the supposed time of the eruption, a sudden hush sped through the hundreds of people waiting, cocking cameras, and vying for the best viewing. Then, only a weak spurt shot upward. The spurt grew in size, and suddenly the heated water gushes high over the white encrusted mound of the geyser. The viewing crowd cheers.

A nearby ranger explained that the water forces its way through the constricting throat in the rocks, then falls from a 300-foot crest, splashes on the rocks below, and changes the emotions of many of the humans gasping in awe while they click and wind their cameras. The eruption lasted about two minutes. The water spilling from the geyser's cone-shaped opening ran and soaked into the mineralized crust, and a cloud of steam puffed the last signal before the next eruption.

15 June 1962

Although the nights are cold, and an early morning hailstorm sent people scurrying, my ice chest was too warm for food. I found a vending machine for ice, but the smallest amount I could buy was about 10 pounds, much more than I needed. I was in luck. A man was trying his best to stuff his newly purchased bag of ice into a too-small bucket of fish. I offered to relieve him of his excess ice for a fair price. He declined but only my money and helped me load up what ice I needed. We were both happy.

The next eruption of Old Faithful would be a while. A visit to a small general store seemed in order. The place was crowded with milling tourists and jingling sounds of busy cash registers ringing up inflated prices. Hurrying to a quiet corner next to a stack of canned beans, I tried to visualize the condition of my provisions. Think, think. I had stocked up in Idaho, but I could use the pre-cooked apple pie waiting for me to buy. No, it cost too much.

Today, I saw and photographed a coyote loping along the edge of the road leading from Old Faithful. According to the literature the ranger handed me at West Yellowstone, coyotes are becoming as bold as the bears, and are commonly near Mammoth in the northern part of the park. Coyotes were not seen again, but I did find a few stale tracks and half-dried scat. Bison were grazing in the meadows. My search for moose was unsuccessful, elk also were missed, and happily, grizzly bears were not there to chronicle today. Few things scare me in nature, but grizzlies and poisonous snakes are worth avoiding.

A concession along the way sold me a very enjoyable strawberry milkshake. Meanwhile, I worked on my notes, lamented about the bad birding, visited with a couple of my camping neighbors, cleaned, cooked, cleaned some more to avoid trouble from bears, and again wondered, Where are all the birds? By sundown, I had zipped myself into my cozy sleeping bag. After nearby campers stopped stumbling over exposed tree roots and each other, a deep sleep dominated the night.

YELLOWSTONE, THE FIRST DAYS

16 June 1962

Today was a busy day. After breakfast, I walked down to watch Old Faithful. I did not take pictures as I needed to save the film for snapshots of other geysers to see on a naturalist tour. The walk started with a small gathering of people sitting on a log that faced Old Faithful. A naturalist preparing to lead our group of about 30 stood watching the last smatterings of the eruption. When all the steam disappeared, he turned to address his audience and gave us a brief summary of Yellowstone, with emphasis on Old Faithful. The naturalist also gave us warnings that the area's yellow crust was dangerous to walk on. He emphasized the point with gruesome examples of people being half-boiled alive or even dying from a foolhardy step from the safety of the boardwalks.

Our group stopped at almost every geyser along our route, where each geyser was different from the others. The variations were shape and size, such as Beehive Geyser and Giantess. Other differences were the amount of water and steam emitted, which was related to the size of the opening of the geyser. There were six major geysers along the walk near Old Faithful, and each one begged to have its picture taken, but that could get expensive. Knowing my budget was already straining from the cost of film and developing, and strawberry milkshakes, I tried to control my zeal for taking so many pictures in such a picturesque place.

The park naturalist explained that, like most geysers, the behavior of Giantess changed after the Alaska earthquake of 17 August 1959. The power of Giantess exceeds that of Old Faithful, although its eruptions are comparatively not predictable and are more infrequent. An eruption of Giantess lasted over 100 hours after the quake. Our naturalist pointed out that other changes occurred because of the earthquake. Dormant Geyser Cone, lying to our right on a hillside overlooking our loop-shaped route, was put in action for the first time since the discovery of the park. Farther along on the walk, the naturalist told us that another inactive mound named Aurum Geyser also began renewed activity. An entirely new geyser was born near Arrowhead Springs, not far from Old Faithful. On the night of the quake, the ground opened, spewed rocks called geyserite and clouds of steam, only to become inactive weeks later. Our group reached Beehive, near the end of our steamy walk. The naturalist explained that the Alaska earthquake disrupted the cyclic behavior of Beehive that now only erupts about two to five times a week.

One of the most interesting features of the naturalist tour was directly behind Old Faithful, the geyser. A small steam vent perched at the towering shoulder of Old Faithful mildly exhaled its gases into the crisp air. The 30 or so members of the tour stared at the little puffs of steam and wondered what was unusual about such a small steam vent. Our guide did not keep us in suspense too long. He explained that each time Old Faithful, or any geyser, erupts, the mineral-laden water from the eruption leaves a thin coat of deposited solid particles on the lining of the vent or inside the throat of the geyser. Each time an eruption occurs, the opening may become smaller and smaller until the opening becomes closed. Our naturalist emphasized that this phenomenon is happening to Old Faithful. He added that in hundreds or thousands of years, Old Faithful will not be erupting from its present vent and that it might be erupting from the little vent on the side of the geyser's mound. Time will tell.

After the naturalist talk, I headed southeast toward Yellowstone Lake and over the Continental Divide at Craig Pass and Isa Lake. At 8,262 feet, or about 1,000 feet higher than Old Faithful, I found snowbanks to use for my ice chest. Nearby Isa Lake presented a unique situation. During spring runoff, the lake drains into both the Pacific Oceans and the Gulf of Mexico at the same time! (And backward, too!) The west side of Isa Lake flows into the Firehole drainage (Old Faithful region) and, eventually, into the Gulf throughout the year. The eastern shore of the lake, during spring, flows into the Snake River drainage and to the Pacific Ocean. Putting a note in a bottle in Lake Isa could end up on either shore. Another location that also drains into two oceans is in northern Montana, which is not on my itinerary.

The cold air was quiet except for the wind sighing in the lush conifers. Not even a bird murmured. Suddenly a car broke the near silence of the surprisingly lonely road with its engine straining as it pulled up the last few yards to the summit of Craig Pass. The car eased down the slope toward West Thumb and Yellowstone Lake. I hurried with my chore of collecting snow and also began the descent to West Thumb. After time negotiating curves, I crossed the Continental Divide a second time at an unnamed 8,391-foot pass just about 100 feet higher than Craig Pass less than 10 miles behind me. I soon reached West Thumb, a western part of Yellowstone Lake. The lake is the largest natural freshwater lake in the United States that is above 7,000 feet. It is 7,733 feet above sea level, covers 136 square miles, is 20 miles long by 14 miles wide, and its maximum depth of 320 feet deep is in the West Thumb region. Probably every 110 miles of shoreline has been fished for the lake's famous trout. The average temperature of Yellowstone Lake is 41°F. It is not a lake to fall in. Besides being vacant of clumsy humans, the lake was birdless.

West Thumb Campground was crowded. Of the few people at their campsites were those polishing their fishing gear or cleaning and cooking fish. I managed to find an unoccupied camping site. It was small and rocky,

YELLOWSTONE, THE FIRST DAYS

but I made it work. About three hours of daylight was all the horizon would allow, so I hurriedly unpacked my equipment and put up the tent. My rod and reel were still in fine shape (this was my first time fishing on the trip). The hard bumps of Red Rock Pass Road had scrambled the contents of my tackle box, but I managed to untangle most of the crucial pieces.

Years have gone by since I last had the excitement of a fish pulling at a bent rod. I used to go fishing every chance I had; birding was only slightly interesting at ages 12 to 14. During those days, something changed. At the edge of a reasonably good trout stream in southwestern Oregon, I happen to look away from the water and my fishing line to see a flycatcher. The bird dove out from an overhanging branch and was intent on snagging doomed insect. Momentarily, I forgot all about the trout that I might catch from the stream below. My next fishing trip included a pair of binoculars handily draped around my neck. That day, as I recall, time spent birding and fishing was pretty much a fifty-fifty situation. Though I continued to go fishing, the more fishing trips I made, the more time I spent birding and the less time fishing. Finally, fishing became as uninteresting to me as once was birding. Now, on this June day in 1962, I found myself gripped with renewed vigor to go fishing. The fishing fever was short-lived, and I soon found myself not fishing, not even birding, as there did not seem to be any birds or fish around, and, with no more ambition than to lie in the warm sun and listen to the small waves lap on the shore, I nearly fell asleep.

After returning to camp empty-handed, a new neighbor in a pickup camper arrived. Two passengers got out and began turning a crank at one corner of the camper. Soon the camper began to telescope upward. A few other campers had taken notice of the newcomers and their unique camper. My thoughts turned to the domestic matter of what I would eat for dinner that I had hoped to catch. A glance into the trusty ice-chest told me that I was again to eat the tired menu of hamburger and a canned green vegetable. In a brief time, my cooking utensils were ready for the decent fire I managed to build. Just as my hamburger began to sizzle, the odor of frying fish drifted my way. That appetite stimuli made even the hamburger seem mouth-watering. I ate every bite and even dipped into the next day's rations, but at least hunger no longer existed. That is when the two guys in the telescoping camper walked my way and introduced themselves. They led me to their camper where they showed me a freshly caught and freshly cooked trout. They asked if I would please take it. After my hamburger/green bean eating frenzy, not to mention eating part of tomorrow's food, I was in no position to eat. They insisted that I take the fish, that they could not eat another bite, and that they had no way to keep it overnight. If I did not take the trout, they would have put it in the garbage. Throwing away perfectly good food went against our collective values.

One way or another, I ate the fish; I was not so full of hamburger and canned vegetables after all. How wonderful to taste a product of Yellowstone NP. Being well over-nourished helped bring sleep so deep that the rocks under my sleeping bag disappeared.

17 June 1962

Most of the people in the campground were gone by the time I managed to unzip my sleeping bag and crawl out of the stubby pup tent. Once upright, I staggered up the important path, the path to the restroom. A stone poking out of the path caught my right foot and almost mooted my mission. Recovering from my stumble, I sped to the waiting room of rooms. On the way from resting, a Ruby-crowned Kinglet was flipping its wings nervously near my campsite. It and two more were feeding in a nearby tree. As with most observations of Ruby-crowns, their fiery red crowns were not to be seen. Maybe all three birds were females but the name characterizing these kinglets is often hard to see.

After breakfast, really brunch by now, I headed south, exited the park, and after about eight miles through national forest land, I entered Grand Teton NP. The Teton Mountains are perhaps the most spectacularly beautiful range in the United States, especially when viewed from their east slope. I soon arrived in Jackson Hole, the name of the 13-mile-wide valley running for 55 miles east of the range. The brochure handed to me at the north entrance informed me that this valley is drained by about 50 miles of the Snake River. The average elevation of 6,800 feet slopes gently to the southern boundary of the park. Grand Teton, at 13,770 feet, and other peaks, tower abruptly 6,000 feet above Jackson Hole. There are 12 peaks over 12,000 feet in elevation in the range. The blue-gray granite peaks are along a fault line and rose partly in response to volcanic activities in Yellowstone. Through the combinations of geologic forces, Jackson Hole sunk, and concurrently, the region west of the valley rose in a gigantic fault block. Erosion, weathering, and glaciation attacked the young mountains to wear the surfaces to pointed spires, with rough up-sweeping contours and sheer and deep valleys. The fiercely steep etched peaks reaching skyward from the peaceful green forest and placid lakes were beyond grand.

The road from the northern boundary skirts along the east side of Jackson Lake for about 20 miles. The Tetons, although not particularly high in elevation compared to other peaks in the Rocky Mountains, especially in

Colorado, seem formidably tall. The range, on their east side, has no foothills. Viewed from Jackson Lake, at 6,700 plus feet above sea level, the peaks are steep and erect, alarmingly jutting skyward while revealing dangerous rocky cliffs formidable to most. Driving a few gorgeous miles southwest took me to Jenny Lake, a locality at the very base of the uplifted granite block forming the Tetons. The lakeshore was complete with a campground and is where climbers converge for equipment and guides to climb the lofty peaks. I had the foolish notion that perhaps I could climb one of the peaks, preferably Grand Teton, the tallest in the range. Reaching its 13,766-foot summit when, at that elevation, spring was yet to come, with the equipment I would have to rent and learn to use, made the idea of a climb unreachable. Because of my lack of experience, I would need a day at the mountaineering school and a guide, which would have cost at least $30. Once again, the budget told me no. Disappointed, I found consolation in blaming my meager budget and found a diversion by poking around in the nearby museum at Jenny Lake. The museum housed the complete mountaineering history of the range with exhibits of equipment used by the early alpinists.

The museum faced westward. From the commanding view, Mount Teewinot's 12,000-foot summit blocked seeing Grand Teton. Grand Teton was three miles from the museum; Mount Teewinot was closer, its bare shoulders spilling into the frigid water of Jenny Lake. The closeness of the mountains made me sigh. Except for the sheerest slopes, snow managed to cling to the hard gray rock of the mountains from their summits downward to about 2,500 feet above the lake. The line of demarcation between snow and no snow was the line between spring and winter. Even if I could not climb a Teton, I must find a way to at least touch one. The park map showed a trail around Jenny Lake that would take me to the base of Mount Teewinot. That would have to do, so I began the trek around the lake. Near the trailhead, I found a male Yellow Warbler pulling at a long strip of bark from an aspen tree. The bird lost its grip on the bark strip momentarily. It then grabbed the strip again, tugged and tugged, and suddenly flew from the tree. Behind the bird streamed the prize of a foot-long strip of bark for its hidden net. Near the northern edge of the lake, the trail began to bend away from the shore. Always ready to take a shortcut, I opted to leave the trail and follow the shoreline. The further I traveled, the more difficult travel became. Soon the gentle lapping of Jenny Lake was drowned by the roaring sound of the rushing white water of Cottonwood Creek. The creek connects several lakes, called string lakes, along the fault line before emptying into the Snake River. The creek was much too wide to jump. The high mountains, with their horizon so close, shadowed the sun. It was late, so I returned to the campground.

BIRDER INTERRUPTED

18 June 1962

Last night I attended a naturalist talk that was on the wildlife of Grand Teton NP. Following the talk, the naturalist revealed where a Great Gray Owl might occur. As the early morning sun bombarded the mountains with a flood of light, I drove north to Signal Mountain and the owl quarry that has so often eluded me. Signal Mountain, unlike the Tetons, is east of the fault and east of Jackson Lake. A five-mile narrow and winding road with its collection of switchbacks brought me to the 7,730-foot summit of Signal Mountain. Signal Mountain did appear to offer habitat for a Great Gray Owl. Once again, scanning for a roosting bird and spicing to create enough excitement that an individual might move did not bring results. Quietly walking through the woods, or, trying a different tactic, noisily walking through the woods did not produce a Great Gray Owl. After the failed search, I entertained myself by taking more pictures of the Tetons looming across Jackson Lake. The trip up Signal Mountain was still well worth the time.

Before leaving the summit of Signal Mountain, I gazed down at Jackson Lake and northward toward Yellowstone NP. Soon my route would cross the Snake River for the fifth time, beginning with the crossing at the Oregon and Idaho border only nine days ago. This would be the last crossing of the winding river. Not far up the road, I would pass West Thumb on my way to the Grand Canyon of the Yellowstone. I gazed down. Eight hundred feet below were mountain roads to travel and complete the second half of the trip, time to act like a tourist, and maybe see a new trip bird or two.

The world's first national park, Yellowstone is near the size of Puerto Rico and ranks as the eighth largest US national park. The park is either so large or so inadequately surveyed, which seems understandable, that the exact size is yet to be confirmed. In area, the park is close to 2,221,766 acres or 3,468 square miles. Yellowstone occupies a humongous caldera that first erupted about 640,000 years ago, give or take a few years. The park is still very active with hot geysers and bubbling mud pots. Registered as the hottest, Norris Geyser Basin, which is about the size of Chicago, has about 500 geothermal features and since 1990 has risen in elevation by five inches. Waiting for Steamboat Geyser to clear its throat in 1962 was in vain, but the geyser has been at a record pace since 2018. Old Faithful, once on a schedule of erupting every hour, has gone astray, and erupts about every

90 minutes, especially since the 1959 earthquake (the one that decimated Anchorage, Alaska). Small earthquakes frequently occur in the park.

The town of West Yellowstone grew from about 500 in 1962 to 1,376 in 2020. Growing numbers of visitors creating traffic backups at the western entrance, and other entrances to the park went from approximately two million in 1962 to three million in 1996 and a little over four million in 2019. That is correct, during the past 60 years, visitation to the park increased by 270 percent. Because of the uniqueness of Yellowstone NP, people are drawn there, but recreationists need to spread out a little and put less pressure on the same places. The increase in people comes at a price. The entrance fee went from the three bucks I paid in 1962 to $35 in the new roaring twenties. A one thousand and change increase in the entrance fee might seem excessive, but the $35 is a bargain and helps pay for upkeep needed from the throngs of park visitors. Today, the park charges a camping fee and a fee for a fishing license. Although visiting Yellowstone costs more today, paying to enter, camp, and fish in Yellowstone NP is truly a gift. The small pittance we pay hardly makes up for the result of loving the park to death.

My 1962 visit was free of those fees, including overnight at the now-closed campground a few steps from Old Faithful and West Thumb campground. The latter campground closed in 1980, but a new campground opened in 1984 when Grant Village was constructed. Tom Thumb has returned to a more natural state sans the campground and outhouses. Now, the grizzly has greater difficulty catching spawning trout, but visitors have more civilized facilities. And those trout, when caught by humans, must be released. Grizzlies and humans are not the only problems to native trout. Non-native trout, introduced to the park after 1962, became problematic, but the Park Service intervened. The interlopers are on the decline. Still, there is always something tipping the ecological scale.

Grizzlies were not seen or heard during my short stay at Tom Thumb in 1962, nor did Linda and I, in 1996, find bears of any species when we stopped at Grant Village to make a small purchase, an emergency chapstick, at the busy general store. The only bears were cranky motorists vying for a good spot in the long lines at the gas pumps. Alston Chase, author of *Playing God in Yellowstone* included in that controversial tome at least 48 different entries about Grant Village, and most of them were not complimentary.[1] I wonder what the twin biologists and grizzly specialists John and Frank Craighead thought about Grant Village. The architects of the village that took away the fish and grizzly habitat must have thought the

---

1. Alston Chase. *Playing God in Yellowstone: The Destruction of America's First National Park*. (San Diego: Harcourt Brace, 1987).

throngs of tourists would appreciate the new human habitat. Grant you, the village may be attractive to visitors with casual minds who like its gas pumps, stores, lodge, and visitor centers, but it seemed to Linda and me as unattractive as it must be to grizzlies.

Grand Teton NP ranks in size as twenty-fifth among national parks. The park includes Jackson Hole and the Teton Range, which is 310,000 acres or 485 square miles. A critical wildlife corridor between Yellowstone and Grand Teton Parks of 640 acres was added to the Grand Teton in 2018. Although next door to Yellowstone, apparently people skip visiting Grand Teton. Visitation in Grand Teton NP was 1,799,400 in 1962. Visitation was 3,405,614 in 2019, which is a small fraction visiting Yellowstone NP.

Birding in both parks was surprisingly unproductive. According to the park checklists, there were 300 species to stumble upon, but not much more than an innocent Ruby-crowned Kinglet crossed my path. I should have heard Neotropical species singing and residents marking their territories. Geology, not ornithology, had my attention and all those gurgling geysers drowned out the birds caroling nearby. Birding in 1996 when Linda and I briefly visited Yellowstone was likewise nearly birdless.

During the 1962 journey, I had two cameras, one loaded with color film, the kind to produce slides, and a second camera loaded with black and white film. Both were 35 millimeter cameras good for snapshots. The scenery kept me busy trying to frame my pictures, and at the same time, I worried about the cost of film and development. Today presents a whole different situation, when camera shutters open and close without worrying about cost or running out of film and editing pictures from framing to changing color to black and white is as easy as a click of a computer.

My early collection of pictures in Yellowstone reflected my fascination with geology. One might think that the geology of a region might indicate different habitats for the residing avifauna. Actually, it does. The original rocks weather and erode to become soil. The type of soil, along with climate, produces habitat. Birds occupy different habitats. I had just been unsuccessful in seeing what birds like which habitats. So, speaking of geology, short-term geological changes have occurred in Yellowstone since 1962. Beehive, in 2004, reportedly erupts twice a day, with hot plumes of water from 130 to 190 feet high for four to five minutes. It only erupted a few times a week in 1962. Who said geologic events take a long time?

My youthful dream of climbing one of the Teton peaks would still strain a budget in the twenty-first century. In 2004, the cost of a climb was closer to $300, but around 2019 the increase from 1962 was about 3,000 percent. Climbers are better prepared and are safer than ever before, but that does not matter now. Although a few years past 1962 afforded me the chance to learn a modicum of climbing techniques from a Crater Lake National Park ranger during employment there, Teton was out of my range. Grand Teton never was checked on my life list of mountains.

Perhaps it is just as well that I did not climb in the Tetons. Too many people today believe they are capable beyond their abilities. Consequently, each year people die while climbing in the Tetons. From 1997 to 2017, seven died on Teewinot, the Teton I tried to touch, the peak supposedly easier to climb than Grand Teton. Seasoned mountaineers surmise that people are less careful on mountains rated easier to climb than on mountains requiring technical skills. This is similar to the fact more accidents occur on straight roads than those with dangerous curves. My failure to at least touch the base of Teewinot was due to my failure to stay on the trail where I could have crossed Cottonwood Creek. Maybe I would have seen a Dipper there. Nonetheless, the whole issue of mountain climbing is moot because of two factors. One, I have inexplicably developed a healthy degree of acrophobia. Two, I am fast approaching octogenarianistic tendencies.

Lest I forget, the fees for climbing Grand Teton are not collected by the Park Service. They are collected by a business, just as are boat rental, a couple of youth backpacking companies, skiing, river cruises, lodging, and more. A similar plethora of concessions also operates in Yellowstone NP. Although concession businesses in national parks pay a franchise fee for setting up business in parks, concessions make a considerable profit, otherwise they would not be in the business and create larger private companies.

During the fall of 1996, Linda and I entered Teton NP at Moran Junction, a little over seven miles east of Jackson Lake. We splurged for a honeymoon night at the lodge just feet away from the lakeshore. The coming and going of boats and people did not detract from our stay. The next morning, but too early, we traveled the John D. Rockefeller, Jr., Memorial Parkway that borders Teton and Yellowstone. The 24,000-acre parkway, dedicated in 1972, offers protection to the ecosystems shared by the two parks. In 1962, the region between the parks was national forests, which were subject to hunting and logging. On our way to Old Faithful, the Rockefeller Parkway offered up my first moose, an animal that took me 52 years to see. I really should have gotten out more.

During our 1996 visit, Linda and I had to use one of the park's "rest" rooms. It was uncomfortably hot that September day. Thousands of people had used the very same "rest" room that we found ourselves forced to use. My early morning visit to the two-holler on that cool June morning in 1962 was nothing compared to the super-heated offal inside our September "rest" room. We were both grateful and nauseated for the facility. We observed others exiting, their faces squinched and blue from desperately trying to hold their breath as they bolted out the door on oxygen-starved lungs. Exchanged glances acknowledged a kind of camaraderie borne from running the gauntlet of the fetid "rest" room. That poorly maintained facility was in a store in Grant Village and was operated by one of the many concessions in Yellowstone.

That was not a great way to recall Yellowstone, but the handwriting was already on the wall, not the restroom walls, but everywhere. It began long before 1962, long before accelerating to 1996, and it has not slowed down (except for COVID-19). According to sources, concessioners and park policies consider what the visiting public wants. There is little doubt that a person parking a rickety food truck at a viewpoint could sell a few hot dogs to visitors. People would like that, others would ignore a food truck, and still others might bring their own food and water and enjoy natural nature. Do we really want parks to be crawling with lunch wagons and other human comforts or do we want parks to stay as wild as possible? National parks are supposed to protect wildlife. Perhaps humans need similar protection from each other.

Chapter 6

More Yellowstone and Big Sky Country

18 June 1962

PASSING WEST THUMB, I drove along the northern shore of Yellowstone Lake to the famous Fishing Bridge, where people crowd the bridge rails, elbow to elbow, their fishing lines dangling down into the lake with great expectations. There was not one angler in sight. Where did everyone go? Just two days ago on the shore of Yellowstone Lake near West Thumb, I saw small hordes of people casting and reeling and casting and reeling or whipping fly lines back and forth from the shore and more expectant fisher folks casting from small aluminum motorboats. What was going on were clouds wafting ominously overhead. By the time I drove about 16 miles down the road following the Yellowstone River, the dark clouds had billowed and grown, then stretched above as if a giant gaseous amoeba. Its threatening arms occasionally opened only to close again, squeezing frigid air over the already chilled Grand Canyon of the Yellowstone. The weather sent the fishing folks scurrying for cover.

Moments of sunshine pierced the clouded sky while driving to Inspiration Point. I wanted to get a look at the Lower Falls where the river plunges 308 feet into the canyon. The river had already plummeted 109 feet just about a mile upstream at Upper Falls. I planned to take a three-hour tour guided by a park naturalist in the morning, but I could not wait to see the region. The shocking beauty of the canyon and the thundering misty roar of Lower Falls overtook my attention that only a bird could interrupt. I spent the remaining daylight taking pictures, gasping at the impressive panorama, and worrying that it had been days since adding a new species to my trip list of birds. Maybe today would be the day for finding a Dusky Grouse. It was not.

19 June 1962

The early morning sky was a rich blue, with only wispy cirrus clouds scattered here and there. A small group of tourists led by a park naturalist ambled through a wooden archway of trees and to a viewpoint where they assembled in the parking lot at Inspiration Point. I followed. A guy maybe five years older than me was just ahead, and we began a conversation. I was pleased to hear of his admiration for the Park Service. The man told me how much he enjoyed Yellowstone, and he was a summer naturalist on his day off. He said, "I enjoy this place so much that I often go along on nature walks disguised as a tourist." He seemed as awe-stricken as I was when we reached the canyon's brink. The bright sun reflected the multi-hued wall made of an igneous material called rhyolite. Every shade of yellow imaginable graced the canyon walls. Pale golds, whites, and the deepest of orange competed with the yellow stone. Ospreys spiraled and soared above the excited water 1,200 feet below. With the help of the naturalist leading the group and the naturalist/tourist at my end of the tour line, I saw several more Ospreys, as well as two occupied nests. The official naturalist ended his talk, and my naturalist, the one on a bus-man's holiday, and I continued down the trail for another hour. We saw more Ospreys, and I learned more about the geology of the canyon.

With reluctance, I moved on. Just minutes from the canyon, I crossed the approximate boundary of the caldera. I had crossed the invisible line south of Madison when I entered the park. The boundary of the caldera nearly reaches the western boundary of the park, and it encompasses thousands of acres to the south on its way to Lewis Lake just off the road to Grand Teton, meanders across Yellowstone Lake and north of the canyon, before completing the circle near Madison. I would see more thermal activity before the day ended, but now it was time for lunch, and I was starving as usual. Tower Junction is a place I shall remember as cold, rainy, but worth the stop. Lunch is at Tower Creek, just before it empties into Yellowstone River and a waterfall, aptly named Tower Falls, drops 132 feet. By now, I had traveled about 20 miles from Canyon Village. I am not sure the distance between the rivers' Lower and Tower Falls, but the difference in elevation between them is about 1.500 feet. Clearly, the Yellowstone River was on a mission, creating falls and rapids on its way northeastward.

After about two hours driving a winding route, I arrived at my last major destination in Yellowstone NP, Mammoth Hot Springs. The first item on my agenda was to stake out a campsite. The campgrounds are just north of Mammoth Village. Mammoth Hot Springs is outside the caldera boundary where most of the explosive geysers, hot pools, and cauldrons of bubbling mud are found. Hot water travels underground from Norris, one of the first places I visited the day I entered Yellowstone, and flows to Mammoth along a fault line. The road from Norris to Mammoth, which I did not travel, generally follows the fault line. The super-heated water at Norris Geyser Basin has tipped the thermometer at 459 degrees. The water is 170 degrees by the time it reaches Mammoth. The hot water travels to the surface through ancient limestone and comes to the surface of igneous deposits. The hot bubbling of 100 or so springs at Mammoth is hot enough to form travertine terraces on the hillsides.

The first buildings at Mammoth Hot Springs were those of Fort Yellowstone in 1891. Sadly, the fort existed because of human pressure on the park. Poachers were killing animals, and souvenir hunters were collecting pieces of geysers. Both factions vandalized the park. Developers were also interested in the park's hot water for assorted reasons ranging from alleged health spas to a cheap way of doing laundry. Fort Yellowstone was constructed on an old terrace formation. Concern that the possibly hollow ground would not support buildings was not later shared when the Mammoth Hotel was built on the same site now called Hotel Terrace. The headquarters of Yellowstone NP and other buildings make up Mammoth Village, a place of administration and a home away from home for visitors.

A look around the sparsely occupied campground revealed that it sits on an old terrace also. My nearest neighbor was three campsites away (usually there were no empty sites by nightfall). The campsites are arranged in rows, parallel and up slope from the peaceful Gardner River, and each row of campsites are on terraces. A closer inspection of the sides of the terraces appeared to be thin layers of deposited strata that looked like the terraces of the active hot springs. Above the clear Gardiner River, heated by the runoff of the thermal springs, are barren hills and the thermal terraces of Mammoth. The whole region is different from most of the park that I have seen. Trees or any tall vegetation was missing. It was like being in the wide-open prairie but without the prairie. It was wide open with the mountains.

Leaving my tent to claim my campsite, I wasted no time driving back up to the hot springs. This area is as different from Old Faithful as Old Faithful is to the Grand Canyon of the Yellowstone. This giant thermal landscape is less dynamic than Old Faithful or Grotto Geyser but the placid water steaming all around, rimmed by clean calcium carbonate borders and towering white terraces, is magnificent to see and to feel. The walk from the parking lot to the top of the Upper Terrace was hot and nearly exhausting. The view from the top of the trail was fraught with the beauty of a rainbow of blues, ghostly whites, and crisp grays. Each brimming pool was a different size, and each spilled over their rims into the pool below. Many of the crusty walls held no water. Other pools held steamy water destined for Gardiner River. The rims of pools of Pallet Springs, a small terrace overlooking the village, are only crusty remnants. Nearby, the depth of brimming and piping hot pools revealed their newness. Far down and past the steam were the buildings of Mammoth Village. The numerous buildings curved around a fat green expanse, and a set of dwarfed, red-roofed structures appearing at the edge of the clustered hamlet sat near the steep road that descended to the campground.

20 June 1962

Awoke with the same strange feeling I had when first arriving at Mammoth Hot Springs. After breakfast, I packed the car for the trip northward through Montana. Just miles out of Yellowstone NP, it hit me. I was beginning to understand what was meant by the Big Sky Country. Mammoth was at the cusp of the big, expansive, and open sky country that people attribute to Montana. The look of the Big Sky of Montana brings with it a feeling, the same that I was feeling at Mammoth, and the same emotion much of the interior West emanates.

From the northern entrance of Yellowstone NP, I passed through a settlement called Gardiner where I pondered if the scientific name of a dark-breasted subspecies of a Pacific Northwest Downy Woodpecker was based on the name of the town. I also wondered why in the world my mind would entertain the origin of the name of a woodpecker in such a beautiful setting. What was I thinking? Before answering that, my mind focused on the surrounding scenery. After about a dozen miles down the road motoring along the Yellowstone River, I stopped at a pull-off to find my lunch, which I kept thinking I had forgotten to put in the icebox. Warm mayonnaise was not on my menu. I also had to check on the name of the woodpecker. I just could not let the origin of the subspecific name go. In my wooden bookshelf rested my very own copy of the American Ornithologists' check-list. In that tome were the latest conclusions on names of birds including woodpeckers. There, at the top of page 327, appeared the name *Dendrogapus pubescens gairdnerii*. No, the eponym had a different spelling. Was the name based on a different person that was honored for the northwestern subspecies, was the Montana town based on a person, or what? I was grasping at straws. Maybe I was spending too much time alone. All those days in Yellowstone and Grand Teton parks had not helped grow the trip list. Sure, I had seen numerous geysers and more scalding hot pools than I had thought possible, but I wondered, am I a tourist or a birder? Would big sky country, with its lack of heart-pounding volcanic activity and soaring Teton Mountains, be less distracting? Would I see more birds, the birds I needed to see for the sake of the trip list, in less dramatic scenery? Was I trying hard enough? Had I planned well? It was beginning to be obvious that I needed help, either from local birders or possibly from an unknown source of literature. Unfortunately, my knowledge of local birders was as sparse as the population of Big Sky Country. As for poor birding results in Yellowstone or Grand Teton Parks, there was no excuse.

After properly stowing the trusty checklist, I continued to drive north. The mountain road meandered, following the twists and turns of the Yellowstone River. At Livingston, the first major town on the route, I gulped down a strawberry shake and bought a few groceries for the total of 97 cents. Keeping track of expenses was a necessity. My melted ice was replaced, which cost 10 cents. About two hours later, I pulled up to the post office at Big Timber. The air had a sultry feel reminding me I was east of the Continental Divide. Because the mail sent to Monida had not been there about a week ago, and because I was anxious to hear from home after 18 days of being on the road, I wasted no time asking for any general delivery for me. It was a relief to see the thick envelope from Oregon forwarded from Monida to Big Timber. There were separate letters from my mom, dad, and even from my sister. Dad reminded me to be careful and eat a good diet. My mom addressed my earlier question about whether sausage spoils more rapidly than hamburger and wondered why I would be eating baloney since I did not like it. She suggested cheese, and, of course, reminded me to be careful. They also sent a photograph clipped from a newspaper. The caption read "Hungary Bear" and showed a bear with an added caption that read "just sizing-up a 'compact' car." The car was a VW Beetle.

I left the Yellowstone River and Big Timber and drove to Harlowton, a small town to the north. I also crossed part of the famous Lewis and Clark Trail, or at least the route on their return east. The terrain on the slow journey north on Montana State 19 from Big Timber to Harlowton began to flatten. I was on the edge of the Great Plains. Harlowton was full of potential. Pettingill's guide stated that Sharp-tailed Grouse perform within easy view from the highway and that early morning was the best time to catch their act. Unfortunately, my noon arrival was not good, and my June visit was seasonally past the best time to see grouse. They were most likely past displaying and were nesting. Pettingill's guide also described a place for longspurs, but no Chestnut-backed Longspurs and no Thick-billed Longspurs were in my sight.

21 June 1962

Although the trip to Harlowton was a washout, I discovered a free campground not far out of town. Apparently, no one had used the campground for quite a time; there were no freshly emptied car ashtrays, dog scats, or any other kinds of litter. The night was peaceful except for an occasional hungry mosquito. Only once was the quiet warm air set in motion as a fast freight rumbled and clanked on the railroad tracks next to the campsite.

Birding in Montana north of Yellowstone was not particularly productive yesterday or today. I decided to drive most of the day. No stops were on the agenda, and as boredom set in, I began to think about the species I am missing. Greater Sage Grouse, Chestnut-collared, and Thick-billed Longspurs continued to evade me despite my route. My path was probably too far east for breeding Mountain Plover. After 300 miles, the most I had thus far driven on any single day, I arrived at Glendive, a town of 7,000 that straddles the Yellowstone River. Today was a long and uneventful one, a time of realization of missing four or five life birds, and a day for thoroughly relishing Big Sky Country.

Since leaving Yellowstone NP just south of Gardiner, I followed the Yellowstone River to Big Timber, then drove north to Harlowton, and again followed the river at Miles City and northeast to Glendive. The river flows well over 400 miles and cascades down 3,245 feet in elevation before emptying into the Missouri River. Lewis and Clark spent their last night in Montana at what was to become Glendive. My last camp in Montana, about 500 feet above Glendive, is in nearby Makoshika State Park. Someone in town said Makoshika is the Lakota word meaning "badlands."

Reaching the park seemed to take too much time driving out of town block after block, turning right and left past house after house. The 5,600-acre park is a landscape carved and gouged by wind and water full of harshly eroded sandstone hills and bare yellowish banks cut into the landscape. Scattered groves of evergreens trees seem out of place. The hillsides are not completely bare by supporting sagebrush, cactus, and yucca. Wild grasses and flowers are scattered everywhere. According to local information, I should have found Prairie Falcons, but I did not. I was beginning to feel discouraged. Camping among the almost grotesque and outlandish formations was an eerie experience, especially as I was the only person in the isolated campground. I felt a little uneasy but was not sure why. Something seemed different. I told myself, as I nestled in the darkness and the warmth of the sleeping bag, that I would soon be crossing the line where western and eastern birds meet, the one hundredth meridian east of here, out in the Plains. Maybe that was it: I am about to leave the West and head into the country completely new to me. Sure, I had crossed but not birded the Plains in years past, but never so far north, and I had never been on the other side of the Mississippi River. I was feeling anxious anticipation.

∽

My experience in Yellowstone and Grand Teton had convinced me to give up the idea of working in a wildlife refuge. Becoming a park naturalist was the new goal.

Yellowstone NP is a fantastic place. Part of its fascination is geological, and the other is ecological or, as people might say, its wildlife. Yellowstone is also complicated and often controversial and discussing more than a few salient points of the controversy is beyond these pages. Actually, problems began from the beginning, the time when saving Yellowstone was but an idea. The mere bringing attention to Yellowstone brought more and more people, curious about the geysers, the animals, and forested mountains. Unthinking curious wanted a souvenir to memorialize their visit to the park, while others wanted more, such as hunting game and logging the forests. In 1886, a US Army cavalry company finally put the kibosh on widespread vandalism to geologic formations, including geysers, poaching, and stealing logged trees. The Army's mission was to administer and guard Yellowstone, which was needed, according to the park literature, for the removal of squatters and ne'er-do-wells out of the park. By 1894 Congress passed a new law protecting the park's wildlife. The army remained as wardens of Yellowstone until 1918 when the newly created National Parks Service became in charge. Park policies and implementing them changed over time. For example, bears, including grizzlies, were fed so that the public might have a closer look. Years pass, and the famed twin biologists, Frank and John Craighead, recommended to the park, please do not feed the bears. I had become familiar with their studies from my high school library that had a copy of one of their several books.[1] In 1971, the Park Service closed

---

1. John J. Craighead and Frank C. Craighead. *Hawks, Owls, and Wildlife.* (Harrisburg, PA: Stackpole Company and Wildlife Management Institute, 1956).

the artificial food supplies (dumps), but dump-dependent grizzlies became more aggressive. After fatal maulings of humans in the 1970s, the park began killing "guilty" bears. While the killer bears were punished, so were the Craighead brothers, who spoke about what was happening to the bears and were not taking kindly to the Park Service overseeing their research. Scientists become unhappy when outside forces want to direct their work. To make more sense from that last sentence, imagine visitors having to have their itinerary in the park approved by the administration of Yellowstone. I know I would not have wanted oversight during my 1962 visit. Recommendations. Fine, but that is it.

Meanwhile, the conundrum of how to be stewards to Yellowstone NP continued. How is the park to be protected and, at the same time, how to make it available for public consumption? The park administrators knew that elk were popular with two-legged visitors. In fact, over decades, earnest efforts to eradicate predators, other than humans, from the park were practiced. The plan worked. Elk populations increased. However, the demise of certain plants and the hordes of munching elk created unbalanced and unnatural habitats. In addition to having fewer predators, changes in the climate may have simultaneously contributed to an expansion in the elk winter range and caused a decline in riparian habitats dominated by willows (*Salix* sp.), with a concurrent significant plummeting in beaver populations. In other words, the superabundance of elk may be responsible for the demise of riparian shrubs, beavers, and other fauna and flora. The ecology of the park was teetering in the wrong direction, but the consensus in the Park Service was to let things be. That is, was it let things be before or after exterminating natural predators? Nature would sort everything out, or would it?

An example of not doing anything was the 1988 fire, the one that burned a whopping 36 percent of the park and presents a long and controversial story. In brief, the policy on wildfires in 1988 was, when fires were caused by the natural phenomenon of lightning, the park staff should naturally sit back and leave the flames to their own devices. That is based on the 1972 "let it burn" policy. It is doubtful that any animal requiring more than a blade of grass or bush to eat, or nest in, hide behind, or shelter from the weather, if they had opposable thumbs and could talk, would have signed an agreement to the wildfire policy of letting it burn. No matter, because the fire eventually became so large that people realized they had made a mistake by not attempting to control the conflagration, but it was too late.

Regardless of the widespread destruction, some thought the fire was beneficial, that the fuel load was too high, that all that lush, thick, and flammable forest needed burning. Notably, limited areas of the burned acres that had begun growing pines became victims of fire years after 1988, so fuel load might be a weak argument for letting it burn. Regarding benefits: More sun-loving wildflowers eventually sprung to life, trails offered better views of the surroundings since all those pesky trees no longer blocked the view, and another one, which I particularly cringe from, is that burning down the forest gives a chance for new growth of trees. What? Okay, deforest the land and give those baby seedlings a chance. Really? Yes, as heard from foresters that will go unnamed. Several researchers said that the burnt land was good as a laboratory to study recovery. Yes, but such laboratories already exist elsewhere. Yellowstone Park once contributed a perfect laboratory for studying climax forests, forests today that are disappearing, rare, or extinct. The perfect laboratory in Yellowstone is an opportunity that went up in flames.

What exactly is recovery, the word circulating 30 years after the fire of 1988? Logically, recovery means what was once there is now on its way of being there again, but the trees existing in the recovered forest are only about 30 years old. The dominant tree was lodgepole pine, a species with cones not releasing their seeds without a fire. Most of the forest that burned in 1988 is being replaced primarily by the same species of trees, but what of the other species of trees, those needing shade, and where is the understory, the ferns, and other plants? True recovery is allusive and difficult because, after the fire, the burnt acres were exposed to the sun, and therefore the region became hotter during subsequent summers. Greater temperatures often lower water tables and tend to favor pines over other kinds of conifers. Heat from fires open up the otherwise closed cones of white-bark and lodgepole pines but so do crossbills and Clark's Nutcrackers. According to reports, Yellowstone is on the mend, but what happened in Yellowstone NP might best stay in the park. What has happened there is not the best blueprint to follow in other regions of the country where less water-dependent pines or worse, maples and various species of shrubs, replace Douglas fir, true firs, and hemlock.

Advancing global climate change will alter the tune of those people evoking the idea that recovery follows wildfires. What follows is change. It might begin with a sprig or two, attractive yellow and red wildflowers blooming on a charcoal-black landscape. Perhaps there will be a recovery of a forest, a return to a normal state of health, mind, or strength, but how many generations will pass before a forest covers the previously scorched earth? Supposedly, some regions will never recover. The Amazon forest, once burned, is gone forever. People might best shelve the notion of recovery and recognize what happens is ecological change and that the change evolves for better or worse.

Animal ecology is also subject to change after a wildfire. According to Yellowstone, fewer than 300 large mammals died in the 1988 fires. Although that number is sometimes repeated as a fact, the unlucky 300 were most likely accompanied by many more individuals of large mammals. We cannot know how many other mammals were fuel to the fire. Some ecologists indicate small mammals might burrow deep enough in the ground to avoid being baked in an earthen oven. Maybe. What of those small mammals burrowing in the ground of a deep forest that survived and find their burrow were in a desert of ash? Nothing now to eat. What of birds? Sure, birds fly. What of the smoke-choked air known to kill not just large mammals, including humans, and birds miles away from the flames? Loss of life continues beyond the immediate fire because scorched land is left bare to erode, water retention is lessened, thus worsening climate induced drought, and fewer and fewer trees are available to perform natural carbon traps and pump oxygen into the environment for all to breathe.

Many claim fire is a way to manage forests, and that idea might help the ecology of forests, but there are limits. Fighting fires is now critical and, during the last few decades, it has become irrational to not suppress wildfires at every opportunity. Mismanagement of forests, rates of forest harvesting, more people in forests who originate wildfires, climate change in the form of increased temperature and drought, and already burned forests are just a few of the reasons why we cannot allow uncontained wildfires. Yes, some wildfires are natural, and studying the progression of ecological change is rewarding, but we can no longer afford that luxury.

If allowing naturally ignited wildfires to burn really means natural regulation of habitats, then why does Yellowstone build roads and erect buildings in the park? There is nothing natural about thousands of vehicles, summer and winter, or the millions of people driving and wandering through like disoriented ants. According to park statistics, natural lightning causes most of the fires in Yellowstone, and most of such fires "never" burn more than 100 acres. The word "never" appears on an official Yellowstone website. How natural is never? We are left with more questions than answers and, specifically with the Yellowstone conflagration, a lack of consensus. Branded experts voice a range of thoughts concerning the recovery of the region. A few investigators believe that park visitors today will not recognize there was a fire, which may be correct and at the same time insulting to visitors. Others believe it will take several decades, not three, but more, before the forests no longer look like the leftovers of a wildfire out of control. Of course, that depends on who is looking. Those "others" might consider visitors to national parks are not stupid and are, instead, informed and that visitors realize, perhaps from necessity for maintaining sanity if nothing else, to appreciate habitat changes occur from the aftermath of wildfires. Or, we can believe the notion that recovery is just around the corner, perhaps in our great-great-grandchildren's life, maybe a generation more or never.

While on the subject in the shadows of doom and gloom is the issue that wildfires and controlled burns contribute to global climate change. Burning is burning, and torching piles of trees cleared with the notion of reducing fuel and thereby decreasing the danger of a more disastrous conflagration is a curious practice. The Bureau of Land Management and the Forest Service frequently burn vegetation removed to thin forests. Commercial forest harvesters regularly burn slash following logging operations. It is a cheap method, damn the soil underneath that is ruined. Sure, controlled burns reduce the fuel loads of a forest but at what cost? Torching the understory is altering the habitat. Not all wildlife like living in a forest without a bush or two to hid behind. In fact, birds that nest in understory habitat or the ground are now often missing. Also, it should not require a PhD to realize that burning a carbon sink, whether a standing forest, understory, or slash, is emitting all kinds of gases including carbon dioxide. Those in the know estimate about eight billion tons of CO_2 from wildfires are emitted per year. I should use an exclamation point here but that punctuation is too weak. Some will point out that wildfires discharge only about 10 percent of CO_2 but any amount is too much. And, there are other harmful chemicals from accidental or purposeful burning of protective trees. Controlled burning versus not lighting that match is a matter of scale. At least that is probably the best rationale for the practice of controlled burning.

I freely admit that a portion of my understanding of wildfires is biased. Three summers during the college years were devoted to fire control in two different national preserves. That was when any fire was to be contained and stomped out as soon as possible. One of the preserves, which was revisited in 2022, had, after a succession of wildfires, lost almost every tree. Several years later, a private company set out to burn slash left from a clearcut too near home. The weather was too hot and dry for burning and the slash burned quickly and so did the nearby standing trees. Control of the controlled burn luckily happened later. Nostalgia is another source of bias about controlled burns and management of wildfires. The coniferous forests in Yellowstone were lush during my first trip to the park just as they were earlier in the late 1950s when my father hurried us to an Old Faithful's eruption and then got the family back on the road before the last camera shutter clicked. The trees were tall, stately, and wild then and in 1962. However, in 1996, Linda and I found an environment quite different from the one so fondly recalled. There was an openness. The air was not cool and fragrant from the smell of evergreen trees and ferns. It was hot and dusty. Billions of conifers and other plants were not there to filter and oxygenate the air, to lend to the headiness we knew mountain air was supposed to be.

A change other than wildfire occurred in Yellowstone NP. In 1962 during my trek north from Grand Teton NP to Yellowstone, I passed the site of Grant Village about a mile south of West Thumb. Tower Junction was renamed Tower-Roosevelt Junction, and several trails were built or rerouted. Compact cars such as my VW became less of a curiosity, eventually rating as commonplace, but lately are gradually replaced with larger and larger vehicles. Most gasoline and diesel-driven vehicles continue to deliver fewer miles per gallon than my trusty 1955 Volkswagen Beetle.

Just a year before my last visit to Yellowstone NP, the Park Service reintroduced wolves. It was a bold and provocative issue and one that made perfect ecological sense. Wolves once roaming the park were hunted with a vengeance between 1872 to 1926. The species was eradicated from the scene. Of course, ranchers outside the park were happy, but the reintroduction of wolves in 1995 made the locals beyond the boundary of the park unhappy. Still, the loss of livestock because of wolves is now paid for by the state governments. That makes the private landowners possibly more comfortable. Attitudes are slowly changing from "kill all those varmints" to a more conciliatory relationship between ranchers and wolves. The reintroduction of wolves has helped change the ecology of Yellowstone NP by decreasing the ravenous elk populations. The partial results show more trees, especially willows, survive the hungry elk and more trees mean more songbirds.

With all that has been and will be said, maintaining Yellowstone and other national parks and monuments is a tough row to hoe, a balancing act, a task possibly impossible. "Maintaining" may not be the correct word. Conserving, saving, perhaps keeping are useful words to plug into the mission of the Park Service. The official mission statement is the Park Service "preserves unimpaired the natural and cultural resources and values of the National Park System for the enjoyment, education, and inspiration of this and future generations." Even in 1962, my undernourished brain wondered about the survival of Yellowstone as it was being trampled by countless people. How will Yellowstone look and feel decades later? It was not so great almost four decades later. What actions might the Park Service implement to "preserve" the park? One tact in Yosemite NP was limiting but businesses outside Yellowstone objected. Fewer people visiting the park meant fewer potential customers. Money does talk, and the idea of limiting visitation was, well, limited to a so-called non-starter position. The maddening hordes of visitors require facilities to enhance their time in the park, but panoramic views should not take to the background for a new concession.

MORE YELLOWSTONE AND BIG SKY COUNTRY

Crowds continue to come, to create traffic jams and sully restrooms. After all, part of the mission statement is for the "enjoyment" of visitors today and those to come. A bladder about to overflow while waiting to access a restroom does not bring enjoyment. Long lines at entrance stations are not enjoyable. Truly, Yellowstone is being loved to death. Parks are known to occasionally adjust their policies for sociopolitical reasons rather than ecological reasons. This is an unfortunate yet necessary step to keep a balance between preservation and people. Criticisms on the care and feeding of Yellowstone NP have been leveled by Chase's *Playing God in Yellowstone*[2] and other publications on the park will come and go. Wildfires will come, and they will hopefully go. Ecological systems will change in time, but human pressures continue the upswing, a reflection on the old adage: there are too many people. Was it the fault of the Park Service that the humming environment of humans even in 1996 seemed to say a food truck would fit in just fine at Grant Village? The answer should be no, though someone has probably suggested a fleet of food trucks ought to help comfort all those hungry park visitors. Perhaps the park should hand out warnings stating "Please, do not feed the humans." Visitors could bring their own food. And pick up after ourselves, especially near park concessions where litter is denser. It costs to pick up after litterers, to pave the roads driven on, interpreting signs and rangers, overrun campgrounds, and more. Everyone from private citizens to government officials should bring to the table ideas and funding to save Yellowstone.

My last days in Yellowstone NP were days spent enjoying the park though I also felt the crush of the hordes of people seemingly looking for the same thing I hoped for, a peaceful scene of beauty that would be enjoyable; would be educational, inspirational; and would be there if I was able to return. Little did I realize what was under the tip of the iceberg.

It was a relief that my very last day in Yellowstone would be less harried, less crowded, and more peaceful than the days since my first busy camp in the park days earlier. Arriving in Mammoth in 1962 was the time I began to sense what people call Big Sky Country. The strength of the feeling, whether real or imaginary, contributed to my sense of unexplained relief as I drove out of the park. It was a feeling of openness, wide horizons, and unhurried tourists, of practically no tourists, and a feeling of being one with the land. That feeling increased during my drive northeastward into Montana along the 692-mile-long Yellowstone River that terminates in the Missouri River. The Yellowstone River, beginning in the Teton Wilderness

---

2. Alston Chase. *Playing God in Yellowstone: The Destruction of America's First National Park*. (San Diego: Harcourt Brace, 1987).

in Wyoming, is the last major river impeded by a dam and a river known by Clark. He stopped at a rock formation with Sacagawea, her infant son named Pompey, and 11 other members of the Lewis and Clark Expedition on the return to the East and took time to carve his name and the date "July 25 1806" on a stone now called Pompeys Pillar. (The useful apostrophe is not used.) The stone is about a half-hour northeast of Billings and has been protected as the 51-acre Pompeys Pillar National Monument since 2001. Today, the monument is accessible from Interstate 94, a highway that was just beginning with limited construction in parts of Montana in 1961. During my trek in 1962, Pompeys Pillar was accessible from US Highway 10, the same road that would take me across North Dakota to Fargo. Although on private property, the owners of Pompey Pillar allowed public access in 1956 and, in 1965, Pompey Pillar became a national historic landmark. One might think an Oregonian would jump at the chance to see where Clark carved his name, but the time in 1962 when I was near that part of Montana was a time for stern driving. I was on a mission—to begin to see eastern birds. It was not until about 30 years later that I saw Pompeys Pillar while traveling with Richard Banks on our way to an ornithological meeting in Missoula, Montana.

Putting the Rocky Mountains in my review mirror so soon was not the best plan for growing my trip list of birds. Rosy-finches (at the time, the three species were lumped into one species) were still missing from my list. I was too far south to try for White-tailed Ptarmigan. Dusky and Sooty grouse were treated as conspecifics in 1962, and I was not concerned about missing Dusky Grouse since I was naively confident that I would see Sooty Grouse when I returned to southern Oregon. There was still a chance to find a Harlequin Duck, but not as a breeding bird, and Boreal Owl would go unchecked. My route in Montana took me too far east of the mountains for a chance meeting of a Spruce Grouse.

In the days of 1962, my bird-finding skills were not terribly bad, but there was always room for improvement. There still is. Also, my zeal for exploration, to discover what was around the next corner other than birds, slowed my birding progress. My impatience to experience birding in the eastern US further hampered me from being a more thorough western birder. Should I audition the Peterson LP of bird songs more than I did? Absolutely. Had I been able to complete the circle around the United States in 1962, I would surely have realized the blunder of not trying harder for the western species I missed during that exciting June. Besides my lack of experience in 1962, bird-finding tools were limiting factors. The local people I contacted along my June route were invaluable for finding birds, but I had no connections in Yellowstone or Montana. In today's birding world, better and more available information is easier and it is faster to communicate information. Today, there are more birders with whom to communicate, whether using email, web postings, or other web-based methods that help birders find birds. Most birders in 1962 were isolated and regarded as odd, even suspicious. Knowledge about the birds of Craters of the Moon National Monument and Yellowstone and Grand Teton National Parks were far from definitive. It would be three decades before a bird-finding guide would cover Montana or Yellowstone NP and a bit longer before a state book documenting the birds of Wyoming would hit the presses.

My twenty-first-century birding in Montana has been primarily limited to the northern part of the state, particularly localities along US 2 during summer but too late for displaying grouse. Breeding Thick-billed and Chestnut-collared Longspurs, Sprague's Pipit, and Baird's Sparrow were there then, and with little effort once I read where to look. *Birding Montana*, the book, mentions finding the two species of Chestnut-sided Longspurs and Sprague's Pipit at Harlowton, but not Greater Sage Grouse.[3] Rumor has it that about a half-dozen leks may be active in the general neighborhood of Harlowton. That is great news since, range-wide, the Greater Sage Grouse population from 1965 has plummeted by 80 percent due primarily to habitat loss. The species in Montana once occurred in the millions but was down to only 44,000 in 2019. Just three years earlier, Montana counted 78,000. The blame for the recent loss of grouse was drought and just maybe wildfires. Habitat loss through fragmentation and just outright destruction are deadly culprits in eastern Oregon to Montana and Wyoming.

High anxiety tempered my thirst to drive eastward and the sooner the better. My last night in Montana, in Makoshika State Park, was in a park known for its dinosaur fossils, but dinosaurs have never piqued my interest beyond a casual acquaintance. My notes reported the size of the park as 5,600 acres, which may or may not be correct. By 2020, the park was 11,538 acres, with an increase of area acquired from a neighboring county, much of which had been held by BLM. Fees for day use and camping are now charged to visitors, but, according to my records anyway, there were no entrance or camping fees during the old days. I should have spent more time viewing the badlands and looking for reported Prairie Falcons, but I was thinking of birds to come and headed east.

---

3. Terry McEneaney. *Birding Montana*. (Helena, MT: Falcon, 1993).

Chapter 7

Mainly the Plains

22 June 1962

THE BRIGHTNESS OF THE sunrise mingled with the wakeful aroma of brewing coffee. Eggs were soon frying in my little aluminum skillet that was not really for frying or anything else. It was part of my mess kit from the Boy Scout days and was great for boiling water in it to help dislodge everything that stuck to its surface. Pushing aside thoughts of cleaning my breakfast dishes was easy as I sipped the steaming coffee and looking out over the steep hillsides and barren multicolored rocks of the Makoshika badlands. What a great way to start the day. In less than an hour, I would leave the West and cross into North Dakota. My route would be a beeline from west to east, a straight as an arrow track connecting Fargo on the east and Jamestown and Bismarck to Medora. Medora was important because it is the gateway to Theodore Roosevelt National Memorial Park, my next destination.

The trek to Medora would require at least an hour of driving, which gave me more time to think about my location. I knew I was in the Great Plains, but where, exactly did the western plains begin? Technically, my arrival on the Great Plains was somewhere east of Big Timber in Montana. I do not recall exactly because white settlers, their cattle, and railroads helped change the face of the land, in many places forever. Because of the settlements and range lands, it was barely possible to think grasslands were part of southeastern Montana. Textbooks I had read divide the plains grasslands into three types, including short, medium, and tall species of grass. This general classification of grasslands begs to be paraphrased with the premise that the further south one travels, the fewer northern birds you see. In the instance of the Great Plains, the farther east one goes, the less one finds short grass. After what we have done to the natural environment, it was hard to detect ecological boundaries. Still, about 30 minutes or less from my destination, I noticed grassland in eastern North Dakota that were tall. The only short grass I saw in the western plains had not reached its potential height, happened to be one of the more diminutive species native to the area, or was a nonnative interloper. For someone other than a botanist, it is difficult to discern the differences between a native grassland and one that has been restored, which is what people who know these things usually call a derived grassland. Moreover, there is a chance that such derived grasslands may have been invaded by Leafy Spurge and Spotted Knapweed. These two aggressive plants can rapidly choke out native grassland species, not unlike crabgrass and dandelions on a lawn.

Prairie and pothole country.

In Montana and western North Dakota, the natural grass consisted of western wheatgrass, green needlegrass, blue grama, needle and thread, and others. Of course, among the natural grasses are bushes (e.g., chokecherry, snowberry, and sagebrush) and trees (Ponderosa pine, juniper, and aspen) here and there, as well as barren, overgrazed, and over paved regions.

Roosevelt Park's three discontinuous units, that add up to just less than 77,000 acres, is located on the Little Missouri River in the North Dakota Badlands. The south unit, where I planned to camp, occupies about 10,500 acres. The formation of the badlands here and those at Makoshika State Park in Montana began tens of millions of years ago, first by sediments deposited from the eroding Rocky Mountains. The lowland sediments later became vegetated swamps, and new layers of sediment formed. Eventually, streams cut through the soft clay layers, carving multitudes of sandstone buttes, tablelands, and valleys. Anyone first seeing such a landscape probably thought the inhospitable scene looked pretty bad.

The flavor of the badlands is one of disbelief that erosion could be so devastating. There also is a taste of fantasy, with people in an old western movie waiting to ambush whoever comes within shooting distance. The badlands embody the tone of Zane Grey and Louis Lamour stories and Hollywood. This was a land of cowboys and cattle. In April 1883, the Marquis de Mores, a French nobleman, tried to establish a cattle empire and meatpacking plant not far out of Medora, a town named in honor of his wife. Theodore Roosevelt first came to the badlands during the fall of 1883 on a hunting trip, and during that time, he became interested in the cattle business. Roosevelt was fresh from college, looking for adventure, and shot his first bison. He returned from New York the next year and established the Elkhorn Ranch. Later he, like others before him, would make and lose thousands of dollars raising longhorn cattle. During visits to the badlands, Roosevelt became aware of the overgrazing cattle damaging the land and its wildlife. Conservation increasingly became a concern to Roosevelt, who once said, "I never would have been president if it had not been for my experiences in North Dakota." While president, Roosevelt established the US Forest Service and signed the 1906 Antiquities Act under which he proclaimed 18 national monuments, 5 national parks, 51 national wildlife refuges, and 150 national forests. Efforts by Roosevelt got the ball rolling, with the creation of the Migratory Bird Treaty Act in 1918 to the Refuge Recreation Act.

The year 1962 was a green year for the badlands, and I hoped for the rest of the Great Plains. After years of drought, the prairie rose bloomed in profusion, and dog-bane daisies, the state flower of North Dakota, were everywhere. Birds were abundant in the park, especially at Cottonwood Campground. Common Grackles seemed especially common, and there were Brown Thrashers and Catbirds to tally. Finally, I had entered the land of eastern birds. This unfamiliar territory was the beginning of what I was so anxious to experience. Now, almost every day, I thought I would find a new species to add to the slowly growing trip list. I could hardly believe my eyes. Both Red and Yellow-shafted Flickers were in the cottonwoods only 20 feet away. (These two taxa are now treated as conspecific under the name Northern Flicker.) I hardly slept that night.

23 June 1962

The morning was quiet except for near peaceful rustles from people walking in the half-empty campground perched near the bank of the Little Missouri River, a shallow meandering stream. Its water was cloudy with sediment, the carving of the badlands being an ongoing phenomenon. The park brochure mentioned it was safe to wade across the river when the water was not high from rain during spring or early summer or during the aftermath of flooding from melting snow. There was not a cloud in the sky, and there likely were no birds on the other side that would entice me to wade into the slow-moving river. It was impossible not to wonder if there were pockets of quicksand out there. Besides, my immediate campsite was rich with bird activity. I could keep my feet dry and watch iridescent Common Grackles scouring the campground for dropped morsels of human food. The two species of flickers were busy looking for ants that were possibly there because of camper leftovers. A pair of somber Mourning Doves was sitting very still in the trees and a House Wren was singing most vociferously near the restroom. The early morning brought the sound of a Common Nighthawk "penting" over the badlands, and the gentle sweetness of bright yellow American Goldfinches.

A male Red-headed Woodpecker called from a nearby tree, then, with a flash of black and white wings, sailed out of sight. A couple of Hairy Woodpeckers pecked almost in a whisper on a trunk of a cottonwood, and its diminutive twin, a Downy Woodpecker, foraged on a small nearby branch. When these two similarly patterned woodpeckers are together, it is readily apparent how they differ in size from one another. Besides the fact that the two woodpeckers were different in overall size, the shape and size of the bill are quite different; the bill of the Downy is small and comes more to a point compared to the larger chisel and almost blunt-ended bill of Hairy Woodpeckers. Of course, the bill is not always easy to see, but these birds like to vocalize and the *pik* sound of the Downy and the *pek* call note of the Hairy are also telling.

From the campground, I drove northeast on the park road that followed the Little Missouri River. Not far downstream from the campground, I came to Peaceful Valley and crossed a shallow Paddock Creek. The land rose about 200 feet above the Little Missouri River to the north. The abrupt rise in elevation revealed layers of color rising from the valley up to a place named Big Plateau. Beyond was the still higher Petrified Forest Plateau, reached only by trail.

Although it was great that there were roads into areas such as the park, not to mention other national parks, refuges, and forests, too many roads spoil the habitat. There was the construction of new roads, more campgrounds, and buildings in national parks. It was, in part, a grand plan to make protected lands accessible to construct buildings for visitors, including visitor centers and museums to preserve and interpret the regions. The plan was Mission 66, a federally funded project implemented in 1956, and that was to run to 1966, the fiftieth anniversary of the National Park Service. Originally, Mission 66 was supposed to improve deteriorated and dangerous conditions in the national parks that were the result of time and neglect, and the pressure from a massive boost in visitation following World War II. The program went beyond mere repairs and prepared for the onslaught of an ever-increasing visitor population to parks and monuments.

There is a pastoral flat on the south side of Little Missouri River near where the stream bends sharply to the north. Called Beef Corral Bottom, the flat was full of burrowing prairie dogs. I wondered about the name of this place. Maybe a corral was located here. In addition to Beef Corral, names such as Paddock for a creek and a trail, Roundup Horse Camp, and numerous names of localities suggested human activity related to the cattle industry. If there was, prairie dogs must have experienced considerable difficulty digging in soil compacted by once residing cattle. However the prairie dogs did it, I enjoyed seeing them much more than cattle, even if they were longhorns. A Kestrel hovered not far from the prairie dog colony. The little falcon did not seem to bother the prairie dogs that watched the hawk from near the entrance of their burrows. A couple of arriving Black-billed Magpies mildly excited the prairie dogs that were more concerned about my two-legged intrusion. Most of the little mammals disappeared underground at my approach.

By late afternoon I had seen several species usually considered eastern birds. Between Cottonwood Campground and Beef Corral Bottom, I tallied Red-head Woodpeckers, Catbirds, and Brown Thrashers skulking just out of sight. Common Grackles continued cleaning the campsites, and several species, which could be either western or eastern species such as Belted Kingfishers, rattled over the river as American Goldfinches and Black-capped Chickadees foraged in the trees. Western birds were also present in the park, with Lazuli Buntings and Western Meadowlarks.

23 June 1962

The night near the bank of the Little Missouri River was restful. After breakfast, I drove into Medora for the car's first oil and lube, costing $3.80. Medora was also where I bought a snack for later in the day, a few groceries, and more ice that cost a total of $2.96. The twenty-second of June was beginning to be an expensive day.

The wait to get the car serviced shot the morning. Starved, I returned to Cottonwood Campground, where my pale green pup tent stood to mark my territory. A quick baloney sandwich and a couple of crackers coated with crunchy style peanut butter put my growling stomach at ease. A hike about a mile down the river was fun. There were no other hikers, just the occasional car touring down the nearby road. I managed to get my feet wet after shedding my hot boots and socks. Getting my feet wet before shedding footwear was too often my plight. Black-capped Chickadees and a Killdeer called their names with their characteristic notes. There were more woodpeckers, including flickers, but nothing new for the trip list. Back at the campground seemed a suitable time to clean out any food crumbs and whatever else did not belong in the car. I also spent time getting these notes up to date, including compiling what I saw in the park. In my list, I noted that although the park had just prepared its first checklist of birds, it needed several corrections. Before the end of daylight, was time to organize the car for tomorrow's destination.

24 June 1962

The overladen VW took me east where I had my last look at the park at Painted Canyon, a vast panorama stretching for miles to the north. Layers of soft red-banded and scarred hills and hummocks were far and near. Roundish dark green bushes dotted a few of the nearer summits and mixed with short grasses on the lower slopes. Whitish and gray mounds and scars contrasted with the greens, reds, and clear blue of the sky. I was alone, the highway empty, while sharing the powerful scene with only the open sky and a magpie that scolded from an unseen perch. What birds, what peace, and beauty. This was not a bad land.

Hurrying east, as if a 1955 VW Beetle could hurry, I drove about 120 miles. Even that short distance proved that the farther east you go, the taller grass you see. Besides watching the grass grow, Yellow-headed and Redwinged blackbirds flitted, gurgled, and rasped from occasional marshy areas. Just west of Bismarck I crossed the mighty Missouri River, the watery route of the Lewis and Clark expedition. My land route was over extremely flat and very straight miles of miles. After a few more miles on US 10 on Sunday afternoon, I turned south to head for Moffitt. Moffitt is a small town just outside Long Lake NWR of 22,310 acres, one of several refuges in North Dakota and the Central Flyway. The refuge is on the mixed-grass prairie and has a few ravines, cultivated fields, planted small trees and shrub, marsh, and, of course, Long Lake. The lake is a natural lake, although regulation of its water levels is maintained at about 16,000 acres to help control botulism, a deadly disease that paralyzes the inner eyelid and neck muscles of waterfowl, especially ducks and geese. That is what the refuge checklist stated.

The checklist had a few birds I hoped to see. It was too late for displaying Sharp-tailed Grouse, but maybe I would get lucky. I was running out of time and range for the species. The manager had written earlier that several species of shorebirds might be possible, but that was before the end of the drought. The grasses had responded to the spring rains, and most of the ponds were full and not leaving much space for shorebirds. Luckily, Lesser Yellowlegs, a new species, which were common, and Wilson's Phalaropes and Willets, were easy to find. Spotted Sandpipers, Killdeers and Avocets, rounded out the small list of shorebirds. A pair of Upland Plovers had nested in the middle of one of the dike roads. The pair had not been seen in a few days, and as luck would have it, the plover was missed. There were several species of ducks, white Common and charcoal Black terns, and Eastern and Western kingbirds. The white-breasted Eastern Kingbird reaches far into the West, all the way to Oregon (the first one on the trip was at Malheur NWR), although I had not started seeing many of them until the badlands. The yellow-breasted Western Kingbirds are truly a western species and do not extend eastward much beyond Minnesota.

Chestnut-collared Longspurs bounded from the roadside in an upland part of the refuge. Most of the longspurs were singing while they wheeled through the air flying a dizzying circle. At least it was dizzy for me. The male's jet-black breast contrasting with the mottled back and chestnut collar was spectacular. The displaying males shared the air with Horned Larks, flying even higher than the longspurs, and foraging Cliff and Bank Swallows. Lark Buntings perched along the fence. The males' white wing patches flashed in contrast to their black bodies and the lush green prairie.

Birding continued until dark and was followed by a night on the floor of the manager's office at refuge headquarters. There, surrounded by tired grays, greens, and browns of furniture and wall, metal desks, and a prominently displayed picture of President Kennedy, US and state flags, books and manuals, and a pair of muddy boots, was a cozy place for me to sleep.

MAINLY THE PLAINS

25 June 1962

By noon, following a couple of hours of birding at Long Lake, I had covered the short distance to Arrowwood NWR located on the James River and north of Jamestown, a major city in North Dakota. The refuge property has three natural lakes and regulated water levels for migrant and breeding birds and control of botulism.

As with Long Lake, my visit to Arrowwood NWR was to find certain species of shorebirds and so-called songbirds. Once again, because of the nearly steady rainfall that lasted five weeks, the water and the grasses were too high to promote good shore birding. The only staff member at the refuge office was a clerk. Unfortunately, I lost his name, but he was an excellent guide. We started birding about 1 p.m. from the west side of Mud Lake, one of the four water bodies backed up by a series of dams on the James River. We purposefully ignored waterfowl, and soon left the gravel road and turned left onto a dirt track marked with two long and obscure spots worn bare from vehicular traffic. An expanse of tall grass that grew on both sides and the middle of the track surrounded us. The pickup we were riding in parted the sea of grass until we, at last, lurched to a stop at a grove of isolated trees. I felt a little bad for the tall grass knocked down by the truck. We got out and waded through the prairie grass. At first, all was quiet but in seconds a strange new sound dominated the silence. It was definitely a flycatcher. By now, we had found three species of flycatchers. Eastern and Western kingbirds were the most common and most visible while Willow Flycatchers were the least visible species. Somewhere in the sea of grass was a new sounding bird, a new life bird, the Least Flycatcher, an *Empidonax* that had eluded me for several hundred miles. A singing bird burst forth a *che-bek, che-bek* from a cottonwood. It finally perched in full sight while continuing to sing. Two others were singing in the distance.

Walking in the tall, six-foot prairie grass is difficult. It is impossible to see much of anything in any direction, but the nearby trees offered perches for birds to see over the grass and a stage to deliver their territorial song. After just a few feet of wading through the grass, I heard four buzzes. The sound was so near and so loud as to be almost ear-piercing. The source was a Clay-colored Sparrow, tidy and trim as any sparrow could be. It is a neat bird, with its unmarked undersides, brownish cheeks, a white line above the eye capped off with a streaked crown. This was a great bird to see. Perched inches away from my first sighting of a Clay-colored Sparrow was a Baird's Sparrow. It reminded me a little of a Savannah Sparrow, only bolder, different. Later in the day, more Clay-colored and Baird's sparrows became available for my viewing pleasure. Both are common species to the refuge.

The Baird's Sparrow was critically good to find; another few miles and I would be out of their breeding range.

Back at headquarters, I cooled down in the shade with a tall glass of cold water or the equivalent that a handy garden hose could deliver. On the other side of the lake were people swimming and I soon joined them to cool away the sultry afternoon and the day's accumulated grime. After the refreshing swim, I drove south to Jamestown and, in the dimming daylight, found a field to pitch my tent. With no idea who owned the field, I took a chance that it would be okay to camp there. Trespassing was not a behavior I felt comfortable doing, but it was late, the field was there and far from any houses. Before the light completely disappeared, I got out the typewriter and pounded out a note to my folks without telling them I was camping on someone's property without their permission.

The constant burning questions from my supportive folks: Are you safe and are you eating well? I wrote: "I am okay, and I am eating well. Probably too well for my budget, but I believe that I am doing better than a German fellow met a few days ago. He was touring the US eating black walnuts and anything else he could find that would not dip into his money."

I paused to cook dinner. After the meal, I finished the note, checking for spelling errors by flashlight. I also sent my parents the following list of items I had for my evening meal:

1 #303 can, Mount Maurice sweet peas 16 cents
1 #303 can, Franco-American spaghetti 20 cents
2 vanilla cream-filled cookies about 10 cents

26 June 1962

Part of the day was to fulfill a promise to visit the father of an Oregonian who lived in the small farm town of Valley City. There seemed to be a bit of consternation and bewilderment among those I visited since they seemed unable to understand me traveling alone just to see birds. Later in the afternoon, I discovered Fargo did not have a YMCA, and I was getting desperate for a shower. Perhaps my Valley View farm host's consternation was not so much about what I was doing but how I might have smelled. I hope not. I had been taking sponge baths daily and changed clothes regularly, but camping is camping. My apologies are to anyone who crossed my path and was encumbered by a hygienic insult. Fortunately, there was a YMCA at Moorhead, which was just across the Red River in Minnesota. It felt great to have the hot water and soap wash over me. It was wonderful to be clean. A shave and change of clothes at least made me slightly presentable.

Still following US 10, I passed Buffalo River State Park where I could have camped, and I could have driven north to Tamarac NWR where Pettingill offered strong assurances of a Red-necked Grebe. I did neither and drove on to Perham, an area all about baseball.

It was getting late again. I had tarried much too long today and had little to show for it. A road leading north out of Perham looked promising for a place to camp. Occasional signs along the way advertised lake resorts. After several turns and forays down side-roads, I began to realize that I was lost or at least had misplaced myself. Finally, a congenially worded sign to Little Pine Lake came in view. Several neat little cabins and a boat dock stood at the end of a driveway. This was not a place I could camp, and as I was turning around in the driveway a tall man approached me. He was bearing a smiling face as peered at me. I told him that I was looking for a campground. He said there was not any close by, but he welcomed me to pitch my tent between his resort and the road. I thanked him and he replied, "Sure, sure. And what about breakfast? Is 5:30 too early?" What luck. After thanking my host, I hurried to pitch my tent. Light was dampened by thickening clouds. I fastened the flaps of the tent and thought about breakfast tomorrow.

∾

The grassland traversed in eastern Montana is in trouble, with 85 percent of the northern biome grazed by cattle or converted to dry-land farming. About 46 percent of the western short-grass habitat is gone, mostly from grazing and drought. The farther east one goes, the more acres of natural grassland are consumed, blotted out, by human creations, with 76 percent of mixed grassland lost and tallgrass prairie obliterated. Besides agriculture, including grazing, a little over one-third or almost 10 million acres of grassland disappeared to exploding populations demanding more and more land for housing, shopping malls, and highway right ways. According to the World Wildlife Fund, Great Plains grasslands disappear faster than the Amazon Basin is deforested. The loss does not appear as dramatic as cutting down or burning up forests, but the insidious destruction of grasslands is dangerous to the environment and ultimately deadly. Part of the acreage used for cultivation continues by what reports called the perverse incentives of paying landowners to convert grasslands to crops they would have not otherwise grown. At this reading, there are ongoing efforts through government grants and private money to save the grasslands.

In the meantime, numerous species frequenting grasslands are at risk of becoming homeless, which in nature equates to nonexistence. Lesser Prairie-Chicken is at the edge of extinction. Baird's Sparrow lost 65 percent of its numbers since 1968, and too many other species are becoming rarer than hen's teeth. How do we know? The declines of grassland species have baseline population studies beginning in the 1960s that show populations spiraling downward to this day. Protection is available by a handful of national wildlife refuges, postage stamps in size compared to the former range of grasslands, and several slightly larger National Grasslands, a classification created in 1960. Unfortunately, according to a National Grassland official website, there are 20 such grasslands that, besides birding, offer opportunities for mining, including extraction of oil and gas.

Reclassification of the monument as Theodore Roosevelt NP occurred in 1978. Reclassification of flickers began in 1965. That was when published results on interbreeding flickers shed light on what would eventually lead the American Ornithologists' Union to conclude the yellow and red-shafted flickers are conspecific. Now we call them Northern Flickers.

While in Roosevelt NP, I took extra time to compare Downy and Hairy woodpeckers. Both species of woodpeckers exhibit considerable geographic variation in size and plumage, and though I was barely aware of geographic variation and subspecies in 1962, I did believe the woodpeckers observed in my native birding patch of southwest Oregon differed from those in Roosevelt NP. I began wondering about confusing species since reading somewhere that birds are generally small in their southern range and larger farther north. What if a large migrant Downy stopped in the park? Would it appear similar to resident Hairy Woodpeckers? Does either species migrate? My trusty fifth edition of the AOU check-list was not clear; some subspecies might migrate. A little information can be a dangerous thing and what was available to me in 1962 was insufficient to satisfy my curiosity. The question concerning migration and thus the need for greater care in identifying the woodpeckers by size was by a woodpecker expert back in the 1980s. That person stated Downy Woodpeckers migrate. However, the more or less short version of the story is that Downy Woodpeckers are permanent residents. Since Downy Woodpeckers do not migrate, separating a large northern Downy Woodpecker theoretically on its way to Canada from a smaller southern Hairy Woodpecker would not likely be a problem.

Enjoying the park and woodpeckers was partially possible because of roads. However, there is a fine line between public access and the protection of a region. The Park Service's Mission 66, completed in 1966, did build and improve roads, campgrounds, and erect over 100 visitor centers in our national parks and monuments. Improvements necessarily continue. My last viewpoint of the park was once a quiet and remote place, but it is now the site of a visitor center constructed in 1978. I am not sure whether to feel grateful or sad.

A lube in the 1960s really meant just that; cars had zerk fittings where a service station person squirted heavy grease to lubricate joints and moving parts of a vehicle. Those too young to know and those too old to remember may, at this point, be confused. First, the term lube is still misapplied to certain facilities that only change the oil. Second, most cars are now factory sealed and thus do not require other lubrication. An oil change now costs significantly more than it cost in North Dakota in 1962. Think a sum approaching $4 back in the day. In the twenty-first century, an oil change, including an oil filter, easily costs more than $50. Most service stations today do not change the oil. The facilities have become gas stations. Forms of service hardly ever extend to cleaning a windshield but there is an employee, usually, to take your money. Drivers even pump their own gas, which I and most drivers usually prefer.

Part of the 8,000 acres of grassland in Arrowwood NWR contained the tallest grasses I had ever experienced in 1962. The nature of the grasslands and other habitats in the refuge are now more under human control. "Controlled" burning has been used in refuges since 1968 "to restore, change, and maintain a diversity of plant communities to restore and perpetuate native wildlife species," according to the refuge website in 2004. Goals of controlled burning include the restoration of native grass species and concurrent reduction and control of non-native species. The refuge also uses grazing as a mechanism to improve the natural state of the habitat. Their website also stated that "sometimes grazing is used in conjunction with prescribed fire to achieve a desired effect." One sure result from the latter practice is burning the hamburger.

Two obvious factors in the ecology of the prairie are fire and grazing, but to what extent is that possible since natural prairie has been so severely reduced. Can we afford to burn the prairie? Yes, probably to a certain degree while attempting "to achieve the desired effect." Grazing, on the other hand, is problematic. Should "controlled" grazing be under the natural spell of bison? Are bison or bovines the best choice for controlled grazing? After all, refuges include wetlands, and cattle habitually hang around the old watering hole and under the shade of trees. In so doing, the life around water and under trees is severely impacted, pun intended. Bison are less likely to clutter up the environment around water and trees, but whether bison or cattle, the grazing acreage in Arrowwood and other refuges is small, which seems to suggest cattle might be the better choice. Bison tend to require more acres per animal than cattle. However, I am familiar with the reluctance of cattle to obey only less than polite directions, and it is difficult to comprehend herding bison. The keyword may be controlled, and the emphasis might be to keep the bovines away from the water. Is part of the answer goats? A few refuges are using them for eradicating invasive plants.

In 1962 I was unaware that building a dam on the James River began in 1955. The dam was completed, and the new Jamestown Reservoir was filled in 1964. Unfortunately, the reservoir severely handicapped the ability of the refuge to manage water, though ironically the refuge was engineered to do just that. Following years of pontification, Congress, in 1986, reversed the negative impact of the reservoir by directing the construction of a bypass channel and better means of controlling water levels. New higher capacity water control structures, initiated in 1987, were completed by 2006.

Since visiting Arrowwood, a series of floods washing the shores of headquarters meant any hoofed plant controllers, be they bison, cattle, or goats, were likely in a sink or swim mode. A new headquarters and other facilities, built on higher ground, opened in 2012.

The checklist of birds at Arrowwood NWR used in 1962 was revised in 1961 and listed Baird's Sparrow as a common summer resident. The checklist for the refuge dated 2012 listed Baird's Sparrow as abundant in spring, summer, and fall. Compared to older checklists, the newer one from Arrowwood defines the terms for frequency, with abundant as "over 600" individuals. The presentation of information in the new checklist is a welcome improvement.

Arrowwood NWR was once a good place for birders to add Baird's Sparrow to their life list. According to current (2021) information emailed from refuge manager Paul Halko, Baird's Sparrow has not been seen in the refuge in the last 10 years. Based on the refuge checklist dated 2012, and the sparrow not being seen 10 years from 2021, Baird's Sparrow was absent in 2011. The reasoning here does not necessarily cause a conclusion that someone made a mistake. Why? Lag times from when a manuscript, in this case, a checklist, is submitted and the time it is printed of course is a fact of life. Still, it is reasonable to believe the checklist was written around 2010 and that Baird's Sparrows could have undergone a population crash. Perhaps there was a major change in habitat structure. Maybe the habitat was heavily grazed. Regardless of who let the cows out, or whatever, Baird's Sparrows no longer breeds in the refuge. They do breed west of the refuge, and, although not listed as breeding in Long Lakes NWR in the 1960s, Baird's Sparrow has since then been listed as uncommon. Another mystery is that my 1962 records of sightings of Baird's Sparrow in Arrowwood NWR also included Clay-colored Sparrows. According to common references, the two species prefer different habitats. Just how different . . . well, perhaps more on Baird's Sparrow another time.

Regardless of all the facts, I was grateful to Theodore Roosevelt in 1962 and presently that public land exists. Once Teddy became president, he set aside 230 million acres of public land. He established the first national wildlife refuge, Pelican Island NWR, in Florida in 1903. Roosevelt did not stop there and established at least 176 different national wildlife refuges, national forests, reserves, national parks, and national monuments. Only two presidents (Bill Clinton and Barak Obama) have preserved more public land than Theodore Roosevelt. Jimmy Carter (a birder) comes in a close fourth in championing public land. All, except Roosevelt, were during my lifetime. This might suggest an improvement since the 1960s, but four presidents serving since that year did not preserve any public land and one actually reduced the size of the protected area. Someone has surely done the math. As for refuges, today over 550 national wildlife refuges dot the land, with over half of them established after 1962.

Over 70,000 acres of public land were set aside as Theodore Roosevelt Memorial National Park in 1947. Before that, the park was designated Theodore Roosevelt NWR. The park had a name change to Theodore Roosevelt National Park in 1978. Since visiting the park in 1962, visitor centers and more trails help accommodate the increase in visitation. In 1962, 245,700 people visited the park. Almost three times that many visited the park in the recent past. The more people, the more public land is needed to accommodate the curious, the adventurous, and those looking for a slice of peace and beauty. At the same time, wildlife requires protection from all those trying to see the fauna and flora. We are going to need a bigger boat.

Chapter 8

Mosquito Coasts

27 June 1962

FIVE THIRTY CAME EARLY. Mr. Jorgenson, my host and maker of congenial signs, was a great cooker of eggs and bacon. He was wide awake and one cup of coffee up on me. We talked through breakfast by first comparing the pros and cons of our respective states. I reminded him that Oregon had far fewer mosquitoes than the millions foraging from every shore of every Minnesota lake. He laughed and scratched an ugly welt on his arm that had grown from an ugly mosquito. I admitted that Minnesota did not have the corner on mosquitoes and that, as a camper, I had the bloodsuckers either constantly on my mind or on bare skin I foolishly exposed.

My host discussed his thoughts on access to Little Pine Lake. He told me that private property surrounds most lakes in the form of homes or as little resorts trying to catch tourist dollars. He hoped to encourage more people to provide campgrounds for tourists and share the lake shores for tourists increasingly wanting places to enjoy the outdoors. I think he may have seen the handwriting on the wall, tourists crowding Old Faithful, vying for campsites, clogging the roadways, and, by sheer numbers of people, ultimately defeating the reason to be outdoors. Overrunning the feeling of remoteness, of peace and quiet, the quest by tourists to get away from it all was in a mode of self-destructiveness. My host frowned at my words but nodded and said there are too many people and not enough good places for them to fulfill the needs to enjoy nature.

I wished my host good luck and thanked him for his generosity and for directions to get back to the highway. Would he open his little slice of shoreline to tourists wishing to wake the next morning to experience a bit of nature? Would he support policies to protect nature as classrooms for tourists hungry for a place to stay and needing to learn what the natural world can teach? I hoped so.

My next stop was Brainerd for my next general delivery mail. Not far west of Brainerd, I crossed the Mississippi River for the first time in my life. I expected the river to be wider though I reminded myself that I was not all that far from its headwaters, Lake Itasca at 1,475 feet above sea level in the northern woods of Minnesota. A brochure picked up at a gas station included interesting facts about the Mississippi. For example, the river flows 2,552 miles before emptying into the Gulf of Mexico south of New Orleans, Louisiana. Mississippi is an Ojibwa (Chippewa) Native American word that means "a great river or gathering of waters." The Nile, Amazon, and Yangtze are the only rivers that exceed the mighty Mississippi River. The watershed of the Mississippi River drains from the Rocky Mountains to the Allegheny Mountains in the eastern United States, a region including 31 states and three Canadian provinces. That is approximately 40 percent of North America. Millions of birds migrate up and down what we call the Mississippi Flyway and some of these birds use the Upper Mississippi River NWR, the longest refuge in the lower 48 states. It extends 261 miles along the Mississippi River from Wisconsin to Illinois and covers 242,400 acres. The only bird I noticed crossing the Mississippi in Brainerd was a lone Rock Pigeon.

At last, I was east of the Mississippi River and could put Pettingill's west of the Mississippi guide in the storage box in the back seat. I had already put in storage my western Peterson, my familiar guide not to be used until my return to the West next year. Reining in my excitement of birding in the East, I followed directions from a service station to find the Brainerd post office. A letter from my parents was there. They each wrote, usually, about what they did individually and together. It is comforting to know your parents are close. My little sister, just barely a teenager, also wrote. There were even a couple of notes from Oregon friends. Everyone was fine. Mail from home was a good thing. Meanwhile, my stomach sent me messages; my early breakfast fooled my system into believing it was already lunchtime. I made the difficult decision to ignore the hunger pangs and wait until my next birding site, which was about an hour away.

It was noon when I arrived at Rice Lake NWR, a refuge of almost 16,000 acres of bog, marsh, and lake in central Minnesota. I checked in with Alex Claud, the refuge manager, who I had written months ago about visiting the refuge. He surprised me by offering their visitor cabin during my stay. The cabin was a little cracker box building known as Antler Inn. An orange and black Baltimore Oriole calling nearby and the idea of four walls and a roof were appealing. Electricity, running water, and a stove were improvements in every way. This was better than the CCC mess hall at Malheur NWR. All those days camping this month made me appreciate even more the comfort of twentieth-century conveniences. More importantly, as I was learning that Minnesota grew voraciously hungry and persistent mosquitoes. After all, I was in the land of a thousand lakes and a zillion mosquitoes. The cabin saved me.

Following a hastily prepared and welcomed lunch, I again met Mr. Claud, who gave me directions and a map for the better birding areas of the refuge. The dusty road from headquarters brought me to a marshy area near the lake shore where I heard a horse-like whinny. I recognized the sound from hours of listening to Peterson's LPs of bird songs and calls. My first Sora was, like most rails, heard but not seen. Practically in the same spot, a Sedge Wren jumped briefly in and out of view. In a field nearby, singing Bobolinks flew all around. Not far up the road, the wetland gave way to a grassy open habitat where I got a good look at a Field Sparrow, in this case, not a life bird but a new species for the trip list.

Common Loon was still not checked off on the trip list though Mr. Claud supplied explicit directions for a guaranteed loon. As instructed, I parked the car at an intersection just west of headquarters. Then, I hiked down an obscure dirt road that angled off the main dusty route. The intersection where I parked baked under the afternoon sun; the route I hiked at first felt cool in the shadows of the tamarack and other hardwood trees. The narrow, seldom-traveled road led to Mandy Lake, small and hidden in the deep-forested ridges of Indian Point. Small pin-sized shafts of sunlight penetrated past the green trees to shine on layers of brown and gray decaying leaves. The air did not move. What might seem a pastoral scene quickly turned to, for a lack of a better word, hell. The mosquitoes that now and then attacked my naked arms began to be more than a little annoying. The farther I advanced toward the unseen lake, the more intolerable the blood-suckers became. Trotting down the road rather than walking might keep the mosquitoes at bay. That did not work, so I tried running until I reached the lake. I stopped, raised the binoculars to scan the lake, and spotted a solitary Common Loon. My arms were held motionless for the seconds it took for my brain to process a confirmation that the bird was definitely a Common Loon, which was more than enough time for hordes of mosquitoes to blacken my bare skin. Each of the countless insects dipped their piercing mouth to quench their thirst for my blood.

My arms were not enough. Mosquitoes unfortunate enough to not make it to my arms, neck, and face, went through my thin T-shirt. Dancing up and down, waving my arms, and screaming words incomprehensible to the buzzing bloodsuckers did not help. My actions probably routed the loon but, by now, I could care not less about the emotional state of anyone or anything but myself. It was fight or flight. Fighting was useless; I was outnumbered. I had earlier noticed that the junction of the main road where I left the car and the road to the lake was a 45-degree angle for a few yards before paralleling the main road. Frantically, I made a mad dash through the forest in the direction I hoped the road to be. Crashing through the underbrush, tripping over occasional rocks, and slipping down the side of a steep bank near the road was part of my great escape. The ground became wetter and spongier. On came the mosquito charge. I soon was in a black bog, where each step from the smelly decay tried to take my shoes. I barely glanced at more carnivorous pitcher plants than I had ever seen. If I did not keep moving, I might be their next meal.

At least the temperature was relatively cool, and it felt welcome compared to the sweat that the exercise had worked up. My progress was slowing, and the brigades of mosquitoes seemed to gather new forces faster than I could wipe away their blacked bodies and my blood. Gradually the rotting ooze of the bog changed to more solid ground. In a minute, I saw the road, dusty and reflecting the hot sun. I jumped into the middle of the road, where no mosquito dared to follow. That was a Common Loon the hard way.

The car was not far from my escape route. The run through the woods left me scratched, muddy, and I itched almost all over. Luckily, the welts and itching disappeared, thanks to my immune system. Back at Antler Inn I cleaned away the adventure and cooked my dinner on a real stove. A familiar buzz of an occasional indoor mosquito turned to silence after a slap of a rolled newspaper. After dinner, the Clauds asked me to join them to look for turtles that were laying eggs. On the way, we stopped at Mandy Lake, driving the road I had earlier walked. Nervous, I rolled up my windows to avoid any misunderstandings with mosquitoes. Mr. Claud whistled an imitation of the Common Loon that was so good that two loons responded by repeatedly calling as they approached him. Mr. Claud did not seem bothered by the pesky mosquitoes; it made me cringe just to see him engulfed by the bloodsuckers.

We found several turtles laying eggs in holes they dug in the soft dike roads. Turtles do shed tears during the process. It must be a strain. Once the female has laid the last egg, the soft earth pushed over the set of eggs, and the cavity she dug filled, the mother-to-be walks, albeit slowly, away. We carefully examined one of the turtles that had just completed its tearful behavior. The intricate lacework of the net-like pattern of the shell suggested that it was the western painted turtle otherwise known as *Chrysemys picta*. If our identification was incorrect, it was of no consequence to the turtle as it ambled steadfastly away from our curious eyes.

A common enemy of the turtles, including snapping turtles, in the refuge is the striped skunk. They eat turtle eggs. The skunks even go so far as to follow the female as she searches for a place to deposit the eggs. Skunks will eat the eggs as they are being laid, grabbing them in their paws and biting into them before the eggs touch the ground. That may sound brutal, but every natural animal must eat to live. Unlike humans who eat more than they need (my apologies to those who do not or cannot), most other animals eat what they need. The turtles lay lots of eggs, some of which do not hatch for assorted reasons, the eggs are destroyed or eaten, the young die or are eaten, and the surviving young gain maturity, reproduce, and lay eggs. The skunk may not find enough to eat, so it cannot produce enough milk for its young, of which most die, some reach maturity and reproduce. It is a balance. Of course, human activities often and universally interrupt the balance. People may be distressed to know that skunks eat turtle eggs. After all, turtles are cuter than stinky skunks.

Did I mention that the tears of egg-laying turtles are believed by the more romantic at heart to be a sign of motherly love? I did not. If the female turtle loved her eggs so much, why did she not defend her nest? We humans are quick to assign emotions to animals out of ignorance and how cute, cuddly, colorful, or an attribute relatable to our own emotions. We are also quick to pave over places where these turtles might lay their eggs.

On the way back to headquarters, we surprised a striped skunk that was digging out a turtle nest on the side of the dike road. Up went its banner tail. The skunk was on my side of the car, and the window was down. Mr. Claud did not see the skunk because of attempts to dodge the dugout nests of generations of laying turtles. He later said that he suspected something was wrong when I lunged forward and away from the window. He said he knew why when we all got a strong pungent whiff of what the skunk sprayed on the side of the car.

It was late, but my host volunteered a little history about the refuge. He told me that Ojibwe and Dakota natives harvest wild rice from the lake. I asked about how they dealt with the mosquitoes. My host answered that people in the region do not let mosquitoes rule their life and then grinned. Mosquitoes were ruling my life and he knew it, mostly from my swatting and itchy-scratchy skin. I also asked about the tree stumps I had seen during my earlier skirmish at Mandy Lake. Mr. Claud said that settlers first came to Rice Lake in the late 1800s and that loggers cleared the white and red pine from the refuge. Timber barons transported cut logs by floating them on Rice Lake to a sawmill or moved them to the Mississippi River 20 miles west. I wonder how many turtle eggs the settlers ate and skunks they killed.

28 June 1962

The morning was cool as I loaded up and headed away from the Antler Inn, and east from Rice Lake NWR. I was happy with the two new trip birds: Blue-winged and mosquito guarded Common Loon. I drove east on state highways to Duluth at the southern tip of giant Lake Superior where the compiler of the Christmas Count might have local birding information. Months ago, the compiler wrote that I should stop by and provided directions to his home. Unfortunately, he was out.

Crossing the southern tip of Lake Superior took me to the city of Superior in Wisconsin. This was a new state for my life list of states and the trip. My route in Wisconsin hugged the shore of Lake Superior as much as possible. The 350-mile-long lake occupying nearly 32,000 square miles with a 2,726-mile coastline was too fascinating for just a glance. Roadside markers along the way told of rich history. Etienne Brule, who discovered Lake Superior around 1620, and Jean Nicolet, in 1634, were the first explorers of the region that became Wisconsin. Both Frenchmen were, what else, searching for the Northwest Passage. Following the early explorers were the missionaries who came to proselytize whomever they contacted. Father Marquette was among the most notable of those lobbying for cultural changes. He was a French Jesuit missionary, who established Michigan's earliest European settlements at Sault Ste. Marie and Saint Ignace in 1668 and 1671. He helped Louis Jolliet map the Mississippi River. Shortly after 1658, even though the French convinced themselves that they owned the Great Lakes region, the English and American fur trade stepped in to build a profit and gained a foothold in the land and lakes. Decades later, the French and English left. Eventually, most things trappable were trapped, and mining became important. The first lure was lead and zinc, followed by iron ore. Much of the iron ore removed from Wisconsin is replaced by dairy cattle manure and the cows that produce it. What they say about Wisconsin cheese is true. It is close to superior.

The first sandy beach that I found was a welcome sight. Late June might not be the best time for a swim in Lake Superior since the lake freezes during winter, and the thawed water might be too cold for swimming. Even so, sun was warm, and a cool swim was inviting. Contorting myself behind the steering wheel while changing into a bathing suit, increased my determination. Walking away from the shore until the waterline and the place where my two legs intersect stopped me from going deeper into the water. It was cold beyond imagination. The opposite of sizzling comes to mind, only more painful. I took a deep breath and took two more steps down the gently sloping bottom. Then, I bent my knees until my head was below the frigid surface. Turning around and gasping, I made my way as quickly as possible to dry land. What part of my body that was not red or shriveled was a sickly bluish white. The only sound on the lonely beach was that of someone foolish enough to think about swimming. That was me, with heavy breathing and chattering teeth. If there were any birds around, I did not notice.

More miles of driving were enjoyable because of the greenhouse effect of the sun shining through the car's rolled-up windows. It was getting late, and I was getting hungry. I had picked up $3.49 worth of groceries and filled the gas tank with 8.8 gallons of regular gasoline for $3.03. The prospect of a bonafide campground was not good. A small farm just above a beach along Lake Superior appeared to be an ideal campsite, and the property owner was most gracious. I was a little cold as I had been traveling in my iced bathing suit. Now I was in the middle of a field and had no place to change into dry clothes. The wet and now itchy suit stayed on during the preparation of a hamburger and heated canned vegetables. In the meantime, a single pesky fly wouldn't leave me alone. Where is a flycatcher when you need one?

At least the stiff breeze was too much for most of the mosquitoes. Those dastardly insects not trying to get to my pearly white legs were lurking out of the wind in the shelter of the hay stubble. Once the meal was over, I unfurled the tent in a wind with a velocity strong enough to blow away that persistent fly, and to nearly dry my bathing suit. The wind increased. Once the little pup tent roof was pushed up, the canvas door flapped hard against the tightening walls. No sooner than when the last tent pole was fully vertical and holding the slanting walls tight did the tent stakes start to come loose from the buffeting wind. Ten pounds of nearby rocks might help anchor the tent stakes. I crawled inside and fastened the door. It was just in time too. Peeking out a hole, I could see that rain was falling at about a 45-degree angle from the bluish-gray clouds over Lake Superior. It was a relief to rid myself of the swimsuit and brush off any misplaced sand granules. Zipping into my cozy and dry sleeping bag, I soon fell asleep in the lull of the rain pelting the tent. Even the occasional cry of the wind was not going to interrupt sleep. However, I half woke up in time to notice that the raindrops were denser, and the wind was blowing harder than ever. A groan from a sudden burst hit the tent hard. The roar of the wind and the pelting of the rain was too loud to hear one of the tent stakes cracking. I did hear and feel the wet thud as the tent came down on top of me. During the rest of the night, I was busy trying to keep the tent upright, at least enough so I could breathe, and keeping outside water from flooding the floor. In the wee hours of the morning, I fell asleep in exhausted frustration, ignoring the rain squall that had unleashed itself. Later, the storm moved on or dissipated enough for hordes of mosquitoes to enter a gaping hole in the door of the rumpled tent. How they managed to escape the storm is amazing, but several did, and they were hungry. Slowly, I woke to a sun that rose in a cloudless sky that warmed the soaked surrounding. The rainstorm was now leaving the wet tent in a flurry of whitish steam racing skyward to form clouds another day.

29 June 1962

The sun was kind as it accompanied a faint breeze that helped dry the tent. An hour passed. The heat from the sun was finally too much for the bloodsucking insects that now lurked in the cool shade. The increase in temperature was perfect by being too hot for the pesky rascals. It was time to prepare a leisurely breakfast of eggs and bacon and to sip a couple of cups of coffee without frequent torment from mosquitoes. The tent slowly dried. That I was in the middle of a field of hay stubble seemed to explain why no birds were around. Although I could have made notes on birds seen yesterday, I was content to take note that the rain squall had done no more damage than a replaceable tent pole and the loss of hours of sleep.

The sun was high in the sky by the time I dragged myself into the packed car and drove out of the field. Back on the highway, the VW was soon churning me across the state line into Michigan, with occasional stops along Michigan Highway 28. There were few cars and few birds or at least places that looked promising to find birds. I drove a little over 100 miles, passing just north of Ironwood, the north end of Lake Gogebic, and little towns like Topaz, Trout Creek, and Covington. On down the highway, US 41 merges with more traffic from the northern tip of Keweenaw Peninsula of Upper Michigan. A ferry from the peninsula went to Isle Royal NP, a wilderness in Lake Superior. The island is famous for its wolves and moose. Months ago, I reluctantly shelved plans to go there.

Late in the afternoon, tired from the night in Wisconsin, I pulled into Van Ripper State Park. As state parks go, it is large, with about 950 acres of pine and deciduous forests and plenty of campsites overlooking Lake Michigamme. My site cost $1 for the night. My arrival was early enough to allow plenty of time to set up the tent and organize an outdoor kitchen on the picnic table. On one end I placed the two-burner stove. It was at the end of the table because it was easier to stand while cooking. About a foot from the stove, where I would sit while eating, was a cup waiting for coffee and an aluminum plate from my mess kit waiting for food. I stacked a couple of books and paper weighed down by a rock at the other end of the table. Next to it and almost opposite my table setting, I placed my typewriter. The latter was for taking advantage of the time for catching up on my notes. I took advantage of a place to shower and used the running water at the campsite to clean away the dirt and grime. There were gratefully few mosquitoes in the park. A flamboyant male American Redstart contrasted with a few yellow-breasted Nashville Warblers topped off the day as new birds for the trip.

1 July 1962

A new month, and maybe today I would find a new species to add to the trip list. Energized by a good night's sleep, I hurried out of the park but stopped briefly at an important historical marker for the Jackson Mine. The marker informed me that in 1844 William A. Burt, a government surveyor, had noticed strange fluctuations in compass readings. This led to the discovery of the great Lake Superior iron ore deposits and the formation of the Jackson Mine, the first mining company in 1847. Remains of the open pits reminded me of the badlands of Montana and North Dakota, only much worse than bad. Any attempt to traverse the mined region would have been far more difficult than crossing natural badlands or even the lava flows of Craters of the Moon in Idaho. Stunted pines and bushes dot the rough gullies and scrapes. The land looked like an easy place to break a leg or become lost because of a confused compass.

At 9:30 a.m., I arrived at Seney National Wildlife Refuge, hopeful for adding eastern birds. The 96,000-acre refuge is important to migrants using the Mississippi Flyway. My day of arrival was a Sunday. Most of the staff was absent though I did get directions for the most recent sightings of LeConte's Sparrows, a species listed by the refuge checklist as rare in summer. I would soon be out of their breeding range, and once during my search thought I heard one. Whatever I was hearing never came out to be seen, and my rule was any new life bird had to be seen to be counted. Unfortunately, the locality of a reported LeConte's Sparrow was occupied by Fox, Lincoln's, and Swamp Sparrows. The refuge checklist considered Swamp Sparrows as abundant, Lincoln's as uncommon, and provided no status for Fox Sparrows. The last species was new for the trip list.

Somehow, I had managed to miss American Merganser on the trip but saw one today at Seney. Rusty Blackbirds were seen for the first time. Harder to see but more intriguing were warblers singing from the dense foliage along the dike road. I wished that I had spent more time listening to Peterson's LP of eastern bird songs. A handful of Black and White Warblers joined my list of abundant American Redstarts, Nashville Warblers, and Northern Yellowthroats.

⁓

The crossing of the Mississippi was a milestone. A lot has happened downstream since 1962. Martin Luther King was assassinated in Memphis, Tennessee. That is where Elvis Presley's career started, and, in the 1820s, where John James Audubon visited. For me, traveling east of the Mississippi in 1962 seemed almost more important than crossing the invisible one hundredth meridian. I then reasoned that crossing the mighty river was akin to entering the true East, not a biological boundary so much, but a cultural and historical boundary. After all, back in the eighteenth century, the river was the boundary between Spain and Great Britain's land grab of North America. Was that fact fresh in the mind of a person recently graduating from high school? Possibly, but probably not, though I did wonder how people crossed the mighty river. Accounts by early immigrants crossing the Mississippi River described the need for travelers to dismantle wagons and cargo in addition to having to force their oxen and horses to swim to the western bank. Of course, getting a bigger boat later helped to cross the river. Crossing the Mississippi River at Brainerd, Minnesota, in 1962, was on a bridge about 10 years older than me. Still standing, it is one of 371 bridges that cross the immense Mississippi. Traversing the river that day in 1962 meant crossing an important landmark, not just for migrating birds but for birders wishing to get to the other side of the west.

Rice Lakes NWR, my first birding location east of the Mississippi River, grew to 18,200 acres in 1970. Other than being painted in 1966, the Antler Inn seems to have vanished by 1979. An estimated 29,000 people now visit the refuge. The only people I saw in 1962 were my two hosts. Visitors today, who might be upset about skunks eating turtle eggs, may rest assured that both predator and prey prosper to this day. Although skunks, and, according to recent information, egg-poaching raccoons, may consume a lot of turtle eggs, their numbers have not taken over valuable natural habitat like their very distant relatives, the egg-eating human species. According to a friend, an average American 70-year-old will have by then consumed dozens and dozens of eggs, 14 cattle, 12 sheep, 23 pigs, 880 chickens, and enough fish to equal 770 pounds. That is pretty much the whole farm.

Although I did not stop in Duluth in 1962, hurried visits in the autumn of the 1980s along Lake Superior north of Duluth were times to see secondary forests of white-barked birch and buoyed Common Loons not far offshore in Lake Superior. The mosquito population was also thriving.

Wisconsin mining is still a business in the state. The last iron ore, once a famous product, was last mined in 1965. Taconite, a low-grade iron product that required huge quantities of water to mine, was a going concern from 1968 to 1983, and mining sulfide ores may occur today. That is a lot of Wisconsin being shipped elsewhere, and as markets change, mining in Wisconsin and elsewhere will change. Linda and I, in 2015, drove essentially the same route I drove in 1962 Wisconsin, only in reverse. Perhaps the most remarkable memory of Wisconsin in 2015 was the possibility of finding Kirtland's Warblers breeding in the state. We were not successful. That species only nested in northern Upper Michigan in 1962!

Seney NWR had a program in the 1960s to help Canada Geese breed where the species had apparently never bred. The effort is amusing because Canada Geese now breed many places where lots of people wish they (geese, and perhaps people too) never bred. Canada Geese now breed and forage in habitats including lawns and golf courses. The latter is especially a problem as their droppings are almost the size of a golf ball and are very mushy.

Authorities claim Seney NWR is the best place in the US to find Yellow Rails. Other locations are laying similar claims for being the mecca for this most secretive bird in North America, but folks at Seney help to find Yellow Rails by conducting guided tours in the refuge. The tours, dubbed twilight tours, may have begun as early as 2015 when Linda and I visited the refuge. Hearing, let alone seeing, a Yellow Rail was not guaranteed. The current checklist, dated 2016, listed Yellow Rails as occasional, meaning only a few are detected in each season. The species was listed as uncommon in a 1961 edition of a refuge checklist I had in 1962. A lightning-caused fire that burned 76,000 of the 96,000-acre refuge in 1978 changed the status of rails and other species. Since then, control burns occur in the refuge and a study in the refuge determined the rails were more likely to be detected vocally within two to three years after their habitat was burned.[1]

Like so many regions in North America, the land to become Seney NWR was ravaged by clearcutting timber barons from 1870 to 1895. What acres could not be cut were drained. Remarkably, the major drainage ditches

---

1. Jane E. Austin and Deborah A. Buhl. "Relating Yellow Rail (*Coturnicops noveboracensis*) Occupancy to Habitat and Landscape Features in the Context of Fire." *Waterbirds* 36.2 (2013) 199–213.

to the refuge was not closed until 2002. In addition to protecting a once pillaged habitat, Seney reintroduced Trumpeter Swans from 1991 and 1993. Linda and I easily observed pairs of adult Trumpeter Swans and cygnets in 2015. The swans at Red Rock Lakes NWR in 1962 were more difficult to see, but their habitat was easy on the eyes.

One species we did not find in 2015 that I found in 1962 was Rusty Blackbird. According to the 1961 refuge checklist, I should not have seen that species. According to two editions of the AOU check-list and text and range maps from other sources, Rusty Blackbirds do not breed in Michigan. Still wondering about my summer record, I eventually unearthed a couple of websites stating Upper Michigan is within the breeding range of Rusty Blackbird. One was from the 2010 breeding bird atlas for Michigan that reported the blackbirds locally breed in western Upper Michigan and recounted a bird found in early July at Seney NWR. Whew. I am exonerated. I think. Breeding Rusty Blackbirds in Michigan are said to be rare. The species, throughout its range, is in steep decline.

My continued experiences with mosquitoes led to discomfort and curiosity. During 1962 and early 1963, I should have had a better insect repellent. There are 3,000 species of mosquitoes worldwide, and 150 of them plunder the United States. Well, maybe I should not say plunder because they do have an important place in nature. The 28 different genera breed in all kinds of habitats including running water, and pools, ponds, lakes, and seas of fresh and saltwater. More than one species lay their eggs in the water collected in old tires. The genus *Aedes* breeds in snowmelt. The little bloodsuckers are everywhere.

Although annoying, wishing that mosquitoes did not exist would be wishing for ecological disarray, maybe even ecological disaster. Sure, mosquitoes bite us, and they bite wildlife, especially naked precocial nestlings. However, mosquitoes are food for many organisms. Mosquitoes are pollinators and thus contribute to plant ecology. We expose our arms, necks, and faces to the hungry beasts for a chance encounter of species of birds that would not be in the vicinity if it were not for mosquitoes. It is hard to accept that while concurrently feeling the itchy-scratchy results of their bites we are celebrating a view of a bird. An anecdotal story supporting the idea that the more mosquitoes experienced, the more birds you see was at Van Riper State Park. My small fee to overnight there probably helped pay for some sort of mosquito be-gone sprayed in the park. I had fewer mosquitoes trying to sip my blood and fewer birds trying to tax my abilities to identify them. Today's state park fees, about 17 times higher than the cost in 1962, continue to keep the pesky mosquitoes (and birds) at bay.

Perhaps thinking of a mosquito bite as a scientific observation might help the conundrum. A course in mosquito 101 would inform us that the females, the only sex that plagues bare skin, bite to get our blood, which is needed to complete their, not our, reproductive cycle. (Anyone attempting reproductive-like behavior in the presence of mosquitoes knows that the mosquito's behavior does not enhance our actions.) When the mosquito bites, regardless of which body part one might have exposed to her, a small amount of mosquito saliva is first injected. This mosquito spit prevents our blood from clotting in the straw-like mouth part that she uses to bloat her body to fullness. About the same time, we feel a slight sting, swelling, and an urge to scratch the point of attack. The symptoms we have after the dastardly deed depends on how much saliva mosquitoes inject into our unsuspecting skin, the species of mosquito, and our physical diagnosis, including how allergic we might be. A mosquito that has not had enough time to inject the full amount of saliva does not leave as much of an itchy welt as one that has a plumped body full of our blood. These are the ones that, if discovered and sent to smithereensville, leave a bloody smear when its meal, our hard-earned blood, is splattered by our deft slap. The itchy welts usually do not persist for more than an hour. However, depending on where I might have been, which likely meant a different species of mosquito, the after-bite of the pesky insects varies from no welt to a welt lasting for hours, and the amount of itchiness varied from none to lots. I have been with people who swell up less than I do, and with people, at the same time and place, who have welts bigger and that last longer than everyone else's bites. The welts may even last several days for those highly susceptible to mosquito spit. Even the amount of pain from a mosquito penetrating the skin varied from no pain to a sting that got my attention and often a mumbled four-letter word or two. The size of the mosquito seemed to have no bearing on its aftermath. The rather large and brownish mosquitoes that bit me in North Dakota were no worse than the smaller and blacker Minnesota marauders.

Mosquitoes, according to the experts, are attracted to us by our breath's carbon dioxide. That means that my heaving and breathing brought on from running away from the mosquitoes attracted more hungry females. The odor of folic acid from our skin is also an important cue for mosquitoes. As for any other smells, the mosquitologist offers no definitive answers about perfumes, hair sprays, detergents, and softener residues in clothing, or other human odors. The odors may either attract or repel mosquitoes that are looking for folic acid fumes and blood. Mosquitoes are attracted to dark clothing because it attracts heat so it is a useful idea to dress in pale apparel or mosquitoes may not snack lightly.

In 1962, the buzzword for controlling insects in your personal space was not DEET. Although DEET, a shortened term for an exceptionally long chemical name, was developed in 1946 by the US Army and was available to civilians in 1957, no one bothered to tell me about it. Perhaps it was for my protection, you know, the old "be careful, you might poke your eye out" advice given by parents at the first sign of perceived danger. After all, you do not want to get DEET in your eyes. Danger or not, in 1962 I had more mosquitoes gnawing on me than the National Debt. DEET, regarded as the gold standard for repelling mosquitoes, is now considered by Consumer Reports as safe and effective when used appropriately. DEET, or maybe a good alternative, is now in my current kit to the outdoors. In 1962, mosquitoes in North America carried malaria, yellow fever, dog heartworm, and viral encephalitis. Now a mosquito can deliver the deadly West Nile Virus. It is a jungle out there.

Chapter 9

Warblering

2 July 1962

The day was uneventful, but the night was unexpected. A campground a few miles east of Seney NWR was nearly devoid of people and mosquitoes. The warm late evening temperature seemed be a suitable time to leave the tent packed in the car and sleep under the stars. Besides, I was tired of unpacking and packing the tent. So far, so good.

When I was ready for bed, a well-dressed and attractive girl jauntily walked up to my campsite. She smiled while sliding her over-stuffed backpack from her shoulders and asked if I would drive her to Lansing. I told her I could not as my car was full. I did not have room for a passenger. She said she could rearrange the car and suggested that I move my ice chest to the left, balance my typewriter on top of the book box, and maybe something else or some other thing some other place. I had by then stopped listening having decided. No. Rearranging the car was not going to happen. After all, I spent almost a year calculating the use of every cubic inch inside my VW. The thought of rearranging the car was not a topic tonight or any other time. I told her no. She put her hand on my shoulder and said please. I suggested she ask the elderly couple at the next campsite. Seemingly wounded for a second, she unrolled her sleeping bag next to mine, saying that we could figure it out in the morning. That seemed harmless enough, especially since I hid a couple of lumpy rocks between our bags that should keep her on her side of the ground. She was not the kind of bird I had on my wish list.

I settled in my zipped and rock-walled sleeping bag. High above, the silvery stars sprinkled light against the blackness of space. The celestial sea of bright stars, stars too far away or too small they barely lit the sky, so many stars, but a faint sound by my neighbor interrupted my stargazing. Except for closing my eyes, I did not move an inch. I must have appeared to be asleep though that did not matter. The good-looking but rather odd female, who did not know me from a cake of soap, talked as if I was awake. Being a great pretender was not my strong suit. No matter, the person in the sleeping bag too close to mine began telling me long and intimate details of her life. Time between mosquitoes gnawing my drowsy brow and three in the morning, she revealed that she was 15. That got my attention, but I kept quiet. She looked older and seemed more experienced than any 15-year-old I had known. Was she telling the truth? She said she had plenty of money. How did she earn it? And why tell a stranger, me, she had money? Was this a person that this 18-year-old should avoid? She finally fell asleep, snoring, and I began easing out of my sleeping bag. I very quietly loaded the car, put it in neutral, and pushed it several yards before jumping in to start the engine for my great escape.

My route was north for hours of nonbirding, to spend money and time touring the waterway of the locks and canals between Lake Superior and Lake Huron. I paid 75 cents for a hamburger and milkshake to go and drove to the American locks at Sault Ste. Marie, Michigan. Hundreds of years ago Chippewa Indians guided their canoes through the roaring rapids of the St. Mary's, the river that connected the two Great Lakes. Standing near the locks, I saw a huge ore ship slowly making its way through the locks. The ship practically scraped the sides of the canal. As the water lowered the vessel down 21 feet to the Lake Huron level, I could see the bins filled with iron ore. The crew scurried here and there, keeping lines secure so that the ship would not bump the thick canal walls.

For a better look, I ponied up $2.75 for the tour of the locks. A small boat quickly filled with passengers and chugged away from the dock. The tour conductor's monotone drowned out the engine as he explained that the locks opened and closed to raise and lower watercrafts from one lake to the other. A Ring-billed Gull followed, and others soon joined it as we made our way into the American locks and back around through the Canadian locks. Our boat seemed to grow smaller as the water lowered us down. The dark wet walls of the canal gradually towered above before the gates of the locks at each end slowly swung shut. The lock was 32 feet deep to accommodate the deep drafts of the huge ships that pass back and forth between the lakes and the Atlantic Ocean. My trip was a two-hour tour, and our skipper returned our little boat to its berth.

Back on dry land, I found a service station employee who would check the ever so leaking transmission. Topping off the transmission cost 50 cents. At a grocery and nearby café, I bought ice, groceries, and dinner for $2.07. Southward bound, I ended up in a free campground in Hiawatha National Forest, or about 25 miles north of the Mackinac (pronounced Mackinaw) Strait, the water body connecting Lake Michigan and Lake Huron. The few campers there were enjoying the peace and quiet that seemed more prevalent than in national park campgrounds. I quickly scanned the area so I could avoid any fast-talking girls wanting me to redecorate my car. I set up an office on a picnic table to write my notes and a couple of letters to Oregon.

3 July 1962

Birding around the campground took time, and I did not leave until 10 a.m. In about 30 minutes, I approached the 26,372-foot steel Mackinac Straits Bridge, the longest bridge in the world. It opened in 1957. Before that, a ferry was necessary to cross the Mackinac Straits. A total of 8,614 feet of the giant structure is a suspended bridge. The bridge has an estimated weight of 1,024,500 tons, has 42,000 miles of wire from the cables, and was built from 4,000 engineering drawings and 85,000 blueprints. The $3.75 I paid at the tollbooth was minuscule compared to the $100,000,000 it took to span the straits. Because I like bridges, I took its picture when I reached Lower Michigan. Had I realized that wind causes the bridge to sway noticeably, I might have liked it less at 199 feet above the water.

Veering off the beaten track in Lower Michigan, I took a less-traveled highway to Pellston and then jogged to the remote University of Michigan Biological Station. Among the 140 or so rustic buildings sheltering students from mosquitoes and the weather were laboratories, classrooms, and dorms. The station, founded in 1909, was in session, and students were everywhere. Students were clustering informally around a teacher, the man himself, Dr. Olin S. Pettingill, Jr. He stood tall and interested, all the while clutching in his teeth a briar pipe. I could appreciate the pipe. My father smoked one. Dr. Pettingill took time from his students to provide me a brief tour of the campus and was pleased and interested that I was using his bird-finding guides. I told him the guides were invaluable. He offered me suggestions on future places I hoped to visit. I showed him my Michigan road map, which I had carefully marked with the locations of nesting Kirtland's Warblers from Harold Mayfield's landmark monograph on endangered warblers. Dr.

Pettingill drew three circles on my map, and, with teeth clinching the stem of his pipe, said, "Try those places."

Not far east of the research station was the summer cottage of Lyle S. and Ester Hubbard on Mullet Lake near the town of Indian River. They otherwise lived in Florida. Lyle was one of several compilers of Christmas Bird Counts who I had written during the planning stages of the trip. He suggested I stop by for a visit to their summer home. Phoning a warning of my pending arrival was impossible, but I had written that I should be in his region in early July.

Lyle met me at the front door of their Michigan home. We talked for about 30 minutes before he suggested hiking through a nearby forest before dark. A few yards from his cottage was an abandoned road. We walked through the grasses growing chest-high in the middle of the old byway. In a couple of steps, the sun-loving grasses disappeared as we entered a tall and darkened hardwood forest full of warblers and vireos. Lyle fondly called the location the Big Woods. A Yellow-billed Cuckoo called from the trees near American Redstarts foraging high in the dim light. It was difficult to see color. Lyle called out the names of three warblers I had not seen. Their unfamiliar songs were a jumble of sounds nearly overpowered by a myriad of Blue Jays, Olive-sided Flycatcher, and others heard over the muffled drumming of a Ruffed Grouse. Was I in heaven or what?

4 and 5 July 1962

The generous Hubbards insisted I spend a few days with them and offered me a real bed, running water, and all I could eat. Before taking advantage of that bed, Lyle and I were up late comparing our local birds and birding and the birds we wanted to see. We viewed a slide show of tantalizing Florida birds and a couple of tours the Hubbards had taken to the West Indian islands. They were planning a trip to Texas next spring, the same time I would be there. I woke refreshed from an indoor mosquito-free sleep and a cool and soapy shower, and rejuvenated by Lyle's enthusiasm about birds. He was nearly as zealous about birding as me.

Almost every waking hour was either talking about birds or looking for them. We visited Reese's Bog and found Canada, Black and White, and Black-throated Green warblers. There also were Yellow Warblers and a rather drab warbler, the Pine Warbler. We saw more warblers with warbler not in their name, including Ovenbirds, American Redstart, and Northern Waterthrushes; the latter species was also seen yesterday following my visit with Dr. Pettingill. The next day and back in the Big Woods was another warbler day. A singing bird had impressed me when I saw it illustrated in my first bird book when I was about 10 years of age. With guidance from my host, we found the bird, a male Chestnut-sided Warbler singing from an exposed perch about 50 feet away. The combination of a clean white breast bordered by chestnut sides and a stylish yellow crown was an appealing array of colors. Maybe it was the chestnut color that was so attractive. Not much later, we heard the high-pitched song of a Blackburnian Warbler. This was another dreamed-about warbler. The singer soon popped into view and, miraculously, it perched in a narrow shaft of light filtering down through the forest canopy. The sight of it seemed impossible. Truly, the illustrations that I had salivated over were nothing compared to the intensity of the real thing. Framed in black, the color of the bird's throat was orange, no, a mixture of red with yellow, but more than that, it was a color to experience. It is beyond description. A lexicon of colors should include one named blackburnian.

These were my best two days for seeing so many species of warblers. Most of my warbler hunting had been limited to southwestern Oregon, where, during June, it would be possible to find nine species by lots of birding requiring forays in riparian valleys and conifers in the mountains. Lyle and I saw nine species of breeding warblers with ease and in only minutes. About 15 more species of warblers probably breed in the region. Including migrants, Michigan can boast about 40 species of warblers. What a mind-numbing thought.

A boat trip to the Indian River Marsh bordering Mullet Lake filled the early morning of 5 July. Our query was the Least Bittern. Luckily, one flew over the marsh, staying in the air long enough for us to confirm its identity. This secretive species usually stays hidden in marsh vegetation. In the vicinity, we found Pied-billed Grebes, Black Ducks, Common Tern, and, best of all, Upland Sandpiper. The birds made up for not finding the Yellow-bellied Flycatchers that Pettingill reported to be at Reese's Bog.

6 July 1962

Bedtime did not come until late last night, a time when we talked more birds and discussed the areas where we might see Kirtland's Warblers. We poured over maps, Pettingill's recent bird-finding information, suggestions he passed on to me a couple of days ago, and sifted through Harold Mayfield's 1961 census of this rare warbler. Sleep that night was five hours, but it seemed like 10 minutes. Even so, I was wired, ready to go. Lyle, though decades older, was wide awake and anxious for finding Kirtland's Warblers.

We gulped breakfast and hurried away from the lake shore cottage. We were soon on our southward journey into jack pine country and the only breeding home of the Kirtland's Warbler. Turning east onto a sandy route, we saw Chipping Sparrows and Indigo Buntings along the roadside and, finally, jack pines. Two cars were parked in single file on the right shoulder of the road.

Mere steps of quiet walking from the car brought us to the sound of a singing Kirtland's Warbler, which provided a glimpse of the bird with a bluish-gray back and yellow front before it disappeared into the pine needles. We left the male singing and soon met Dr. Pettingill and one of his students from the biological station. I was surprised to see them walk to a nest they knew about. Surely the incubating bird would bolt, making the nest harder to find. What I did not know was that Kirtland's Warblers were unafraid of humans, almost tame. The female, slightly drabber than males, did not leave the nest until practically touched, and then it stayed just feet away while the four giant humans towered over the nest. The mate of the female kept singing as if nothing was happening. The nest contained a young cowbird and two cowbird eggs. While examining the obscurely located nest under a jack pine, I happened to look over two feet from the nest and found a smaller egg quite unlike the cowbird eggs. Dr. Pettingill looked, picked it up, and identified it as a Kirtland's Warbler egg. He said the egg was needed for the station's museum. A cowbird had pecked the egg before or after it was removed from the host nest. Later in the day Lyle and I found a nest with three young. This time the nestlings were Kirtland's Warblers. We found six more singing males before the sun began to set.

We felt lucky to observe Kirtland's Warblers, a species with a population of only 502 estimated in 1961. These rare warblers nest on the ground under five- to seven-foot-tall jack pines (*Pinus banksiana*). Once trees grow to an older and taller age, the ground under them becomes littered with needles. Kirtland's Warblers do not like the bed of pine needles. The species does not do well with aging jack pines or nest parasitism from Brown-headed Cowbirds.

7–16 July 1962

The morning of 7 July was full of gratitude from being introduced to so many warblers, the conversations, a cozy bed, and great meals. That time was also full of hope since the Hubbards insisted I stop by their home in Florida, where I would be in December and January. How could I resist an insist? The kindness of strangers was amazing. On the night of 7 July, thanks to my hosts Mr. and Ms. Gerlock in Michigan's capital, Lansing, I enjoyed another mosquito free night. They earlier said I should stop on my way south the day I met them in upper Michigan.

I drove south and out of Michigan to Indiana during the morning, where birding was put on hold while I made an obligatory visit to two families of relatives in Fort Wayne. At my aunt's old neighborhood, I added Northern Cardinal to the trip list. On the other side of town, my cousin and her family lived in a new but treeless and even bushless community where I saw only Starlings. I spent a lot of time visiting, listening to my cousin's stereo, a new and exciting wonder, and worrying that the porcelain plates hanging on the wall would vibrate to the waiting floor. There was always plenty to eat. One day, I ate at least my share of a chocolate layer cake though I do not like chocolate. Not caring for chocolate almost always evokes a look of "are you crazy?" Then there were the colossal strawberry pies topped with whipped cream. The decadent pies were available at a drive-up window, and we did drive up on multiple occasions. Because of enjoying the stereo, clean sheets, hot water, strawberry pies, and potato salad, I was almost in heaven. I also gained four pounds since leaving home. Thankfully, there was time for swimming and boating in a city park lake, or I would have gained more. I bought a stereo record for $4 as a gift to my cousins. One day we toured Gene Stratton Porter's summer home. She studied nature and wrote 12 novels during the twentieth century. My aunt and uncle thought I got more out of the tour than I did, no offense to Gene Stratton Porter or her descendants. I was more than ready to be on my way to birds and more birds.

17 July 1962

At Waterville, Ohio, a small town about halfway between Toledo and Bowling Green, I was hoping to visit Harold Mayfield. We had an appointment, but he was still at his Toledo office upon my arrival at his home. To fill in the time, his 17-year-old daughter and I rowed across the Maumee River in search of Prothonotary Warblers and Carolina Wrens, species at their northern breeding ranges. The Maumee River, which much of my route from Indiana had followed, flows north, and empties into Lake Erie at Toledo. The banks from the slow river water seemed lifeless in the steamy afternoon. Back on shore an hour later, we turned up a Wood Thrush and a couple of Carolina Wrens.

In the evening, I listened as Dr. Mayfield talked about Blue-Gray Tanagers to Pacific terns. Naturally, Kirtland's Warblers came up and he seemed pleased to hear about my experience with the rare bird. My host spoke of Golden-cheeked Warblers of the Edwards Plateau in Texas and an ornithologist he knew who was planning to study the life history of this rare warbler. With information for finding Golden and Blue-winged Warblers, I was on my way.

18–20 July 1962

Southwest of Toledo, I set up camp in Oak Openings Park. Birding in the park was uneventful. I had entered the summer doldrums. It was too hot and sultry for even a mosquito. Whether I was in optimum habitat or not, elusive Prothonotary or Blue and Golden-winged Warblers were not singing, and they seemed not to be moving. Yes, this was the doldrums, with no wind for a sail. In Oregon, late July and August are also lousy months for birding, especially passerines. I still had nearly half of a continent to cross before being in position for fall migrating shorebirds. I was beginning to worry.

On 19 July, I left the oak and prairie region of northwestern Ohio, carefully skirted Toledo to avoid any unseemly traffic, and arrived at Marblehead, a point jutting into Lake Erie. I swam in Lake Erie to rinse away salt deposits and cool down.

With a slightly sullen birding spirit, I made or fought my way into the Cleveland traffic. Traffic in Cleveland was tantamount to running from, with, and away from the bulls. The four lanes started with vehicles moving at a reasonable speed, but as more lanes became available to the speedway, the faster everyone drove. Crowds of vehicles clogged the highway. Eight lanes seemed ridiculous, but that was not enough. The order of the day seemed to be to go as fast as you can, watch out for anyone changing lanes, keep one foot hovering over the brake pedal and one foot on the throttle. Because I was used to more open spaces and fewer people and cars, I was mortified and petrified by the domestication of the land brought from around 890,000 (as of 1960) people. The hundreds of thousands were all driving their cars when I arrived. I finally made it to Lakewood, a suburb and the home of John Smitty, a person I had corresponded with months ago. He was not going to be available until tomorrow but handed me notes to review. He had copied them by hand and told me to keep them. His notes included lists of birds he recorded during an April trip to Texas in 1962 and Florida in April 1961. The two lists revealed he was extremely lucky by finding most of the specialties I hoped to see. I was not that lucky, and I doubted that I would find two species of redshanks in Texas, as did Mr.

Smitty. His Texas list even included Eskimo Curlew! For his trip to Florida, I was suspicious of his sightings of Iceland Gull and Bewick's Wren. Maybe he did see all those oddball birds, but I felt a little unsure about the sightings of Mr. Smitty, whose real name is not used here.

Mr. Smitty also offered a large assemblage of information for finding birds for the Cleveland Park system called the Emerald Necklace. I hoped the information was accurate. That would have to wait until after a night at the Cleveland YMCA where I showered and slept for $3.

On the morning of 20 July, I awoke refreshed, clean for a change, and free of fresh mosquito bites. I ate eggs, bacon, and toast for a $1.24 breakfast. I was ready to go birding in Cleveland's Metropolitan Parks, the Emerald Necklace, circling the city. What a wonderful treat after my seemingly harrowing experience on the highway yesterday. The city park system, started in 1917, administers 14,000 acres that include riparian and upland forests, lakes, fields, and are crowded with human visitors.

My host yesterday thought Rocky River Reservation might yield birds to add to my trip list. The reservation is a 2,572-acre western piece of the Emerald Necklace. I strolled several miles of trails straining to catch a glimpse of anything through bits of cooling shade. The heat and rigors of molt invite most birds to the quiet recesses of big, leafed trees and away from the noise and bustle of people jostling the air. An unwary parent Tufted Titmouse, along with four fledglings tagging along, whistled loudly just off the trail. After about three hours, I realized my time might be better spent elsewhere, and just as I turned back, I heard a soft peaceful sound. This was not the peace of rest or as in peace and quiet, nor was it the call for peace needed in the burgeoning war in Vietnam. This was the peace I had heard numerous times listening to an audio recording of good music, and that I heard on earlier visits to the Midwest. Soothing, reassuring, and exciting was the sound I was hearing. On a bare limb, perched upright in the sun was an Acadian Flycatcher. Not more than 20 feet away, I spied another flycatcher, silent and with buffy wing bars. It had an eye-ring like the adult Acadian, but this young bird could have been any one of several species in the pesky and difficult genus *Empidonax*.

∾

Changes have occurred in Upper Michigan. For example, the cost of the tour boat through the locks went up about 1,100 percent. Camping fees have risen by about the same percentage. The cost for a passenger car crossing Mackinac Bridge has gone up by only a quarter. One cannot help but wonder if the kindness of strangers would be so open-heartedly offered to an 18-year-old male today as it was to me in 1962.

My interest in bridges continues, though acrophobia now dampens my wiliness to cross high bridges. Since 1962, the status of the Mackinac Bridge has diminished, not in height but rank. It now is tenth in the world by having the longest span. The recently built Millau Viaduct toll bridge spanning the Tarn Valley in France is 1.6 miles long and 891 feet high. Yikes. Regardless of dimensions, bridges are often beautiful and inspiring.

Regrettably, I smoked cigarettes in the sixties, and later, during part of my college years, I also picked up the briar. At 50 years of age, after prevailing common sense and watching scary slide shows, I finally gave up tobacco. I did see, nonetheless, numerous birds through the veil of tobacco smoke as I am sure did Pettingill through the smoke from his pipe. If only I could make it to 94 as he did. Had it not been for the man with the briar and Lyle Hubbard, a person who always said, "wallet, keys, cigarettes" when leaving home, I might not have seen so many Kirtland's Warblers. I hasten to say that the three of us smokers were careful not to set these rare warbler's habitat ablaze.

Kirtland's Warblers were nearly extinct 50 years ago. In 1961, 501 breeding pairs were counted. The US Forest Service set aside 4,000 acres for habitat management in 1963. The species was listed on the rare and endangered list in 1967. Only 201 singing males were detected in 1971, which, if the males attracted mates, there were 201 pairs. In 1972 the US Fish and Wildlife Service, US Forest Service, Michigan Department of Natural Resources, and Michigan Audubon Society joined forces to protect the breeding population of Kirtland's Warblers. Efforts to control cowbirds were instituted that same year. In 1973, Kirtland's Warbler was listed by the newly enacted US Endangered Species Act and, in 1974, the species was listed by the Michigan Endangered Species Act. Warblers reached an all-time low in 1974 when only 167 singing males were counted. In 1980, a controlled burn designed to improve habitat for the warblers became a 25,000-acre uncontrolled inferno that destroyed 44 homes and killed James Swiderski, a US Forest Service biologist. During that same year, the Fish and Wildlife Service established protection to 125 separate tracts of 6,784 acres in northern Lower Michigan. Seney NWR administers the tracts. The number of managed acres was bumped up to 219,000 acres by the joint effort from the US Forest Service and the state of Michigan. In 1987, the count of birds matched the record low of 167 in 1974. From that low, the number of warblers slowly began to increase. For the first time, breeding Kirtland's Warblers were detected in Upper Michigan in 1994, and Wisconsin and southern Ontario in 2007.

Why did Kirtland's Warblers almost go extinct? Part of the answer is the nesting habitat required by a picky species. The warbler-specialized habitat requirements, if not met, place the species at risk. A pair of ground-nesting Kirtland's Warblers need about 30 to 40 acres to raise their young, but that means acres of suitable habitat. The jack pines cannot be too tall or too short. The problem of habitat was solved by controlled burning so that tree heights and understory could be regulated. However, these controlled burns sometimes got out of control, so a plan of staggered forest harvesting became a way to manage the fussy habitat requirements of the warblers. A second cause of the decrease in Kirtland's Warblers is Brown-headed Cowbird parasitism. Years of study and years of Kirtland's Warblers hosting cowbirds eggs and young show that one cowbird egg in a warbler nest means one to three of the warbler chicks could survive. However, if two cowbird eggs are laid in a warbler nest, none of the warbler chicks will survive because they cannot compete with the larger and more aggressive cowbird young. Cowbird parasitism occurred in 69 percent of warbler nests in 1966–71, with only one fledging per pair. Concerted efforts to control pesky cowbirds continue.

The 2018 census tallied 2,300 pairs of Kirtland's Warblers. All was right in the Kirtland's land. Having surpassed the recovery goal of 1,000 individuals, Kirtland's Warblers were removed from the US endangered list in 2019. Nonetheless, Kirtland's Warblers are in danger from off-road vehicles, the possibility of a disease destroying jack pines, the persistence of lazy cowbirds, climate change, and too many other factors including human visitors. Now, to see a Kirtland's Warbler you cannot just point yourself to the likely places as I did in 1962. Access is understandably regulated and the best way to see the warblers is by a tour. The first tours began in 1966. Tours might be more productive for birders than birds since there are lots more birders now than in 1962. This increase in birder traffic could cause an inverse in the population gains of the rare and conservation-reliant Kirtland's Warbler by disrupting nesting birds by just being there or worse, a misplaced foot. If we terminate habitat management, including cowbird removal, it is highly probable Kirtland's Warblers would be in jeopardy.

My first warblers in early June included Wilson's and MacGillivray's warblers. Except for Yellow Warbler and Common Yellowthroat, my warbling results were measly compared to the warblers found in the Great Lakes region. The Big Woods at the Hubbards,' Reese's Swamp, and other haunts of northern Lower Michigan were rewarding.

Olin Pettingill's pioneering bird-finding publications pale compared to the birding publications now available, but it should never be forgotten that he is the father of bird finding guides and that he was a great and revered teacher and author of ornithology. Taking a course under his tutelage would have helped anyone.

Swimming in Lake Erie west of Cleveland possibly put me at more risk than driving the fast-paced lanes funneling my white knuckles into the heart of the city. In the 1960s, Lake Erie was declared dead. Algae had robbed the water of oxygen and slimed the beaches. Phosphorous from detergents and fertilizers, heavy metals, sewage, and other gross and poisonous additions poured into the lake. In 1969, the Cuyahoga River, flowing through Cleveland on its way to Lake Erie, caught fire because it was so polluted. In 1962, I noted nothing unusual about swimming in Lake Erie. Although teenagers may often be oblivious to their fate, I was a picky nerdish kind of guy. More than likely, I would have avoided being slimed by Lake Erie. I recall my submersible experience as refreshing, but I hope I did not swallow. In the twenty-first century, Lake Erie is monitored and, although perhaps better off than in 1962, is declining in health.

Having avoided most cities during the trip, Cleveland seemed to me rather large. Remarkably, the population of Cleveland in 1950 was about 914,000. It has dropped by 58.4 percent since then despite the notoriety from the Rock and Roll Hall of Fame and Drew Carey. The Emerald Necklace, a series of city parks, was 20,000 acres by 2004, a 6,000-acre increase since the sixties. For reference, New York's Central Park is only 843 acres.

It turns out that the unnamed birder in Cleveland was a well-known observer and frequently reported his local sighting and even photographed a Painted Redstart in the region. An unaccepted report of a Common Redshank in Texas might have been by the unnamed birder who I called Mr. Smitty. Now, in the twenty-first century, I wonder if some of his records would have been verified or dismissed. He could have been an outstanding and lucky birder who saw an Eskimo Curlew the last year the species was in Texas. Certainly, I planned to look for the curlews in 1963. Did he see two species of redshank, the curlew, Gray-breasted Martin, and other great species in Texas? Did he find a Common Raven in Florida? A correspondent's reply to my inquiry about Mr. Smitty in 2014 revealed at least a portion of his identifications of local birds created legendary disagreements between him and local birders.

Mr. Smitty, whether being truthful or not, offered to introduce me to Harry C. Oberholser. Unfortunately, I was then ignorant of Oberholser's standing in ornithology, and, also, I was told he was not well. Bothering an ill senior was a reason for me to decline the chance to meet him though I regret not ever meeting the man. Little did I realize that the name Oberholser would be a common name during my career at the museum in Washington, DC. This was especially true concerning his taxonomic concepts.

One of the more frequently observed warblers I had been seeing across the country in 1962 was the ubiquitous Common Yellowthroat. Oberholser once described and named 12 subspecies in a 1948 paper he privately published. The American Ornithologist Check-list Committee did not recognize the proposed names. There is one subspecies of Common Yellowthroat generally recognized today that Oberholser described in 1899. As for a thorough and sound review of the Common Yellowthroat, that remains a future task. The thought of trying to discover a better truth about the geographic variation of Common Yellowthroats is somewhat frightening, even to a seasoned taxonomist such as myself. What I did discover about their kin is that warblers in 1962, especially in Michigan, had nothing to do with their taxonomy. The discovery was the feeling of excitement about seeing these gems up close and personal and the anticipation for what warbler was around the next bend.

Today, most any species of North American warbler would be harder to find than decades ago. Why? Presently, there are about one-third fewer birds than 50 plus years ago. Some species are doing better than others but the overall picture is horribly grim. In July 1962, the last reported North American Bachman's Warbler was just one more example of handwriting on the wall. Still, there were more warblers to see during my early journey, and I was looking forward to Prothonotary, Cerulean, and Colima, and more warblers.

Chapter 10

A Stint in Time on the Way East

20–22 July 1962

AFTER A SHOWER AND a night in a real bed at the Cleveland YMCA, it was time to do some plane spotting. On the northeast side of Cleveland, the Burke Lakefront Airport's departing prop-jet airliners screamed off the runway while others roared down to a stop at the terminal. Huge cumbersome-looking trucks traveled in and among parked planes. Their engines were muffled silent by the roar of the airplanes. It was a noisy experience, the near-deafening screams of the propeller grabbing the air, and the roar of the engines burning more fuel at the time than my VW would probably use in its lifetime. The smell of fuel and exhaust was everywhere. I wondered if the noise and fuel consumption were proportional to the speed of travel.

Soon tired of the featherless fliers, I drove from the city in my quiet and high mile per gallon VW. It was a relief to escape the traffic as I drove east and just south of the shore of Lake Erie. With a few miles to travel in thinning traffic, I took mental stock of my situation and tightened up plans for the next few weeks. In my last letter home, I wrote that my next general delivery address would be Bar Harbor, Maine, where I planned to be on 1 August. Being on a schedule should help catch the shorebird migration along the shore. I also wanted to be north of the dog days of summer to try to escape the hot and humid nights and days I knew to be so unpleasant.

Last night, I reviewed my ledger of expenses. My goal was to stay within budget, not look for a job, and thereby take away time for birding. So far, I was financially okay. By the third week of July, I had spent about $40 for food, or about 80 cents a day. Of course, there were those days that people had fed me. I budgeted $150 for miscellaneous expenses. Any budget should have a section that covers unexpected or unclassifiable costs. Mine included postage, film, and film development, lots of ice, camping and YMCA fees, and anything else that did not fall under food or transportation. By now, I had spent almost as much on miscellaneous expenses as I had on food. The transportation part of the budget took into consideration distance traveled and the going price for gasoline. It also allowed for oil changes and lubes, and even topping off the slowly seeping transaxle. By late July 1962, I had spent about $61 to get myself to the east side of Cleveland.

After putting my worrying mind at ease, I was ready to meet Paul Savage, a birder and long-term resident of Ashtabula, Ohio. We had exchanged letters before I left Oregon. He had written that I should look him up when in town. I ended up as a guest for a couple of nights. Paul's wife, Lois, although not a birder, was great company and a gracious host. Paul told me this time of year was a good time to see Ruddy Turnstones, a Willet or two, and "most of the common sandpipers."

Starting on the afternoon of the twentieth and during the next day, we scoured Walnut Beach of Lake Erie for shorebirds. Ruddy Turnstones, as promised, were foraging with Sanderlings, Semipalmated Plovers, and both species of yellow-legs standing side by side. It is reassuring to know for sure which bird is the Lesser and which is the Greater Yellowlegs. Dunlins were dotting the sand and were new for the trip. The plovers and a Stilt Sandpiper were life birds. Besides the shorebirds, a couple of early blue geese, a dark morph of the Snow Goose was on the shore. Herring Gulls shared space with smaller Ring-billed Gulls, and a new species for the trip, Bonaparte's Gull.

After sleeping on a clean and comfortable bed and a hearty breakfast, we hit the beach again. Joining us was Jon E. Ahlquist, introduced by Paul as a young high school student who painted birds. I discovered later that he and I were surprisingly the same age though he seemed socially younger than me. Jon did not seem particularly happy that I was in the car. Ignoring Jon's conduct, I was soon in full birding mode. Over half of the birds we encountered were nonpasserines, with Great Blue Heron topping the list by its rank in taxonomic sequence and overall height. Everyone was enjoying the Green Herons and a Least Bittern, two species of geese and four species of ducks, Turkey Vulture and Kestrels, and a couple of species of woodpeckers. Gulls, three species of terns, and 13 species of shorebirds waited to be noticed.

Paul warned that we cannot be too careful when it comes to identifying shorebirds, especially during this time of the year when the more distinctive breeding plumages are replaced by drabber fall plumages. Taking Paul's comments to heart, we identified every individual of the shorebirds and soon realized that one of the sandpipers was different. About the size of the Semipalmated Sandpipers, our mystery bird was far more rufous than any of the other shorebirds. The three of us watched from inside our car/blind and were only feet away from the bird with the other peeps that were incessantly jabbing the sand for morsels. We could see eyes blinking, the sand stuck to damp scurrying feet, and, from our vantage point, we noticed that most of the Least and Semipalmated sandpipers would peck at our mystery bird if it tried to come as close as their own kind were allowed. The lone bird was not in Peterson. We did not know what it was, but we knew it was unusual, or like so many birders, we hoped it was unusual. With no other choice, we left Walnut Beach for reinforcements.

A couple of unsuccessful phone calls to other birders meant we were on our own. I grabbed a couple of books from the back of the VW parked in the driveway and jumped in Paul's waiting car. While Paul drove to the beach, I flipped through pages of a Pough field guide I snagged from my larder of books.[1] Although mostly using Peterson's illustrations showing birds in profile, I liked the painting by Don Eckelberry in the Pough guides. Eckelberry's illustration of a bird in full breeding plumage fit our bird perfectly, but how could an Asian species get to faraway Lake Erie?

Part of the adventure of birding is that almost anything can happen, and we were anxious to have another look. We were soon back on the beach. At first, we were more nervous than the shorebirds scattered along the sand but relaxed a little when we relocated our strange bird. The three of us quickly decided it matched Pough's illustration of the plumage and the toes. Those toes were not partially webbed. Our mystery shorebird was a Red-necked Stint. Who would believe us? Jon said he would photograph the bird later today.

23–24 July 1962

It was raining while Paul and I toured Pymatuning State Park in Pennsylvania. The park and reservoir by the same name border western Ohio. We also drove to Presque Isle, a point of land jutting into Lake Erie and famous as a migrant trap. Both places were washouts; the wet deluge drenched everything under the dark sky. There were essentially no birds of any kind. Back in Ashtabula, I thanked Lois and Paul for their help and

---

1. Richard H. Pough. *Audubon Western Bird Guide: Land, Water, and Game Birds.* (New York: Doubleday, 1957).

hospitality and drove east along the Lake Erie shore on US 20 to Buffalo, New York.

The rain had stopped by late afternoon when I drove to Humboldt Park to meet Dr. Harold Axtell, the curator of birds at the Buffalo Museum of Science. He had authored a paper in 1938 on the song of Kirtland's Warbler, and he was the first curator of a museum that I had ever met. Dr. Axtell included a local checklist of birds with his lengthy April reply to my questions about birding in the Buffalo region. The list promised few species that would be new for the trip. The rest of the afternoon was devoted to planning an all-day birding foray tomorrow.

By earlier invitation, I stayed the next two nights at the Axtell cottage located just across the Peace River in Ontario. By now, we were on first names bases. To Harold's surprise, several relatives had also planned to stay at the cottage. I said I would be happy rolling out a sleeping bag on the lawn. To Harold, that was not an option, nor was it an option to sleep on the porch. I ended up in a comfortable bed.

The next day began with a satisfying breakfast in an all-night café. I had Canadian bacon in Canada with two eggs and toast. It was nice to have lean meat. For an unknown reason, the toast was a special treat. Trying to hold a slice of bread over a camp stove burner just did not achieve any sort of idealized toast, the golden brown and buttered toast my mother served with breakfast back in Oregon. I was missing the toast of my dreams, but this morning's breakfast was perfect.

It was 5:30 a.m. and the day was just beginning. After the last crunchy bit of toast, we drove back to Buffalo to pick up Kenneth P. Able, who has lived in the region for about a year, but Dr. Axtell said Kenneth had a remarkable knowledge of local birds. Yesterday Ken completed leading a local bird group counting shorebirds. A Ruff was among 18 species of shorebirds. We combed the locality where the solitary European waif was last seen. We revisited the site three more times, but we did not relocate the Ruff. We did manage to find 65 species, including 11 species of shorebirds foraging along about 50 miles of the northern shore of Lake Erie. It was entertaining to see the sandpipers fly in their tight formations as they wheeled back and forth in zig-zags swooping up and down over the flat. How they do that without crashing into one another was amazing.

A little after a quick lunch, clouds rolled across the sky, but that did not dissuade us as we continued to bird the shore of Lake Erie, marshes, and nearby deciduous forests. We saw only two species of warblers, no vireos, all possible swallows except Cliffs, but only one kind of flycatcher. We found one thoroughly dead Black-billed Cuckoo nearly flattened on the pavement. Besides the shorebirds, the highlights were two new birds, Great

Black-backed Gull, and Mute Swan. As the light faded in the west, we hurried one last time to where the Ruff was sighted last. Again, the beach was empty.

After dinner, Harold talked about his plan to turn the acreage around his newly purchased property into a sanctuary. He already had planted 600 evergreen trees and several species of plants that would produce seeds to attract finches. Bird feeders and baths dotted the land. He also talked about the difficulty in chairing list committees, stating that the "big shots" would threaten to leave the local group if their records were not accepted. He also recalled his 1949 birding hitchhiking tour of the US. Later, as I lay in a cozy bed, I thought about the birds we saw, and Harold in his fedora sitting at the wheel of his sedan. He had the annoying habit of pumping the accelerator. The car's small engine and being in high gear probably kept us from lurching back and forth from slow to a faster speed. I ignored the pulsating sound of the car's engine as much as possible until the behavior seemed normal to me as it was for Harold. Back at his home and after dinner, we had talked until 2 a.m.

25 July 1962

Before leaving the region, I drove to Niagara Falls, the town, in Ontario, Canada. At the shoulder of the city were the river and the world-famous falls by the same name. Niagara Falls was well known to Iroquois Indians, who informed French explorers about the landmark. It was later, possibly 1615, when Etienne Brule, the first European to see all of the Great Lakes but Lake Michigan, also became the first tourist to view Niagara Falls. This is where the Niagara River, flowing from Lake Erie, jumps downward abruptly before emptying into Lake Huron, the last lake before the St. Lawrence River.

The immensity of water plunging over the edge of the Niagara Escarpment at Horseshoe Falls was breathtaking. I can still hear the liquid roar pounding the rocks below. The plummeting water travels vertically only 177 feet from the top of the 400-million-year-old escarpment that existed about 350 million years before dinosaurs were extinct. Anyway, moving ahead millions of years, Niagara Falls begins to form. That was only about 12,000 years ago. About 7,000 years later, thousands of tourists enjoy the postcard panorama of thundering Niagara Falls, complete with thousands of tourists. Tourist attractions lined every shore of the river and the falls. The Canadian and American shores were crawling with people and everything that the civilized world brings with them. In this case, it was places to eat, buy souvenirs, film for more and more pictures, boat tours and any other tours that might bring a profit, and more places to eat. I succumbed to the so-called tunnel tour. Draped in an oversized and heavy raincoat and boots, I joined a similarly yellow-clad group of tourists in an elevator that would lower us through part of the 400-million-year-old rock. After a long ride down several feet, the door opened to a tremendous rumble and a tunnel draped in a thick cool mist. The wet rock walls of the dark corridor led to an area of muted natural light behind an opaque curtain of water racing vertically to the talus below. The mass of roaring water was frightening. The thick watery flow, the cold billowing mist, and the thunder of the Niagara River rushing past seemed another world. Back on the elevator, its doors closed, someone announced that 90 percent of the six million cubic feet of water plummets over the three Niagara Falls. The thunderous rumble of Horseshoe Falls came into the closed elevator and hushed the chattering tourists.

Although the rain gear kept most of my clothes dry, I became drenched around the edges. Even though I have avoided most tourist attractions, other than National Parks, I was happy with my subterranean experience. Getting so close to the falls was fantastic. There was so much water. The force was humbling. As I walked back to the car parked in the acres of paved parking lots, I glanced back at the falls, held my hands up to frame my view as if a movie photographer, and took in the panorama. My hands purposely blocked out the human-made structures for a more natural Niagara Falls. What a beautiful sight. Too bad there was so much commercialization in what should have been preserved as a national park.

26–27 July 1962

Yesterday my plan for camping somewhere between Buffalo and Rochester was not possible along the route. I pushed on to Rochester for a bed at a YMCA. It was just about my usual bedtime when I found a YMCA for the night. Before turning in early (I usually was asleep before most since I was usually up early), I made a couple of calls to Rochester birders that Harold mentioned. My potential guides were busy; Rochester was not going to be a birding location.

When the morning broke, I bought 7.8 gallons of gas for $2.35, food for $2.00, and ice for 25 cents, and headed east to Montezuma National Wildlife Refuge. The refuge is on the north end of Cayuga Lake near Seneca Falls. It contains 6,432 acres of marsh and swamp, and even the cultivated fields offered good birding. It was windy, with the threat of thunderstorms. A Semipalmated Plover at refuge headquarters perked me up. Three people down one of the dikes were glassing over a group of Gadwalls. By coincidence, the three were the very same people I had phoned last night. A few feet down the dike, they identified the squawking call of a Green Heron as a Pileated Woodpecker. That is when I decided to go solo for the remainder of my visit to the refuge. I managed to find 34 species that balmy afternoon.

Not far from Montezuma NWR was Cayuga State Park where I spent the night. I should have gone fishing. Cayuga Lake beckoned those imagining a northern pike or large-mouthed bass hooked for breakfast, but not today. The Rochester group at Montezuma yesterday suggested I drive down to Cornell University to visit Sapsucker Woods. Anyone who listens to recorded sounds of birds has heard of Sapsucker Woods. The place is famous. By the time I rolled into Ithaca, New York, the sun was baking the Finger Lakes region. The only thing that prevented the hot rays from drying everything to a crisp was the heavy, overbearing humidity. My first set of directions from a student I snagged on campus turned out to be directions to one of the dorms. The second, third, and fourth sets of directions from students were useless. The hot sun bearing down and my heated frustration got the better of me. Giving up, I drove east, ending up at a YMCA in Amsterdam northwest of Schenectady. The sultry night was uncomfortable. I looked for an all-night movie theater hoping for air-conditioned relief, but there were none.

28–29 July 1962

Vermont was another new state. It was by far the most mountainous state since leaving Montana, and it was the greenest eastern state yet. Not far east of Rutland, I hiked part of the Appalachian Trail to look for Blackpoll Warblers and Boreal Chickadees. The southern part of the trail doubles as part of the Appalachian Trail and the Long Trail. The former begins in Georgia and ends 2,159 miles to the north at Katahdin in northern Maine. The Appalachian Trail probably originated in 1921 whereas the 265 miles of Long Trail, extending the length of Vermont, began in 1910. I hiked to the fork where the Appalachian Trail continues northeast, and Long Trail bears left and north toward Canada. I opted for Canada but only for a couple of miles. The cool forest was full of deciduous trees that seemed huge when compared to the scrub oaks and madrones of southwestern Oregon. The wide leaves of these Vermont trees could not stand the searing dry summers of the West. Fire danger, according to a local warden, was low. Out West, the dehydrated pines and firs were experiencing summer fire danger levels of high to extreme. Some were burning. The New England forest floor was thick and moist, with matted ferns and shaggy mosses. There was a soft rustling breeze along the deserted trail.

Appalachian Mountains.

Birding was not great today. Three species of warblers were okay, especially since two were Blackburnian and Canada warblers. Black-capped Chickadees, Eastern Wood-Pewee, a couple of finches, American Robin and Dark-eyed Junco rounded out the short list. Today was the third day since not seeing any species new for the trip. I was becoming discouraged.

The drive north to capitol Montpelier was grand, and almost wild except for the frequent New England hamlets, with white church spires and small, neat fields nestled between the wooded slopes. There was more of the same east to the Fairbanks Natural History Museum in St. Johnsbury. The museum is like the one in Buffalo but smaller. Both began in the nineteenth century, were crowded and poorly funded. I spent most of my time in the cool halls of the natural history exhibits, something I had not taken time for in the Buffalo Museum. I also peeked in their one-year-old planetarium that was a new and almost unbelievable experience. I could almost hear the faint calls of thrushes and warblers migrating in the night sky.

A STINT IN TIME ON THE WAY EAST
30 July 1962

I woke in a campground in the White Mountain National Forest in New Hampshire. I hoped to take the cog-driven train to the top of 6,288-foot Mount Washington, the highest point in the Northeast. Reading the brochure about the mountain revealed I might be just one of many tourists since the first train, called Old Pepperass, made the climb in 1869. The last page of the brochure revealed the fee to the top was beyond my budget. I supposed I could have hiked the trail to the summit. Remarkably, Mount Washington has one of the highest human casualty rates in the world, with inexperienced or out-of-shape people thinking they can accomplish the deceptively easy trek to the summit. Hikers often misjudge rapidly severe weather changes on its slopes. People going up Mount Washington have died from several causes. Death came from an overturned carriage (in 1880), from avalanches, getting lost, a Pepperass engine accident, heart attack, and among others, drowning. I do not understand drowning, but the guy who died of hypothermia in June 1962 is understandable to a westerner who has experienced extreme cold in the mountains. According to the brochures, the killer weather on Mount Washington is the worst in North America and even rivals that of Antarctica! I reasoned that it was not the risk but the time it would have taken to hike to the summit.

Not far from the Mount Washington trail, I managed to find three chickadees. My first view of these birds was their backs and crowns, which resembled badly faded Black-caps. About the time I saw the dark flanks of the bird, I heard the nasal call known from my Sapsucker Woods recording. The New England woods gave me my first Boreal Chickadee. Try as I did, Blackpoll Warblers or Gray-cheeked Thrushes were not to be found.

It was early, with anxiety to reach the Atlantic growing. With almost two months and a continent nearly behind me, I decided this is the day for arriving on the Atlantic shore. Maine and the Atlantic Ocean would be lifers. I was excited, but before I got there, after traveling almost across the United States, I was stuck behind what appeared to be an overloaded truck of cattle on a narrow two-lane highway. It was bumping along about 25 miles an hour. Finally, and after a couple of miles, I chanced to pass, but an oncoming car caused me to duck back behind the cow brigade. After another slow mile, I looked in my rearview mirror to see a car speeding toward the mooing bovines and me. Would it stop before rear-ending me? I was not sure if I should go for the shoulder or try to pass. The car was rapidly filling my rearview mirror. A sickening screech of tires quickened my pulse. The rearview mirror revealed the driver's pursed lips and wide eyes. By then, the shoulder was gone, so I swung out into the oncoming lane, which I hoped would remain empty for a while, and I stepped on it. Not much happened; my vintage car was slow to respond. Luckily, no one was in the westbound lane. The speeding car behind me twisted and dipped to a tire-burning 25 miles per hour just inches from on-looking cows at the rear of the truck. After overtaking the beef, I discovered a slow car directly in front of the truck hauling the bovines. Somehow my little engine could get me a couple of car lengths ahead before I pulled into my eastbound lane only seconds before the arrival of an oncoming vehicle. The car that nearly rear-ended me was barely staying on the cambered road as it went careening past doing over 70.

⁓

In that letter home mentioned earlier in this chapter, I wrote that I was alternating the use of the two gas credit cards I carried. Two different gas companies were involved. The cards were really in my dad's name but sharing first names helped avoid any confusion. In 1962, at least in the circles that I was familiar with, just any old credit card would not work at any of the gas stations as they do today. Customers used gas credit cards that were specific to a particular gas company. Furthermore, teenagers very rarely own regular credit card accounts. Before leaving Oregon, my savings account was made accessible to my dad, who paid the gas companies from the money I had earned from work in orchards, ranches, and, what else, service stations. When I needed money for food and other items, I would ask my dad to wire me the amount from my account, which was then converted into travelers' checks. Today, one card fits all, which makes life less complicated.

In a September 1962 letter, Paul Savage partially satisfied my anxiety about reporting the rare sandpiper we found near Ashtabula, Ohio. Could the identification of our sighting be proved? Paul wrote that Jon Ahlquist obtained photographs of the bird and that the company Jon sent the film to had taken extra long in processing the pictures. Paul added that only one slide showed relevant characters to enable identification and that he planned to send copies of the slide to Ira Gabrielson and Harold Axtell. Ira N. Gabrielson was a name I knew well; he was the senior author of the 1940 *Birds of Oregon*, the definitive work on my state. I met Ira N. Gabrielson in the late 1960s when discussing my intention of drafting a new book on Oregon's birds, an insurmountable project that I never accomplished. My principal interest was the taxonomy of the birds, and being the taxonomic editor of the 2003 *Birds of Oregon* more than fulfilled my original goal.[2] Dave Marshall, who preceded Gene Kridler at Malheur NWR, was senior editor of the 752-page tome on Oregon birds that held several records of Red-necked Stints.

Paul later wrote me that Dean Amadon, Lamont Curator of birds at the American Museum of Natural History in New York City, Alexander Wetmore of the National Museum of Natural History, and Harry Oberholser at Cleveland had examined Jon's photograph. The three ornithologists agreed that the bird was a Red-necked Stint. Since our sighting, the first in the contiguous United States, Red-necked Stints have occurred at localities on the East and West Coasts. The species now appears in most editions of the various field guides.

Jon reported the stint in a paper in *The Auk* that hit the finer newsstands in 1964.[3] Funny though, Jon's accounting of the stint differs from my notes. He claimed that he was the person first to notice the prized shorebird and that he pointed the bird out to Paul and me. If anything, the three of us saw the bird together, but I might be wrong. Maybe Paul did, or was it me? Perhaps Jon's claim of being the first to see the bird and alleging he pointed it out to Paul and me related to Jon later admitting he was a "loner who fundamentally did not trust other people."[4] According to my notes, the three of us tentatively identified the bird seconds after I displayed to Paul and Jon a plate in my copy of the Pough field guide. The illustration in Pough brought a consensus; we were sure our bird was a Red-necked Stint. However, Jon wrote in *The Auk* that "after careful study, we tentatively identified" the bird as a Red-neck. Of course, our identification should have been tentative as should all identification until there is proof. Although more than one photograph was sent for experts to examine, Jon did not mention in his published note that only one photograph was diagnostic, and he stated nothing about what was between the toes of our Ashtabula accidental. What was between the toes is a difficult character to see. However, from our vantage point of being in a car and looking down on our bird, it was possible to see there was nothing but sand between its toes. Jon closed his paper by stating, "Study skins sent to us by Amadon further aided in our making the identification." I must have been elsewhere when such an event occurred.

2. David B. Marshall et al. *Birds of Oregon: A General Reference*. (Corvallis: Oregon State University Press, 2003).

3. Jon Ahlquist. "Rufous-necked Sandpiper, *Erolia ruficollis*, in Northeastern Ohio." *The Auk* 81 (1964) 432–33.

4. Jon Ahlquist. "Charles C. Sibley: A Commentary on 30 Years of Collaboration. *The Auk* 116 (1999) 856–60. It was 27.

By now, you might wonder why quibble over such seemingly minor differences in chronicling the first contiguous US record of a Red-necked Stint. After all, any birder worth their salt and more than a few years old would have realized the identification of the Ashtabula bird if they had been armed with a copy of Pough's field guide. Jon's omission of Pough concerning our shorebird was a disservice to a contribution too often unappreciated. Pough's guides were excellent. Giving credit where credit is due is the responsibility of anyone profiting from another's contribution. Bibliographers reading Jon's account might conclude Pough's guides are of little to no consequence. Again, Pough was not mentioned by Jon. Not one reference was mentioned, so how did we, after "careful consideration," come to any conclusion? What in the world were we considering since none of us had ever seen a Red-necked Stint? Additionally, readers might also summarize that Paul and yours truly were mere bystanders of the event guided by Jon.[5] Furthermore, and more importantly, was the bird positively identified and subsequently reported so that anyone reading about the bird would have sufficient information to be assured of the stated identification? Was there anything in Jon's 1964 paper verifiable? The strongest support for the identification is that Wetmore, Amadon, and Oberholser were said to agree it was a Red-necked Stint. They are surely correct, but where is the proof?

My offering this sin of digression might appear to go beyond the purpose of these pages, but the issue about the stint was part of my growth, an evolving development alongside the trip in 1962 of traveling from place to place, seeing birds and locations, meeting new influential people, and learning methodologies. Birds and birding were ever so slowly becoming less of a casual muse to one more serious, still fun, but leaning toward science. Of course, I did not realize the growth part at the time.

During discussions on my last night at the Savages, Paul and I discussed the best ways of documenting a rare bird. We both lamented not taking pictures. I did not even try. My snapshot cameras were nothing like the digital cameras of today, and Jon promised us he had the gear and ability to properly capture the stint. Of course, lacking a decent photograph could have called for a specimen, the ultimate proof of any pudding, but no one of our stint trio wanted that. Nonetheless, Paul and I agreed that specimens were the preferred means for documenting and confirming bird distribution. I came to agree even more with our decision during my career.

Admittedly, I did not like collecting, and I was a minor practitioner of collecting specimens during my career.

5. Jon passed in 2020. Though he is best known for his work with Charles Sibley that led to a revolution in avian systematics, Jon later turned to creationism. He began his association with Sibley in 1962.

A STINT IN TIME ON THE WAY EAST

Paul and I kept in touch until 1965 when Lois, his wife, passed. Our favorite shorebirding sight, Walnut Beach, prohibited vehicles on the beach starting in the 1970s. That might make birding difficult, but the closure is best for the birds.

Meeting Harold Axtell was more good fortune than I realized in 1962. At that time, I did not appreciate the extent of his expertise, especially concerning identifying and documenting identifications of birds. I also did not know of his early history as a musician, when for 12 years he toured, playing trombone. Piano and banjo were his other instruments. His position as a curator intrigued me the most. But I could not imagine at that time what a curator did. About nine years later, I began learning about curators, curation, and museums. I also began meeting curators. They are keepers of the treasury of specimens that continue to teach us the many facets of biology. Curators, caretakers of collections of birds, are orderly and well-organized. They might dress formally and wear suits and real shoes. Others are more laid back and might wear sandals, shorts, and Hawaiian shirts in the summer and flannel shirts with jeans in the winter. Most bird curators are in-between formal and informal. Harold Axtell was in the middle.

Shorebirds flying as if in a ballet also intrigued me. Kenneth Able, years later, would write that slow-motion photography revealed that the whirling flocks are led by different individuals during a flight and, that as a leader changes course, the entire flock cues on the leader. The change in direction and speed takes place in microseconds. If humans could react as rapidly, there might be fewer auto accidents and just think about how much fast reaction time would enhance our birding. As for the Ruff we never found, the first and only bird of the species that did grace my binoculars occurred in mid-1990 when Linda and I saw a lone bird at an interior location in southwestern Oregon.

A few years after first meeting Harold Axtell, this time in a different VW Beetle, and with my daughter, who at the time was modeling her swaddling clothes, I left Washington, DC, to attend an AOU meeting in Buffalo, New York. I was excited for the chance to meet Harold again. I wanted to ask him about the stint and, more importantly, to tell him that he influenced me to become a professional ornithologist. Planned time to relate a conversation fell short when my daughter's mother took over the drive from Arlington, Virginia, to Buffalo while I slept. Waking, I realized we were off course and almost in Ohio. Backtracking left little time, but Harold and I managed a brief reminisce about when we first met and birded in 1962. Our too-brief visit ended before I could ask if he finished turning his property into a sanctuary. As part of the local committee hosting the meeting, he had much to do. That was the last time seeing Harold.

My brief encounter with Harold Axtell steered me not only toward ornithology and working in a museum but that birders need to be careful when making field identifications. To that end, I must add ornithologists need to be careful when identifying specimens. I will save the specimen misidentifications mishaps, but a story about field identification and Harold Axtell bears attention. Briefly, dozens of birders descended on Brigantine NWR in New Jersey to see a Spotted Redshank. As related by Kenn Kaufman, Harold also made the trip to see the rare Old-World shorebird, but after careful and detailed study, he convincingly reidentified the redshank as a Greater Yellowlegs that got in oil.[6] Harold was widely accepted as an expert in field identification, which harkens back to a part of the unfinished story about Jon Ahlquist. As mentioned earlier, Paul Savage wrote me of sending a photograph of the Red-necked Stint to Harold. I do not know the date of that communication, but clearly, Jon ignored or did not understand Harold's abilities. I also do not know if Harold identified the photograph as a Red-necked Stint though I cannot ignore my suspicion that he might have disagreed with Amadon, Wetmore, and Oberholser, or he concluded the bird could not be positively identified, possibly because the photograph did not illustrate unwebbed toes. There is no available information to confirm or dispute this. Finally, of all the individuals that were stated to have seen Jon's photograph, Gabrielson was likely the more qualified person to identify the bird because of his fieldwork in Alaska. He may have had conclusions similar to that of Harold Axtell. Jon did not mention Harold or Ira Gabrielson, but he did list the other higher-profile individuals. Based on plumage, the Ohio bird matches Pough's illustration and specimens I later examined during my museum days and live examples I observed in Alaska after retirement. However, I cannot prove the Ohio shorebird's toes were or were not webbed. My notes and memory support the bird to be a Red-necked Stint, but no one needs to take my word for it.

What is left, at least to this questioning mind are, well, questions. Why did Jon state the Red-necked Stint is smaller than Semipalmated Sandpipers when the two are similar in size? Why did he not discuss the important character of toe webbing? Why did he not include Axtell and Gabrielson among those who examined the photograph? Why did he omit important information later in his career that, as stated by Fred Sheldon, "raised a cloud over themselves [C. Sibley and Jon] and their remarkable genomic

---

6. Kenn Kaufman. *Kingbird Highway: The Story of a Natural Obsession That Got a Little Out of Hand.* (Boston: Houghton Mifflin, 1997).

method"?[7] I wrote Jon a letter a few years after our observation. He never replied.

People sometimes shoot themselves in the foot. Is any of the forgoing about Jon and the stint relevant to these pages? Again, I believe so. Based on Jon's paper, there is no stated evidence to definitively equate the visiting shorebird with an individual Red-necked Stint. So, why not discuss the toes? Webbing, what some give the fancy word palmation, is a character that at once separates Semipalmated Sandpiper from Red-necked Stint. If the photograph was diagnostic, why was it not published or at least archived? It appears that Jon's paper did not come under peer review or a serious critique by the journal editor. Today, shorebird identification is taken as seriously as Harold would have liked. For a rare bird, the standards are high. The shorebird, which I believe but do not positively know was a Red-necked Stint, was my first experience with such a rare occurring species. In 1962, I was on the path of appreciating the importance of accuracy of information, that science should be factual, unadulterated, repeatable, and, therefore, verifiable. Was I prepared for early sixties shorebirding on the coast of Maine? At the time, I hoped so.

In reality, I was not prepared for early sixties shorebirding in Maine. However, I had expert help from local residents, and I am still learning. There is a reason these birds are often called chore-birds. I continue to worry about the identification of the Red-necked Stint in Ohio. It was not so much that I doubt the identification, but that I wonder why anyone believed what we saw was a Red-necked Stint. No, I cannot find any fault with Wetmore's conclusion. However, because Jon's 1964 paper provided no definitive information other than the distinctive plumage, I was later surprised that our sighting made it into the official list of birds of Ohio. Bruce Peterjohn, senior author of *Birds of Ohio*,[8] emailed me in 2021 that "given its overall size, bill shape and head/neck/throat/upper breast pattern, everyone who reviewed this slide readily accepted the report as a Red-necked Stint. Nobody expressed any reservations about this identification." Bruce also informed me that the slide is in the Ohio archives. That could be too much information, and I apologize to inducing possible, maybe even probable, boredom. So, present knowledge taken collectively allows for an identification accepted without reservation. Okay, but I still regret lack of what was between those stint toes and what Harold Axtell had to say. I can be happy,

---

7. Fredrick H. Sheldon. "Jon Edward Ahlquist, 1944–2020." *The Auk* 137.4 (Oct 2020) 1–3. DOI: 10.1093/auk/ukaa050.

8. Bruce Peterjohn and William Zimmerman. *Birds of Ohio*. (Bloomington: Indiana University Press, 1989).

by consensus, to count the species as one of the rarer birds during my trip even though I cannot prove what I saw was what I saw.

Shorebirds and their proper identification aside, I continue to worry about pollution. After all, that stint might not have been on Walnut Beach had there been contamination by oil. Dirty greasy oil and other toxins get everywhere, even at and in Niagara Falls. In the early sixties, chemical and human waste was documented at the falls, a fact making me think less of repeating a visit. In 1984, up to 9,000 pounds of chemicals were illegally dumped into the Niagara River per day. Pollution seems to be a given, something ubiquitous, a part of our history, and our future.

Aside from the ability of humans to ruin such a phenomenal locality, it is hard to not notice the importance of the history and geology of Niagara Falls. A geologist named Lyell was interested in the rate the Niagara Escarpment was eroding. In the mid-1800s, he surveyed people living in the area about how quickly they thought Niagara Falls was eroding the escarpment. They told him that it was wearing away at about four feet per year, but that was not what Lyell wanted to hear. That rate meant Niagara Falls was too young to support his theory of deciding the age of the earth. And here is the rub. Lyell fabricated the facts and published an erosion rate of one foot per year. He claimed that the falls were 35,000 years old or too old to conform to biblical times. Oh well. Erosion is the primary factor that will change the falls. The average rate of erosion is now believed to be about five feet per year, which means it will take between 8,000 to 12,000 years, give or take a few months, before the falls erodes all the way south to Lake Erie. In the meantime, an average of 212,000 cubic feet of water per second falls 325 feet from Lake Erie to Lake Ontario. Power companies have harnessed the flow and in doing so have slowed some of the erosion either by happenstance or on purpose. Slowing the rate of erosion would benefit the production of 5,965,600 kilowatts of electricity and keep the tourist facilities standing.

Ontario's Niagara River is reputed as being an excellent place for gull watching but where I saw few birds in 1962. Millions visit the falls each year and among them must be a few birders. One estimate counts 8.91 million visitors in 2014. Places along the river in southern Ontario provide habitat for interesting gulls, including an occasional visit by Arctic nesting Thayer's Gull, a taxon with a long and controversial taxonomic history. Part of that history is chronicled elsewhere.[9]

The increasing human population spilled across the land from Niagara Falls and westward. Having crisscrossed New York, Vermont, and New Hampshire several times since 1962 and as late as 2015, it seems parts

---

9. M. Ralph Browning. *Rogue Birder*. (Eugene: Oregon Review Books, 2018).

of the country changed more than others. Aside from strip malls, many of the smaller towns in Vermont and New Hampshire are altered less than are large cities. That might mean fewer acres of bird habitat were swallowed for domestic and commercial enterprises prevalent in more heavily populated regions. One factor that has especially changed is the increased cost of transportation and tourism, with the latter predicted to climb higher. And those 50 cent strawberry shakes I so enjoyed in 1962 are history.

I made no record of the fee to get up Mount Washington but, recalling my tight budget, the fare was probably around $5. A round trip drive today costs over $35 per car and driver. Add $10 per passenger. The cog-train ride costs $70 a person. As for driving, I wonder if my heavily loaded and under-powered VW would have made the climb. A count of 12,800 vehicles summited Mount Washington in 1961. Currently, about 45,000 drive to the top. When Linda and I visited the slope of Mount Washington in 2015, we had a 23-foot RV. Our dual-wheeled vehicle was not allowed on the road to the summit.

It may be lucky that I did not try to hike to the summit of Mount Washington. A round-trip hike would have taken eight to ten hours, with little birding time. The average temperature at the top is only 26.5 degrees Fahrenheit, with a range from -47 degrees to 72 degrees. The average wind chill in July is five degrees below freezing. After 1962 there were more deaths caused by hypothermia.

Since 1962, a once considered subspecies of Gray-cheeked Thrush was treated as a distinct species in 1995. Mount Washington now offers special auto tours for the newly recognized Bicknell's Thrush for a $50 per person fee. From the base of Mount Washington in 2015, Linda and I gazed up the slope while longing for a Bicknell's Thrush. We later made a successful hunt in Vermont requiring a little hiking, patience, and a small fee.

Chapter 11

Remembering Maine

31 July 1962

LAST NIGHT'S RESTFUL CAMP in an eastern New Hampshire forest prepared me for a day of driving, and in a brief time, the little VW whisked me into Maine. My road map, like maps of other and larger states I had already traveled, was marked with my route highlighted and indicated potentially good bird localities gleaned from Pettingill's guide. The better birding spots were on the coast, which was slightly over 200 miles away. That distance would require more than four hours of steady driving, which should put me in Acadia NP in the afternoon. However, in my anxious state to reach the park, I forgot that the gas tank was getting low. As a reminder, vintage VWs did not have a gas gauge but did have a little lever under the dash that, when turned after running out of gas, would provide another half a gallon to go. I had already turned the lever. In the heart of Bangor, Maine, going up a hill during the beginning of their evening rush hour was when the car stopped. I ran out of gas. This was a first, but nothing to celebrate a foolish and embarrassing moment that cost an hour of walking to a gas station and returning the gas can they reluctantly loaned.

Back on the road and about 50 miles to go, the highway would soon end at near sundown on Mount Desert Island and in Acadia NP at Seawall Campground. If only there was sun. The landscape was cool and fog-shrouded during my first view of the Atlantic Ocean. I strained my eyes as I watched intently for oncoming cars and hoped not to drive off the edge of the misty veiled road. To the left as I approached the turn into the campground were flat sheets of darkness that appeared through occasional holes of the murkiness. Those darkened areas were the ocean, the cold water of the Atlantic. A spot where the pavement was close enough to the sea allowed me to detect an object floating on the water. Was I seeing a bird? What would be lounging on the ocean in late July? I would have to wait for better weather.

Atlantic shore near Seawall, Maine, sans fog.

I planned to stay two weeks in Acadia NP. For what was left of my first hours of the day, giving in to the weather seemed a good idea. Before the last light, time was devoted to learning something about my new location. A park brochure related that Acadia is the easternmost national park in the United States. It occupies about 47,000 acres of a cluster of islands and peninsulas, with steep rocky shores, headlands, cobblestoned beaches, and mountains draped by deciduous and coniferous forests. Rocky faces of the mountains look down on glacial valleys and lakes. Remarkably, the rocks that contribute to the wild beauty of the island are from river deposits hundreds of millions of years ago. Periods of erosion and even volcanism occurred before moving ice carved and polished the land with 20 to 30 glacial sheets that invaded New England. Only a short while ago, geologically, the last glacier pushed past Acadia about 18,000 years ago, and only 4,000 years ago, it retreated from Maine. The U-shaped glacier valleys, running from north to south, and the barren slopes scored by the grinding ice left the mountainous landscape the French so aptly named *Isles des Monts Desert*. The park brochure also explained that when the glacier melted sea level went up. However, with the heavy ice gone, the land rose. Although this rise and fall eventually stabilized, sea-level still rose a little leaving a sunken coastline much like what I was seeing in 1962.

In 1524, people called the area L'Acadie or Acadia, a word from the native Wabanaki Indians or corrupted from Arcadia of ancient Greece. Possession of Mount Desert Island a.k.a. Acadia bounced back and forth between the French and English. Homesteading, this time by Americans, was going strong in 1820. The region was saved from the loggers' ax and developers by the tireless efforts of George B. Dorr. Most but not all of Mount Desert Island that he salvaged would become the first eastern national park, initially known as Sieur de Monts NM in 1916, then Lafayette NP in 1919, and finally Acadia NP 10 years later.

The park brochure promised bogs, meadows, and rock-covered mountains, including 1,530-foot Cadillac Mountain, the highest point on the US Atlantic coast. I was excited about the potential of finding Spruce Grouse, Black-backed Woodpecker, and White-winged Crossbill. All that would have to wait, partly because the dense fog was going to make birding difficult, and a heap of dirty laundry needed attention.

1–6 August 1962

Laundry or no laundry and fog or no fog, exploring the campground, a walk southward to the rocky shore, and a brief foray into Big Heath, a bog, filled my first day. No fog was not possible. My view was grayed with fog too heavy in the air. Fog obscured the tops of the tallest conifers in the campground and dampened the sound of any calling birds. A Common Raven remained quiet as did a flock of usually twittering Cedar Waxwings. Fog was a common winter condition in my home turf in Oregon and was not productive for birding so it would likely not be here. The best use of time would be to catch up on the chore of laundry, so, on my second day, I drove about an hour to Bar Harbor.

The air is not so foggy in Bar Harbor, which was bustling with tourists. I think I can almost classify the types of visitors to national parks. There were the few dressed as if doing business, their neckties hanging limply in the fog-laden air. More looked like they were dressed for the beach. They were wearing short sleeves, some with shorts and sandals, and they looked and were surely unhappily cold. Such tourists looked outlandish, which recalls what a friend once said. "You shouldn't wear something you wouldn't wear in your hometown." Most of the tourist were somewhere between tropical beachgoers and those with jeans, a warm top, and sturdy boots. The laundromat, which seemed the only one in town owing to the crowd there, was teeming with all types of tourists. It was laundry day, and almost everyone was in an impolite rush. If one of several washers stopped before the owner retrieved their wet clothes, the next in line would plop them on top of the dirty washer tops. There was no good clean fun here. Compared to western parks, even at busy Yellowstone, people at Bar Harbor seemed not at all glad they were in such a beautiful setting as Acadia.

One hour later, I was shoving my clothes into a huge drier. Every 10 minutes the drier would stop, and every 10 minutes I fed it a dime. While I waited between dimes, I guarded the drier door and read welcome mail I had picked up at my general delivery at the Bar Harbor post office. Stuffed tightly in a single envelope were separate letters from my parents and sister and a card from an aunt congratulating me for completing high school. My mother wrote she would send a shirt appropriate for Florida at my next general delivery location. I wondered what "appropriate" meant about the time my drier went silent. It spun its last cycle, so I stuffed everything in pillowcases to make a hasty exit from the overcrowded laundromat and Bar Harbor. Fog-drenched Seawall Campground and my little green pup tent welcomed me back to pastoral comfort.

The next days at Seawall were cold and dank beginnings for birding the eastern shore. Peep sandpipers, mostly Semipalmated and a few Least, fed along the seaweed and rocks. Ravens croaked and Herring and Great Black-backed Gulls called hoarsely in the gray fog. Once the fog cleared, a Black Guillemot still in breeding plumage swam into view. A small crow appeared in a window of the murkiness. Perhaps a Fish Crow, but its silence did not identify the lone bird. About the time the guillemot appeared I realized that the objects I had spotted on my arrival at Seawall were buoys marking lobster pots. Two men in a small boat were checking the traps.

There were plenty of granite boulders along the shore for sitting and having lunch. Much of the granite was in nearly symmetrical blocks, broken and carved from thousands of years of wind, water, and glaciers up to 9,000 feet thick. The rocks were cold and wet in August. By the second night, the fog had made its way to every fiber of my clothes and sleeping bag.

The next day hike was a visit to nearby Big Heath, a 420-acre bog full of peat moss, orchids, pitcher plants, and more. The area hosted five species of warblers, most still feeding young as evidenced by caterpillars or other insect hanging from their thin bills. Magnolia Warblers were new life birds. The crisp nights, low daytime high temperatures, and fog created a lag in time. The plants seemed behind. Blueberries one month ago in Michigan boasted ripe fruit; the Acadia blueberries were just beginning to ripen. Bunchberries were already white in Wisconsin and just starting to turn red in the bog in Maine. In the cooler spruce bogs, the season is even later, with *Mimulus*, my favorite wildflower genus, and orchids blooming. Although the fog helped delay the season in Big Heath, the sunnier and warmer days there were absent in the campground. Even though my clothes were soaked by the wet fog, I enjoyed repeated hikes to Big Heath. I enjoyed just being in the park. My continued search for crossbills was to no avail but I did find my first Broad-winged Hawk. That bird brought visions of thousands I might see at Hawk Mountain.

In a letter home, I wrote about how intriguing it was to listen to New Englanders talk and that I had met several French-speaking campers. I told them about a service station attendant in Maine who asked, "All the way from Pennsylvania?" The color patterns of the license plate for Oregon and Pennsylvania were identical. I wrote to my parents that I had to pay an extra 5 cents to have ice cream in a milkshake (the term *frap* was apparently synonymous with milkshake sans ice cream). To my parents, I declared that I am going to give up bacon because it was too difficult to keep from spoiling. Giving up bacon to my folks was a foreign concept. A final food-related sentence in my letter to them stated I might give up cooking altogether since my white gas-fueled camp stove had burst into flames for the second and last time when I singed the hairs of my right hand. I planned to live mostly on canned tuna and peanut butter for my breakfasts, continue to make baloney sandwich lunches, and stop at cafés for dinner.

7 August 1962

Arrival at Black Woods Campground early in the day was necessary to assure obtaining a campsite. This was the sunny part of the island, and it was also the more crowded part. However, today, I experienced Seawall weather, cold and foggy. Campers accustomed to typically warmer weather shivered while gazing skyward as if praying for the sun. At 10 a.m., a park naturalist was explaining the fine art of catching crabs while I stood under a dripping stand of overhanging black spruce. Crabbing. What a cold and hard life, yet a life of freedom, with no boss, but the weather and the sea. No matter how cold or rough, checking the crab traps regularly prevents the cannibalistic crabs from eating one another. After removal of the crabs, the traps are re-baited, thrown back in the water, and the removed crabs are marketed. What spare time the crabs man might have had was spent repairing and maintaining traps and marker buoys that look like birds in a fog to a novice like me. The naturalist skipped to tidal pool flora and fauna. At one point, the naturalist passed around a small sponge that he produced from a pool. He suggested to the 135 listeners that each should smell it. I could see people wince. The sponge, we were told, had a combined odor of dirty socks, rotten egg, and spoiled milk, an odor I tried to avoid on this trip. Later, a Herring Gull flew over. Our naturalist revealed the plastic rain cover stretched over his flat wide-brimmed hat, which he said was not so much for rain as it was for gulls flying overhead.

The naturalist talk ended at noon, and, once again, I was having lunch sitting on a grand block of granite listening to the faint sound of the Atlantic lapping at the hard shore. The granite provided a cold and solid balcony as the fog ebbed and flowed while letting me snatch views of the ocean. Just as I finished the last bite of peanut butter on whole wheat, a White-rumped Sandpiper landed on a nearby rock long enough for me to look it over. Recalling lessons from Harold Axtell, I checked for all the salient field marks before satisfying the accuracy of my identification. The single sandpiper then flew and joined six other identical birds that had been apparently foraging just out of my view.

The sandpipers wheeled away as I left my rocky perch to continue to Thunder Hole, a small dead-end channel where waves crash and, of course, thunder. The trail went through spruce and deciduous understory. The thick conifer canopy chilled everything in the subdued light. A dark, colorless bird flushed from a dead bush and stopped in another bush 50 feet away. It was a thrush, perhaps a Swainson's, but it did not quite fit anything I had ever seen. I overcame the problem produced by the shadowy lighting with my trusty spotting scope. What could be better, a Gray-cheeked Thrush?

An hour later on a stretch of the shore, I discovered a painter gathering up his paints, canvas, and brushes. As he stood, a sparrow flushed almost at his feet. The bird had a most faint breast streaks but I needed a view of its crown. Was this the elusive LeConte's Sparrow? Not likely, but anything is possible. A closer look revealed a definite gray crown strip. My first Sharp-tailed Sparrow.

Feeling chipper over my three new birds, I practically skipped down the road on the way back to Blackwoods. In the excitement of finding the bird, I skipped a wrong turn, and only after two foot weary hours of correcting the error did I find myself busily and very hungrily preparing dinner.

8 August 1962

Today began at 6:30 a.m. while a passenger onboard the M.V. Bluenose, a 346-foot passenger-auto ferry traveling from Bar Harbor to Yarmouth, Nova Scotia. This was my maiden pelagic trip. For the first time, my trusty car and its pantry of food are not handy. Luckily, the ferry was not to leave Bar Harbor until 8 a.m., which left me time for breakfast in the ship's cafeteria. Plenty of time for eggs and bacon. After the checker rang up my purchase, I paid, and before I could pick up my tray a staff person carried it to a waiting table. I should have tipped him, but I did not have it to give.

The service, not to mention the bacon, was impressive. I was also impressed that of the 600-passenger capacity Bluenose, almost all the women wore dress hats, high heels, and a suit or dress. The male attire included sports coats and slacks or suits and ties. There I stood, blue jeans, flannel shirt, high top lace boots, in a need of a haircut, and I had not shaved for a week. With my telescope mounted on a rifle stock slung over my shoulder, binoculars around my neck, a Peterson sticking out one pocket, and a sack lunch poking out the other, I must have looked as strange as they did to me. However, I was not completely shunned and conversed with several passengers. They were probably curious about what I was up to, and one fine lady and her husband invited me to New York City where she would show me around.

The Bluenose left Bar Harbor on schedule. A few Herring Gulls followed as the ship moved east into thick fog. The maximum speed of the Bluenose, about 18 knots, caused the frigid wind to bite through my layered clothes. Unbearable as was the fog and intermittent rain, I was determined to see as much as I could. Only the two heavy showers of rain drove me off the forward deck. The gulls eventually peeled away from the stern and flew back toward the mainland. I moved to the bow where the speed of the ferry cut through the colder and hard bracing wind. Most of the passengers seemed overdressed, whereas I was most definitely under-dressed, especially temperature-wise. Regardless, I remained steadfast to the day's mission: to see as many birds as possible. Fortunately, there were a few minutes from time to time when the fog cleared. About halfway to Nova Scotia a bird representing a new family glided out of the fog. A Great Shearwater, my first tubenose, was one of 21 observed during the cruise. About an hour later a Cory's Shearwater coasted through a trough in the waves. Soon I began to glimpse petrels flickering past. Under the circumstances of weather and inability to see enough of any one individual meant identifying these small birds was impossible. However, on the way back to Maine, when the fog at least partially cleared, I was able to identify Wilson's Petrels. By the end of the day, I had seen two species of shearwaters, about 45 petrels of which I can say with certainty were Wilson's, a Northern Phalarope, a Black Scoter, and four flocks of unidentified sandpipers hurriedly racing to Maine. Seasickness never reared its ugly head, but before docking back at Bar Harbor, I began to take more breaks inside. The foggy and frigid and windy air was stretching my limitations. That night, snug in my sleeping bag, I detected a sore throat. The average summer temperature of 67 degrees was not going to help and my skinniness was not keeping me warm. Although, according to my weight taken back in Vermont, I had gained three pounds since leaving the strawberry pies in Ohio. Of course, tipping the scales at 146 pounds was not going to help keep me warm.

9–19 August 1962

I planned to be in Biddeford Pools, an important shore birding site on the coast of Maine, in late August. With time to spare and a worsening sore throat slowing me down, I settled in Black Woods camp life. Two days were devoted to fishing, with one day off the rocks when I caught 12 pollock in two hours and, another day, I caught 10 off a beach. All but five of the fish were released. Those five were breakfast. Another breakfast was blueberry pancakes, made with blueberries I picked the day before and pancake mix from a campground neighbor who wanted a couple of my eggs. It was a good trade. Because of my sticky skillet, the meal ended up as scrambled blueberry pancakes. During the next few days, I met another camping neighbor, Mark, who had watched me cook my canned dinner one evening. He observed, "You're all alone, aren't you?" I said yes, and this guy, about 10 to 15 years older than me, said that he and his wife were cooking steaks, and they had more than they could eat. "Would I please join them?" With grateful shyness, or was it apprehension of being in the company of people, I joined the Raymonds that evening and for several other meals as well as sailing with them in a small skiff in Bar Harbor.

During the time nursing my troublesome throat and a bit of fever, I was busy writing my notes on observed birds to be submitted to six different regional editors of *Audubon Field Notes*, fishing from the rocks, picking blueberries, and not much in the way of real birding. After the Raymonds left the campground, a neighbor at a nearby campsite took pity on me. They invited me for a dinner and overnight at their home in Schenectady, New York, a city on my route south.

Trot Larson, another camper, told me about a fishing trip he planned and asked if I wanted to go. I agreed, paying my $3.50 fare. We headed out for four hours from Seal Harbor with six ardent sports fishermen. Trot caught haddock and cod, including the largest fish of the day. Just before our 30-foot cruiser turned inland, Trot hooked a fish and quickly handed me his pole and told me to reel in prize. Struggle and perseverance allowed me to reel the fish to the edge of the boat. An angler to my right snagged my line with a pole and drug on board a long, streamlined three-foot sand shark. Its snapping and twisting stopped after the captain efficiently broke the shark's head open.

I was not sure how I felt about the incident. Even more difficult to weigh was that several of the caught fish were returned to the water but most did not appear to recover. The anglers simply threw stunned fish back into the ocean either because they did not want to eat them or legally could not keep them. Many of these fish died anyway as soon as their dazed bodies hit the water when waiting gulls made them an easy meal.

On the night of 19 August, I drove to the top of Cadillac Mountain, the highest point on the Atlantic coast. Named for Sieur de la Mothe Cadillac, a French nobleman, who founded the city of Detroit, the 1,530-foot mountain nearly matches the elevation of my home residence. Just five days earlier, I hiked to the top when fog enveloped most of the view. Not today. From the vantage of the summit of Cadillac Mountain, the half-light of the setting sun exploded through the clouds to reveal the details of the land of Acadia below. The smooth glaciated terrain, dark green coniferous forests, gray granite slopes, and the dark water of the Atlantic was a scene not to forget.

20–21 August 1962

The departure from Acadia NP seemed like the end of the journey from the West. Leaving Acadia was my turning point for the south, even though on the coast of Maine going south will put you in the Atlantic. So, I headed west again, but on southbound US 1 and, if I stayed the course, I would end up at Key West, Florida. I camped on a back road near Camden State Park not far from Rockland where I hoped to catch a boat to Matinicus Rock to add Razorbills and Atlantic Puffins to my trip list.

Last night's camp, the tent pitched on a dead-end road just off US 1, was a soggy end of the day. The rain pattered on the canvas nearly all night. As the skies dried to a cloudy gray, I pulled into Rockland just in time to see the mail boat to Matinicus Island leaving a noisy wake at the dock. The next mail boat to the island would be in a couple of days. As I began to fret and kick myself for not being on time, I looked in the review mirror and saw a shaggy head of hair. I did not need to sit there and worry; worrying is a waste of time. What I needed was a barber. Coming from a small town, I pondered that the local barber might have information on how to get to Matinicus Island. He did. A call to a lobsterman promised a trip to the island in "a day or two," and a hefty quoted fee. At the ferry terminal, I was given the name of someone who could take me today, but the price was higher than the first and out of my budget. Matinicus Island was not in the cards but a shorter trip to Vinalhaven Island, about 14 miles east of Rockland, looked promising. That might be just as good if I was extremely lucky. Europeans first knew Vinalhaven and some of the surrounding islands as early as 1500. Its long history brought loggers, farmers, and anglers, and industries including granite quarries, the stones used all over the country including the Washington Monument in Washington, DC. The trip to Vinalhaven was plagued by fog and cold. I was wearing a T-shirt, a flannel shirt, a hooded sweatshirt, and a coat. Including pants and boots, my garb kept me barely close to comfortable. The visibility was not much over 300 yards. Birds on the cruise included Black Scoters, Double-crested Cormorants, Black Guillemots, two of the usual species of gulls, and a Ruby-throated Hummingbird that rested on the mast. Perhaps I should have soaked in Vinalhaven's history, but I took the next ferry back to the mainland. I consoled myself that the last week in August might have been too late for puffins and Razorbills off Matinicus.

Driving in the fog was more hazardous in the sixties than today. The wonderful "invention" of painting a solid white along the edge of a highway lane did not become a national standard until the 1970s. Although my little VW was solidly constructed, by today's standards, it might be regarded as dangerous to one's health. There were no seatbelts, no airbags, and essentially few safety features found in more modern vehicles. That red light I mounted to the center of the back may have prevented a driver from rear-ending me. I could not complain and enjoyed hearing the whine of the air-cooled engine struggling to get me to birds.

The car that could took me to Maine, where only 5 percent of the state is public land. That is surprising compared to western states where there are millions of acres of national forests and other public lands. Slightly over 53 percent of Oregon is federal land. That translates to far more public access in Oregon, which is far more land to roam and enjoy without fear of trespassing compared to Maine. Those few publicly accessible acres in Maine are heavily used. Only 47,000 acres (various sources report different acreage) comprising Acadia NP occupies half of Mount Desert Island, Isle au Haut, and several acres on the mainland. Starting in 1989, additional tracts of land have been purchased by the Park Service. Acadia NP was ranked as the eighth most visited national park in 2020. Approximately 1.5 million visited in 1962, and most of them were hovering around the laundromat in Bar Harbor, a hamlet of 3,807 in 1962 that has grown to 5,611 in 2020. The town also has more visitors, since about 3.5 million came to Acadia NP in 2019.

Taxonomic changes after the early 1960s meant I could not count the thrush; it could have been a Bicknell's, then, in 1962, a subspecies of Gray-cheeked Thrush. The same day I saw the thrush, I found a sharp-tailed sparrow. At the time sharp-tailed sparrows up and down the Atlantic coast were a single species. Because my notes mention diffuse breast streaks, I am now fairly convinced the Acadia bird was a Nelson's Sharp-tailed Sparrow.

The passenger fare for the Bluenose ferry in 1962 was $11.88. In 1998, the Bluenose was replaced by the "Cat," a 319-foot catamaran that makes the 116-mile trip from Bar Harbor to Yarmouth in 3.5 hours compared to 6 hours in 1962 and charges approaching $200 for a round-trip passenger. Birding from the speedy catamaran would have been bitterly cold if impractical since its design disallows being on an open deck except for the stern. Still, hardy birders are said to expect to see shearwaters and petrels. Maybe the speed overtakes them just as I found a speeding pickup on a dike road in Idaho turned out to be a dangerous but productive way of seeing surprised waterfowl. Although I was not dressed formally or in the latest beachwear, the passenger inviting me to New York City must have overlooked my birder garb. I did not go to New York until about 10 years later while conducting research at the American Museum of Natural History. One evening, John Farrand gave me my first tour of Manhattan.

The research project concerned the geographic variation of Red-footed Boobies, a seabird occurring almost all over the world. Seabirds, often called pelagic birds, sometimes present questions about their taxonomy, not just at the subspecies level, but at the species level. For example, the Cory's Shearwater treated in 1962 as one species is, according to recent studies, possibly two or three species. How many species are in the complex depends on whose taxonomy one follows, and most North American references recognize only one species. Was the 1962 Cory's Shearwater different from any of Cory's Shearwaters I later witnessed? I cannot be certain. If two or three species are officially recognized, the Bluenose individual will have to be relegated to shearwater (?).

REMEMBERING MAINE

Linda and I visited Maine in 2015 while traveling from western Maine and then west to Mount Washington or essentially a route similar to mine in 1962, only in the reverse direction. We did not see any wayward shearwaters but, from a small 67-foot boat, viewed alcids including Razorbills and Atlantic Puffins, and other littoral species offshore from nearby Bar Harbor. Our list of birds, especially the alcids, was an improvement over the 1962 trip. We also did laundromat time, but close to Seawall Campground. Overnight fees at the campground were $15, but a senior pass cut the camping fee in half and the entrance fee to zero. Camping 1962 was free.

One day in 2015, I attempted to enter Big Heath, but the southern trail was grown over from neglect and lack of use. At the edge of Big Heath, I managed to scare up a Swamp Sparrow and out of place Boreal Chickadees and a Northern Waterthrush. Perhaps it is a good thing that entering Big Heath is difficult. It is a fragile habitat and Acadia is being overrun by people. The park needs millions of dollars just for repairs.

Chapter 12

August Assemblage

22–23 August 1962

RAIN BEGAN FALLING EARLY last night, but that was not going to prevent sleep. Tired of the wet ground, I decided to sleep in the car. The last time I did that was to escape the hordes of mosquitoes at Red Rock Lakes, Montana. This time was also not comfortable. Cramped and aching from contorted positions, I vowed not to do that again, at least not confined to the driver's side of the car. I had an idea. After breakfast of four donuts, I headed for the nearest lumberyard in Rockland. For $1 I constructed a shelf using two boards called one by twelves, positioned them side by side from a wooden bookcase sitting on the back seat to the front windshield. Luckily, the heights of the bookcase and bottom of the windshield were the same. The 24-inch-wide boards, braced in the front with two smaller boards that extended to the left and right sides of the car's interior, supported the front end of the bed to be. Behind the seat, my two suitcases stood on their hinges, both equal in height to each other and remarkably to the new bed resting on top of the bookcase and braces at the front windshield. On that platform, I placed my sleeping bag and air mattress. From the driver's seat, I could easily squeeze onto the bed that was about 15 inches below the ceiling of the car. If I felt claustrophobic, I needed only to slide the sunroof open slightly and lock it in position. Now I would have a clean, dry, and warm, and possibly safer, place to sleep.

Christmas Cove occupied the remainder of the day. What a beautiful place. The body of water must have been a welcome sight when Captain

AUGUST ASSEMBLAGE

John Smith steered his crippled and nearly sinking ship into Christmas Cove. The present Christmas Cove was full of boats today, boats ranging from dinghies to small sloops. One of these boats tied up at the dock where I stopped belonged to Aaron M. Bagg, who I had corresponded with about the birding trip and who lived in Dover, Massachusetts, and summered at Christmas Cove. I knew of Aaron Bagg only as the editor of the northeastern maritime regional report appearing in *Audubon Field Notes*, a journal I read from cover to cover for years. Aaron had taken the Bluenose ferry the day after I had and experienced similar weather and birds.

The Baggs graciously offered me a bed in their small cottage for the night and extended their hospitality with dinner, evening conversation, and a chance to browse through their extensive ornithological library. The next morning and just after a hearty breakfast, the Baggs launched their 15-foot inboard from Christmas Cove to a trip to Damariscotta Island. Laughing Gulls and Common Eiders were everywhere. Three Arctic Terns, their bills blood red, were new life birds, a species that migrates from the Arctic to the Antarctic. On the seaward side of the island was a Great Shearwater that glided toward us for a close-up, then wheeled about and out to sea. Being in the company of a more seasoned birder than me and seeing the Great Shearwater together gave me confidence in the shearwaters I identified from the Bluenose ferry.

Back on the mainland of Maine, I thanked the Baggs for their kindness and drove about 10 miles to Reid State Park, where Aaron suggested I would begin seeing more shorebirds. The 800-acre park offered access to the shore of the ocean and at the mouth of the Little River. Unlike most of the rocky coast of Maine that I had so far experienced, the shore was sandy and teeming with shorebirds. The tide was coming in and crowding the birds in tighter and tighter congregations, forcing them to compete for higher ground while avoiding the throngs of swimmers and sunbathers. The great thing about shorebirding is the birds are out in the open, like sitting ducks. My trusty scope, an incoming tide, and plenty of time to check each individual bird was a treat. This was what I had read about, dreamed about, and finally was experiencing. This was why I was in Maine in August.

There were more Semipalmated Sandpipers and Semipalmated Plovers than I had ever seen, and they were in a feeding frenzy. Also scurrying about were flocks of surf-dodging Sanderlings, Ruddy Turnstones, and spotless Spotted Sandpipers, and two new life birds, a single Red Knot that joined a flock of at least 50 Black-bellied Plovers. I recounted the shorebirds an hour later and discovered that the number of plovers did not change but 85 percent of the Semipalmated Sandpipers had disappeared. Perhaps the migratory flock departed southward or found a nearby foraging area away from the numerous people that were competing for the sand.

24–27 August 1962

It was late so I spent the night in Reid State Park. The next day I got my notes up to date, and cleaned and organized the car. By now, I realized that in the heat of birding, various articles of clothing and papers tossed in the car landed in the wrong places. Keeping organized meant keeping a certain amount of sanity. I also attempted to contact Chris M. Packard.

The next evening, I discovered that there were no places to camp. With permission, I slept in my VW bunk behind a service station in Brunswick. Getting in and out of my bunk was a little tricky even for my skinny six-foot frame, but that was not nearly as difficult as dressing and undressing. My midget mobile home was without drapes and that created a risk of being caught in my underwear. As far as I know, no one observed me slinking out of my sleeping bag and sliding from the berth and into the driver's seat. Once extricated, the next step was to get out of the car and find an appropriate place to unburden my bladder. Then, I could move the back of the driver's seat forward and lean into the back toward the rear seat to access books, a blank piece of paper or an envelope, a typewriter, items of clothing, food, first aid kit, whatever I needed. Everything had its place for easy retrieval. The freezer chest that held most of my daily food sat on the back seat. Though I had by now officially given up cooking bacon and eggs, the chest was still useful for storage and keeping any food free of bugs. Breakfast was three, no four, sugar-coated donuts and a slather of peanut butter. A few people, I imagined, might call what I ate a continental breakfast, but that did not make it any more nutritious. Donuts are donuts but mostly the peanut butter did the trick. Before getting back on the road, I rolled up my sleeping bag, let most of the air out of the air mattress, removed the front cross-piece supporting the two wide boards and slid all three pieces toward the rear window, secured the three pieces to the right side of the interior, and was off to the races.

Later, I found Chris Packard, the director of the Maine Audubon Society and Portland Natural History Museum, at Mast Landing, a 160-acre sanctuary in a coniferous forest and marsh near Yarmouth. He was conducting an insect survey. Volunteers were busy inventorying the year-old sanctuary and cataloging plants and animals of all kinds and surveying for potential interpretative trails. Chris, as he preferred, took time from the insects to fill me in on recent bird finds in Maine. We discussed the puffins

AUGUST ASSEMBLAGE

I missed. Chris tantalized me with a list of what I could see in the winter, including such chilling species as Razor-billed Auks and Great Cormorants.

Following our talk, Chris and his company of volunteers went back to surveying insects, but one person begged off and went up one of the newly built trails. He said he wanted to photograph a pinesap, a plant resembling the ivory-colored Indian pipe. An unexplored trail seemed more interesting to me than looking for insects, and maybe a new bird would be around the corner. In the meantime, I watched a meticulous photographer hovering over a pinesap on the forest floor just off the sunny trail. The deep shade subdued the honey hued color of the plant nestled in the deep shade, but in a moment the forest floor was lit by the bright August sun, which was just enough for a mirror to capture and reflect its rays to the pinesap. After a few quick manipulations of the camera, the shutter began snapping to finish the job. It was then my companion apologized for concentrating so intently on the plant and explained that in a few more minutes the little spot of sunlight would have been gone. He preferred not to use flash and said the pinesap color would change with age. Today and the time of day were perfect. Introductions were in order. This was Harry Chadbourne, whose primary interest was birds.

We wound our way through the aspen and willows to a saltwater marsh, arriving at a narrow strip of mudflat bordering a channel. Semipalmated Sandpipers pattered back and forth, pulling what looked like tiny worms from the sticky muck. Nearby, we discovered three different-looking peeps. They were Baird's Sandpipers. The next day we returned to the mudflat with Chris where three Baird's Sandpipers foraged. Maybe they were the same birds. Chris was excited, as the peeps were new species for Mast Landing Sanctuary, as was a sharp-tailed sparrow, possibly a Nelson's Sparrow. We also found Lesser Yellowlegs, Semipalmated Sandpiper, and Spotted Sandpiper migrants.

Before the day was complete, Harry, Chris, and I traversed through a wet marsh at Mast Landing. I told them that whenever I get near water, I manage to get wet. About six feet farther along, as I trailed just yards from my companions and much to my surprise, or was the prophecy coming true, my right foot kept going down into mud. And down. In seconds, I tilted forward, catching my plunge to the center of the earth with my left leg and hands. Next was a roar of laughter. Chris and Harry just happened to turn as I went down. The tall marsh grass folded over my sinking body, and I waved madly as I attempted to right myself. It was funny, even for me. Harry laughed the most and offered his home where I could wash the marsh ooze away. On the way, we found a Magnolia Warbler in a tall fir and talked about shorebirds, flowers, hawks I might see at Hawk Mountain, and Harry's dream trip, a chance for birding in Florida.

During the last three days, Harry and his wife, Virginia Chadbourne, were my generous hosts. The couple took me into their home, Ginny, as she preferred to be called, fed me, and the two helped me find birds in the area. They showed their love of nature and life. They were wonderful and genuinely encouraging toward my travel goals. Harry's day job was delivering fuel oil to residents. He liked it because it got him out of doors, which gave him time to look for birds or flowers to photograph. The hard winters and dragging a smelly fuel hose across icy snow was not his favorite activity but he probably saw more Snowy Owls, Snow Bunting, and redpolls than most Down Easters.

28–30 August 1962

Yesterday, Robert Gobeil greeted me at the doorway of his home in the town of Biddeford Pool. He was highly recommended by Chris and others as a good guide to Biddeford Pool, and the locality was highly recommended by Pettingill as an important stop. Biddeford Pool, not the town, is a tidal basin occupying roughly a half-square mile of prime habitat for migrating shorebirds. Robert, just two years older than me, was enthusiastic about birding. He related that he had spent the summer as a counselor at a boy's camp in Vermont and was anxious to see the shorebirds his region in Maine was so famous for. The light was going so we talked about the shorebirds we would see tomorrow.

Almost all our time the next days was spent shorebirding Scarborough Marsh, Hills Beach, Higgins Beach, and the famous mudflats of Biddeford Pool. We made three visits to Biddeford Pool during the day. Although aiming for incoming tides, our first arrival at Biddeford Pool was during low tide. Our first visit yielded a smattering of Semipalmated Sandpipers and plovers, knots, Greater Yellowlegs, Ruddy Turnstones, altogether 11 species of shorebirds. Highlights for the day were four new trip birds: White-winged and Surf scoters, Roseate Tern, and Northern Mockingbird.

The next morning was one of rain and the stiff wind blowing about 30 miles an hour. We ate our breakfast to the sound of the rain pelting the windows. A few minutes and miles away, we arrived at Biddeford Pool. Shorebirds covered the mudflats. Bob and I splashed through the area, glassing almost everything until the rain soaked into our water-resistant but not waterproof jackets, rain flowing down the collar. What mattered was keeping our optics dry. After all, we were there to identify birds. Sandpipers and plovers crawled around us, some almost too close for binoculars. A few shorebirds ran away as we approached them while others reluctantly flew to the other side of the short marsh grass that bordered the mud. They seemed to realize that taking wing in the stiff wind might be hazardous and therefore stayed grounded. The short grass borders were already full of groups of standing shorebirds, little two-legged trees forming an oasis of birds waiting for identification. We found several Whimbrels and three Long-billed Curlews. Robert was elated to see the curlews. The species is rare for coastal Maine. I had seen the curlews out West and did not appreciate fully that these birds were way out of their normal range. On the other hand, I was happy to see the Whimbrels, a new species for the trip. The amount of rain and the intensity of the wind, brought courtesy of Hurricane Alma, increased. It became impossible to use our scopes. During the day I had soaked two pairs of socks, two pairs of boots, one pair of pants and most of another pair, and two shirts, a jacket, and, of course, my underwear.

After the tide went out, the shorebirds dispersed, and so did we. There was daylight left so we looked for land birds. We found a couple of Eastern Phoebes and a small flock of Barn Swallows trying to ride out the blustering rain. A couple of warblers were lingering in the bushes including a yellowthroat and my first eastern sighting of a Wilson's Warbler. Back at the house, in dry clothes, we pored over field guides, making sure we knew the salient field marks to be ready to identify terns that the hurricane might blow northward, and looked over gulls, pondered the prospect of an early Black-headed Gull.

Our last and third day was under calm skies and Biddeford Pool was again loaded with shorebirds. We glassed each standing Black-bellied Plover and mostly waited for them to fly, which allowed us to check the color of the axillaries. All were black, but finally, a winter plumaged plover flew directly overhead. The axillaries were not black. It landed among the Black-bellied Plovers where we could compare bill size (we could use our scopes today). My first American Golden-Plover! Soon, several more birds joined the foraging Black-bellied Plovers. More searching revealed a Pectoral Sandpiper, a trip species. Just as we were about to leave a group of nine birders arrived, the first seen these last three days. The group, well equipped with high-powered scopes mounted on the heaviest of tripods, parked themselves on the flats and began identifying the birds. Unfortunately, the golden-plover had departed just minutes earlier.

Still dry from outer to inner wear by the afternoon, and happy with shorebirding in Maine, I thanked Robert for his hospitality. It was a relief to be away from Hurricane Alma although the wind and what birds it brought were at the same time exciting. It was my first hurricane. Luckily, it was a weak one and left less than two inches of rain on the coast of Maine. Of course, the entire storm seemed to be at Biddeford Pool, with much of it in my underwear. After not finding a place to camp, I got permission to park on a service station lot near Portsmouth.

31 August 1962

Chris Packard had suggested I try to meet Dr. Arthur C. Borror, an internationally known ornithologist living in Durham, New Hampshire. Unfortunately, he was out of town, but a secretary permitted me to browse one of his libraries. I never realized there were so many different publications sponsored by so many birding organizations. Besides the big three, *Auk*, *Condor*, and *Wilson Bulletin*, there was the *Delaware Naturalist* and *Chat* that covered the regions to the south. *Audubon Field Notes* filled several shelves. In fact, volume one of most of the journals stood at the beginning of rows and rows of shelves of journals from all over the country. Skipping the *Auk* and *Audubon Field Notes* seemed prudent since, beginning in 1962, I had become a novice member of the American Ornithologist's Union and was regularly receiving *Audubon Field Notes* that were mailed to my Oregon home. Once on the road, my parents sent current issues of the two journals to me via general delivery. There was so much to read and so little time to learn. It was tempting to browse early editions of those and other journals, but that would eat up time that I did not have. Instead, reading was limited to journals from regions on my itinerary that might offer clues for good bird localities.

Part of my day in New Hampshire was devoted to the mundane. It was time for a lube and oil change that cost $4.40. Worst of all, time was spent watching my dirty laundry become clean and dry for the next day's birding. After laundry and groceries, which came to $1.09, I headed west, ending up at a deserted side road about 30 miles east of Concord.

1–3 September 1962

Awake at my peaceful camp at the deserted side road out of Concord, I realized that it was Labor Day weekend, a time when more than the usual number of people are driving the highways. It is a time when more auto accidents occur than any other time of the year. Like my parents and a few others, Labor Day weekend was a time to stay off the roads, be safe, and be alive. For a few seconds, the realization of what my calendar revealed sent a wave of feeling trapped. What should I do? Should I stay put at my location?

Stay off the busy roads? My answer was yes, take the time for cleaning, reading, writing, and, of course, birding.

Spending four nights in one locality was okay at a few localities, but here, on the deserted road, just feet from the highway did not seem ideal. Fortunately, the thick understory of bushes and seedling trees competing for overhead sunlight hid my car. The vegetation also dampened the sounds of the light passing traffic, but not completely.

On 2 September, a car pulled up behind my parked VW. It was a police car. One officer exited his vehicle and strode up to my car. My driver's door open, I sat in the seat, with my legs out of the car, my typewriter balanced on a metal TV tray for a desk, and my fingers poised over the keyboard. The officer seemed to be both confident and cautious as he approached me. We were both perplexed and a little unsure what might happen next. Was I trespassing? How much trouble was I in and why am I being the subject of a law enforcement officer? He probably was wondering if I was a criminal who might be armed, or maybe he was laughing internally at what he saw. He asked me what I was doing and, observing my sleeping bag inside the VW, added that it was illegal in New Hampshire to sleep overnight in a car. So, what was I doing? Did he want the whole reason or a condensed version? I condensed it and stressed that I wanted to avoid the dangers of being on the road during Labor Day weekend. Luckily, my concern about safety on the road was also his concern. Satisfied with my reply, although I could see he was puzzled, the officer told me he would look the other way regarding sleeping in a car, wished me luck, and off he went. Relieved, I returned to writing a column about my travel for my high school newspaper.

Not much was going on during the dog days of birding at my tiny spot of woods in New Hampshire. Restlessness set in. By now, the local birdlife had been seen and re-seen, I was tired of writing and reading and anxious to get on the highway. Bored, I turned on the radio and found a disc jockey announcing that over 400 people were highway fatalities so far. Luckily, I had driven almost 5,000 miles without being in an accident. Tomorrow, the weekend would be over and the drive to my next birding location would be accident-free.

4–5 September 1962

Having avoided trouble sleeping in my car, I drove out of New Hampshire on 4 September and into New York near Albany before heading south to eastern Pennsylvania. That day, I veered a few miles north and stopped at Elnora, New York, the home of Fred and Margaret Denner. We met in

Acadia NP, and they invited me to stop. Fred and Margaret reminded me of my parents, and I suppose I was a little homesick even though the birding kept me from thinking about home. The Denners seemed truly happy to see me. I momentarily worried why. Even their son, about two years older than me, was interested in my travels. We all talked about Acadia, and I told them about Biddeford Pool. Being non-birders, they were curiously bewildered but accepting that someone would travel the country just to see birds. At the same time, I enjoyed their company, focusing our conversation away from birds and, before I left, they even encouraged my traveling. However, convincing as I might have been, information about my diet was met with a degree of almost parental style scolding and admonishment for maintaining a diet of donuts and canned vegetables.

During my early years in Oregon, shorebirding was limited to a few interior migrants since I never made it to the best Oregon coastal shorebird locations. I was too busy, mostly working to save money for this trip. So, Ohio and Maine were shorebird treats. While during all the hours watching sandpipers and plovers, I was surprised that no one seemed to take a second look at my telescope mounted on a rifle gun stock. Perceptions change. A scope on a gunstock today might be celebrated by certain factions and considered suspicious if not dangerous by others such as law enforcement.

Nothing particularly rare was found at Biddeford Pool although since then notable species have been recorded there. Part of the shore of Biddeford Pool is privately owned and some is owned by the Rachael Carson NWR, a refuge established in 1966. The fragmented refuge has a projected acreage of 14,600 acres along 50 miles of coast from New York to Maine just south of Scarborough Marsh and a tract south of Portland. In 2003, the refuge purchased nearly a half-mile of frontage of the pool. Parking is limited and no longer free.

Visiting Maine in June 2015, Linda and I skipped Biddeford Pool, thinking shorebirding there would not then be fruitful and, being put off by the heavy traffic, drove to Scarborough Marsh for a few days looking for sparrows. In 1962, I skipped going to Scarborough Marsh for landbirds because sharp-tailed sparrows had not been treated as two species. However, according to the seventh edition of the AOU check-list, two species overlap between the easily accessed Scarborough Marsh near Portland and Popham Beach, just north of Reid State Park. More recent studies show that the zone of overlap of the two species is expanding; a recent report put the zone from near Rockland to coastal Massachusetts. The zone of overlap probably has changed at this very moment. At any rate, the sparrows seen at the Scarborough sanctuary could have been either species. In 1962, few if any birders were checking bill lengths and head shapes, and whether the buff color of the face contrasted sharply with the paler underparts or any of the other subtle differences between what then were only separate subspecies.

Fortunately, several field guides today help identify subspecies, especially ones that are easily recognizable in the field, and occasionally those sets of subspecies might be suspected to comprise distinct species. Examples include certain gulls, Spruce Grouse, Yellow Warbler, juncos, Fox Sparrow, and other field recognizable taxa that might represent multiple species. Are there two species of birds that North Americans call Yellow Warblers? Several authorities believe there are. Are the morphologically and vocally different taxa of Fox Sparrows different species? Then there are more difficult taxa to identify such as warbling vireos that contain eastern and western taxa identifiable by subtle morphology, but separable by noticeable differences in vocalizations and behavior. Observing these differences and similarities adds to the knowledge base as well as the challenge to observe and record the world of birds. Perhaps I should have been a better student of my subject in 1962, but I accepted whatever the checklist stated. Science builds on facts and new information sometimes alters earlier conclusions. Checklists are based on scientific studies and hopefully change as new information becomes available, which is a situation recognized concerning the Scarborough sparrows.

Maybe I should have taken detailed notes or a good photograph of that sparrow at Mast Landing. Then, it might have been possible to identify the bird to what were, in 1962, regarded as subspecies. My Mast Landing sparrow, if identified to subspecies, could have gone on an escrow list. That is a list of birds that are not officially recognized by the American Ornithological Society (formerly the AOU or American Ornithologists' Union). Once such a listed taxon is officially treated as a species or its status is accepted as an established bird, the taxon can be removed to the escrow list to the list of countable species. For example, almost everyone realizes there are probably several species treated under the name of Red Crossbill. As studies refine what is known about crossbills, many birders are placing on their escrow list the different song and morphological types of crossbills. One of them has relatively recently been officially recognized as a species distinct from the other red crossbills. Another example that primarily concerns introduced birds might be Rose-ringed Parakeet that for years, although observed by numerous birders, was not countable until the taxon met certain criteria allowing it to be considered established and therefore countable. Removing the parakeet from an escrow list to a main list became possible only after the hundred, if not thousands of birds, were recognized as established species. Of course, not everyone follows the rules, which is okay too.

When Hurricane Alma hit Biddeford Pool, thoughts of storm driven tropical birds came to mind. What Alma brought was lots of rain, rain that fell sideways in the wind as drops larger than the average cloud might produce. Very wet Hurricane Alma, the first named hurricane in 1962, began in Florida as a tropical storm. Despite my comment that Alma was a weak hurricane, the storm became more destructive as it worked itself up the coast. At the time, I was clueless that damage was beginning to add up in North Carolina and as it moved north, harm to property, utility infrastructure, and trees was increasing. Alma became a category one hurricane with wind speeds of up to 85 miles per hour, but it had quickly weakened by the time the storm hit New England. Rain pelted the region including Maine before Alma moved further offshore and fizzled out near Nova Scotia.

Surviving Labor Day and possibly being a highway fatality seemed to be an important accomplishment in 1962. The radio announcer heard from my parking spot on Labor Day exaggerated the death toll, but not by much. Not being one of the official 392 souls that were highway deaths in 1962 was a good thing. I had avoided a catastrophe that fretful relatives often imagine. Having to explain that not every bear is going to maul or every stream is hiding deadly quicksand is tiring, but my parents were far more forgiving and trusting. Nonetheless, they did instill fear of highway accidents during holidays. Taking their advice brought me a peaceful and restful Labor Day weekend. I needed it. After all, I had lived through a hurricane. Today, the Labor Day death toll is higher than in 1962, with 448 killed in 2019. However, any comparisons need to consider several variables. Equivocating death rates in 1962 and the last few years must consider there are now more vehicles on the road, many positive safety features are installed in vehicles today, and, on the negative side of life, a plethora of drivers are distracted by the belief they must stay in constant phone contact with everyone they know. High rates of traffic fatalities are not limited to Labor Day. In 2019 more people died during the Fourth of July. Like reports of mortality in wars, the number of the dead does not reflect the near-death of those suffering from wounds from car accidents and war. My VW, much smaller than most vehicles in 1962, and without seatbelts or airbags, would not have done well in keeping me out of the statistic books had I been so unlucky as to drive into a mauling bear, quicksand, or an oncoming vehicle. Insofar as being a wartime statistic, I knew in 1962 I would soon be facing down that barrel all too soon.

In the meantime, I was enjoying life and friendly conversations with strangers I met. Some people may have viewed me as needing help. Was it my youth and innocent-looking face? Was it my way of living? What of my little oddly shaped vehicle turned into a teeny-tiny motor home? My goal was independence, but I did enjoy talking to people. Was I too trusting? I almost was in Michigan, but I escaped. Being taken advantage of had not occurred to me. Would situations involving strangers today as they did nearly 60 years later have similar outcomes? People in campgrounds generally do tend to let their hair down, be less cautious and more friendly than they otherwise might behave. Would similar outcomes involving strangers occur then or today if I met people at my current septuagenarian age? Would I be regarded as the gray old man of the campground or the silver-haired birder to invite for a fireside dinner? So much is relative. One Acadia camper in 1962 once observed that I was alone, but fortunately, I was not lonely.

Chapter 13

Hawk Mountain

6–7 September 1962

SEPTEMBER, ACCORDING TO MY plans set in motion months ago, was to be the month for raptors, hawks, falcons, and eagles migrating south along the ridges of the Appalachian Mountains. Specifically, Hawk Mountain in eastern Pennsylvania, I hoped, would be an unforgettable lifetime experience.

A camper at Acadia National Park told me he would introduce me to Hawk Mountain. The person, Rev. George Deisher, turned out to be among the august individuals I had earlier met. George, as he asked to be called, had a day job that was more soul-related than it was to birds. He invited me to visit his home in Kingston, Pennsylvania, a city just north of Wilkes-Barre and down the road from Scranton and where I had weeks earlier arranged for a general delivery of my mail. There was a promise of good birds to see, but with houses and businesses crowding in every direction, where could birds find habitat to fit their needs? It was nice to be wrong. By 7 a.m. on the sixth of September, we were searching a marsh near Kingston where we found an immature Virginia Rail and, in a small wood lot, my first Cape May Warbler. Nothing was confusing about this autumn observed bird. A few other warblers were found but not as abundant as there used to be according to my host. Insecticides were the prime suspect for the population declines.

By late morning, George, Howard Allen, a birder friend of George, and I arrived at Hawk Mountain, a sanctuary set aside to protect migrating raptors. Here, the ridges of the Appalachian Mountains are oriented in a northeast/southwest direction, the direction followed by migrating birds and most known for migrating raptors. At the headquarters of Hawk Mountain near the base of the mountain, George introduced me to Alex Nagy, assistant to Maurice Broun, caretaker, and curator of the sanctuary since 1935. Minutes later the man himself showed up, Curator Broun, not a curator of museum specimens, but a curator who had seen more hawks than anyone in the world. The five of us were soon on our way to the lookout to count migrants.

George warned me that our time on the mountain was limited since we had to return to Kingston. We did see a few raptors, including an immature and adult Bald Eagle, migrants that usually pass the sanctuary later in the year, and several smaller Broad-winged Hawks. It was a taste of days to come.

Before leaving, I picked up a couple of free pamphlets about the sanctuary for night reading since tomorrow I would be back and thought I should be prepared. One brochure stated that Pennsylvania's Game Commission once placed a $5 bounty on Northern Goshawks. The bounty was a great amount for people during the Great Depression, and those eager to collect hardly cared whether they were shooting a goshawk or any kind of hawk. The bounty on goshawks was finally terminated in 1951. Most hawks, then and even decades later, were often called chicken hawks and placed in the general category of varmints to kill. Prompted by George Miksch Sutton, Richard Pough, then a graduate student in 1932, visited the site of the carnage at what locals called Hawk Mountain. He tried to stop the killings to no avail. However, Rosalie Edge, a New York conservationist, saved the hawks by purchasing 1,398 acres, including Hawk Mountain, and hiring Maurice Broun, with his wife Irma, as caretakers. The shooting stopped and the new sanctuary was open to anyone wishing to watch hawks. Broun's 1949 *Hawks Aloft* chronicled the years on Hawk Mountain.

7–14 September 1962

About 8 a.m. on the seventh, I thanked the Deishers for their hospitality and drove southward to Hawk Mountain Sanctuary. The sanctuary is on part of the Kittatinny Ridge, one of the prominent ridges in the Appalachian Mountains. It is deciduous country: the land had experienced deforestation from logging and charcoal, burning to preserve blueberry habitat, and a blight that destroyed the dominant American chestnut by 1950. The surviving trees are about 100 years old, with secondary growths of Red Maple, birches, hickory, Black Gum, and several species of oak. The shortness of the trees was a result of their age and the shallow rocky soil.

Maurice Broun, telling me to call him by his first name, permitted me to park my car behind the museum just across the road from Schaumboch's, the Broun residence. He knew I could not afford the fee for the nearby campground, and he may have thought I would be a good night watchman. For whatever his reason, I was grateful.

Once settled, I followed my host's lead and hiked up to the lookout. For about a mile, the dirt trail climbs nearly 300 feet before opening to the lookout at 1,521 feet. The view is glorious by eastern standards; the grandeur of the West spoiled me, but Hawk Mountain is exciting. The lookout is a jumble of massive gray boulders that provide great seats and backrests for hawk watchers peering northeast in the 180-degree viewing window. Below is the River of Rocks, and further away are the tops of summits forming landmarks when spotting oncoming birds. There are four of these summits that appear as small bumps in the horizon, each numbered from left to right. A bird seen over the easternmost summit was announced as coming in over four. This helped everyone locate a bird, which at first might be a dark speck. Maurice could identify, and always correctly, these raptorial specks with lightning speed. I had to wait for a closer view. From 3:30 until 5 p.m., the time the lookout usually is closed, I saw only an Osprey, a couple of Cape May Warblers, and several Broad-winged Hawks. It was a slow afternoon, but Maurice was enthusiastic.

My first full day, 8 September, at Hawk Mountain was almost as described in Pettingill. Broad-winged Hawks dominated the air with 111 birds migrating overhead. Sixty of these soared by during the first hour. One lone Northern Harrier added to the list of birds flying over birders perched on Hawk Mountain. By eleven o'clock, activity became quiet, although my stomach was growling. The sandwich I packed did the trick while I took time trying different boulders for a seat that might offer the best viewing and comfort.

After lunch, a few Broad-winged Hawks trickled over. I became a little birding lazy at that point. As a few ardent observers were faithfully keeping an eye on the horizon, I decided to read the literature I had stuffed in my lunch bag. I also was rereading *Hawks Aloft*, a book that now took on greater excitement than even the first read during rainy winter days back in Oregon. It was also a good time to scout for confusing fall warblers. One such bird was a warbler in drab and olive plumage that was at first glance confusing. The warbler's telling white wing spot at the base of its primaries identified the bird to be a Black-throated Blue Warbler.

Back home, at my parked VW behind the museum, I barely got the car door open when Maurice came around the corner to invite me to the little cottage called Schaumboch. Irma, Maurice's wife, and partner on the mountain since the beginning, enticed me with a home-cooked meal and a huge piece of freshly baked apple pie. During the evening, I described my trip itinerary, and casually mentioned that I might try to find a job so I could extend my travels. There was a noticeable pause then I was to hear almost harsh words. There was no cursing but there was a stern look from Maurice who blurted, "People would give their eye teeth to do what you're doing, so don't spoil it by working." He said a few other things that questioned my intelligence, but he complimented me for making the trip in the first place.

At daybreak the next morning, I ascended the last steps to the lookout expecting to see songbirds; the hawks would begin migrating later with the sun-produced thermals. The sun rose like a fiery red ball. The gray clouds' glow bounced the sunlight down to the fog-draped valley below. What a beautiful setting for seeing migrating warblers and thrushes resting and foraging after a long night of migrating. However, there were no chipping birds, no leaves stirring; there were no warblers, just a lonely Wood Thrush scolding and a distant Blue Jay giving a tinny trumpety cry far below the summit. Maurice was down the slope and also searching for songbirds. Were the warblers late or was it the pesticides?

Back down from the summit I happily joined the Brouns for an invited breakfast. After delicious hotcakes fresh off Irma's griddle and a good cup of coffee, I was ready to walk the mile again to see what hawks might be flying down the ridges. It was a slow day bird wise this Sunday. Between birds, I visited with a few of the birders including a lady who had about the same bad luck seeing birds in Yellowstone that I did. I also continued rereading *Hawks Aloft*. Just before closing the book, I glanced again at Maurice's inscription he offered last night. It read, "Inscribed for R.B.—with greetings and special salute on a year-long journey of 650 birds! Good Luck!" I appreciated the confidence but knew I would be lucky to break 500. A Black-throated Green Warbler flitting at the edge of the trail topped off the day.

The tenth day of September started with a feeling of stiff and sore muscles. It was not the two miles of hiking each day to the lookout. It was my not-so-precious air mattress that had developed a slow leak. I had to reinflate the partially deflated mattress more than once last night. Wake up, blow up the mattress, sleep for a while, wake up, and blow up the mattress, sleep for a while . . .

The local meteorologist predicted rain for today. I debated with myself. Should I make the climb or catch up on my notes and reading? While waiting for the clouds to brew or blow, I used the morning hours reading.

Especially interesting were the recent reports on the problem flaring up in parts of Texas. Ranchers, farmers, a Texas senator, and generally ignorant trigger-happy raptor haters decided Golden Eagles should be killed. Conservationists believed eagles should not be killed. Maurice had just received a letter about the controversy concerning a misinformed and biased opinion of one of the local Texas politicians, who sided against the conservationist, blinded by reality, and influenced by the twisted truth that these birds were stealing calves. Perhaps a calf was lost to Golden Eagles but man's best friend, the domestic dog, is known to harass cattle to death. No one was suggesting wholesale killing of dogs.

By afternoon I was up at the lookout. It never rained although a southwest wind was blowing hard and steady. Hardly any hawks were migrating. A Kestrel zipped by, and I found a lonely Ovenbird as the token warbler for the day. Darkness was coming earlier as the season advanced, leaving me less and less time to update my notes and any domestic chores such as blowing up my air mattress.

The eleventh of the month was by far my best day on the rocky outpost of Hawk Mountain. It was not that there was a great number of individuals that had scudded southward, but it was the variety of species. At least it seemed so to me. At the end of the day, eight species of hawks were identified. Finally, a Sharp-shined Hawk appeared. This was a new species for the trip and I asked myself how in the world had I missed such a widespread bird. Maybe I should keep this to myself. Anyway, what a bird today. The Sharp-shinned Hawk, an adult, soared high overhead, which was not the usual quick glimpse I was accustomed to as a bird dove into the trees after its prey. The bird today surprised everyone watching as it broke away from its circling route and dived from the sky at falcon speed. It made a pass at a slightly larger migrating Broad-winged Hawk. The Sharp-shinned Hawk's talons were extended and ready for the strike, but the Broad-wing swerved, just missing death.

Besides raptors, there were more warblers, including two Cape May and one Black-throated Blue Warbler. I overheard a staff member comment that fewer warblers were seen this year.

My fifth full day at Hawk Mountain was a great day. Today I checked off Cooper's Hawk. It was first spotted far in the distance between bumps one and two, the hawk watchers' reference points. The first identification yelled out was Broad-winged Hawk. My trusty 20x scope revealed the bird to have a tail much too long for the sturdy Broad-wing. My reverence of the other birders caused me to keep quiet about my suspicions. Would I get over the embarrassment of being wrong? Moments later Maurice took a glance and confirmed my identification.

HAWK MOUNTAIN

As the day progressed, several Broad-winged Hawks and Turkey Vultures winged past. Someone called out "Cooper's Hawk." Instead of the earlier adult, less than 50 feet above us soared a magnificent immature. Before the bird was barely out of sight, two Sharp-shinned Hawks darted overhead. These birds apparently did not notice the Cape May and Black-throated Blue warblers foraging below.

That evening, Alex Nagy invited Seal Brooks, a visitor from Wilmington, Delaware, and I for an owling trip into the Pennsylvania Dutch darkness. Screech Owls were our target, and Alex knew where to find them. He has a mammoth project studying these little-eared owls. The owls were using most of the 50 nest boxes he had placed three years earlier. He plans to extend the project so he will have five years of data on nesting behavior. Mr. Brooks and I were amazed as Alex whistled one answering owl after another. Alex had the uncanny ability to know exactly where a bird was by its sound alone. It was as if he could see in the dark. Once a bird was close, he switched on a flashlight and its unwavering beam was a perfect aim at the owl. Alex showed us over a dozen owls, more than I had seen in any one night.

The hot sun bore down on the watchers waiting on the rocky outcrop called the lookout the next day. There was little breeze and several of us, including myself, were more than discouraged. At 9:40, a small vanguard of broadies (that's Hawk Mountain talk) got everyone's attention. Soon a real flock or kettle of about 31 Broad-winged Hawks wheeled gradually to the south. By the end of the day, I had counted 114 Broad-winged Hawks, and an assortment of Sparrow Hawks, Ospreys, and Sharp-shinned Hawks. This was not the big flight expected. Once that happens, I will leave Hawk Mountain. I was willing to wait another week then I would make my way south also. When hawks were not waiting to be identified, the hawk watchers at the lookout discussed the fall plumage of Cape May Warblers (I saw 10), delighted in the southward passages of two Pileated Woodpeckers, about 50 Rose-breasted Grosbeaks, and around 75 Cedar Waxwings. They also talked about local politics (I just listened), and whether Cuba was going to be a Communist foothold in the Western Hemisphere.

There were a few other migrants including more Black-throated Green Warblers and, new to me, two Palm Warblers. The real high light of the day was two Red-headed Woodpeckers. An observer two boulders to my right announced that the woodpecker has been declining for years.

That evening Seal Brooks and I ate campfire food consisting of potato and eggs, with a dash of onion and black pepper. We talked about the prospect of the big day when thousands of Broad-winged Hawks might soar over Hawk Mountain. It was a crisp and dark night lighted only by twinkling stars and our flashlights. No screech-owls were heard although we could hear the faint calls of warblers and thrushes as they made their nocturnal journey southward. Back at my car, I hurriedly inflated my unrepaired air mattress. By now, the crisp air had evolved to cold. I was willing to wait a few more days for the big Broad-winged Hawk migration, but the next morning made me wonder just how many more days the wait might be. The thickening clouds soon began releasing a drizzle.

15–18 September 1962

The fifteenth began 12 feet from the lookout summit. That is when six Broad-winged Hawks rode a thermal southeastward. Shortly after, a few more trickled by, and it looked as if today was going to be the big day. Maurice and several others at the summit thought so too. John Alderman was among us, a lobbyist for the pending "Golden Eagle Bill." I had met John the night before while he and other volunteers worked until midnight on posters illustrating raptors and raptor watching. The "Golden Eagle Bill" represented raptors, and more specifically, it was to protect eagles from being shot. Maybe the hard work would be rewarded by a couple thousand hawks winging by Hawk Mountain.

Not so. By noon we found ourselves staring into empty air. Forty Kestrels rocketed down the Kitanny Ridge. A few southbound Northern Harriers and seven Ospreys scudded just over the treetops. The warm sun joined my boredom; I almost fell asleep on my rocky perch. If anything happens, surely one of the 250 visitors would let me know.

The next day was the day. By the end of the day, 3,200 Broad-winged Hawks made their way over the lookout. Never had I seen so many birds of prey in one day. One large swirling mass gathered overhead at first with 20 birds, which were joined by 50, then 20, then 50, then 250 or more, all streaming from the north and into the swarm overhead. It was a humbling experience. It was life-affirming to know that so many Broad-winged Hawks had survived DDT, habitat destruction, and illegal shooting. Before the day was over two Bald Eagles, two Northern Harriers, and 22 Osprey had coursed over the lookout. A single Pileated Woodpecker seemed unaware of all the carnivores overhead.

The seventeenth began full of clouds and doubt. Was yesterday the big day for the year, the high count for Broad-winged Hawks? Maurice thoughtfully scratched his head, paused, and gave his answer based on 28 years of watching hawks. "Yes, the big flight has gone." He was not entirely satisfied with the answer; he had stationed hawk watchers on several known hawk-watching sites north of Hawk Mountain. Alex monitored Hawk Mountain, Darwin Palmer from Wilmington, Delaware, kept watch at Owls Head, a rock outcrop about a mile and a half south of Hawk Mountain. Would counts from those localities offer a better count of the Broad-winged Hawk migration today?

Anxious to discover the count at Bake Oven Knob, a promontory east of Hawk Mountain and near the Appalachian Trail, Maurice, with three others and me, piled into a couple of cars and drove 16 miles north to the site. Rain pelted our windshield as Maurice steered the car to the valley floor, talking birds, mostly hawks, at every milepost. The rain drenched our optimism as we sped across the rolling Amish farmlands, and even more drops fell as we arrived at the top of 1,500-foot Bake Oven Knob. Now fog clung to us as we slipped out of our vehicles to discuss our next step. I mostly listened. The weather was terrible for hawk watching and even worse for grounded migrating hawks. It was not long before the huddle of dripping people agreed to opt for a day of armchair ornithology back at Hawk Mountain. The consensus was that the last big flight of Broad-winged Hawks was over. That was what was keeping me at Hawk Mountain, the big flight, and now it was time for me to move southward.

On the drive back "home," Maurice and I stopped so that I could pick up a few groceries should I stay at Hawk Mountain a few more days. I certainly did not want to leave for points south in the rainy drizzle and besides a talk of a trip to the New Jersey coast was in the air. With that thought, I hurriedly picked up my rations. The little general store, similar but different from the one in Monida, Montana, required the same rules. As the customer, I needed to spot the item I needed, such as brand x beans, then tell the clerk the name and brand of the item. The storekeeper would follow along the big wall full of shelves decorated with can goods until he found the brand x beans. After he found the item, including the brand name, I would announce the next needed item. There was some communication problems owing to the fact that brands in the East were not always the ones familiar to me.

My last day on the lookout, 18 September, was rainy and cold. Gusty northwest winds swept over the rocky outpost, but it was a good day for at least hawks. About 850 Broad-winged Hawks passed by at eye level as they skimmed the treetops on the west side of the ridge. Kestrels zipped by so fast and so low that individuals were probably being missed. Alex and I stationed ourselves on the windward side of the lookout and were able to pick up more Kestrels and Sharp-shinned Hawks. I wondered if this cold and wet weather would cause migrating Broad-wings to pile up as they waited to the north for better weather. It felt like winter when I crawled into bed. Thank goodness, I had finally patched the leaking air mattress.

19 September 1962

This would be my last day at Hawk Mountain. Tomorrow I would join Maurice and others on the trip to New Jersey. Today, for the first time in 12 days, I would not ascend to the lookout. This time I birded down in the Kettle, the valley directly below Schaumboch's and the immediate area around headquarters. Although Broad-winged Hawks and Kestrels were found, I was enjoying looking more for Passeriformes. In four hours of searching, I managed to scare up 30 species, including Wood Duck, Ring-necked Pheasant, several resident species such as Tufted Titmouse and Northern Cardinal, but also migrant Rose-breasted Grosbeak and Indigo Bunting. A Red-eyed Vireo was still around as well as four Black-throated Blue Warblers and one each of Nashville and Magnolia warblers and an American Redstart.

Ever since that night when Alex Nagy demonstrated the ease of calling screech-owls, I wanted to try my luck. My feeling of slightly self-consciousness about whistling weird sounds in the dark kept me quiet. Now, alone, I could try whistling all kinds of owl notes, even though it was perfectly light. I reasoned that I might be able to fool other birds. Standing still near a small creek, I puckered and slurred a whistle barely resembling a screech-owl. Following a couple of these sorties, and just before I was about to embarrass myself further, I began to be swarmed by Blue Jays, all screaming madly. A few Black-capped Chickadees joined the fray, followed by a lone Wood Thrush adding its distinctive guttural scolding call. I felt a little proud that I was finally successful with my ruse, but also a little guilty for exciting so many birds. Still, my owl imitation was a good way to find birds.

20 September 1962

The group going to Brigantine National Wildlife Refuge on the New Jersey coast gathered at Hawk Mountain at 4 a.m. An hour later, Maurice, Darwin Palmer, Erwan, and Eve Cobb from Toronto, Ontario, and I folded into a car for the long three-hour journey east. Our first major stop was after a nourishing breakfast at Holgate. Since I was not driving, I sat back and enjoyed the scenery, so just how we got to Holgate was a mystery. The small 256-acre unit of the entire refuge was a gift from the National Audubon Society. Bordered by the Atlantic Ocean and channels, it is technically a barrier island. Out the door from the cafe were Herring and Laughing gulls sailing in a cool wind strong enough to whistle in our teeth. The birding group crossed a stretch of sand dunes where we began combing the marsh grass for anything there. A Seaside Sparrow jumped up as we, a split second later and in unison, announced its identity. A Clapper Rail flushed within feet of our faces and sallied past the rest of the crew as we swept the grass. Two Black Skimmers cut the water surface in the channel. There were numerous unwary sharp-tailed sparrows, most of which were approachable within a few feet.

Two hawks I missed at Hawk Mountain were at Holgate. An adult Merlin swooped by us as it chased a flicker into a bayberry bush. The speed falcons fly is amazing, but most falcons are slow when compared to the huge falcon that flew above our heads, even catching Maurice off guard but only for a moment. It was a Peregrine Falcon, new to the trip list, and capable of about 200 miles per hour in a dive. Luckily, our falcon was just cruising at a slower speed; otherwise, we might have missed such a magnificent species.

We were soon on our way to Brigantine's 13,310 acres of coastal marshes interspersed with channels and open bays. Along the dike roads, we found several more species on our growing list. On a bush at the edge of the dirt road were hundreds if not more of Monarch butterflies. Maurice said they were migrating. Fish Crows, hundreds of them, gathered on one of the pumphouse roofs. This was a new life bird, and what a funny crow, much quicker in flight and with a strange nasal call. We found Carolina Chickadees near headquarters, a new bird for the trip. By the end of the light, I had seen 12 new species for the trip of which seven were new for my life list. The 17-hour round trip, with 72 species on our list, and great birding companions, was a wonderful treat.

Clear and dark skies dominated as we rolled back to Hawk Mountain. Darwin, still wound up, had borrowed Maurice's giant 20x binoculars for stargazing. He was more than happy to point out Jupiter, the brightest planet in view. What was most amazing was that the binoculars' magnification was sufficient to see two of the giant's moons and the rings of Saturn. Years earlier, I had spent blinding hours on the roof of my parents' carport in Oregon looking for the silhouettes of birds as they passed between my precarious perch and the full moon. Looking at planets was even more amazing.

21 September 1962

During a wakeful night, I reviewed my long stay at Hawk Mountain, the opportunity to see thousands of hawks, the developed friendship with the

Brouns, Alex Nagy, and others. The falling temperatures urged me to move southward, as did the prospect of new birds to see.

My day started with one last breakfast with the Brouns. It was a quiet breakfast interrupted by Maurice's enthusiasm for my birding adventure, where I should go, who I might contract, what new birds I would add to my growing list. I returned to my little home, the VW tucked behind the museum, where I typed my notes covering the last couple of days, stowed my stuff for traveling, pored over maps, and prepared myself for a long goodbye to Maurice and Irma. By now, it was noon, so we had one last meal together. Not until 2 p.m. could I bring myself to leave. Part of me wanted to stay, but I also hoped I would be in Washington, DC, in two days.

Before jumping into changes and reminiscences about Hawk Mountain, a comment concerning the trip to New Jersey is in order. In 1962, Brigantine National Wildlife Refuge was high on the list for a good birding locality. It still is. In 1984 the refuge and nearby Barnegat NWR that was established in 1967 were combined under the name of Edwin B. Forsythe NWR. Most of the 47,000 acres of the fragmented refuge property are salt marsh on the mainland, but some of the refuge, including the Holgate Unit, is insular. The size of the Holgate Unit, especially valued for protecting Piping Plovers, went from 256 acres reported in 1962 to currently 400 acres. The refuge, about an hour and a half north of Cape May, is also important to a population of brant, a species of goose on the decline as rapidly increasing populations of Cackling Geese and especially Snow Geese compete with brant for nesting habitat. Beginning in the 1960s, the latter species population exploded to the point that bag limits for Snow Geese were, well, unlimited.

Since that whirlwind trip in 1962, I visited New Jersey only twice, once at Cape May, unfortunately in late summer and not during migration, and once north of the Cape at Egg Harbor to search for brant during the winter. Egg Harbor is the type locality of birds often hailed as Black Brant (*Branta nigricans*), formerly and quite likely a separate species from the other brant (*Branta bernicla*). More on the taxonomic controversy elsewhere.[1]

Reading the history of Hawk Mountain decades after my first visit brings to mind some of the people of that history. George M. Sutton, who encouraged Richard Pough to visit Hawk Mountain, decades later encouraged

---

1. M. Ralph Browning. "Three Taxonomic Goose Issues to Gander." *Oregon Birds* 46 (2020) 16–18.

me concerning a study I completed on the taxonomy of Rock Ptarmigan. Pough, the founder of The Nature Conservancy, was a familiar author of a set of field guides I owned, and, in the 1960s, about the only competition to the Peterson guides. A few associates have remarked their puzzlement that Pough's guides did not gain more popularity. Peterson owned those little lines pointing to the salient field marks; Pough could not use them so, before the trip, I meticulously copied field mark pointers onto the illustrations in my Pough guides. This seemed to improve the illustrations and help sharpen my ability to identify birds. Of course, *Hawks Aloft* became one of my favorite books. Maurice autographed the copy that was one of my most cherished belongings but was lost or destroyed.

One of the topics discussed among birders on Hawk Mountain in 1962 was the declining populations of birds. I had heard this earlier from people such as Harold Axtell, Aaron Bagg, and Harry Chadbourne, and some of my older bird friends in Oregon. Often associated with the topic of dwindling numbers of birds was a new book, Rachel Carson's landmark *Silent Spring*. In 1962, I had not read it, nor did I realize its importance. Her book has been reprinted countless times, including a fortieth anniversary edition. Those that maintain it is possibly the most significant book in our nation's history are probably correct. It was not until 1973 when widespread use of DDT was finally banned in the United States, but the half-life, the time one-half of the DDT becomes something else, is about 15 years. The picture gets worse since studies show DDT remains in humans for generations after initial exposure.[2] Evidence to this day shows DDT is present in the Great Lakes. It is no secret that US companies, along with India, China, and North Korea, still manufacture and export DDT to other countries. A number of those same countries ship vegetables and fruits consumed in this country. DDT continues to be used in some countries, at the recommendation of the World Health Organization, as an indoor spray to control malaria-carrying mosquitoes. Not addressed here are at least a couple of questions. How many people are harmed by the indoor spraying of DDT? How much illegal DDT waste in metal barrels will seep into the environment?

Fortunately, authors continue to draw strength from Carson's *Silent Spring*. Conservationists inheriting and acknowledging responsibility to the planet, just as did Sutton, Pough, and the Brouns, continued to struggle to save the environment. Today, the battle is even more imminent as we grapple with climate change, another deadly arrow from the recklessness of humankind.

2. Michele A. La Merrill et al. "Association between Maternal Exposure to the Pesticide Dichlorodiphenyltrichloroethane (DDT) and Risk of Obesity in Middle Age." *International Journal of Obesity* 44.8 (2020) 1723–32.

Hawk Mountain sanctuary provided a window into the plight of saving habitat and wildlife, but I admit that, at the time, my thoughts and appreciation focused more on the quiet nights behind the Common Room, mornings with the Brouns, and birding from the top of Hawk Mountain. I did not miss a day. Sometimes, the trail was empty, just me and the trees, with memories of each out-of-place rock or tree root ready to trip the unsuspecting. The hike up to the lookout was usually quiet, punctuated only by my footsteps as I navigated the trail alone to the remote summit. Numerous trips to the lookout were to count birds, which I later reported to Maurice on days he was busy with administrative chores. The trips gradually began to wear thin just as, according to Maurice, administrative chores wore thin. My earlier entries stated that the trail was one mile to the lookout, but on 12 September, I wrote, "I trudged up the rocky one-and-one-half mile trail . . ." I must admit that the hike up had become less and less inspiring, but that once at the summit I decided getting there was worth every step.

Hours watching the sky begged for creature comfort such as a seat flat and big enough for the buttocks and a backrest. In 1962, it was possible to select your seat, when only 19,100 people visited the mountain during the year. Only 10 years later a virtual lion's share of the Division of Birds and friends including Fran James, Marshall Howe, Storrs Olson, Dick Zusi, and yours truly hunted unsuccessfully for a place to sit. By the late 1980s, crowding on the mountain was worse than standing room only. I could not face even more people and have not been back since. About 60,000 now visit Hawk Mountain annually. I wonder if Maurice had a place to sit. The Brouns and I maintained correspondence for several years and a letter from them once confided, as much as they loved people, they missed the quiet of their early years on the mountain.

The owls Alex Nagy called Screech Owls were Eastern Screech-Owls. In 1962, these owls were treated as an eastern subspecies, but it and the western subspecies were found to be separate species. That taxonomic split was based on research by Joe Marshall, one of the 1970s Smithsonian contingent visiting Hawk Mountain. Changes in taxonomy caused changes in my trip list, including adding a second species of screech owl. On the other hand, the merger of the red and yellow-shafted flickers was a loss of one species. Taxonomic relationships of birds are in flux and as new knowledge accumulates, a better understanding of birds grows. As recently as the roaring twenties, the 2020s that is, new information on the hybrid zone of flickers suggest the possibility that the two taxa are separate species.

Besides owls at night and diurnal raptors after sunup, other birds migrated past Hawk Mountain. I did not appreciate the significance of seeing some of these, including Red-headed Woodpeckers, which I believed were common, at least in part of the country. These colorful birds too often ended up on women's hats (along with egrets and others). The woodpeckers were also killed by farmers protecting their crops of berries and fruit, and their nesting cavities stolen by European Starlings. Red-headed Woodpeckers were also killed because of the bird's damage to power and telephone poles. Red-headed Woodpeckers are now considered rare in the Northeast.

On 18 September 2004, 42 years and two days from the date in 1962, the big day at Hawk Mountain for Broad-winged Hawks yielded 2,596. The annual average of 8,164 is a paltry sum compared with a record high of 29,519 in 1978. Much higher numbers have been reported from Hawk Ridge Nature Reserve near Duluth, Minnesota, where, in a recent mid-September, over 102,000 Broad-winged Hawks streamed their way south. Even larger swarms, called kettles, have reached up to 400,000 over Veracruz and elsewhere in Middle America. Broad-winged Hawks are one of the most common eastern forest raptors, but reported declines since 1980 are probably the result of forest fragmentation in Quebec, New England, and the southern Appalachians. Data from various sources are but an indication of population dynamics and constant habitat degradation among factors that dictate the need to protect Broad-winged Hawks and all the creatures of their domain. For example, at Hawk Mountain, the forests, as at other places in Pennsylvania, suffer from a lack of plant regeneration. Recent studies revealed that heavy browsing of small young trees by essentially predator-free White-tailed Deer cancels the possibility of older trees being replaced and produces an understory that is too sparse for shrub-nesting birds and small mammals that raptors might relish. Conservationists plan to reduce the deer population to recover the forest and understory, which likely will benefit hawks and other wildlife.

Hawk Mountain was a turning point for me. The Brouns' invitation into their home showed me their love of history and how they cherished Schaumboch's, their revolutionary-era cottage. They would have appreciated Schaumboch being listed on the National Register of Historic Places in 1979. In the meantime, the cottage was a cozy retreat, a place where the Brouns tended to administrative chores of Hawk Mountain, and where meals and conversation within its walls continued its history. One of several nights at a home-cooked meal was followed by a generous slice of pie and a talk. Maurice and Irma convinced me, contrary to my earlier plans, that I really should go to college. They also advised me, if at all possible, do not take time during the trip to work. I took their advice. Another evening, as I was gaining weight from all those great meals, Irma got after me because I smoked. Maurice told her to let me alone, "after all, he's got to have at least one vice." Eventually, I also took Irma's advice.

Continuing to think of the Brouns never stopped and I should have kept better in touch. It was disappointing not to see them at Hawk Mountain during my next visit there in the early 1970s. My generous and caring friends retired in 1966, moving one mountain ridge away from the maddening crowds, and at which time Alex Nagy became the curator of Hawk Mountain. The sanctuary grew to 2,600 acres, a significant increase since 1962, which must have been welcoming to the Brouns, but the increase of around 60,000 visitors per year would not have suited them, at least privately. Maurice died of cancer in 1979, Irma in 1997. It is too late to tell them that, without their guidance, my path would have been different. If only all those that the legendary Brouns touched with their wisdom, hospitality, and happiness could once again thank them.[3] The lessons of observation, the value of keeping a journal, conservation, the importance of education and knowledge, and the conversations during cool nights inside their welcoming home was Hawk Mountain. The warmth of this remarkable and loving couple was my personal Hawk Mountain.

3. Michael Harwood. *The View from Hawk Mountain: The Story of the World's First Raptor Sanctuary*. (New York: Scribner's, 1970).

Chapter 14

Capital Birding

22 September 1962

HAWK MOUNTAIN WAS GREAT, but I was looking forward to time alone for a couple of days with only the hum of my little VW Beetle before entering the densely populated Washington, DC, region. Time alone was not in the cards. The drive yesterday took me farther south and into a region wherever I looked, there were houses, businesses, and far more people than I wished. Traffic was heavy, even in the late darkness that dictated a stop for the night. I was just south of the Mason-Dixon Line. Sleep on a wide grassy area several yards from the hard surface of Interstate 70 in Maryland was mixed with roaring diesel engines of trailer trucks thundering by as each pushed through the air that shook my car. More annoying were their bright headlights. About 3 a.m. and finally sound asleep, I was awakened suddenly by the deep-throated rumble of an idling car. Then I heard heavy footsteps followed by sharp knocking on my rolled-up window. Thank goodness the window was up, but I worried what might happen next. I was just about to slide out of bed and into the driver's seat. I knew I could do this rapidly. The keys were in the ignition. Could I start the engine and escape whatever was confronting my innocent slumber? Before I could make a move, a demanding voice asked what I was doing. Hell, it was obvious what I was doing, but what was the person outside my car up to? About the same time, I realized that the rumbling car was a police car, but was this person a real police officer? For an unknown reason, the person thought that shining his flashlight directly in my eyes made it easier for me to answer his repeated questions. A glimpse of a shiny badge relieved my suspicions. My answer to the impatient officer was that I was traveling and unable to find a spot other than my present location for sleep. The answer satisfied the officer. Without further ado, the long nose of the law left, and I settled back into slumber.

Following a breakfast of the usual half dozen cake donuts, I looked over the road map, which revealed I was much closer to the Capitol Building than I had thought. Back on the road, the car was nearly pushed along by the traffic. It was worse than Cleveland, it was worse than anything ever experienced. Before I knew it, I was in a bustling metropolis "full of sound and fury," and did not have the least idea where I was or where I should go. A service station attendant saved the day, at least for the moment. In a brief time, I again became lost and stuck in traffic entanglements but, at last, found a needed YMCA. A hot shower and clean clothes suitable for city life replaced the body grim, dirty blue jeans, and worn T-shirt. A bank of vending machines not far from the shower sold food, and with the correct change, I purchased a stale hamburger. I also got a $1.25 haircut, including removing the hair on my neck that the patrol officer caused to stand upright.

People at the Y directed me to a tourist campground not far away. Of course, I got lost again. I was not accustomed to so much traffic, and the streets radiating out from the traffic circles like spokes of a wheel completely befuddled me. Driving in what I heard was the best-planned city in the United States was no easy task. There were no left turns and getting on and off a traffic circle put a new meaning to the word merge. Another problem I was facing was the confused driving by tourists. So far, I had been relying on the position of the sun and time of day to help guide me in the right direction, but the amount of fast moving traffic prevented a glance of the sky for any meaningful navigation.

After what should have taken only a few minutes, I finally made it to my destination, East Potomac Island campground. For a small fee, I had a campsite with a cold-water faucet, picnic table, and a place to take a hot shower. The site was enclosed by a tall cyclone fence and could be entered only by passing through a guarded gate. The island was quiet, green with scattered trees and only a 20-minute walk to the historic Mall. With time to spare, I hurried to the Museum of Natural History.

23 September 1962

The morning pitter-patter of rain splashing on the car's fabric sunroof accompanied the light of dawn at East Potomac Island campground. Just inches from my head, the sound reminded me of rain hitting my now obsolete pup tent. I tried birding on the island, but the area seemed void of variety. In a place like the capital, there should be plenty of nonbirds to see. Being Sunday, I thought that the streets would be full of tourists, so I walked leisurely along the cherry tree-bordered Potomac River sidewalk, just following my nose. Today I would try to be just a tourist, but I could not help trying to identify almost every bird flying my way. I was a committed capital birder.

The first stop, the first national monument on my life list was a domed building standing in the background of a view of a Northern Mockingbird perched in a tall bush. Sun reflected the white of the Jefferson Memorial and inside stood a giant bronze statue of Thomas Jefferson. I felt I had suddenly stepped inside a high school textbook. To the north were the White House and the 555-foot monolithic Washington Monument. The Lincoln Memorial was to my left, but a good hike away. There were so many beautiful buildings, so many recognizable from those textbooks studied back in Oregon. History was everywhere.

On I walked, leaving Jefferson behind, and entering the Mall, a park-like section of lawns and trees running from Washington Monument to the Capitol. I had heard the Mall was "alive" with birds, but today I think I would have been excited if I had seen a robin. Birds might have livened up the Mall once planting American elms occurred there and elsewhere and before detection of Dutch elm disease. The disease, an introduced fungus, swept across the Northeast in the 1930s, but it was not detected in Washington, DC, until 1947. Controlling the disease by removal of infected trees and by spraying began in 1952, the decade when there were over 38,000 American elms in public areas of the city. Perhaps there was a healthy number of birds in the elms at given times, but the throngs of people strolling under the trees were not likely contributing to avian privacy, whether it was for nesting or migration. Probably all that spraying depleted any chance for a bird to have a fulfilling snack. The surviving American elms did provide great shade, but not great birding.

Before ending my day, I walked up the gentle hill to the base of the Washington Monument. There are few areas in the city where I could not see the giant white spire that helped me navigate the streets. I was not sure I would have time to walk the 896 stair steps to the top. I took the elevator. During the 70-second ascent, I glanced through a pamphlet outlining a few brief facts about the Washington Monument. It was hard to believe that construction began in 1848, a time when my home would not be a state for 11 more years. Completed in 1885, building the monument cost less than it now costs to maintain. At the top, a tiny pyramid-shaped area accommodated only a few people at a time and people vied for a position at the thick windows facing out in four directions. The view revealed an amazing perspective of Washington, DC. The green scene, expansive lawns, and tree after tree were gratefully startling.

My camera seemed heavy with film exposed to the four cardinal directions from each of the monument's windows. As I made my descent by the stairs, I noticed the stones of the walls represented every state in the Union as well as localities worldwide. During the long way down, several weary climbers struggled for the pinnacle. Several were shedding clothes; I wondered how much they were wearing once reaching the top.

Back home at the campgrounds, I rested my weary feet. How much of the grandeur of the city could I enjoy before my planned two-week stay ended? I had met a few long-time Washingtonians today. They said they could never see it all. More importantly, what birds would I find here?

24–28 September 1962

The next five days were spent in the Division of Birds at the National Museum of Natural History. I wanted to use the library, especially for information on the breeding behavior of Western Bluebirds, a species I thought of studying when I returned to Oregon. Digging back in old, timeworn volumes of the *Auk*, *Condor*, *Wilson Bulletin*, and other journals and books revealed much new and exciting information about bluebirds. Occasionally, I found myself gazing at accounts entirely unrelated to my subject. It was hard to stay focused in the quiet room holding 6,000 books and 20,000 author separates that Pettingill had described in his bird finding guide.

Before starting with my library research, I made a phone call from a phone in the central part of the museum. My explanation for using the library was sufficient for the person on the other end to tell me, "Sure, come on up." However, I was not sure how to get from the ground floor to the Division of Birds on the third floor. I asked a uniformed guard, who surprised me by telling me all I had to do was take the elevator up and turn left or was it right. Off the elevator, I wandered about, looking for the library. The hallways were empty and noticeably quiet. Eventually, I found an open door, and inside was shelf upon shelf of books and journals. Finally, the library, but was it? I picked up a tome, but before I could open it, a tall, whitish-gray-haired man appeared in the doorway. He wore a white shirt, conservative tie, dress pants and shoes, and a comforting smile. The imposing figure, who had been just around a corner examining bird specimens from Panama, did not speak. I did, and said, "Surely this isn't the complete library."

"That's my personal library," he replied. Embarrassed, I quickly told him who I was and why I was wandering around the Division of Birds. He extended his hand, laughed, and introduced himself as Alexander Wetmore. The extent of my knowledge of the person was he was a famous ornithologist and that he was a kind gentleman for not calling security. I did not realize at the time that he was the sixth Secretary of Smithsonian. He introduced me to Phil Humphrey, the curator of birds, who took me to the library, told me where the local restroom was located, and left me in the awe of all those printed pages. I worked, taking notes on bluebirds until about 4 p.m.

It was time to replenish my food supply, so I headed out to find a grocery store. It would have made more sense to ask at the museum for direction to a store within walking distance. Instead, I drove. Then I drove some more, being pushed west across the Potomac River by the steady stream of homeward bound cars. Everyone was exiting the city at the same time. The further I got from downtown, the lighter became the traffic. I accidentally ended up across the Potomac River in an undisclosable location in Arlington, Virginia. At the time, I did not know where I was. I spotted the store, got my food, which cost more than what I had been paying, and, with a clerk's directions, carefully navigated east to the campground on East Potomac Island.

The next day I pored through as much material at the Division of Birds library as time allowed. My hand ached from writing notes on what I might use for my research. That afternoon, with directions from Dr. Humphrey, I headed for Georgetown. Historically, Georgetown was in Maryland. Washington, DC, was first conceived by none other than George Washington. I had grown up thinking that the late 1800s represented history, as that time did for Oregon, but the history in the East was nothing that new. Georgetown was founded in 1789, but I got lost today before finding it. Finally, I reached Wisconsin Avenue, a narrow main street that took me to the Audubon Center bookstore and my appointment with Dr. Joan Criswell. During the planning stages of the trip, I read she was the one to ask about birds of the region. We had corresponded about a year ago. She read my complete wish list, naming the species that could be found in the area. Most of the birds were those at their northern limit of their breeding range while others could be found wintering southward, maybe in Florida. Later, I managed to navigate back toward the museum and eventually up Pennsylvania Avenue where I had time to tour the inside of the Capitol Building.

Cool rain fell most of the twenty-seventh, but it was warm and dry in the Division of Birds. The day started with a visit with Dr. Wetmore. We discussed education and ornithology as a career. His advice, along with that of Maurice Broun, was swaying me away from working for either the refuge or national park systems. During our discussion, I learned that Dr. Wetmore was working on a reference book on the birds of Panama. It was exciting to listen to his accounts of research in the tropics and see the smile in his eyes as he spoke of plans to return to Central America. He gave me four reprints, what Pettingill called separates, which I read from cover to cover, back at my camp for the evening.

On the last day at the Division of Birds, 28 September, I had copied volumes of notes from more than 25 references. Drs. Wetmore and Humphrey helped steer me to certain reprints that I might have otherwise missed. The staff was small, with Theodore Bobber, formally dressed in a snow-white shirt, but with sleeves rolled up, working in a corner near a window where he cataloged incoming specimens. Other staff kept to themselves. Dr. Humphrey told me of an expedition he would soon be taking to Brazil, and that he needed about six employees to send to various parts of the world to study and collect birds. If only I had college behind me.

During the afternoon, Dr. Wetmore remembered an inquiry I made about Barn Owls in towers of the original 1847 vintage Smithsonian building now called the Castle. He said he would show me one if there was one to be found. It was a rather strange birding affair, without binoculars, in street clothing, and inside the attic of a tower of a museum. We climbed a ladder from within one of the offices, and then up several staircases. There, we found nothing but the strong and disagreeable stench of layers and layers of bird droppings. To our displeasure, the openings where a Barn Owl might enter had been boarded over. Dr. Wetmore told me that he had had the same entrances cleared a few years ago when he was secretary of Smithsonian and, even though retired, he was going to have the boards removed.

29–30 September 1962

The twenty-ninth was a welcome change. I went on a scheduled bird outing with the Atlantic Naturalist Society to Monument Knob, Maryland, a birding site featured in Pettingill's guide. The area is in Washington Monument State Park on a spur of the Blue Ridge Mountains. The Appalachian Trail winds through the park, not far from the rough 75-foot-tall rock structure built in 1827 to honor George Washington. Vandals had reduced the structure to rubble by 1882. The local Odd Fellows Lodge of Boonsboro began rebuilding. The finished product of today looked very much like a milk bottle. For birders, this was a good place to watch migrating hawks and eagles.

I was more excited about the prospect of passerines than migrating hawks. The area would not hold a candle to Hawk Mountain. I set off with a couple of guys to search the nearby scattered woods but found only two species of warblers, no flycatchers, and no thrushes. I did find a Red-bellied Woodpecker, a species I had met in Arkansas, but new for this trip.

By noon, I was inside the monument itself, climbing the narrow dark stairs to the top. From this vantage, I observed a few Turkey Vultures sailing over, along with a few more Broad-winged Hawks and lots more Rock Pigeons. A couple of birders in the group identified a bird as a Peregrine Falcon, which I did not see well enough to call. By early afternoon, the leader apologized for the bad day and left. I soon followed. My chilled core and hunger were soon relieved by a quick dive into my larder inside my waiting tiny motor home.

When I got back in town, my luck of the day had not changed as I rear-ended a car. Luckily, neither car was damaged. The next day I spent getting my notes up to date. I used the picnic table at my camping site. The picnic table offices across the country worked well despite the lady in Michigan who thought I was strange enough to use up a few feet of movie film and various people, especially children, who wanted to know what I was doing. Occasionally I spied a curious highway police officer parked at the roadside, radioing to check out my license plate and me. My Potomac picnic office was quiet on this last day of September. Most everyone ignored me as I banged away on the typewriter, shaping a column about the trip to be published in my high school paper. A call home was welcome, from both ends. I reassured my parents not to worry and they reassured me that they would continue to worry but at the same time remained supportive of my adventure.

1 October 1962

The first day of October was spent on the historic Chesapeake and Ohio Canal, a system completed in 1850. A towpath, about 10 feet wide, flanks one side of the shallow canal. This was where mules pulled the slow, heavily laden barges that navigated the narrow canal from lock to lock, from Seneca to Georgetown about 600 feet below. The towpath is a favorite for strollers, bikers, and birders. Before those leisurely pursuits, the C and O, as the locals call it, carried everything from people to coal. In 1924, the construction of a railway and a major flood ended the commercial importance of the canal. Since then, much of the canal dried up, washed away, or became filled in by the Potomac River that runs near it, or became overgrown by reclaiming vegetation. The federal government has been responsible for the canal since 1938 but almost lost it to a highway. William O. Douglas, Supreme Court justice, along with the editor of the *Washington Post* and others, walked from Seneca to Georgetown in 1954 to publicize the importance of the C and O as a recreation site. The highway was never built. Before and after, parts of the C and O required restoration from the aftermath of floods.

The towpath led me from nearby Key Bridge in Georgetown to about five miles west or just outside the Washington, DC, boundary with Maryland. On my return, I began to worry about getting a parking ticket and less about the fact that I was able to scare up only 17 species. About a half-mile from my car, I spotted a couple of vultures. Ordinarily, I would have ignored them, but I still had not found Black Vultures, a species most likely south with the warblers and flycatchers I could not find. As I looked them over a voice behind me announced that the birds were Turkey Vultures. I introduced myself to Dennis Sherwin, formerly from Cleveland, who lived in Georgetown and loved birdwatching. We traded stories about birding in Ohio, where he had earlier met Paul Savage and Jon Ahlquist in Ashtabula. I bragged about our Rufous-necked Stint and asked questions about birding in the Washington area. Dennis suggested a day trip to check out the Chesapeake Bay and parts of the coasts of Maryland and Delaware. The grass is always greener on the other side of the fence.

2 October 1962

My last day of taking in the historical sites of Washington, DC, included a climb up the stairs to the top of the Washington Monument and quick visits to all the Smithsonian buildings, except the National Gallery of Art. At the White House, I was herded with a group of tourists from the Red to the Green, Blue, and other rooms. No pictures were allowed but carrying a camera was okay. It tangled from a shoulder strap and I sneaked a couple of shots even though I knew they would be crooked and dark without the benefit of aiming or a flash. After the big house, I trudged back to the Mall, saw Whistler's Mother in the Freer Gallery, ate lunch, and walked to Lincoln Memorial. On the way, I passed the Reflection Pool that contained blooming water lilies floating above what someone said were goldfish. Then, back on the Mall, I stared at the Wright brothers' Kitty Hawk, Lindbergh's Spirit of Saint Louis, old cars and farm machinery, costumes, and more. I planned the National Museum of Natural History to be last and took a few minutes of marveling at fossils and skeletons of extinct prehistoric animals. (I was taught that these animals' small brain capacity was the reason for their extinction.) At 4:30 p.m. sharp, the museum closed, but by then I was standing comfortably in an ascending elevator. At the top, I met and said goodbye to Phil Humphrey and curator George Watson.

3 October 1962

The great expectations of a trip east began when I slid out of my berth, the warm cozy sleeping bag, down to the open driver's seat, and out the door for a sprint to the restroom. The lights that had illuminated Washington Monument had been turned off, and only the dim neon lights of the city outlined the black spire of marble in the 5:30 a.m. sky. Dennis Sherwin arrived at the campground at six, and we roared eastward in his rear-engined Chevy Corvair. We soon crossed a massive bridge yawning over the Chesapeake Bay, the largest estuary in the US, and motored onward to Ocean City, Maryland. According to Pettingill and a couple of local birders, we should have good birding at Kent Island, Ocean City, and, in Delaware, Rehoboth and Lewis Beaches.

We managed to find 39 species by working hard. Probably our best birding was when we kicked up Seaside Sparrows, which was a new life bird for Dennis. It is a pleasure to bird with people who, at the time, see a new life species.

4 October 1962

The rains came down Oregon style, a slow and steady drizzle under the shrouded dark gray clouds too thick to allow much light to penetrate. This was at first a day typical of the most winter days back home, but the raindrops became bigger and more numerous, changing to Virginia-style rain. Water then fell in a steady deluge. Dennis and I drove to Roaches Run, a backwater adjacent to and within the ear-splitting sound of Washington National Airport. Roaches Run attracted waterfowl.

By now, I had found most of the ducks excluding some of the southern species such as the whistling ducks and Mottled Duck. At first glance, through the windshield and glaze of fallen rain, there was not much to excite until we saw a demure duck with a creamy-colored crown and forehead. Our first thought was European Wigeon, but our bird clearly had a dark green stripe running through the eye. The rest of the head was dark, but not the rufous of the European bird. However, the head was not grayish as would be an American Wigeon. Roaches Run was a short drive to the Division of Birds, which we drove in record time. George Watson gladly showed us a specimen that appeared to share characteristics of both species of wigeons. Even so, our bird did not look like the specimens.

We were barely out of the heavy glass and bronze doors of the museum before we decided to take another look at our wigeon. This time our mystery duck was out on the water. Now, the clouds were breaking although it was still pouring rain. Maybe we could photograph the bird. However, we lacked a camera. As we rushed out of the parking lot to retrieve Dennis's camera in Georgetown, the windshield wipers stopped suddenly. Frantically, we traced the trouble to a loose screw. With the screw tightened, our nerves stretched as we rushed up the Potomac River to Georgetown. While double-parked I noticed a police officer becoming interested, but before he got to the car Dennis came running out of his home, camera in tow. Returning to Roaches Run, we saw our questionable wigeon drifting away. As if modeling itself, the bird turned to one side then the other. One side of the bird resembled a typical male European Wigeon whereas the other side was typical of a male American Wigeon.

Just how I got from Hawk Mountain to Washington, DC, is not clear. The wide shoulder of what highway I spent the night on and what route took me into Washington, DC, is a mystery since my notes are unclear and my maps have long since been lost by decades of too many moves. My night was likely off I-70 as stated. I later crossed a northern section or a construction zone of the 64-mile beltway, the interstate now encircling Washington, DC, and adjacent communities. Construction of it, I-495, began in 1957 and was completed in 1964. Although a traffic jam reportedly occurred on the beltway shortly after five from its opening date, people continue depending on the multiple-laned highway. Today, around 225,000 vehicles per day clog the busiest part of the beltway, an estimate that seems reasonable when Linda and I drove part of the eastern beltway in 2015. Inside the beltway, the part of I-95 near the city was being built in 1962 when I hiked a shortcut through the construction zone to and from my campsite and the National Mall. In 2015, Linda and I discovered I-95 in the downtown region was redesignated as I-395 and that numerous significant changes had occurred, with such familiar intersections as the dreaded "Mixing Bowl" south of Alexandria reengineered for safer driving. Nonetheless, traffic speed was fast, and it may have been luck that we were in the correct lane at the right location, which shunted us to our chosen exit in Alexandria.

CAPITAL BIRDING

Not long after my 1962 visit, the East Potomac Park Campground disappeared, and tennis courts, golf greens, fairways, driving ranges, and well-manicured lawns appeared. By necessity, I even had a second job at the golf course during the late sixties when I was in the Navy while at the Pentagon. Touring the big city today is not possible on the cheap, at least not as cheap as I enjoyed it in 1962. Since my visit to Washington, DC, in the early sixties, more museums have sprung up; never mind the countless memorials, statues, and monuments. Eventually, the prohibition of most vehicular traffic on the Mall helped provide a more park-like environment. A subway system constructed from 1969 to 1976, and millions of tourists growing in number created a steady hum along the Mall from the US Capitol to Lincoln Memorial. During my nearly 30 years of living in the region, I learned to drive in traffic, including navigating easily around much of the city. Of course, I had favorite routes that I usually traveled, but there were alternate routes just in case the usual lanes became unusable, as they often did by snow, accidents, especially on the bridges, and occasional blockages by dignitaries being whisked to wherever they were whisked. The traffic circles became more negotiable but still places to avoid. I learned to go with the flow and take gridlock and snarls of stationary cars in stride. After all, almost any direction I looked at was beautiful, historical, and inspiring.

Many of the trees viewed from the Washington Monument in 1962 are gone. From the 38,000 American elms in 1950, the number of trees dropped to 18,000 in 1983 and 10,699 elms in 2002. Satellite images reveal that acres and acres of city neighborhood trees have vanished. Worse, only 32 percent of surviving trees remained healthy. Methods of control of the elm disease have varied from the removal of infected trees, spraying, which was rightfully ended in 1964, and of late, injecting trees with fungicides. Of course, Dutch elm disease is not the only enemy of American elms. Soil compaction from visitors, sidewalks and roads, other diseases, and more continue to hurt the elms. People better at math than me estimated that 10,000 trees would have to be planted for 10 years to reach the number of trees in 1970. Perhaps the loss of trees and so much spraying was why the Mall and East Potomac Island are not the birding hotspots they could have been.

In the 1970s, eighties, and nineties, it was common to find members of the Division of Birds enjoying lunch under surviving American elms growing in front of the museum. The leaves shaded us from the sun. In all those years of bag lunches underneath the elms, I never detected any birds breeding in the trees. Possibly some migrants foraged in the elms. Migrants certainly occurred in the Mall as evidenced by dead birds, victims of running into buildings and monuments. Some things never change. Most species ignore the Mall and take advantage of the numerous postage stamp city parks, including those of Alexandria and Arlington. Barn Owls have not been seen in the original Smithsonian building since a little while before Dr. Wetmore and I tried to find them. On a positive note, Osprey, hard hit by DDT, have increased since 1966 by 3.07 percent per year. Bruce Beehler, retired from the Division of Birds, pioneer student of Birds of Paradise of New Guinea, and resident expert on the local avifauna, emailed me that American Crows and Blue Jays might now nest on the Mall.

The view from the Washington Monument helped me realize that the city could be greener, but it required work, funding, and diligence so that the whole region is not paved over. The human growth of the metropolitan region has been a steady climb of about 1.5 percent per year. In 1962, there were almost 2 million human residents in the Washington, DC, metropolitan region. The population was 3.7 million when I retired and was 5,378,000 in 2021. The differences between traffic, new roads, and recently constructed buildings were shockingly remarkable when Linda and I visited the region in 2015 and when we enjoyed a lively migration of spring warblers in a tiny but productive park in Alexandria.

During my fortunate tenure at the museum, I can say that the only time I observed Dr. Wetmore exhibit anger was the time when learning the access holes used by Barn Owls in the Castle had been boarded closed. He was otherwise most cordial and gentle, an imposing man. He frequently asked me to comment on geographic variation of specimens from Panama and offered countless and welcomed stories on his remarkable life. Dr. Wetmore died in 1978 before completing his magnum opus. The fourth and last part was realized in 1984 when I contributed information of the taxonomy of a few North American species, especially concerning Yellow Warblers.[1]

The staff at the Division of Birds naturally changed since the early 1960s. The museum was always understaffed and underfunded, with people in the Division staying there out of love and a certain degree of stubbornness.

Linda and I visited the Division of Bird during a year of contiguous US birding by RV in 2015. Since my retirement, Birds, as we usually called the really important part of the museum, had a face lift. Most obvious was the type and spirit collection were more secure. Mistakenly wandering into someone's office was not likely in the new order of security.

Though many believe museums are places of little change, the bird collection of the Division of Birds was in the 1910 section of the museum and, in 1962, and was moved to the newly constructed east wing. The collection continues to grow not just in size but in importance. Yet,

---

1. Alexander Wetmore et al. *The Birds of the Republic of Panama*. Vol. 4. (Washington, DC: Smithsonian Institution, 1984).

underfunding continues. At the time of my visit in 1962 and until 1967, what I like to call my museum was officially the US National Museum of Natural History. In 1969 the museum took the name National Museum of Natural History. Specimens continue to be designated as USNM. Alexander Wetmore retired as secretary of Smithsonian in 1964 and was replaced by Leonard Carmichael and later by S. Dillon Ripley, the latter of whom had a research office next to the Division of Birds. Mr. Ripley, as he preferred over Dr. Ripley, named a subspecies of kingfisher after me. That is another story.

Around 1972 when I curated the 8,200 specimens of ducks, geese, and swans at the Division of Birds, curator George Watson told me that he was embarrassed that he did not acknowledge Dennis Sherwin and me for helping draw attention to a Florida hybrid wigeon, which George published a detailed description in the journal *Auk*. Incidentally, Roaches Run, where the hybrid wigeon resided, is technically Roaches Run Waterfowl Sanctuary. The airport near the tiny sanctuary, reported as the Washington National Airport, was renamed Ronald Reagan Washington National Airport in 1998. Both localities are in Virginia, adjacent to the Potomac River, and just down the road from the Pentagon.

Insofar as birding in the Washington, DC, region today compared to 1962, I believe that technology and communication have improved so that visitors might find and identify birds. Of course, and yes, I am repeating myself, there are fewer birds than decades ago. Having worked on the Mall for years, I gave up expecting to see a lot of birds but I never tired from watching my city.

Chapter 15

Dismal, Hatteras, Mattamuskeet

5-9 October 1962

EARLY OCTOBER SUN WARMED the East Potomac Island campground as I rearranged the inside of the car for travel. I would miss Washington, DC, even though my birding experiences had not been particularly rewarding, but the city itself, Smithsonian, and the people I met were worth the well-spent time. I would even miss, a little, the roar of airplanes taking off from the airport across the Potomac River, watching tourists as they displayed their excitement, the scenery, and just being in such a place. It was late in the day when I checked around my campsite to make sure it was clean and neat, the same way it was when I arrived in late September.

Before leaving, I had to do a load of laundry (80 cents) and pay for my 13 days of camping ($6.50). After crossing the Potomac River to Arlington, I found the same grocery store I accidentally ended up at on 24 September, bought $2.59 worth of food, and, nearby, enjoyed a coke and hamburger for 25 cents. I filled the gas tank for 32 cents per gallon and was soon on my way south.

After only 20 miles south on US 1, I pulled off at a wide place on the road. Compared to the daytime hum of Washington, DC, my new location felt unhurried and peaceful. A picnic table became an office and for the rest of the day and the next, I pored through brochures, maps, and pictures that helped me update my notes for the past several days. When the notes were complete, I placed the brochures and other materials and a letter into a homeward bound envelope to Oregon.

DISMAL, HATTERAS, MATTAMUSKEET

On the second evening at my picnic site, I had a can of chili and polished off the last piece of shoofly pie, a taste I learned to love while in the Pennsylvania Dutch country of Hawk Mountain. I looked over a list of what I had been eating for the past week. For breakfast, I had the usual six cake donuts, for lunch crackers and peanut butter and often an apple, and my evening meal varied but usually included beans and canned meat such as tuna, fruit occasionally, and maybe a candy bar. I hoped my folks would approve.

The next two days were uneventful and almost boring as I leisurely drove a few miles each day. I was too late for most migrants and too early for wintering birds. I had almost two months to bird before getting to Florida. I wondered if birding between Virginia and Georgia would be worth nearly two months.

The monotony was broken on the ninth when I heard a harsh rasping sound like *scrripp*. Having arrived in southern pine country and hearing the unknown sound of a woodpecker got my adrenaline flowing. Creeping into a thicket and on into a small opening got me closer to the sound. A few squeaks on the back of my hand caused the bird to pick up the tempo of its call. A Red-cockaded Woodpecker soon tumbled from a tall pine and into plain view. This was a new lifer. Historically, Red-cockaded Woodpeckers ranged from Florida to New Jersey and Maryland, Tennessee, and Kentucky, and as far west as Texas and Oklahoma. My Red-cockaded Woodpecker was just off US 1 about 20 miles south of Richmond, Virginia.

In Petersburg, I took a tour of one of the major cigarette manufacturers. The guide proudly told the touring ensemble that the average annual sale of tobacco was over $7 billion and that over 65 million Americans used one form or another of tobacco. I also toured part of the 2,600-acre Petersburg National Battlefield. The park is administered by the National Park Service. The longest and bloodiest battle of the Civil War happened here, with 70,000 causalities wasted during a nine and a half month siege in 1864 and 1865. The Union army took over, Lee took off, and not much later, the Civil War was over. If there had been a Red-cockaded Woodpecker around it surely left the area. The tour guide, apparently a local docent, was more than happy to give her audience a spiel strongly suggesting an edge of bitterness about the outcome of the war. The person also offered a few wry comments about what she called Black people, such as where their station in society ought to lie. I bristled on hearing the hateful comments but kept quiet while staring daggers that I hoped were read by this awful person. Most everyone in the tour group, all of whom were snow-white, thanked the guide, but I could not. I had been raised to thank hosts, but I knew if I had spoken to this hateful person, I would have unleashed my viewpoints, which were opposite of her diatribe. I also reasoned my own well-being might best be served by maintaining a low profile. The handwriting on the wall had already made it clear once I was but a few miles south of Washington, DC; I was in a different land. Travel farther south revealed individuals, not unlike my tour guide, advocating a society with segregated restrooms, drinking fountains, and more. Although I read about segregation, witnessing it was disgustingly shocking.

10–11 October 1962

A highway took me away from US 1 and Petersburg. Heading southeast, I drove closer to the coast and for a while, according to maps, my route would not be near US 1. My confusion rested on the fact that US 1 took me along the Atlantic seaboard in Maine and I knew would be much of my route along the Atlantic coast of Florida to Key West. Had I made a mistake? Why was US 1 a coastal route and other places an interior byway? In the West, US 101 is unquestionably the Pacific coast route from California, Oregon, and Washington. The highway east of US 101 is US 99 and the highway east of there, on the east side of the Sierra Nevada and Cascade Mountains is US 97. Most highways are numbered simply and straightforwardly. In New Jersey, the birding party from Hawk Mountain traveled along the coast on US 9, on the coast of Maryland I noticed the north-south coastal route was US 113, and today, according to my maps, I will intersect with US 13, which is a few miles west of US 17 that will go inland.

Much to my surprise, I discovered there was a reason why US 1 did not follow the coast, although none of the reasons are particularly geographic. Beginning north of Washington, DC, in the state of New York, US 1 follows a geological feature, the edge of the Piedmont and the Atlantic Coastal Plain. The is the Fall Line. The Piedmont is the plateau region between the Appalachian Mountains and the Atlantic Coastal Plain and rises just west of the Potomac River and includes a large part of Alexandria and Arlington. The Plain, a region of low elevation, begins in New York and includes all of Florida. Somewhere in South Carolina or Georgia, US 1 leaves the Fall Line and heads southeast. Looking ahead on my road map, I would pick up US 1 just north of Okefenokee Swamp in southern Georgia. I was relieved that all those hours spent months ago marking road maps now saved me the headache of deciphering how to get to my destinations.

I soon ran out of time and found a wide place in the road for the night. Once again, during the early morning, I was awakened by the rumble of the deep-throated exhaust of a car idling just feet away that suddenly awakened me. Was it the KKK sent to punish me for not thanking the middle-aged Southern belle tolling her misguided humanity? Was it one of the people who laughed at me for working at the picnic table? A bright light flashed in my face, a pale face that must have satisfied the onlooker, who said nothing, turned back to his vehicle, slammed the car door, and sped away. My blinded eyes recovered just in time to see that it was a Virginia State Police car.

It was late afternoon when I arrived in the heart of the Great Dismal Swamp in southern Virginia. According to bird finding information, getting into the swamp would be a problem. While driving US 17 on the east side of the swamp and paralleling the Dismal Canal, I wondered how I could see birds in such a densely vegetated place of bamboo, oak, mangrove, cypress, and other trees, vines, and bushes. A long canal aptly named Feeder Ditch runs east from Lake Drummond; deep in the swamp to the west might be where I could start my jaunt but first, I had to get across the 40-foot wide Dismal Canal that runs north to south. There were no bridges. Additionally, there were numerous big signs with bold lettering announcing no trespassing and no hunting. Several people I contacted were unimpressed that I just wanted to look at birds. A lady at a restaurant was kind enough to give me a clue to where and whom I should talk. I found the person and told him why I wanted to enter the swamp, and that I could only pay him a few bucks for the favor. Lank, with a hatchet nose, the weather-worn man looked at me with suspicion and amusement. Standing back to size me up, I could see the shiny dirt on his overalls reflecting the evening sun. His colorless ragged ball cap was pulled down to obscure his eyes and his pursed cracked lips seemed to signal an unwillingness to help me. Again, I told him that I only wanted to see the birds in the swamp. He seemed reluctant to commit. I practically begged. I needed only to cross 40 feet of water. He finally decided and said, as if giving up to a possible enemy, "Meet me at my dock at six and I'll row ya cross. Jest up an' from the feeder ditch."

Early the next morning, the dock seemed lonely and a little foreboding. The man arrived a few minutes later, seemingly annoyed that I got there first. In minutes, he directed me to a small unpainted boat. I later learned the shallow-draft craft is called a lighter boat. Without a word, he rowed me across the dark canal water. In a thankfully short time, the small boat reached the other side of the canal. Before I could be on my way, my chance to enter the swamp began to rail for about 10 minutes about how I was not to vandalize his property, what a big gamble he was taking by letting me step on his land, and what a huge favor he was providing. I assured him I would not harm his property and thanked him again and again for rowing me across the canal. Asking about getting back across the canal changed his anguished face. He smirked and said that maybe I could hitch a boat ride from someone coming down from Lake Drummond. The lake was my ultimate destination for birds and not so much for finding someone there who might help me get back to the car. Before my angry oarsman departed, I quickly asked for directions whereupon he made a weak gesture toward the northwest before silently rowing back to the other side. He did not look back. It was as if I did not exist. As far as I was concerned, it might be best if he did forget me. Maybe it was best to be on my own.

    I followed a farm lane that meandered further into the swamp. The ground was hard from years of compaction by rolling wagons and tractors. An Eastern Meadowlark flushed from the edge of the lane. After an hour, I found a trail, a two-foot-wide path leading straight as an arrow southwest and away from the farm. For the next four hours, I threaded deeper and deeper into Dismal Swamp toward, I hoped, Lake Drummond. Hiking was relatively easy as I followed the trail cleared by hunters. In some places, a couple of inches of water covered the ground, but in other areas, it was bone dry. I heard no eerie sounds, saw no snakes, and the only trouble was countless spiderwebs crossing the trail about every 10 to 15 feet. I was glad not to see snakes, especially water moccasins, but I had hoped to hear the day-calling cackle of a surprised Barred Owl. Except for an occasional spider occupying one of the webs, any kind of weird life in the Great Dismal Swamp remained hidden (maybe too hidden). This was not what I had thought I would experience. The spiders, about an inch in diameter, with brilliant yellows, oranges, and blacks, were strangely beautiful. The big mystery was that I could not be certain about my location and where the trail would take me.

    Fortunately, there were lots of birds to see. Migrant Cape May Warblers filled the trees almost everywhere. Carolina Wren's cheery rhapsody echoed from the shadows and Carolina Chickadees twittered at my intrusion. There were no Parula or Prothonotary warblers although there were Black-throated Green and Pine warblers as well as American Redstarts and yellowthroats. A Yellow-billed Cuckoo skulked in a tree overhanging the trail and Eastern Towhees foraged the forest litter. There were no Barred Owls to give the swamp an accent of misgiving. A calling Pileated Woodpecker might have provided a flavor of intrigue, but I recognized its sound instantly. One Black Vulture, my first on the trip, rode a thermal with a few Turkey Vultures. A Bobwhite, with five young, scurried in and out of the understory. The young appeared about two weeks old.

    About the time I ran into a den of copperheads was when I found the shore of the Feeder Ditch and soon was at the Army Engineer Corps building near Lake Drummond. By now, an hour past noon, I opted to forgo the short walk to Lake Drummond, reasoning that I probably would not see any new species for the day. Besides, I shuddered at the thought of spending the night, without food or shelter, with or without accompanying Barred Owls or snakes of any kind. I was happy for the chance to hitch a ride on one of the Army Engineer Corps boats. The sputtering outboard motor ended the possibility of hearing birds as its sound muted the gentle slap of the flat water against the bow. The breezeless air was broken ever so little as blue engine smoke settled in a fog over the boat's narrow and disappearing wake. Soon, the tiny craft had plied through the 50 or so foot wide Feeder Ditch to a dock at US 17. My car was just a short hike up the road.

It was a relief to return to the car, be out of the swamp, and I was grateful that I was snake free and saw a few birds. In the mix of species that I found were White-throated Sparrows, winter visitors to the region. The Eastern Wood-Pewee, abundant in spring and summer, should not have been there. Soon the flycatcher and all the warblers would be gone, and winter would dominate Great Dismal Swamp. It was time to keep going south.

12 October 1962

Last night I was on the Atlantic coast. I had driven south into North Carolina through the remainder of Great Dismal Swamp, then east to a spit of land jutting between Albemarle Sound and the Outer Banks. Driving south took me through little towns called Bertha, Mamie Harbinger, and a roadside sign pointing to Spot, a shore hamlet just across Currituck Sound north of Bodie Island's towns of Sanderling and Duck. I drove off the road just a little too far, got stuck, and dug free before settling in for the night. Because the days were getting shorter with the season, I ate in the dark. This gave me more daylight hours for birding, but birding was not over. In the darkness, I picked my way to the east side of the spit. With the help of a flashlight and a bright moon, I identified several Sanderlings, a kind of peep and a plover, all scattered on the sandy beach. The plover was probably a Black-bellied, the same species I saw along with my first Royal Terns just before dark. The spotlighted plover seemed intrigued by the narrow beam from my five-cell and allowed me to approach it within about 30 feet. The other shorebirds were not so impressed and flushed at the first glimpse of the flashlight. A curlew called through the moon shining on several foraging Black Skimmers that cut the glassy water.

The morning light brought more birds, including more Royal Terns and Black-bellied Plovers and a handful of Sanderlings, at least 30 cranky sounding Forester's Terns, and a few quiet Black and Surf Scoters. A steady wind blew the terns from side to side, and it still blew as I approached Kill Devil Hill at the Wright Brothers National Memorial. Everyone knows the story of their great experiment. A lofty granite monument swoops 60 feet up from its gray 1932 base. I wondered why memorializing the brothers' 1903 achievement took so many years. I also thought about their plane, the Kitty Hawk, I saw at Smithsonian.

In a few miles, I had entered Cape Hatteras National Seashore, a park that includes Bodie, Hatteras, and Roanoke islands, a 70-mile stretch of barrier islands occupying 31,000 acres. It is the nation's first such recreational area. My destination was a campground near the south end of Bodie Island. I marked my campsite by leaving a note under a rock on the picnic table, trusting the rock would keep the note from blowing away, and that no one would lift it and my campsite. I was anxious to visit Pea Island National Wildlife Refuge just to the south on the north end of Hatteras Island. Refuge headquarters, in the small town of Manteo, on Roanoke Island was easy to find. Charles Noble, the manager, told me that the refuge included 5,800 acres of the barrier reef, with fresh and saltwater marshes, which attracted mostly migrant waterfowl. About 25,700 acres of water are part of the 1937 vintage refuge that has yet to wash away from hurricanes. The refuge was the Atlantic's southern terminus for wintering Snow Geese, which I was about one month too early to witness. Mr. Noble told me that although 172 species had been recorded on the refuge, most birders avoided what he considered to be limited habitat and hordes of mosquitoes.

13–15 October 1962

Yesterday evening I met the Levinsons, who were camping site neighbors at Pea Island. They were from Portsmouth, a city in the Norfolk and Newport News region of Virginia, not far north of Great Dismal Swamp and not far west of Virginia Beach, home of Edgar Casey. When I mentioned that I was birdwatching and planning to try my luck at Pea Island NWR, they asked to come along. I explained that my stuffed car would not accommodate passengers. They said they would drive their car. Ms. Levinson was especially anxious to learn birds although she had "Double-crested Gulls and Black-backed Cormorants" confused. It was agreed that we start the next morning. At least for me, the start was when the Levinsons' seven-year-old accidentally dropped a large piece of driftwood on the boardwalk. Thump! It was time for me to get up anyway, so I slipped on my clothes and crawled out of my VW berth. Most people usually get dressed after they get out of bed, but my berth had windows. Mrs. Levinson offered me a hot bowl of oatmeal and steaming coffee, which I gladly accepted.

Birding started with the free 40-minute ferry ride across the Oregon Inlet to Hatteras Island courtesy of North Carolina. Flocks of Laughing Gulls followed us across. Several people were tossing chunks of bread in the air and the gulls were wheeling around while attempting to rob the individual that caught the last piece. A man told me dredging the ferry canal of the shallow Oregon Inlet is a constant job. In fact, the whole area is shifting, eroding, changing, with each day and especially during storms. Entire islands may be flooded during severe hurricanes.

The starving gulls soon disappeared as we landed on Hatteras Island and drove to Pea Island refuge. Mr. Noble explained yesterday that Pea Island was years ago an actual island separate from Hatteras Island. The inlet separating the two islands eventually filled with drifted sand.

Once on Hatteras Island, we stopped to check out the beach. Only Mrs. Levinson, who, unfortunately, I did not record her first name and I ventured east over the dunes and through the beach grass and sea oats that had been planted to stabilize perennially shifting sand. What we did not realize was that mosquitoes were bracing themselves from the heat and wind by inhabiting the vegetation. Wind or no wind, the hungry hordes were soon biting us, penetrating our summer clothing, and making us generally hate them. I spotted a couple of small birds in the dunes. My first thought was Savannah Sparrows, but, despite the mosquitoes, the sparrows begged a closer look. The birds seemed ever so slightly larger and noticeably paler than any Savannah Sparrow I had seen. They had to be Ipswich Sparrows, a subspecies of Savannah Sparrow confined to Nova Scotia that winters south along the Atlantic coast. This subspecies was once believed to be a species distinct from the darker Savannah Sparrows. A hasty scan of the beach revealed a Black-bellied Plover and a smattering of Sanderlings. This was not what Mrs. Levinson had hoped for and I was far too miserable from the hordes of mosquitoes to provide help in showing the salient differences between plovers and sandpipers let alone to discuss the details of separating Savannah and former Ipswich sparrows. We retreated as fast as possible across dry loose sand. Minnesota and Michigan paled at hosting the densest flocks of mosquitoes.

We found a couple of Tricolored Herons, a new life bird for both of us. So far, my list of herons was still missing Little Blue Heron, a species that, because of its similar size and dark plumage, reminded me of today's new bird. I was yet to see Yellow-crowned Night-Herons. Reddish Egrets would come in Florida. We saw a small flock of Canada Geese, early migrants that would later join other flocks of geese and ducks.

The mosquitoes followed us around the refuge with such diligence that we were happy to leave. We ended up at Cape Hatteras Lighthouse near the south end of the island. The 208-foot lighthouse, activated in 1870, helped lessen the frequency of shipwrecks off the outer banks. Laughing and Herring gulls milled about, as did a few tourists, several who were on the ferry when we crossed Oregon Island on our return to Bodie Island campground. They probably did not see the pair of reddish orange billed American Oystercatchers standing on their pinkish leg and calling noisily above the rumble of the ferry motor. Doubtless they missed seeing over 300 nervous Black Skimmers landing and taking off again in one tightly organized flock.

The day for birds was not over. The Levinson's invited me for an evening meal of fried chicken. The next morning, I birded around camp. There were fewer mosquitoes and more time to help Mrs. Levinson hone her birding skills. She complained that fall warblers were difficult. I told her that I had much to learn about the fall plumages of warblers and other eastern birds. We also birded north at Kill Devil Hill, looking for birds on the seaward side of the inland brackish shores of Albemarle and Roanoke Sounds. The uneventful search went on until late evening back at the campground. The Levinsons were preparing to head home. Mrs. Levinson and Ned, the seven-year-old who dropped the driftwood, and I walked the beach. A big adult gull appeared to be courting a first-year bird, believed to be a female even though mid-October seemed an unlikely time for gull courtship. The supposed male kept busy chasing away other adults and returning to the younger bird that tried to ignore the adult. This time Mrs. Levinson got the name correct. A Great Black-backed Gull. I hope that she will enjoy birding at least half as much as I do.

On 15 October, I returned to Hatteras Island. A single oystercatcher sat at the water's edge and gulls chased the ferry across Oregon Inlet. I combed the beach grass for another look at the pale Savannah Sparrows. Much of the beach and grassy habitat was located at what had been a campground that was demolished by a nor'easter just a few months ago in March. I found the sparrow as well as a few Prairie and Palm warblers and, on a nearby mudflat, flushed a Piping Plover that landed a few feet away. Minutes later I was looking seaward when a Herring Gull came screaming toward me. I had never heard this species of gull make such a frantic sound. The term frantic was not anthropomorphic because not far behind the fleeing gull was a bird that I first took to be a first-year Herring Gull. I quickly realized that the pursuer was too dark to be that species. That is when I also noticed the white patches on the wings and the rounded central tail feathers protruding beyond the rest of its tail. My pulse accelerated as I put it all together. I found a new life bird and a completely new family. My first Pomarine Jeager!

16–18 October 1962

Before leaving the Outer Banks, I compiled a list of nine sightings that I thought were significant to pass on to the appropriate regional editor of *Audubon Field Notes*. Then, I tried to sweep a sandcastle's worth of sand out of the car. I crossed the bridges to Roanoke Island and east across Croatan Sound to the mainland of Dare County occupying part of the 3,200 square mile Albemarle-Pamlico Peninsula. Croatan Sound is part of the Atlantic Intracoastal Waterway, part natural and part artificial water route from Cape Cod to Florida Bay. The 1,700-mile route of the waterway that began in 1919 is routinely dredged to maintain a minimum depth of 12 feet. Ever onward, I drove deserted US 264 through acres and acres of marsh. I did not want to arrive at my next destination late in the day and pulled off the lonely road not far from the little hamlet of Engelhard.

The sun eased over the flat eastern horizon the next morning. In just a few miles, I was at Mattamuskeet NWR. Mattamuskeet is an Algonquin word meaning "dry dust," which is what the lake site might have been long before the basin, which, someone said was possibly formed from a burned-out peat bog. Maybe the refuge could be a place where I might pick up a few southern species. As I usually did before entering a refuge, I scanned the checklist I had in a file inside the bookcase sitting on the back seat of the trusty VW. The checklist for Mattamuskeet listed 216 species. I optimistically highlighted 21 species, but reasoned, based on experience, I might find seven or eight of them. I discussed the list with Charlie Cahoon and Bob Brown of the refuge. They were not as optimistic as me but escorted me to a couple of prime birding areas. We saw Canada Geese. A couple of early Snow Geese were found two days ago, and a King Rail recently discovered were not found. Nor did we find hoped for Anhingas or Yellow-crowned Night-Herons, two of the species I had highlighted earlier. We did find Little Blue Herons and throngs of Myrtle Warblers (=Yellow-rumped Warbler). Three yellow bibbed Parula Warblers perched in the open shortly before flitting out of sight.

Woke up on 18 October in Mattamuskeet refuge with strong winds and a heavily overcast sky. Hurricane Ella was only 300 miles south of Cape Hatteras. I was glad to be off the Outer Banks. As Mr. Cahoon put it, "one good wave would melt the sand like sugar." Ella seemed to stop to rest out in the Atlantic, and meteorologists believed the storm would continue seaward in a northeast direction. Even so, boats were brought inland to safer water, and small craft warnings were enforced from Miami to the New Jersey coast. Yesterday, I had helped the refuge staff lash down the big cabin cruiser they used at Swan Quarter, a nearby refuge that Mattamuskeet administers. The refuge staff had earlier weathered Hurricane Alma, with its category two winds (about 85 miles per hour) in late August and early September. That hurricane slipped just offshore of Cape Hatteras, and damage was relatively minor. Hurricane Ella, with its category three winds (111–130 miles per hour) and tide surges of nine to twelve feet could wreak havoc in its path.

19 October 1962

The morning wind was blowing stiffly. Hardly before I was able to become awake, I saw a male Yellow-headed Blackbird. Staff at headquarters were excited to see this western waif. My goal was to find more of the 21 species I checked off the checklist a couple of days ago. Bob suggested I try the end of a narrow road, the road where I have been parking the last two nights. Dust blew in my face and the trees bent in the noisy gale. I checked over a group of waterfowl swimming in a shelter. Ring-necked Duck was still missing from my list. A mixed flock of Gadwalls, Black Duck, along with silly coots and a Common Gallinule huddled together allowing my approach to be far closer than normal. The swaying trees at refuge headquarters were alive with warblers, mostly Palms but a Magnolia Warbler was among the huddled masses. I tried to identify every individual while also maintaining my balance and keeping the flying dust out of my eyes. It paid off when I found two new species, Yellow-throated, and White-eyed vireos. Most of the 21 species I wanted to see were listed by the refuge as transients or would most likely have moved southward before October. I was happy with four new species. Maybe the next stop would bring more birds, and, after all, there is always the remainder of the day.

~

The Red-cockaded Woodpecker near Richmond possibly bred there then but not more currently. The last known breeding population of Red-cockaded Woodpeckers in Virginia was at Pine Grove, a Nature Conservancy property in Sussex County about 60 miles south of Richmond. That may have changed by now, and most likely not in favor of the species. The woodpecker has been an endangered species since 1970. The species no longer occurs in New Jersey, Maryland, Tennessee, and Missouri. Presently, there are only about 12,500 individuals representing about 1 percent of the species' original range since clear-cutting, forest fragmentation and disease, and inappropriate fire management contribute to the slow demise of the woodpecker. Although the population of the woodpecker is now reportedly growing, one source nonetheless estimated that 70 years would pass before the species recovery was sufficient to remove it from the endangered list. I can hear Woody the Woodpecker laugh. In 70 years, the human population may be on the list.

Any sane Red-cockaded Woodpecker would have avoided the battle-grounds at Petersburg, just as I wished I had not heard the hateful docent. What I naively did not realize was that to a lot of people the Civil War was not over and that those same people continue to think people of color should not have the same rights as others. Various post-Civil War states enacted laws that legalized segregation, which prevented persons of color from employment, education, voting and more missed opportunities at the risk of fines, jail, even death. The laws were called Jim Crow laws that officially ended in 1964 and unofficially have not ended.

It is likely that the docent in Petersburg, if knowing my next destination was the Great Dismal Swamp, would have thought my interest was appropriate since I did not embrace her prejudicial garbage. That is because, back in the days that this twentieth-century docent was wishing to return to might have been when George Washington and business partners wanted to drain the 1.28-million-acre Great Dismal Swamp. Accomplishing the task was to be on the back of slaves. Ironically, the swamp eventually became part of the Underground Railroad and a place for escaped slaves to hide and build communities within the region.[1] Of course, just how George and his buddies owned what was once the property of American Natives is not apparent and, although not readily reported, the situation is par for the course concerning confiscated Native land.

Over the years, more than 59 drainage canals reduced Dismal Swamp to one-third of its original size. Drainage produced more arable land and access for timber barons ready to cut the virgin timber, including cypress trees. The region was eventually heavily logged. No virgin trees were left standing. Union Camp Corporation, a large wood products company, purchased much of Dismal Swamp from George Washington's heirs about 1900. Founders of Union Camp produced the first machine that mass-produced paper grocery bags. That was in 1852, but the bags were not the flat-bottomed brown bags we all know and love today. Those were patented

---

1. Marcus P. Nevius. *City of Refuge: Slavery and Petit Marronage in the Great Dismal Swamp, 1763–1856*. Race in the Atlantic World, 1700–1900 35. (Athens: University of Georgia Press, 2020).

by Margaret Knight in 1872. More and more paper products required more and more trees, but at least Union Camp donated 50,000 acres to The Nature Conservancy in 1973. The Conservancy then turned that over to the newly created Great Dismal Swamp NWR in 1974, which now contains 107,000 acres of the swamp in Virginia and North Carolina. The refuge, including the 3,100-acre Lake Drummond, one of the two largest freshwater lakes in Virginia, is protected from additional commercial exploitation. It is an area of the leftovers, which is less than half of the swamp's original acreage.

In the realm of conservation and commercial exploitation, the larger picture may overshadow the contribution of Union Camp Corporation, which, incidentally, garnered them a $12 million tax deduction. In 1998, Union Camp was acquired by International Paper, a $25 billion dollar a year company that has operations in 40 countries. International Paper purchased Weyerhaeuser's pulp business in 2016 and continues to grow. Several operations by International Paper in Canada include various subsidiaries that "harvest" two million cubic meters of boreal timber annually according to Forest Ethics' July 2004 report. That is a lot of nesting sites. More recently, it was estimated that one million acres of forests are clearcut in Canada per year. Canada has approximately one billion acres of boreal forest, which could mean we have 1,000 years to cut all those trees. Maybe, but just one variable could change that. Wildfires and disease are two that have already decimated forests. What happens if the human population increases and global climate change? Only 8 percent of the Canadian boreal forests are presently under protection, and we have all witnessed the demise of natural habitats when not protected. Following clearcutting, a slow-growing Canadian forest will also never return to its former self.

In the meantime, birds travel through highly fragmented habitats to their nesting grounds that are being diminished by a million acres per year. Sure, companies might plant new trees, but what is a bird to do in the meantime?

The remaining populations of birds in Dismal Swamp are easier to see. It is now possible to drive in the refuge and dry trails are maintained for walking and biking. There is even a boardwalk, features also found in Great Dismal State Park in adjacent North Carolina. It is now possible to drive to Lake Drummond. Although I have not revisited the Great Dismal Swamp, a map of the refuge revealed that close to 2,500 acres on the east side of the swamp and north of the east-west ditch flowing from Lake Drummond are still private land. This is where I entered the swamp in 1962. From satellite photographs, it appears that much of the area I traversed is now heavily cultivated and much of the forest has been "harvested."

Cape Hatteras National Seashore now has a new visitor center, built in 1999. Another major change was moving the Cape Hatteras Light Station. When activated in 1870, it was 1,600 feet from the water, but the encroaching sea was within 120 feet before the whole structure was moved a half-mile inland in the late 1990s. Although the islands are "protected," vehicles are permitted to drive on parts of the beaches. I do not recall vehicles on the beaches in 1962. Of course, the average tourist was less inclined to drive any and everywhere as so many want to do today.

Most touristy birders birding the beaches, especially the dunes, will not be as excited about extremely pale Savannah Sparrows as I was in 1962. Back then, those handsomely bleached-out sparrows were recognized as a distinct species, the Ipswich Sparrow. The birds breed in Nova Scotia and were known to move along the Atlantic coast as far south as Georgia. The ebb and flow of the taxonomy of the Ipswich Sparrow, which is now relegated to a subspecies of the highly polytypic Savannah Sparrow, is a story to tell, but it is better told in a later chapter.

Oregon Inlet, crossed by ferry in 1962, has a history tied to the ebb and flow of sand. Formed in 1846 from a hurricane, the inlet was later crossed by boat and, in 1941, by a ferry operated by the state of North Carolina. A 2.7-mile-long bridge spanned the shifting sands of the Oregon Inlet in 1963. In 1990, a dredge destroyed a section of the bridge, which was rebuilt years later. Because of shifting sand, the new iteration of the bridge was closed in 2013. Finally, a new bridge crossing the Oregon Inlet was opened in 2019. The newest bridge comes with what bridge engineers call "scour countermeasures." Unlike cattle, people do not like the term *scour*. I wondered what bridge builders meant since, recalling my old ranch hand day, I thought any situation involving scours was not pleasant and may require rubber boots. I was wrong. Regarding bridges, scour countermeasures prevent soil erosion around piers and abutments. This is particularly important because the Oregon Inlet has moved south over two miles since 1846. That is about 66 feet per year, which partially explains why the Coast Guard Station finally gave in to the ebb and flow and abandoned their station in 1988.

The giant shifting sandbar, the 200 miles of islands of the Outer Banks, was originally flat. Tide surges from storms rolled across the islands, flooding everything in its path. In the 1930s, the CCC and the WPA (Works Progress Administration) placed fences that slowed blowing sand that gradually formed dunes. Once dunes began to develop, the roots of planted cordgrass and sea oats further stabilized the sand, not to mention provided shelter to those pesky bloodsucking mosquitoes. Many of those dunes exist today and rebuilding damaged ones is an ongoing effort. Sea-level at Oregon Inlet, separating Hatteras and Bodie Islands, has risen by nine inches since 1977. Tropical storms and hurricanes continue to batter the Outer Banks with increased frequency and magnitude. Not just flooding, dunes, and sea-level changes, but all of the above might explain why the plight of the Outer Banks is in peril.[2] It seems that the dune-building has blocked the natural movement of sand across islands, and, on the seaward side, the islands continued to erode, thus narrowing the beaches. At the same time, the islands could not grow on the interior or sound side. To make matters worse, engineering projects thought to protect human activities (dredging, jetties) actually increased erosion.

Pea Island NWR, so long as it exists, now has a checklist of about 365 species strong or more than twice the total in 1962. Although Canada Geese were on the old list, their status has changed in the last 40 years. In 1962, the species was a winter resident in the eastern United States. The southern breeding range has since pushed southward. Following better habitat management and introductions, the species exploded to become the urban goose, the bane of golfers and barefoot children. The species now breeds as far south as northern Florida.

Had there been an opportunity for pelagic birding off Cape Hatteras in 1962, such a trip would have been beyond my budget. Pelagic trips began about 25 years ago and attract birders to the nearby Gulf Stream. These pelagic trips have added new species to the US checklist.

Leaving the Outer Banks required crossing a bridge over the Intracoastal Waterway. A single pleasure cruiser would occasionally hold up traffic for 30 or more minutes as it slipped past a raised drawbridge. The Army Engineer Corps maintains the toll-free system as well as 1,300 miles of the Gulf Intracoastal Waterway. Funding this infrastructure has become a problem and, in 2004, there was concern that the system might be abandoned. However, the waterway is currently viable.

Once landing in Dare County, I was in what some considered a wasteland worth only the time to attempt to drain it. Fortunately, several refuges protect a hefty part of the Albemarle-Pamlico Peninsula. Alligator River National Wildlife Refuge, which also administers Pea Island Refuge, was established in 1984 to protect and restore its 152,000 acres. National Wildlife Refuges of Swanquarter and Mattamuskeet, both established in the 1930s, and almost shiny new Pocosin Lakes, established in 1990, protects 176,696 acres of the peninsula.

As with most marshes and swamps, people wanted to drain 40,000 acres of Lake Mattamuskeet. During 1914, large-scale drainage ditches

---

2. Sara Peach. "Rising Seas: Will the Outer Banks Survive?" *National Geographic*, Jul 24, 2014.

dried enough land to establish the aptly named town, New Holland. However, Pamlico Sound, only about five miles away, continues to have problems during higher high tides. Meanwhile, unlike most refuges, especially western ones, freshwater Lake Mattamuskeet has too much water. Because the lake is at sea level (a couple of sources said three feet below sea level), the refuge maintains flood gates to prevent tides from entering it. Figures vary widely, but Lake Mattamuskeet is about eighteen by seven miles and averages only three feet deep. Recent reports describe the troubled waters of the lake as plagued with cyanobacteria and overrun by invasive carp.

Speaking of fish, the establishment where I purchased a hamburger and coke on the day I left Arlington, Virginia, is familiar. Although I cannot be absolutely certain, I believe the establishment is the very same one where I briefly was employed about six years later. My primary duty was to make fish sandwiches, a job that helped boost my military income.

Chapter 16

Whiskers and Doing Charleston

19 October 1962, the Afternoon

A WASHINGTON, DC, BIRDER suggested I check Swanquarter NWR for Ring-necked Duck and Brown-headed Nuthatch. I found neither and was more than embarrassed that after about five months I still had not seen a Ring-necked Duck. Maybe at my new location there would be nuthatches. The duck was surely around the corner waiting to grace my trip list.

Yesterday, I had phoned Geraldine Cox, a schoolteacher, who was on my list as a Christmas Count compiler, and a local birding expert of Washington, North Carolina. The town sits at the head of the Pamlico River, not really a river but the name of the estuary of the Tar River. Though Ms. Cox had written I should contact her when in the neighborhood, she must have forgotten about a possible meeting since the telephone call at first seemed as if I was intruding. Showing up at someone's doorstep was always a bit awkward to me as it must have been to others. I did not want to intrude, but the conversation soon turned positive once I reminded her that I was just out of high school and trying to see as many birds as possible. The teacher at the other end of the line apparently could not resist a potential student, and I was eager to learn. Geraldine, a few years my senior, lived with her parents in the quiet outskirts of town. Remarkably, the family invited me to bunk in the spare bedroom.

WHISKERS AND DOING CHARLESTON

20–21 October 1962

Geraldine told me that for the last two months other obligations allowed for only casual birding out her backyard and from her classroom. I told her that I hardly ever saw any interesting birds from my school windows but that I had spent plenty of time trying, or at least dreaming I would see something beyond my classroom. Her two months of not birding had reached their limits and she was ready for some serious birding. I mentioned that I was looking for Brown-headed Nuthatch and was instantly pointed to the door. There it was. My first Brown-headed Nuthatch was foraging at a suet feeder in a tree just a few feet from the house. I did not mention my failure in finding a Ring-necked Duck.

After just a few minutes of driving from the family dwelling, Geraldine introduced me to a new birding term. We had spotted something perched on a branch of a tree. Closer examination revealed our subject was nothing more than an oddly shaped wooden knot. She said, "Oh, it's just a whisker." She explained that something that looks like a bird but is not a bird is a whisker. I wondered why Pettingill, Peterson, and others had not publicized such a useful term. Perhaps I should be spreading the news. A whisker is something every birder has seen, been fooled by, and left explaining what they saw in what could easily be condensed into one word. Whisker. That's it.

While birding with Geraldine, I noticed she was interested in the mount for my scope, my hand-made rifle gunstock that I fashioned in high school wood shop. She also had a similar stock, which she had purchased through a company advertising in *Audubon Magazine*. Geraldine said she liked the feel of my stock, and we agreed to trade. The longer commercial stock also had a nice sling that made it easy to carry.

The next day, Geraldine introduced me to her friends the McLarens, who owned a tract of land full of bird feeders and plants to attract birds. That is where I found my first Bay-breasted Warbler. The four of us, Mary, Mac, Geraldine, and I also birded a nearby marsh where a strange plumaged sparrow caught us off guard. I first thought it was a species I had never seen. Luckily, the bird was very cooperative, allowing close observation from all angles. It was a Swamp Sparrow, between juvenile and immature plumages. We continued following the deserted road through the marsh. Except for the strange sparrow, our stroll was uneventful until we returned to our car. I jumped on a mound of dirt that was stacked high with big chunks of asphalt. I stood astride a broken painted yellow line of a former highway for one last scan over the marsh. From my vantage, I spotted a big King Rail sauntering across an open stretch of shallow water. Mary scurried to the top of the mound just in time to see the regal rail slip into the dense reeds. That was number three for new life birds.

Before midnight of my last night in Washington, Geraldine hauled her portable record player out into the backyard. We hooked it up to a long extension cord and cued the needle at the beginning track for Barred Owl of Peterson's guide to bird sounds. Twice we thought we heard one or two half-hearted hoots. Maybe it was wishful hearing. We tried the screech-owl track and were happily successful. The next morning Geraldine was about to leave for her classroom. She remarked that maybe it was a good thing that she did not bird too often because it would not be so enjoyable if she did it every day. After almost five months of birding, I very rarely thought the last day was any less enjoyable than the first.

22–25 October 1962

The Maurines relayed me south to New Bern, a town with about 5,000 more people than Washington's 10,000, and to their friends, Fred and Margaret Conderman. The hosting abilities of the Condermans were wonderful, with breakfasts just a window pane from red cardinals, Carolina Chickadees, Redwinged Blackbirds, and Red-bellied Woodpeckers. The Condermans later followed breakfast with nutritional lunches and dinners and a clean, soft bed, all of which was warmer than my usual fare.

We were skunked on the twenty-third when they tried to show me a Wild Turkey. We looked for a Purple Gallinule at Lake Ellis, a small lake dotted by stunted cypress and bordered by a promising marsh. Water lilies grew but the leaves were not the big round ones that would provide a floating perch for our bird. Or so we thought. Again, we failed to find our query. We did find Common Gallinule. Our fortune looking from shore was not working so we paddled a small boat along the shore, in and out of cypress and lake vegetation, looking for whatever we could find. Little Blue and Great Blue herons lumbered away, and I saw more Wood Ducks here than any one place I had been. Over 40 Turkey Vultures and a single Black Vulture milled around the shore. A few were preening, others seemed to be sunning in the warm afternoon sun.

The next day, after breakfast, we drove to Beaufort and Moorhead City, coastal towns west of the southern end of the Outer Banks. Being back on the Atlantic shore felt comfortable. I wondered how the birding was on Pea Island, but just for a moment. We were now scouting Beaufort's reef for Cattle Egrets, a sure thing according to Margaret Conderman. Though there were plenty of cattle, egrets were not found. Inquiries to a couple of roadside farmers said no large white birds had been near their cows since Hurricane Ella.

At Fort Macon State Park, near Morehead City, birding got better than our peak of zero Cattle Egrets. First, a Western Kingbird, becoming less of a rarity of the East Coast, popped up on a wire. I had not seen one for three months and over 2,000 miles. Shortly, we found a straggling migrant female Rose-breasted Grosbeak. Overhead several gulls and a hawk were wheeling in an updraft slightly over the water. The white windows in the hawk's wings, its banded tail, and reddish underparts fit the Peterson field guide as a Red-shouldered Hawk, a new bird for my life list. The grosbeak, possibly unnerved by the new lifer, scurried into denser vegetation as several pugnacious mockingbirds began mobbing the hawk. All but their chatter disappeared in the understory. Not far north of Morehead City, we stopped to check out a new promising area. A sparrow popped up and froze on an open perch just long enough for us to come to the collective conclusion that it was a Henslow's Sparrow. Minutes later, we practically bumped into an immature Yellow-crowned Night-Heron. The day was leaning toward night, so we hurried back to the car just in time to spot a different sparrow. Unlike the clear-breasted Bachman's Sparrow, the new bird had streaks on its breast. The streaks were too broad for a sharp-tailed. Seaside, Savannah, the usually streaked sparrows were ruled out. It reminded me of a Baird's Sparrow, but it was too brown, and the bill appeared large for the size of the bird. We added up the field marks but had to flush the bird one more time to be sure, and we were. Another life bird, a Bachman's Sparrow.

26–30 October 1962

Yesterday evening, at the Condermans' home, I met medical Dr. Sam Holmes. He stated assuredly that visiting Wilmington would add to the trip list Gull-billed and Least terns, Purple Gallinule, Cattle Egrets, and a couple of other species. I found none of the species he listed. My confidence was shaken, but the day was not over. Other local birders might guide me to new species. However, the person I had corresponded with months ago, as he had previously warned, was off attending a faraway college. He had suggested an alternate contact, who I tried to reach by phone. No one was home. I had the contact's address and drove a few miles east. I knocked a couple of times, but no one answered. A next-door neighbor said the person I was looking for was out birding and that I should wait. Only two minutes later "Dot" Earle drove up. She had heard I was coming, and right away offered me a guest room. I wondered what she had heard. My original contact would have told her about my visit and my friends from up the Carolina coast might have called ahead. "Take pity on the skinny kid from Oregon."

Dot suggested a quick trip across the Intracoastal Waterway to Wrightsville Beach where a beach and town share names on a barrier island. The place, including the ocean, island, and sound, was once alive with birds and mammals, even alligators. Unlike the protected Outer Banks, flat concrete and asphalt and vertical buildings cover most other barrier islands. The island hosting Wrightsville Beach is a reconfiguration of islands, a few bulldozed to form one long narrow strand. Habitat alteration, mostly destruction, began early, in the nineteenth century. It has never stopped. I wondered where, in this mess of human habitat, it would be possible to see any birds. Still, I had faith that my enthusiastic host knew of one or two undisturbed bits of sand and marsh.

Crossing the waterway on our way back toward Wilmington caused me to wonder how many of the southbound yachts carried birders. It was getting late and evening traffic slowed the pace. A tern, a gull or two, and a distant shorebird interrupted my thoughts. The birds remained unidentified as we crept back to the house. Black-eyed peas, freshly caught mullet, and hushpuppies capped the day.

The next morning was barely above freezing as we searched the sea beyond Wrightsville Beach. We were looking for Gannets, but the horizon was cold and birdless. For the next three days, we scoured the region from the causeway east of Wrightsville to Carolina Beach, Fort Fisher, just north of Cape Fear, and back to the mainland. Luckily, a few feet from the sand and reeds, we found one of those confusing fall warblers, a bird allowing us to stare at it long enough to be sure it was a Blackpoll Warbler.

On the last day, Dot planned a trip to two new areas south of Wilmington: Orton Plantation, a rice plantation circa 1700 loaded with formal gardens and ponds, and Long Beach, on a long offshore barrier island separated from the mainland by the Intracoastal Waterway. As we drove into the plantation, which reminded me of a city park, I began wondering if this was such a good idea. It was. Anyone's first Anhinga overpowers all trepidations about birding in such a well-manicured place. Further south, at Long Beach, we found a White Ibis. A Long Beach resident told us that immature White Ibis, like the one we found today, wander north to visit nesting Glossy Ibis.

WHISKERS AND DOING CHARLESTON

31 October 1962

Mail from Oregon was waiting for me at Shallotte, a hamlet not far north from South Carolina. The last mail from home was picked up at Suffolk, Virginia, only 20 days ago, but it seemed longer than that. In 20 days, I had been in Great Dismal Swamp, the Outer Banks, North Carolina marshlands and estuaries, more and more Spanish moss, and hospitable people. In the mail at Suffolk, my mom wrote that she enjoyed the last phone call (called from Petersburg), and ever the teacher and librarian, commented that my writing and speech was improving. My dad wrote, "It seems like you are having good luck with your bird count." They wrote that the family parakeet, Billie, had died. She and I had little mumbled conversations as she perched behind bars. Whatever I did or said led to the strange behavior of her periodically laying a single egg. If I ignored her, she did not lay eggs.

The new mail, at the Shallotte post office, started with a description of a windstorm that killed 48 people in Oregon. No one died in my home area. My mom had read the autographed copy of *Hawks Aloft*, which prompted her to read parts of it to my dad, who could not manage the fine print. She also wrote, "I will admit I was very apprehensive about you making this trip, but now I think it has been the best thing that could have happened to you." I could not agree more.

My mom wondered if the Cuban crisis was going to be a problem while traveling and wrote that my sister cried because she believed I might have to go into the military. What Cuban crisis? My mom briefly outlined the problem, which then began to worry me. No one had mentioned it, or maybe I just was not listening. I rarely turned on the car radio, my only source for news other than that relayed to me by people I met. Almost immediately, I began searching the stations on the radio. Surely, every station will be jammed with news about what was going on. Today, the radio, on the last day of October, was quiet. No one announced that we should get under our desks and wait for a survivor to tell us it was all clear, that we could come out and life would go on. Everything seemed normal.

There was a long paragraph in my mom's letter about my eating habits. My mom was worried that I was not getting enough protein, even going as far as suggesting a kind of canned meat (I will not mention the name, but it is well known, hated by some, and loved by others. Several books and essays have been written about it. A reviewer of one such book referred to it as the Cadillac of canned meat, but others comment about the conglomerate meat charged with sugar and sodium nitrates). My dad wrote that he no longer was working at the sawmill. He had gotten a job with the school and had a conversation with my former high school principal, the very person that told me during my senior year that I would never make anything out of my life. What led him to such a conclusion? I never even had the pleasure of toilet papering his home but I was not one of his best students. Nevertheless, he changed his tune when he told my dad that I would learn more on the trip than most "boys." My dad also wrote a long paragraph chastising my eating habits and sent a five dollar bill to me to get a couple of hot meals. Really, my plight was not that pitiful.

The mail also included a letter from Alexander Wetmore. "Dear Ralph: In response to yours of October 10, I have identified your slide as showing *Erolia ruficollis*." The Ashtabula, Ohio, sighting was now confirmed thanks to Jon Ahlquist's photograph.

Although I had planned originally to stop at Myrtle Beach, South Carolina, I drove on until I located a place off US 17 to hide the car behind a grove of bushes. It was dreaded Halloween, and I did not want any trouble from trick or treaters.

1–4 November 1962

Last night was uneventful, thank goodness. Waking was difficult. I was tired from lack of sleep. The boards of my berth were hard compared to the real beds I had been sleeping on for the past several days. The air mattress needed repairing, again. It was cold, nearly 32 degrees. I was spoiled and had become soft. All those breakfasts of eggs, bacon, toast, hot cereal, hot coffee, and all those warm soft sleeps had taken their toll. Getting back to the simple life, the cold and often too wet buggy nights, was what I knew I must get used to again. Still, the living condition of essentially living in my car was far better than sleeping in a tent.

Today would be a tour of Brookgreen Gardens, a 4,000-acre sanctuary full of formal and informal gardens, ponds, sculptures, and natural habitat. Pettingill mentioned Wild Turkeys and numerous species of ducks could be found in the garden. Past the open rustic gates were Ring-necked Ducks, Canvasbacks, and Canada Geese. The elusive Ring-neck was new for the trip, and so were the Wild Turkeys that strolled unconcernedly about 20 feet from my gaping mouth. Should I count the new duck and the turkeys? They seemed too unafraid to be wild. I certainly did not count the Flammulated Owl freshly captured in eastern Oregon, the toucan my cousin jokingly showed me in a grocery store in Ohio, or the Golden Eagle in a Vermont zoo. None of those birds could, at the instant I saw them, fly free from their captivity. However, would I count them if suddenly they escaped? The *Audubon Field Notes* recorded a "Harlan's Hawk," a dark northern subspecies of

Red-tailed Hawk that was wearing leather jesses. Should it be counted? I finally rationalized that Pettingill would not have mentioned the waterfowl and Wild Turkeys unless they were wild. I was still suspicious. When I was sure no one was looking, I rushed the ducks and turkeys to make them fly. They flew and the two species were added to the trip list.

"Camp" was made a few miles down the road near the town of Georgetown on the banks of the Great Pee Dee River. What a terrific name. A large part of the day was used to bring my notes up to date, write four letters, and plan my next stop. I decided to visit McClellanville, a small town surrounded by the Francis Marion National Forest that is dubbed the gateway to Cape Romain NWR. The refuge occupies about 60,000 acres of marsh, forest, and water on a 20-mile stretch of barrier islands. One of the refuge staff had supplied a name and address of the leading birder of the region. Unfortunately, I had not made any previous contact, and he had no phone, which meant if I wanted his help, I would have to show up at his house, unannounced. As the late afternoon ushered in thick clouds threatening more rain, I drove down a remote road on a small farm aptly named Ardea, a generic name for several species of herons, to make my unexpected visit.

The house, sitting alone in the long shadows of a setting sun, was dimly lit by the puny flicker of kerosene lamps. A storm had knocked out the electricity, or, for a fleeting moment I wondered, was this the aftermath of the Cuban Missile Crisis? No one seemed particularly excited by the routine power outage. My contact, Robert Edwards, responded to my knock. "In the light of things," I was invited to spend the night. While we discussed where the best birds would be tomorrow, I noticed strange shadows on the walls. They moved, stopped, pounced, and made loud noises. The shadows had tails. At least five Siamese cats were climbing and jumping from ceiling-high bookshelves. They also liked jumping into laps, with needle-sharp claws extended. Tropical finches of all sorts chirped faintly in the kerosene rhapsody and a lone brownish cocker spaniel pup crouched in a stuffed chair. A Barred Owl hooted just outside the door. Wow, a new life bird. Then I was told that the owl had been a captive of the family for 10 years. The next morning the sun revealed a pair of American Kestrels, three species of pheasants, two huge parrots, and, more interestingly, several caged Painted Buntings. Robert told me that when he was not teaching high school chemistry and physics, he studied the eclipse plumages of these gaudy buntings.

Our birding day started at Blake's Reserve, part of the Santee Gun Club. I instantly thought a gun club is not where I want to be, but we saw a variety of birds in addition to the mainstay of the club, plenty of ducks. Soras winnowed from the marsh vegetation. One foraged calmly in the open about 40 feet from where we stood, the first Sora I had ever seen. We had already flushed Virginia Rail at the farm. Herons and egrets were abundant, and two adult Glossy Ibis wheeled so low overhead that the air could be heard rushing through their wings.

We headed down to Moore's Landing. That is where the ferry departs for Bull Island, part of Cape Romain NWR. Pettingill recommended Bulls Island, but we confined our birding to the vicinity of the dock. Mr. Edwards brought his grandson, and in no time 12-year-old John spotted five Marbled Godwits, a species I had been chasing down the Atlantic shore. The godwits were foraging with American Oystercatchers, Short-billed Dowitchers, and Dunlins. We later rowed along the marshy shore near Moore's Landing looking especially for rails and found plenty of Clappers. The Black and Yellow rails would have to wait. During the day, we managed to find 72 species, two of which were new trip species.

Our arrival back to Ardea was just in time. Mrs. Edwards had prepared a hot, sumptuous meal accented with a fresh apple pie. The next morning, I thanked the Edwards family for their kind hospitality and said goodbye to the captive Barred Owl, at least five Siamese cats, assorted tropical finches and parrots, and Painted Buntings. It was Sunday, an inconvenient time to be arriving in Charleston. There were plenty of notes to type, and a roadside park looked good for paperwork and a night for sleep before Charleston.

5–7 November 1962

In less than an hour, I would be in Charleston. To me, this Charleston, not Charleston, Vermont, or any one of several other Charlestons, was THE Charleston. Reaching Charleston meant crossing the wide swath of the Wando and Cooper Rivers that spill into the Charleston Harbor between Mount Pleasant and Charleston. It meant driving the infamous Cooper River Bridge. A couple of my North Carolinian birders chuckled about the bridge and warned me to keep my fingers crossed. I stopped about a quarter of a mile east of the bridge to snap a picture. The Mackinac Bridge in Michigan was impressive in structure, but the Cooper River Bridge seemed impressively scary because of its aging structure. The South Carolina bridge opened in 1928. It was constructed high over a windy expanse of nothing but water and its aging structure sounded danger. I had read that by 1957 the bridge had claimed 27 lives. People then were, well, scared to drive over it, but told that it was "safe" to cross. Hearing that did not help me feel less afraid today. The wind alone could be a problem for my little VW, but I was more concerned that the bridge might fall. The crossing was a white-knuckle affair that required my fullest attention as I tried to ignore the creaking sounds of a bridge in distress. Luckily, I managed to make it to the other side without getting wet or seeing the bright light of doom.

The fifth day of November was still young. I telephoned B. Rhett Chamberlain, who was the local regional editor for *Audubon Field Notes*, recognized preeminent Charleston birder, editor of the *Chat*, the bird journal for North and South Carolina, and, with Alexander Sprunt, author of *South Carolina Bird Life*, published in 1949. How could I miss? By earlier correspondence, a birding plan was set in place, but a close friend of Rhett's had just died. Nevertheless, he took time to pore over my worn trip list and remark that most of the missing eastern species this time of year would be easier to see in Florida. He said I should meet Edwin Blitch, the curator of vertebrate zoology at the Charleston Museum of Natural History. The institution was founded in 1773 and it is the country's oldest museum. Dr. Blitch and I made plans to meet in three days to do Charleston.

I left the museum with directions to Magnolia Gardens and the name of the manager who, the curator told me, would be happy to help me find local birds. Considered America's oldest man-made attraction, Magnolia Gardens was founded in 1676 and has been open to the public since 1860. Today, I hoped the region would still be an attraction for wildlife. Arriving at Mr. Ted Beckett's manager's residence, I was greeted by one of his daughters who could not believe anyone would travel to see birds, and who was flabbergasted that I would drive all the way from Oregon to see tree ducks in Magnolia Gardens. Mr. Beckett chuckled. He managed the plantation's 464 acres of stylized gardens, low arching bridges reflecting from the dark water of lily ponds and, I hoped, a few good birds. In size, the region was near the size of the Oregon ranch I worked to help pay for my trip. The region of Magnolia Gardens I was most interested in was the "unimproved" acres. Ted showed me a list of about 300 species he had seen during several years at Magnolia Gardens. That was most of the species on the checklist of birds from the whole state excluding a few normally found along the Atlantic shore. He penciled four additions: House Finch, Evening Grosbeak, Cinnamon Teal, and Fulvous Tree Duck. Ted allowed me to park off the beaten path on one of the dike roads for two nights and provided detailed directions for the best birding locations.

For the next two days, I wandered freely around the property, searching huge oaks, heavily laden with cloaks of gray-green Spanish moss, thick leathery leafed magnolia, palmetto, bushes, ponds, and marshland. I hardly saw anyone although a man, who introduced himself as Mr. Hastie and owner of the plantation, asked me to show him the tree ducks. I did, even though I had read upon entering the property that the Drayton family owned the plantation.

Anhingas, herons, and egrets were everywhere. Ducks swam in the water not choked by cattails and lily pads. As promised, 15 Fulvous Whistling-Ducks exploded into the air, with a weak goose-like squealing gabble, circled, and flashed their white rump band before disappearing in the afternoon sun. At night, I prepared supper (opened a can), with the voices of coots, gallinules, and ducks.

The cold of the night felt piercing, and my makeshift bed was unforgiving. My thoughts took me elsewhere. The pretty girl whose picture keeps my wallet open called to my heart. What was Linda doing tonight? I also thought of less spiritual longings. Running water would be nice. A warm bathroom and soft bed would be great. Home in Oregon rolled through my brain. The temperature hovered just above the magic number between liquid and ice. I must be crazy. Could I keep going until next June?

Sleep was intermittent; I woke a little tired and freezing. I gulped down the six breakfast donuts and headed out for Yellow-throated Warblers, but only occasional kinglets flitted in the loblolly pine. I worked a freshly plowed field for a possible Grasshopper Sparrow and found five American Pipits. A little after a peanut butter sandwich, I took a short ride in a skiff Ted mentioned I could use. Paddling down a canal toward the whistling-duck area and nosing the boat into edges of remote pools might surprise a Yellow Rail. No luck. By early afternoon, the temperature was up to about 65 degrees. Rowing in the hot Southern sun was not much fun, and birding from a boat, as I had found on other occasions, was not especially productive. After returning the boat to the dock, I trudged back to the car on a dike road. I needed to shed some of my layers, and the car contained food. A few yards from the docked boat, I barely glimpsed an animal slink through the dike grass. Maybe it was a mouse or a snake. I picked up a few golf ball-sized dirt clods and lobbed one to the left. Miraculously, a small chicken-like bird moved to the right and into a bare tire track on the grassy road. The bird stopped just long enough to get it in my binoculars for a few seconds. There was no doubt about it. The diminutive bird disappeared about the time guilt swept over me. Thank goodness, I had not beaned my first Yellow Rail.

8 November 1962

Edwin Blitch was waiting for me in the morning at the Charleston Museum. We loaded into his station wagon and headed for Folly Beach under an overcast sky. Stops were first made to check a small city woodland and

WHISKERS AND DOING CHARLESTON

the city sewage treatment area. At Folly Beach we picked up Semipalmated Sandpiper and two species of gulls at the last site. A weedy field on the way added three skulking sparrows, the usual suspects according to my guide. Except for a couple of Ruddy Turnstones, Folly Beach was empty. Not even a whisker. So, that was doing the Charleston.

Mr. Blitch and I returned to the Charleston Museum. He had told me that before visiting the Savannah region and Okefenokee Swamp, I should visit one more place in South Carolina. My Charleston guide phoned John Henry Dick, who agreed to meet me at his home, the 880-acre Dixie Plantation a few miles south of Charleston and near the Stono River. Rain dominated the day. The decision to make today a nonbirding day seemed a good one. Besides, I was anxious to see the live waterfowl collection and curious to meet such a famous bird artist.

Glistening sheets of water were pouring down the windshield as I followed the directions to the old plantation. The route, well off the beaten path, finally led down a long oak-lined driveway. Thick dark trunks supported limbs of the giant old trees that, draped in Spanish moss, arched over both sides of the straight drive. The limbs had grown and met and formed a long-woven tunnel around the drive while the heavy branches opposite the drive hung low to the ground as if bracing against their own weight and heaviness of the thick clinging mosses. Robert E. Lee or Clark Gable, or both, would have felt at home. On the other hand, I felt out of place until, the car window partially rolled down, I heard a friendly voice put me at ease.

Two big but friendly brown boxers pounced on me the moment I stepped out of the car, almost knocking me to the drenched ground all the while licking my hands. A tall, husky man stepped forward and introduced himself. His thick heavy hand, as we shook, felt more like that of a laborer than imagined of an artist. This was John Henry Dick, whose superb work I had appreciated in books including *A Gathering of Shorebirds* and Griscom and Sprunt's *Warblers of America*. Especially impressive was the art and, even more, he had observed every species of North American warbler. The rain flowed and ebbed the rest of the day while John revealed a personality I instantly liked. Between the falling rain, we toured the duck pond where I saw live mandarin, Shelduck, Pink-footed Goose, and more. Of course, these did not go on my trip list. Most interesting was a living collection of all the subspecies of Canada Goose. We saw the usual non-captive herons and sparrows and listened for Great Horned Owls that had been plaguing the waterfowl.

Although not the original plantation house, which burned, John built a new modern house and separate studio in 1939. The interiors were amazing and shocking. A zebra skin dressed a hallway and, in the middle of the main room, a large Indian tiger skin covered the floor. Indicating regret for killing the tiger, my host directed me to two large and recently finished watercolors of the Flightless Cormorant and Galapagos Albatross that casually were supported by the back of a sofa. My host had been in the Galapagos this year. Inside a fireproof room were countless ink drawings covering a cabinet top and part of a wall. Many of them were to be in a forthcoming book on the South. A collection of old, out-of-print bird books lay in metal racks. Stacks of books hid the tops of tables and chairs. Bird study skins from various parts of the world occupied the largest space. Several heavy volumes containing thousands of personal photographs of birds, mammals, and places recorded quests for wildlife. His passion about the excellent photographs seemed greater than about his superb paintings and drawings.

Although John Henry Dick was leaving for Texas tomorrow morning, he offered a meal and a spare room. That evening, we enjoyed a sumptuous meal of hamburger, potato cakes, and Jerusalem artichokes or sun roots. John explained that sun roots are a relative of the sunflower and there is a taste like jicama. I was too embarrassed to ask about jicama. We talked more than we ate. John had the habit of commenting to himself about the taste of his food. He punctuated every mouthful with an audible "mmm" or "mm-mm" that I easily ignored. I learned my host liked Stravinsky and old bird books and marched to the beat of his own drum. He loved to travel and considered himself an artist-naturalist more than a bird specialist. He talked about birds, travel, music, and conservation until midnight. He asked me questions, wanted my opinion, offered ideas. Midnight was too early.

The useful term *whisker* caught on. Well, just barely. In early January 2015, my friend and former colleague Marshall Howe just happened to be visiting Buenos Aires NWR in Arizona the same time my wife Linda and I were birding by RV. Marshall, who also retired from the Biological Survey at Smithsonian, and I had not been in contact for 18 years. He had moments earlier explained the term *whisker* to his wife. It was a happy circumstance visiting with Marshall and a reminder that a perfectly good and time-saving word was not completely forgotten.

Another word, actually a group of words, that some people have forgotten is the "Cuban Missile Crisis." The mess came to a boil on 16 October 1962 when intelligence revealed to President John "Jack" Kennedy that the

Soviet Union had started building missile bases in Cuba, just 90 miles from Florida. In a nutshell, Kennedy and Premier Nikita Khrushchev, the guy in charge of the Soviet Union following Stalin's murderous reign, were at odds with one another. The general US public did not know about the crisis until 22 October 1962 and, fortunately, after debating and teeth-gnashing went on until 29 October when the missiles were to be removed. The imminent threat of nuclear war was averted.

How I managed to avoid hearing about the Cuban Missile Crisis amazes me, but in the sixties, 24-hour television news, hours and hours of talk shows with pro and con political railings dripping out of the audio speakers did not own the airwaves. CNN did not have a reporter embedded on the scene. CNN did not exist. Sure, there was the nightly network news. I could have listened to David Brinkley, who was from Wilmington, or tuned in another source, or one of my birder friends could have warned me. They may have talked about the crisis, but I had birds on the brain to hear any bad news. Cuban missiles were not going to dampen my spirit, whether I knew about them or not.

Although I did not fully appreciate how close the USA and then the Soviet Union came to blowing each other to smithereens, lurking in the deep recesses of my brain of denial was a question. How soon would I be scooped up and sent to a military camp where I would become the soldier I did not want to be? Vietnam and now missiles about 90 miles from Florida, where I was heading, was not good. Typical of my youthful optimism, I decided to ignore those dangers and see more birds. I never appreciated the graveness of the threat and reality of nuclear war, although living in the Washington, DC, region for 30 years raised my fears. How can anyone sanely survive entertaining the complete horror of a nuclear weapon? Talk about habitat destruction. The aftermath of a nuclear blast puts to shame any habitat alterations dreamed up by commerce and allowed by governments.

Another reason to wonder about my lifespan was the frightening bridge to cross when entering Charleston from the north. The John P. Grace Memorial Bridge, called the Cooper River Bridge by most, opened in 1929. It arched high over the water, was narrow, steep, with a 6 percent grade, bumpy, dangerous, and no longer suited for the Ford Model As it was built for. By 1964, shipworms were caught chewing away at the Cooper River Bridge supports, which caused sections to buckle and lean. Regardless, traffic continued to flow. The Silas N. Pearman Bridge opened in 1966. It had modern 12-foot-wide lanes but was only open to northbound traffic. South bounders had to use the old bridge. Finally, the eight-lane Arthur Ravenel Jr. Bridge replaced both older bridges in 2005. Locals call the new kid on the river the Cooper River Bridge. It is 366 feet closer to the water than the

Mackinaw Bridge in Michigan, a bridge my developed acrophobia causes more fear than I felt on the old rickety bridge entering Charleston in 1962.

Most birding localities I visited in South Carolina continue to exist. Cape Romain NWR, in addition to protecting a significantly large population of loggerhead turtles, remains a good birding spot. Over 154,000 people visited the refuge in 2010. At least some of the more recent visitors reported additional species of birds that brought the refuge checklist of 1959 that I used to the current total of 293 species. Access to the refuge is still limited to boat travel just as it was about 300 years ago when Bulls Island was reputed to be a hideout for pirates. The moniker for Moore's Landing was changed to Garris Landing since 1962. A ferry now docks there and for $40 will transport an adult to Bulls Island. The Sewee Visitor Center began in 1996, which now offers interpretive information on the refuge and national forest.

My 1962 notes recorded that my time at the Magnolia Gardens was free. Things change. As of 2004, a fee just to get on the property was $13— additional fees would get you to special places that sound great for birds. Brookgreen Gardens still exists and, in 2021, has an entrance fee of $18. Many popular places in the twenty-first century require reservations, something I did not concern myself with during the sixties travel. Unfortunately, making reservation takes away any spur-of-the-moment activity, which can remove the freedom found in more impromptu travel such as that enjoyed in 1962.

Edwin Blitch retired from his curatorship to a high school teaching position. In 1968, William Post became the curator of ornithology at the Charleston Museum. We talked on the phone numerous times and met at Smithsonian during his several visits. His accent was even more Southern than Mr. Blitch's. Through conversation with now-retired curator William Post, I learned that the Charleston Museum, as of 1980, had a new building. Someday, I will do Charleston, again.

A little background about John Henry Dick taught me more about this unique and impressive person. Prior to his birth, his mother was then married to John Jacob Astor, and was a survivor of the ill-fated Titanic. John Henry almost did not exist. Although already well-known, John's artistic prowess was better noticed when, in 1952, he won the competitive annual Duck Stamp Contest. The US Fish and Wildlife Service has sold duck stamps since 1934 that permit hunters to hunt waterfowl and to gain access to national wildlife refuges that charge entrance fees. Stamps are a reproduction of a species of duck or goose found in North America based on artwork submitted in an annual competition. John's victorious entry in 1952 was a black and whitewash of a pair of Harlequin Ducks flying over a rocky ocean surf. The stamp was sold to hunters and others for $2 and collectors today might pay $90 for the same issue of the stamp in mint condition. Other issued duck stamps for different years can be worth hundreds of dollars. For a current stamp (2020), the Fish and Wildlife raised their price from $2 to $25. John painted 2,500 separate birds for the 1983 book on birds of India coauthored by Salim Ali and Smithsonian Secretary S. Dillon Ripley.[1] I was often reminded of John especially when various contenders for a duck stamp would bring their entries by the Division of Birds for a critique from willing museum staff members. The staff had no connection to the judges of the contest and questionable influence on the artists. In addition to his work with Peterson and others, John illustrated Pettingill's *The Bird Watcher's America*.[2]

John Henry Dick was aware of environmental changes, not just in the vicinity of his home near Charleston, but everywhere. We talked about some of those changes, the habitat loss and conservation of birds in 1962 and the future. I mostly listened and knew this was a person on the side of nature. We also talked about the loss of numerous habitats and discussed a couple of sparrows I saw earlier. Both the grassland Bachman's and the pine forest Henslow's have major habitat problems. The former species lose habitat to grazing and urban sprawl. Henslow's Sparrows, the only sparrow endemic to the United States, has had a downward spiral in population since Audubon discovered it in 1820. The usual culprit to the demise of most species, habitat loss comes from clearing pine forests and the growth of trees, even in a protected area.

John later commented about the Indian tiger and related that the skin was a reminder of the time when he realized he should stop hunting, but be watching, photographing, illustrating, and, thus, conserving. Before 1995, the year John died, he set up protective easements around his valuable habitats, the Dixie Plantation, and left his collection of rare books, other collections, and land to the College of Charleston. The college, which conducts numerous classes on the property, now calls the Dixie Plantation the Stono Preserve.

Besides the rickety bridge into Charleston, the region sometimes offered a sighting of the rare Bachman's Warbler, but I never got that dance. Ever since Audubon described the warbler in 1833 from a bird discovered in a swamp near Charleston, people have traveled thousands of miles to catch a glance at this black-bibbed yellow warbler. It was not photographed until 1958 when John Henry Dick and H. P. Staats recorded an elusive male

1. Salim Ali and S. Dillon Ripley. *Handbook of the Birds of the Indian Subcontinent*. (Delhi: Oxford University Press, 1983).

2. Olin S. Pettingill. *The Bird Watcher's America*. (New York: McGraw Hill, 1965).

on film. Had I planned better, I believed I might have had a chance to see Bachman's Warbler, but it was November. Birds would have migrated south.

Bachman's Warblers declined because of the usual culprit, habitat loss in its breeding and wintering ranges. This small warbler also suffered because of its dependence on bamboo, from women's hats depending on cute and colorful birds to mix in with feathers of egrets, herons, and other easy targets, and by hurricanes. The last known nest of the Bachman's Warbler was in Alabama in 1937 and reported by H. M. Stevenson, a fellow correspondent during my Smithsonian days. The last confirmed record of any kind of this rare warbler was in 1962 near Charleston. In 1962, I did not know that the last confirmed record had been made just months before my November visit to Charleston. In addition, I did not realize that that sighting was at Moore's Landing by none other than Robert Edwards. I recall thinking I still had a remote chance of seeing Bachman's Warbler in the spring of 1963. There had been later unconfirmed sightings from Cuba, nudging a wish to go there to see a species before it was too late. Of course, the pesky missile crisis, not to mention my budget, would prevent getting to the winter territory of the warbler. Bachman's Warbler was placed on the federal list of endangered species five years later, or is that five years too late? The species is probably extinct.

Chapter 17

Okefenokee on My Mind

9–10 November 1962

With gratitude, I reluctantly end the abbreviated time with John Henry Dick and his haven south of Charleston, South Carolina. Our conversations were forced to end; he soon had to be in Texas and me in Georgia. To paraphrase a popular song about Georgia, I had Okefenokee on my mind. When I was a kid, before I started birding, I loved reading Walter Kelly's comic strip *Pogo*. Appreciation of the political nuances and social commentary came later. The comic strip gave notoriety to Okefenokee Swamp, and Pettingill recommended it as a great place to see birds. Visiting the land of Pogo, I thought, would be another milestone of the trip, ranking up there with Yellowstone, coastal Maine, Hawk Mountain, and Washington, DC, the source of much of Pogo. I was eager to bird the wild swamp. The closer I drove to Okefenokee, the more anxious I became. However, I was not there yet.

Before Okefenokee, I had other stops. A cold rain fell most of 9 November. About halfway between Charleston and Savannah was a good place to stop, catch up on my notes and correspondence with a few birders, some who I had met and others who might help in my quest for birds. Also, I had bitten my tongue, which made chewing an ordeal, and developed a sore throat, which made swallowing painful. Perhaps my parents were right; maybe my diet was not the best for my health. Regardless of who was correct, I hoped not to spread my germs and decided to lay low for a while, take time to reflect, and wonder about the Cuban Missile Crisis. Maybe it was already over, and no one pulled the trigger. Surely John Henry Dick would have warned me not to head for Florida. Even so, I had heard travel on the Florida Keys was restricted because of the missiles. Was that a rumor? I began to wonder if my roadside camps would soon be restricted. Poor communication and hearsay did not calm my apprehensions, but I decided no news must be good news.

11–13 November 1962

The skies cleared on the day I arrived at Savannah NWR. The approximately 12,600-acre refuge straddles the South Carolina–Georgia boundary. At headquarters, on the South Carolina side of the meandering Savannah River, I met Mell Millinger, biologist for the refuge. From my wish list of birds in the refuge checklist, he indicated the few species I had a slim chance of adding to the trip list. We also discussed the fact that camping in national wildlife refuges was usually prohibited, as it was at Savannah, but he had a place in the refuge where I could park my car and probably hear Barred Owls during the night.

After lunch, Mell and I took a trip on a few of the dike roads of the refuge on the South Carolina side of the Savannah River. At last, no rain, but a slight breeze blew in a few harmless clouds. Our route took us across acres of marsh, burnt fields full of starlings and hordes of blackbirds, a few Mourning Doves, and American Pipits. We did not realize until we stopped that one of the fields was teeming with thousands of pipits carpeting the ground in a pulsating mass of hungry birds. Freshwater marshes were dotted with island oases of live oak, other hardwoods, and pine. The islands were probably ancient sand dunes. Because I had already found most of the waterfowl possible in the refuge, we concentrated on the wooded sections for gnatcatchers and owls. No luck.

Late in the day, we arrived at Mell's house to the aroma of food. He and his wife insisted I join them. I could not refuse free food. About an hour before dark, I hurried off to the parking spot Mell had suggested and where I might find Barred Owls. The site was surrounded by tall trees on one of the old dunes. After about two hours of deep sleep, all hell broke loose. Less than 20 feet away a strange and eerie sound disturbed the silence. About 40 feet away an answer to the first bird sliced the humid air. It was an almost sinister cacophony of otherworldly calls. Now, fully awake, the hair on the back of my neck was standing at attention. Two birds were calling back and forth, occasionally overlapping their barks and cries, until a sudden silence. A good likeness of what I heard on my Peterson LP back in Oregon had broken the stillness. I eased out of bed, down to the driver's seat, and out the car door. With a flashlight at the ready, I aimed the beam at one of the birds. The dark eyes and round face of a Barred Owl stared back. I eased quietly back in the car and into bed. The unsettled owls started calling again about 30 minutes later and continued until about an hour before sunrise.

The next two days were discouraging. The refuge checklist contained 10 species that would help my trip list, but most of the species on it had departed southward. I tried but none of the 86 species I found during the two days were new; only the Barred Owl was an addition. In the evening, I met Ivan Tompkins at Millinger's dinner table. In addition to being an expert on Georgia's birds, Ivan was keen to go birding and offered to take me along. Ever eager, I accepted.

14 November 1962

The early morning hour was, for lack of a better word, nippy. I was warm inside from a hearty Millinger breakfast of bacon and eggs. I sped the few miles to the city of Savannah where I met Ivan Tompkins at his home. We drove in his car east to Tybee Island, a 3.3-square-mile barrier island, which was replete with the usual beach houses, tourist cafés, and other buildings crowding out most natural habitat. Ian knew all the nooks and crannies that might offer enough undisturbed habitat for a few good birds. We parked at a cold and windy spot near a wooden jetty hunched in the wind. Icy salt spray soared high over our heads in vertical plumes each time the Atlantic came crashing into the worn jetty. The wind blew most of the spray away from us as we looked over about 50 Ruddy Turnstones. Ivan announced casually that this is the spot for Purple Sandpiper and, in minutes, he calmly pointed out a Purple Sandpiper, then two more, three, until we counted an even dozen. The new life bird felt good. We birded most of Tybee Island, finding three more species of shorebirds, three species of gulls, and a Western Kingbird just to make me feel at home.

15 November 1962

The next day Ivan and I drove north to his favorite birding location, Hilton Head Island, South Carolina. The island, about 30 miles, as the Fish Crow flies, from Savannah is a foot-shaped mass of land about 42 square miles. Luckily, my guide knew just where to go. One of the first stops was to look out to sea. I was still hoping to find gannets, and Northern Gannets we found. Far out to sea two large white birds soared high over the water, folded their black-primaried wings, and dove into the dark ocean. Just after getting my breath, a loon surfaced between the gannets and us. Its upturned bill and white on its face and back were telling. In a hunchback flight, the snaky necked Red-throated Loon disappeared to the south. Finding two life birds within brief minutes of one another was exciting. Throughout the day, we found 14 species of shorebirds, Anhinga, an immature Red-headed Woodpecker, and about 40 others during our visit to Hilton Head.

16–17 November 1962

Last night, I called home to let them know I had survived the missile crisis, that I was enjoying the Southeast, and would soon be in Florida. Mention of my bitten tongue and sore throat, which were now hardly noticeable, was left out of the conversation.

According to my calculations, I was 10 days ahead of schedule; I had planned to be in Florida on 1 December. Departing Savannah, I drove only 15 miles where I found a roadside park. Two other campers were there enjoying the short-sleeve temperature. I spent the next two nights at the park, catching up on notes and correspondence and planning my next stop. After reviewing my list of birds so far found since early June this year and the new species I might see, the prospect of finding my goal of 572 species looked impossible. It now appears I will find close to 500. That is not so bad. Meanwhile, I had Okefenokee on my mind.

18 November 1962

Today's drive southwest in a light rain took me to Waycross, Georgia, the town just north of the famed Okefenokee Swamp. With one eye kept out for a good place to look for birds, I checked out a couple of likely places for a roadside pull-out for the night. One seemed exactly right. The remaining daylight went to writing a letter to my parents and to Linda, and to catch up on reading. An *Audubon Field Notes* that covered the winter season invited a read and I was especially eager to peruse the Florida region. The sporadic sprinkle of rain stopped and so did my peace and quiet. Before five minutes passed, a Georgia state trooper rolled up beside my car. I was sitting behind the wheel reading. A portly uniformed man eased out of his car, walked over, and asked for a driver's license and car registration. He then demanded I tell him what I was doing, where I was going, and why. I attempted to explain that I was catching up on my reading about birds, that

I was going to Okefenokee National Wildlife Refuge tomorrow, and that I hoped to see more birds there.

"You what?"

I tried again, explaining that I had a list of birds and that I was trying to see as many of them as possible.

"The f— you say." Big sigh. "Okay."

He drove off. "Hell," I muttered to myself. I continued reading and salivating from reports of winter sightings in Florida.

It was time to eat once it became too dark to read. Eating in the dark is sometimes difficult, but that is just as well. When I reached the halfway mark on a can of tasty beans, I was again interrupted. This time two men got out of a state police car. Gone back for reinforcements, I thought. Both challenged their belts, the new guy being as wide as the first. They were a matching set, like a decorative set of salt and pepper shakers, except both were snow-white. One officer, different from my first visitor, approached my side of the car, and the other uniformed cop went to the other side of the car. They dwarfed the little VW. I told them I had already been checked, but this time with the aid of a bright flashlight shining in my eyes was again interrogated. It is amazing how these people think shining a bright light in someone's eyes is supposed to help anyone.

I explained what I was doing, why I was doing it, or at least the best I could, and where I was going.

"Hm. You have any cigarettes?"

By then my nerves were being calmed slightly by a cigarette that I gratefully inhaled. Stupid me, I said yes.

"Humph. How many?" Now the other officer started aiming his flashlight beam inside my car, sweeping back and forth across the still unread *Audubon Field Notes*, an ice chest, and the big wooden box that held my books and papers. The box occupied about two-thirds of the back seat, and, with its door closed, looked suspicious to the overzealous cops. Everything looked suspicious to them, but so did they to me.

"Yeah. How many? Lemme see." It was not a curious "lemme." It was more of a demanding "lemme."

I told them they were in the big wooden box. That excited them. They had caught me red-handed. Three-quarters of a VW back seat full of cigarettes. Even if it was full, I wondered what the big deal was. I only had the four cartons that I had purchased in North Carolina. They were cheaper there than any place I had been. The four cartons totaled $9.40.

Both officers placed their hands hovering over the handles of their holstered guns as I slowly opened the wooden box. Beads of sweat apparently forming under the wide brim of the serve and protect guy nearest me were beginning to run down his round pale pink cheeks. The first objects in the wooden box to come into view were my field guides and other books. "Well, I'll be," muttered one of them. I will be what, I wondered. They wanted to see the state stamps on the individual cigarette packs. Fortunately, each one was stamped properly. They seemed satisfied and drove off.

I went on about my business of finishing my can of baked beans. Later, I had dessert, then an after-meal cigarette, and spent 30 minutes listening to the radio. I was curious if there was any news about the Cuban Missile Crisis and if law enforcement had caught the dangerous ring of cigarette smugglers. I crawled into my berth, went to sleep, but was awakened by the same troopers. Once again, I explained myself but this time I did not talk about birding so much for fear they would lock me up. Another man, who I could faintly see in the edges of the customary blinding flashlights, stood silently while frequently adjusting his necktie and buttoning and unbuttoning his suit jacket. Finally, I was told that the suited person had seen me sitting in my car and reported to the police that he feared I had pulled off the road to die. I choked to hold back laughter and disgust at their lame story. There was enough light from the pesky flashlights to reveal the suited man, also white. He did not at all appear concerned about my well-being and in fact seemed to enjoy watching the badgering police officers. Maybe my interrogation would have gone better if I had been willing to offer a few of my breakfast donuts.

19 November 1962

Waycross beckoned. At last, I was reaching my destination, the Okefenokee Swamp, a 700-square-mile bowl-shaped depression straddling the boundary between the coastal plain of Georgia and Florida. Stephen Foster's Suwannee River begins from the southwest corner of the swamp before emptying into the Gulf of Florida. Information I picked up at Waycross explained that the swamp was 25 miles across and 40 miles long. The Miccosukee Indians called the region Okeefologee, which meant "funnel of water," although some sources state that Okefenokee is a European rendition of an Indian word meaning "land of trembling earth." Funnel of water or trembling earth, the swamp was huge and powerfully thrilling regardless of its etymology. About 331,000 acres of the 400,000-acre swamp were protected by the Okefenokee NWR in 1937. In addition to huge patches of open, slow-moving, brown-stained water are 60,000 acres of what locals call prairie, that is, an open marsh. Huge cypress and understory also occupy this fascinating place. Historically, like everywhere, native use of the region was taken over by European settlers. The Okefenokee Swamp is generally said to be discovered by Europeans, specifically by Spanish explorer Hernando de Soto in 1539, which was centuries after the native discovery and occupation.

Ivan Tompkins told me before I left Savannah to look up Eugene Cypert, the refuge biologist in Waycross. He was not in, but one of the staff told me to call Mrs. Cypert. She said to call Roy Moore, a retired refuge manager, who told me to call Mr. Cypert at 6 p.m. and to wait right there. Mr. Moore said he was planning to be in Waycross soon. Before I could blink, Roy Moore was rushing through the headquarters' front door. We discussed the birding possibilities in the refuge. He seemed disappointed that previous commitments would keep him too busy to help me bird the swamp. Roy was a wealth of information, and even though retired, he clearly had Okefenokee on his mind. He guided me to a nearby roadside picnic area where I could spend the night.

20-21 November 1962

Eugene Cypert answered my 6 p.m. call last night. He told me to meet him early in the morning at refuge headquarters. Following hasty introductions, I was once again a passenger riding in a refuge vehicle and on my way south to Fargo, then up a road paralleling the Suwannee River to, appropriately, Stephen C. Foster State Park. No other roads penetrate Okefenokee. This is a place for boats, and Eugene and I were soon skimming the black water in a small craft powered by a tiny outboard and a long push-pole in case of an emergency. That the top of the gunwale was only about eight inches above the water surely hinted being swamped in the swamp. Fortunately, alligator feeding time was not today, and our gentle wake barely disturbed the dead-calm surface. Not a drop of Okefenokee water came on board as we sliced deeper and deeper to the heart of Pogo land.

Our cruise had a mission. We were not just going on a casual tour; we were going to count everything we saw. The official census began at Billy's Lake near the boat dock. The "lake" was a narrow channel of open water surrounded by towering cypress and a thick understory of deciduous brush. Our goal was to count the big birds, the ibises, herons, ducks, and hawks. Little time was allowed for small birds, but I was still looking for gnatcatchers and Yellow-throated Warblers.

We entered Floyd's Prairie about five miles from the boat dock. The 60,000 acres of prairies are wet marshy areas once ravaged by drought-induced fires that not only destroyed most of the trees but also smoldered into the thick peat below. A large white bird, with black flight feathers and large oversized bill, flew from one lone tree to another. The bird, a Wood Stork, is locally called flinthead. We found more flintheads, all of which, like the alligators, allowed us to approach closely. The survey included every Anhinga splash, every egret flying, and every kingfisher rattle. Surprised Black-crowned Night-herons, Great and Little Blue herons, Sandhill Cranes rattling their rolling *kerooo* just out of sight, and flushed Wood Ducks were all tallied. We estimated the number forming the chorus of Carolina Wrens that filled the air during our journey of pastoral beauty and delightful awe.

Strange panoramas changed constantly. The dark water formed a polished glass surface that reflected every detail. It was as if we were skimming through the swamp on a horizontal mirror. We could look up or down and enjoyed the same view, the reflection, and the actual scene. Even birds flitting in the moss-draped cypresses reflected in the flat glassy water, as did every brilliant hue of the black gums and blue sky. Cypress knees spiraled above us in the shade of their own trunks, and alligators slowly sank below the peaceful surface as our boat approached almost too close for their comfort as well as mine. Shadowy pools, little islands of peat 15 feet thick, cypress and other trees, and more of the same stretched for miles in all directions. We motored north through Minnie Lake and beyond to a place marked on the map as "Dinner Pond." By boat, we had traveled about 12 miles. If we got into trouble, we were on our own, with no walkie-talkie or anyway to call for help.

Besides birds, we surveyed alligators for number and length. Determining length was accomplished by measuring, at a distance, of course, the distance from their nostrils to their eyes. Every inch between those features, attractive only to another alligator, is supposed to equal a foot of actual length. Judging from the nose to eyeball equation, several were longer than me. I kept my hands in the boat, especially at Dinner Pond.

Before turning back, we stopped to check a refuge cabin that was built on a hammock at the edge of Big Water. We glided into shore. Because I was at the bow, I jumped out on what appeared solid land to secure the boat. The Indian gods must have laughed. The land of trembling earth taught me a lesson as I began sinking fast. From the corner of my eye, I saw something move. Was this a time to apply the nose to eyeball equation? The soft wet peat sucked at my legs. I grabbed at a slippery cypress knee, and then pulled one leg at a time to the surface. I did not lose my boots, and I did not lose my life.

With humility and mucky wetness, but with an eye for birds, we returned to the dock at Billy's Lake. Back on firm land, Eugene and a state park official discussed refuge boundary. While I waited, six raccoons suddenly appeared. It was time for their appointed feeding by one of the park employees. Deer also showed up for snacks, and skunks roamed the parking area looking for crumbs. All but one skunk was black and white striped; the odd one was brown and white. I kept a respectable distance from the skunks, thinking that my rotten peat smell might seem competitive.

Luckily, I was able to find a place for a shower and changed clothes before driving southeast of Waycross. On 22 November, I found a suitable place for the night north of a little town called Mattox, over 10 miles east-southeast of Big Water and on drier and more solid ground. My notes were up to date, it was getting dark, and I was hungry. However, a patrol car pulled up. It was the county sheriff, who said he was just checking, and, with a grin, suggested I drive into Folkston to tell the "boys" at the office that he sent me in "to fix me up for a place to stay." Maybe it was a gesture of kindness. Maybe being fixed up was an invitation to sleep where I did not want to sleep, a place known as jail. Since it was only a suggestion, I decided to stay put. During the night, I wondered if my decision would be changed for me or was the sheriff actually protecting and serving. Sleep finally came but not before I entertained the thought that the regional constabulary were following Georgia's nineteenth-century history and, because of months of my outdoor suntan, had mistaken me for a native that should have been on the Trail of Tears.

22 November 1962

It was Thanksgiving Day, and I was out of breakfast donuts. Instead, I ate sweet rolls to the sound of traffic zooming by and faint singing of distant Carolina Wrens. I was halfway through my oh-so continental breakfast when a dark green Ford came to a screeching stop. A man jumped out. It was Eugene, who said he had seen my car and stopped to invite me to accompany him on a short excursion into Okefenokee Swamp. I was delighted and glad I had not taken the suggestion of last night's lawman.

We launched a boat from Camp Cornelia, traveling west in the Suwannee Canal, south to Chesser Prairie, and east of Seagrove Lake, about a 12-mile round trip. The mission was to band Wood Ducks and open the traps since no one could check them during the remainder of the day. The wind blew through our clothes and buffeted the water. Our boat had a deeper hull than the one yesterday. I was relieved. There were only five traps to tend and each one was empty. I was disappointed at not having the opportunity to band Wood Ducks but grateful for the two-hour cruise into the swamp. For the second time, I thanked and said goodbye to Eugene Cypert.

The remainder of 22 November was the end of my time in Okefenokee Swamp. I drove south from Folkston, Georgia, on US 1 to Callahan, Florida, leaving behind the mysterious beauty of tea-colored waters, cypress knees, alligators, and birds. I would never read *Pogo* the same way again. I was lucky that I had Okefenokee on my mind.

∽

With considerable apologies to the great Ray Charles, I admit my favorite crooner singing "Georgia on My Mind" is Willie Nelson. The song "Georgia on My Mind" was composed in 1930 by Hoagy Carmichael, who wrote the music, and Stewart Gorrell, who penned the unforgettable lyrics. Written with thoughts of Carmichael's sister Georgia—or was he thinking of the state of Georgia, a location neither Carmichael nor Gorrell were from—the song became the official state song of Georgia in 1979. A check of the lyrics reveals no mention of Okefenokee or even Savannah. Having the memory of being hounded three times by Georgian law enforcers is part of Georgia's Okefenokee on my own mind. Of course, there were some good people, including everyone at Okefenokee and Savannah refuges and Ivan Tompkins.

Besides having Okefenokee on my mind, I did have those pesky Russian missiles in Cuba on my mind. I missed the news and the people I met along the way were not discussing what was particularly good news, that being we were out of danger of being blown to smithereens. Luckily, by 2 November, cooler heads prevailed, and I would live to see another bird.

One situation that the lyrics of "Georgia on My Mind" does not address was the law looking askance at young teenagers suspiciously stalking Okefenokee birds. I wondered if my perceived untrustiness was a southeastern law enforcement thing. Maybe the problem was my vehicle, a German product in the land of Fords and Chevys. Could there have been an issue concerning the color of my face and arms? Maybe it was my dark brown eyes, always searching the trees and sky. Although somewhat of a mutt, I have been told that the bulk of me, my genes, come from people once residing in the mountains of northern Georgia. And, it so happens that with just a little sun, which after about a half-year I had plenty, my tanned skin becomes washed with a reddish tone. Was I rousted by the long arm of the law because I looked like the people once forced from native homeland? Was I identified as an ancestral stray? Maybe I was targeted by the law only because I was looking for birds.

Among the 14 species of shorebirds seen with Ivan Tompkins was the rather nondescript grayish Willet that reveals itself best by its flashy black and white wings and loud and distinctive call. For those paying attention to the taxonomy of Willets, Ivan played a significant role in 1955 and 1965 when he published two major papers on Willets. Two populations of Willets occur in North America. They look and sound different. The western population breeds from the southern prairie provinces of Canada to parts of the northern US prairie west to eastern Oregon and northern Nevada, and the eastern population breeds along the coasts of Newfoundland southward along the Atlantic coast. The breeding ranges of the two populations are separate. The keepers of checklists, in this case, a committee of the American Ornithologists Society, rather than ruffle the feathers of the status quo, have thus far been reluctant to accept published evidence that two species of Willets should be recognized.

Not surprisingly, the Willet was considered rare in Okefenokee NWR, a refuge full of other Georgian wildlife. One of the opossums I saw in Okefenokee might have been related to Walter Kelly's popular comic strip *Pogo*. During the stay in Okefenokee, I did manage to find 48 species, which must have included a few of the several depicted in the comic strip. However, my overall effort to see as many species of birds as possible was not panning out. At the time, I wondered why. When I arrived at Okefenokee, I pulled out from my magic wooden box in the back seat of the VW the checklist of birds of the refuge that was mailed to me months before leaving Oregon. Sixteen of the 201 species in the 1960 checklist were species I needed to see; species required to boost my trip list. Only two species were contenders, the rest were marginally possible, but their occurrence was sparse, and some species had migrated southward. Today, I would have planned better by considering the frequency of occurrence and abundance of any given species at any given locality. During the planning stage of the trip, Okefenokee Swamp was added to the itinerary more as me wishing for a chance encounter with a legendary place. From studying the checklist while back in Oregon, I reasoned Okefenokee would not be a hotspot for birds, but it would be a fantastic spot to visit and enjoy the essence of the largest swamp in North America. Looking back, I made the correct choice.

Changes have occurred since visiting the two refuges and part of coastal Georgia. Hilton Head's population of about 40,000 is increasing annually by 32 percent and is visited by 2.5 million tourists in recent years. Much smaller and less beleaguered Tybee Island's population has almost tripled since 1960, going from 1,385 to 3,093 though a hydrogen bomb was misplaced nearby in 1958. The truth of that scary thought remains lost. Oh well.

Savannah NWR grew from over 12,000 acres to 28,000 acres. Okefenokee NWR grew from 331,000 to 353,981 acres, with a large part designated a National Wilderness Area in 1974. The population of Waycross, just north of Okefenokee NWR headquarters, peaked to about 20,000 in 1960 and dropped to an estimated 13,354 in 2021. In the meantime, Okefenokee Swamp was, in 2019, threatened by outside forces. An Alabama company planned a strip mine for heavy metal in a region bordering Okefenokee NWR. DuPont Company once made a similar plan in the late 1990s but abandoned the idea after widespread opposition that eventually led to DuPont donating 16,000 acres to The Conservation Fund, which, in 2005, transferred 7,000 acres to the refuge. It appears that the Alabama company, experiencing considerable opposition, has, as of March 2021, withdrawn its destructive mining plan. Okefenokee Swamp, everywhere really, is also under constant threat from wildfires. Hundreds of thousands of acres of the refuge burned just a few years ago. What habitat is not drained, logged, mined, or otherwise severely altered is kindling forever for frequent wildfires.

As Rosanne Roseannadanna warned, "It's always something" and that holds true to Savannah and Okefenokee swamps, along with Great Dismal Swamp. These world-class habitats have one thing in common: manipulated water levels. Savannah Harbor expansion will lead to too much water in the Savannah NWR. In the case of Okefenokee and Great Dismal Swamps, people wanted to remove water to access land and timber. Plans to drain Okefenokee began in the late 1800s. Logging the cypress began in 1900. Over 431 million board feet of timber were removed from Okefenokee by 1927 when logging operations stopped. Ten years later, a large part of the swamp was protected as the Okefenokee NWR. The same timber removing forces, once the Union Bag and Paper Corporation, later called Union Camp acquired by International Paper around 2004, were instrumental in donating and selling land to the Okefenokee refuge, although usually timber rights to such transactions were retained.

The thousands and thousands of acres of Great Dismal and Okefenokee swamps and boreal forests in Canada look different partly because of our consumption of paper. In 2020, 461 million metric tons of paper were predicted to be consumed, give or take a ream or two. A recent source decried that a US citizen would consume 680 pounds of paper per year. I find that hard to believe although I do notice that each new edition of my favorite field guide is heavier with more pages than the previous printing. Nonetheless, I sure do not want to use a lot of paper explaining my disbelief that I and others used that much paper. The use of computers was suspected to cut the use of paper, but the paper consumption and computers are both increasing. That would mean everyone now is using even more paper, and we are. Even e-commerce consumes it by the ton. Most of the paper we consume, about 90 percent, is from virgin tree fibers. Although the fibers can be recycled about a dozen times before becoming too short for paper production, and, although the quality of recycled paper is comparable to paper from virgin fibers, less than 10 percent of the paper we use is recycled. Once used, we flush it, shred it, and fill 40 percent of landfills with unread and unwanted catalogs, advertisements, newspapers, old bird books, you name it. Some of it goes up in smoke, and I am not going to contribute to paper use about what burning does to the environment. Paper is supposed to be biodegradable but that depends on exposure to environmental elements. If scattered loosely, paper might biodegrade in two to five months, but much more time is required if compacted.

With all that said, COVID-19 changed the dynamics of paper consumption. It is said that consumption of paper, in general, went down between 2019 to 2020 as the virus ravaged the planet. Well, maybe, but what about all that hoarded toilet paper?

Chapter 18

Florida, the Early Miles

23–25 November 1962

After the barrage of billboards at the border crossing, I entered Jacksonville, Florida. Many Carolinians had insisted I look up enthusiastic Mrs. Edna Appleberry, better known as The Fabulous Mrs. A. She answered my phone call with an invitation and directions to her home. In a few minutes, I was there, where I was given several names and addresses of people to see down the Florida coast followed by her offer of her kitchen and a spare bedroom. Mrs. A might have thought my skinny frame needed help. Unfortunately, a field trip was not possible since Mrs. A and her husband did not have a car and my thoroughly packed home on wheels had stuff right up to the bottom of the windows. We talked birds into the night.

The next morning Mrs. A sent me to the Jacksonville Zoo where I would meet a local birder she knew. While waiting for my contact, I had a surprising conversation with an employee of one of the concessions. A merry-go-round operator saw me and asked why I was wearing binoculars. I told him I was looking for birds. He said, "You mean you're a birdwatcher?"

"Yes," I replied.

"Oh," he blurted, adding, "I ain't never seen one before, but heard a lot about 'em."

I laughed. "Well, how do we look different?"

He stammered. Evidently, he did not expect me to say what I did. Finally, he said, "No, I didn't mean a difference, I just can't see lookin' at birds, that's all."

After some questions, I discovered his hobby was watching baseball games. We then exchanged comments on our passions, and I think he realized that bird watchers were not strange people after all.

The contact did not appear but the day was not over. As earlier arranged through Mrs. A, I arrived at the home of W. C. Davis. Hardly had I gotten out of the car when I began seeing birds. Pine, Black and White, and Myrtle warblers joined 27 other species found on the property during the next 45 minutes. Mr. Davis and I then walked toward Fort George Island, once land for a small fort, plantations, a country club, and finally a state park. North of the St. John's River huge heaps of shells along the road were possibly once large sturdy burial vaults made of whole oyster shells mixed with sand that Native Americans called tabby houses. Natives also used oyster shells for money. Today, I was told, the shells are important for road surfaces, chicken grit, and more. Four Common Ground Doves were life birds. These small doves were reluctant to fly, allowed close observation of their pearly necks and their deep monotoned voice. Blue-gray Gnatcatchers were still missing from my trip list, and the growing wind made it difficult to hear or to see bird movements.

The sun was going down as we arrived at Davis's neighbors who were hosting an oyster roast, a novelty for the Davises and certainly new to me. I tried a couple of raw oysters and did not care for more. Getting roasted oysters was a slow process since only two people could eat at a time. When my turn came, I increased the food value by adding tomato sauce and crackers. Everyone there, and certainly the Davises and I, hurried home to bolster what really had been an appetizer.

Before we left, a hunter fired a gun near the house. Mr. Davis, 54, although not in good health, walked with long purposeful strides as he stormed out of the house toward the sound of the gun. The property had "No Trespassing" signs and it was, I was informed later, against the law to shoot near a house or a road. Noticing that Mr. Davis had been gone a long time, I stepped out of the house to see what was going on. Mr. Davis and the shooter had been talking and as I arrived, Mr. Davis called the mid-twentyish shooter a liar. The young man called Mr. Davis an SOB. In heated seconds, Mr. Davis jumped the man who defended himself by socking the 54-year-old. Both were scuffling as I tried to stop the fight. It is not easy to try parting fighting men. I squeezed in and out between them, pulling, tugging, and talking to them as I hoped to calm them. At first, they did not seem to realize I was even between them, but eventually, they calmed down, perhaps not wanting to sock the skinny kid from Oregon. No one was hurt. The young guy even apologized for unlawfully firing a gun near the house and for fighting Mr. Davis. In the fracas, I thought I heard a Barred Owl.

My third day in the Jacksonville region included a hike on the two-mile-long north jetty of the St. John's River. Horned Grebe or a new tern seemed possible. Sunday anglers decorated the huge boulders. Ocean waves colliding against the huge granite rocks sent spray across my path and onto the placid riverside of the jetty. Constantly wet, some of the rocks of the jetty were said to weigh up to seven tons and were green with slippery algae. The wind blew hard, softened only by a sea mist picked up from the growing whitecaps. Brown Pelicans and gannets seemed unconcerned as anglers and one birder struggled on the narrow knife reaching seaward. The irregular and sometimes slippery footing made me feel vulnerable and appreciative of a simple stroll on the sandy beach. No grebes or terns were found.

The ferry crossing the St. John's River to Mayport was uneventful. South on Highway A1A, the road closest to the beach, brought me to a wide shoulder for the night. Before sunset, I hiked over the dunes and down the beach for about a mile looking at terns. Most of them were in small flocks mixed with larger gatherings of Ring-billed and Laughing gulls. The terns were all Forester's. Then I got lucky. While glassing over another gathering of gulls and terns, a strange bird flew into view. My trusty 20x scope on its rifle stock magnified a small crested tern with a yellow-tipped black bill. At last, I had a new tern, a lifer, a Sandwich Tern. The name and the hour reminded me to get back home, my VW parked on the sandy shoulder of the now deserted highway. It was time to eat and sleep to the rustle of the wind and surf of a growing storm.

26–27 November 1962

A wind woke me in the gray light of early morning. It shook the VW, overhead palms swayed, and the stiff palmetto leaves rattled together as a definite nor'easter breathed its damp chilly air on the cloudy Sunshine State. Discouraged, I went through the motions of eating, stowing my bed, and headed for the nearest and out of sight place to pee. The road now carried a few cars at the time. Otherwise, I would have reversed the last activity with the first and it was far more comfortable too.

Dubious about looking for birds in the unfriendly weather, I drove south to meet Mrs. Victor Rahner, the club president of the St. Augustine bird club. I hoped to join a field trip planned for tomorrow. While waiting, I strolled around the old Castillo de San Marcos, aka the Castle of Saint Mark. A brochure I picked up earlier informed me that the castle was built to protect St. Augustine from raids by the English pirate Sir Francis Drake. Constructed in the late 1600s from shell and mortar from shell lime, the structure was under several flags, first under Spanish, then British for 20 years, then again by the Spanish from 1783 to 1821, the United States and briefly by Confederates in 1862, followed by the Union flag. The US flag was now straining at the flagpole as I waited for my contact and details for the field trip tomorrow. I walked around the castle, reading plaques, and wondered what birds had passed by during its history. There was not anything to see today. I also wondered where I would spend the night and found the deserted information center parking lot was perfect.

The next morning's weather was better than yesterday though the wind continued to bluster and the temperature was too, too cold when I crawled out of bed. In a few minutes, I was at a grocery store parking lot waiting for the field trip group to arrive. Finally, a car arrived, and a little old lady walked up and asked who was leading the trip. Later, a car from New Jersey arrived. They said they heard about the trip on the radio. At last, Mrs. Rahner arrived. She had an apologetic expression when she announced to the small group that the trip was called off because of weather. She then approached me and asked questions about my trip. The wind continued to continue its blowing, carrying stinging sand through my denim jeans. Mrs. Rahner and I continued talking for an hour in the shelter of her car while poring over a local map where I might try my luck.

During the next five hours, I searched for birds in an unsuccessful housing project called St. Augustine South. Roads, some of them paved, were laid out in right angles, and inside the blocks were live oaks, pines, and dominating palmettos. Although I was about a mile inland, the northeast wind blew cold and harder than at the beach. The vegetation shook. Finding a dainty Blue-gray Gnatcatcher was not going to be easy. In the end, I identified only 14 species and let one possible life warbler get away. It was either a Connecticut or Mourning Warbler, but I could not get a sufficient look at its eye-ring if it had one. The plate of confusing fall warblers Peterson illustrated was confusing.

28 November 1962

Leaving last night's roadside parking, I arrived at peaceful Crescent Beach on Anastasia Island where submarine springs 2.5 miles offshore discharge 10 to 300 cubic feet of freshwater per second. Mrs. Rahner suggested I might find a stray Wilson's Plover there. The wind carried the white beach past my feet as smaller grains of sand bit through my clothes and into my skin. The damp veil that shrouded the car overnight was heavier at the beach and it clung to my clothes, making them heavy with cold moisture. High tide was now four to six feet above normal. Six species of shorebirds huddled together in a flattened cove of dunes. Even the robust Sanderlings were not charging back and forth at the edge of the surf. Gulls and terns stood in rows, facing into the wind. Black Skimmers were grounded as the powerful northeaster bore its brunt.

At the Matanzas Inlet Bridge more gulls, terns, and skimmers sat out the storm. A Brown Pelican turned its back to the wind only to have its feathers stand on end, nearly pushing over the hapless bird. A feisty Sanderling was keeping other birds, especially other Sanderlings, away from itself until a Ruddy Turnstone, seeking shelter, landed. The Sanderling scuttled toward the turnstone, but the larger bird pointed its turnstone beak at the attacker and quickly ended the Sanderling's little dictatorship.

The timing could not have been better today if not for birding. It was almost too windy to see birds and Marineland was just down the road. At least I had something to do while waiting out the storm. Coughing up the $2.75 for admission and a booklet on the facility was hard on my budget. Ignoring that the amount could buy a tank of gas, I immediately began to enjoy the 2,000 species of fish, turtles, porpoises, and whales. The porpoise show started a few minutes before my arrival. Portholes allowed viewing the animals before they jumped out of the water for their fish reward. At one tank were sharks, curious black drum, a member of the croaker family, angelfish, with black and yellow spots and stripes, rock beauties full of gold and black hues, the yellowtails, and my favorite, the queen triggerfish. This oddly marked reef fish is striking, with its several brilliant blue lines in contrast to its charcoal upperparts that blend gradually onto a soft cream-colored breast. I toured and revisited tanks and the water show for three hours. On the way back to the car I found 15 Palm Warblers crowding a bush just out of the force of the northeaster.

29–30 November 1962

After a roadside stand for the night north of Daytona Beach, I spent the morning typing the notes for the last couple of days. As I wrote, I was surprised to hear a strange noise sounding like a sick grackle. I turned toward the sound and saw a Florida Scrub-Jay sitting on a palmetto.[1] If I had not seen the bird, I would not have believed it was the same species as the western birds I watched stealing almonds from my backyard in Oregon. The morning was also occupied with trying to clean the worst of the inside of the car, including sweeping out about two cups of sand, inventorying my

1. In 1962, Scrub-jays in Florida were treated as a conspecific of all other scrub-jays.

food supply, and determining how many more days I could go before having to do dreaded laundry.

Atlantic shore, Flagler Beach, Florida.

On the way south, I stopped at Flagler Beach, where an apparent storm-driven Sooty Shearwater skimmed near the shore. At Daytona Beach, I called the person Mrs. Rahner had recommended. Unfortunately, the contact did not have a car, and, if I made space for a passenger, where would I temporarily store all that filled the jump seat? I apologized that I could not make the room in the VW and drove back to Ormond Beach where I met George Williams, director of the Halifax River Audubon Society's weekly field trips. An English accented voice directed me to a small house where George and his wife Kay asked me to be their guest. It was soon revealed they were from Boston, not England.

The next morning and the last day of November started with a few fleecy clouds and a sunny blue sky. It was a relief after the northeaster. At a designated meeting place, the bird club gathered for a half-day trip in the Daytona Beach region. George wrangled us in four cars, with the lead car piloted by Conrad Ekdahl, the car I was riding. Of several stops, one was at a slaughterhouse. Doomed bovines were surrounded by Cattle Egrets, an alien species wandering to the New World under its own power. The egret's yellow bills flashed in the sun as they walked as barnyard chickens, their heads moving back and forth in perfect unison with each step. On our way back to the car, I mentioned hoping to see gnatcatchers and Yellow-throated Warblers. As I finished the sentence, something moved in a palm nearby. A couple of Blue-gray Gnatcatchers foraged just overhead. Several more were seen before the trip ended. Back at the car, someone yelled "Yellow-throated Warbler." I hurried toward the observer, got directions where to look, and was soon looking at my third life bird for the day.

The last stop was at Orange Point where a Bald Eagle was seen circling over the water and where milling gulls and tern followed a shrimp boat into the harbor. We were about to leave when someone saw a Horned Grebe. I aimed the scope and found a second bird matching the other by its winter plumage. I thanked the group for showing me the new birds and tallied the list of 72 species, a total not too bad for a few hours of birding.

The kitchen at the Williams home had been freshly painted and friends, knowing this, thoughtfully invited everyone to dinner. It was a fish fry.

1–2 December 1962

Yesterday must have been a lull in the storm. Today the wind was again from the northeast, and it was cold, accompanied by a mist tumbling down from the heavy gray clouds. It was a day to stay indoors. However, by evening, we left to brave the weather and a dinner invitation of one of the groups on yesterday's field trip. I felt hesitant to join, but the Williamses said they considered me a grandson. That embarrassed me, but I was grateful for their generous friendship. We dined in what I consider a formal cafeteria, even though the establishment let me in. After dinner, we joined our host in his home where we were served tequila and coffee brandy purchased by our host in Texas at a National Audubon Society convention. I was interested in the birds seen in Texas and tried not to be too annoying with questions. As we were leaving, our host asked what I was going to do for a career. I told him ornithology. Very seriously, he said that he was sure that everything about birds had already been learned and that the only thing to expect is changes of opinions. I hope that I did not offend him or humiliate anyone when I told our host, very seriously and as politely as possible, that he was wrong.

The next morning's weather looked good for the trip to the interior of Florida from Ormand Beach to Osteen Marshes and Wikeva River north of Orlando. We also stopped along the St. John's River, the same stream that terminates at Jacksonville and originates 310 miles to the south. Limpkins were promised. We stopped along the road bordering the river several times, once when five Hooded Mergansers floated into view. I had missed them on their breeding range. Anhinga, ibis, two species of vultures, Tree Swallows, Eastern Meadowlarks, and more were checked off. By 2 p.m., our stomachs began to protest not being fed. Ignoring hunger and when on a bridge spanning the narrow Wikeva River, we heard an unforgettable call. A large brownish bird with a slightly down-curved bill fluttered from one riverbank to the other. Then another bird landed on a nearby island and began searching for what I knew to be snails. It was joined, but not by the first bird, which called a loud *kra-ow* from the opposite bank. Limpkins, their look, and sound made me feel I had entered the tropics.

3 December 1962

Kay and George Williams and I stood at the edge of the driveway. Before saying goodbye, they invited me for Christmas. I said I would but was not sure where I would be at that time, and I thanked them for taking me into their home and showing me the local birds. We were all a little teary-eyed as I crawled into the car. I drove only about 10 miles out of town, found a wide pullout, and bore down on getting my notes up to date. Tomorrow, I hoped to be at Audubon House in Maitland. Laundry was still on the to-do list.

4–6 December 1962

Maitland, a small town of people and orange groves northeast of Orlando, was home to the Florida Audubon Society. Margaret Hundley, director of field trips, publications, and research, outlined where I might find Dusky Seaside Sparrows and good places to visit in the Keys, and introduced me to Russ Mason, the boss of the place. A live White-bellied Stork, an African species that someone caught in Massachusetts, had been sent for rehabilitation. There were other birds worse for wear, the worst being a supposed Cory's Shearwater that was dug up from its grave. Mrs. Hundley wanted to open the packaged corpse but was afraid of what awful smell might waft its way into the office. I was curious, but several tiny and possibly hungry gnats buzzing around the package seemed a good sign that the carcass would stink up the whole place. The job of feeding the stork was offered so long as I kept my hand clear of the long bill. By the end of the day, someone suggested I could find a corner in the building for my sleeping bag. That was a fine idea.

The next morning brought a surprise. Russ and Margaret, as it now seemed okay to call them, wanted to interview me for a taped radio program.

Stage fright was immediate, but I agreed. The interview started: "This is Margaret Hundley, and the program is Audubon Highlights presented by the Florida Audubon Society in cooperation with the Rollins College Radio Department and coming to you through the courtesy of your local radio station." After being introduced, Russ and Margaret alternately asked me questions such as what am I doing, where am I going, what outstanding species were seen, how much time in Florida and elsewhere, and are you keeping records? The broadcast was statewide, but I never heard it.

The remainder of the day was much easier. I spent time browsing the wonderful library and earning my keep by carrying boxes, sweeping, and totting for the industrious staff. Being slightly embarrassed was not over. The day after the radio interview Russ surprised me by introducing me at an Audubon benefit. There I stood in my faded sports shirt, worn jeans, and ragged shoes. Thank goodness speaking was not required.

The radio interview and introduction at the benefit were difficult, although I otherwise enjoyed everyone and every minute at Audubon House. I could have learned so much, but I needed to move on.

7–8 December 1962

Pettingill recommended Merritt Island was the place to see Dusky Seaside Sparrows, and my arrival there yesterday was early enough to look for birds in the nearly cold 40 degrees and strong wind. That did not discourage an attempt to find a Dusky Seaside Sparrow but my effort was futile. Temperatures rose and the wind slowed in the morning. Again, finding the sparrow was unsuccessful.

Giving up, but only momentarily, I drove south to Rockledge and, by invitation, to the home of Allan and Helen Cruickshank. Allan had suggested in a letter that I stop by. He had just returned two hours earlier from New York attending the funeral of Mrs. Rosalie Edge, founder of Hawk Mountain. The Brouns must have been there. It had been a little over three months since seeing them. My world seemed smaller.

At first, it was Mr. Cruickshank, but soon Allan seemed appropriate. He went over my trip list while keeping an ear open for a Painted Bunting, a species I had not yet seen. Allan told me that I had seen most of what should be expected in this area and named off several species I could pick up if I was further north. I commented that I should have reversed my route and he assured me that it was impossible to be in all the best places at the right time, a paraphrase of advice Peterson wrote earlier to me. Suddenly, Allan stood up and told me to follow him to the scope aimed from the living room to a bird feeder in the yard. Squinting through the scope, I saw my first Painted Bunting, a species I dreamed about since becoming a birder. The bunting was mostly green, not the bright male I imagined would be my first sighting of the species.

The bird feeder, which was called a cage feeder, was a wooden frame about 20 by 20 inches draped with one-half-inch mesh wire. Wary House Sparrows stayed out because they felt enclosed, and larger birds, of course, could not get to the food. Buntings could slip through the wire and did not seem bothered by being enclosed.

Allan invited me to take part in the Cocoa Christmas Bird Count, the count he led and that has, for many years, recorded more species than any other count. Last year (1961) the Cocoa group found 191 species. The chances of seeing any new trip birds were remote, but it was an honor to be a member of the group. Just before leaving the Cruickshanks, Allan went over a few details of the count and urged me to come back a day ahead of the count to "get our signals straight."

Allan called W. Foster White, resident of Merritt Island, the hamlet, to arrange for me a tour of the northern end of Merritt Island, the island. The next day, I met Foster at his home, where three male Painted Buntings were at a feeder three feet away. What a brilliant spectacle. Minutes later, we were traveling north on highway A1A and back to State 402 where I had earlier searched for Dusky Seaside Sparrows. The wind calmed to a breeze and to a warmer day today. We followed the dike into the Merritt Island marsh another mile and stopped. A bright yellow truck belonging to the mosquito control division drove up and Chuck Trots leaned out. "You don't look like duck hunters to me." Though young, Chuck was locally known as the leading authority on the Dusky Seaside Sparrow. Foster, Chuck, and I began scanning every piece of marsh dominated by *Juncus*, a genus of grass and other short saw grasses, spishing between about two dozen periodically heard shotgun blasts from hunters. Chuck said that in the summer squeaking would bring the birds up, that is if they were not already singing in plain view. He had completed an ecological study on the sparrows and mosquito control and said that by next year the birds will be protected, even from birders, when the Bureau of Aeronautics-Space Division will restrict public access to Merritt Island.

Several times, we glimpsed birds that could have been our quarry. Suddenly something dark fluttered across an opening in the grass and just as quickly dropped out of sight. I was practically on top of it when the bird flushed. Luckily, I saw the black plumage and rufous nape. The Black Rail was not a bad bird to find, but I was intent on finding the sparrow. Eventually, we turned back toward the vehicles where a pair of hip boots might help me find the elusive main event. The idea of wading in the marsh was not appealing, but I was still high from seeing the Black Rail and had high hopes for the sparrow. On the way back, two Mottled Ducks flew in for a landing runway between the saw grass, unnoticed by the platoon of great white hunters.

The necessity of pulling on the dreaded hip boots was becoming more and more likely just before Foster yelled out "Dusky." With binoculared stares, a bird filled the lenses. The striking bird was similar to the regular Seaside Sparrow that I first observed on the New Jersey coast months ago. However, the Merritt Island bird lacked the blended hues of the northern sparrow by having an obvious black and white pattern, but it had the seaside mark, the yellow area in front of the eye. [The yellow region is known by the fancy term supraloral spot.] Although it may someday be regarded as a subspecies of the regular northern birds, I feel lucky to see it.

Chuck later drove Foster and me into more inaccessible parts of the Merritt Island marsh. Our bumpy ride put us a few feet from a nesting pair of Bald Eagles. Chuck hoped the rare eagles could successfully produce young, but the use of insecticides had caused low reproductive rates in birds, especially birds of prey. We also found numerous individual wounded ducks, carcasses of less edible coots, and dead and wounded gallinules, a Great Blue Heron, a Red-shouldered Hawk, and various other birds of varying degrees of injury and decomposition. All were near empty shotgun shells.

Later, I drove just outside of the town of Cape Canaveral near the restricted southern boundary of Cape Canaveral Air Force Station. On a dike just off a sandy road, I found an incoming tide and finally, a Wilson's Plover. There were three of them and they were alive.

Ever since arriving on the Atlantic coast, I marveled at the numerous jetties formed from dark chunks of rocks stacked in piles from a beach and extending seaward. Of course, I had noticed jetties up the Atlantic coast, but for some unexplained reason, the jetties in Florida piqued my curiosity beyond normality. Perhaps it had something to do with the fact I was 18 and still circulating teenage blood in a brain not sure where I might land. Maybe the fascination about jetties somehow related to the several tall bridges crossed along my path. There are few tall bridges in Florida so perhaps the jetties were replacing my interest in bridges. I do recall not being so enamored when revisiting a jetty or two in Florida as a seasoned adult. Had a jetty then been under construction, I believe I would stop and watch the process. People do appreciate those viewing spaces at construction site, those windows allowing us to watch others change a landscape. Is that morbid curiosity? Man-made jetties, by definition, are not natural and what is unnatural often has a harmful consequence, one that might mean life or death to the environment. Perhaps my interest in jetties was wanting to know how man constructed something that, by consensus, is adversely changing the coastal environment. I wonder how jetties will weather rising sea levels and try to imagine our coastal waters unimpeded by jetties and their smaller relatives, groins and seawalls.

Most jetties are on both sides of rivers, extending the riverbanks away from land, thus allowing water craft to avoid dangerous surf and to safely navigate the course between the river and the sea. Jetties might function as barriers to alter water movements and thereby help control erosion. Of course, any diverted sand must go somewhere and the end result might not be beneficial. That is when it is time to bring out the dredges and other earth-gouging devices invented for alteration of the natural environment.

At 18 years of age, my recollection of jetties and groins was limited. What I then wanted to know was how are jetties constructed? How did those huge boulders get there? Jetty 101 tells us jetties are piles of rocks hauled from some rocky locality and placed perpendicular to a sandy beach. Rocks of assorted sizes were first delivered to otherwise rockless beaches by wagons and later by rail car, the temporary rails built on the top of a jetty as it was extended further and further seaward. Trucks and cranes might be used today.

The north jetty of the St. John's River juts over a mile from the sandy beach of Huguenot Memorial Park, a city park of Jacksonville. The region was settled by French Huguenots in 1564, and construction of the jetty began in 1880 and may have been completed by 1892. It was planned to be 1.8 miles in length, but it is closer to 1.6 miles long. Standing between 6 to 14 feet high, it is 10 feet wide at its top or crown. Its base, like that of an iceberg, is much wider. Originally, brush and wood formed a mat for the heavy rocks. Later, jetty builders realized that invertebrates were eating the mats and the builders discovered that it was best to start with smaller stones and place larger ones on top. The stones are called rip rap and armor stones. Larger stones, during the early building, weighed about 4 tons, and by 1928, they were using 7-ton boulders. During a major repair to the north jetty in 1934, 25- to 100-pound rocks were placed on the ocean side to fill in voids and arrest shifting sand, and in 1938, a concrete cap was added. Some repairs were made the year before my visit. Around 21,500 tons of stone for $398,000 was added to the jetty in 1969.

In my journal, I reported the north jetty as about two miles in length and did not state how far I hiked on it. Repairs were made in 1961 so I likely hiked seaward as far as humanly possible being the fearless young Danny McSkunk I was in 1962. According to recent satellite photographs (e.g., Google Earth 2015), the jetty is in considerable disrepair and missing the smooth and walkable concrete cap. The north jetty is mentioned as a place to possibly find Purple Sandpipers in winter. As with most jetties, birding the north jetty of the St. John's River may be hazardous to one's health and is likely dependent on weather and conditions of the sea, the surface of the jetty itself, and the birder. Those giant jetty boulders, often challenging the surest of foot, may be slippery when wet and hard to resist since they are often great places for wintering Purple Sandpiper, turnstones, and who knows.

The St. Augustine South failed housing project did not last forever. By 2019, 5,431 people lived in the once quiet acres of palmetto and pines. Nearby Crescent Beach in 1962 seemed desolate; by 2019, 1,118 people lived there and the region thrives with places to feed and house throngs of tourists. Florida, like so many states, loses scores of acres of natural habitat per hour. The bulldozer brigade plunders on to make room for an ever-increasing population. In 1962, only 5,258,000 lived in Florida. That is fewer people than live in Greater or Metro Miami today. In 2015, when Linda and I birded in the state, 20,219,111 resided in Florida and about a million and a half more occupied the state only four years later. Even though a tropical storm was brewing in April 2015, Flagler Beach was crowded with people spilling from the burgeoning population of the state.

Fortunately, the state of Florida has purchased thousands of acres designated as preserves and management areas that protect natural habitat. One such preserve north of St. Augustine was designated in 1984. Bird finding guides, something not so available in 1962, help find the surviving geographic gems and the birds occupying them.

Marineland has been resold several times. The general admission fee has sky-rocketed to over $50 if you happen to be over 13 years of age. As for sleeping in a car along A1A or any other highway, it might best be regarded as inadvisable.

Margaret Hundley told me about birds being killed from collisions with various man-made impediments ranging from radio and TV towers, lighthouses, and buildings. She joined Herbert W. Kale II in a 1969 paper reporting tower kills of birds from Grand Bahama Island. On the morning of 22 October 1966, the authors found 137 dead individuals of 22 North American breeding species. Many of the birds were sent to the National Museum to be identified by Roxie Laybourne. Years later, Roxie was still receiving packages arriving via the post office of dead and decaying birds found below the guy wires of a communications tower, a cattle trough, embedded in an airplane windshield, you name it. Sometimes the whole of the Division of Birds would reek of some foul odor. Herb Kale's occasional visits to the museum reminded me of my early days in Florida.

Besides holding directorships of the Massachusetts and Florida Audubon Societies, Russ Mason was an extraordinary conservationist in numerous countries in Central America and helped establish the Asa Wright Nature Center in Trinidad. He also helped start the Cerro Punta Sanctuary in Panama and founded Audubon Societies in Mexico, Belize, and Panama, the latter a birding destination for Linda and me in 2005. Russ was also probably the first to initiate natural history tours in Central America. In 1962, I met a gentle and humble person and I had little inkling of the important force of the man.

Energetic Allan Cruickshank was an icon, who was often called a modern Audubon with a camera. He told me he hoped to photograph every North American breeding bird. He had a good start in 1962 and, by 1974, the year he died, Allan had taken thousands of photographs. He would have probably loved digital cameras. His career with the National Audubon Society allowed him to teach millions. I was lucky for the brief moments we shared.

Twenty-five years after I visited Merritt Island, the Dusky Seaside Sparrow was extinct.

Ivan Tompkins, who I birded with in Georgia, talked about researching the sparrows. He studied them from the terra firma, but some census takers later used helicopters to find Dusky Seaside Sparrows. I am not making this up. The chopper thumps 30 miles per hour and 100 feet over the marsh, causing every flying thing to flush. An experienced observer then identifies what is described as the distinctive dorsal pattern of flying for its life Dusky Seaside Sparrow. However, the method admits that carelessness might lead to confusion with female Redwinged Blackbirds. On my walk to the Pentagon day job many years later, I had to walk under the flight path of approaching helicopters. I felt the need to take flight also.

The hapless Dusky Seaside Sparrow's demise was rapid, especially when construction of impoundments of the salt marshes of Merritt Island began in 1957. Optimum habitat, 10 to 15 feet above sea level where cordgrass (*Spartina bakeries*) grows, was drowned. Chuck Trot's hope that the marshes might be better protected by what is now the Kennedy Space Center was not realized. It did not take a rocket scientist long to realize that flooding the breeding habitat to control gnawing mosquitoes, building a road through the marsh, setting legal fires by ranchers adjacent to sparrow habitat, and any other destructive process that comes to mind would, in a word, kill the Dusky Seaside Sparrow. The sparrow population spiraled to only 70 pairs by 1963. By 1968, only 33 to 34 males were found on the island.

The Dusky Seaside Sparrow was a charter member of the Endangered Species Act but attempts by the US Fish and Wildlife Service were a day late and several sparrows short. Through the dogged persistence of Allan Cruickshank, Merritt Island National Wildlife Refuge, on the north end of the island, was established in 1963, the year the marshes were regrettably flooded. A population of 372 males was discovered in the marshes of the St. John's River west of Merritt Island in 1968. St. John's NWR was finally established in 1971, but eventually critical marshes of the St. John's were drained, more roads were built, more marshes drained to fulfill real estate ventures, leaving fires, introduced pigs, and Boat-tailed Grackles to reduce the crippled population to six sparrows by 1979. Five were captured and brought to Discovery Island at Disney World. A captive breeding program ensued, but that was not going to work since the five birds were males. Cross-breeding with other subspecies of Seaside Sparrows might have preserved some of the genetic diversity of the dusky birds, but the experiment failed. The last male Dusky Seaside Sparrow died in 1987.

The sparrow was treated as a species in 1962 but was relegated to the status of subspecies by the AOU in 1973. The reason for the decision is weak at best. Deciding whether it is a species or subspecies when actually based on data versus assumption (=guessing) has been slow. Bob Zink and my late friend Herb Kale commented in 1995 that the absence of genetic differences found in morphologically distinct subspecies of Song and Swamp sparrows lends little basis to argue against species level determination of a morphologically distinct taxon and does give pause to the birds being treated as species.[2] However, even in death, a decision on the Dusky Seaside Sparrow's taxonomic standing is grinding slowly. In a popular publication, the late sparrow expert and taxonomist James D. Rising reviewed the various populations of seaside sparrows and aptly pointed out that subsuming the Dusky Seaside Sparrow into the rank of subspecies is based on little to no information and the Dusky and Cape Sable Seaside Sparrow (also once a

---

2. Robert M. Zink and Herbert W. Kale. "Conservation Genetics of the Extinct Dusky Seaside Sparrow *Ammodramus maritimus nigrescens*." *Biological Conservation* 74 (1995) 69–71.

species) do differ genetically.[3] Did we lose a subspecies or a species? Current literature indicates the jury is still out.[4]

Charles H. Trots was in fact Mr. Dusky Seaside Sparrow. In 1968, Bent's *Life Histories* included Chuck's chapter on the doomed bird. Chuck recently wrote me that "the whole affair [of the sparrows' extinction] leaves me saddened and wishing I could go back and change the past."

3. James D. Rising. "Ecological and Genetic Diversity in the Seaside Sparrow." *Birding* 37.5 (2005) 490–96.

4. Kathryn E. C. Davis et al. "Range-Wide Population Genetic Analysis of Seaside Sparrows (*Ammospiza maritima*) Supports at Least Five Distinct Population Segments That Do Not Align with Current Subspecies Descriptions." *Ornithological Applications* 123.4 (2021).

Chapter 19

The Florida Keys and Christmas Count Fever

9 December 1962

My great luck of meeting Allan Cruickshank and being invited to participate in the Christmas Bird Count he leads was my first morning thought. Sponsored by the National Audubon Society, these counts began in 1900. The rules are simple. Count individual birds in a prescribed 15-mile-diameter circle in one day during a period around Christmas. I was excited. However, the early freezing temperatures near Melbourne did not exactly make crawling out of bed pleasant, and I was feeling a little self-conscious as the traffic zipped past. My drive south on Highway A1A along the barrier islands, with the Indian River, the longest saltwater lagoon in Florida, to my right and the Atlantic Ocean to the left was uneventful except traffic sometimes came to a halt because of raised drawbridges.

10–12 December 1962

Shamelessly not turning down help during my travels, I took Lyle Hubbard up on his invitation he offered when we birded in northern Upper Michigan. He welcomed me to stay with his family when I was in Florida. So, upon arriving at Fort Pierce, I found the post office where my general delivery mail was waiting and a barber who would cut my hair. Trusting that I was presentable, I located Indian River Drive, the Hubbards' residential street. I had not seen Lyle since July after we found Kirtland's Warblers in Michigan. Unfortunately, he was home-bound for a couple of days while recuperating from recent minor surgery.

The next morning, 11 December, after a night in a real bed, was a busy time with writing letters and checking the bird feeders around the Hubbard residence. The Hubbard property once belonged to a prosperous citrus packing company, but for reasons unknown to Lyle, the business was abandoned years ago. The slowly dying fruit trees attracted many Red-bellied Woodpeckers and those trees still fruiting provided tree-ripened oranges and grapefruit for birds and humans. I even liked the tree-ripened grapefruit, a flavor I could not tolerate earlier. Edges of the property are thick with palms, vines, a few scrubby deciduous trees, palmettos, and spiny cactus. The front yard offered a wide view of the Indian River. In 16 years, the Hubbards tallied 175 species on their property.

In the afternoon, Jenny, Lyle's daughter, guided me around Hutchinson Island, a barrier island just across the Indian River from Fort Pierce. In three hours, we found 50 species of birds, none of which were new for my trip list. Nonetheless, it was great seeing more Painted Buntings and Yellow-throated Warblers. Back at the Hubbards, the family invited me for Christmas, and because Lyle and I planned to bird so many Christmas Counts, I accepted. We talked birds into the night, made plans for field trips, and went over Lyle's notes about birds in southern Florida.

The weather on 12 December began pleasantly warm and sunny. Of course, it might have felt cooler if I slept in the car. A warm bed and hot meals can change a person's outlook, but outside was where I belonged. By noon, clouds grayed a windy sky. The temperature plummeted 15 degrees. Spishing along the vegetated sides of a nearby railroad track brought in six Florida Scrub-Jays. I wanted to hear their sick grackle call again. These amazing birds perched in plain view and one hopped to within arm's length. Swiping its bill back and forth, it stared my way. I froze and stared back. Who was going to blink first? The jay suddenly flew, either because I had nothing to offer, or was it that I blinked?

The remainder of the chilly day was spent planning a trip south. Lyle assured me that I would be safe from Cuba and could go to Key West.

13–15 December 1962

After a leisurely morning with the Hubbards, I headed south to Lantana, home of Howard P. Langridge. We had previously exchanged letters a couple of times beginning in January 1961. Howard teaches high school

English and is the compiler for the West Palm Beach Christmas Bird Count. He invited me for dinner and later offered the guest room, supplied maps for finding birds tomorrow, and asked me to participate in the local count.

The fourteenth was a school day for Howard. Alone, I followed his maps to various places to scout for birds in the count circle. One of the maps was directions for a Spot-breasted Oriole recently reported in the region. The bird was on a residential street. I felt a little uneasy looking for birds where people live; a friend in Oregon was nearly arrested for accidentally pointing his binocular at a house. Putting on my best nonchalant look and trying not to appear like a molester or peeping tom, I pretended to be a lost tourist. The ploy worked; the police did not show. However, neither did the oriole. I waited about an hour before returning for another round of searching. Again, no police or an angry mob, but this time I saw the large fire-orange Spot-breasted Oriole. Now, it will not be necessary to look for the oriole in the more congested Miami region where it was introduced a few years ago.

Chuck-will's-widow was supposed to be in the count circle, but I could not find one today. At Boytan Inlet, I scanned for reported Dovekies and Magnificent Frigatebird to no avail. A flock of phalaropes was too far from the beach for me to try to identify. A sick Great Blue Heron lying on the ground had a stick through one wing, which I carefully removed. The bird was too weak and starved to fly and soon died. Other than the oriole, the day was not going well for birds or me.

In the afternoon, I noticed a small obscure bird lying on the pavement. I swerved to a stop, jumped out of the car, and quickly scooped up the carcass before I or the bird was flattened by a tire of one of the too many vehicles rushing by. A few hours later Howard measured the find and after looking through references we concluded it was a female Black-faced Grassquit. Of course, if the identification is confirmed, could I count it? I believed that a specimen record is better than a sight record. However, the bird was dead.

My last full day in Lantana was an improvement over yesterday. It started with a plan of attack by Howard that related to scouting for the coming Christmas Count. Howard used the term *cryp* for species that were difficult to find. Of course, cryp was short for cryptic, and included, for example, Chuck-will's-widow, Grasshopper Sparrow, and Smooth-billed Ani. Phil Allan would join us to find as many cryps as possible while walking through muck and cold icy water, skirting rattlesnake-infested palmetto scrub, and trying to avoid being impaled by briars, thorns, and matted with burs and stickers. While running the gauntlet, we found a Barn Owl, a species I thought was ordinary, but Howard thought was a great find. Not all the 80 species we saw were difficult. From the comfort of the car, we saw a Greater Scaup. An effortless walk on the beach revealed a flock of birds that we were sure were Red Phalaropes. Later in the evening people reported to Howard of seeing Northern Phalaropes. Pangs of doubt set in. We could not be 100 percent sure but we were sure of Smooth-billed Anis seen by walking a section of railroad track, and certain of a surprise species, a White-winged Dove.

16–17 December 1962

Howard and I checked the nearby beaches for shorebirds on the morning of 16 December. By 9:30 a.m., I left Lantana and drove south to Fort Lauderdale, did laundry, and found a service station manager who allowed me on the lot for the night.

Florida weather had returned to normal on the seventeenth. It was 75 degrees, perfect for a threadbare T-shirt. A quick telephone call to the local bird club provided directions to Hollywood, a town south of Fort Lauderdale where Blue-gray Tanagers nested. These birds were escapees or introduced and nested for two years on Thomas Street. I had the street number but no idea what the tanagers looked like. Just before noon, Ms. Ida Arnold, who discovered the new Florida species, showed me a picture of them and described their song. Again, I was using binoculars in a residential area, but this time I decided not to worry about the police as I paced two blocks for four hours and 30 long minutes. During the time, four Smooth-billed Anis relieved my impatience. Finally, a pair of beautiful steel Blue-gray Tanagers appeared.

However, time was not standing still. I needed to be south of Miami before the five o'clock rush hour and in Kendall before dark. Miami traffic was not bad, and Horace Johns in Kendall showed me Red-whiskered Bulbuls. These birds, native to Asia, probably escaped from a local business and now nest in Kendall. The first bulbuls I identified were too far away to see field marks, but Horace and his wife said that the noisy birds were bulbuls and showed me pictures. Soon I was seeing real Red-whiskered Bulbul field marks of real birds.

18 December 1962

A large vacant lot hidden by tall grasses and covered with palmetto and pines was home last night. In the distance, I could hear the rushing traffic of the Miami megapolis. Soon joining the fray, the VW hummed down the main drag, US 1, crossed a bridge onto Key Largo, and the trip to Key West began. My route was built on the bones of a 1912 railway to Key West that was destroyed by a hurricane in 1935. Ahead lay 113 miles and 42 bridges.

Allan Cruickshank told me to look for Roseate Spoonbills at the tiny resort of Jewfish Creek. None were there. A nearby bridge keeper said he had never seen the pink birds and that I should ask the fishing camp manager. As I walked back to the car, a large pink bird with a scarlet shoulder patch flew over. Amazingly, so many people are blind to so much.

By now, it was time for a snack, and I ate several peanut butter and cracker sandwiches. Luckily, I had just replaced my stash of peanut butter, and luckier, the store carried the crunchy style. It is my firm belief that anyone preferring the creamy style required social adjustment. My favorite snack was followed by a few coconut macaroons and a glass of water.

By mid-morning, I pulled into Tavernier on Plantation Key and down a gravel road to a small house, the residence of Sandy Sprunt. A tall lanky man, technically Alexander Sprunt IV, dressed in an Audubon Society uniform, came to the door. His huge smile under thick red hair welcomed me indoors. He was waiting for a phone call, and I excused myself for outdoor birds. While I waited, a strange dove landed in a short, maybe 15-foot, tree at the edge of the driveway. I could not identify it until turning to the back pages of my Peterson where a few accidentals were described. Meanwhile, the dove stayed in the same tree. According to the description, I decided the bird was a Zenaida Dove. I ran back to the office and knocked on the door. Sandy had just completed his call, walked below the tree, glanced up, smiled, retrieved his camera, and took about five pictures.

Finding a Zenaida Dove may have paved the way for a boat tour from Sandy. The small outboard motor pushed our skiff less than a mile over the flat water of Florida Bay. Our liquid route was dark, then blue, no, turquoise, often clear, and sometimes a different and beautiful blue or green. This must be what people call tropical water. Our destination was Cowpen Sanctuary, a three-acre mangrove island protected by the National Audubon Society. As we approached Cowpen Sanctuary we could see a male Magnificent Frigatebird perched about three or four feet on a sturdy mangrove. The bird nonchalantly inflated its throat pouch that became an intense red orb of skin stretched tight and, well, magnificent, toward a nearby female. Possibly because of our presence, the displaying male deflated its balloon-like pouch and seemed to fall from its perch, catch a breath of air about a foot above the water and sail away. We also found Great White Herons[1] and four spe-

---

1. Although officially treated as a subspecies of Great Blue Heron, the Great White Heron should be regarded as a distinct species. A paper by yours truly and Jim Kushlan discusses why the herons are separate species.

cies of egrets including a Reddish Egret staggering in water up to its knees. We cruised around the small mangrove thickets where more egrets, herons, bald Wood, and red-legged and red-faced White ibises, gulls, shorebirds, and more pink and red spoonbills graced the bow.

One of the main things the birds had in common, even the shorebirds, was the mangroves. I had been noticing low-growing bushes before today, but the cruise with Sandy brought me closer to defining such strange plants. Mangroves grow in water, mostly salty but sometimes in brackish water, which for a woody plant is unusual. Above the tide line, mangroves spread in every direction, forming a tangle of branches and stems and green leaves. The plant stands on roots that are exposed by the tide going out and that are often visible through the clear water where they grow. The roots burrow into the ground, holding the plant upright and solid in place. Some of the roots form arches, others bend this way and that, forming an impenetrable barrier to our boat, but Sandy explained that mangroves provided a suitable place for fish and invertebrates to live, an important way to keep the ground from shifting, and a way to slow storm surge. I was beginning to appreciate mangroves but had more questions. What were the numerous small, cone-shaped objects pointing up from the ground? Sandy had an answer. The little cones helped acquire oxygen. He also volunteered that there are three native species of mangroves in Florida and that we were looking at red mangroves, the most salt tolerant species, that differs from the other species by its aerial reddish arching roots. Sandy said black mangroves have opposite leaves, which often have salt crystals on them. Opposite leaves? I had to think back to my high school biology class. White mangroves have rounded leaves and grow more inland than other species. By the time we docked back at Tavernier, I was ready for solid ground, the ground enjoyed by the shorebirds we saw, and ground that existed because of mangroves.

19 December 1962

Last night I parked on a deserted road near Tavernier, and at 5:30 a.m., I crawled out of my bunk. By six, Sandy and I were driving southwest to meet Ms. Francis Crane, the compiler for the Lower Keys Christmas Bird Count. There, we talked strategy, said hello to Margaret Hundley, met Everglade's biologist Bill Robertson, and picked up the rest of our team, George Avery, bridge keeper on Seven Mile Bridge, and Russ Mason.

Sandy, Russ Mason, and I were assigned Big Pine, Middle, and Big Torch Keys for the count. Our first good bird was a dark-phased Short-tailed Hawk. That was a life bird for me. A Chuck-will's-widow was found but it was dead. I wondered if I was ever going to find one alive. Russ and Sandy's abilities to identify birds were amazing and I felt bad that our total for the day ended with only 56 commonplace species. Our team did find a species no one else in the count saw, an immature Cedar Waxwing that brought cheers during the compilation of 91 species. Beside birds, a tiny key deer jumped from a narrow dirt road. The six-point buck was the second key deer for Sandy and a first for Russ and me.

The compilation dinner was a new experience since I had never been in such a lavish residence. We drove into a driveway wider than most streets and got out of Sandy's car. I followed 6'6" Sandy through an open tile-floored garden to a ramp leading to the front door. A smiling uniformed woman opened the door. Inside, I could see a formally dressed man, who I was told was the butler. The maid was just taking up the slack. The house was huge. The ashtrays were so large I was afraid to use one until I noticed other guests stubbing their butts in them. The butler asked what I would like to drink. I settled on bourbon, and long before my drink was empty, someone was there to fill it. A sort of fishy appetizer covered with what must have been green-colored shredded coconut was passed around. When the delicious appetizers were served to Sandy he gasped, "What are those things? They look like they're camouflaged!" I think I was the only one who laughed. I was disappointed that the butler did not announce that dinner was served. The host did, and I was eager to enjoy a meal though I was feeling that all this was too much and was ready for fresh air and fewer people. Finally, Sandy and I said goodbye and thanked our host. The round doorknobs centered in the middle of the oversize door were unfamiliar and I narrowly missed tripping as the opening door grazed the tip of my nose. I kept walking as if nothing happened.

20–21 December 1962

Key West continued to beckon, and I left my overnight parking site outside of Tavernier and drove farther southwest and out to sea. I could not help but feel a little vulnerable to the long ribbon of highway, hopping from island to tiny island. Thanks to Bill Robertson, I relocated a Worm-eating Warbler, and I found a displaced Scissor-tailed Flycatcher on the way southwest. A few more stops along the way made for a late arrival to the end of US 1 at Key West. I looked up my only Key West contact, Mrs. Francis Hames, who drew a map where I might find Mangrove Cuckoos.

It was getting late, and I needed a place to park for the night. Spotting the sheriff's office, I asked if I could park on the beach for the night. Asking first should be better than being rousted by authorities later. However, I could not be sure. The hesitant clerk asked for my driver's license, picked up a microphone, and proceeded to bark a code number and information from my license. Anxious minutes dragged by. What had I stepped into this time? Finally, returning my license, the clerk provided directions where I could park. I asked what code number 49 meant. Unsmiling, he said it was routine to check individuals like me since a young fellow once asked about sleeping on the beach. The police approved but later found the guy was wanted for robbing a bank in New York.

The beach lodging worked out. The night was pleasant, the morning was hot, humid, and beautiful. Ms. Hames and I met as arranged and we birded several places on the island. Our first stop was a surprise. We were greeted by a reporter from the *Key West Citizen*, the local newspaper. A photographer wanted me to pose with binoculars at the ready while I searched the sky. It was all a little silly, but I was searching the sky. One skyward search later did reveal White-crowned Pigeons, but we never found the cuckoos. Near the end of the field trip, we toured Audubon House, a two-story mansion built by John H. Geiger, a wealthy harbor pilot and salvager. John James Audubon stayed there in 1832. A tree in the elephant folio of a White-crowned Pigeon grew in Geiger's front yard. I would have liked to visit the Dry Tortugas where Audubon, Peterson, and Fisher and so many others have birded, but those islands were beyond my budget.

Mangrove Cuckoos demanded a stop on Stock Island, just east of Key West. Searches for the birds on my way to Marathon were also without a cuckoo. While on the way back to the mainland, I stopped where Ms. Crane and a friend had baited another Zenaida Dove. They wanted me to verify their identification. A soaking deluge that began earlier in the day accompanied the confirmation. While looking for and finding the dove, a young woman continually tried to get my attention. She finally began screaming that I must see her unusual find, hustled me into her car while telling me the bird talked to her. We drove a short distance and the bird was a first-year Herring Gull. I kept a straight face and feigned wonderment, primarily to get a ride back. I finally did see a cuckoo.

The rain poured as I slowly drove along the highway, barely able to see the car in front. Fortunately, I took a picture of the Seven Mile Bridge yesterday; the bridge was now out of sight. The emerald green water lost its color as big drops hammered the formerly still surface. The wind increased and sunlight dimmed. Farther up the island chain, I arrived at my familiar parking place at Tavernier where not a drop of rain had fallen.

22 December 1962

Sandy had convinced me that I should help in the Key Largo-Plantation Key Christmas Bird Count. I agreed, but I could spare only a couple of hours since I wanted to be in Lantana by the afternoon. Sandy piloted our boat out to sea where we saw frigatebirds and two Portuguese man-o-wars, a graceful but toxic jellyfish. We landed on Tavernier Island and waded through mangroves where we found Yellow Warblers. These were the Cuban Golden Warbler. Our best bird was what Sandy called an "eyebrow-raiser." It was a Red-necked Grebe. Robert P. Allen greeted us on our return to the boat dock. He and Sandy would finish the count. After about a two-hour-and-thirty-minute dash north to Lantana, I met Howard Langridge, who showed me two new birds, Purple Gallinule and Grasshopper Sparrow.

23–26 December 1962

Howard and I were up early for more scouting the upcoming Christmas Count. We searched for Bachman's Sparrows a couple of hours in local pine woodlands west of Lantana. We succeeded and Howard returned home. I spent the last two hours of morning searching for a female Black-faced Grassquit reported by a dependable observer. The only interesting bird found was a confusing fall warbler that remained unidentifiable.

It was just after noon when I stopped birding, ate a lunch of peanut butter, crackers, and an apple. During the drive toward Fort Pierce, I began noticing blackened vegetation along the road. I had escaped a rare and frigid cold front by going to the Keys. In slightly over an hour, I was back at the Hubbards. By previous agreement, they were acting as my general delivery, and Lyle handed me a stack of mail that included Christmas cards and letters. There was nothing from Linda, but I was sure there would be next time.

On Christmas Eve, Lyle, Jenny, and I scouted part of the Fort Pierce Count area. Most of the morning was spent at a residence where a Black-headed Grosbeak, White-throated, and White-crowned Sparrows were reported. Lyle had already confirmed the grosbeak. The White-throated Sparrow appeared just before lunch when we had returned at the Hubbard residence. A telephone message reported a rare Dickcissel seen at a feeder with House Sparrows and Redwinged Blackbirds. I missed Dickcissels in the summer and had not expected another chance to see them until Arkansas or Texas. I saw the new bird hold its ground as it ate among the larger blackbirds.

That evening we enjoyed a scrumptious dinner and were entertained with a slide show on birds by Grant McNichols, US Fish and Wildlife biologist and regular on the Fort Pierce Count. Later, the Hubbards asked me to join them at church from 11 p.m. to midnight. I wore my only suit, the one my mother insisted I pack. The air-conditioner, if there was one, was off, the windows were shut, and it was hotter than Hades.

Christmas Day seemed strange; it was my first time away from home. I gave the Hubbards a book on Audubon in Florida. They gave me two pairs of socks, candy, pencils, and a carton of cigarettes. Part of my day was used to continue scouting the region for the Fort Pierce Count. The next morning, I birded around the Hubbards' property, feeling the pace quickening as multiple Christmas Counts loomed on the horizon. In the afternoon, Lyle and I drove to Lantana. Excited Howard Langridge welcomed us for the night where Bill Robertson had earlier staked a claim in the corner of the living room floor.

27 December 1962

Today the pace of birding intensified as the West Palm Beach Christmas Count started. Bill Robertson and I were up, flushed, dressed at 4:15 a.m., and out of the house when our party stopped down a darkened road. We listened in silence, but the quiet was broken by a rough voice coming from a nearby darkened house. The voice told us where we should go. We left but thankfully did not end up where we were directed by the disgruntled resident. Instead, we went back to Howard's place for an allotted 45-minute breakfast. At 5:30, Howard, Lyle, Bill, and I rushed to a nearby marsh where Howard, while banging on a garbage can lid with a steel pipe, hit his thumb. His yell or the banging produced a King Rail. Bill kept mumbling that if the police come, he would be the one arrested. Dawn found Phil Allan and me in a large cypress forest, accompanied by five yelping coon hounds and their master, a grizzly old man leaning over his shotgun barrel as he tied a loose shoelace. We were more concerned that he would shoot himself than us. His crazed dogs ran into a thicket where a woodcock had been yesterday and near a site where an American Bittern and a Redstart had been staked out. None of the much-needed birds were found. We hoped a different party in the count did better. Soon more dogs and hunters tramped through, each barking at something or maybe just to hear their heads rattle.

Noon was approaching; we had missed our three cypress birds, now we could not locate the Burrowing Owls. We had met with Howard, who was now peering into every culvert he could find for the wayward owls. We then scurried to the beach for gannets, and later rechecked a pinewood for Bachman's Sparrows and a small cypress area for woodcock. No luck. We took 40 minutes to eat lunch and to go over plans for the afternoon. Unfortunately, Lyle and I would have to leave by 3 p.m., but before departing, we joined a party of three people to check a couple of places for shorebirds. After missing Dunlins, being stuck in loose sand, digging to solid ground, Lyle and I headed north to Cocoa for Cruickshank's count. Lyle and I arrived at Allan's house to get our orders for tomorrow's big day.

28 December 1962

A hazy ring of the alarm clock shook us at 3:45 a.m. Somehow, we staggered out and to the car and drove to an all-night café in downtown Cocoa where we met Allan. Birdwatchers took every seat. The first bird had already been recorded by Allan when he left home. Allan quickly introduced me to my party leader, Joseph Howell, professor at Knoxville, Tennessee, his son, and another fellow, who, with me, formed a team.

Our party soon sped in Dr. Howell's car to a designated spot east of the café. We parked to listen for owls. No one said a word for several minutes, and then Dr. Howell asked me the usual questions, such as where Phoenix, Oregon is, where will I go to school, and more. It was still pitch black as we waited in the pines, hoping to hear birds. To speed things up, Dr. Howell gave incredibly good imitations of screech, Barred, and Great Horned Owls. The chilly air carried silence until a cacophony of two Barred Owls broke the calm. Morning light revealed a marsh that gradually came alive with King and Virginia Rails, Soras whinnying, American Bitterns, both marsh wrens but nothing particularly critical to the count.

Allan assigned us to bring back Red-cockaded Woodpecker, Brown-headed Nuthatch, and Bachman's Sparrow so we headed farther west into the pine forest. Failing to locate any of our assigned species, we began working our way toward the Atlantic. During one stop we searched for Tufted Titmouse and heard one. The tide was out at Turn Basin. Unlike my mid-tide visit there on 9 December, birds were scattered over the vast mudflats. I picked out a Marbled Godwit, which I tried to show Dr. Howell. He spotted a Long-billed Curlew, which he thought was the bird I found. I began to worry that he would say that I could not identify a godwit from a curlew. Shortly, Allan's team arrived and, armed with scopes, picked out curlews and godwits.

Our next mission was to find seaside and Sharp-tailed Sparrows that might be about a mile from Turn Basin. Grassy tufts bordered a mudflat.

I asked Dr. Howell about walking the flat while he walked the dry side. Surely, we would find something. He said that the flat could occasionally be treacherous. I took a few test steps and found it to be solid. It did not seem treacherous today; it must be safe. Three yards farther, my right leg suddenly was completely under a mucky sulfurous gray mud. I managed to twist around, throw my left leg flat over the surface and grab a tuft of grass. Somehow, I kept my scope and binocs out of the smelly mess and freed my right leg. I tried to go back but my left leg sunk deep into the soft clay trap. Finally, I managed to get to dry land. A gravel company office was nearby and so was a hose and running water. The manager there told me that the area was extremely dangerous and that I could have gone over my head. Surely, the good doctor knew that also since I learned he had birded the same basin on many previous Christmas Counts. In the meantime, Dr. Howell, apparently impatient with me, drove down the road about a half-mile to check out a new area. I had taken off my sunglasses after getting out of the mud and laid them on top of the car. Luckily, they had not fallen off when the car was moved. By then I was mad that Dr. Howell had been so nonchalant about the dangerous mud and driving away and leaving my glasses on the car. He seemed shocked that I dared to tell him I was not happy with the way he treated the situation.

The 13-hour day ended with our party logging 109 species. I saw 94 of them, including two, Virginia Rail and Sedge Wren, which Howell refused to believe. Overall, our party rated badly, having missed most of the needed assigned species. The compilation party at the Cruickshanks' was noisy and crowded. Despite hosing off my Turn Basin muck, I knew I smelled like a rotten lagoon. Allan called off the species, beginning with loons and ending with finches. The 100 species mark came quickly. Then 150 and finally 46 more species were checked. We reached 196, more than last year, and ranking second to the highest count of 200 set by Cocoa in 1961.

Before leaving, I had a polite chat with Howell when I censored my view of his arrogance. I wondered if he still thought I did not know the difference between a godwit and a curlew. Why should I care? Allan backed me up when he saw both species at the basin. I talked briefly to Margaret Hundley, Russ Mason, Foster White, and others before driving south to be ready for the next Christmas Bird Count.

29 December 1962

The Vero Beach Christmas Count was unlike the other counts in that no one started until around 8 a.m. I was paired with Grant McNichols and the compiler. The local newspaper sent a reporter to cover the new count. Grant and I covered the western part of the circle, the pinewoods. We searched the habitat most of the day for Red-cockaded Woodpecker by walking five miles and, although we saw only 57 species, we found 10 that no one else saw. Lyle and I did not stay for the Vero Beach compilation party. We were anxious to return to Fort Pierce and to get needed sleep.

30–31 December 1962

Wakeful morning arrived around 9:30. We were tired but scouted the Fort Pierce Christmas Count circle and found Eastern Bluebirds, Chipping Sparrows, and Brown-headed Nuthatches. All were good birds for tomorrow's count.

Howard Langridge arrived at the Hubbards late in the evening. He had been on a count 150 miles to the south. We asked him why no one ever finds snakes during the counts. Howard laughed and then told us a birder actually stepped on an Eastern Diamondback Rattlesnake during the West Palm Beach Count. Luckily, the person was not bitten.

The last day of 1962 began with early breakfast and, with a packed lunch in hand, we rushed out the Hubbards' door for owls. I called up Barred and screech owl, checked a barn that was owless, and by 7:45 met my party, Fred Harden, director of the mosquito control unit near Fort Pierce, and Bob Bergan, WIRA radio announcer. Bob began birdwatching only a week ago and was remarkably good. He especially had a knack for identifying shorebirds, a group of birds many experience as trouble. While loading our gear in a small boat, a reporter and photographer from the *Miami Herald* arrived. Our birding trio obliged them with a brief interview and made a couple of circles in the boat while the photographer shot away. The tide was coming in fast. A northeaster had been blowing since yesterday and the brine sprayed off the bow and blew into our faces. It was sticky, and Fred said the salt content was unusually high. We clicked off the customary four species of gulls, heard a Clapper Rail, but could not find Marbled Godwits that Lyle and I earlier staked out. I finally found a Short-billed Dowitcher that I could, with certainty, separate from the Long-billed Dowitcher. Shorebirds are not easy.

Before we knew it, the sun went down. By 8 p.m., the compilation began. We missed many of the birds staked out earlier. Lyle noted that hummingbirds were missed and that the only duck found was Red-breasted Merganser. The Indian River is usually full of scaup. I was a little sad that this was my last Christmas Bird Count for the season. Although I did not find any new trip birds, the experience was fun. There was a sense of accomplishment. Of the four mainland counts, I saw 119 species. The list of all those species made me realize Florida in the winter is great for shorebirds, with 16 species, and pretty productive for terns and wintering warblers. The long days and miles driven were behind, and there was a sense of relief.

∼

Over 75,000 people participated in recent Christmas Bird Counts that took place in numerous countries, but mostly in the US and Canada. Additional 15-mile diameter count circles and eager participants join the fun every year. Fees are no longer collected, and the journal reporting the results of the counts, formerly *Audubon Field Notes*, is now known as *North American Birds*. Participation dropped during the COVID-19 pandemic, which everyone hopes is over.

Being in a count is mostly fun, but it can also be challenging work depending on the seriousness of the observer. Back in Oregon, I was the compiler for the local count for a couple of seasons and quickly learned that leading a count is fun, but it is also work if one desires a thorough count. It can also be numbing cold, wet, hot, buggy, disappointing, great, and educational. Marshall Howe, one of my former museum bosses, Dick Zusi, and I froze from the icy wind howling along the Maryland shore of the Potomac River on Christmas Counts. Marshall, along with Chan Robbins and others, formed a panel to make recommendations to enhance the scientific value of Christmas Counts. Published in 2004, their promising ideas would have been lost in the brain of my skinny youth. Having met Allan Cruickshank, Mr. Christmas Count Editor himself, the heat of the moment swept me on to a goal to enjoy as many Florida counts as I could. I was especially excited to be on the Cocoa Count—it always topped the nation in the number of species.

Participants in the Cocoa Count did not have to worry about introduced birds, but that was not true in southern Florida. Especially today, Florida, along with parts of Texas and Southern California, is known for harboring numerous species of birds that occur in the state by introduction, either by accident or on purpose. Species that breed and that independently support viable populations for 15 years are considered established and are species that birders can add to their lists. During my 1960s visit to Florida, introduced Red-whiskered Bulbul and Spot-breasted Oriole were countable species. The bulbuls continue to breed in Kendall, and Spot-breasted Orioles are more widespread now than in the sixties. I recall in 1962 mention of introduced Scarlet Ibis but never saw them. It never occurred to me to look for Budgerigars in Florida, what used to be called dime store parakeet escapees that might be found anywhere. As for the breeding population in Florida, those little parakeets died out in 2014. Budgerigars may be gone from the Florida birdscape, but dozens of species of non-native avifauna are alive and well, with confirmed and self-sustaining breeding populations. Many of these include members of the parrot family. More species of birds are now qualified as countable in Florida than were in 1962, several of which Linda and I located during an April 2015 visit to the state. We saw Nanday Parakeet, Purple Swamphen, Muscovy Duck, Red Junglefowl, even peacocks, Egyptian Geese, and others, including Whooping Cranes. We looked for the oriole and bulbul but found neither and did not bother searching for Blue-gray Tanagers, a species that disappeared in the mid-1970s. Of course, we saw House Sparrows and European Starlings, species most of us love to hate, that, with other non-native species, regardless of their countability, pose threats to native birds.

Besides all those introduced birds that trick and confuse birders, there are plenty of chances of strays from the Caribbean showing up in Florida. The one waif of a species that did turn up during sixties trip, other than Zenaida Dove, was the Black-faced Grassquit that I found smashed on a street. Even though I found the bird, which became an undisputable specimen, I cannot count the species on my list because the bird was dead.

Live and countable species were found in the Florida Keys in 1962. The time in the Keys was like a dream. It happened too fast, the Christmas Counts, the people, the rain, and fear of arrest. And, finding the Zenaida Dove, a naturally occurring species, was exciting. The two doves I saw in 1962 stayed around until March the next year. Since then, there have been records of individuals in 1988 and 2001, 2002, 2004, and 2010. Audubon reported the species breeding in the Keys during the 1830s. Zenaida Doves of late are possibly pioneers that might recolonize Florida just as likely is occurring in the state by White-winged Doves and that has occurred throughout the country by Eurasian Collared-Dove.

The chance to meet so many great people in Florida ranked right up there with new life birds. I recall Sandy Sprunt seemed happy when I told him one of the books I had in the VW was a tome on birds of prey by conservationist Alexander Sprunt, his father. He also had big smiles when he took pictures of the Zenaida Dove and when showing me close-ups of displaying Magnificent Frigatebirds in Florida Bay. Sandy became a biologist for the National Audubon Society in 1952 and was the research director at the long-established Audubon's Everglades Science Center. Time with Robert P. Allen, author of all those monographs I read and reread in high school, helped establish the scientific baselines for the recovery of endangered species. If only there had been time to hear more from Allan Cruickshank, Bill Robertson, and others. Many of the people I met in 1962 would be seen again, others would not. Most have passed.

Several kinds of birds that I had been seeing in 1962 have changed in terms of their names, distribution, and taxonomy. The scrub jay in Florida was later realized by taxonomists to be specifically distinct from interior birds and those on Santa Cruz Island off California. By convention, the jays also gained a hyphen in their English names, thus becoming scrub-jays. The Great White Heron, a bird with a dwindling population, was considered by the AOU, in 1973, to be a subspecies of its dark brethren, the Great Blue Heron. Several ornithologists outside the checklist committee disagreed. Also, the checklist committee continues to not believe the bird currently known as Yellow Warbler comprises more than one species, one or two of which occur in mangrove habitat.

Mangroves were a new species of plant for my young birding self. It did not take me long to realize that mangroves offered a unique habitat for unique birds. In the Keys, mangroves provided habitat for the Yellow Warbler populations that differ morphologically from the northern mainland Yellow Warblers. The mangrove habitat is important to other kinds of birds and other organisms, including commercial fish, and protects shorelines from erosion by slowing the brunt of waves, especially when driven by hurricanes. Despite the importance of mangroves to man and beast, the destruction of mangrove habitat has been considerable since 1962. Between the years 2000 to 2015, 1,300 square miles of mangroves worldwide were lost, with 62 percent of the loss human caused. Obvious human causes to the detriment of mangroves are related to shipping that involves dredging and filling, oil pollution, herbicides, and urban blight. Too many people often do too many injurious things. Shooting oneself in the foot comes to mind. Florida laws, enacted in the mid-1990s, protect mangroves. Yet, according to a 2021 report by the Florida Department of Environmental Protection, Lake Worth near West Palm Beach has lost 87 percent of its mangroves over the past 40 years.[2] Private land that grows mangroves is not fully protected since landowners are allowed to trim and even remove mangroves.

The mangrove islands Sandy Sprunt showed me have also changed administratively. Cowpen, split by the Intracoastal Waterway, has its western part inside Everglades National Park and as of 1990 the eastern part, no longer administered by the Audubon Society, is in the Florida Keys

---

2. Florida Department of Environmental Protection. "Florida's Mangroves." Last updated August 14, 2023. https://floridadep.gov/rcp/rcp/content/floridas-mangroves.

National Marine Sanctuary of NOAA (National Oceanic and Atmospheric Administration). Peter Frezza, formerly with the National Audubon Society's research office, wrote me that most of Cowpen's nesting birds moved to the Everglades National Park side and that spoonbill populations have declined since the sixties. He also said his office was across the street from Sandy Sprunt's place.

Chapter 20

Everglades and a New Plan

1–5 January 1963

It was New Year's Day and the Hubbards and I huddled around a radio. We were listening to a taped program with Bob Bergan asking me questions about my trip. He recorded the interview during the eleventh hour of yesterday's Christmas Count. It was uncomfortable to be interviewed and embarrassing to hear it.

The Everglades beckoned, but Lyle had arranged for me to speak to the St. Lucie Audubon Society in five days. I planned to talk about the trip and that I enjoyed the local birding, Until now, Lyle and I were in the field every day. Shorebirds were plentiful and we found the Marbled Godwit missed on the count. One morning I amused myself watching a Blue-gray Gnatcatcher chasing tiny pieces of bread flipped in the air. Once the airborne bread landed, the gnatcatcher lost interest. Eight nearby ovenbirds, on the other hand, chased the morsels to their landing place and ate them. Besides tricking innocent gnatcatchers, there was plenty of time to get my notes up to date, write letters, and make notes on my talk to the Audubon Society members.

On the afternoon of 3 January, Lyle and I searched Hutchinson Island and found 50 species. Strong gusty winds blew hard, but Lyle and I managed to find plenty of birds in three hours. Pelican, heron, a Clapper Rail, several species of shorebirds, gulls, and terns, and three species of woodpeckers made up half the list, with Blue Jay, Fish Crow, three species in the thrasher family, four of the usual warblers, an Eastern Meadowlark, a couple of Painted Bunting, and an Eastern Towhee making up the second half of our list.

The northeaster was still blustering on 5 January, but Lyle and I combed the neighborhoods of Fort Pierce for birds. The most remarkable find among our list of only 39 species was a Black-headed Grosbeak. It felt good to see an old familiar species, a bird I expected on any given summer day back home in southwestern Oregon. At 2 p.m., I began speaking to the St. Lucie Audubon group, which was an outline of my trip so far, and where I would go before returning to Oregon. I did not have slides although I had a map of my route. After 30 minutes of talking, I attempted to answer questions. A member of the group made a motion to help my trip budget, someone seconded the suggestion, and hands were raised. I was impressed that Robert's Rules of Order worked beyond the high school classroom where I was first exposed to the way a meeting should be run. I was surprised and grateful when the treasurer later presented me a check for $25. The amount could cover the cost of about 75 gallons of gas!

6 January 1963

The Hubbards and I were on our way southwest to Lake Okeechobee, a place high on my list for good birds. Earlier, I had visited the edges of the Everglades, but today, I am smack in the middle of the huge habitat stretching from central Florida to the very southern shore of the state. Lyle explained that the number and kinds of birds in and around the Lake Okeechobee were diminishing because of various agencies manipulating water levels, and too many people in boats, fishing, and hunting, and arguing about water flow without caring for the demise of the Everglades and the Snail Kite. The chances of seeing a Snail Kite would be slim, but we stopped frequently to scan the marshes for one of the reportedly eight kites left in North America.

It is about a 100 mile drive around Lake Okeechobee, farther than we had time, but Lyle hoped we would be lucky on the north end of the lake. South of the town of Okeechobee at the dikes at the north shore was our destination. Excepting Snowy Egrets, all the usual wading birds, a couple of species of ducks, seven species of raptors were all busy foraging. We scanned with our binocs then with scopes until our eyes hurt, but a kite did not appear. Getting nowhere, we drove southwest along the lake to Fish-eating Bay, near Lakeport. Still scanning for kites, we also checked vulture flocks for caracara. At one stop, Black and Turkey Vultures were feeding on a dead cow that had fallen into a shallow ditch. Lyle told me that although thousands of vultures help clean the cattle-rich region, Florida offers no protection to these beneficial birds. Even I knew that the 1918 Migratory Bird Treaty Act protected migrants and that vultures were migratory. I also knew that certain people look for excuses to shoot their guns and kill something just for the "sport" of it.

As we later glassed a small flock of Black Vultures a bird flying much faster came into view. It was a Crested Caracara, finally a new life bird after searching for days. After our brief glimpse, we retraced our route from Fisheating Creek to the town of Okeechobee where a caracara flew near the road. It stopped and boldly posed, revealing a red face, long legs, and striking black and white plumage.

7–10 January 1963

The morning was gloomy. It was time to say farewell to the Hubbards, who had been my hosts, friends, and invaluable guides. Deciding not to drive far from Fort Pierce on the seventh, I found a narrow dead-end road leading into the pines about a half-mile from busy US Highway 1. At the end of the sandy road, I explored the surroundings before settling in for the late afternoon. A narrow path hacked through a palmetto thicket led to a pile of what looked to be junk. Adjacent to the heap was a table, a lean-to, and a few fresh human tracks. A leather shotgun carrying case draped over a bush. Rain had fallen last night but the case was completely dry.

That was enough for me to try a different place. A quick backtrack to the highway and another dirt road, this time near the beach, was my new temporary home. I snacked on the Christmas candy and cookies I hoarded for the New Year, slapped mosquitoes, and slept for 12 hours. Maybe those Christmas Counts were more exhausting than I thought.

Refreshed by morning, the sound of waves crashing on a few offshore rocks and the sight of the bright eastern horizon was inspiring. I wrote Linda about the sunrise and the last several days in Florida. In nearby Jupiter, I found a much-needed laundromat; the washing and drying cost 80 cents. The only way to avoid the expense was doing laundry at the Hubbards, but it was embarrassing because of the degree that my pile of clothes needed washing. My boots were wearing thin. I later spent $5.10 on a sturdy pair of shoes. The first sand in the new shoes was on a beach with an immature Great Black-backed Gull.

Late in the afternoon, I arrived at the Langridges' home in Lantana, talked birds, ate dinner, and attended a meeting at the Everglades Audubon Society. A couple of members there gave me a contact who might know where to find a Snail Kite. Howard went over details for finding birds in the Everglades.

On 9 January, I left the Langridges' home for Fort Lauderdale, where I phoned a contact for information on locating kites. I was anxious and pessimistic about seeing the rare bird. The directions given were to drive west on State 84 to its junction with US Highway 27 to a gas station and restaurant called Andy Town, then to the first left and stop at a parking lot. Once there, I began walking the northern dike to look for the kite seen there last week. A three-hour search brought only darkness. A security guard at the parking lot had permitted me to park in the lot for the night.

A six mile drive the next morning took me to another possible location for kites. There, at a flood control pump house sitting astride one of the Everglades dikes were two workers. They looked at me curiously when I asked if they had seen Snail Kites. "You mean one them paper . . ." I interrupted and tried to explain but got nowhere. My last chance to see a kite required hiking down the dike two miles west to the next pump house. Two kites were there a month ago and I knew finding them was a long shot, but I had to try. All I saw was the immense Everglades, the miles and miles of flat green grass, and an occasional shimmer of water. The dike was the only way out or into this lonely and empty vastness.

The day was half over as I rushed back to civilization. In Oregon, I had enjoyed televised horse races and wanted to see the Hialeah Racetrack in Miami. Much like the bad luck of not finding a Snail Kite, the track was not open. Not giving up, I had another and different lead. Following a phone call, I visited Louis Stimson, who had recently published a paper on the distribution of Cape Sable Seaside Sparrows. I took detailed notes. Although I felt certain of finding the bird, I was not certain about getting to Everglades National Park before dark. Somehow, I took a wrong turn on the way to Homestead, ending up on Old Cutler Road instead of US 1. By the time I found the correct road, it was too late to get to the park. The back of a service station provided a place to park my mobile VW home.

11 January 1963

Passing the town of Homestead, I was soon in Everglades National Park, the third-largest park in the system, and walking the Anhinga Trail at Royal Palm Hammock. The hammock, the island of trees in the ocean of saw grass, was crowded with people and birds. Also known as Paradise Key, the region is a bundle of life, with the straight white trunks of royal palms towering over wet tangles of vines and bushes. Compared to the seemingly chaotic growth, the trunks of the palms appeared perfectly round, their shape seems unnatural, akin to white concrete poured into a long and straight mold that held up decorative fronds that could have been manufactured at a commercial shop. Royal Palms are almost too perfect for nature.

Below the towering white trunks were irregular shapes of green, the predominant color that soothed the eye with varying shades. Colorful butterflies and dragonflies darting everywhere bejeweled a backdrop of tropical plants and heavy humid air. A breeze weakly stirred the 80 plus degree day. A huge alligator, known as Old George and estimated to be 14 feet long, dozed in the sun, unconcerned with human noises across the water. Safe on the wooden boardwalk, I joined the amazement of the tourists as gallinules and yellow-footed Snowy Egrets and other species of herons were too busy foraging to notice the tourists jostling along the boardwalk thinking they might capture a photograph as good as one they saw taken by Allen Cruickshank. Herons squawked and croaked with the chorus of frogs as silent snakes slithered from sight. Fish splashed to the black surface of the still water where, concentrated by winter's dry season, they end their life by feeding the avian and reptile menagerie. Sleek Anhingas graced their trail, the Anhinga Trail, some swimming in water teeming with alligators and Anhinga food, unsuspecting fish. Other Anhingas waited on perches in full view as if posing. More than one impaled fish, their sharp bills pierced through the side of a fish's abdomen. A water-soaked Anhinga flipped a two-inch fish from its bill, repositioned the prey so that it could be swallowed headfirst, gulped several times, and then proceeded to spread its wings and tail to dry in the sun.

Hours slipped by before leaving Royal Palm Hammock and finding a campsite at Long Pine Campground. Surrounded by saw grass, the pines of the hammock remind me of the lodgepole pine left behind six months ago in Crater Lake NP. "Remind" might be a generous word since my botanical knowledge needs work. The two pines have very straight and small in diameter trunks and therefore fit more than one species of pines. Shade from the pines in Florida was beneficial, not just to me but mosquitoes. One or more of the 50 species of mosquitoes inhabiting the park came from the shadows of the pines and other vegetation and they all sampled me during the evening while I attended a naturalist talk. The naturalist said that during the summer, rains bring the water level of the park to the edge of the paved park road. He hastened to add that the water also produced lots more mosquitoes than what the audience was slapping now.

BIRDER INTERRUPTED

12–13 January 1963

The temperature and humidity raced upward, pushing the morning from hot to miserable. I decided to find a shady spot, write a few letters, and plan the rest of my time in the park. Birds around the campground were the same species I saw in other pine forests in southern Florida. No new birds and unbearable weather were not what I had dreamed. Sundown was welcomed. Well, almost, but the mosquitoes also liked sundown.

The next morning, I left Long Pine Key Campground to drive south to Flamingo, at least 30 minutes away at the end of the park road. Stops along the way, including Pinelands Trail, took me through a section of shortleaf figs, buttonwood, and bayberry. I made the summit to Rock Reef Pass, 3.1 feet above sea level. The vastness of the park, 1,400,533 acres, could only partially be appreciated. The river of grass, what Indians called pa-hay-okee stretched for what seemed forever. It felt lonely being the only human on the road and boardwalk at Pahayokee Overlook. Every direction was open and flat. To the south, I entered Mahogany Hammock, a lush jungle containing the only mahogany stand in our country. Plants surrounding a boardwalk created a dense shade that was cooler than anything offered by overhead pines. Tree branches were full of orchids and ferns. Huge strangler figs encircle thick branches of trees as plants compete for sun and space, creating a tangle that would have been impenetrable had it not been for the boardwalk. The mahogany trees were impressive. The largest one measured 12 feet and 6 inches in circumference at 4.5 feet above the ground. The crown of the 70-foot-tall tree spreads out 75 feet.[1] A sign along the boardwalk stated visitors might hear Barred Owls. I tried to imagine owls calling in the night, as I tripped over strangler figs and trees downed by Hurricane Donna in 1960. Leaving the mahogany forest, I enjoyed the beauty of a stand of paurotis palms. Their graceful trunks are covered with a fur-like matter, which produces a soft and delicate appearing tree, with pale green and fan-shaped leaves. If only there were birds around.

Late in the afternoon, I met Richard Cunningham, author of 1961 *A Field List of South Florida Birds*. His publication, along with Pettingill and local bird watchers, were my sources for finding birds in Florida. Since entering the park, I had not seen any new trip birds. Dick had some leads. With a key that he loaned me, I drove through the gate and down the narrow-shaded road to Snake Bight. Slightly over an hour of daylight remained. A brant was there last week, but not today. Plans to search for Mangrove Cuckoos on the way back to the main road ended abruptly as

---

1. Dimensions of this tree, standing since well before 1963, are actually based on 2020s measurement. Any information I had from the 1963 visit has since been lost.

black clouds of mosquitoes entered the open windows of my car. Stopping was out of the question.

In a few more miles on the main road, I arrived at Flamingo. There seemed to be considerable activity, especially among people with boats and fishing poles. Flamingo, I soon learned from visiting the visitor center, was once a remote fishing village. I also learned that the campground was a short distance away, sitting at the edge of Florida Bay. Once it was dark, it was very dark, and I was treated with a night sky the likes I had not seen since leaving the West. Silvery stars sparkled from the Milky Way that arched overhead with dazzling crisp light.

14 January 1963

The inside of the car quickly heated the next morning. I crawled from my bunk to escape to the relatively cooler outside air at the Flamingo campground. A few shady spots were under a strange tree sporting smooth reddish bark. The trees, Gumbo Limbo, reminded me of the madrone back in Oregon, but with more delicate leaves, and range from southern Florida and the Caribbean. A park brochure stated the tree bark has medical benefits.

Flamingo, Everglades NP.

A drive east of the campground took me back to Snake Bight Road, where I slathered my bare skin with mosquito repellent. I was again ready to take on all 1.6 miles of mosquito-infested road. This time I would be walking the road, which should increase my chances for birds. I parked near the gate, walked a few feet along the dirt road, and stopped, squeaked, and listened. Clouds of mosquitoes swarmed all around my invisible barrier of repellent. Snowy Egrets and Wood Ibis fussed at my intrusion. I walked 20 more feet, stopped, squeaked, and listened. The cloud of saltwater mosquitoes followed. The cloud could have been shaped like a thunderhead, one ready to release thunder and lightning. I was not sure but feared the misery about to come. About 450 feet from the beginning of the road, an animal moved in the otherwise still vegetation. Searching, I saw a bird, at first mostly hidden by the dense green and gray vegetation. The bird moved and became a cuckoo skulking 25 feet away. It peered around a thick branch, revealing its black face patch. The bird seemed as curious about me as I was interested in it. We both did not change perches, and eventually, I could see its buffy belly and white-tipped tail feathers as sweat began to drip from my nose and wash away my mosquito repellent. Satisfied I had seen a Mangrove Cuckoo, I walked further through the tunnel of frustrated mosquitoes that were getting closer and closer to my skin. Before it was psychologically unbearable and while it was possible to see beyond their hungry six-legged bodies, something much larger than an insect stopped me in my tracks. The horde of mosquitoes hovered, waiting as sweat washed away more of my protective shield while I put the binoculars on a Red-eyed Vireo foraging just off the trail. What? That species should not be here now. Could it be a different kind of vireo? A few mosquitoes breached my bug-be-gone armor. Ignoring increasing blood loss, I strained to see the suspected field mark, which was there. The aptly named Black-whiskered Vireo and the cuckoo were observed within minutes of each other. I hurried back to the car.

Dick had suggested another place to look for birds, and on my way there, I ran into Bill Robertson. I must have been the first one to speak. "I saw a Mangrove Cuckoo." Bill congratulated me but did not seem terribly impressed. We chatted about Christmas Counts and birding in the Everglades. He asked where I was going. I told him Dick Cunningham suggested Bear Lake. Bill said, "While you are there count the number of adult and immature Roseate Spoonbills there; something funny is going on there." He explained that most of the spoonbills are adults, which is not encouraging if the species is expected to continue to live in the park.

Bear Lake was slightly over one and a half miles from the main road. It was late morning. An almost white path reflected into my eyes as I squinted to check every step in front of me and search the low green bushes and trees at my side. Snakes might be on the trail, sunning under the dappled light, or snakes might be waiting in the shade, only slithering out for their prey. Reptiles need to get their temperature just right. An alligator might be exploring the old canal near the trail. Any evidence of recent human activity that might scare off unwanted reptiles away from my route was days old. I needed to be extra careful and be alert of a new bird, one of several other than the usual suspects might be lurking in the tropical vegetation. As it turned out, nothing out of the ordinary was observed.

Hunger struck at the lakeshore. It was high noon and time for a few peanut butter and cracker sandwiches. Along with rising temperature and humidity, a little water from my canteen and I was ready for spoonbills. I found only 19 spoonbills, all of which were adults. Of course, that is only a sample, since Bear Lake occupies about 800 acres and miles of the shore where other spoonbills might occur. Even so, the flock I did see should have had a few subadult individuals to replace the aging adult population.

15–16 January 1963

The morning at Flamingo was filled with writing several postcards to people north of Florida. Several brief showers of light rain fell the rest of the day. I again reviewed my trip list. Allan Cruickshank had mentioned I would be missing several northeastern species if I stuck with my plan to bird Florida and slowly work my way to spring in Texas and the Southwest. There seemed only one answer to the problem. I would find those missing northeastern birds by going to them. After Florida, I would drive north as far as coastal Maine during February. There would still be enough time to make it to Texas for the spring migration.

At noon, I met Dick Cunningham, to who I returned the key to Snake Bight Road and thanked him for information on the cuckoo. He wished me luck on my venture. By late afternoon, I was at Long Pine Key Campground, where heavy dark clouds later obscured the next morning sunshine. I aired out my bedding, made sure I had winter clothes, cleaned the inside of the car, and repacked for the trip north. While cleaning, collections of crumbs, mostly ex-Christmas cookies, were spread out on the picnic table. An American Crow, Northern Mockingbirds, and even a Palm Warbler visited the table.

17 January 1963

On my way from Long Pine to park headquarters, I stopped for a second look around at Royal Palm Hammock. The usual herons, egrets, and gallinules clamored for food, an eight-foot alligator was sunbathing 20 feet from the boardwalk and, surprise, an Anhinga had just caught a fish. Only the bird's neck was visible. It truly looked like a snake. I noted its metallic green skin around the eyes.

Just one of the many Florida herons and egret.

Nearby Gumbo-Limbo Trail was fascinating, but not for its birds. The half-mile winding trail was under a deeply shaded canopy of oaks, mahogany, poisonwood, and gumbo-limbo, lush ferns, and mosses. Epiphytes were everywhere. This was a place for a botanist, but I imagined it crawling with birds during migration.

Bill Robertson was at park headquarters. He was standing over a large table examining specimens of birds collected over the years in the park. These were small samples of the 206 regularly occurring species recorded since 1947 when the park began. I was embarrassed that I saw only 75 of the species during my short visit. I reported finding only adult Roseate Spoonbills at Bear Lake. Bill said he was not surprised and told me the green skin of the Anhinga becomes more noticeable during the progression of the courtship of the species.

The next couple of hours were spent driving, first to Homestead, then due north to the famous Tamiami Trail, the only highway, the only road, across the Everglades. My home for the night was a few miles west at a wide spot along the highway.

18 January 1963

Limpkins calling during the night kept me pleasantly awake part of last night and lulled me to sleep the remainder of time. Mosquitoes found their way through the cracked car windows during the cooler morning hours. The sun quickly warmed the car, and the mosquitoes began to search for darker and cooler nooks and crannies in the car. After the heat from the sun rousted me out of bed, I rolled up the windows of the car to let the sun heat the car to kill any trapped mosquitoes. That way, I could start fresh, with a new and annoying population of mosquitoes for the next night.

Just west of the western sign announcing the boundary of the hamlet of Ochopee was a left turn and a place to park. As instructed by Mr. Stimson, I walked a side road for about a quarter of a mile southward where sparrows began flushing. There were five and they were ducking and covering too fast to identify. It was frustrating. Walking back and forth through broom grass finally panned out when one of the wily birds stopped long enough to identify it as a Cape Sable Seaside Sparrow. Feeling great about a new life bird, I headed to Marcos Island on the Gulf of Mexico. I drove a short distance down the beach, then, because the tide was in, I waded through waist-deep water to the north bar of the island. A walk of about 100 yards, dripping warm water on the dry pale sand, was where I found my first Snowy Plover.

My second crossing was slightly drier; the tide was going out. The warm marine breeze dried my clothes while I photographed several of the attractive shells that I had read were on the Gulf beaches. At nightfall, I pulled to the side of the highway.

19 January 1963

In the western Everglades and not far inland from heavily populated southwestern Florida is Corkscrew Swamp Audubon Sanctuary, a 13,000-acre region of virgin forest saved from the ax of loggers. Thousands of acres of cypress and pines had been cleared from southern Florida in the 1940s and fifties. By 1954, the National Audubon Society began acquiring what untouched land remained. When I arrived, Hurricane Donna had blown hundreds of trees to the ground, but the guide I met seemed optimistic. As for birding, I was not optimistic, but the experience rivaled only my time in Okefenokee. Three species of herons, Limpkins, Chuck-will's-widow, five species of woodpeckers, seven species of warblers, flaming red Northern Cardinals, and more filled my day. While leaning on the rail along the 2.25-mile-long boardwalk, I felt the whole structure first vibrate slightly, and then it began to shake from a person walking just out of sight. The shaking became stronger, and I looked up. The heavy footsteps were those of Sandy Sprunt, now a couple yards away. He smiled and said the Zenaida Dove was still hanging around his home. Sandy offered hints about birding in the Northeast in winter and was supportive of my plan to concentrate on the coast of Maine. Alexander Sprunt, Sandy's father, was also in the swamp, somewhere, and busy leading a nature tour. He eventually came in sight, but not wanting to interrupt his tour, I never got to meet the man, the author of my book on birds of prey, and who curated the Charleston Museum that I visited not long ago. Leaving Corkscrew Swamp, the Sprunts, and cypress, I drove north to Fort Myers where I parked for the night. It was time to get serious about my winter plan.

Lyle Hubbard and others complained vociferously about the tortured plight of the Everglades. Since the discovery of the great marsh, people have cursed it and have tried to drain it. Canals were dug, new land became settlements and farms at the expense of the Everglades from its headwaters, the Kissimmee River to Lake Okeechobee, and the vast sheet of water to the shores of Biscayne Bay and Florida Bay. The US Congress, in 1948, authorized the Army Corps of Engineers to construct a system of roads, canals, you name it, to, so it was said, to provide water and flood protection to save the Everglades. Not surprisingly, the plan backfired. Damage ensued. In 1962, the Army Corps of Engineers destroyed 48,000 acres of marsh when they began to channelize the Kissimmee River and in 1963 the Everglades was divided by levees and canals into three so-called water conservation areas. In early 1963, I was oblivious that a year earlier the floodgates along the Tamiami Trail were closed, further restricting water flow to Everglades National Park.

The mighty Everglades has naturally changed. Some of the obvious changes, for example, were in 1979 when stormwater from the Everglades Agricultural Area that should have been pumped into Lake Okeechobee was pumped into the marshes, resulting in the spread of cattails into the normally saw grass habitat. The complex chemical balances of water flowing from agricultural and urban regions continue to evolve. The Everglades is heavily channeled and how much water flows where is controlled by man, not nature. Nature continues to lose.

Interstate 75 crossing southern Florida before going north to Michigan obstructs part of the southern flow of water to Everglades NP. How could it not? Of course, building a road across southern Florida was not new. The Tamiami Trail, aka US Highway 41, was completed in 1928. Originally built to allow the flooding summer water to flow over the road, at which time the route was closed, changes in traffic demanded the road always be opened. That meant building up the road, constructing canals to protect the road, and thereby impeding the flow of water. Replacing sections of the roadbed with long bridges began with a mile-long bridge in 2013 and a 2.3-mile-long bridge in 2019. More of the Tamiami Trail is planned to be raised for a better flow of water. When? The projected deadline is 2030.

To prevent the occurrence of a dull moment, the federal government in the 1960s pushed to have a giant international airport constructed in the Everglades. The plan was defeated by 1968. In 1971, the Army Corps completed engineering a straight Kissimmee River. The project caused the major depletion of waterfowl and fish. Over 90 percent of birds were gone. About 20 years later, Congress authorized the Kissimmee River to be restored to its former meandering self. More to the story includes good, bad, and ugly changes, including agricultural by-products getting into the water and a $7.8 million federal restoration program. Plans to increase the water flow to Everglades NP also include construction south of Lake Okeechobee of what is dubbed the Everglades Reservoir. The project has not received good reviews by those outside governmental entities,[2] including scientists and representatives of the Sierra Club and executive director of the Friends of the Everglades and Florida Director of the Center for Biological Diversity.[3] Regardless, so much historical and ongoing damage, the continuance of human pressures, and climate change will hinder restoring the Everglades.

Another issue affecting the Everglades and the park is hurricanes. For example, in 1992, Hurricane Andrew devastated parts of southern Florida.

---

2. William J. Mitsch. "Restoring the Florida Everglades: Comments on the Current Reservoir Plan for Solving Harmful Algal Blooms and Restoring the Florida Everglades." *Ecological Engineering* 138 (2019) 155–59.

3. Letter from Diana Umpierre et al. to Andrew LoSchiavo and Amy Thompson, February 24, 2020. https://everglades.org/wp-content/uploads/2020/05/EAA-Storage-Reservoir_Final-EIS_Joint-Comments_Sierra-Club_Center-for-Biological-Diversity_Friends-of-the-Everglades_02-24-20-3.pdf.

Bill Robertson's home, including his library, was ruined. Portions of it were replaced by the ornithological community. Of course, not much could be done about the destruction of the habitat by Andrew and other major hurricanes (Katrina and Wilma in 2005, Irma in 2017) that shredded trees and bushes of their leaves and trimmed the canopy trees down three to five feet. Loss of vegetation, the worst including downed trees, some of the unique mahogany trees, continue as wind strength from hurricanes increases in response to global climate change.

Of course, restoration of Everglades NP should include eradication of the introduced Burmese pythons, one animal likely unaffected by hurricanes. The proliferation and damage by the snake is an ongoing issue. Had those awful, introduced predators been around in 1963, I likely would have kept the windows rolled up. The snakes have slithered their way over the park and have depleted populations of raccoons and anything they can wrap around. Even alligators are on their menu. Besides the pythons, about 250 species of invasive plants and around 50 nonnative animals have occurred in the park. Nineteen of those are reported as maintaining populations. One is enough to cause irreparable harm. Luckily, most exotics introduced on purpose or accidentally in southern Florida do not survive.

On a positive note, Everglades NP has grown. Extensive details about the park appear in Robert W. Blythe's web-based report.[4] Beginning in 1945, the 400,000-acre region was known as Everglades NWR and was patrolled by the US Fish and Wildlife Service. Dedication of Everglades NP occurred in December 1947. About that time, the Park Service relocated residents of Flamingo to the present site. The last permanent resident of Flamingo vacated the park in 1951. I learned that the Flamingo campground was built in 1958. I was unaware or have no memory of the RV campground, which was constructed in 1963. Linda and I resided in our RV in Flamingo Campground during part of April 2015 and were relieved that electricity had been installed around 1986. Overflight of military jets and sonic booms were a problem in the park in the 1960s. The fast flying was stopped by 1987. Anyone experiencing sonic booms knows the sounds are at the very least disturbing. Other and varied military activities that, according to Blythe, involved infrared experiments during the Vietnam War, low-flying bombers, a missile base during the Cold War, and the Cuban crisis have taken their business elsewhere over time. Everglades NP contains 1,542,526 acres that includes the 109,500 acres added in 1989. Most of that is designated as a wilderness. The park has also had important designations such as a

---

4. Robert W. Blythe. *Wilderness on the Edge: A History of Everglades National Park.* https://evergladeswildernessontheedge.com/

EVERGLADES AND A NEW PLAN

Biosphere and World Heritage Site in 1976, a World Heritage Site in 1979, and a Wetland of International Importance in 1987 by UNESCO and the Ramsar Convention. Unfortunately, those designations may not save the Everglades, the endangered wood stork, and other birds living in it. Declines in Roseate Spoonbill populations that Bill Robertson worried about in 1963 were not ill-founded and continue. Several sources have concluded the decline is a result of current water management practices. Designations also have not increased the progress of the Comprehensive Restoration Plan, a program of millions of dollars, a cast of thousands, and decades in operation, or so it appears.

When I was in the park in 1963, 626,100 people visited there. In 2015, considerably more people were made happy or contributed to the happiness of mosquitoes by visiting the park. Why the third largest park is visited by so few people is not clear. Perhaps it is the bugs, now it might be the pesky Burmese pythons, the heat, that there is only a single road in and out of the park, and did I mention the bugs? If no other reason for visiting Everglades NP, visitors often consider the winter sky. Deep into the park is where star gazing is at its best. It is a place to see the Milky Way, a sight that in most parts of the world is out competed by the lights of cities and towns. In the park, the natural darkness and stars above allow sea turtles and other wildlife to live unencumbered by artificial lighting. An obvious problem caused by artificial lighting is the creation of a false horizon that misdirects hatching sea turtles. There are so many good reasons for going to the park. Birds are posing, orchids and other unique flora are blooming, there is peace and quiet, camping, panthers, and bears, oh my, so much that needs the water held upstream.

People wanting more from the water originating from the Everglades watershed now have the 729,000-acre Big Cypress National Preserve, established in 1974. Unlike a national park, hunting, mining, off-road vehicles, and personal real estate are allowed. Snail Kites occur in the preserve.

The total population of endangered Snail Kites in Florida in 1962 was dangerously low. Estimates then ranged from as low as 50 up to several hundred. Someone I met during my travel suggested there were only 200 kites in the state. Population estimates in 1972 included only 65 birds. It is no wonder I missed one of so few birds living in such a vast area of potentially good habitat. Kite populations thwarted by drought and more importantly habitat alteration have increased since then, despite the continued loss of habitat. Based on systematic surveys of the University of Florida, around 3,500 kites occurred in Florida in 1999. A severe drought in 2001 was responsible for the kite population to plummet to only 700 birds. A decade later, the Snail Kites population was estimated to hover at 2,600 birds. I feel lucky having seen one in Kissimmee Prairie Preserve State Park in 2015, though estimates by the University of Florida demonstrate a gradual and unspectacular increase in kites beginning in 2009 but petering out about 10 years later. Audubon Florida recently agreed with the National Research Council of the National Academies that restoration of the Snail Kite garners a failing grade, a big F.[5] Could better marks for saving Florida's Snail Kites ever be achieved? All is not good in the land of kites and snails. Unstable water levels create a feast and famine situation whereby low water leaves snails high and dry, something a slimy snail cannot afford and continue living. Water levels that are too high puts the snails below the surface and thus inaccessible to the kites. What might, no, what will happen is human induced weather changes will continue to deteriorate. Water levels will continue bobbing up and down. Another issue is simply snailessness. That is correct, some part of kite habitat is devoid of snails, either because of erratic water levels or some unknown cause.

There is more to the story of Snail Kites and snails. It seems that the natural diet of the kite, primarily the apple snail, is competing, at least as of 2004, with an invasive species of snail from Middle and South America. A correspondent wrote that the invasive snail "got loose," which evokes a Jurassic Park scenario in slow motion. No matter, those alien snails are out there, everywhere, and not as susceptible to changes in water level compared to the native apple snail. The southern snail is three times larger than the apple snail. Of course, bigger prey equates to a bigger meal, and it is not difficult to imagine Snail Kites likely eyeing the apple snail with less gusto than the invasive snail. The larger species is apparently out competing the small apple snails, which at first sounds positive to the kites, but populations of the larger snail, for whatever reason, are subject to the boom or bust syndrome. Like sudden eruptions of overpopulated lemming, the large snails could be here one today and gone tomorrow.

Early studies suggested Florida Snail Kites were having difficulty capturing and eating the new food source. The Florida kites were not too big for their snails. So, what is a Florida Snail Kite to do? It seems simple. To capture and eat the larger and heavier snails, the Snail Kites needed to be larger and have a larger bill than their ancestors, and that is what the kites did; the birds became larger, including their bills.[6] Not the same birds but their descendants were better equipped for the larger fare. That is a remarkable

---

5. Audubon Florida. "Everglade Snail Kite Receives 'F' Grade from National Research Council." Jun 21, 2012. https://fl.audubon.org/press-release/everglade-snail-kite-receives-%E2%80%9Cf%E2%80%9D-grade-national-research-council.

6. Paul Hess summarizes the kites, snails, and research on them in *Birding* 50.4 (2018) 24–25.

feat owing to the brief time between about 2004 to present. My first thought was Holy Darwin, I thought evolution was a slow process. It normally is, but there is a process called phenotypic plasticity, which means the response of an organism to environmental change can occur without a genetic change of that organism. I would add that there probably is genetic change, but we just do not currently understand detecting it. Nonetheless, the Florida Snail Kites seem to have a chance to thrive if only fluctuations of water (floods and drought) and other pesky habitat problems were measurably abated.

Speaking of something measurable, the Snail Kites of Florida were originally described by Robert Ridgway as a new subspecies. Ridgway, a famous ornithologist beginning in the late nineteenth century, is one of my heroes who worked at Smithsonian decades before me. He named the taxon of kite *plumbeous*. Some later investigators decided Ridgway, the man who authored the book on coloration of birds, was wrong about *plumbeous* being grayer than other subspecies of Snail Kites, but that differences between the four recognized subspecies could be based on size alone. Now, enter the invasive snail and the alleged increase in size of Florida kites. This is a recipe generating innumerable questions. One of the larger questions is if the Florida birds, aka *plumbeous*, are getting bigger by the snail if not the year, how can the characters of size remain useful for identifying subspecies of kites? Another issue is whether Ridgway was wrong about characterizing Florida Snail Kites as grayer than nearby subspecies. A long-time colleague and avid birder questioned ignoring coloration. As a long-time practitioner of identifying subspecies, including qualitative determinations of color, I believe Ridgway was probably correct, but I would like to see for myself.

Lyle Hubbard, ever optimistic, was genuinely disappointed when he introduced me to the heart of the Everglades and could not show me a Snail Kite. I will always remember him for showing me a plethora of warblers in Michigan and his enthusiasm and dedication while participating in so many Christmas Bird Counts. I also remember Lyle for another reason. Before leaving his home, both in Michigan and in Florida, he had the habit of saying "wallet, keys, cigarettes, fly" so as to not leave behind something important or exposed. Even to this day, although I stopped smoking three decades ago, I occasionally catch myself reciting Lyle's important checklist before leaving home. Lyle died several years ago. When visiting near Fort Pierce in 2015 I wondered what footprint he might have left in Florida or at least at his home turf at Fort Pierce. Sadly, the local birders I spoke to did not know his name. Besides the history of Lyle, much of Fort Pierce that I came to know was gone in 2015, unrecognizable, replaced by different storefronts and a population that exploded from 25,256 to 46,270.

On my way to Everglades National Park, Howard Langridge, another person who tried to help me find a kite, asked if I had heard anything from Smithsonian about the dead grassquit. I had not. Not much later, in a 16 March 1963 letter from Smithsonian to Howard, George Watson stated that the bird I found was a female Black-faced Grassquit representing the nominate subspecies, a resident to the Bahamas. Howard wrote that he would send the information to the regional editor of *Audubon Field Notes* (=*North American Birds*), "with the understanding that you (Mr. Browning) will write the article for the Auk as suggested by Mr. Watson. Therefore, Ralph Browning added a new species to our local list. Congratulations." Had I not been swept up by what I perceived as more important than it was and not felt rushed to get into print, I would have insisted that Howard be one of the authors. After all, it was a tiny note documenting the third specimen for the United States and Howard was instrumental in the initial identification and sending the specimen to Smithsonian. It was not the first grassquit for the country. Howard wrote me more than once when the note would be published. The duration of time from submitting a manuscript to an editor to the printing is generally called "turn around" and it can be considerable, depending on the journal. Editing, peer review, possibly more editing, it all takes time. The Black-faced Grassquit I found was the first specimen in Smithsonian that I ever collected. The publication on it appeared in an issue of the *Auk* in 1964.[7]

Birding almost every day is bound to reward a few rare or unusual birds. Although I did not question the identity of the grassquit, I began doubting my identification of the Black-whiskered Vireo I found along Snake Bight Road since the species is not known to winter in North America. However, I think I can recall that bird back in 1963. My recollection of the event, mosquitoes, and all, somehow is focused as if it happened yesterday, well almost yesterday. It is hard to explain, but the degree of clarity of my memory of the vireo ranks with my first kiss with Linda at age nine (an altogether different story), summiting Mount Shasta, Alexander Wetmore standing at his office door, other kisses with Linda (which is still another story) and so many more memories sometime gratefully recalled with uncanny clarity and others that were not so pleasant, such as the death of my parents and fear that first night of the trip when I huddled in a freezing tent and heard something sniffing on the other side of the thin canvas. Did I see a Black-whiskered Vireo, or should I remove it from my list of birds

---

7. M. Ralph Browning. "Third United States Record of the Black-Faced Grassquit (*Tiaris bicolor*)." The Auk 81 (1964) 233.

observed in Florida? Since then, I have seen numerous Black-whiskered Vireos. The one I am sure I saw in 1963 and the later ones are identical.

William B. Robertson, who I enjoyed visiting during his trips to Washington, DC, worked almost 50 years for the betterment of Everglades and Dry Tortugas National Parks. He died at 75 in 2000. I still recall Bill laughing when Howard Langridge hit his thumb that early morning looking for rails. The late Dick Cunningham, who began working in Everglades the year we met, sent me an email in 2004 about working on a book on the birds of Everglades National Park. One of his co-authors was Bill.

My effort to find a Cape Sable Seaside Sparrow near tiny Ochopee, a small unincorporated town of possibly 150 people, was all for naught. Oh, I found the taxon, but later had to discount it as a species. The federally endangered Cape Sable Seaside Sparrow taxonomically traveled in the same direction as the famed Dusky Seaside Sparrow. Both came to be treated as subspecies of Seaside Sparrow though I am not so sure the last large-sized singer has delivered the last note on these sparrows. Meanwhile, Ochopee became the headquarters of the Big Cypress Preserve. Ochopee's 1953 post office, a former tool shed measuring eight feet and four inches by seven feet, might need a new wing.

Leaving the waters of the immense Everglades in 1963 then seemed tantamount to leaving Florida. Nearing the end of January brought me closer to going north to find birds wintering in coastal Maine. My 1962 autumn in the North garnered several acquaintances that might help me in my goal, but detailed plans to get there were based mostly on guesses and little regard that I would be heading into bone-chilling temperatures and ice and snow that could make driving hazardous. With a rudimentary route mapped out, a few phone calls to northern contacts, a lack of adequate winter clothes, absence of snow tires or chains, it was not a great plan. Still, if a Snow Bunting, an alcid or two, maybe a Great Cormorant showed, the plan could be worthwhile.

Chapter 21

Going North, Going Home

20 January 1963

WIND-DRIVEN WAVES SPRAYED HIGH over the long causeway at the mouth of Tampa Bay. The high bridge across the bay, the Sunshine Skyway, was 15 miles long. The height of 150 feet above the bay and a buffeting west gale made for a nervous crossing in the lightweight VW. Maybe having a year's worth of pounds of clothes, food, books, and notes kept me from flying into the bay. How many more white-knuckle-producing bridges will I have to cross?

St. Petersburg, at the north end of the bridge, was a breeding location for the introduced Ringed Turtle-Dove. The AOU check-list stated the species breeds in Los Angeles and Miami. Florida birders told me St. Petersburg was the place to look, and I did not want to wait until Los Angeles. They said I "would have little trouble finding the doves in the city parks and that they practically feed out of your hand." I fought Sunday traffic into town and checked a couple of city parks. No turtle doves were in sight. Three different birders I phoned for new information were not home.

21–23 January 1963

The night east of Lakeland, away from the warming Gulf of Mexico, was cold. Arriving at Orlando in central Florida and not so many miles from the northern Everglades, I was supposed to meet my aunt and uncle from Indiana whom I last saw in July. Because they were a month behind schedule,

I continued eastward to pick up my general delivery mail at Cocoa. While there, I paid $9.61 for a mechanic to winterize the VW by installing new points put in the distributor and adjusting the timing. The mechanic also sandblasted the carbon off the electrodes of the four spark plugs. That was one of many of the jobs I once performed to collect money for this trip. The transportation budget, starting at $185.00, was now down to a balance of $60.65. With little over four months of travel left, I would come close to staying within budget although my detour to Maine would put my transportation budget in the red. Thankfully, there was the $25 for my talk at the St. Lucie Audubon Society. I told myself everything would be okay. After all, the transmission suddenly stopped leaking and the long underwear I packed back in 1962 and never wore were going to come in handy. The car and I were ready for northern weather, but the waves of cold fronts sweeping southward did worry me.

Before leaving Florida, I had a few stops and more time to reconsider driving north. One stop, fulfilling a promise to an aunt in Oregon that I would look up her sister and family, could no longer be avoided. They lived in Eau Gallie, which I heard should be pronounced as "oh golly." It was a good name since it was hard to locate on a road map. My hosts insisted that I stay a couple of days, one of which was for a visit to Patrick Air Force Base a few miles south of Cape Canaveral. It was interesting, but I preferred to witness a rocket launch or another Dusky Seaside Sparrow.

24–27 January 1963

Leaving the east coast of Florida, I drove west to Maitland to visit the Audubon staff who might offer advice about birding New England in winter. Mo Oliver, the bookkeeper, and I got into a lengthy discussion about the value of studying birds as a profession. She could not understand how anyone could enjoy watching birds. She asked questions about ethics, such as ornithologists disturbing the birds that they are studying; does ornithology really help the health of the environment and the health of the ornithologist. I told her ornithologists did help save birds and that if doing so made them happy, maybe it helped the health of ornithologists. For me, a bird watcher, I was happy and healthy.

After my last night sleeping on the Audubon House floor, I was greeted by Mo, Russ Mason, and Margaret Hundley returning to work. Russ and Margaret were encouraging about my northern detour and offered places to look for birds. Mo had already told me I was crazy. After a final cup of coffee, I headed northeast past acres of orange and grapefruit orchards.

Unfortunately, most of the fruit was on the ground, lying in the mud of flooded trees. Trees were leafless and blackened by the cold wave I felt nipping at Fort Pierce in December. By afternoon, I arrived north of Daytona Beach at the Williams in Ormond Beach. I had not seen them since before Christmas.

A cold light rain fell in the morning. The phone rang. A Brant, a species I needed for my trip list, had been spotted in the area. The Williams couple and I headed to the Halifax River near downtown Daytona Beach, where we found a single Brant preening itself on a small outcrop of beach rocks. I wondered if this waif of a Brant was the one reported earlier from the end of Snake Bight Road, the Brant I searched for amid the hordes of mosquitoes. The Brant today was bug-free.

Later in the day, I was riding a car on the famous flat sands of Daytona Beach for the first time. There were no speeding cars. The posted speeds limited daytime driving to 15 miles per hour and 25 miles per hour at night. Car traffic was light, and in one and a half hours, we found 45 species including eight species of shorebirds with the expected gulls and terns resting on the hard sand. It felt good to be birding again.

The next day's field trip ended abruptly when the Williams' car began to sputter. We turned to their home. The cold rain continued to fall as I started to have doubts about going northward.

28–30 January 1963

My VW motor home seemed cold as I drove east from the Williams. The blower that cooled the engine also was the source of air from the heater vents. The faster I drove, the stronger the flow, but the faintly warmed air barely helped my cold fingers. Today's destination was on the other side of Florida at Live Oaks, a town west of Tallahassee and home of Elisabeth Ball. Geraldine Cox of Washington, North Carolina, the person introducing me to the term *whisker*, suggested Ms. Ball would likely know of places to look for birds in St. Marks National Wildlife Refuge.

I spent a chilly night parked behind a service station eight miles east of Tallahassee. Once out of my sleeping bag, I realized just how frigid it was. I hurried to drive west through the rolling hills of Tallahassee. For the size of the city, the YMCA was tiny and without shower facilities. Luckily, there was a sink and hot water. I suppose it is fortunate that I am traveling alone; at least I manage to tolerate myself.

At Florida State University, I hoped to meet Dr. Henry Stevenson although an exact date and time were not scheduled. I found the biology department, but he was in class. Instead of waiting there, I drove to the post office to stock up on the new 5 cent stamp. On the drive back, the snarl in traffic caused me to miss Dr. Stevenson. He had moved on to a different building. I missed him there, so I left him a note apologizing for my poor scheduling.

Driving south from Tallahassee, the fiery glow of the sunset to my right, I found a wide shoulder off the road north of St. Marks National Wildlife Refuge. The night's thoughts were on what a Florida birdwatcher I met in the Everglades told me. They were directions to a locality in St. Marks where someone reported the rarest of North American birds. The remote possibility of seeing an Ivory-billed Woodpecker kept me awake almost the entire night.

Sunshine seeping through the car windows warmed the morning of 30 January. Excited, I followed my directions, ending up at a building and a sign advertising boats for rent. An old gent standing near the door looked up. Tobacco, wet and disgustingly stuck on his stained lips, oozed down his bristled chin and onto brown spotted overalls. "Yes," he told me, as he wiped his chin with a sleeve and spit. "They arsome big peckerwoods 'round." I quizzed him, showed him my field guide, and everything he said led me to believe he had seen, years ago, an Ivory-billed Woodpecker. I decided to use the rest of the morning to search the dense woods he described. I walked, listened, walked, and listened, hearing and seeing no shortage of Pileated Woodpeckers.

Back at Tallahassee, I picked up $4 worth of groceries for the next several days and paid $1.60 for an oil change and lube. Darkness was falling as I drove north following headlight beams on US 319. Pockets of fog, constant rain, and wet roads were unpleasant for driving. Sadly leaving Florida, I decided to call it a day at a service station in the southern outskirts of Thomasville, Georgia. Falling asleep behind the garage was not easy. My trip list, standing at 340 species, was small and not what I had expected it to be by the end of January. I hoped that the gamble to return to Maine would be worth the pain of cold and risk of driving in ice and snow. I also hoped the Georgia law would not pester me again.

31 January–2 February 1963

The cold and being behind the wheel left aching muscles. After driving all day, I crossed Georgia and most of South Carolina. Only 30 minutes of daylight, I found a place at Cheraw, South Carolina, just off US 1 to park for the night. I wrote Linda an airmail letter. Ice covered every alley and side street.

The first day of February was freezing. Much to my relief, the car started, and I was soon crunching ice along the street to the highway. The windshield kept icing up while frozen snow began gathering in the wheel wells and undercarriage, which increased the car's weight. Donning long handles after a hot shower in Raleigh, North Carolina, was an absolute necessity. Before leaving town, I spent $2.88 on new wiper blades. Near Petersburg, Virginia, two large birds flying overhead invited a closer look. Sudden stops were impossible on the glazed road; I had already witnessed several cars abandoned in highway ditches. Inching to a stop, I jumped out of the cramped car, and with tired eyes saw two Black Vultures. My night was a time for shivering in my VW behind a service station in Richmond. On 2 February, I decided to drive to Shenandoah National Park but got as far as Charlottesville. Because the icy roads were even icier to the northwest, I decided to take a right on US 29 toward Washington, DC.

3 February 1963

Yesterday evening I arrived in Vienna, Virginia, and phoned George William's daughter Francis. She was expecting me and gave me instructions to her home. It was wonderful not to sleep in the car. With her children, we toured the newly opened Dulles International Airport. The sweeping architecture was stunning, and it was warm inside. Huge and very unsightly buses ferry passengers from the terminal to the airport runways, about a half-mile away. Later, we visited Great Falls on the Potomac River where George Washington surveyed and where few birds shivered. Before the day was over, we were standing in line at the National Gallery of Art to view the Mona Lisa. A Marine guard kept everyone moving though I took as much time as possible staring at the wistful expression of the famous face.

4–6 February 1963

The early morning temperature dipped to around five degrees. Dennis Sherwin, who I met last fall and was alerted that I was traveling through, had planned a trip to Ocean City, Maryland, tomorrow. In the meantime, he had arranged for me to stay at his vacationing aunt's house in Georgetown where I spent a cozy evening working on my notes and wondering if I had made a mistake coming north. Maybe tomorrow would help decide the usefulness of entering the boreal landscape.

The promising trip to Ocean City, where 142 species topped their Christmas Bird Count, was disappointing. After driving over 300 miles, paying the dollar toll twice to cross and re-cross the Chesapeake Bay Bridge, Dennis and I entered the city just in time for rush hour traffic. Still, Tundra Swan was added to the trip list. On the next day, 6 February, we headed toward the Chesapeake Bay again and birded on the west side at Sandy Point and Kent Island and added Long-tailed Duck to the trip list. White fog hid the strangely mysterious calls of the swans. Ever slowly, the fog lifted, revealing over 100 of these white birds. As the day progressed, a freezing wind became almost unbearable.

7 February 1963

I visited the Division of Birds at Smithsonian. Drs. Humphrey and Wetmore were away. George Watson was there and right away told me that he and Dr. Humphrey were considering me for a position for work in the Pacific. I could not believe it. After a few years of college I could be working for Smithsonian.

8 February 1963

Dennis, a fellow named George, and I checked for waterfowl on a pond at Roaches Run near the airport. The next day the three of us drove to Kent Island, where we met a couple birdwatching. They had seen several American Tree Sparrows, one of the northern species I hoped to find on Sandy Point. Forty minutes later, we arrived at the described place and found a flock of American Tree Sparrows.

9–10 February 1963

Dennis and I drove to Patuxent Research Center near Laurel, Maryland, on the ninth, where we found closed gates. It was Sunday. We birded around Alexandria and found a few of the usual suspects. The next morning, we drove back to Patuxent. This time, I followed Dennis since I would be driving north later in the morning. We searched for longspurs but found White-throated Sparrows, a single American Tree Sparrow, and ponds too frozen for anything but ice-skating. We met Chandler Robbins in the warmth of his office and his smile. He also lamented that birding on the center was dismal.

In the early afternoon, I headed north. Before reaching Baltimore, the right front brake developed a loud grinding noise.

11 February 1963

Today was car repair day. I had already found many mechanics unwilling to work on foreign vehicles and was relieved that someone would look at my brakes. The worn right shoe would not keep me safe. I was shocked that replacing one shoe and the labor came to $7 and even more shocked that I had to use my last travelers check to pay the bill. Even though I was using a gas credit card that my father paid from my bank account, I had only $5 in my pocket and enough food to last 10 days. If anything else comes up, I could be in trouble. I was thankful for a handy phone. My father would wire money from my Oregon bank account.

12–13 February 1963

It was a frigid night, with a low of 15 degrees, in a noisy parking lot of a service station in Wilmington, Delaware. After the morning restroom run and eating nearly frozen donuts, I was on my way. The drive north on turnpikes took me west of New York City and took a chunk of my $5. Slippery roads became worse close to Boston while the temperature hovered slightly above 20. I located the Massachusetts Audubon Society office to see what birds might be in the area. It would be exciting to see a Tufted Duck, Glaucous and Iceland Gulls, Snow Bunting, and a King Eider they listed. Unbelievably, after all the miles driven from warm southern Florida, those rare birds were all somewhere other than Boston. Near Gloucester, I found two Harlequin Ducks and searched for new gulls. A breeze sent cold needles to the bone. When I reached Newburyport, a coastal town a few miles south of New Hampshire, daylight and my eyes were growing dim. At the YMCA, I got a room for $1.75. I could not afford to buy anything to eat. Luckily, I had a little food in the car. Because bringing food inside the Y was prohibited, I had to smuggle the food from the car into my room. A can of beans was heated on my room's radiator.

14 February 1963

The warm bed in the YMCA was difficult to leave but life birds were waiting, or so I believed. A check at the local sewer outlet was birdless. My drive to Parker River National Wildlife Refuge on Plum Island slightly south of Newburyport might have yielded longspurs, but it did not. When asked about Snowy Owls, the manager told me I should have been there last year.

Birding was not good, and the weather was too uncomfortable to keep birding. What had I gotten myself into?

Driving nonstop for about three hours, I arrived at my August friends, the Chadbournes in Yarmouth, Maine. They were one of the recipients of a postcard from Florida, my brief warning that I was coming back. The Chadbournes welcomed me back with smiles, questions, and a glowing fire warming the inside. Outside, the snow was almost three feet deep while the thermometer was holding in the teens.

15–18 February 1963

The next day I rode shotgun on Harry's stove oil delivery truck while searching for Snow Buntings and redpolls. We saw only three crows chasing a Red-tailed Hawk and gulls with black wingtips. Harry asked why a man who made homes warm and comfortable had to be so cold doing it.

The temperature dropped to zero in the early hours of the sixteenth. Ginny had an electric space heater blasting in the kitchen, and then pushed down the toaster. A fuse blew but there were no replacement fuses. I offered to go to the store for fuses, but my car would not start. We tried pushing it into the warmer garage, but the snow and ice were too slippery. A neighbor, with his pickup, pushed the freezing VW out of the frigid wind. He also picked up the necessary fuses. Later, my car that could did, and I picked up the needed money from home.

On the third day at the Chadbournes, Ginny, their young son Brian and I toured backcountry roads north of Yarmouth. The bright sun reflected off immaculate snow, snow that had glazed over by repeated thawing and freezing. The narrow, marginally plowed byways and snow banking high at the edge of the pavement were unlike any winter I had experienced. Most of the birds we saw were concentrated around houses, with starlings and chickadees dominating the scene. A man clearing his driveway looked up as we slowed to check a Hairy Woodpecker. He seemed to be rambling, but I heard the words "snow birds." He might have meant juncos but said they were close to the size of a robin and mostly white. A Brown Creeper spiraled up a tree followed by a massive flock of birds exploding from the man's backyard. "That's them, snow birds," he said. Snow Buntings at last!

That afternoon we drove to Portland's Back Bay. Buffleheads, Common Goldeneyes, and Oldsquaws dotted the water. The next day, the eighteenth, we returned to Back Bay where I found a Bonaparte's Gull, a new trip species. Harry had taken off the afternoon and was eager to check birds south of Portland at Pine Point near Scarborough. Before leaving Yarmouth,

Harry wanted to initiate me to wearing snowshoes. I first learned how to fall face-first into the snow. A few yards of walking taught me I lacked certain leg muscles needed for traversing any distance beyond the length of a garden hose. Pine Point, on the other hand, did not require snowshoes as long as you stayed on the snow-packed roads. There were no new birds to add to the trip list.

19–21 February 1963

The road leading to Bailey Island, southeast of Yarmouth, was full of frost heaves, one of which sent my head to the car roof. At the end of the road, in the town of Bailey Island, I parked and walked part of the rocky shores. A large, white-throated cormorant shadowed a Common Eider. An hour later, I saw my second Great Cormorant swimming near the shore. Finally, efforts to find a different gull paid off, but the bird was not a large bird with white wings, but a small delicate Black-legged Kittiwake.

When I was about to leave Bailey Island, a pickup backed up to the edge of the ocean, a man exited the vehicle and began shoveling out trash and garbage. This was his second such trip. I jotted down his license plate on his third trip and confronted him about his abuse. His annoyance boiled to the point I felt in danger. On the way back to Yarmouth, I stopped at the Brunswick newspaper office to discuss my experience. As luck would have it, I talked to the editor, who seemed interested. He said he planned to write an editorial and would send me a copy.

That evening and back at Yarmouth, Harry and Ginny were planning a trip to Portland. Snow began falling. Harry, used to driving in all sorts of weather, drove us to Portland for the Maine Audubon Society and Portland Natural History Society weekly meeting. The only ones attending the meeting were Chris Packard, who I met last fall, the Chadbournes, and me. The snow kept falling. Soon, adjourning the meeting was the only sensible choice that would allow escaping the slick Portland streets. It took us an hour to drive the 11 miles back to Yarmouth. Every few minutes, we needed to stop and scrape the blowing snow that was collecting and freezing on the windshield. A few inches of snow covered the shoveled driveway, with the rest covered with two-foot snow dunes. Harry blasted through the snow, but the last icy drift stopped the car. We jumped out quickly and began shoveling the choked path to the long garage. We finally spun Harry's big Buick into the sheltering bowels of the building. Ice caked our hair, and my windward ear was numb by the hardened snow.

The next day it snowed even more to shovel, and provided time for chatting and listening to music (Ginny sings and plays the guitar). I planned to start heading southward today but the Chadbournes advised against leaving. They were right. It snowed even more.

On the twenty-first, the snow had stopped falling and the roads were plowed. After breakfast, the blue sky blackened as snow began falling again. I planned to leave today, but I wondered if I was making a mistake. Ginny fretted while Harry said I would be all right. I hated leaving such gracious and caring friends.

Chris Packard had earlier suggested I stop at York Beach on my way south to Portsmouth, New Hampshire. It was rated as a good place to look for gulls. I spotted a strange bird from a high perching and ice-glazed residential street overlooking the pounding surf and rocky shore below. It had a telling white line on the edge of its bill. It was a Thick-billed Murre. A Barrow's Goldeneye came into view as life bird number 351. If only a Glaucous or Iceland Gull would appear. Portsmouth did not have a YMCA, but Manchester, New Hampshire, did. Dinner was across the street at a Woolworth department store.

22–24 February 1963

Minus 10 was too cold for the car battery to turn over the engine, but a pedestrian helped me push the car fast enough for the car to kick to life. Driving across New Hampshire was uneventful considering bone-chilling temperature and snow were the norms. I wanted to experience winter in the Northeast and add winter birds to the trip list. I had not done well adding new birds and I had enough of winter. Early February in Oregon is usually the beginning of spring.

Dennis Sherwin wrote his friend Warren King that he had convinced me to stop in Williamstown in the northwestern corner of Massachusetts. Warren was a student at Williams College and finding his dorm almost required snowshoes. I was invited into a crowded three-room dorm full of heavy coats and boots and stacks of books and papers, and one vacant set of bare bedsprings and a thin mattress was a welcoming place for my sleeping bag. Next to the nicest piece of furniture, a record player, was a set of cement blocks and boards holding up around 150 LPs of classical music. A Mahler symphony strained the speakers. Warren had other obligations on Saturday and arranged for Woody Hartman, another student, to help me look for birds. Woody wore a long fur coat, jeans, and hair covering his ears. Although we attempted to locate redpolls and a Great Gray Owl, we failed.

That evening, Woody invited me to dinner at his fraternity house. At the time, Warren was obligated to attend a banquet for a motorcycle association with his physics teacher. What was the common denominator between physics and motorcycles? I told myself to ask Warren.

The next morning, Warren and I rushed to the cafeteria for breakfast. Heavy snow fell as we ate scrambled eggs and hot buttery pancakes. Warren was not sure we should go birding until the last snowflake drifted to the white ground. Once that happened and only a second later, we were in Warren's classic Porsche, my first ride in a sports car, and in my favorite car. Warren nudged the throttle causing the car to fishtail, then dug in and pushed us past trees bent from heavy snow and mountains draped in white. Nearby Mount Greylock, with its 3,491 feet and the highest point in Massachusetts, allowed us to bird its shoulder. We stopped in a silent forest and then drove to a small mountain town to the east called Florida. Maybe a resident there had an active bird feeder, but once again, in the muffled snow, we heard only a few humans venturing into the cold. Still, I was thrilled to ride the car of my dreams until more snow began falling and the road began to become dangerously slick.

Warren and I spent part of the evening going over birding locations in Florida, the state where he and Woody would be next month. I looked out the window thinking I might go south again. I was not careful about what I wished for, but I did find a few northern birds. Anyway, Warren was a good host and I hoped I was returning the favor by telling him about birding in Florida.

The rest of the evening was attending dinner. The university had ruled students must wear a coat and ties for Sunday evening meals. I joined them and wore the same tie I wore in Florida, the same tie my thoughtful mom insisted I bring so many warm months ago. As suggested by Warren, I also wore my jeans and boots as a protest against the impractical dress code.

25 February–5 March 1963

Thinking I might have a chance at northern finches, I drove north from Williamstown to Burlington, Vermont. Missing from my trip list were redpolls and Pine Grosbeak. At Rutland, south of Burlington, the cold and snow changed my mind. I turned west, arriving at Elnora, a town north of Schenectady, New York, and home of the Denners, who I met last fall. We had stayed in touch, including a hastily written postcard when I left Florida almost a month ago. They welcomed me to show up on their doorstep.

During the next several days, while searching back roads for winter finches and being stuck in the snow more than once, I found a new trip bird, a Saw-whet Owl. Crossbills and redpolls were never found. Plans to leave Elnora were ended when I pushed on the brake and nothing happened. Fortunately, I was not driving fast, traffic was light, and my emergency brake worked. My thinking that I just needed new brake shoes was too optimistic since the master cylinder had to be replaced as well as new rear shoes. The mechanic charged $35 and diagnosed the knocking sound that I had been hearing since Maine: the flywheel was loose. My car was falling apart. Without the car, my motor home, I would have no means of transportation. I would be homeless. I wondered if I should head directly to Oregon before the car broke down completely.

6–15 March 1963

During last night or this morning, my mind churned away, with the focus on what to do. What should be my next step? Should I drive across the middle of the country, the Great Plains, the Rockies, and home in Oregon? No. Giving up while there is life in the car is not the best decision. Maybe I could fix the problem. My dad had taught me a thing or two about mechanics. The inside of the engine of a VW was not foreign to me. Once deciding not to throw in a greasy towel, I had to have a place to do the work on my car. A place like the backyard almond tree in Oregon, the tree with the block and tackle that was exactly right for plucking the engine out of the VW a couple of years ago would help save my car. I decided relatives in Arkansas might have a backyard tree where I could perform some of the mechanical wizardry handed down from generations of Brownings. Spring in Texas was still on my agenda if I could only get to Arkansas.

A local meteorologist reported that a snowstorm was on its way, but I needed to leave Elnora for points west. Nearing western New York, the storm had turned into a blizzard. Keeping the windshield clear of snow was almost impossible, especially when the slow crawling traffic came to a complete halt. Meanwhile, the caravan of idled cars was becoming covered with falling snow. My VW would soon look like a pile of snow. After several minutes of not moving and accumulating snow, I got out and wrestled the wind and snow to find the car blocking the way. The wind cut through my coat like a thousand knives and plastered snow hard against my face. The driver blocking the way was panicked, afraid to drive in the blizzard. I told him he had to keep moving; otherwise, about 10 cars behind him would become buried by the snow. "You have to move!" I fully expected him to ignore my teenage request. He gradually calmed down and agreed to keep moving. Finally, I was able to drive onward.

West of East Aurora, I topped a small hill and was surprised to see a driver attempting to turn their car around in the middle of the road. There was no time to stop on the snow-packed highway and I skidded into the car. Luckily, there was no damage. Visibility by now was about 20 feet. Not a bird was in sight. A mailbox on the road indicated there might be a house in the vicinity. A farmhouse across the road momentarily showed a ghostly frame as the wind-driven snowflakes no longer seemed delicate. Blowing snow then blurred the view but we found the front door and knocked. With a borrowed phone from the occupant, a call to the police was moot. We were told that they were too busy to come to the scene. The police dispatcher added that if the vehicles were drivable, for our safety, we should come back to East Aurora. The other driver, who was the head caretaker at the East Aurora high school, agreed neither of us should be on the road and I should follow him back to town. Once in town, he first took me to dinner at a local bar and then to the gymnasium where hundreds of stranded motorists were camping for the duration of the storm. The snow stopped falling by the next morning. The car started but the knocking flywheel sounded seriously worse. No doubt about it, I was in trouble. Birds had to take the back seat since I must get out of this storm. Secondly, I needed to try to repair my old faithful VW.

Fearful of being trapped by more snow, I headed southwest to Springfield, Missouri, where my favorite cousin and family lived. I drove all day and the next night, stopping only for pie and coffee and the used coffee department. My arrival at 5 a.m. at my cousin Bonnie's was early but expected. After a couple of days of recuperating and visiting, I drove south to Harrison, Arkansas, where I could stay with my favorite aunt and uncle. During the drive, each time I decelerated, the flywheel would bang loudly on its housing.

On 12 March, I located a garage that would allow me to use their space and a block and tackle free of charge. By the fourteenth, I had pulled the engine and discovered the problem. The flywheel had oblong holes that allowed it to move and bang against the housing. A local mechanic told me it could be repaired. I hired a machinist to bore new holes and to reattach the flywheel. By the next day, I had the car back together and drove to my paternal grandparents a few miles on country roads from the garage.

GOING NORTH, GOING HOME

16–24 March 1963

Now, I knew I could complete my trip, and began dreaming of migrants on the coast of Texas, and flocks of birds in the desert Southwest and California. The next day, Saturday, everyone planned the customary trip to town. My grandparents and an uncle squeezed in a small pickup. I decided to drive into town separately. When I was a quarter of a mile ahead of my uncle, a loud sound, a cross between a pop and a thud came from the engine. Before there was time for an echo, the car stopped abruptly in the middle of the dirt road. My legs, weak from anticipation, barely carried me to the rear of the car. A few feeble puffs of smoke wafted upward as oil poured from the bottom of the broken motor.

Lee, my uncle, towed me back to his home. Days later, I discovered that when the flywheel was re-bored, the machinist did not bother to check whether it was balanced or not. After all, it was just a VW, a vehicle considered most foreign in northwestern Arkansas. Hardly anyone in this part of the country wanted to be associated with foreign cars, especially those from Germany. Because of that, I had difficulty selling the car for junk. Fortunately, I found someone who towed it away. It was worth more than the $100 I was paid. My old friend, my traveling companion, shelter from all kinds of weather, had kept me safe day and night. It had transported me to new places, wonderful and interesting people, and took me to birds that a year ago were but dreams. My powerless home was being dragged away to be scavenged for parts while the remainder would be tossed in a heap of oily rust.

My favorite aunt and uncle stored the car's contents in their garage until I decided what to do. On the twenty-fourth, I knew what was next and purchased a bus ticket back to Oregon. Most of the contents of the car were shipped, along with my defeat.

25 March–3 April 1963

The bus route first took me to Little Rock to visit another uncle and aunt before heading west. I was looking forward to seeing them and birding with a cousin still in high school. She tried to help find species missing from my trip list, but it was too early for migrants. One day the family and I visited Hot Springs National Park. My uncle suggested the park, which was about 5,500 acres and had at least 50 hot springs. A brochure I picked up, along with their bird checklist, indicated the region was set aside as federal land in 1832, though the thermal features were nonetheless privatized, with bathhouses built over the springs. Maybe my disposition was no longer enthusiastic about most things, but what happened to the hot springs in Arkansas reminded me of how commercialization had spoiled Niagara Falls to the north. Even the birds were forced into unnatural settings. A Downy Woodpecker was excavating a nest hole in a tree no doubt planted by an ancestor of one of the early 1807 people who wanted to capitalize on the springs. A Tufted Titmouse was marking its territory, using a planted rosebush. Back at the house in Little Rock, Northern Cardinals and Brown Thrashers signaled spring was on its way, but I was not on the way to coastal Texas. I could not become excited about this spring. It was an effort to remain positive, but I would see something new during the bus trip home. The fact that my adventure was actually over hit me hardest as I boarded the bus home. As consolation prizes, I did see a Prairie Falcon in Texas and long tiring miles farther in central California I saw the last new trip species, Yellow-billed Magpie. On the second of April, the day of the magpies, I began to be anxious to be home. At 10:29 p.m., the bus rolled into the Medford, Oregon, terminal. The only entry of my journal on the third was "Saw some friends, Linda, especially."

Ringed Turtle-Doves, a common cage bird worldwide, was breeding in St. Petersburg in 1953. Alexander Sprunt documented that occasion. The dove was more recently confirmed to breed in two other counties in Florida by Florida's breeding bird atlas, a publication full of old acquaintances in its bibliography that included Allen Cruickshank. Not finding the doves was not such a loss since, in 1962, the American Birding Association (ABA) removed it from their official list. Really. Communication systems around then were not so great, and I was clueless about the removal. Anyway, it turns out that the doves, which may or may not have been derived from the African Collared-Dove (*Streptopelia roeogrisea*), are completely domesticated. According to the ABA, anyone leaving Ringed Turtle-Dove on their life list should add Barnyard chicken. Now, I do not feel so bad having missed my St. Petersburg target bird. I am glad that I did not cross the Sunshine Skyway in May 1980 on my way to St. Petersburg. That is when a freighter crashed into the southbound part of the scary bridge and when more than 1,000 feet of the structure, with cars and a passenger bus, fell into the mouth of Tampa Bay. Thirty-five people died. By 1987, a new bridge was built.

GOING NORTH, GOING HOME

Leaving Florida was not easy. First and foremost, Florida is a very birdy state. Second, Florida is not cold, usually. It was mostly warm and comfortable. I knew that leaving Florida would be cold, that my car, my wardrobe, and I were not ready for winter north of the border of Florida. However, the contacts I made when traveling south during the autumn helped make the northward journey possible and worthwhile.

Before leaving Florida, I was able to find more birds and had more time to ask myself, Why spend so much time looking for birds? The long and essentially birdless trip back to Oregon punctuated the fact of why people are interested in birds. I missed birding. Birding was not only entertaining, but it might also have a greater value. A chance conversation at Maitland, Florida, with Mo Oliver taught me that the importance of what birders and ornithologists discover should be conveyed to conservationists and the public at large. Thankfully, since 1963, the gap between scientists and others has narrowed and information about birds helps in decisions about habitat preservation. As for the question whether studying birds improves an ornithologist's health, it may. Birds get us outdoors, require us to hike, maybe climb a mountain slope, to jump over a stream on the way to birds. Certainly, the premature ending of my trip affected my well-being. I was depressed, maybe not clinically, but I felt bad. Birds and birding are inspiring. During my career, the time when I visited the National Museum of Natural History and stayed a few years, I met many happy birders and ornithologists. One of the things I remember the most about Dr. Wetmore was his laugh. It is easy to recall the hearty laughter of most of my colleagues, including the whispery chuckle of the late Herb Kale and the raucous laughter of Roxie Laybourne. Warren King, who I met in snowy Massachusetts, worked at Smithsonian in the Division of Birds when I started there. He was happy. Warren authored for the International Council for Bird Preservation the first *Endangered Birds of the World: The ICBP Bird Red Data Book* published in 1981, that made everyone smile. I feel lucky to have rubbed shoulders with so many, who have, through studying birds, contributed to avian conservation and who are happy for it.

One study by ornithologists in the name of bird conservation was by Margaret Hundley and Herb Kale in 1966 that documented bird mortality caused by communication towers. Had Mo Oliver checked the background of another important colleague, she would have realized that banding efforts and other studies conducted by Russ Mason led to bird conservation. Russ did not seem one to brag, but he could have told Mo that he also protected Burrowing Owls at the Miami airport, convinced Florida landholders to protect then diminishing Bald Eagles, and establish reserves from here to

Trinidad and Mexico. As of this writing, the Miami airport owls and Bald Eagles almost everywhere are doing very well.

While I was inside discussing the pros and cons of birds with Mo, I was appreciating being warm. The freeze of December 1962 and 1963, with a low of 18 degrees in Tampa and 20 degrees in Lakeland, had made part of my visit to Florida colder than usual. Record lows were not limited to Florida and were reported from many places around the world, notably in Great Britain. In Florida, damage to nearly 50 percent of their oranges and tangerines began on 14 December when temperatures plummeted below freezing. Winter vegetables were severely damaged, with 70 percent of the cabbage crop destroyed, putting a whole new meaning to what people call coleslaw. Quite possibly that cold front influenced any possible tropical waifs from traveling to the peninsula. A Thick-billed Vireo, Bahama Mockingbird, perhaps a grassquit, almost any species from Cuba or the Bahamas, would have been nice.

An Ivory-billed Woodpecker would have easily made up for the lack of any waifs from the Caribbean. Reports of Ivory-billed Woodpeckers from Highland Hammock in south-central Florida in the 1950s or 1960s were seductive. Henry Stevenson, who I never physically met, and I later discussed the woodpeckers once during one of our many phone conversations. As for Ivory-billed Woodpeckers, the only individuals I ever saw were specimens at the museum. Years later, an alleged Ivory-billed Woodpecker was pecking around northeastern Arkansas. A few people argue that the species still lives while others disagree. More on that in the next chapter.

News in 1963 of possible employment with the museum was tantalizing but first I needed a few years of higher learning to qualify. In 1967, with sheepskin in my pocket, a letter from Smithsonian arrived. The letter offered me a position in their Pacific Ocean Biological Survey Program. Unfortunately, I was in San Diego attending classes directed by the Navy. In fact, the Navy directed most aspects of my life then. I was in the Navy, but I would rather have been in Smithsonian seeing the world or at least part of the Pacific islands. About a half-year later, the Pentagon became my Navy duty station. Between my Navy responsibilities and a part-time job, I volunteered at Smithsonian's Pacific Project measuring specimens and collating data. Termination of the Pacific Project in 1969 came as a stunning loss to science. Luckily for me, I was already working with Richard Banks of the Biological Survey, the organization administered by the US Fish and Wildlife Service. I stayed.

Chan Robbins and I met on and off during our careers. Visits with Chan were always inspiring. In 1997, Chan received the Elliot Coues (pronounced cows) Award from the American Ornithologists' Union. It is the most prestigious award in North American ornithology. In 2000, he received the Audubon Medal in recognition of his contributions to conservation and protection of the environment, joining Roger Tory Peterson, Rachel Carson, Jimmy Carter, Ted Turner, E. O. Wilson, and others. Although it was cold when I first met Chan, it was much colder on the coast of Maine where I witnessed garbage being dumped into the Atlantic. The newspaper editor I contacted did write an editorial about dumping garbage into the ocean.

Linda and I visited Maine in 2015, spending most of our time in Acadia National Park and Scarborough Marsh. The Chadbournes and I had briefly visited the marsh in 1962. Generally regarded as healthier now than it was 100 years ago, the marsh is at risk from invasive plants and other infringements. I wonder what the marsh would look like after a snowstorm like the one in 1963. In 1964, the Chadbournes moved to Mast Landing Sanctuary where they were caretakers for five years. Our correspondence continued and one day Ginny wrote that Harry had died unexpectedly. He never made it to dreamed about Florida. Ginny remained in touch and kept me apprised about birds in Maine. She wrote that Chris Packard, 12 years my senior, died. Harry, Ginny, and Chris showed me the possibilities, the intrigue, and the fun of studying birds. The assembly of people in Maine and elsewhere, and the assembly of birds they shared, helped shape me.

The forbidding sight of snow in 1963 might have made me rethink the winter part of my sixties trip. That wintertime in Maine was the last time I saw the Chadbournes. There was opportunity to meet with Ginny in 2015 though she declined to meet face to face to preserve 52-year-old visual memories. We chatted on the phone, avoided seeing one another's wrinkles, recalled the snowy Maine landscape, and said goodbye.

Woolworths was a department store and diner that closed their doors in 1997 (they still operate in Mexico). I had my first banana split, the ultimate dessert, in a Woolworth in Oregon and an inexpensive dinner in wintery Manchester, New Hampshire, in 1963. I am not sure if Williams College continues to hang on to their 1963 dress code. Warren and I both dressed in coat and tie attire during my early career at the museum. It was not a dress code thing, but some fun competing for who had the most outlandishly loud tie, but that is another story.

The last few days of my trip ran a gamut from dress codes, blizzards, friends, and car trouble. Most worrisome was the bitter cold and car trouble. What was I thinking? Were the few winter birds added to the trip list worth it? My answer is yes. As for the car, it was dying a slow death no matter the location. I met part of my goal, to bird around most of the country, but the remaining precious months were impossible. Experiencing spring migration and the Southwest would not happen during this trip. I reluctantly accepted the end. There was nothing left but to try to resist the disappointment.

Chapter 22

Forty-Two Years Later

NOT THAT I HAD ever thought of picking up where my broken VW left me, not that the birds of Texas and the great Southwest beckoned me, but where would I find time to do justice to such birding areas? I had not allowed myself to think seriously about completing what I had started so many years ago. How could I, with college, military duty and war, work, and more work, and family? Then one January day in 2004, retired from my day job at Smithsonian, something changed.

Linda, that girl I left behind in 1962, and I were in Austin, Texas, a few days before my beautiful daughter would give birth to her and her husband's baby girl. The couple chose to name their daughter Sabine, the name of the Sabine River separating Texas and southern Louisiana, and the name of an ancient tribe from central Italy. I had nothing to do with choosing the name Sabine for my granddaughter, but the name had special significance. That is because after repairing my VW in Arkansas in 1963, I planned to drive south to Sabine NWR near the Gulf Coast of Louisiana. There I would see fabulous birds to add to my life list, and then I would cross the Sabine River and see thousands of spring migrants dripping from the trees on the upper Gulf Coast of Texas. However, my car died. I had put the ill-fated trip behind me, that is, until January 2004.

During the wait for the birth of Sabine, I discovered a book in the library of her soon-to-be parents. The pages were full of information about hiking in Big Bend National Park, where Colima Warblers nest. I could feel the urge to see Colima Warblers, to go around the Big Bend. One day during the pregnant pause, I visited an Austin bookstore and purchased a bird-finding guide for Texas. That was it. I was in, hook, line, and sinker, with no going back to days missing live birds. Someone had to see all those places and birds. Why not me? And, better yet, with that girl once left behind, now my full-time partner. The new Sabine meant an adorable granddaughter and it meant birds. The name of a new life and a place I once thought I would bird 42 years ago was now even more important and no longer an impossibility. I could hear a little traveling music.

All this catapulted the idea of more than just visiting the Sabine region of Louisiana and birding in Texas, but sowed the seed to complete the trip, the one started so long ago, the one back in the twentieth century. The fuse was burning as Linda and I talked it over. Yes, I could go back to Arkansas and follow the old route I planned to travel in. This time, Linda, my soul mate, and I would travel the route not forgotten and complete the trip that my broken car abruptly ended decades ago.

Unlike the earlier part of the trip, plenty of sources for discovering additional sites to find birds had become available. Even recent sightings could be communicated through computer websites and by cell phone. I eventually collected three bird-finding guides just for Texas and one each for Arizona and Southern California. Besides publications, a plethora of information lay waiting on the internet. Amazing! It is possible to email birders for local bird-finding information and to check the latest bird sightings in most regions. That sped things compared to the postal mail that I used in the early sixties. Internet sites on individual species provided information varying in detail on identification problems, behavior, distribution, you name it. The internet still was not as good as the Smithsonian's Division of Birds library, but it was quick and available in Austin and back in Oregon where most of the planning took place. Replacing my LPs of the 1960s were bird sounds over the net; I could record them either to tape or to CD for study or playback, and along with my Geographic field guide, identifications were waiting to happen. In addition, more and more people are out there birding, including highly organized commercial bird tours led by legendary Jon Dunn and other friends. Current observations by birders often end up on the net or otherwise shared via emails across the country. The results from mining so many sources for finding birds ought to improve my sixties plans for Texas and the Southwest.

Linda and I began preparing for the second and final leg of the trip near the end of January 2004 when we were home in Oregon. We would restart the trip in April in Arkansas where my car had died in 1963. However, plans to begin the trip in April 2004 were impossible. Our multiple family members were experiencing health problems. We decided to wait one more year, which was a good decision. We were not ready in 2004. A serious itinerary began to grow then blossomed into a detailed and optimistic plan. Hope was eternal that every i was dotted, every t crossed, and that all target birds were listed with details on where to detect them. The itinerary listed birding sites, page numbers of bird-finding guides that provided the details concerning the location and its birds, the number of miles from the previous birding localities, and the target species. An entry in the new itinerary looked like this:

North Fork Taylor's Bayou (21 **map,** 25) [30]
Swainson's Warbler—nesting (Patterson Bridge)
Swallow-tailed Kite
Mississippi Kite
Prothonotary Warbler—nesting

The locality is about 30 miles from Sabine Woods and west of Sabine National Wildlife Refuge. The target species are those not seen in 1962–63. Jon Dunn, who looked over the itinerary, had several productive suggestions. I attempted to have at least three localities per missing species since any species might be missed at any given locality. Of course, as Jon warned, some targeted species might be missed altogether.

Kenn Kaufman, in *Kingbird Highway*, a delightful and inspiring chronicle of teenage birding, considered listing will shift from planning and knowledge to communicating with others and money.[1] The first leg of the listing journey, in 1962 and 1963, was based on meager knowledge, considerable planning, although not enough, contacts, and truly little money. Although I never counted on the kindness of strangers in the 1960s leg of the trip, I definitely benefited from meals and a place to sleep offered by so many. Now, decades older and looking less needy, I knew Kenn was correct.

Part of the recipe for our birding trip is money though we crafted our itinerary for getting the most bang from our expenditures. That meant watching our food expenditures by avoiding eating out and staying in clean and safe but not necessarily five-star motels. Part of the bang for your buck formula is importantly related to new species for the trip list. We also based our itinerary on more knowledge but never enough, more planning and experience, and fewer contacts than in the sixties. As for birder hotlines, we will evaluate some of them as we travel. Still, we were looking not just for a big list, but also for the adventure of the unexpected, and to see what is around the corner, not just birds but panorama, and other wildlife. The unexpected did not have to be a rare or hard-to-find species. It could be in a person met, a landscape, sunset, or another surprise of nature.

The master list of bird species Linda and I would follow was an ABA checklist of birds found in North America. Red checks were marked next

---

1. Kenn Kaufman. *Kingbird Highway: The Story of a Natural Obsession That Got a Little Out of Hand.* (Boston: Houghton Mifflin, 1997).

to the species seen during the first leg of the trip. The optimistic total for the 1962–63 trip had been 572 species. Only 384 were seen from June 1962 to the unscheduled vehicular meltdown in March 1963. We optimistically hoped to find about 200 new species on the second leg of the trip. If so, the combined legs might hit a grand total of 584. Beginning in Arkansas and traveling south would prevent us from picking up many of the species embarrassingly missed earlier. Still, this was not a competition, but a goal, a target number that would keep us alert, not to mention increasing our life lists. The real competition was with us. The goal was to complete the unfinished business of birding until we dropped or at least for about 45 days.

Our mode of travel by a little SUV was not in the economic spirit of the old VW. However, the newer vehicle could hold enough clothes, food, bird references, and maps for two, could fit easily on the shoulder of most narrow roads and could turn around on a dime so that the "what was that" bird could be identified. Everything we needed, and then some, was in the vehicle. We tried to maintain our food supply so that no matter our location, we would not starve. Gone were the donuts and canned meat, both of which we replaced with healthy nutrition morsels chosen under the good auspices of Registered Nurse Linda. We would eat and drink well, with a jar of peanut butter, plenty of water, cereal, and fruit. It was all there.

Not to be entirely outdone by the center brake light I installed on the old VW in 1962, I put multiple stripes of reflective tape on the back of our SUV, so much so that someone asked if we were rural mail carriers. Incidentally, our SUV already came fitted with a center brake light. Who knew? We also designed front and rear bumper stickers that read "ABA Birder." Our thinking was that the labels might improve trading critical birding information with other birders. I am not sure any birders noticed. One person asked, "What was an aba birder?" Linda looked at me and said, "Well Yogi, what should we say?" Maybe most people thought we were lawyers and ignored us.

Now, in our sixties, we were confronted with travel expenses several times greater than I found in the 1960s. We are still highly dependent on fossil fuels. In 1962 and 1963 I paid around 31 cents per gallon. In 2005, gasoline averaged $2.74 per gallon. Surprisingly, a vehicle's ability for increased miles per gallon had not improved in the last several decades. The old VW got 30 miles per gallon; our small SUV attained an average of 26 miles per gallon. Also, after 40 years, the comfort of camping night after night or sleeping in a car night after night is no longer appealing. Camping fees today would have quickly chewed away my 1960s budget, when most state and federal camping was then free. Our comfort level, in the sixties (we are talking age here), begs for running hot and cold water, a real bed, and a door that locks out everything from bugs to whatever. We might camp occasionally, but only infrequently. Therefore, infrequent camping means frequent motels. Add that to the inflated cost of transportation, user/entrance fees across the country, and food, and the total is up there. Of course, we had to get to the starting gate, where the VW motor shattered in Arkansas. That required driving 2,200 miles from southwestern Oregon to northwestern Arkansas. Being past the age of endurance driving, we chose to use five days to reach the starting point of the second leg of the trip. Regardless of economics and the need for a real bed, our sixtyish age held a spirit of the 1960s. We knew the trip might turn back time and that it would also bring adventure to our future.

In late February 2005, we allocated a back room of our Oregon home to lay out everything that might go in the vehicle. We made lists of what we still needed, including plenty of batteries for flashlights, a camera, and a tape player, as well as dried food, an air mattress with a pump, and a new bee-sting kit for my allergy developed in 1968, new socks, and the cash registers kept ringing. I began finalizing our itinerary, with bird-finding directions from people emailed and added contact information and last-minute sightings of rare birds reported on the net.

Although my dad and my mom suffered from forgetfulness and other ailments, they held their own most of the time. It was during one of the more lucid moments that I told my dad about the trip. His eyes widened as he said, "Good, I'm glad you are going to do that." Ever supportive, he asked specific questions about the trip. Sometime later, my mother's health began to deteriorate, and my dad's well-being followed. By early 2005 my parents, who had suffered for years, suddenly became more ill. They were extremely close and died within four days of each other. Linda and I knew their fate was near though it was a shock and a relief. Their suffering and my dad worrying about his mate had ended. Still, Linda and I had earlier hoped my parents would be there when we completed our travel.

The loss of my parents was more than difficult, but I knew they would have wanted us to continue with our plans. We wanted to be in Arkansas to begin the second leg of the birding journey by 3 April. We left our nest in Jacksonville, Oregon, on 28 March and headed south over the Siskiyou Mountains for the long journey through the greater length of California before turning east. Our southern route would help us avoid any late winter storms. On the way, we veered north to the south rim of the Grand Canyon. Linda had earlier seen the chasm. I had, gasp, not. Just as James Fisher in *Wild America* had experienced, the view brought tears to our eyes. Before leaving, we looked down on the backs of three California Condors soaring below the South Rim.

In shock.

We sped onward, stopping briefly at Sandia Crest near to Albuquerque, New Mexico, to see rosy-finches. In my earlier birding days, I had seen two species, but Linda had seen none. The unseasonably late snow and cold at 10,678 feet awarded us all three species of rosy-finches. They spiraled down from wind-buffeted conifers, cascading earthward as if autumn leaves to join gray-headed Dark-eyed Juncos at a bird feeder. Farther east on the eastbound interstate, my back decided to exercise its periodic caravan of pain. Meanwhile, we careened across the Panhandle of Texas to meet Tom Smeltzer at Black Kettle National Grassland in eastern Oklahoma. Just to the north of headquarters, before sunrise, and after my throbbing lower back made it difficult to walk, Tom showed us our first Lesser Prairie-Chickens. That was my first and, hopefully, only life species accompanied with wincing pain. It was too bad we could not include the rosy-rosy-finches and Lesser Prairie-Chicken on our trip that we were about to complete. At the time, California Condors were not countable by ABA rules, but the rules eventually changed decades later.

Harrison, Arkansas, was not only the location where the sixties leg of the trip terminated and where my car died, the region was also where my parents once lived and where I was born. Decades later, I was lucky enough to join a few other Arkies in the ornithological community, including the James family. Douglas A. James, professor at the University of Arkansas, was not far west of Harrison. He started teaching there in 1953, but it would be nearly 20 years before we would meet at Smithsonian. A prolific writer of numerous papers ranging from bats in the Ozarks to Great Pied Hornbills in Africa, Doug coauthored *Arkansas Birds* with Joseph Neal in 1986. The first day I met Doug was when he left the Division of Birds late one evening. He had forgotten to get a property pass so he could leave the museum with his luggage without delay. Just as a museum guard was about to stop him, I grabbed his two suitcases and told the guard, who knew me, that the luggage was mine. No pass was required. Security today is, of course, much stricter. More recently, Doug was senior author on a paper on Cerulean Warblers in Arkansas, a species missed on the first leg of the bird trip.

Francis James, who left Arkansas for points east, is a renowned avian ecologist and conservationist. Despite my best efforts, Fran was not convinced that the study of subspecies of birds (a large part of my day job) might be interesting. The third James, daughter Helen, is a prominent avian paleontologist, working at Smithsonian's Division of Birds. Helen's colleague down the hall was Arkansas son Gary Graves. Gary was one of the curators I used to tease when he was the new person in the Division.

The 1960s journey was near the northern boundaries of what I call southern warblers, species including Yellow-throated and Prairie warblers that regularly winter in Florida where I saw them. When I departed Arkansas in 1963, I headed west on a Greyhound with my hat in my hand, leaving without seeing any remaining southern breeding warblers, including Prothonotary, Cerulean, and Hooded warblers. Linda and I would be too early in Arkansas for most warblers. What we would find in Arkansas and beyond inevitably would be the adventure of surprise, learning, and just plain fun, chiggers, sunburn, and maybe a few warblers. Whatever might happen, we would relish trying. We would soak in the landscape and the birds.

3 April 2005

We found our reserved motel in Harrison, Arkansas, and made a couple of phone calls. The first was to my surviving northern Arkansas relatives who lived several miles northeast of Harrison. Another call was to Sheree Rogers, who lived just out of town and had staked out a Harris's Sparrow. I will visit her tomorrow.

Before the sun fell below the western horizon, Linda and I rushed to our first official birding site, Baker's Prairie. Once 5,000 acres, Harrison swallowed up all but 71 acres of Baker's Prairie, now preserved by The Nature Conservancy and Arkansas Natural Heritage Commission. Spring was only beginning to arrive in the cold April wind. We parked in the lot of a giant new high school where Vesper Sparrows foraged on the edge of the lawn. Linda crossed the busy street at the edge of the prairie while I gleaned the sparrows. Northern Bobwhites called from a briar tangle. At the edge of the open prairie stood a grove of low trees not quite ready to put out leaves. Singing from them were our first Eastern Towhee and tail-wagging Eastern Phoebe. Not far were Eastern Bluebirds, and over the spring wind, Eastern Meadowlarks were singing from the brown winter grass. Baker's Prairie was the place to start our trip list.

4–5 April 2005

Sheree Rogers's place near Harrison was alive with birds. About a dozen feeders attracted Red-bellied Woodpeckers, Blue Jays, Mourning Doves, Purple Finches, and more. White-throated Sparrow grabbed our attention; the target sparrow had been foraging near them. Thirty minutes later, a buffy female Harris's Sparrow popped up for identification.

The morning was young, and more importantly, the wind was still in the breeze stage. Another walk-through of Baker's Prairie yielded more meadowlarks and bluebirds. Prairie flowers had yet to spring up, and last year's grass was dead and prostrate. We were too early for Grasshopper Sparrows. Barn Swallows flew by, turned in the speeding breeze, and circled back again. A Willow Flycatcher clung to a wind-blown perch at the edge of the preserve near a stunted woody tangle. Before the flycatcher vanished, a rusty Brown Thrasher added color to the grayish brush.

We visited my aunt, her son, and her brother, my uncle, in the remote rocky hills several miles northeast of town during the afternoon. My uncle was in physical if not emotional distress. He was unable to work his beloved farm, the place he had lived since birth, and the place where my paternal grandparents once lived. Usually talkative, he remained stoically silent except for asking how I was doing, and saying that Linda and I were welcome to visit the old farm. My aunt had once been on the staff of the US embassy in then West Germany, but preferred the solitude of the Ozarks, rebuffing even Harrison. I could understand the snub. Sleepy Harrison, with its two traffic lights, had changed. It had become engorged with people, commerce, especially fast-food joints, and needed even more traffic lights than the dozens I counted. What happened?

From age three to eight, I visited Harrison every Saturday when my folks, and everyone else, went to town to shop and visit. Anything shoppers needed could be purchased from stores built around the old brick courthouse centered in the town square. I spent most of Saturdays watching movies, Flash Gordon, and travelogues in one or both big screen theaters that faced the solid courthouse. Today, old men sat on park benches outside, whittling and talking about bygone days. Indeed, those are bygone days. The two theaters are closed. Harrison's population had more than doubled since my youthful movie days, and the county count had nearly tripled its population. The town blossomed like a dandelion. The city line sprawled across much of Baker's Prairie and encompassed a typically blighted land of too many shopping centers and houses with unnecessary square feet. Only small areas of Harrison held on to the rural charm I remembered, especially the large town square and Crooked Creek drifting nearby. I wondered if the little house of my birth was standing. Was it a historical landmark, a museum, or was it a corner of a superstore selling discounted paraphernalia people likely do not need? We all think we need more stuff. I let my curiosity gravitate to when we would find our next trip bird.

During the next morning, we attempted to complete our laundry at the motel while we birded around the property, adding a couple of new species to our trip list, most notably a Mississippi Kite. At the time, we were unaware that the driers were not heating. We piled our clean but soggy clothes into plastic bags and hunted for a fully functioning laundromat.

While contemplating our laundry tumbling in a couple of driers, I reviewed that state of my back, which was, after carrying wet laundry, ever so slightly better. There had been a toll of all those days sitting, driving grimly across uneventful and stressful interstate highways. Those hours were beginning to be happily replaced with walking, standing, and, most importantly, birding. In the 1960s, my back never bothered me. My body was lean, and my eyes were like a hawk. In 40 years, I had gone from a skinny ectomorphic kid to almost pushing too many pounds for my six-foot frame. My ribs were no longer showing. I am using the same belt and belt hole that kept up my pants 10 years ago but fitting the same size as 1963 is impossible. Consuming the almost daily milkshakes as I birded across the country in 1962 and 1963 would be a mistake today. Maybe all those skinny months were why people so graciously fed me. Now, I no longer appear like a starving kid and my adult demeanor may not paint me as anyone that needs saving. My smile is a big one, but, so I have been told, my deportment could be determined as negative, ranging from sad to almost menacing. Once, riding the metro home from the museum, a man asked me if it was all that bad. Most likely I was deep in thought, perhaps ruminating a yet unsolved taxonomic problem, but I must have appeared depressed. As for menacing, that look came in handy more than once when in potentially dangerous situations. Of course, that is another story belonging elsewhere.

Compared to the good old days, my vision had changed. Much to my chagrin, my arm length could not keep up with my inability to read. Now, reading glasses became within arm's length. Months later, I realized I needed help reading a few small road signs, and worse, my vision was becoming a problem while birding. So, very recently, I gave up squinting at hawks and warblers. Glasses became part of the accoutrements to carry around and lose. I was surprised the power-line wire along the local road was not a double strand, and how much easier and farther away I could distinguish perching Kestrels from Mourning Doves with my new spectacles. However, the glasses did not go well with my binoculars. Whether on and off meant dropping or misplacing them. I purchased a glasses strap that allowed me to throw the glasses off and then look through the binocs. That worked well except for the glasses tangling with the binocs, and until an earpiece poked me in the eye. Identifying the bird through the tears was difficult.

For years, my dear dad offered a particular greeting. It was "Ralph, don't get old." Out of respect, I really tried. Part of the punishment for my failure has been years of looking for my glasses.

After drying and folding the laundry, we left Harrison and turned off scenic State Highway 7 a few miles south of town. I wanted to show Linda where I had lived during the days of Saturday movies. The road, a narrow paved lane, led through familiar country. One stretch had been particularly good for Scissor-tailed Flycatchers during earlier visits, but instead, Linda and I found a barren fence on both sides of a once vegetated roadside. Houses that I once knew were gone completely, whole farms abandoned, but new homes had sprung up in old fields and leveled woodlands. The road, now dirt, turned, crossed a creek, up a slight grade, and made a 90-degree turn to the right. Those hard turns were marking property lines. The house of my early youth was enlarged from the original structure built by my father, his half-brother, and father. Vegetation once lining the intermittent creek had been stripped from the banks. Two sycamores below the house and a large black walnut were a memory. We drove on.

A mile to the west was a 90-degree turn to the left. Inside the fence was a corner of my uncle's property. It contained about three acres of huge oaks and cedars, trees he loved and hoped to preserve. I saw my first Hooded Warbler there back in the day when my first binoculars had training wheels. Down the road, past the woods was my uncle's house and the home of my late grandparents. The old house stood relatively straight, but the front porch sagged from the combined weight of discarded furniture, obsolete and rusting tools, and general well-worn debris under layers of road dust. The grounds surrounding the house also were decorated with discarded junk, including a horse-drawn hay rake and a couple of dead vehicles. We had witnessed familiar scenes in Oregon and in every state that we have ever visited. Still, when a hoarding relative is a perpetrator, it is at least embarrassing.

Remembering a pond and nearby barn were about 500 yards from the house, I dodged the cow pies while hoping for a Barn Owl in the aged rafters. There were no owls though four male Blue-winged Teal flew from the pond. There were two males and a female Harris's Sparrow in the bushes next to the pond. I quickly retrieved Linda, who was busy photographing the outside of the house. We relocated the sparrow. A fourth bird, briefly seen, appeared to be a female.

Later in the day and miles south of Harrison, we traveled an hour on a winding State Route 7 and 30 minutes of tighter turns on a different and narrower road to small stream near Ponca in remote Lost Valley. Trees were leafless and silent. No warblers, but a shallow stream looked promising. A minute had barely passed when we spotted a bobbing brownish bird at the edge of the water. The clean buffy flanks clearly marked the Louisiana Waterthrush, our first eastern Warbler.

We drove back to Route 7, continuing south in the mountains before descending to the Arkansas River at Russellville. We then mounted I-40, the highway we traveled earlier from California to Oklahoma. Today, we sped eastward to Little Rock where we arrived at another uncle and aunt's residence south of the city. They lived in the same spotless home near where I caught a bus to Oregon on 31 March 1963.

6 April 2005

A thunderstorm had lightly touched southern Little Rock. I searched the trees around our host's home, but I could only hear the hum of cars joining the morning commute. I stood in the same yard 42 years earlier and heard only traffic. Wishful thinking would not silence the traffic or hurry the migration.

After breakfast and goodbyes, we found the interstate to Texarkana, cruised through part of Hope, home of Bill Clinton, who retired from his Washington, DC, day job a few years after I retired from my post. We never met though I saw his limousine during our numerous commutes. Linda mailed a couple of letters from the Hope post office before we caught the highway south for our night in Sulphur, a town west of Lake Charles in southern Louisiana.

My impression of Sulphur was that it had two sides, one that was a nice small town (about 20,000 or about double of what it was in the 1960s) populated with people enjoying a slow and comfortable pace, and another that was startling. A brochure picked up at a local restaurant revealed Sulphur began as a mining town for, what else, sulfur. One problem though, quicksand thwarted the mining efforts. Upon reading that, Linda and I instantly recalled the times our parents warned us about the dangers of quicksand. Sulphur's quicksand was nowhere to be found, but the immediate landscape was enough to poke out an eye. What was startling about Sulphur was the starkness and noise that dominated our attention. The shiny metal pipes, tanks, and all kinds of plumbing steamed, smoked, and snaked up and down in large and small pipes were an eye-sore. Petroleum was its name and sweating men in hard hats scurried by foot and truck through the gray and hard landscape of the refinery. Except for the humidity of the Gulf rolling inland, nature had been removed. The place seemed extraordinarily weird. It was an ugly reality. The human consumption of rotten subterranean juices obliterated the immediate smokey view. The prehistoric fluids, the rotten ooze of tiny dead bodies, would flow on, into our car and other machinery, to leave an indelible mark everywhere. The infrastructure that spewed itself over the land was stupendous. It was shocking. Our road wove through the bowels of the steely gray place. How vulnerable we felt. Not a bird was in sight. It was too harsh.

Sabine National Wildlife Refuge was on the itinerary tomorrow, which sounded like a reward for the punishing sight of a refinery. Linda mentioned that the landscape of refineries, oil pumps, and the like was part of the economy of the Gulf. She had seen it before. I had not, and her words helped me brace for more to come. In the meantime, there would be the refuge to explore and new birds to discover.

7 April 2005, the Beginning of the Day

South of our motel night in Sulphur and onward to Hackberry on Highway 27, we began to fully appreciate we were in the Gulf Coast wetlands. The ecosystem in Louisiana makes up about 12 percent of the nation's wetlands. It is twice the size of the Everglades, and, according to *National Geographic*, is disappearing under the Gulf of Mexico at the rate of 33 football fields per day. Put another way, a football field of wetland habitat is destroyed every 100 minutes. Dredging, digging deep shipping channels, levees, the introduction of nutria, and other man-made manipulations is causing the demise of an ecosystem that provides natural habitat for countless species. That same ecosystem also protects human habitat, including petroleum concerns, from flooding especially during hurricanes. There are so many examples of humans shooting themselves in the foot.

So, at last, on the shrinking marsh, we watched a Roseate Spoonbill fly high over Sabine NWR. Sabine country at last. We breezed through the refuge, hardly experiencing its 125,000 plus acres. No cars were on the road as we continued south as far as possible, then turned west on Highway 82. We were barely above sea level.

Eastern Towhee, Harris's Sparrow, and others back in Arkansas had been the prelude of birds to come, and today and in the lower watershed of the Sabine River would be the day new birds might be tripping over each other. We stopped only a couple of times along the road, once to check for migrants in willows growing on a levee. We found burnt tinted Orchard Orioles. Later we stopped to glass White and Glossy Ibis as they foraged the shallows. Glossy and the similar White-faced Ibis overlap in coastal Louisiana, and we were sure of our identifications. Our next scheduled stop was Peveto Woods (pronounced peva-toe, with emphasis, according to locals, on the toe). However, we never found it, although we must have been close. A sign reading "Peveto Woods Migratory Bird Sanctuary" guided the way for a short distance though the lack of additional signs left us unsure. The only person to ask directions was a confused tourist. Maybe a birder could have helped but no one else was around. We birded a spot that partly fit our emailed directions and found Yellow-throated Warblers in an otherwise quiet set of trees. The site was private property, a home site ready for placing a house on about 10-foot-tall power-pole-sized stilts. The extra height is to help avoid floods. Flooding from ravaging hurricanes has happened repeatedly, and everyone hopes to be prepared. In 1886, the thriving town of nearby Johnson's Bayou, along with tens of thousands of cattle, were wiped from the face of the land. On this dry day, our trespassed home site was not acting as a migrant trap.

We still had daylight as we crossed Sabine Pass and at the south end of Sabine Lake, a wide part of the Sabine River. Texas was now on the agenda.

∽

Much to my chagrin, Harrison, Arkansas, and numerous other settlements openly considered itself a sundown location. As a youth, I was ignorant of that fact and no one mentioned it during frequent visits there. Fortunately, by at least 2005, integration appeared to have occurred.

The farm in Arkansas that my uncle had to leave was less cluttered with old farm equipment and broken vehicles than it was on my last memory of the place. I recall my uncle complaining to his father, my granddad, that the farm was junky. However, my granddad believed almost anything might come in handy someday. He was right some of the time and not so much most of the time. My uncle eventually gave up and by the time the farm was his, he discovered cleaning and hauling away all that stuff would cost more than he could afford. He was stuck, but he did have the trees, which he spoke of with fondness during phone conversations. He declared that the three or so acres of deciduous trees would never be cut. Those trees were standing tall in 2005, but most of the trees disappeared a few years after my uncle succumbed. The house and outbuildings, and scattered junk, everything was gone between 2012 and 2014. Only a few bushes near the pond remained.

Lots of trees have perished by the ax ever since people saw them. Even so, in 1963, I thought there might be a forest where I might be lucky enough to see an Ivory-billed Woodpecker, the grandest of all North American woodpeckers. I tried in western Florida and had planned to try again in Louisiana. However, my optimism of the sixties disappeared. Scattered reports that the species was not extinct seemed anecdotal, and I was reluctant to spend time following what seemed to be an exceedingly long shot. After all, the last confirmed North American Ivory-bill was observed in Louisiana in 1944, the year Linda and I were born. Even so, when we arrived at Tom Beatty's place in Arizona's Miller Canyon on this trip, we were stunned when he handed us a print-out from a website. The sheet of paper announced that an Ivory-billed Woodpecker was videotaped in eastern Arkansas. What exciting news. Just 20 days earlier, Linda and I were near the location of the bird not far from Little Rock. Even so, I did not believe we had missed anything. Being a museum person, I appreciated that hard evidence of photographs supposedly supported the claim. So did John Fitzpatrick of Cornell University, Van Remsen of Louisiana State University, and 15 others, in an online Science Express report that soon to appeared in the prestigious publication *Science*.[2] Van has been a long-time member of the Committee on Classification and Nomenclature of the American Ornithologists' Union; Fitz was a former member of the committee. Both were known from my museum days. The authors of the report were convinced the evidence of the rediscovery of an Ivory-billed Woodpecker in the Big

2. *Science*, Jun 3, 2005.

Woods (aka Bayou de View) of eastern Arkansas was solid enough to confirm the big woodpecker was not extinct. The Nature Conservancy, Cornell University, and the US Department of Interior were on board with the notion of rediscovery. Had there not been a leak of the find, First Lady Laura Bush was prepared to make an official announcement that the Ivory-billed Woodpecker was found in Arkansas. How could those pillars in ornithology and organizations be wrong?

During the next days and months, people searched for, talked, and wrote about, but did not detect any Ivory-bills. They did everything but put the bird's picture on a milk carton. Woodpecker specialist Jerome Jackson, in his insightful review of this and past Ivory-billed Woodpecker reports, seemed to exert a more measured interpretation of the situation and was not convinced the woodpecker was found.[3] My evaluation of the photographs, the so-called evidence, was likewise not favoring the alleged sighting. Others were likewise not convinced. As much as I, along with others, might want to believe, I remain skeptical. Good irrefutable evidence should not be overridden by exuberance for the existence of what has been exterminated by the hand of man.

Not long after the sighting of something said to be a woodpecker, the southern region of Louisiana was ravaged by record breaking hurricanes in 2005. Following Hurricane Katrina that hit New Orleans was Hurricane Rita that blew with 155 mile an hour winds over Sulphur. An estimated 30,000 acres of Sabine NWR were flooded with water and covered with seven million cubic meters of debris that included refrigerators, parts of buildings, junk, you name it, and not less than 115,000 gallons of toxic waste. Damage to wildlife populations from hurricanes may be direct but habitat destruction in the form of physical alteration and pollution causes mortality possibly lasting for years after the meteorological event.

---

3. Jerome A. Jackson. "Ivory-Billed Woodpecker (*Campephilus principalis*): Hope, and the Interfaces of Science, Conservation, and Politics." *The Auk* 123.1 (Jan 2006) 1–15. https://academic.oup.com/auk/article/123/1/1/5562496.

Chapter 23

Texas Migrants and Chickens

7 April 2005, the Remainder of the Day

IN A FEW MILES, we were in Texas at Sabine Woods, a 32-acre motte or grove of oaks and the property of the Texas Ornithological Society. My birder expectations were tingling a signal that this was the day to see spring migrants. However, the steadiness and power of the strong south wind indicated otherwise. What was needed for a day when warblers, tanagers, and orioles dripped from the trees was a cold north wind. Of course, that kind of wind is difficult to fatal to birds migrating north. The migrants that survive crossing the Gulf of Mexico are starving for food, water, and rest. They would head straight for the nearest land that has trees and bushes that could provide localities to forage and to rest and a place to avoid predators. Sabine Woods is one such place, but fortunately for the birds, they were flying on by, buoyed by a nice tailwind. Their miles per calorie would allow them to go farther inland where suitable habitat was more continuous than often narrow and fragmented habitat on the Louisiana and Texas coasts. We did find a few Northern Yellowthroats, Yellow-rumped Warblers, and several male Blue Grosbeaks. Also present were five birders walking slowly and quietly, with binoculars at the ready. A birder's muffled voice told us that Worm-eating Warblers were found in the morning. Two apparent Gulf Coast veterans shook their heads, lamenting the southerly sea breeze. On our way out of Sabine Woods, Linda and I met three birders who were anxiously trying to decide if the waterthrush they were seeing was a Louisiana or Northern. I pointed out the white flanks, narrowing eye band, and dull leg color. It was good to see a Northern Waterthrush again.

Passing through Port Arthur for the second time, we left behind the petroleum-formed landscape of white sky, metal tanks, pipes, smell, and noise. We got a room in a Winnie motel just early enough to double back to the north fork of Taylor's Bayou for a chance at Swallow-tailed Kites and Swainson's and Prothonotary Warblers. The directions painted an accurate picture of the area, and as promised, a couple of Barred Owls conversed in the distance. Wood Ducks swam around cypress knees where a golden-yellow Prothonotary Warbler sang above the black mirror of swamp water. The pale ghostly green of the Spanish moss kept the gilded warbler hidden almost beyond my patience and the dimming sunlight. Herons traveled up and down the bayou, including members of a colony of chunky, red-eyed Yellow-crowned Night-Herons. Kites never appeared. The sky dimmed, frogs tuned up, and mosquitoes began their happy hour of drinking. It was time to retire to Winnie.

8 April 2005

Anahuac NWR loomed far on the predawn horizon. Pronounced anna-WHACK, the name of the refuge is Aztec for watery plain. However, the first people to the area, the Atakap and Akokisa nomads, had no connection with the distant Aztecs. The refuge began in 1963 with 12,000 acres. With the help of The Nature Conservancy, the refuge encompassed 27,506 acres by 1993 and grew to its present 37,000 acres. My trusty Pettingill guide, in 1963, listed Anahuac as an important birding place, and my ABA finding guide devoted a whole chapter to birding in the refuge. It is especially famous for its Yellow Rails. This secretive species occurs at Anahuac as a winter resident and migrant. Birds are then often seen by scores of birders participating during the Yellow Rail Walk. That is when a band of people tromping abreast through the Yellow Rail Prairie try to flush a yellow Yellow Rail. (Note to non-birders: I am not making this up.) I saw this tiny straw-colored rail in 1962 and did not want to panic another individual to fly any more than I wanted marching giants to frighten me to flight. Whether I would walk the walk if I had never seen a Yellow Rail was moot. Finding a Yellow Rail on the Yellow Rail Walk in the Yellow Rail Prairie was not on today's itinerary. There was no time.

Migrant LeConte's Sparrow was the mission. In the meantime, a brief stop at the East Bay Bayou Tract, a continuous parcel of the refuge, was profitable, with Scissor-tailed Flycatchers on fence lines and American

Golden-Plovers in a freshly plowed field. A volunteer at the information booth at the main part of the refuge was not confident about me finding Neotropical migrants at The Willows. Nonetheless, I drove the short distance, parked, and searched the branches in an otherwise warbler forbidden zone. A couple of audacious Palm Warblers were the only birdlife. A nearby wetland attracted plenty of yellowlegs, both the tall and short variety, and a Whimbrel that made me wince when the thought of the demise of the Eskimo Curlew tugged at a feeling of loss. Bill probing Long-billed Dowitchers held my attention as I tried to no avail to tease out Short-billed Dowitcher. On the dike roads was the namesake of the road, a gathering of Northern Shovelers. Near the intersection of the western end of Shoveler Road was West Fence Line Road. A couple of Savannah Sparrows popped up from the taller grass tufts along the narrow road, but a different bird caught my attention on the other side of the tight wire fence. Perched for an easy view was a LeConte's Sparrow, a species I missed from my 1962 trek across the southern tip of its breeding grounds. The now cooperative life bird revealed its white central crown-stripe, orange-like face, pale straw-colored back, which were all the field marks I had mentally stored. Of course, being a new lifer, I confirmed my sighting with a quick consult of my trusty field guide. Still, if only I could hear that buzzing call, but the bird remained quiet, then it disappeared in the grass.

Back at the Winnie motel, we regrouped and headed southward to High Island. Terra firma surrounds 32-foot tall High Island, not water. The "island" is a salt dome, a region where ancient salt deposits 30,000 feet below push up toward the surface. The resulting elevated landmass, with trees, is essential for food and shelter to northbound migrants. The groups of trees or mottes are the first trees birds find since beginning their 400-mile journey across the hazardous Gulf of Mexico. The woods of High Island are also the targets of birders. Sources stated that optimum birding on High Island would be in the afternoon, and we were right on schedule. It was shortly after lunch when we arrived at Boy Scout Woods, one of the many patches of woods on High Island purchased by the Houston Audubon Society. We happily paid the entrance fee to support the organization's important endeavor. So far, our luck in finding migrants was about the same as the dozen birders milling quietly in the sanctuary.

There were barely more birds than birders. A Blue-headed Vireo sang near the entrance of the 42 acres of woods. The vireo's message buoyed our eager optimism. However, only four Summer Tanagers, a Gray Catbird, a few Common Yellowthroats, and just enough chipping Yellow-rumped Warblers to be distracting adorned Virginia Live-Oaks, hackberry, and other plants. Somewhat disappointed, we left, thinking the time must be good for the well-being of migrants since the weather must have allowed them to fly over High Island. Of course, that was not good for us. We then drove up to the larger Smith Oaks Sanctuary. More birders and even fewer migrants were there. Several Roseate Spoonbills were flying overhead, but we found none of our targeted warblers.

We headed west to Bolivar Flats, which was crawling with Friday afternoon tourists scurrying about in anticipation of the weekend. Billed as a great place to see migrant shorebirds, the only shorebirds we saw were on the road to the beach where a couple of Pectoral Sandpipers and several Greater Yellowlegs were needling the mud. Just to the south, we lined up with pickups, cars, SUVs, and motorcycles for the free ferry ride to Galveston Island. Laughing Gulls followed the crammed ferry, hoping to catch leftover picnic fodder from tourists. Great-tailed Grackles, a species we saw everywhere, rode the ferry. Although typically noisy, the half-dozen birds were relatively quiet but called wildly to grackles riding the ferry traveling in the opposite direction. Linda and I were the last on and last off the ferry. The grackles stayed onboard. Birding Galveston would have to wait; we needed to get to our Dickinson motel early. A steady hum of traffic from I-45, only partially damped by the walls of the motel, reminded us to be thankful we were not traveling north to gargantuan Houston. The behemoth is alive with over two million people occupying around 656 square miles. Half the size of Rhode Island, Houston is the fourth most populated US city but sprawls over 200 more square miles than the second most populated US city, Los Angeles. Linda had previous and not joyful experiences driving in Houston. Thankfully, we had no reason to go north into the storm of urban sprawl where you can drive forever and still be inside the city limits. Little old Dickinson was close enough.

9 April 2005

The alarm sounded at 3:30 a.m. for some serious birding. Yesterday evening I made a dry run to the Texas City Prairie Preserve, 2300 acres of coastal prairie owned by The Nature Conservancy. We did not want to chance being lost and late for the tour to observe Greater Prairie-Chickens. Linda's enthusiasm for seeing members of Galliformes, especially lekking species, is beyond reproach, and being early was important.

Our target birds belong to the southern coastal subspecies known as *attwateri*. The Texas taxon, *Tympanuchus cupido attwateri*, was declared endangered in 1967 and put on the endangered species list in 1972, the same year Attwater Prairie Chicken NWR was established. Wildlife managers call the birds Attwater's Prairie-Chicken though English names are no longer officially used for subspecies. The coastal birds are known as the Greater Prairie-Chicken. To confuse matters worse, Heath Hen is the English name for the extinct northeastern subspecies of Greater Prairie-Chicken, aka *Tympanuchus cupido cupido*. English names for subspecies are often unnecessary and confusing to most, including birders and museum folks, even retired ones. The 1957 AOU check-list, which refrained from English names for subspecies, stated the southern subspecies ranged from southwestern Louisiana to Arkansas and Texas. Odds on seeing the species in 1963 would have been better than now since only a few birds now remain in the wild and only in Texas. Our chances today increased only because of the goodwill of someone saving a few known survivors. Thanks to The Nature Conservancy, first for the preserve, and second for allowing us access, we had a great chance of seeing Greater Prairie-Chickens.

As planned, we arrived at the locked gate, the same one I found yesterday evening on the 15-mile dry-run between the motel and preserve. Except for faraway lights, we waited in our vehicle engulfed by pitch darkness. After several minutes, two vehicles carrying more birders and then Brandon Crawford, our host, joined us. The gate was unlocked and the caravan behind our guide slowly crunched along a gravel road to a building. Brandon went in to unlock the restrooms so that everyone could prepare for a long session in a blind where any used liquid had to remain on board. One by one, individuals of the group gathered in a huddle, ready to be shown the rare chickens. While waiting in a darkened circle of people, I asked if anyone had seen a Buff-breasted Sandpiper recently. No one had. I added, "I suppose no one has spotted an Eskimo Curlew." In the dim reflection of flashlights, I could see a family of silent reactions ranging from incredulous to "should I believe that?" and "you must be pretty stupid for even asking." Linda softly chuckled. Perhaps it was too early to joke about the death of a species.

Each person took their turn in the restroom, knowing that it might be hours before another opportunity. Following the last flush, we were bouncing down a dirt lane in a giant SUV that took the group deep into the preserve and to an 8 x 25-foot blind. One by one, we stumbled past the blind's unseen door while we felt the cold inner walls as if reading braille. Linda and I held on to each other. Brandon told everyone which wall to face and to select a viewing hole. A viewing hole? By now, it was possible to discern the dim outlines of holes on the viewing side of the blind. Some of the holes were higher than others. I chose an opening that fit my height. Another nearby opening a few inches below mine fit Linda's height perfectly. A few lawn chairs came to the rescue during the long wait and a propane heater in one corner took the edge off the cold morning. A few minutes passed before the first bird began to call. Linda and I immediately noticed the differences in the calls between the Lesser Prairie-Chickens observed in Oklahoma and today's lower-pitched Greater Prairie-Chicken.

The morning light was ever so slowly becoming brighter and the temperature edging toward comforting warmth. At first, it was impossible to see anything, including the birds, even each other. Seconds later, after a slight turn of our planet, a smidgen of light hinted what Brandon, using a scope, had found. He spotted a prairie chicken. It took me a couple of minutes before seeing the bird, which suddenly jumped from the grassy twilight. The sun, rising east-northeast of the blind, gradually revealed a reddish glow that lit the distant oil-scape that drives so much of this part of Texas. A grayish fog appeared and hung over the lek. By now, 10 displaying males were in view. Finally, enough light allowed us to see that Greater Prairie-Chickens are distinctly darker than the Lesser Prairie-Chickens. The dark barred plumage and golden neck sack of individual birds burned into our memories as the sun also revealed our smiling faces. Individual birders were posturing and so were the prairie chickens. The birds puffed themselves up to appear larger, which enhanced their bold horizontal strips and bulging yellow orange, no, golden, neck sacks. Hormones were racing as the males lurched into a stiff dance to signal their intentions, which was to mate with an onlooking female. It was magical, but out of nowhere, a half-dozen cows on their way to water ran through the displaying lek. Two calves stopped to notice the gathering of birds. Otherwise, neither the birds nor the bovines paid attention to the other. Brandon told us calves are often interested in the chickens. Surprised to see bovines, Linda and I had to ask why cattle. Our guide informed us the hoofed beasts were substitutes for bison, animals once part of the ecology of prairies.

Could we count the dancing birds? Could we add Greater Prairie-Chicken to our lists? According to ABA rules, there must be wild individuals. Brandon said the lek contained both reintroduced captive-reared individuals and luckily, originally wild birds. With that information, Linda and I accepted our new life bird. By 9 a.m., the birds flew from the lek, and we left the blind, happily loaded back into the SUV, and, with considerable relief, returned to the restrooms. Before Brandon escorted us back to the entrance gate, our group was talking to each other, smiling to one another, pleased with their experience, and knowing everyone was also sharing a joy that created a collective bond.

Our drive back to our motel in Dickinson included a view of three adult White-tailed Hawks and a stop at a local grocery store. The beautiful hawks were too distant to appreciate that they are the longest legged of any North American buteo. While the birds hunted for a meal, Linda and I quickly performed our aisle hunting and drove back at our motel. We promptly nuked lunch in our motel microwave, ate, and physically crashed our tired selves to bed. We were bushed and grateful to assume a horizontal position between clean sheets.

We had been traveling, birding, visiting relatives, and up too early too many mornings. Our trip list now stood at a lowly 114 species since 3 April. Our total is several dozen short, but that was okay. We were still hoping for Neotropical migrants though a northerly wind was not, well, in the wind.

We needed to catch up and slumber came as a remembered prairie chicken dance gave way to a deep sleep. Our afternoon slumber stopped abruptly when I woke upon hearing the motel door partly open. That was not supposed to happen. Fortunately, the safety chain prevented anyone from entering. A woman's face, appearing in the cracked door, belonged, I assumed, to a member of the motel staff. I asked her to heed our "do not disturb" sign, but she persisted by attempting to hand us clean towels. We already had clean towels but needed sleep. Maybe I needed to sound meaner, more urgent and demanding, but I could not persuade the giver of towels to cease and desist. The only way to get the person to understand was for me to get out of bed, take the damn towel, and shut the door. Without thinking, I jumped out of bed in my usual sleeping garb of nothing. She jumped back, I shut the door, was not arrested for accidental exposure, and I fell back to dreaming about Neotropical migrants.

10–12 April 2005

People fishing this Sunday lined the Texas City Dike. Most had five or more poles in the water. Two is the legal limit, but no one was counting. The multiple fishing lines shook in a stiff southerly 15 to 20 mile per hour wind. Besides a place to fish, the dike or levee, as it is also addressed, was built in 1935 to protect Texas City from flooding. It is 19 to 23 feet high and is also a fine place to see birds, including a raft of unwary Eared Grebes that floated near the dike road, their red eyes and flared golden ears making them look surprised. A second raft of Eared Grebes had two Horned Grebes in tow. A handful of Neotropical Cormorants waited for a meal. Little Kelp Gulls, seen on the dike in past years, were not around today. More searching yielded two Common Loons. Electricity lines supplied power to a café at the end of the five-mile dike where the wind was brisker in the middle of Galveston Bay. Two Least Terns paralleled the dike on my return to natural land.

TEXAS MIGRANTS AND CHICKENS

Death and destruction have plagued Texas City and Galveston. A shipboard of nitrates that exploded, killing 576 people in 1947, and a 1900 hurricane, killing 8,000 Galvestonians, were the most dramatic disasters. Several storms in Galveston have annihilated hundreds and destroyed whole parts of the city though the estates near Galveston's Kempner Park seemed to survive just fine. Eurasian Collared and White-winged doves cooed in the park. A walk around Hasting Estate was worth one-half of a life species, a Gray-cheeked Thrush. In 1962, I recorded the same name, but since the splitting of Gray-cheeks into Bicknell's and Gray-cheeked Thrushes, I felt compelled to delete both from the trip list. Because of the season then, I might have observed either species. This time, I am reasonably confident about the identification. The late Henri Ouellet, who had proposed recognizing Bicknell's and Gray-cheeked thrushes, and I had discussed these two birds over coffee and trays of specimens. Bicknell's Thrush migrates along the eastern seaboard and the Appalachian Mountains, whereas Gray-cheeked Thrush migrates along the Gulf of Mexico. Of course, anything is possible, which is part of what makes birding fun. Do those Bicknell's Thrushes that winter in the Greater Antilles all avoid Texas? Because of its small breeding range, Bicknell's is surely far less abundant than Gray-cheeks. The chance of finding a Bicknell's Thrush on the coast of Texas is remote but possible. The only definite way for separating these thrushes is voice, and my Galveston thrush was silent. As taxonomic editor of *Oregon Birds*, published in 2003, I noted that the two-state records were not, with certainty, Gray-cheeked Thrushes though most likely the two birds were that species. How could I be sure of my Galveston thrush? I could not. However, as a birder, but with trepidation, I joined most other listers of the upper Texas coast and added to the trip list Gray-cheeked Thrush.

After passing the crowded Galveston beaches, probably populated with Houston escapees, I turned north to check the inland marshes and tidal flats. None of the places I checked produced new birds. Farther along the coast at Clapper Rail Trail in Galveston Island State Park, the temperature turned from overly warm to hot and windy but improved with fewer people. A flock of eight male Orchard Orioles and a female Baltimore Oriole were the only migrants found. Two Crested Caracaras were waxing amorous in a distant tree, and I finally heard the insect sound that only a LeConte's Sparrow could love.

Galveston on Monday was less crowded than yesterday, but the beaches we checked were mostly birdless. Our best birding was at San Luis Pass, where Piping, Wilson's and Semipalmated Plovers, Dunlins, and Western and Semipalmated Sandpipers mingled on the sand. Many individuals of the sandpipers were in grayish winter plumage though a few were rusty breeding birds. The two plumages required us to work twice as hard to separate drooping bills from stouter bills. Herons were abundant east of the beach, including an unafraid white Reddish Egret. It had the same unbalanced foraging behavior as its rufous and dark morph.

The closed tollbooth on the long bridge across San Luis Pass meant a free ride onto the Texas mainland. With so much activity by so many birds, we had to force ourselves to leave the pass. South of Freeport, we crossed a high arched bridge over the Intracoastal Waterway onto Quintana Island. Our destination was the Quintana Neotropical Bird Sanctuary, a four-acre grove of mostly salt cedars preserved by the Houston Audubon Society as an important migrant stopover. A Yellow-green Vireo, one of few found in the United States, was found in the sanctuary in 1998. We did not expect any rarities, but the north wind fed hope for finding the Neotropical migrants that so far had eluded us.

The sanctuary has trails, a couple of fountains with artificially running water, and park benches for the weary birder. The trees, barely exceeding 15 feet in height, moved slightly under the northerly wind. The branches also moved under the steady flutter of groups of migrants. We ticked off Blue and Golden-winged warblers, species I missed from Ohio to New York in 1962. The two are famous for interbreeding, but we did not see any of their hybrids. We finally saw a Cerulean Warbler among the 17 species of Parulidae. Several yellow-faced Hooded Warblers swarmed the fountain about 15 feet from the park bench. While waiting for the next species to appear, a female Northern Parula foraged on a limb overhanging the bench where we were sitting. I pondered the bird's strength and perseverance. The four-and-a-half-inch long waif appeared unafraid as her barred wings carried her from leaf to leaf. She was most likely famished from the long 500-mile nonstop flight from the Yucatan. Like the Parula, most of the birds we found in the Quintana woods were ignoring the humans.

Indigo and Painted buntings and three species of vireos had crossed the treacherous gulf today. Exhausted Common Nighthawks and a larger Chuck-will's-widow trying to sleep dwarfed the diminutive and brighter warblers and vireos. A splash of a couple of orange and black Baltimore Orioles caught our eyes. A singing Swainson's Thrush did not sound anything like those breeding in western Oregon, but I ignored what is a taxonomic issue to admire a baker's dozen of Orchard Orioles. These were lucky birds, and we were lucky to see them. It was a smorgasbord to delight our eyes and ears.

Astounded by the little woods that could, we had finally witnessed a Neotropical fallout. Warblers and tanagers were not dripping from the trees, but there was plenty of action. Owing to the north wind, we briefly wondered if we should drive back to High Island. Deciding against it might have been a mistake, but we needed to keep moving westward.

We drove inland, essentially up the winding Brazos River to the small town of West Columbia, the chosen capital of the once fledgling Republic of Texas that had declared its independence from Mexico. Sam Houston was inaugurated as president there in 1836. The capital of the Republic of Texas was Columbia for three months, then moved to Austin in 1839, then to Houston in 1842, and finally back to Austin in 1844. The new republic, like the duration of each capital, was short-lived, lasting from 1836 to 1845. Linda and I were at first unaware of the historical aspects of West Columbia, the new name for Columbia. We nonetheless enjoyed a quiet slumber in a local motel. The price, $58.89 including tax and a continental breakfast of waffles, cereal, and/or fruit, was near average for the franchised motels we had so far frequented. That single night was a huge portion of my entire budget during the 1960s leg of the journey.

A Streak-backed Oriole had been reported about 30 minutes north of West Columbia at the 5,000-acre Brazos Bend State Park. The aptly named oriole, breeding from Costa Rica to northwestern Mexico, is only occasionally a visitor in California and Arizona, and only in fall and winter. Today was 12 April, and the week-old sighting held promise of orioles to come. After all, rare birds might stay put for weeks, even months, although many are one-day wonders. A ranger at the visitor center handed us a map labeled Streak-backed Oriole, with an arrow pointing to the Hoots Hollow Trail. The ranger added that the last unconfirmed sighting was of a female observed last Friday. Five days from an unconfirmed sighting was not encouraging though we hiked Hoots Hollow armed with hope.

A half-dozen birders crept around the trail, looking intently in bushes and high in the sycamores and cottonwoods. No one had seen the rare oriole today. Linda and I searched for the oriole and for warblers, found a female Cerulean Warbler, not so much sky blue but a drabber bluish-green bird. Linda located a striking male Black-throated Blue Warbler. We eventually gave up Hoots Hollow Trail for a hike along the shore of 40-Acre Lake. A sunning Anhinga, with outstretched wings, perched on the opposite shore. Linda said this was her first since she did not count the one at Disney World seen a few years ago. In 1962 and 63, orange groves and natural habitat flourished where the Disney amusement park would be built. I never saw an Anhinga in that part of Florida; Linda's suspicion that her early Anhinga was an import was correct.

American alligators were foraging among the Purple and Common Gallinules, funny long-toed birds reminiscent of barnyard bantam chickens gone aquatic. One seven-foot alligator lurking in the flat dark water appeared slow and cold. Its mouth formed a smile, almost, as it lay waiting for a careless duck or heron. Gallinules stepped lightly. A pair of Least Grebe, a first, watched us stroll by, then kept one eye out for food and the other for alligators. The two grebes also kept their golden eyes on two chicks. An observation tower afforded a better look at the smallest of grebes, almost three inches shorter than the small dark-eyed and nearly ubiquitous Pied-billed Grebe. Several Black-bellied Whistling-Ducks graced the scene. Two took to the air, with reddish bills ablaze and their white wing stripes contrasting with the black trailing ends of powerful and sturdy flight feathers. I caught myself calling them by their old name, tree-duck. We also could see a heron and spoonbill rookery not far away to the north. Several more Prothonotary Warblers nipped at insects in the moss-draped trees along the dike. I would have enjoyed Brazos Bend in 1963, but about 20 years would pass before the region became a state park.

The hot and humid climate of southeastern Texas was beginning to compete with our zeal for birding. We made one more try to find the Streak-backed Oriole but found only a disappointed birder looking for shade. Our vehicle, the Birdmobile, was steamy hot, but thanks to the air-conditioning that my old VW did not have, we traveled comfortably. Last night we were in the former capital of the Republic of Texas, and tonight we will be in the present capital of the state of Texas. We would also be at our daughter and her husband's home, and the home of little Sabine, the granddaughter whose name rekindled the completion of the birding trip.

Thankfully, our first few days in Texas were accompanied by good directions to localities that had been preserved from conservation efforts managed by the Houston Audubon Society, The Nature Conservancy, the Fish and Wildlife Service, and others. Many of the localities were unknown or inaccessible to birders during the early 1960s, at least unknown by then young Danny McSkunk, a.k.a. this writer.

The good work of preserving habitat by the Houston Audubon Society began with the 1969 establishment of the society, which now owns and manages 17 sanctuaries of 4,171 acres of protected habitat valuable to birds, birders, and anyone who enjoys the outdoors. Most localities were not under the umbrella of the society until the 1990s. The Quintana Neotropical Bird Sanctuary, owned and maintained by the town of Quintana and the Gulf Coast Bird Observatory, opened in 1994. These saved remnants, these leftovers from human occupation, help wildlife and are reminders of what once existed.

Our testing the waters of Rare Bird Alerts did not help produce a Streak-backed Oriole. We tried. The alert on 14 March, the one read before leaving Oregon, listed the oriole. However, the oriole was not mentioned in the next two alerts, the last dated 12 April. An alert 10 days later stated that the elusive visitor was last seen six days after we visited Brazos Bend. We missed a chance meeting. Other Rare Bird Alerts were consulted during parts of the remainder of the trip. The reports mostly tantalized us and we did not have the time to be at the right place and time for rarities scattered here and there across a state as vast as Texas. Primarily, we stuck to our researched itinerary, trying to find the maximum number of targeted species in the shortest time. Wearing binoculars helped. They are a badge that often indicated either the need for or a source of knowledge. Most birders like to share, and we benefited from the polite camaraderie of strangers with binoculars.

Our visit to Brazos Bend State Park in 2005 helped add several new life birds not just by different species but an abundance of those sought-after species. Linda and I revisited Brazos Bend in late March 2015 just on a whim, perhaps to satisfy a measure of nostalgia. After all, we saw our first Least Grebes there. Although the grebes and many of the same species we saw in 2005 were present, the number of individuals was surprisingly low. Hopefully, the difference was in our timing.

When visiting Texas City Prairie Preserve (hereafter TCPP), Linda and I had no idea we were stepping into a land fraught with controversy. The 2,300-acre preserve was gifted to The Nature Conservancy from Mobil Oil in 1995. The Nature Conservancy is the largest nonprofit environmental organization in the world with about $6 billion in assets and 20 million acres under protection nationwide. Mobil Oil declared their donation was to help for the last chance for the Attwater's Prairie Chicken suffering from loss of habitat. Of course, much habitat loss was from activities by the petroleum industry already laying waste to acre after acre of coastal grasslands. Mobil's concern for the prairie birds may have been a day late and a chicken short since they had been drilling on the property up until 1995. In 1996, The Nature Conservancy began introducing captive-reared birds from zoos that were co-mingled with the extant wild individuals, keeping in mind the genetics of all individuals to maintain viable populations. Anyway, trouble reared its ugly head when The Nature Conservancy began drilling for oil in 1999. The august organization reasoned the operation would demonstrate drilling was possible without causing harm to the environment. However, the Conservancy's claim of no foul to our subject fowl was questioned and the story was punctuated by a nearby explosion and several oil spills,[1] never mind prairie chickens dying from neglect as reported by expert Stan Temple. Holes larger than from drilling for oil riddle the story of the prized grouse at TCPP. First, Stan wrote that the prairies chicken population was "hopelessly small" with "a very low probability of succeeding in the long term, but not because of mismanagement, oil wells, poorly designed pens or other issues . . ." He also pointed out that small populations such as the one at the TCPP were doomed because of inbreeding, demography, and hurricanes.[2] Stan and I have communicated on several occasions and subjects, and I thoroughly trust his expertise.

Regardless of what experts knew and did, the fact that The Nature Conservancy drilled for petroleum raised eyebrows. For example, the National Audubon Society made it clear that activities involving petroleum on their property are not acceptable and that The Nature Conservancy made a mistake. Kierán Suckling, executive director of the Center for Biological Diversity, a group that works extensively on endangered species, stated, "The very idea of oil drilling inside a reserve is utterly wrong, and it is especially disturbing in this case because the Attwater's prairie chicken is one of the most endangered species in the entire country. It could very well be the next species to go extinct in the United States."[3] In the same article in the *New York Times*, the author also reported internal Nature Conservancy documents "suggest" drilling was disturbing the chickens. The Conservancy made $8 million from the well, whose profits were to be for conservation issues. However, most of the plunder from the well went to the slippery slope of lawsuits concerning mineral rights. Since 2003, "The Nature Conservancy has maintained an explicit policy against entering new oil and gas leases on its preserves" and closed operation and removed the infrastructure associated with the 1999 well.[4] The 1999 well was actually closed in 2006 due to mechanical failures. In 2007, the leaseholders (not The Nature Conservancy), took advantage of their legal rights and drilled a replacement well under the watchful eye of The Nature Conservancy. That well was plugged in 2015.[5]

1. Naomi Klein. *This Changes Everything: Capitalism vs. the Climate.* (New York: Simon and Schuster, 2014).

2. 8 May 2003 letter from Stanley A. Temple to Mike Coda, The Nature Conservancy director of external affairs, regarding *Washington Post* articles.

3. Justin Gillis. "Group Earns Oil Income Despite Pledge on Drilling." Aug 3, 2014, *New York Times*.

4. Letter emailed 24 June 2021 from Suzanne Scott, Texas state director, The Nature Conservancy, to M. Ralph Browning.

5. Letter emailed 19 July 2021 from Anne Zuparko, director of marketing and

But, what about the Greater Prairie-Chicken? It is no surprise that energy development practices negatively impact prairie-chickens.[6] Sure, there are exceptions to that, but despite the best efforts and well-wishes (pun possibly intended) by those concerned, playing chicken with actual prairie chickens was not a good idea. Biologist Val Lehman reported oil development was one of the several reasons for the decline in the Greater Prairie-Chickens.[7] I have no reason to doubt the decline in population or the reason for it. However, based on a small and anecdotal sample, I must acknowledge that Linda nor I were aware of the 1999 well during our 2005 observation of lekking birds. We believe the birds were.

Meanwhile, the infusion of captive-reared birds continued although a 2010 Fish and Wildlife report stated birds in the TCPP had limited recruitment.[8] The TCPP population was not increasing, which could have been for many reasons ranging from teeny-tiny fire ants to colossal hurricanes. Despite periodic and severe hurricanes such as Hurricane Ike in 2008, most birds apparently survived severe weather, including flooding. For example, 23 birds at TCPP were monitored before Hurricane Ike, whereas 19 were monitored after the hurricane.[9] On the other hand, Hurricane Harvey in 2017 drowned bird after bird. An estimated 800,000 Attwater Prairie chickens historically thrived on the prairies of coastal Texas and survived hurricanes but added together, modern disturbances by introduced ants to humans and more severe weather, including climate change, are not on the side of the birds. The cited Fish and Wildlife Report also stated the release of captive-reared birds at the TCPP was terminated in 2011 and, by 2012, Greater Prairie-Chickens no longer roamed the preserve.

Though mistakes were made, so were corrections. The current policy of The Nature Conservancy should prevent repeating their historical faux pas. Today, the organization focuses on prairie chickens from captive-reared populations breeding on private land under the Refugio-Goliad Prairie Project managed by the Conservancy. Captive-reared birds at the Attwater Prairie Chicken NWR also benefit from research by the Conservancy. As of April 2021, the Conservancy estimated there are at least 178 Attwater's

---

communication, The Nature Conservancy, to M. Ralph Browning.

6. David W. Londe et al. "Female Greater Prairie-Chicken Response to Energy Development and Rangeland Management." *Ecosphere* 10.12 (Dec 2019) 10:e02982.

7. V. W. Lehmann and R. G. Mauermann. "Status of Attwater's Prairie Chicken." *Journal of Wildlife Management* 27.4 (Oct 1963) 713–25.

8. U.S. Fish and Wildlife Service. "Attwater's Prairie-Chicken (Tympanuchus cupido attwateri) Recovery Plan, Second Revision." Albuquerque, NM. April 26, 2010.

9. Texas Parks and Wildlife. "Adopt a Prairie Chicken." Fall 2008 newsletter. Austin, TX.

Prairie Chickens on the privately owned Refugio-Goliad property and the Attwater Prairie Chicken NWR. That is still a frighteningly small number but shows at least a greater trend than exhibited by interior populations of Greater Prairie-Chickens occupying fragmented ranges in the Great Plains.

Would I have found Greater Prairie-Chicken in coastal Texas in 1963? Less than 1 percent of the original six million acres of coastal prairie currently exist and the percent of extant prairie might have been slightly greater in 1963 than today. Attwater prairie chickens in 1962 included 1,335 individuals according to the FWS. More habitat and a larger population might have increased my chances of detecting these elusive birds, but in 1963 I did not have any leads where I might look for the southern subspecies. Of course, my petroleum-propelled VW had traveled its last mile before I could get to Texas, but it is doubtful I would have found prairie chickens. I had missed seeing the birds earlier when I crossed North Dakota. It was past lekking behavior. Perhaps I could have found the species in the central US in the spring of 1963 but traveling there would have been too distant from my planned spring route that year. Most likely, I would have missed the species.

Since all the original wild Attwater prairie chickens no longer exist, is the Greater Prairie-Chicken seen in coastal Texas countable by ABA standards? ABA rules require a bird to be established and to demonstrate a viable breeding population for at least 15 years. Currently, the Attwater subspecies of Greater Prairie-Chicken exist only because extant populations are infused by introducing captive-reared individuals. The birds cannot self-sustain their existence. That is, if it were not for those introductions, the species would likely become extinct in coastal Texas. All the 2021 estimated 178 birds are the progeny of introduced birds and no originally wild birds are alive today. Since the Texas populations are not established, birds observed from coastal Texas cannot be counted. They are no more countable than domestic chickens, which agrees with the official Texas checklist that considers the species not established at this time. The species was once upon a time established, and a few were alive and active participants in lekking at the TCPP in 2005 when the species was countable.

Inquiring minds probably want a better explanation about the various capital cities of the ephemeral Republic of Texas. Linda and I thought West Columbia, remember the new name for Columbia, was the first designated capital of the want-to-be nation. There seemed to be considerable political activity in deciding the location of the capital of the Republic of Texas. Sources vary, with some considering the existence of at least five different capitals of the republic. Washington on the Brazos, now a historical site northwest of Houston, might be the first capital of the Republic of Texas but not everyone agrees. West Columbia appears to win as the first capital by consensus. We are not sure which was first, though we were certain there must have been more individuals of Greater Prairie-Chickens than people or capitals of the short-lived republic.

The population dynamics of *attwateri* deserve a little more attention. Readers of bird literature may recall that Cleveland Bent wrote that the coastal prairie-chickens were extirpated in that region because of civilization and hunting.[10] We now know that he was incorrect about the taxon being extirpated. He was on the mark about why the birds were thought to be extirpated. They were hunted, but what he did not mention is the prairie chickens were also targets in a sport that might have been called "Let's see who can slaughter the most." Reportedly, the targets were left on the ground where they fell.[11] The birds were possibly being enjoyed as a sight to behold, substitutes for clay pigeons, and as the main ingredient in a prairie-chicken pot pie. At the time, 1836 to 1845, the birds were relatively abundant though beginning to suffer from the introduction of cattle, the plow, and the gun that did in the innocent birds. Also, no one took a scientific interest in the edible fowl until 1893 or well after Texas became a US state. One person noticing was none other than Charles Bendire, father of Oregon ornithology discussed way back in chapter 1 when I was freezing in his old haunts in the Klamath Basin. Bendire, who was at the National Museum of Natural History from 1884 until his death in 1897, formally named and described the coastal prairie birds (*attwateri*) that he based on specimens donated by conservationist and naturalist Henry Philemon Attwater, who lived in Rockport, Texas. The specimens were collected from Aransas and Refugio counties in 1893, the same year Bendire published the original description of *attwateri* in *Forest and Stream*, a popular outdoor publication focusing on hunting, fishing, and camping. Printed in a newspaper format (11 inches by 16 inches), *Forest and Stream* was an unusual place to formally name and describe a new kind of bird, though Ridgway published descriptions of two new grouse in the same publication's first volume in 1873. There are commonalities here. The birds described by Ridgway and Bendire are in the same taxonomic order, they are huntable and edible, and both men worked for Smithsonian. As for the publication *Forest and Stream*, it merged with *Field and Stream* in 1930, a magazine sold at your finer newsstands and sometimes found in my local barbershop until a few years ago when the

10. Arthur Cleveland Bent. "Life Histories of North American Gallinaceous Birds: Orders Galliformes and Columbiformes." Vol. 162. (US Government Printing Office, 1932).

11. B. C. Robison. *A Haven in the Sun: Five Stories of Bird Life and Its Future on the Texas Coast*. (Lubbock: Texas Tech University Press, 2020).

publication became digital only. The loss of "Forest" to "Field" happened as a huge chunk of eastern forest became, huh, fields.

As is usual, there always seem to be more questions than answers. One such question is why did it take so long for science to recognize differences in some of the grouse roaming the land? Bendire surely heard about the grouse in coastal Texas before 1893. Maybe not, but according to the specimen database of Vertnet, the oldest specimens of *attwateri* were two collected in 1850 and housed in the collection of the University of New Mexico in Albuquerque, New Mexico. Even the year 1850 seems a late time for the edible prairie chicken to be collected as a scientific specimen since human settlement had already begun decades earlier. David Douglas collected and described Mountain Quail in the early 1800s. It is easy to assume that the citizens of the Republic of Texas were too busy to think of sending a specimen to a museum. After all, it was a time for choosing a capital and partaking in fried prairie-chicken dinners.

Chapter 24

Austin City Limits and Southward

13–14 April 2005

AUSTIN, NOW RECOGNIZED AS the capital of Texas, was cold and nearly birdless in January 2004. Today it was warm, almost hot, and hormonal White-winged Doves were cooing from hidden perches of leafed trees in the backyard of our daughter's home. Rowdy, almost comical Great-tailed Grackles shrieked, as Blue Jays joined in the dissonant clamor. Except for the doves, we were very much in eastern bird country. The west was not far away. As previously arranged, I called Balcones Canyon NWR to make plans for a visit tomorrow. Realizing that our schedule was running behind, I also phoned our Harlingen motel to move our reservations ahead a couple of days and add an extra night. There were so many birds to see and so little time. I began to worry that we would not be able to be home by our scheduled 15 May.

Earlier in the day, I walked a few blocks from the house to a city park. Maybe a Neotropical migrant or two would heighten today's birding. I was surprised that numerous Ruby-crowned Kinglets were still wintering. Most were singing but would be gone sometime in May. In 90 minutes, I found a few Neotropical migrants that included our first trip White-eyed Vireo. It was also singing, which was a typical vireo sound, loud and not at all sweet like a Ruby-crowned Kinglet.

The next morning was an early one to beat the Austin rush hour and arrive at the Balcones refuge at a suitable time. Linda stayed with her beloved daughter's baby Sabine, trying to teach her to coo softly like a dove. I filled the 13-gallon gas tank of the Birdmobile for $21.27. The pump's gauge turned so rapidly that it was hard to round off the cents when gas costs more than $2.00 per gallon. That $21.27 could have purchased 64 gallons of gas in 1962, enough to travel almost 2,000 miles in my long-gone VW. We had already spent $77.66 on gas in Texas, where the price per gallon is cheaper than most other states. Perhaps it was more important to worry about the cost than meeting our timetable. I mused that we are here now; this is time to fish or cut bait, a time to bird or not.

The drive from Austin to refuge headquarters should take an hour, but I was an hour into nowhere. I had become lost in the rolling Texas Hill Country. Although not a huge fan of cell phones, I was glad I had one with me. A call to refuge headquarters resulted in detailed instructions. By accident, it turned out I was not far from the Shin Oaks observation tower. The gate was locked, and a sign announced public closure to the tower. I decided to walk on in since the biologist of the refuge had emailed months earlier that I should not be concerned about the closure. Just inside the cable gate, I heard a Black-capped Vireo sing but could not locate the vocalist in a frustrating 45-minute search. Though once widespread from Mexico to Kansas, the vireo now occurs locally in Texas and three counties in Oklahoma. The dwindling population is victim to people, cowbirds, and cattle.

Just as I returned to the Birdmobile at the edge of the main road, a Texas car roared to an abrupt stop a few yards away. That momentarily hushed the out-of-sight vireo. Three men jumped out of the car and two males shut their vehicle doors quietly. The other person slammed his door and then looked at the others as if apologizing. The three appeared as if they had been caught stealing. Maybe they had not expected to see anyone. Noticing their binoculars, I wondered if they were anxious about finding the vireo. They continued searching past the fence and glancing up and down the empty road. One of them looked at me strangely and with what appeared to be unfriendly glances. These guys reminded me a little of a few of the secretive people I met when I was indentured to the Pentagon. For some reason, being an ex-patriot Fish and Wildlife employee and feeling protective of the vireos, I blurted that the area was closed. One of them snapped, "Well, we can look from the road, can't we?" He seemed defensive and perturbed. In a minute or two, the three jumped back in their car and roared away. Were they bonafide birders in a rude hurry on a big day or disgruntled local landowners in disguise? Not all residents were happy about the refuge. They considered the vireo and the warbler competition for the land they wanted to build upon or a place for their cattle to graze. Too much of that urban sprawl had already harmed the environment. As to cattle, their history of befouling the landscape is long. Possibly only historians

AUSTIN CITY LIMITS AND SOUTHWARD

have discovered who let the cows out, who decided the Texas Hill Country should be rangeland, but no matter. It is no longer the late nineteenth century. Pickup trucks have replaced horses, and once in a while, thanks to conservation efforts, struggling vireos and warblers have replaced cattle. As for the three anxious guys at Chin Oaks, I never saw them again.

A stop southward at the Doe Tract of the refuge looked promising. I reasoned that a hike to a stand of oak and juniper might produce Golden-cheeked Warblers, and after only walking a few yards from the parking lot, I heard the rare warbler. As with the song of the Black-capped Vireo, I had listened repeatedly to recordings of the song of Golden-cheeked Warbler. Again, no amount of searching would produce the bird. Frustrated, I left, nearly tripping over a pair of Black-throated Sparrows.

Not much later at refuge headquarters, I met Chuck Sexton, the refuge biologist. He asked if I had seen the vireo or the warbler. I told him I had heard them but not seen them. He said, "That's not good enough—let's go for a ride." In minutes, I was jumping into a refuge pickup. Not since the early sixties part of the trip had I been a guided visitor riding in the jump seat of a refuge truck. This time the trucks were larger, far more comfortable, and air-conditioned.

While on the way to Shin Oaks, we stopped at a culvert where Cave and Cliff swallows were nesting. Chuck identified a few of the individuals as they flew overhead. I was much slower and less accurate in my identifications of these similar-appearing birds. We arrived at Shin Oaks as a Black-capped Vireo was singing. In a couple of minutes, Chuck spotted the bird. It remained in view long enough to see its black head and white spectacled eyes. The rarest of North American vireos soon disappeared in the thick leaves of the shin oak thicket. The twittering song did not stop. The bird's territory is in a 200-acre plot known as Eckhard, one of several discontinuous tracts of the refuge scattered around the Edwards Plateau. Much of the region is or was cattle country. Before that, the region was the last bastion of Comanche and Apache until 1848, a time when there were more proto-Texans than American natives. Brown-headed Cowbirds came with the settlers' cattle, and vireos have suffered ever since. The refuge now attempts to control cowbird populations and maintain shin oak suitable to vireos by controlled burns and pruning. The oak, actually sand shinnery oak (*Quercus havarti*), is a natural climax plant. Removal of it by cattle owners allows grass to grow, cattle to fatten, hamburgers to make, and people to fatten. The process then requires longer leather belts from those tasty bovines. I like a good hamburger, but I also hope to live to enjoy vireos, the Brazilian jungle, and other beef-independent animals and plants.

We returned to the swallow colony and drove up a nearby driveway to a former working ranch house that had become accommodations for one of Chuck's research assistants. The building sat high on a hill, overlooking Ashe juniper stands that Chuck thought might host Golden-cheeked Warblers. We did not hear any warblers but did hear the plaintive song of local Canyon Wrens and singing Rufous-crowned and Black-throated sparrows.

It is harder each year to find Golden-cheeks. The entire population took a plunge from an estimated 15,000 to 17,000 birds in 1974 to only 2,200 to 4,600 in 1990. The population drop most likely started earlier, when, in the 1950s and 1970s, over 50 percent of the warbler's juniper habitat was bulldozed and burned to make way for urbanization, cattle, and cowbirds.

Chuck and I zipped past headquarters to a new refuge endeavor, Warbler Vista, and a wooden observation stand in the making. The contracted carpenters grinned as we looked at the progress, and they stared at our binoculars. My interpretation of the encounter was the carpenters were glad to have a job but resented the two birders taking away the land of their rancher friends. Hopefully, I was wrong. Brushing off the grins, I followed Chuck down the nearby slope on a trail recently constructed through junipers. That is when we heard the familiar refrain of a Golden-cheeked Warbler. We located the singer with little difficulty. A different song came out of the junipers further down the slope. Chuck announced that we were listening to song "B," a song I would not have recognized. Again, we located the male, and watched it sing.

During the drive between tracts, I learned that Chuck, who said he was "a sixties surfer-guy from Orange County, California," worked in the field with Joe Marshall on Botteri's Sparrows and knew my former next-door office mate, Roger Clapp. We stopped on the return to headquarters at a private residence driveway where Chuck showed me the plant that he discovered in 1989. The small whip of greenery known as *Croton alabamensis* var. *texensis* is a variety of Alabama Croton, a rare shrub confined to none other than Alabama. I thought he was kidding when he laughingly called it the Texabama Croton, but that seems to be its "official" English name.

Departing Balcones NWR was almost as difficult as finding it. Failing to negotiate Chuck's direction on my return to the city center of Austin, I had to backtrack to find the Town Lake area. Monk Parakeets had nested there. I found an old nest heaped over a floodlight of a ballpark. The nest and the clean ground below suggested the site was abandoned a considerable time ago. A passerby, curious about my binoculared attire and without a sly carpenter's grin, asked what I was looking for and, when I told him, commented he had seen the birds a week earlier. I searched for an hour before giving up and threaded my way to the southern side of the city. Road construction in Austin offered many unique opportunities for getting lost.

As I rushed from traffic light to rush hour traffic light, I wondered why people often underestimate how much travel time is needed to go from A to B. Finally, I arrived back at my daughter's home and my Linda after the long trip back to the Austin city limits. I lamented that too many people, excluding Chuck, have lost the ability to give proper directions and do not know north from south or the names of roads. Linda and I were becoming sadly aware that asking most people under 30 was asking for frustration. We once met a birder who planned to be in southern Oregon and was looking for Mountain Quail. We, I hope, told him correctly how to find a remote covey not far from our home.

15 April 2005

Linda's generous birthday present for my sixty-first was a paid birding tour on the King Ranch that would start around dawn tomorrow. The prudent thing to do today would be to leave Austin and make a few stops along the way to the ranch headquarters.

So, I thanked Linda and first headed to Aransas NWR, which was not that much out of the way, especially if a late Whooping Crane was hanging around. Approximately 80,000 people visit the refuge each year. A volunteer at the visitor center said apologetically that the last birds left yesterday. Maybe if I had just looked skyward from the hills yesterday, I would have seen Whooping Cranes flying northbound over singing Golden-cheeked Warblers. A search from the Aransas refuge's 40-foot observation tower looking over Hog Lake was indeed crane-free. The stiff south wind shook my binoculars as I scanned the lake and adjacent marshes. Far on the southern shore of Hog Lake was a huge black animal, a hog of sorts, a javelina. Others joined it. The view was almost birdless.

Happy that the pendulum was swinging favorably for the Whooping Crane, I could tolerate missing a species. Birders need to be optimistic. Maybe the old sand dunes jutting into San Antonio Bay, the partly wooded Dagger Point, would be crawling with Neotropical migrants. All that needed identifying was a White-eyed Vireo. It was time to leave the refuge.

While driving north of the refuge on Farm Road 774, two bumps on a perfectly flat field moved just enough to catch my eye. I quickly made a U-turn on the almost deserted road. The bumps were Buff-breasted Sandpipers, a life bird that would soon be winging north, traveling on a 2,500-mile route like that of Whooping Cranes. Another surprise was a roadside

Ferruginous Hawk, the largest of North American species in the genus *Buteo*. The driver of a long and wide RV traveling in the opposite direction noticed me gazing at the raptor out in the recently plowed field. They slowed. Maybe they were birders also looking for Buff-breasted Sandpipers or Ferruginous Hawks. Apparently, they realized that parking their motor home on the narrow road would not be safe and drove on toward the refuge. Several miles down the road, the same vehicle caught up with me just as I turned south on the highway to Rockport. Maybe they just missed their turn.

The steady south wind at Rockport did not promise Neotropical migrants. This area would have been a major stop in 1963, but today I needed to hurry on. Connie Hagar had made Rockport world famous for viewing migrants. Peterson and Fisher in 1953 visited there. I glanced east toward the Connie Hagar Wildlife Sanctuary but stopped only near Cape Valero, where a few Red Knots were resting with a handful of assorted herons and egrets.

My next mission was finding a Masked Duck. After a crowded and uneventful ferry crossing to Port Arthur, I drove down Mustang Island to Padre Island. The Masked Duck, reported on a recent Rare Bird Alert, was supposed to be on a pond south of the road to Bird Island Basin in Padre Island National Seashore. The duck was not there or at least I failed to find it. I rushed back to the main road to the visitor center to check if there had been a sighting of the bird today. However, it was late, and the center was closed. No one was stirring except a couple of relieved people sauntering out of the restroom. I emptied some sand in my shoe and headed south to Kingsville.

16 April 2005

The alarm sounded at 5:15 in the dark and lonely Kingsville motel room. It took about 45 minutes to revive my sleepy brain to wakefulness and complete all the necessary morning duties. Shaving was barely needed in the sixties leg of the trip. It was also not required on this or any other morning since becoming a bearded one in the late sixties. I was the first tour member to arrive at the King Ranch office. By 6:30, seven other birders had gathered around a big tour van. Tom Langshield, our guide, confirmed our names on his checklist much like a birder ticking species. As a former student at Texas A&M University at Kingsville, he inventoried the birds on the vast ranch. He loved the area, and King Ranch hired him to develop and lead nature tours. That was 10 years ago. While I conversed with Tom, a Houston couple a few years my senior, I think, two brothers from Ontario, a man from Arizona, and a father and adult son began piling into the van. They politely took the rear seats, leaving the front jump seat unfilled. Maybe they thought whoever had that seat would be the one jumping in and out to open and close gates. It was great luck for me to fill that seat since I could see ahead easily, and it was easier on my protesting back that had recently announced I was not the master of my back.

The 10-passenger diesel-powered van made more noise than I would have expected for a birding vehicle, but that was never a problem as we roared from place to place. Our first stop was almost an hour south of Kingsville on the Norias Division, just one of the several huge units of the 825,000-acre ranch. A square mile contains 640 acres; we would barely skim the surface of the vast ranch. A separate headquarters occupies each of the several huge divisions. The colossal property was once over a million acres, gradually built in size from the original 1852 purchase by Richard King, a steamship captain. As for opening and closing gates, most of them were so-called bump gates, a device that replaced the traditional cattle guard. Jumping out of a vehicle to open a gate is not required. These unique gates open with a slow gentle bump by the vehicle that causes the gate to swing open. The heavy flat gate pivots on a center spring-loaded pole. Once opened, it is necessary to drive quickly through the gate to avoid it hitting the vehicle on its return to its former closed position. It gave new meaning to close the door and do not let it hit you in the rear extremity on the way out. For inquiring minds that might want to know, W. H. Bachler invented the bump gate. He is also known for the "ALL-IN-ONE" Castrator, advertised as "a proven instrument that is mechanically sound and has positive feedback." Feedback from whom? Nonetheless, I did not have to be the gate guy.

Tom drove about 30 minutes through the flat sandy mesquite before stopping. Everyone piled out. It was cool and quiet at first. Tom directed the group to the buzzy trill from a bird hidden higher in the Spanish moss dripping from the oaks. In seconds, a Tropical Parula appeared. Tears pooled in my eyes, not because it was my first Tropical Parula, but it was my first Tropical Parula without Linda. I missed her on the sixties trip, and I missed her today. Two Northern Beardless-Tyrannulets whistled a few yards from the warblers. Our birding group barely noticed Bewick's Wrens; we were on a trophy hunt. There were Harris's and White-tailed Hawks, Verdins, and more. The mournfully plaintive Audubon's Oriole proved to be a difficult bird to see as a pair ducked from one side of a grove to the other. I volunteered that I would function as an oriole hazer on the opposite side of the grove. Two others from the tour joined me. Our idea was to help the others have a better chance of seeing these black and yellow blackbirds. However, the orioles kept a close eye on us. We saw them better than ever. The most important trophy was the small Ferruginous Pygmy-Owl. We located three birds, their buffy tails accompanying monotonous calls. They seemed more annoyed than afraid of the binoc and scope totting, camera clicking, and whispering throng of salivating birders.

The tour group gathered around a picnic table for chicken and potato salad at noon. Before turning to food, a question about cattle came to mind. Perhaps my curiosity was piqued because of ranch work during my spring chicken days. Those were the days of the running of the bulls, with time for keeping clear of them and always having an exit plan at the ready. Even cows are sometimes cranky and want to hurt you. Should our birding group be concerned by the tens of thousands of cows and bulls on the King Ranch? The cattle had a familiar name. That was Santa Gertrudis, a breed developed by the ranch in 1910. They are part Brahma and part shorthorn Herford, and I was once informed the breed was introduced to a favorite winter birding area near my home in Oregon about 40 years ago. Those huge animals were the talk of local barbershops for a few years. My recollection of the new bovines was of large and not particularly friendly animals that, though formidable, were likely not to attack. Today, it seemed odd that the lunch menu did not include part of a Santa Gertrudis but that was okay. I munched my preferred chicken and listened to a distant Ash-throated Flycatcher. Nearby was a small barn with a resident Barn Owl and outside were Vermillion Flycatchers flashing red against the blue of a clearing sky.

Tom asked if anyone needed Sprague's Pipit. I did, and the brief foray into a field near the Norias Division headquarters produced the bird. The group needed to see Buff-bellied Hummingbird, Brown-crested Flycatcher, Couch's Kingbird, Green Jay, and Long-billed and Curve-billed Thrashers. With so many pairs of eyes, and our guide knowing the best places to look, we kept busy looking and ticking. Someone would yell, "There's one," Tom would slam on the brakes, and we would have a good look. Often it was necessary to angle the van in the road or back up for the best view. This would not have worked in one of those bird tours via a caravan of cars. Good friends of ours, let us call them S and J, once witnessed a vehicle inadvertently crunching expensively into the rear of a suddenly stopped lead tour car. Except for a pickup or two at headquarters, our van was the only vehicle in the immense garden of birds. Our vehicle served as a near perfect bird blind during the nine-hour tour that became eleven hours by the time we rolled back to Kingsville. My list tallied to 87 species. I missed only the Least Sandpiper among the eight other shorebirds at a couple of ranch ponds.

I grabbed a hamburger in the land of beef and went to the only place where I could have the Birdmobile's oil changed. Once finished, I drove south following information provided by Tom to where I might find Common Pauraque around dusk. The directions were a little vague, so I stopped at one of those little mart-stores for more details. For lack of willpower, I picked up a small pack of donuts that suddenly transformed me back to the early sixties and found a person for detailed directions. Better yet, a man told me to follow him down the main highway, and he would point to the turn. He did, and by dark, I was listening to the weird whistle of my unseen targeted pauraque. One seemed to be about 10 feet from the edge of the narrow paved lane.

17–18 April 2005

Yesterday inadvertently marked my face red with minor sunburn. It did not hurt, but now the strawberry complexion clashed with my sun-bleached hair. Near my other end were three round and reddish welts on my lily-white legs, evidence of chigger bites. Most of my western friends had never experienced the treat of chiggers. I had that treat and hoped that keeping my jeans tight around my ankles and a good dose of DEET would keep the red devils at bay. My tactics helped, but not completely. The tiny mites are about 0.16 millimeter in diameter in their pesky larval stage and are too small to notice until it is too late. They jump on you from vegetation, find the skin around a hair follicle, and bite. That is the beginning of the itching, the allergic reaction to the saliva from chiggers as they inject the site. Maybe Brer Rabbit was not worried about the thorns of the briar patch but might have been concerned about the chiggers living there.

I checked Kingsville Cemetery for Grove-billed Anis, produced a Greater Roadrunner, and saw what appeared to be a beginning of a Sunday funeral. Not wishing to intrude, I departed, drove to a take-out sandwich shop, and found a gas station. The price for gasoline in Kingsville was the lowest on the trip, yet it was above the national average. I wondered where that mystic average place might be. The 200 plus mile drive back to Austin went as quickly as my above-average gas would allow. It was early afternoon when I arrived at the doorway where my wonderful Linda stood. I told her about the last two days and the hope that we would later find most of the species I witnessed as we journey west.

The next morning was time for sad goodbyes to our granddaughter Sabine and her wonderful parents. Southwest of Austin at Alice, we asked at a local establishment for the location of Alice's restaurant. No one even blinked. Were we that old? There must have been a restaurant in Alice frequented by someone named Alice. If we could have found the place, we could have gotten anything we wanted. Instead, we dipped into our peanut butter jar, ate an apple, and gave a moment of silence to Arlo Guthrie. On down the dry highway, we stopped at Kingsville Cemetery, this time finding a Greater Kiskadee nest and three Golden-fronted Woodpeckers. Yesterday the two species were new; today they are new for Linda. The well-kept cemetery of tombstones memorialized mostly Latin names etched in the headstones displaying dates from the cradle to the grave of citizens from decades past to yesterday. We wondered about the stories and history of those outlined in stone.

We arrived at our motel in Harlingen late in the afternoon. The heavily overcast sky and blustery wind suggested we might be dealing with harsh weather for the first time during this trip. It was out of our control. We optimistically planned the next four days of birding in the lower Rio Grande.

19 April 2005

The weather was much better than last night's forecast. It was morning, and the south wind was humid under the pale gray clouds. The temperature was pushing upward as we rolled into the parking lot of the Frontera Audubon Center in Weslaco, our first lower Rio Grande birding site. Only 12 acres, the native trees and wetland of the little oasis attract birds that are easier to find south of the border. People were everywhere, stealthy birders armed with binocs and expectations. We joined in, creeping around the tangles until we could not find the feeders. I doubled back, partly for new directions but also for a bug-be-gone we left in the Birdmobile. While at the visitor center, I talked to a very elderly man who had trouble walking. He announced proudly that he had watched a male Crimson-collared Grosbeak for as long as he desired, and that now he was walking home to fix his lunch. With new information, hope, and poison on our skin, we forged on to the feeders where we inhaled the gorgeously colored grosbeak. Paying attention to RBA reports had paid off. The Crimson-collared Grosbeak seemed enough to satisfy our rare bird appetite since we opted against going to a private residence not far up the road where we might see a female Crimson-collared Grosbeak, a Rose-breasted Becard, and an expensive Blue Mockingbird available for viewing for a fee. There was a good chance to find becards in Arizona. We would save our money.

Santa Ana NWR was on the after-lunch agenda. Our Golden Eagle Pass took care of the entrance fee. The 2,088-acre refuge of tropical thorn forest is a small part of the remaining natural habit in the lower Rio Grande Valley.

Over 95 percent of the valley has been cleared or altered. The refuge was closed to all but foot traffic and a tram. The sun filtered through the white sky, quieting birds and birders. It was too uncomfortably hot to walk, so we took the tram. Before embarking on the open-air vehicle, a staff member penciled an "X" on a map showing where a Roadside Hawk once recently occurred. However, it was difficult to see beyond a few yards down the narrow byway that we traveled because the densely growing thorn forests blocked our view of birds. We tried for the hawk, even where the vegetation nearly arched over the road and even when the tour guide reminded us that the thorns on all that jungle out there could poke out your eye. Would there also be quicksand and cougars? Maybe. Would there be a Roadside Hawk?

The tram bumped along at a surprisingly fast clip. Linda and I were the only binoculared guests and rode in the back, away from the windshield. We craved the breeze that cooled and dried away the steamy weight of humid air. By the time we arrived at the penciled "X" I wondered what Roadside Hawk would allow the giant tram to approach it, and if it did, could anyone see it at tram-warp speed? We might have seen it if we had gotten off and waited quietly. Linda was especially a proponent of sitting quietly, waiting for a bird to show itself. I generally did not have her patience. Today, neither of us was willing to wait in the still heat for a bird that might not be there, even if it was an exceedingly rare Roadside Hawk.

Although cooler than walking, the tram was not for us. Back at the visitor center, we heard that a Kentucky Warbler was near the outside door. We sat in the cool of the shade, waited, and soon a long-legged bird with a yellow belly appeared on the ground under a small thicket of brush. We watched, along with three other birders. Most of the birders had walked most of the trails. We could tell this by their flushed and sweaty faces, wet shirts, propensity for water and shade, and disappointed expressions. By now, the sun was beginning to dip ever more westward, and the temperature must have dropped maybe a whole degree. Our enthusiasm, buoyed by the Kentucky Warbler, was gaining weak strength to the point of hiking the trail toward Pintail Lake. We had seen some of the species we targeted for Santa Ana during the last couple of days. The rest, the Hook-billed Kite, Muscovy Duck, Red-billed Pigeon, and others, remained unmarked on our trip checklist. Surely, we could stand the heat and get lucky. Couch's Kingbirds, Brown-capped and Scissor-tailed flycatchers were familiar family members along the way. By now, Harris' Hawk and Green Jays were no longer eye-catchers. We limped back from Pintail Lake with one new trip bird, a Yellow-billed Cuckoo, that we could have found almost anywhere.

The remaining daylight shimmered through thickening clouds as we drove down the Rio Grande to Progresso Lakes to find Tropical Kingbirds.

We had seen Couch's Kingbird, and our target now would not have been treated as a species if I had birded Texas in 1963. My old first edition of *Birds of Texas* by Peterson listed Couch's and Tropical under the latter species name. The short-billed birds were *Tyrannus melancholicus couchii*, and then considered a subspecies of Tropical Kingbird a.k.a. *T. m. occidentalis*. According to the fifth edition of the American Ornithologists' Union checklist, published in 1957 and sitting in the back of my VW in the sixties, the only subspecies found in Texas was *T. m. couchii*. It was not until 1983, following research in 1979, that the AOU recognized two distinct species. A half-mile from the lakes our target bird, an unafraid Tropical Kingbird, posed on an electric power line.

20 April 2005

Today, we meandered through the road construction at Harlingen, hoped that we could find our unmarked exit for our motel tonight, and again drove south. Two stops at a couple of intersections where Tamaulipas Crows had recently been reported rewarded us with unwanted views of Great-tailed Grackles and people. The last intersection was bustling with garbage trucks on their way to the Brownsville Dump, a famous place, or a place of infamy, depending on the state of mind and efficiency of olfactory glands. We followed one of the trucks, and according to the rules, we were waving our binocs as we passed the office, which is the landfill office, not the dump office. Therefore, as we politely toured the Brownsville Sanitary Landfill, we braced ourselves for the odor of unsanitary dumped stuff. We followed the dusty main drag, making sure our dwarfed vehicle was well out of the way from the large roaring trucks. A lone Horned Lark foraged a few yards from the powdery dirt road. Near the top of the heap, the landfill, trucks regurgitated their contents. Then, the mass of refuse was attacked by grinding yellow caterpillars with snowplow blades and thousands of birds. The birds, mostly Laughing Gulls, dodged the trucks and caterpillars while searching for edible morsels among the discarded plastic and paper. Cattle Egrets and grackles joined the pack. The sound of birds' cries was nearly silenced by diesel engines that continually roared as the machines sculptured the incoming refuse into giant heaps.

There was not a crow to be seen. Luckily, a supervisor parked nearby in his not-so-white pickup yet impeccable uniform gave us polite directions to find our birds. We dodged more trucks as we drove up a side road created in the mountain range of the landfill. At the top, we turned onto a narrow track astride a manufactured ridge. There was no place to turn around or for a vehicle going in the opposite direction to pass. We drove on. While

I kept us from going over the steep barren sides, Linda did most of the looking and, though she might have enjoyed a perfumed handkerchief by now, cheered us on for our target bird. A few yards to our left were trees and bushes. Snagged in branches everywhere were plastic grocery bags flapping in the southern breeze. We vowed not to step out of the car for health reasons. Taking pictures seemed important. After all, we could show our friends and relatives how we spent our summer vacation. A few yards on the narrow dirt road and in a short wait, a Chihuahuan Raven croaked by, and, moments later, three Tamaulipas Crows flew in front of our binocs. We heard the frog-like croaking and noticed the distinct flight of such distinguished birds. They appeared to be coming from the newly dumped refuse we had seen earlier. Satisfied, we found our way out of the Brownsville Dump by driving a dirt track mounded on both sides by packing crates and discarded pieces of wood, saw more ravens and another Tamaulipas Crow, and hoped our tires did not meet with a nail.

It was early but not nearly early enough to hear Botteri's Sparrow. This would be our last chance to see them in Texas, but all was quiet on our way toward Boca Chica. There was only the wind, the usual Eastern Meadowlarks, and an occasional Savannah Sparrow to keep us alert. We turned back after a few miles. The only surprise was the border patrol checkpoint. They asked about our citizenship. We were birders without a Botteri.

Entering Sabal Palm, Texas.

With time to spare, we drove to Sabal Palm Audubon Center and Sanctuary. The sanctuary protects native habitat, including Sabal Palms, a tree once common along the lower Rio Grande. It also potentially harbored a half-dozen species on our list of target birds. Two of those species were rare, but we hunted the Blue Bunting and Gray-crowned Yellowthroat anyway. At the end of the boardwalk, the wetlands bridge, something moved. A glancing view of a yellowish bird got my attention, but a better look proved it was a chat. It was not a Ground Chat, the old name for the Gray-crowned Yellowthroat. It was the common, usually noisy Yellow-breasted Chat.

The afternoon temperature was edging into the high eighties. The bright sun was great for enjoying the wide array of birds. We had seen all colors and sizes, including Green Herons and Green Kingfishers, Purple Gallinules, Blue-winged Teal, Olive Warblers, and Scarlet Tanagers with Least Grebe and Great Kiskadee. Back at the feeders near the center were screaming Plain Chachalacas, an assortment of doves, and at long last, two Altamira Orioles. I was especially excited to see these large black-backed orioles. Their pattern of black and orange is similar to the smaller Spot-breasted Oriole of Florida. However, Altamira Orioles lack the spots.

What also excited me about the new oriole was its old name, Lichtenstein's Oriole. The name had once struck my youthful imagination as amusingly unusual and too long for any bird. Later, yet still a juvenile person, I discovered that a tiny European country established in 1719 between Austria and Switzerland is called Lichtenstein. Still later and as a bird person at the museum, I learned that Martin Hinrich Carl Lichtenstein, living from 1780 to 1857, had penned scientific names to numerous birds. Several times, in a run to the Division of Birds library, I would consult his *Verzeichniss der Doubletten des Zooligeschen Museums* published in the early 1800s when Lichtenstein was director of the Berlin Museum. Nonetheless, Johann Georg Wagler was the first to publish the specific name *gularis* for the dream oriole. He was at the Zoological Museum University in Munich, or about 375 miles down the proto autobahn from Berlin. Wagler had found the name *gularis* in a manuscript by Lichtenstein, who published the same specific name a year too late to be the author of the scientific moniker. That honor went to Wagler. The oriole probably became known as Lichtenstein's Oriole in recognition that Lichtenstein first used the name for the bird, even though he was not the first to use the name in a publication. Perhaps someone did not want the bird to be known as Wagler's Oriole because Wagler, while collecting, was so careless that he accidentally and mortally shot himself with his own shotgun. How embarrassing. Wagler's Oriole would not have held my attention for four decades even though Wagler was far easier to spell than Lichtenstein. The long name for the oriole caught the attention of a band, described by several as rootsy and rocky. The music group named their second album Lichtenstein's Oriole. However, the American Ornithologists' Union, likely without the knowledge of the album, did not like the name Lichtenstein, so they called it Altamira Oriole. That name is a derivation of Altamira, a city in Tamaulipas, Mexico, which is the type locality of the northern subspecies of the oriole. A type locality is where a bird was collected. A type specimen from the type locality represents a named species or subspecies. Although certainly easier to spell than Lichtenstein, would Altamira be a good name for an album? Probably.

I was elated. The Altamira Orioles were shameless as they let the small crowd of birders drink them in as they foraged on a grapefruit half at the sanctuary feeder. Linda and I proceeded to the edge of an area called the Butterfly Garden where we made another futile search for the Blue Bunting. Instead, we discovered several new trip warblers including Tennessee and Worm-eating. That went well with the new Blackpoll Warbler at Frontera yesterday. Our list of eastern warblers was filling in.

We decided not to look for parrots in Brownsville, drove back to Harlingen, and barely managed to exit near our motel. The feeder road had no exit sign that we could find. Thanks to our high clearance and following the tracks of other frustrated motorists, we were soon rolling over a 10 to 12-inch-high curb to reach our motel. Sundown, shower, dinner, and sleep soon were to follow.

21 April 2005

Yesterday, I talked to Woody Franzen, who I met birding at Santa Ana and Sabal when Linda and I visited there. We compared lists as if anglers were talking about pounds and inches. Our successes and failures were similar. He did have one up on us, an Aplomado Falcon in Laguna Atascosa NWR.

The refuge, located on a former delta of the Rio Grande, contains 45,187 acres of subtropical vegetation. Linda quickly found two Clay-colored Thrushes and a Wood Thrush behind refuge headquarters. Both birds were new trip birds; the robin was a new life species for us. Green Jays, Bronzed Cowbirds, Brown-capped Flycatchers, and Great Kiskadees were common near the building.

After apparently exhausting possibilities for new species, we headed around the 15-mile Bayside Drive. The one-way paved loop travels west through thorn forest before angling southward in coastal prairie and scattered scrubland. Years earlier, most of the region had been tromped, grazed, burned, and generally domesticated by hordes of cattle and people. Wild long-horned cattle, thundering from four to six million in Texas by 1860, were descendants of progeny brought by Spanish centuries earlier. The cattle business was profitable and common in southern Texas long enough to employ Rowdy Yates and too long for the environment. Only 5 percent of the native plants survived the onslaught of cattle and agriculture. Today, the lost native vegetation of Laguna Atascosa is being restored.

About where Woody suggested was where we stopped. It was also time for a nourishing peanut butter fix. Hardly before the nutty gold hit the cracker, an Aplomado Falcon swept by, turned sharply behind the scrub, and vanished. Five minutes later, it, or another bird, suddenly appeared low over the terrain and just as quickly disappeared. I would not likely have seen this species in 1963. The last nesting of these unmistakable falcons in the United States was in 1952. The cooperating Peregrine Fund, US Fish and Wildlife Service, Texas Department of Parks and Wildlife, and others reintroduced birds from young captured in Mexico from 1978 to 1989. At least 39 pairs fledged 179 young in Texas in 1995. Regrettably, Aplomado Falcons in Texas, according to ABA rules, are not countable.

∾

Not so many years after our trip to Laguna Atascosa NWR, the ABA allowed Aplomado Falcon to be counted on a life list. Even so, I was inclined to count the species anyway since we never detected bands, which could indicate wild birds.

Upon returning to Oregon, I phoned Tom Stehn about Whooping Cranes. He keeps track of them at Aransas NWR, and he told me that 12 cranes occupying winter territories were visible from the observation tower on 8 April. These birds migrated before I arrived at the refuge. The remaining winter birds were accessible by boat only. All the cranes migrated after my visit, except for one injured bird that probably would spend the summer in the refuge. Years later, I took a boat tour and had ample views of several wintering Whooping Cranes.

In the early 1970s, Roxie Laybourne, remember, the feather lady, encouraged me to visit Patuxent Research Center in Laurel, Maryland. The center, a few miles from Smithsonian, held several captive Whooping Cranes for propagation. Roxie had earlier developed an external method for determining the sex of cranes, a technique probably less amusing to the birds than to the museum staff. So, Roxie called her old friend Ray Erickson. At that time, he was the chief of the Rare and Endangered Species Program. Roxie told him that the new kid at the museum would like to see Whooping

Cranes. Dr. Erickson, as I knew him in the youth of my career, had been the biologist at Malheur NWR near the time of my conception. The survival of Whooping Cranes and California Condors are examples of his recent work. He walked me to the Whooping Crane pens. It was a freezing January day, and the cranes shivered as they strolled with stiff legs on the hard ground. The cranes were so impressive that I hardly remembered what Dr. Erickson said, but I do recall a kind man with unflagging enthusiasm.

Patuxent Whooping Cranes that died ended up as museum study specimens in large specimen cases not far from my office. At least one was a bird I met on that cold January day years ago. Incidentally, Roxie, who began her career at Smithsonian the year I was born, taught a class on preparing museum specimens. She called it her skinning class. She and Claudia Angle, one of her A students and my younger colleague, made sure anyone viewing the deceased would see a Whooping Crane worthy to rest in the museum.

Whooping Cranes were once widespread. By 1937, only two flocks of less than 20 each wintered in Louisiana and Texas, the year Aransas NWR began. Populations ebbed dangerously to 15 birds in 1941. By 1963, when I hoped to see the Whooping Cranes, only 32 adult birds were known. The lack of immature birds meant the Whooping Crane was in grave danger. The next winter census revealed that six adults had died but seven young replaced them. In 2020, 826 Whooping Cranes occurred from reintroductions in Florida, Louisiana, and Texas. Of the total, 504 birds are from the population breeding in Canada and wintering in Texas.

Bird tours continue at the King Ranch. There are even tours that last three days and two nights, but the one-day tour to the Norias Division looks to be the best bang, or bird, for the buck. Brownsville Dump, or Brownsville Sanitary Landfill as it is dubbed in modern lingo, is also called the Mexican Crow Park. Laguna Atascosa NWR grew from slightly over 45,000 acres to 97,000 acres. Santa Ana NWR remains at 2,080 acres and Sabal Palm Sanctuary, reported as encompassing 172 acres in a 1993 bird finding guide, is only 60 acres strong. Both Santa Ana and Sabal Palm are on the Rio Grande, which means they are adjacent to the US–Mexico border and subject to habitat loss because of border barriers. More on that dreadful conundrum later.

As for missed birds on our list of targeted species in 2005, the search for a few continues and are good for more stories about Texas birding. Groove-billed Ani and Masked Duck continue to elude us. We count ourselves lucky on finding Tamaulipas Crows, a species no longer so easily detected in Texas. Oh, a Gray-crowned Yellowthroat was finally checked during an RV trip in 2015, but we are still looking for a Blue Bunting.

Chapter 25

Up the River and Around the Bend

22 April 2005

Heat and humidity surrounded us during our early morning at the Harlingen motel. The unpleasantness permeated our clothing. It was oppressive. We momentarily recalled our welcome swim in the pool late yesterday and entertained another cooling dip before checking out of our room. Instead, we headed up the Rio Grande, traveling on US 83, passing through Weslaco, near Pharr where we passed on the chance of seeing a Blue Mockingbird, drove beyond McAllen, and onto Mission, and then to our first objective of the day, Bentsen-Rio Grande Valley State Park. Four target species might be there, waiting, and ready to show themselves. At least that was our fantasy.

Movement in the 587-acre park was confined to walking, biking, and a tram. The sun biting through the steamy air ruled out walking. As for a tram ride, we convinced ourselves that we could do better on bikes. We thought biking would involve two separate bikes, but the available side-by-side bikes welded together were like an oversized toy. We were not happy about the mode of transportation, but we could not keep the target birds waiting. We paid the rental fee and pedaled fast, which increased airflow. That was cooling, but the effort to pedal was not. Pedaling was harder than pedaling a standard bike. Pushing on, we arrived at our first stop, Kingfisher Overlook. Three British citizens birded there while a Green Kingfisher foraged. I then proceeded to get Linda and me lost by insisting on going in the wrong direction. After that unnecessary pedaling, we arrived at the trail to our goal, the old trailer loop. The park closed the loop recently, but I wanted to see where RV birders once lived and attracted chachalacas, Green Jays, Altamira Orioles, Blue Buntings, and other lower Rio Grande specialties. Those were just a few of the diurnal birds former RVers detected. They also found nocturnal rarities, including Mottled and Stygian Owls. Closure of the RV park sealed opportunities to discover what comes and goes so close to the Mexico–US border.

Today, the area was an RV ghost town, devoid of people and birds. We parked our transportation in the scarce shade and found the tree a ranger said was home to an Elf Owl. If the owl was there, it was not going to come out in the hot sun. Linda found a javelina, and while ogling it, the beast made its displeasure known by walking uncomfortably toward her. Linda and I eventually trudged back to our four-wheel hell on wheels, which was no longer in the shade. We climbed on, gripped the hot handlebars, and pedaled with our last moment of strength. Of course, we missed target species; no Blue Bunting and no Grove-billed Ani. We did manage to see 13 species of birds before pedaling back toward the visitor center that included a rewarding view of Least and Pied-billed Grebes side by side, Great Kiskadees, Brown-capped Flycatcher, and White-tipped Doves. Returning to the center, we collapsed in the cool air-conditioned room. I sped my recovery by standing in front of a huge roaring fan, not caring that the heat and odor from my body were wafting out into the room. Linda and I, with one employee, were the only people in the center; the heat had driven everyone away. While I was beginning to feel better, Linda stared out a window at a White-throated Thrush, a bird looking similar to a white-throated American Robin with an unfamiliar color. I prefer the moniker White-throated Robin, a name strongly suggesting the species does not appear like all the other thrushes but more like our northern brick-red bellied birds, the American Robin, also a species in the genus *Turdus*. Anyway, by the time I dragged myself to the window, the bird had disappeared. Barely invigorated by the new species, we braved the outside, thinking we could relocate the bird. We could not find it, and we were soon numbed by the heat so much that we forgot to walk the few yards back to inform the park employee about the rarity. Even though we were cognizant of keeping well hydrated, the temperature was becoming too dangerous. The heck with a White-throated Robin, I mean Thrush. All we cared about was dragging ourselves to the car and turning on the air conditioner.

In two days, Linda had seen two species that I missed. Yesterday was a Zone-tailed Hawk at Laguna Atascosa that she kept asking me to check. I didn't even take a close look and dismissed it as a Turkey Vulture. Because the thrush was new, Linda pored over the details of her sighting and the field guide. Although neither Linda nor I had ever seen a White-throated Thrush, her identification stands in my book.

The day was not over though the increasing heat had become more hazardous. Rather than risk our health, we departed Bentsen Park and continued up the river. From our vehicle, its air conditioner roaring at top speed, we spotted a Ringed Kingfisher on power line wire paralleling the highway. In a few miles, we were east of the Falcon Dam, a locality according to our bird-finding guide that offers exceptional birding opportunities. However, months ago, I had made inquiries about the region. It seems access to areas near the dam is restricted. We did not stop and sailed onward to San Ignacio.

Perhaps our bodies had acclimated when we reached San Ignacio. Or was it being closer to the Rio Grande? Whatever the reason, we felt less oppressed by the heat. Although we missed finding Morelet's Seedeaters, we did witness a flock of a half-dozen Red-billed Pigeons fly over. The pigeons are larger than Rock Pigeon and are uncommon in the region. Use of the nebulous term uncommon comes with apologies since I am not sure of its meaning. Based on our time along the river, that flock of six was our only observation of the species, which is declining in Texas. An air-conditioned motel rounded out a rather good day.

23 April 2005

A quick check at the local cemetery in Zapata for the Morelet's Seedeater was a dead end. South of town near the post office, we identified an immature Gray Hawk. From Zapata, we backtracked south through the heat to bird the 0.85-acre Kepler Tract, a US Fish and Wildlife Service woods located adjacent to the famous Salineño Birder Colony on the Rio Grande. Naturally, we became lost or at least unsure of our location, and we simply did not want to waste time taking wrong turns. We stopped at a small grocery store in Salineño, a town populated with under 200 people. After asking about the birder colony, a clerk walked me out to the road and pointed. After a couple of miles, I thought we made a wrong turn and stopped at a local fire station. If they did not know, who would? A staff member not only told me the directions, but he also came out to the road and pointed. We had earlier met people who did not know north from south, but here everyone seemed to go out of their way to get us to our destination. Thanks to everyone, we finally arrived at the bank of the Rio Grande. It was no wonder that the fire department knew of the place. Much of the birder colony site, including some of the outbuildings, burned a month ago.

The Salineño Birder Colony donated their two-acre plot to the Lower Rio Grande Valley Land Trust to ensure the property remains untouched. In return, the previous owners, including Pat and Gale DeWinds, who were permitted to use the region, had vacated for cooler climes. The bird feeders were pecked clean. We were on our own. Because the area might be one of the best places to see Muscovy Ducks, we spent about an hour scanning up and down the river. I then decided to walk through the charred woods down the river but did not see anything to write home about and joined Linda's river vigil. If anyone were to find the rare duck it would likely be her. Ten minutes passed before my impatience took over and I left our observation post in Linda's good stead. Walking upstream might be productive. The woods were unburned and occupied by a pair of Brown Jays tending an adult-sized, yellow-billed juvenile. I rushed back to retrieve Linda.

Besides the Brown Jays, we saw people's activity in the form of a big car parked a few yards from the edge of the river. Through the closed windows we could see a bird field guide. Two people returned while I was sifting through the burned Kepler Tract. Linda thought they might have been father and son. They nodded to Linda and hurried away. Minutes later, we heard a motorboat start up from the other side of the river. The small boat held two men, one operating the motor, the other looking at the banks. A few minutes later, the craft disappeared only to return loaded with three women with anxious faces and a small child. The boat landed near us, the women disappeared into the vegetation, and the two men and the boat returned to the other side of the river. We pretended not to notice.

A quick tour at Chapeño, up the river from Salineño, included Bronzed Cowbirds, Long-billed Thrasher, and Green Jays. Dwarfing them were eight Brown Jays, including a couple of yellow-billed juveniles. Altamira Orioles drifted through the vegetation while Black Vultures reminded us to stay healthy. We then hurried up the river through Zapata, north to Eagle Pass, and left the tropical lower Rio Grande behind. The West and western birds were ahead. Our trip list, standing at 258 species since Harrison, Arkansas, was growing every day though we were missing a few southeastern species. There was no reason to complain. We had a profusion of sun-borne vitamin D, toned a few hiking muscles, and taken several chiggers on board thereby aiding in the spread of the pesky stowaways. I had 21 bites and was still counting. DEET harnessed the mosquitoes to a modicum of our tolerance, but the bug-be-gone did not agree with certain T-shirt dyes. We were closing in on a month of fun on the road together. Our night at a motel in Eagle Pass was welcome.

24 April 2005

The morning air was less humid than yesterday. Our route had taken us from the tropics to the arid West. We nuked our morning oatmeal in the motel, made a couple of canned chicken and lettuce sandwiches for lunch, and filled the gas tank for a 180-mile nonstop trek to Sanderson. The oatmeal and a couple of sandwiches meant not wasting time waiting in restaurants. Besides, we worried that the signs in most restrooms had to remind the staff to wash their hands. Perhaps we were also saving our health, not to mention that preparing most of our meals saved money. We ate fruit and salads kept fresh in our cooler, cooked with motel microwaves, and "cleaned" by using paper plates. Alcohol gel from a handy dispenser substituted for water and a sink. The trade-off was guilt that those throwaway items added to the Brownsville dump of the world. We also had to freeze our blue ice packs in motels freezers, and occasionally partake in dreaded grocery shopping. The grocery shopping on hot days was a treat, especially in the frozen food section. Our motel at Eagle Pass was $63 including taxes, which was $10 higher than the motel under the same franchise in Harlingen. Filling the 13-gallon gas tank this morning swelled our plastic account by $24.28.

A handy sack of Linda's blend of trail mix, sturdy, non-crushable cereals, nuts, and raisins fortified our way across the western part of the state dubbed the Trans-Pecos. We were entering the northern Chihuahuan Desert, a parched land of mountains and flats dotted with creosote and grasslands. Sanderson, the Cactus Capital of Texas, was our next stop. The old storefronts, an 1800s Spanish mission, adobe, and faded wooden buildings gave us a definite feeling that we had arrived in the West. The lack of a mall enhanced the quiet and isolated town. If there was a coffee-to-go establishment, we did not see it. Desperadoes, including Pancho Villa, had toured Sanderson many decades before our arrival. I would have traveled through Sanderson in 1963 when the population was slightly over 2,000. Two years later, flooding Sanderson Creek killed 24 and destroyed part of town. High unemployment, closure of the train depot, and construction of nearby Interstate 10 were factors to bring the 1990 census down to 1,128. Bids for tourism and ads for real estate may contribute to growth in a town now needing to sell fancy double espresso to take in tourist dollars.

A Curve-billed Thrasher foraged among buildings needing repair. The bird's breast was pale, with prominent spots, and the ends of the underside of the tail feathers were obviously white. That would make it a member of the eastern subspecies group; birds of a western group that reside in Arizona have indistinct breast spots and less white on the underside of the tail. We will look for the differences when we are in Arizona. We had been keeping a separate list of birds that are represented by distinct subspecies. Why? Some of those subspecies may be species. There was talk of the two Curve-billed Thrashers representing two separate species. We even made a point of looking for the subspecies *texana*, which might be specifically distinct from other interior scrub-jays. Jays of any kind were not patrolling Sanderson, but House Finches were abundant. Replacing the raspberry color that we were accustomed to seeing was a cardinal hue of the southern subspecies *potosinus*. How do I know? Working on Oberholser's birds of Texas during my museum days had exposed me to a few species. It was good to see them as live birds.

The landscape west of Sanderson was more open, less populated, and wilder than most Hopalong Cassidy and Roy Rogers's westerns I saw at the movies years before becoming a birder. The forbidden panorama reminiscent of scenes behind Clint Eastwood and Tom Selleck westerns faded on the horizon. The region was also a great area to drive like hell, which we did, except for watching the rear-view mirror and slowing down to spend $25 for gas in Marathon. The town of about 800 souls had grown by 200 since the early sixties.

With no time to spare, we headed south to Big Bend NP where the Rio Grande's essentially southeastward flow bends south and further upstream bends north to draw on the arid landscape a giant horseshoe shape. The park is about 25,000 acres shy of being as large as the King Ranch. Big Bend NP protects 118 miles of river shoreline and 801,000 acres of wild desert and mountains ranging from nearly 2,000 to 8,000 feet in elevation. Big Bend is one of the least visited national parks. In 2004, 360,087 people visited the park, which is fewer than tourists visiting the more accessible Bentsen-Rio Grande State Park on the lower Rio Grande. Only slightly over 114,000 visited the park in 1963. Almost half of the visitors came to the park during our April tour 2005, and most of them were at our first stop in the park at the Panther Junction Visitor Center. A majority of the visitors were on big motorcycles filling the sound with unmuffled bike engines, several idling, others roaring louder with decibels cracking the air and assaulting ears. A quick check inside the center for recent sightings of birds was tantalizing. Common Black-Hawks were at Rio Grande Village, and Colima Warblers were singing in the Chisos Mountains. One of the rangers at the desk said that the warblers were two miles up the Laguna Meadows Trail. Only two miles sounded good. Outside the center were an abundance of House Finches, a Curve-billed Thrasher, and roaring hogs of the gas-powered variety.

Our immediate destination, a wide place in the road just west of the park, was about 30 minutes from Panther Junction. Emmons Peak loomed above us, reaching 7,852 feet skyward from the shoulders of the Chisos Mountains. We passed the Santa Elena Junction where the road wanders south past Sam Nail Ranch, a site on our itinerary. After a few more miles, we descended past the Maverick Mountains to the north and to the settlement called Study Butte. Someone at the visitor center told us that the Study part should be pronounced "stoody." However, we found the local people said stoody while others pronounced Study as study for an exam or used the name Terlingua. Most referred to the area as Terlingua, even though the official Terlingua is a nearby ghost town. Still other residents claimed the area was called East Terlingua. Both towns are the products of mining, mostly cinnabar to extract mercury, which may account for the confusion of the names of the two settlements. However, most everyone we met in the area seemed sane. As for our location, wherever we were, we were there.

We found a room at a local motel and waited for darkness. Passing up a chance for Buff-collared Nightjar would not be, well, passed up. As the sun began to set, we left the smooth pavement and began bumping along the gravel of Old Maverick Road bordered by ocotillo, agave, and others that revealed our severe botanical handicapness. Before we would lose the ability to detect color, we stopped in the waning light to admire the salmon blooms of spiny ocotillo. Several of the agaves were blooming, their last act before death. The plants have tall stalks bearing mostly white blooms loved by Scott's Orioles and migrating hummingbirds. For us, the agaves became silhouettes that disappeared as the full force of the black night dominated everything, even the dust kicked up by our vehicle. As darkness progressed, more and more stars sparkled. The park's night sky, after all, is the darkest of any national park in the lower 48. With the aid of the headlights, we continued southward toward Santa Elena Canyon of the Rio Grande. Watching for eye reflection from a potential nightjar and stopping, the motor off, and listening did not produce any birds or other life, not even a mouse, a kangaroo rat, or anything. After a mile or two of not finding any wildlife, we turned around, leaving the solitude, the quiet wilderness with its open sky, and the brightness of the starry night.

25 April 2005

Linda spotted our first Scaled Quail yesterday. I had not seen the species since, when practicing my day job at Smithsonian, I evaluated a proposed new subspecies of Scaled Quail. Of course, the Scaled Quail at the museum were study specimens and did not count on my life list. The birds today were less interesting from a taxonomic perspective and more fascinating as living and beautiful entities. I marveled at how they blended into the gray-brown desert but could not help thinking about their reported hybridizing with Gambel's Quail. Once a taxonomist, always a taxonomist I suppose. In 1963, Scaled Quail were in a genus separate from Gambel's, California, and Elegant quails. However, Lester Short, who held my friend Dick Bank's job a few years earlier, had supposed that interbreeding of these quail was evidence to recognize only one genus. Thus, the genus *Callipepla*, which represented the Scaled Quail, and *Lophortyx*, which represented the other species of quail, must have as their generic name the older proposed genus *Callipepla*. Actual data would later support Short's idea. As for me, Scaled Quail appeared uniquely fascinating, even though they occasionally fool around with Gambel's Quail in western Texas.

This morning, I birded near the motel. What a pleasure. Most of the motels we had stayed in were in no bird's land unless you count grackles, starlings, and House Sparrows. I recalled road trips with my parents too many years ago. Back in those days, habitat suitable for birds other than introduced starlings and House Sparrows surrounded about 50 percent of the motels we then lodged in. I would bird a compound while the folks were packing up for the next round of miles. Frequently, I would find new species to add to my then burgeoning life list. People now crowd out those habitats of my youth. Today, I would enjoy where time had yet to leave its unrelenting mark. Once exiting our Terlingua motel room, I crossed a worn board walkway. From the adjacent sandy parking lot, I turned to catch a Cactus Wren growling its song from the apex of the roof. A soft breeze perked up as the sun blazed from the horizon. Walking toward the Rough Run and Doggie Mountains on a dirt road, I soon saw several Black-throated Sparrows, Pyrrhuloxia, and a Scaled Quail, which was singing from the top of a cactus. The museum side of me instantly thought that these remote quail must represent pure strains. Populations of upland game birds often consist of introduced birds of mixed subspecies, making later identifications to subspecies difficult to impossible. That is because game bird biologists often did not consider reestablishing birds representing the subspecies that once occupied a region. Worse, introductions and reestablishments sometimes were fueled by releasing birds representing more than one subspecies. The quail I was watching was most likely unadulterated by non-native genes. One roadrunner stood as a sentinel on a high barren mound overlooking a dry wash and the motel beyond. A Cassin's Sparrow was a surprising addition just before a couple of four-wheelers, those noise-sputtering little off-road dirt bikes for people with balance problems, scared the sparrow and made the roadrunner run. For several minutes after the engine noise of the machines abated, the disturbed birds were stone quiet. No more singing, but, as I hurried back, the quail called.

The drive back to Panther Junction was uneventful birdwise. Of course, the stone mountains and flowered desert were a major event, but we rushed to get to Rio Grande Village. We knew the lower 1,850-foot elevation would be hot. It was. Mark Flippo, a park naturalist, had emailed us a couple of months ago directions for our target, a Common Black-Hawk. More up-to-date directions at the visitor center sent us down the road past an RV camp to Daniel's Ranch and a set of lofty cottonwoods. Linda, ever sharp-eyed, spotted an adult hawk and the nest. After directions, including "no, not that tree, the one to the right," and the "third branch from the . . .," I finally saw the adult. Eventually, we located a second bird. We were happy to add the species to our life lists. Moments later, two Black-tailed Gnatcatchers and an unexpectedly yellow Bell's Vireo revealed themselves. I was more used to seeing the pale grayish and white western subspecies of the vireo.

The heat and humidity were wearing us down as we drove to the end of the road and walked the short distance to the Rio Grande. South of the border, on the southern bank of the river, was a Black Phoebe, just like the one wintering in our backyard in Oregon. We could not count it. Finally, the southern phoebe flew the short distance across the river and perched on a stem growing from US soil. It became number 279 on the trip list.

Rio Grande River, Big Bend NP.

Why was that Mexican Black Phoebe seen from the US side of the river not countable? Were the criteria for not counting it based on a story told to me 43 years ago? Maybe. Harold Axtell, who I met in western New York in 1962, so the story goes, would not count a Brown Jay until it flew north, across the Rio Grande into the US. Admittedly, Harold had influenced my thinking and helped steer me to a life of museum ornithology, but the decision to not count the Black Phoebe until after it made the border crossing could have just been one of a nest full of my nerdy quirks.

On the climb back up the road to Panther Junction, we stopped at K Bar to look for a power pole Jon Dunn emailed to check. An Elf Owl had used an old woodpecker cavity. It was 4 p.m., which was, of course, much too early for seeing the smallest of North American owls. We bumped back to the pavement and stopped at the visitor center. Panther Junction was again abuzz with motorcycles and their friendly pilots. A Cactus Wren was barely audible over the racket. I asked at the desk if Mark Flippo was there. He soon appeared. He looked busy. Recalling days at the museum, enduring budget cuts, and increasing workloads, I understood and tried to be brief. Mark was enthusiastic but probably tired of people asking the old questions about finding Colima Warblers. Fortunately, he did have new information, which I would try tomorrow.

26 April 2005

The alarm clock shook me awake in the early morning darkness. Linda decided to take the day off. I left Terlingua following the headlights into the park. Phainopepla wings flashed in the rising sun a couple of miles west of the junction to the Chisos Basin. Turning right, I headed up Green Gulch and toward the strange rough mountain oasis. The origin of the name Chisos varies from a spelling after the Chizos Indians to a Spanish corruption from *hechizos* meaning "bewitchment or enchantment." The Chisos Mountains are like a stony phoenix rising from the parched ashes. A geology 101 text might describe the range using terms about the time of the rough terrain. The mountains are the product of an eroded Cenozoic volcanic uplift that, 26 million years ago, slid downward several thousand feet. Erosive forces continue in the austerely beautiful landscape.

The car heater melted the early morning chill during the six-mile climb up to Green Gulch. The park map marked the road to the basin as too winding for trailers over 20 feet and RVs over 24 feet. The twists, turns, and climb brought an ever-changing panorama that competed for the need for attention to safe driving. During the ascent above the desert, I noticed the larger and darker green plants fond of cool and wetter environments were replacing the gray-green leaves of the dry, hostile desert. Split-second glimpses of Canyon Towhees and Mexican Jays slipped into my view before the next curve. I loved the mountain driving and marveled at how blue-headed the Mexican Jays were. With thoughts of an old sports cars once owned, I began wondering how far I would have to hike to find Colima Warblers, would I even find the warbler, should I brake just before the next corner, what other birds might I see today, should I slow down, did I have enough water, and would there be snakes? Luckily, the swirling thoughts did not overpower the embarrassment of a wreck. During the roller coaster ride, I had forgotten that the eastern Mexican Jays are bluer than those from Arizona. I did remember that the Canyon Towhee would have been Brown Towhees in 1963.

Chisos Basin was deep in the shadows of the mountains that virtually encircle it. After days of thorn forest and hot, dry desert scrub, the comfort of high mountains and tall trees provided unexpected pleasure. The basin was awash in green lushness amid the rocks and clean mountain air. Thin soil supported Douglas fir, ponderosa pine, and madrones familiar to a Pacific Northwesterner. I was energized because a life-long dream was about to become a reality. Even before I planned the sixties trip, I had daydreams about hiking in the Chisos Mountains where I would find a Colima Warbler. During the planning of that early leg of the trip, the Colima Warbler was the species that most compelled me to bird the United States. Beginning in 2004, I often joked to Linda that finding a Colima Warbler was maybe the most important reason for the trip. Now, I know that it was not. The most important part of the trip was the whole trip. However, standing in the Chisos Basin, staring up at the face of the mountains, and knowing a Colima Warbler was within reach was exciting. It was a beautiful time of expectations and unsurpassed scenery. In my early dreams of this event, I was alone, but, today, this was a moment to share. I pretended Linda was at my side.

Deep shadows of the mountains, 2,000 feet above the 5,400-foot Chisos Basin, produced a pleasant chill to the morning. Because of the steep high-rising peaks, sunrise would be hours away. Two hikers tightening their bootlaces were in the parking lot. I said hello and mentioned Colima Warbler. "The what?" I explained that a Colima Warbler was a rare species of bird breeding in northern Mexico and only in the Chisos Mountains in the United States and that I was looking for the bird. "Oh, well, huh, good luck." I walked a few yards to the trailhead and began the trek to my dream bird.

At first, the Laguna Meadows Trail was straight and easy and bordered by vegetation and rocks mostly taller than me. The trail seemed almost confining in contrast to the open and relatively flat desert terrain below. Sun was reflecting from the summits of the peaks ahead as a surprised Canyon Towhee jumped from the dimly lit trail. Loose rocks crunched underneath each booted step. Soon I was climbing stairs that had been cut into the trail. Small plateaus, flat and grassy, were interspersed between long and steep inclines. I read somewhere the grade of the trail ranged from 8 percent to 23 percent. I also had read that decades ago cattle and horses grazed over much of the park, including the Chisos Basin. I did see old but familiar horse and mule droppings along the trail and in contrast, less than halfway to the summit, a pair of Scott's Orioles entered the panorama. The dry air was beginning to change from comfortable to hot. I needed to divert my mind from wondering which might happen first, running out of water or physical stamina. Despite earlier exercise, this was the first non-horizontal hiking I had done in a month. The old lure of what was around the next bend and the possibility of a Colima Warbler kept me going. Before I could say switchback, I was climbing higher and higher, and in the region where Mark Flippo said the warblers might occur. That is when a largish bird flew across the trail. What was the silent bird? I could not relocate it. During the drive from Terlingua, I listened to the CD track of the target warbler about 20 times. The pay-off was recognizing two Colima Warblers singing from the oaks bending over the trail between the fifth to eighth switchbacks. I am not sure which switchback since I lost count between grappling for rarefied air and hearing my first Colima Warbler. Ultimately, a male came into view. It reminded me of a large and faded Nashville Warbler. I knew Nashville Warblers, but the bird I was seeing was no Nashville Warbler. It was larger, not nearly as colorful, and, for a warbler, almost lethargic compared to the more typical nervousness of a Nashville Warbler. Colima Warbler was my dream warbler, better, I imagined than a Kirtland's Warbler and possibly just as exciting as the Bachman's Warbler I missed by months in 1962. Well, maybe not Bachman's. Was part of the excitement the remoteness and hard hike to see a Colima Warbler? Was self-sacrifice part of the joy from observing the warbler? What causes emotions to peak from seeing a new and difficult bird?

By 11:30 a.m., I had witnessed Spotted Towhees that were more spotted than most subspecies, saw numerous White-throated Swifts twittering in and around the cliffs, heard Canyon Wren songs reverberating off the hard Chisos rocks, and met a couple of hikers on the trail. The two thirties-something men were the first humans since leaving the basin. We talked briefly about the difficulty of the trail. They trudged upward while I ate a snack and let my pulse get back to normal before hiking onward. By earlier standards, the trail was relatively flat just below what appeared to be the summit, but I had other places to visit today.

With reluctance, I headed down to the basin. On the way, I met a couple a few years my senior. They were from Alexandria, Virginia. He volunteered in the Botany Department at Smithsonian. Small world. They missed seeing Colima Warblers. Most no one else I met that I talked to had ever heard of the warbler. Not far below, I met a ranger wrangling four mules carrying concrete for repairs of a relay station on Emory Peak. The sheer footed mules explained the old droppings I had seen since these quadrupeds had hiked the trail more than once.

About halfway down my knees began to react to the steep descent. Annoyance became wincing pain to genuine worry. This would not have happened in 1963. I had pushed myself physically and I stopped to rest. Perching on a relaxing rock, I realized I had been sitting behind the wheel much too long and that descending the trail was using different muscles than when climbing. I should have had a pair of trekking poles, but I was stickless in the Chisos. The respite on the rock helped a little and cutting through the more gently sloped grounds near the lodge helped more. Finally, at the bottom, I observed a Canyon Towhee foraging at the feet of a man sitting in front of the store. He said his hip replacement would not allow him to hike. How could I complain? The Colima Warbler was finally found, and my knees were already feeling better.

At the visitor center I learned that a Lucy's Warbler was reported to be at Cottonwood on the Rio Grande southwest of Chisos Basin. Although tempted, driving to Cottonwood was shelved. I did go as far south as the Sam Nail Ranch, found Bell's Vireo and Virginia's Warbler, and turned around at Sotol Vista just past the old Homer Wilson Ranch.

Peterson remarked to Fisher on their trip to Big Bend that the grass was beginning to recover. He meant the vegetation was recuperating from cattle, goats, sheep, and horses owned by several ranches that occupied the region before it became a park in 1944. Sam Nail did not leave the park until 1946. The ranchers are gone, and by 1972, the Park Service had purchased 8,562 acres of ranches and other private lands within its borders.

Linda and I tried to imagine the rough beauty of Big Bend NP before the non-native settlement of the region and before the park came under attack from so many sides. Of course, before settlement by non-natives and their bovine trade, it must have been more stunning than it is today. Preserving a national park once ruled by ranchers and their livestock must be challenging. We pondered on the difficulties rangers had when dealing with the illegal smuggling of candelilla wax made from a plant in the genus *Euphorbia*. The wax, once used in making phonograph records and packing rifles, is now in cosmetics. The practice of digging or pulling up plants, roots and all, left thousands of acres of an already near barren desert virtually denuded. Even residents once living on private parcels within the park sold the wax. In addition, airborne pollution, mostly from US sources, sometimes chokes the air and stains the view with a haze of sulfates, nitrates, acid rain, and other unhealthy man-made by-products. Before the environment was completely hoofed to death, Sotol, a xeric succulent, almost became extinct in the park. The sugary trunks and the bases of the leaves of the tall spiky plant fed cattle while the flower heads formed the basis for an alcoholic beverage. Sotol is recovering. Today, illegal drugs and immigrants are problems in the park, but auto accidents by drivers ogling the panorama, bears, dehydration, and sunburn head the list that warn visitors with hints on how to stay safe in the park.

My day no longer was holding morning's chill and the ruthless desert heat reminded me to hydrate and slather on the sunscreen. The drive back to the motel was too long. Because of my late arrival, Linda began to worry that I had fallen off a cliff or been bitten by a rattlesnake and then fallen off a cliff into a pit of rattlesnakes. The very worst thing that happened was my failure to understand Linda's new camera that I borrowed for today. Being digitally stupid, I had not depressed the shutter button past the focusing sound. Any pictorial record of my Chisos Warbler Day was only in memory.

Once back in Oregon, we learned more about the Kepler Tract and its fire that burned and scorched riparian trees. Like the majority of wildfires, the Kepler Tract fire was caused by human behavior; in this instance it was caused by a runaway trash fire. According to a posted newspaper article on the web, the result of a wind-driven fire on 26 March 2005 destroyed two empty homes, then moved to the birder colony where it burned vegetation around the vacated lots in the birder colony, an outbuilding, an owl house (not a typo for outhouse) and part of the habitat of the Kepler Track. The owl survived as did a building containing birdseed worth about $1,000. The 80 years of age DeWinds, who had evacuated the colony, moved back. The DeWinds reported seeing several Brown and Green jays, Altamira and Audubon's orioles, and a Hook-billed Kite a few days after the fire. David Blankinship, a wildlife biologist for lower Rio Grande Valley and Santa Ana NWR, emailed me in early June that the vegetation of the area was recovering. He also related that the resident starting the fire was attempting to burn trash that was illegally dumped on his property. The resident received a citation for the damages. I visited the same region in 2010. Vegetation had recovered to the point I hardly recognized the place.

There is more to the story concerning birding near Falcon Dam. During the planning stages of the 2005 trip, we thought of including a visit to sites below Falcon Dam. Birding localities near the spillway and about two miles downstream are well-known places to find species that might be difficult to locate elsewhere in the lower Rio Grande Valley. However, information becoming available during the planning stages of the 2005 journey suggested that the region might be closed and, as stated, we skipped past the dam site because I could not discern whether the region was closed or open to the public. I emailed and phoned a few local birders. No one was sure. Finally, I found the International Boundary and Water Commission Public Affairs Officer. An email reply stated that the area at and below the dam was closed. Dam. Reasons for closure were not provided, but after digging through layer upon layer of cyberspace, I found that all dams on international borders were apparently closed "for reasons of national security." Life experiences had taught me that the quoted phrase is bandied by officials who cannot think of something better say and want you to go away. Granted, that is not always true, though the information I was getting was not confirming anything. Maybe the closure was announced on CNN, but I could not be sure. Not ready to give up and as a firm believer that it never hurts to ask, I inquired about permission to access the area. Of course, who to ask was unknown, so I tried several likely sources. Unfortunately, my old Navy days in the bowels of the Pentagon or years at Smithsonian were of no help to influence anyone to at least reply. Finally, my last attempt to learn about the closure was met with an email from the dam public affairs office. The river downstream from the dam was closed to protect "sensitive structures and instruments." Of course. Why did I not think of that? In addition, "they" wanted the region closed to "prevent traffic from bypassing Port-of-Entry." Accessing the region below the dam may now be possible since bird-finding information published in 2008 suggests the regions below Falcon Dam are open to birders. I would check before going assuming that someone now knows what is accessible and what is not.

Thankfully, Big Bend NP does not limit access to the Colima Warbler. What is limited, without some digging, is why the scientific name of the Colima Warbler keeps changing. Granted, not everyone is aware of the change, but it happened and this old taxonomist noticed. Colima Warbler is usually placed by taxonomists in the genus *Oreothlypis*. Colima Warbler's closest relatives include Nashville, Lucy's, and Virginia warblers, which most authorities place together in the genus *Leiothylpis*. Why even mention genera? The Colima Warbler and its closest relatives are also considered by some taxonomists as being in one genus and by other taxonomists as in a different genus. Yes, not all scientist agree any more than dentists agree on a particular product. Sure, mostly we agree, but ornithology is not math. However, it is sometimes approaching the old adage that two plus two equals four since so many taxonomic conclusions rely on genetics. Although I agree with the *Leiothylpis* camp, I will not let who belongs to which genus derail this chronicle. At least I hope not too many eyes are now glazed over. Subjectively, Colima Warbler seems a different beast from the other warblers. I must admit that I might be better off not worrying about taxonomic issues and accept whatever relationships are posited by keepers of the list, even if they are wrong. With that said, as an offering on a taxonomic issue, it is a given that taxonomy is in a state of change as is often reflected in new editions of field guides. Although it is annoying to me that hummingbirds occur before instead of much after shorebirds, the changes in the sequence of birds is supposed to reflect the best and most current information about their relationships.

Also in a state of change is the numeric status of Colima Warblers, though sifting through information on populations did not reveal any major concerns about the number of Colima Warblers in Big Bend NP. Populations of the warbler in Mexico are not known and the breeding range there is not protected. Wildfires could impact the species, and one in the park, like the Kepler Tract fire, was suspected to be human-caused.

What is protected is the boundary between the US and Mexico. We noticed the border was more intensely regulated just five years after visiting Big Bend. For example, border security was ramping up then. I personally was made aware of the increase in security when two border patrol agents in Texas picked up my riverside tracks while I was searching for seedeaters. I became hunted while I hunted. The two-man patrol, who I spotted before they saw me, met on the shore of the river. I was relieved that I did not fit an arrestable profile.

Linda and I have revisited the Rio Grande downstream from Laredo more than once since 2005 but have not yet made it back to the likes of Sanderson, Marathon, and Big Bend NP. The park needs revisiting. I would like to show Linda a Colima Warbler, see Santa Elena Canyon, camp under the stars, and soak in the desert flowers. Those places and times are on our list, and maybe, even after the COVID-19 pandemic and its aftermath, we just might renew old acquaintances. We wonder what happened to Sanderson, a town with such a rapidly dwindling population. Sanderson citizens stood at 861 in 2000. In 2016, the population was 616, grew inexplicably to 759 the next year, 893 in 2012, and was down to 774 in 2021. As of this writing (2023), Sanderson is down to only 613 resident.

What most people who care about the environment are not looking forward to is visiting many of the sites along the Rio Grande that are ruined by some kind of obstruction constructed at the US–Mexico border, be it a wall, fence, or other obstacles that destroy wildlife and access to habitat. Yes, and as promised, here is a concise summary of how border security is detrimental to the environment. Barriers are built on the US side of the legal boundary, which means a large parcel of land once in the US is now south of the border obstruction and therefore US property is on the Mexican side of the barrier. Rumor has it that the patrol roads and wide zones of devegetated area on both sides of border barriers improve detecting smuggling traffic. Proposed barrier sites are sometimes a mile north of the Rio Grande, which equates to US farmers and ranchers losing their land and conservation entities forfeiting their efforts to restore the land to its natural state. The land becomes inaccessible to everyone, including birders. That land south of a barrier might be plundered or otherwise abused. For example, during construction, waivers were granted that allowed contractors to ignore the National Environmental Policy Act, Clean Air Act, and Endangered Species Act. In the process of building the barriers, water is siphoned wherever contractors can find it. Also, the apparent right-away on the US side of the barrier is a nice road used by patrol agents only. The roads, often wider than a four-lane highway, create a broad devegetated region that a mouse would be frightened to cross and the barriers are higher than several species of birds fly. That is correct. Not all birds fly high in the sky. Roads are also built to access the roads paralleling the barriers. The combination of barriers, roads, and other devegetated regions prevent wildlife on the US side from accessing the river that provides sources for drinking water. Proposed barriers through Santa Ana NWR along the northern levee would cause most of the refuge to fall on the Mexican side of the barrier and therefore be unprotected. US land is forever changed. Incidentally, rumor once circulated that the offices and visitor center at Santa Ana would become offices for the US Border Patrol. Similar disastrous losses of land and property might happen to Bentsen-Rio Grande State Park or other conservation areas that have as their boundary the Rio Grande. What dire plans might wait for the 118-mile boundary in Big Bend NP? The remoteness and the steep inaccessible geography of the park will hopefully keep proponents of a wall at bay.

Of course, the boundary wall extends farther west through New Mexico, Arizona, and California. Portions of the wall have already been constructed and are easy to view from points along I-8. There are parts of the border marked with broken barbed-wire fences in Arizona like that in the remote California Gulch region where Five-stripped Sparrows, Montezuma Quail, and Buff-breasted Nightjar are almost certain. Anyone going there should probably carry their passport and driver's license, especially if you are dressed in comfortable clothes and sport a deep tan. And keep in mind, border patrol agents seem suspicious of anyone driving anywhere near their new boundary barriers. For example, I've been stopped while driving the Geronimo Trail, a public road, which, in places, is only yards away from border barriers. The rough dirt and rocky public road leads to the Slaughter Ranch, which lost thousands of acres to the wall effort. The Geronimo Trail road continues to San Bernardino NWR, where Mexican Ducks are known, and east to the historically famous Guadalupe Canyon. Farther west in Arizona, Organ Pipe Cactus National Monument, a place on my 1963 itinerary, did not escape the indelible damage from border barrier construction. There is more about the Southwest border in the next chapter. For anyone thinking too much has already been said, what is in these pages is only the tip of the thorn.

Peterson and Fisher would have been shocked by the aftermath of the mostly politically motivated destruction of so much borderland habitat. It is one more sad situation joining so many other destructive forces that will forever alter our landscape. For those willing to brave our southern border states and try to see the great birds the region offers, be prepared to be pulled over by a border patrol agent and make sure your papers are in order.

Chapter 26

Go West ... Man

27 April 2005

We left the Big Bend of the Rio Grande and followed a northerly route to New Mexico where we would soon be on a westward track until reaching the coast of California. The West was familiar territory. It was where I started my life list. Going west this time, I was not young, but was ready to accept a paraphrase of advice originally penned by John Soule, a writer for an Indiana newspaper. Horace Greeley made famous Soule's "Go West, young man." As a young boy, I had gone west when my parents drove part of historical Route 66 to move to California. It was only for a year and months later I went west again, this time to Oregon, all of which is another story. I also went west as a young man in 1963, with my field guide closed and binoculars hung low, a victim of mechanical meltdown. As a retiree from the Biological Survey at the Division of Birds on the Washington, DC, National Mall, I again went west to Oregon. Now, packed up to leave Big Bend NP, I was going west as a sexagenarian and would soon hear the surf of the Pacific Ocean.

Today, this day in 2005, Linda and I will drive west with young hearts but wishing for a time that had not so quickly aged each day. Though competing with only our collective selves, we could not help but regret not finding the eastern species we missed. In a 1961 letter, Roger Tory Peterson replied to me that "it is difficult to be at all the best places at the best time." We followed some of Peterson's advice, especially by spending so much time along the coast of Texas where eastern migrants might arrive. Peterson also wrote that I should spend more time in the interior of the continent than Fisher and he did. To emphasize the point, Peterson seemed to lament that Stuart Keith's "mother apparently owns a ranch in Alberta and that is where he scooped us." My 1963 journey did include time in the interior, but I skipped Peterson's recommendations to visit the Bear River Marshes of Utah for breeding birds and Point Pelee on Lake Erie and Cape May for the fall migration.

Missed species and found species are the yin and yang of birding. It was time to move on, to continue the chase, to go west. Departing the grandeur and birds of Big Bend left Linda and me full yet empty because we could never know it all. While in the Big Bend NP, our trip list increased by about 20 species. However, targeted Elf Owls, Varied Buntings, Black-chinned Sparrows, and Western Screech-Owls did not make themselves known. We missed the Broad-winged Hawk Jon Dunn identified three days after Linda and I visited Rio Grande Village. We never saw the species during the trip. I missed Zone-tailed Hawks and White-throated Thrush, and Linda missed Colima Warbler. We potentially missed several species by not visiting Boot Springs. Most of all, now miles away, we missed the feel of Big Bend, its geology, its vastness, and its history. Linda said she even missed its strangeness as an earthling might miss beautiful Mars.

Somewhere southeast of the park, maybe back at Del Rio, we had entered the largest North American desert, the Chihuahuan Desert. Big Bend NP punctuated the feeling of being in the Chihuahuan Desert. Our time offered but a taste that begged for more experiences in the Chihuahuan Desert. Today we would drive across the northwestern range of the desert, not stopping, but mentally recording the immensity of it vastness. Perhaps the attractiveness of the great Chihuahuan Desert, actually any desert, is our own history of living in wetter climates. Something different could be attractive. Even so, deserts, regardless of their deadly heat, seemed inspiring to us, amazing, mysterious, and pulling us forward into the West.

As we drove from Terlingua, we vowed to revisit Big Bend, relive its desert wonder, and thrive under its sun and the clear night sky. There was just not enough time to do it even a modicum of justice, and we now realized we would have to skip the Davis Mountains and stops we planned in New Mexico. Lesser Prairie-Chickens near Roswell, New Mexico, would not make it on the trip list. Would the other target birds be in Arizona? Time would tell.

Our route today was to Alpine, more precisely once the candelilla connection. Peterson and Fisher traveled the same route, but the road was then gravel, not paved as it is today. The more graveled roads connecting to Big Bend NP to the north, the less remote it will become. Still, Linda and were grateful that our journey was not accompanied with flying gravel, dust, and those little rocks that quickly eat the tread from a healthy tire.

We estimated we were about three days off schedule, so there would not be time to set foot in Guadalupe Mountains NP in Texas for Gray and Plumbeous vireos. There would not be time for bats at Carlsbad Caverns NP in New Mexico. That will have to be another trip to witness more flying creatures, especially the feathered variety. So, our northwestern route sent us past three mountain peaks over 6,000 feet and to the town of Alpine and 34 miles west to Marfa. In 1963, Alpine was about 4,700 strong and Marfa 2,800 in number. Since then, Alpine has gained another thousand people, but Marfa has lost about 600 citizens. We wondered about that, thinking there must be a story there, but we had miles to go before the end of the day. Regardless of our curiosity and the birds we hoped to find, we realized we were gaining in elevation; Alpine and Marfa were in the neighborhood of 4,500 feet in elevation, which is higher than Terlingua's 2,891 feet. Maybe the more rarefied air would be cool.

The drive from Marfa to Van Horn on Interstate 10 and along the Rio Grande to El Paso was a long and uneventful three-hour drive. The temperature was not cooler even though we had climbed past 4,000 feet in elevation. Impatient traffic filled the interstate between Van Horn and El Paso sitting on the river a little over 3,700 feet above sea level. Spilling outward and upward, El Paso doubled in size from its 276,000 people in 1960 and since the 2000 census was still growing. We located a suitable motel in the city, and once situated, we took advantage of the later afternoon for a journey across the Rio Grande, across the border into Mexico. Neither of us had been in Mexico for a few years, and walking into Ciudad Juárez, one of the country's largest cities, was a surprise. The main street near the crossing had crowds of busy stores selling pharmaceuticals. The stores were well-organized, clean, neat, and ready for business. They were not full of sunglasses on turnstiles, candy bars, postcards, or anything we would expect from a drug store north of the Rio Grande. Establishments in Ciudad Juárez did not sell what we thought would be easy to find, simple tourist souvenirs such as a postcard offering evidence of our south of the border excursion. There were none. Maybe further from the border, we might find what we were looking for, or we might find something we had rather not wanted, such as trouble. Even though we thought it might be fun to explore a city of 1.5 million people, to find a suitable trinket to send home, we opted to heed warnings we had heard months ago and spend the remainder of our day in little El Paso. Most of all, we wanted a good rest and a fast morning escape from the metropolis to a country setting.

28 April 2005

Once again, we drove like, well, as fast as we dared and still keep our licenses. Again, we crossed the Rio Grande, but this time we remained in the USA. Today, we needed to travel 305 miles or almost the exact miles traveled yesterday. Three hundred miles has been more miles than we usually drive per day, but we had to try to maintain a schedule.

Signs along I-10 continuously warned drivers of dangerous wind. The warnings were correct west of Las Cruces, New Mexico, but two illiterate pale-phased Swainson's Hawks ignored the signs. We carefully tacked across New Mexico to the junction of the highway to Rodeo. Along the way, we left the Chihuahuan Desert and entered the Sonoran Desert. We are not sure where. There were no signs welcoming us to the Sonoran Desert, no speed bumps, no change in the quality of the road often obvious when crossing from one state to another, nothing. Various sources seem to agree the Chihuahuan Desert is south of Rodeo, New Mexico, and Cochise County of southeasternmost Arizona. The remainder of southern Arizona is in the Sonoran Desert. Parts of the northwestern part of the state are in the Mojave Desert. As expected, the three deserts differ in vegetation, temperature, and more that I am going to entertain on another day.

Originally, we intended to turn west to Portal, Arizona, bird Cave Creek in the foothills of the Chiricahua Mountains, then head south through Rodeo on our way to Douglas and Guadalupe Canyon, which is in the Chihuahuan Desert. Instead, we headed for Sierra Vista, our headquarters the next few days, which is in the Sonoran Desert.

We arrived in Sierra Vista at 3:30 in the afternoon. The town, established in 1877, began as a hamlet outside Fort Huachuca, an army base also established in 1877. The base is currently operational. Officially founded in 1927, Sierra Vista grew with the fort, which, after languishing, was reactivated in 1954. I would have found a relatively small town in 1963. The 1960 census tallied only 3,121 Sierra Vistians. Annexation of Fort Huachuca into Sierra Vista occurred in 1971. The 2000 count was 37,775 individuals, a 14.5 percent increase since 1990. The close association of the fort and the town relate to our birding itinerary. Sierra Vista, often called the hummingbird capital, stands at 4,623 feet in elevation and is near four mountain ranges, one of which is the Huachuca Mountains, a range with several birding sites on our agenda. Many of our prospective birding sites are also inside the boundary of Fort Huachuca. Anxious and tired from the long drive, we found a motel, and after a couple of hours of unpacking and a brief rest, we were ready for Arizona birding, starting with a few southwestern hummingbirds.

It was too late to bird the canyons in adjacent Fort Huachuca, though Beatty's Guest Ranch in Miller Canyon held promise. I phoned ahead. Tom Beatty said to come on up. The paved canyon road climbed westward past modern houses and desert to a rough dirt road with taller and taller oaks standing to the sides. Gambel's Quail zipped across the road, and an Arizona Woodpecker stopped us in our tracks. What a beautiful shade of brown and a new life bird for me. Vociferous Mexican Jays were paler blue than those in Texas. Tom Beatty greeted us at the end of the road. Standing erect on an agile graying frame, dressed impressively somewhere between birder and beekeeper, was Tom Beatty. He immediately exuded pride about his hummingbirds, rare frogs, cabins, and orchard on the 10 acres nestled at about 5,750 feet elevation in Miller Canyon. Tom, and his wife Edith, moved to the canyon in 1967, grew apples and bees, and opened their hummingbird feeding stations to the public in 1997. The Beattys maintain about 45 feeders and hold the US record for the most species of hummingbirds, 14, in a single day. Eager to begin the hummingbird safari, Tom led us up a steep and rocky slope to a set of feeders. For no reason, I thought the Miller Creek area would be flatter. So, we left the motel wearing sandals. The rough terrain was far from flat, and our feet begged for boots. We barely managed to keep pace with Tom as he practically scampered up the rocky trail and arrived at the first level at the main string of feeders above a parking lot. Shortly, a large male hummingbird arrived that looked unlike anything I had seen alive or in the museum. Tom announced that the strange bird was a hybrid Rivoli's X Berylline Hummingbird. At that moment, I had seen neither species. Gary Graves, the younger Smithsonian curator I used to tease, liked hybrids. He especially relished ones difficult to identify. The hybrid du jour was easily identifiable as it sported fairly equal amounts of plumage characters of the two species. There was no need for a complicated and detailed hybrid index like those Gary might devise. That parents of the hybrid belonged to different genera suggests further studies of the systematics of hummingbirds are warranted. I was also curious about the size differences of the parent birds. Rivoli is roughly 1.25 inches longer than the smaller Berylline Hummingbird. That is a three centimeters difference for those metric speaking individuals, and, since ornithologists would express these measurements in millimeters, the difference in length between the two species is a whopping 30 millimeters. That hefty difference made for an odd couple. Tom said publication of a photograph of the hybrid was in the wind. The story in *Birding* would arrive in our mail before our return to Oregon in mid-May.

The hybrid was extremely aggressive, which is not necessarily the mark of hybrid vigor. We left it tilting at windmills for another seemingly vertical march behind Tom's quick footsteps. We arrived a few yards from one of Beatty's cabins and a set of feeders and chairs. Two people sitting near the feeders interrupted the quiet by occasional gushes and faint *Star Wars* sounds emanating from a large digital camera. Sharp high-frequency bird tinks, squeaks, assorted chips, and lower raspy sounds also broke the silence. Naturally, there was plenty of humming, mostly from the birds, but also from the birders. The feast was on. The big ones, not the birders but the hummingbirds, were those Tom called Mags, which were absolutely magnificent and are known as a Rivoli's Hummingbird. The most abundant were the smaller, Black-chinned Hummingbirds. Joining the palate of hummingbirds were violet crowned and throated Costa's, rosy red-throated Broad-tailed, Calliope, with streaked red and white throats, Anna's, with a rosy head and throat, and true to its name, Rufous hummingbirds.

An early sunset caused by the tall Huachuca Mountains to the west and a chance to see a Blue-throated Hummingbird lured us to the lower feeders. Tom had seen one there during the last two evenings. On the way down, we learned that the two birders at the upper feeding station had just flown from Harlingen to El Paso and driven to the Beattys, where they were staying. The four of us joined others who were waiting for a Blue-throated Hummingbird. The bird never appeared.

We arrived back at the motel in Sierra Vista for some close-up R and R, updating our trip list and planning tomorrow. What an incredible day.

29 April 2005

Leaving our Sierra Vista motel, we drove to Bisbee, once known for mining and ranking as the largest town between St. Louis and San Francisco in the early 1900s. A jolting stop at the edge of the famous Lavender Open-Pit Copper Mine opened a vein of despair. It is amazing what humans can do to the earth. The 2,000-foot hole began in 1951, and 46 million tons of removed earth dumped everywhere, was profitable to some, perhaps for a few generations, and ecologically disastrous for perhaps ever. Linda recalled, in the early 1970s, the massive earth-gouging machines and huge, overgrown trucks mounded high with Arizona's flesh. Noisy machines rumbled, and smelly burnt diesel blackened the air. Profit dried up by 1975 when Bisbee's mines were joining 100,000 closed mines in Arizona. By then, eight billion pounds of mined copper and tons of other minerals left water sources toxic, the land profoundly wounded, and that is just in the Bisbee region. World-renowned turquoise and other minerals contributed to the making of Bisbee, now 5,900 strong, a town of art galleries and gourmet restaurants.

In 1963, I would have seen a smaller Lavender Pit, about 4,000 more people, and probably the same number of birds as today, that being zero.

It was difficult not to be impressed by Bisbee. However, what lay ahead was even more impressive, the famed Guadalupe Canyon. For decades, birders had been coming to the canyon in the extreme southeastern corner of Arizona and the southwestern corner of New Mexico. The canyon was high on my list of locations in 1963. In the 2004 planning stage, I was slightly disappointed to learn the canyon was no longer such an important birding site. Nevertheless, I felt compelled to drive the long and dusty road from Douglas to the locality where several species were first detected visiting the United States. Although we had 16 target species for Guadalupe Canyon, I was there more for the history and the nostalgia than the birds.

Time, always at our heels, was gaining as we drove east of Douglas on the Geronimo Trail, the only practical way to reach the remote Guadalupe Canyon. In a cloud of dust and bouncing gravel, we barely slowed while passing Slaughter Ranch. The property was owned once by John Slaughter, a Wild West lawman contemporary with Wyatt Earp and Pancho Villa. We passed the road to San Bernardino NWR, established about 20 years after I would have traveled the road in 1963. We followed the unimproved road more miles and time than we could afford. Geronimo, famed leader of the Chiricahua, an Apache group, probably also thought the route was too long when he was avoiding the cavalry in the 1800s.

The road is remarkably wide, possibly to accommodate the large trailer trucks laden with cattle. We dodged the speeding trucks and saw border patrol vehicles numerous times. Because of my usual propensity of wanting to be sure we were on the right road, we flagged down a ranch pickup. A man, in neat cowboy regalia, was on his way to town. We had just passed a road leading to the north, so I asked if the road east was the correct one. He said yes, and when I mentioned that we had earlier received permission from the landowner to bird the canyon he looked me in the eye and said, "Of course." We hoped he believed us. We rushed onward, passing Chihuahuan Desert creosote and cactus while speeding to around 50 miles per hour, though often necessarily slowing to 10 miles per hour to avoid our teeth rattling from the bone crushing bumps. On the way to the canyon, we were followed, mostly well within our cloud of dust. We thought the driver was possibly a fellow birder. Finally, after about 30 long miles of rocky road, we headed down a hill toward the gate I had seen photographed in the bird-finding guides. As we parked just off the roadway, the vehicle once trailing us traveled past, stopped at the gate, then a man, again clad with cowboy boots, hat, and big decorative belt buckle, dismounted his trusty pickup, did not look our way, unlocked the gate, drove through, locked the gate, and hurtled up the canyon. A stiff breeze soon blew away the dust and Linda and I walked around the gate and entered the inner sanctum of Guadalupe Canyon. The locality that I had waited 42 years to see had become a reality.

We soon glimpsed a large hummingbird, possibly a Rivoli's, and a smaller, Black-chinned hummer. Flycatchers seemed everywhere, perching in the sycamores, cottonwoods, and lower growing shrubs in the riparian canyon. Abundant Vermilion Flycatchers dotted the gray-green trees with bright red, and Brown-crested and the paler breasted Ash-throated flycatchers snagged aerial insects. Western Kingbirds provided a little more yellow, and Dusky-capped Flycatchers provided a new life bird. A breeze was gaining speed, and the sun brought hotter temperatures and still increasing wind. House Finches and Gambel's Quails were at home in the drying heat. Bridled Titmouse added to the mix of black-bibbed Hooded Orioles and migrant Wilson's Warblers.

A Yellow Warbler sang from a high sycamore. I had seen the same subspecies, *sonorana*, in the Mojave Desert in the late seventies. Years later, I assembled thousands of specimens of the Yellow Warblers while enduring a study of geographic variation. To paraphrase a well-known politician, it was hard work. Although the process necessitated naming new subspecies and confirmed, as most modern field guides illustrate, birds breeding in southern Arizona have faint narrow chestnut markings on the back and underparts. Naming the new subspecies and reviving ones not recognized for years serves to draw attention to geographic populations and their need for conservation. During the 1960s parts of the trip, I found Yellow Warblers at several localities. Linda and I were now seeing our first Yellow Warblers for this leg of the trip. We may have been too early for arrivals of many migrants elsewhere and too late to see destroyed riparian habitat that the species once frequented.

We walked as far as a windmill before returning to our dusty vehicle. A Rock Wren called through the now steady wind, and an Arizona Woodpecker gave us a good look. A few white puffy clouds were thickening in the western sky. It seemed a long drive back to Douglas and north to Portal. The wind was steady and strong, gusting to around 25 or more miles per hour. Surprisingly, it began to rain. Dark bluish-black clouds were brewing over the high Chiricahua Mountains. For the first time in weeks, I had to switch on the windshield wipers.

East side of Chiricahua Mountains, Arizona.

Portal Road climbed steadily from US 80 north of Rodeo to Portal's 4,773-foot elevation. We parked near the tiny store just as the mood of wind and rain became serious. I jumped out of the car and onto the worn wooden floor of the general store. High noon had passed. We knew that doing justice to the Chiricahua region would be impossible. The wish list would have to be limited to only a few species. I asked about Blue-throated Hummingbirds. The clerk and a single customer said the species had been seen at the American Museum of Natural History (AMNH) Southwestern Research Station up Cave Creek. Because of the worsening weather, I dismissed trying to check local bird feeders, though Juniper Titmouse might have been possible. The wind was blowing harder.

We were unprepared for the beauty of Cave Creek. As the splendor increased, the weather improved. At 5,400 feet, we reached the research station, where the wind seemed to have vanished. We parked and asked a couple of different people where the feeders were located and would it be all right to view them. No one seemed to mind what we did. This was a more laid-back situation than the required security I experienced decades earlier as a visiting researcher at the American Museum of Natural History in New York City. Memories of my early visits there included meeting the late Stuart Keith, a world-class birder who held the 1955 Big Year of 594 species, 26 more than Peterson during the *Wild America* marathon. Dean

Amadon, truly a gentleman and scholar, wonderfully frank John Bull, John Farrand, my friend, and roommate when he worked at Smithsonian, Bob Dickerman, who later went to New Mexico and a mutual friend to irascible Allan Phillips, generous Mary LeCroy, and memories of others flooded my mind. Central Park West in the city of New York seemed not so far away.

While approaching the feeders a few yards down from the parking lot, we heard a loud sound that only a hummingbird or a birder could love. Split seconds passed before a large hummer came into view. The bird was blue-throated, and it was another new life bird for Linda and me. As more threatening clouds skimmed overhead, several Yellow-eyed Juncos began foraging below the feeders. Their pale eyes suggested anger compared to the docile eyes of Dark-eyed Juncos. Of course, both species were prone to attacking each other if one violated the space of another.

Grudgingly, we left the station and headed up Forest Road 42. Rich Hoyer and Alan Craig had generously provided me locations where Mexican Chickadees might be. The panorama up the dirt road was increasingly beautiful with mammoth 3,000-foot cliffs, looming groves of green pines and oaks. The region was national park quality. We stopped at the junction of Paradise Road to listen for chickadees. The only sound we heard was the wind blowing through the pines, the sound of forested mountains breathing. We hurried onward, following the twisting road around blind curves and dizzying vertical drops. An oncoming car crowded the narrow road, but slow maneuvering allowed two meeting vehicles to pass. My knuckles were whitening. We stopped to take only pictures until we reached the summit at 7,600-foot Onion Saddle, where a cold, stiff wind howled loudly through the trees. I was beginning to feel frantic—all this way and no Mexican Chickadee. Just as my sky seemed to darken, I heard the unmistakable call, the same one heard on our CD. The gusts kept the trees moving so much that it was a while before one of the chickadees was visible. Blustered but not flustered, we were ready to head back down the mountain. Not far from Onion Saddle, a flurry of bird activity stopped us for an unbelievable feast for our eyes. Grace's Warblers, similar to eastern Yellow-throated Warblers only more yellow, less white, and with faces less contrasting, first got our attention. Linda spotted a Painted Redstart among the fray. The bird's mostly black plumage was accented with a red belly and large white wing patches. A Greater Pewee whistled before showing itself and looking superficially like our Pacific Northwest Olive-sided Flycatcher. Amid the Grace's Warbler, a small flood of Olive Warblers appeared with a dark-billed male Hepatic Tanager balancing the red spectrum set off by the redstart. The group of Olive Warblers, not warblers at all and belonging to the family Peucedramidae, was represented mostly by tawny headed males and a few more yellowish headed females. All but the pewee was new. Perhaps there is something to the descending method of finding birds.

Satisfied we had identified all members of the mixed flock of birds so luckily witnessed, we kept the Birdmobile in first gear and foot over the brake during our descent, stopping only to take more pictures of the outstanding views. Halfway between the saddle and the research station, Linda identified a Buff-breasted Flycatcher. I was glassing a different bird that got away. Mexican and Steller's jays grouched from the slopes. We hated it, but we had to leave the Chiricahua Mountains. The drive back to Sierra Vista was long, a fight with the gusting wind, and comparatively boring.

30 April 2005

Yesterday's almost brutal itinerary was hard emotionally because we knew there was much more to see in the Chiricahua Mountains. The day was difficult physically because of the long hours and too many miles driven. Our minds were numb; our eyes burned. Linda took the day off. I slept late, getting up about 8 a.m., packed a lunch, kissed my bride, and drove north on Highway 90. There were intersecting roads named Bobcat Lane and Camino de Tundra not far north of Sierra Vista. At milepost 300, I turned onto a narrow dirt track and crossed a cattle guard just north of the highway. A road climbed gently up the alluvial deposits washed from the heart of the Whetstone Mountains through French Joe Canyon. There was nothing gentle about the road. Littered with large and small rocks, the route, the water-eroded ruts, holes, everything but quicksand, was challenging. An empty pickup sat just past the cattle guard. The driver was walking with a small dog as I inched a few hundred bumps up the route. Catching up to him, he told me he was a volunteer at nearby Kartchner Caverns State Park and that he was out exploring.

After a jolting half-mile of dodging the larger boulders, the kind that hate oil pans, and deeper ruts that grabbed the tires, I decided to follow the volunteer's lead, parked, packed a bottle of water, and walked toward French Joe Canyon. I read that about 29 Arizona residents die annually from heat-related causes, mostly because they are not sufficiently hydrated. Linda, my very own personal nurse, who is an RN of considerable expertise, makes sure we drink more water than our thirst demands or at least eight glasses per day. As for waterless birding, or any other activity, I would not want to be suffering from thirst. According to a few sources, half of the people dying from desert thirst, for example, perish in 36 hours, a quarter die in 48 to 50 hours. No one makes it past 80 hours. It is not a pretty way to die.

Following the feeling of thirst, a victim goes through stages ranging from water-treatable cottonmouth and shriveled tongue to the untreatable blood sweat phase. That phase is when mental capacity is unclear. By then, the pain of thirst is gone, the body shuts down, and you die. Yikes.

I am glad to carry an extra bottle of water. Plastic water bottles gurgled from the back of my vest, the vest that held a compass, field guide, paper and pen, whistle for emergencies, an energy bar or two, camera and tape recorder, and more. I trudged up the last remnants of the dirt track to the creek bed of French Joe Canyon. Reliable sources outlined where to look for targeted Rufous-capped Warbler seen in the canyon last year. I also kept an eye out for Fan-tailed Warblers, but what was I thinking? The species had not been seen there for eight years. A flash of bright yellow teased my wishes, but it was a male Yellow Warbler foraging abnormally close to the ground. Rufous-capped Warblers were not for the finding. Black-throated Gray Warblers were abundant. A pair of Scott's Orioles swooped by to identify me. The water bottles in my vest were becoming lighter and the day hotter. I turned back.

After bouncing back to the highway, I threaded through Saturday traffic of Sierra Vista and south to Miller Canyon where Flame-colored Tanagers were once seen on the trail above the hummingbird feeders. More cars and people had converged at the end of the canyon road than two days ago. Tom Beatty was busy directing visitors to hummingbird feeders and informed me that no new species had arrived since the day before yesterday. When I told Tom about hiking up the canyon, he offered me the shortcut through his property. The gate he directed me to was locked. Turning back, I saw Edith Beatty, who unlocked the gate and told me the combination number of the lock for opening the gate on my return. What generous and trusting people.

An old access road reaches up the canyon toward the trail and a spring that supplies water to Tombstone about seven crow miles to the northeast. Water pipelines from Miller and Carr canyon and three other sites in the Huachuca Mountains have supplied water to Tombstone since 1882. The springs in Miller Canyon still help keep the dust down in the O.K. Corral. Ruins of buildings sat just off the trail. An exposed pipe appeared, then disappeared under the rocky surface of the narrowing trail. Loose rocks littered the steep climb. A binocular-bedecked couple coming down told me they had photographed a Flame-colored Tanager in the canyon in 2002. I asked how far up the trail. Months earlier, a friend confessed that the trail to the tanagers was physically demanding. Could my sixties-something self meet the demands of Miller Canyon?

Onward and upward, I slogged past trees reaching from the deep canyon floor. Towering Douglas fir stood high above me, many growing taller and wider in girth than most Oregon loggers (and lawyers) would allow to stand. Cool air from the riparian lushness of Miller Canyon was nearly canceled by the rising afternoon temperature. The roughness of the canyon trail contributed to the rise in my own temperature and the beat of my heart. I needed to see a bird just to slow me down to a healthy pace. Finally, I reached the location on the trail where the couple photographed the tanager three years ago. Sweat was running into my eyes, and my pulse was slowing from a freeway to a reasonable speed. My brain was telling me I was crazed.

Expecting to see a Flame-colored Tanager at the very spot where one was photographed three years earlier was ridiculous. Further, some of the tanagers more recently reported were hybrids between Western and Flame-colored tanagers. I could not count a hybrid, a point I considered as I turned downhill. Descending was a welcome trend albeit a little treacherous because of so many loose rocks. I hoped my Big Bend rubber knee syndrome would not rear its ugly head. Just as I decided to face the music that a Flame-colored Tanager would not be possible, I heard a loud Western Tanager sounding as if it was on steroids. A bird flew from one thickly branched tree to the other. It was reddish, not yellow and red, and it flew out of sight. I froze, shuffled a few feet up and down the trail, waited, and then I saw a loud gray-billed and streak-backed tanager. It matched its mug shot in my field guide of a Flame-colored Tanager. If it was a hybrid, it was not obvious to me.

The remainder of the trip back to the trailhead, though tanagerized, was long and physically arduous. My knees began to protest, and my water bottles no longer gurgled. The well was dry. By the time I arrived at the upper gate, I had forgotten the combination to the lock. I never was much of a student of math. Besides, numbers are much harder to remember than are field marks of birds. The fence appeared too difficult to cross. I had no choice but to take the trail around the Beatty property. It seemed a long way; I should have written down the combination. The car was a welcome sight, where a cool bottle of water waited in the icebox. Before reaching the car, I saw the female side of the couple who gave me directions about the tanager. She was sitting in a chair next to an open vehicle. I thanked her, told her I saw a tanager, but could not be 100 percent sure it was not a hybrid. That might seem ridiculous, but I had observed many specimens of hybrids that, if seen in the field, would have been identified as one of the parent species. The woman said, "Oh, don't you have Sibley?" I said no, whereupon she said, take a look at theirs, "it's in the car." A large dog, the same one that accompanied them on the trail, was in the back seat of the open vehicle. I rethought reaching for the book, telling her I was not too sure if her dog would be happy about my intrusion. Debbie Parker walked past the dog and handed me the book. Jim Parker walked up about the same time I had decided the bird I saw was a pure Flame-colored Tanager. We exchanged emails and good birding salutations. Soon I was back at the motel. After a hot, yes hot, soak for my tired muscles, Linda and I went over our notes.

1 May 2005

We registered our vehicle and ourselves at the Fort Huachuca gate and headed into the inner sanctum of the army base. The fort occupies 113 square miles on the east slope of the Huachuca Mountains. During the 1970s, Linda picked up a privately published history of Fort Huachuca and she told me that Huachuca, in Indian language, means "thunder" or "stormy," and that a careful listener could hear "Troop ho!" and horse hooves pounding the ground. I doubt that was what the Apache had in mind. To us, Huachuca meant canyons and birds. We were happy that the Fort tolerated birders visiting Garden, Scheelite, and Sawmill Canyons within the boundary of this historical and currently active military installation.

Our first destination was Garden Canyon. Below the mouth of the canyon, we encountered Bullock's Oriole and Gila Woodpecker. At the upper picnic grounds, several cars and more people had converged. We parked, walked to the creek, and heard the unmistakable sound of a trogon. It is not the sound associated with demure beauty or even average good looks. In moments, we saw an Elegant Trogon mapping out his territory from a tall sycamore growing from the bank of the creek. The bird did not seem to mind the milling throng below, who acted as if they were witnessing a fireworks display. One group of the gushing dozen across the creek went into such a state of audible awe that the male flew away from them and perched obligingly for Linda's waiting camera lens.

We rushed from Garden Canyon to Sawmill Canyon. About a quarter-mile hike from the cable-gated road, we discovered a Buff-breasted Flycatcher. One of the easiest species in the genus *Empidonax* to identify, it is also possibly the prettiest. Red-faced Warblers added to the excitement, as did skulking Mexican Jays and more flycatchers. Back at the trailhead and the cabin where we parked, we broke for a quick lunch. A van of three birders soon arrived, parked, and set up a table for their lunch. At the same time, Linda and I, after so many miles and birds, realized we still did not have a picture of ourselves together during our trip. We asked our neighbors for help. Two of them chimed that the third was a great photographer and would be happy to accommodate us. As we posed, but before we could explain anything about our camera, the accomplished photographer announced his success. Wonderful, we thought, as we returned to our vehicle. A check of the results disclosed nothing. Seems the volunteer photographer did what I did when looking for Colima Warblers. At any rate, we were too shy to ask for a second sitting.

Several minutes later, we parked at the entrance of Scheelite Canyon, famous for Spotted Owls, a species we needed. As an ornithologist, a long-time birder, and resident of the Pacific Northwest, I was slightly embarrassed that I had never encountered a Spotted Owl. The late Robert T. Smith, former caretaker of Scheelite Canyon's habitat, had guided thousands of birders to their first Spotted Owl for 20 years since 1978. In 1963, I would have had to negotiate a trailless canyon. Today, Linda and I checked the log sheets at the beginning of a real trail. Rich Hoyer logged that he saw one on the upper fork. One owl? Only one? I had envisioned Spotted Owls dripping from the trees. Even so, one Spotted Owl was better than no owl at all, but would there be even one?

Compared to what lay ahead, the beginning of the trail was relatively flat. Beyond, it was a steep rocky scrape, with several places requiring sheer footedness and good handholds. In little over an eighth of a mile, we began to scour the trees for owls. The trees were birdless. Not far ahead, we met a couple coming down the trail. The man of the couple was constantly talking inanely about how easy the trail seemed. His mate, with a tired expression of jumbled embarrassment, anger, and detached sadness, was speechless. He was as nimble as the intoxicated donkey he emulated. I knew it was no point in asking them about owls. The hapless couple continued down the trail and Linda and I worked our way upward. We decided to turn back between what our trail map called the "Jaws" and a cliff. Hiking down had often been lucky for finding the prey. Yesterday, in Miller Canyon, was a good example of the so-called descending technique. We were not giving up; we were changing the angle of our view.

In a few steps, we met the Parkers coming up the trail. Although their owl list today was spotless, they were reasonably certain they could show us our target bird. We followed, or at least the best our bodies would allow. If their aging dog had not slowed them down, we would have had more difficulty keeping up on the ever-steeper rocky canyon. The five of us, counting the dog, arrived at the middle roosting area where the guides had seen owls the previous year. The last few yards were a real puffer. After all, the trailhead, the start of the trail, was 5,521 feet in elevation and we were slightly beyond the fork in the trail and within what the map designated as Middle

Roosting Area. We had trekked only a quarter of a mile and reached an unknown elevation. If only a sighting of a Spotted Owl had replaced our oxygen starvation, but, again, there were no owls. When the Parkers said they were heading down the trail, Linda and I decided to wait, rest our lungs, and avoid hypoxemia. The Parkers said they would mark the trail if they found a Spotted Owl. We thanked them and eventually began our descent. I looked at the trail that goes to the upper roost. It appeared steeper than any part of the canyon, and I knew we had to get to the car. The sun would soon be setting.

While on the Scheelite trail, we noticed a couple of recent fire pits, not the kind constructed for recreationists, but a few rocks and charcoals were there from somebody. We also found empty water bottles and garbage in several places along the upper part of the trail. A birder related that they had encountered about a dozen immigrants on the trail, probably from the 21-mile Crest Trail that has connecting trails north of the US–Mexico border. Linda and I worried about the potential of wildfires and hoped no one would ever find a Spotted Owl reduced to mere drumsticks.

∽

There is not enough time for revisiting southeastern Arizona, a place that keeps on giving. I can only claim two other visits since 2005. The first was in 2009. I surmised a July visit could add several species to my life list. The journey meant several days apart from Linda, a duration we had never endured since reuniting in 1994. Usually separated no more than six feet, we managed though missing one another. Of course, the 2009 journey was much easier on me; I was birding. During my 2009 time in Arizona, plus a day at the Salton Sea, I racked up 13 life birds.

At Miller Canyon that July, I found Berylline and White-eared hummingbirds within minutes of one another while in the company of Tom Beatty and old friend Jon Dunn, who was leading a group of birders. Miller Canyon did not offer Flame-colored Tanagers, but it did provide more than satisfying views of a pair of Spotted Owls and more than one rigorous trek up and down Miller Canyon Trail. The Huachuca Mountains also provided Lucifer Hummingbird and a species then not on the ABA list, a Brown-backed Solitaire. Other new lifers were added during that 2009 visit and during winter in the Southwest in 2014–15, but that is another story.

Insofar as changes that might have been responsible for any of the new birds seen in 2009, it is not possible to unequivocally state that climate change was the force driving the Brown-backed Solitaire north into

Arizona. It probably was a contributing factor. Less gradual changes in the various mountain ranges occur from wildfires and subsequent water erosion, especially from flash floods. The frequency and severity of wildfires and meteorological events, including lightning, are certainly correlated with climate change. Also, more and more people frequenting the out of doors increases the chance of wildfires in the US since 84 percent, country-wide, are human-caused.[1] That is a shocking percent. Whatever the percentage, any figure is too high although it may be a good indicator for measuring human carelessness and downright stupidity. Sure, human-caused wildfires could be accidental, such as parking a vehicle over flammable fuel. Think red-hot catalytic converters. And, how about the age-old practice of setting off fireworks to celebrate the Fourth of July? Just how patriotic is it to burn down a forest? Operating machinery that might cause a spark such as when mowing a lawn and hitting a rock could be a fire starter. Mowing a pesky lawn might seem innocent enough but really, is it, in these days of rising temperatures and chronic drought? There are many ways humans can cause fires, including on purpose. Regardless of how human-caused fires are started, probably 99.9 percent of the 84 percent of fire starters should not be walking upright, let alone be permitted to have matches or allowed to reproduce.

Once the forest floor is exposed, water erosion usually runs rampant. The Beatty property was devastated by flash flooding and debris flows, the aftermath of a 2011 wildfire. That fire and its outcome of the alluvial flow of boulders and sand even threatened Sierra Vista. The cause of the wildfire was reported to be human-caused. Carelessness, leaving a campfire unattended, smoking, any number of ignorant behaviors, either by immigrants crossing the southern US border or by resident hikers out to inadvertently burn down the forest they came to enjoy will and have destroyed countless acres, townships, and watersheds.

Flash floods almost destroyed campgrounds in the low elevations of the Chiricahua Mountains. The campground I stayed at in 2009 was closed when Linda and I looked for a camping location in 2015. The devastation from eroded debris filling culverts, covering recreational infrastructures, all of which was the result of a wildfire in 2011, was so horrific, and restoration was beyond the underfunded budget of the Forest Service, that the campground may remain closed for years. The fire of 2011 covered 222,954 acres or burned 70 percent of the Chiricahua Mountain range, cost at least $50 million to suppress, and was human-caused. I wondered if there were

---

1. Jennifer K. Balch et al. "Human-Started Wildfires Expand the Fire Niche across the United States." *Proceedings of the National Academy of Sciences* 114 (2017) 2946–51.

any surviving Mexican Chickadees at burned-over Onion Saddle. Recent reports indicate the species miraculously continues to occur in the region.

Four pages in the bird-finding guide Linda and I used in 2005 are devoted to the historically famous Guadalupe Canyon. Modern guidebooks allow about a page for the same place. While visiting the Slaughter Ranch considerably north of the US–Mexico border in 2009, I saw construction of patrol roads and barriers that diminished access beyond the Geronimo Trail. Also, I witnessed border patrol agents ranging in behavior from intimidating puffery to semi-polite border humans, heard complaints about losing land because of the barriers, and breathed lots of dust and attitude blowing in the dry wind. The patrol roads are wide and smooth compared to the rocky, bone-jarring road civilians must travel.

My 2009 revisit to the Geronimo Trail was to the Slaughter Ranch, where reports of the demise of the region are not pretty. For example, concrete is required in construction and valuable water from San Bernardino NWR was just a perfect source. Another disturbing element is that the border project requires an estimated $41 million per mile to build the barriers.[2] That is considerably more than the amount to build a six-lane interstate in average rural America, which is only $7 million. Really? Besides US land becoming inaccessible by being south of border barriers, even small mammals and reptiles can no longer travel across the border. Even before wildlife approach a border barrier, they must cross 300 or more feet of disturbed habitat, which is often bathed in bright spotlights and border patrol vehicles. Birds are also victims of border barriers. Sure, most birds fly, but several species do not fly high off the ground. Those suddenly confronted with a 10-foot, or worse, a 30-foot barrier, might not fly over such a height. Flying high may not be in their genes. The rare Ferruginous Pygmy-Owl avoids flying much higher than 4.5 feet above the ground, something they do to avert being eaten.[3] How many of us have seen our resident Song Sparrow population performing high aerial bounds over a few feet? What about Greater Roadrunners? And, what if that roadrunner was south of the barrier but north of the official border? Will the ABA consider the bird countable in ABA land or will the bird be a candidate for a checklist of birds in Mexico? Of course, an answer to such a sad question may be moot since my last visit near the border had to be at an unspecified distance from the

---

2. Maya Kapoor and Ariana Brocious. "In Arizona, Building a Wall—And Destroying a Canyon." *AZPM News*, Oct 30, 2020. https://news.azpm.org/p/news-splash/2020/10/30/183147-the-borderlands-boondoggle/.

3. Aaron D. Flesch et al. "Potential Effects of the United States-Mexico Border Fence on Wildlife." *Conservation Biology* 24.1 (2010) 171–81.

border barrier. Why? US border agents do not allow anyone to approach the region of the barrier. Why? It was for our safety.

Our safety is endangered from many sources, including populations of birds that are trending downward. Not seeing Yellow Warblers until Guadalupe Canyon might have been a fluke but believing that is difficult to accept. Data from the Breeding Bird Surveys indicate Yellow Warblers are down by a whopping 26 percent since 1970. As for Yellow Warblers in Guadalupe Canyon, I can only imagine the devastation to them and any other wildlife in the canyon when, in 2020, sections of the canyon's sides were dynamited to make way for the destructive border barrier.

Chapter 27

Arizona Byways

2 May 2005

It was dark when we collapsed in our motel bed last night. Although tired, my mind would not be quiet enough for the slumber I needed. Thoughts of changes in scenery, habitats, birds, and plants flashed in my mind like a newsreel seen in the days of big-screen movie theaters. This was not the Old West. It was the New West, with businesses and homes along highways and suburban streets. The same theme was coming to my thoughts. Too many people. Habitat loss. Somehow, I needed to calm my mind and, in one of so many motels dotting the landscape, find sleep. The motel we chose was quiet and dark, but my mind was full of sound, no, not tinnitus, but awash with sights of the past and birds of the future. I needed sleep but sleep would come later.

Gazing up at the faintly lit motel ceiling, I continued to worry. The new potential problem was related to timing. Are we too late in the season to avoid the boiling heat and dehydrating air that is so famous in the Southwest? Salton Sea was on our agenda. Could we take it, would the Birdmobile overheat? Would Linda and I succumb to the scorching heat? Would a cactus thorn poke out an eye or might quicksand smother us?

Continuing to allow my mind to churn away, I began to worry that we would not be in San Diego on 7 May. How could we possibly be in California in five days? We would be late. Either the time in Arizona had to be brief, or the time in California must be short. We were reluctant to short-shrift fabulous southeast Arizona. We had good information on where to look for Arizona birds and most of the localities were concentrated in the southeastern part of the state. Additionally, the region was heavily birded so if something rare was found, we might hear about it and thereby benefit from other birders. Yeah, that's it. We will spend more time in Arizona and hope for the best in Southern California.

Way back in 1963, I had a 1959 version of the Tucson Audubon Society's "Field List of Birds" that included only 261 species, counting accidentals, that I was hopeful for finding. Of course, using a list from any finding guide and expecting real live birds is not guaranteed. In 2005, a "Checklist of Birds of Southeast Arizona," updated in 2003 and published by the Tucson society, listed 482 species. Even allowing for taxonomic splits since 1959, the difference in the total number of species in the new list is remarkable. The approximate 185 percent increase in known species likely reflects the higher number of people interested in birds and known places to find birds. Linda and I were enjoying the knowledge of those birders and ornithologists. Of course, we would only see a small portion of the possible species, which we realized was a perfect reason for returning to Arizona another time.

Arizona birds have long been a magnet for birders and ornithologists. In 1964, my old friend Allan Phillips, a short welterweight with a giant mind, led ornithological gurus Joe Marshall and Gale Monson to author the landmark *Birds of Arizona*. Even though I had planned, in 1963, to find every specialty possible, which meant birding every locality Pettingill and others ever mentioned in print, I would not have known to look for species now regularly observed by birders in Arizona. I would not have targeted Thick-billed Kingbirds or walked up Miller Canyon for Flame-colored Tanagers in 1963. I would not have abused myself and my vehicle in French Joe Canyon to search for Fan-tailed and Rufous-capped Warblers. Perhaps the biggest difference between the possibilities of sixties birding and now is the number of species of hummingbirds. The old list included nine species; the new list has 17 species. An obvious reason for such an increase is the increase of hummingbird feeders. Feeding hummingbirds in the last decades has become almost commonplace. Humans love the antics of these adorable and sparkling birds. People might feed because their neighbor does, and neither may know the difference between a Ruby-throated and a Rufous Hummingbird. In fact, too many Westerners are convinced that the hummingbirds they see are Ruby-throated and all jays are Blue Jays. That was what they learned, and that is that. What a terrific way to see hummingbirds. People have learned that maintaining their feeders beyond usual hummer departure dates will increase their chances of luring an accidental during winter. The increase in sightings of Rufous Hummingbirds east of the Rocky Mountains possibly reflects an increase of feeders, people to see them, and less obvious reasons. I wondered if birds have and will change their distribution, without our help.

Human activities have caused changes in vegetation that may be adverse or beneficial to different species. When I studied the geographic variation of northern populations of Wrentits, a species breeding from Baja California to western Washington (not Arizona), it was obvious that fewer trees and more brush meant Wrentits in new locations. The change was the result of fire and logging. Brushy plants are often the vegetation growing from disturbances that remove trees. Several species have progressed northward over several decades as brushy habitat has increased. Incidentally, fewer trees equate to warmer ambient temperatures. Could changes in vegetation and global warming be pushing species toward cooler habitats? Anna's Hummingbird in Oregon first showed up about six decades ago, bred in the 1980s, and is now a resident over much of the western part of the state. It now breeds as far north as British Columbia and wanders to Alaska. Why? Was it feeders and ornamental flowers reflecting an ever-increasing human population? Probably, but vegetation and climate surely contributed.

Eventually, I fell asleep, possibly by counting hummingbirds. Morning came too early as I slipped out of the motel room to find a facility to wash and vacuum the Birdmobile, thereby removing part of southeast Arizona dust that was hitchhiking on our dime. Linda and I left Sierra Vista, proclaimed as the Hummingbird Capital of Arizona, and, without ever seeing a hummingbird there, headed west to the Paton's, where we should find the whirring wings of hummingbirds and promise of new trip birds.

We first drove south of the Whetstone Mountains, home of erstwhile warblers of yesterday, and motored north of the wonderful Huachuca Mountains to Sonoita Creek near the southeastern side of the Santa Rita Mountains. The high desert and all that came before it was a blur. We had been on the road for 36 days, pushed the speed limit most of the time, and stayed in more motels than we cared to count. More mosquitoes had bitten and more chiggers crept on board than should. We had looked into the abyss of the Grand Canyon, drifted across the high plains, reckoned our way through the Ozarks, glided quickly along the Gulf Coast, and ticked off birds from there westward. Travel the last five weeks seemed to be at warp speed. In the sixties, age-wise, time often hurtles past, whether you want it to or not. Now, we were actually racing time, inflating gas prices and rising digits reported by local meteorologists. I am not sure whether we had seen too much country in a too-brief time, or we were tantalized and frustrated by what we did not have time to see. One thing was certain—we missed the

Montezuma Quail. The revenge for missing Montezuma Quail and other species was the feeling of guilt from not trying harder and the frustration of rushing time. Gratefully, we managed to stay healthy while on the verge of birder exhaustion.

Perhaps we had met a level of saturation. If so, it was akin to too much good food when already full, but even so, we wanted more; a new lifer or at least a new trip bird would help maintain what we had become used to. Were we spoiled by too much good birding? Expecting all that wonderful birding to last forever was unrealistic. I had waited for this trip, but now, I was beginning to realize that all good things have a limit. A state of fullness was approaching. Maybe there were too many interstate miles, or too many stints of packing and unpacking the vehicle, way too many bugs to scrape from the windshield, and too many depressing scenes of human impact on the land. A tremendous amount of fun still electrified our emotions, but there was not enough time to soak in completely all that we experienced. There seemed too little time to realize that this was actually a fantastic trip and not a dream.

Linda and I took a moment to smell the roses today by stopping at Paton's Hummingbird Haven, a well-marked plot of land in the outskirts of the small town of Patagonia just off Sonoita Creek. Thousands of birders visit the Paton's 24–7 hummingbird smorgasbord annually. Unlike Beatty's place, Hummingbird Haven is on flat even ground. I could have worn my beloved sandals but prepared for rougher terrain and wore boots. Once inside the backyard, Linda and I encountered a canopied rectangle replete with chairs for hummingbird birders. We selected a couple of shaded seats. Behind and to our left was a garden fountain, in front were a row of hummingbird feeders hanging from the back of the house, and far to our right were more feeders for hummers and non-hummers. The hot dry air blew delicately enough to not disturb the birds but hard enough to almost cool us.

Two contented-appearing birders were leaving the area when we arrived. Our meeting was a silent nod. For a half-hour, we had the place to ourselves. The show began with Broad-billed and Violet-crowned hummingbirds buzzing from feeder to feeder. The two were life birds. A mostly reddish-billed bird swooped to a close feeder. At first glance, I thought it was a White-eared Hummingbird. Its throat was plain, and its tail forked. It was a female Broad-billed hummer. Big Anna's Hummingbirds evicted smaller Black-chinned Hummingbirds and Violet-crowned Hummingbirds. We were on the edges of our seats. A Green Violet-ear, a hummingbird rarely found only in Texas, was at the feeders during the week, but it is not for our eyes today. There were plenty of non-hummingbird tantalizations though a Thick-billed Kingbird was in the neighborhood but not today. Sparrows, hawks, and a cowbird were for our viewing pleasure.

By now, there appeared to be two groups of people, totaling about nine individuals. Their level of excitement depended on where they were lived. William L. Murphy was particularly interested in a male Lazuli Bunting, whereas Linda and I jumped out of our seats to see an Abert's Towhee scratching for dropped seeds below a feeder. Linda divulged to the group that I retired from Smithsonian, whereupon Bill Murphy acknowledged helping on bibliographic details from my former next-door office neighbor Roger Clapp at Smithsonian. Had I known Murphy was the author of a bird-finding guide on Trinidad and Tobago, I might have discussed Caribbean avifauna and my bird survey on St. Kitts in the northern Lesser Antilles. I was an et al. author, number three of four of a paper published in the *Caribbean Journal of Science* 20 years after my fieldwork. If that seems to be a long time between fieldwork and publication, James Peters, of the famed Peters Checklist of Birds of the World, was on St. Kitts in 1922 and never published his survey.

Just as there is more work and less time for ornithologists to devote to their trade, time today was ticking away, and there were plenty of birds yet to see. Linda announced seeing a Zone-tailed Hawk, a species I failed to see in Texas. In seconds, I joined her and the group to ogle the hawk gliding low overhead. Another few days and time would have ticked away the opportunity to see that bird. The sight of White-crowned Sparrows and Bronzed Cowbirds near the fountain produced a strange picture of an odd couple. Strafing hummingbirds zipped in and out of view. The show of birds and birders was going strong when, after three hours, Linda and I grudgingly departed.

The next stop was the Patagonia Roadside Rest Area, famous for several Arizona specialties. The day's heat and excitement at Paton's had drained us, but not enough for a hike across the road from the rest area. Except for the busy highway, it was quiet. I was determined to scour the region for Varied Bunting and Rose-breasted Becard. A female becard did finally reveal herself, and a pair was calling across the tight fence between the road and Sonoita Creek. In the meantime, Linda located Yellow Warblers and saw a male becard. About that time, long shadows enticed mosquitoes to patrol our bare arms.

Almost desperately, we scurried into Patagonia Lake State Park. Black-capped Gnatcatchers breed there, and I had a map of the precise locations of the last known nests. The sun had long since set. The rough terrain and hard stickery brush along the trail would not be forgiving after dark. I walked a few yards above the man-made lake, then a few more before accepting gnatcatcher defeat. Neon lit the Nogales streets where we rested the night.

3 May 2005

Today would be more of a day of rest. A kingbird called from its electric wire perch behind the motel. Like a wish sandwich, the one without meat, it would have been great if the bird was a Thick-billed instead of a Tropical Kingbird. It is amazing how fast listing creates a skewed attitude. A few weeks earlier, I would have considered a Tropical Kingbird as a must-see bird. It depends on where you are from or where you have been.

Hankering for an authentic Mexican meal, we decided to make one more visit to another border town, drove to the edge of Nogales, Arizona, and walked into Nogales, Mexico. Linda visited there in the 1970s and was surprised about the growth. Pharmacies dominated the scene just as they did in Ciudad Juárez on the Rio Grande. In fact, by lunchtime, we had to return to Nogales, Arizona, to find a Mexican restaurant. It would have been easier to settle for a hamburger, but our taste buds were ready for authentic, albeit north of the border, Mexican fare.

By the time our lunch was well into our systems, we were primed to motor up the Santa Cruz River on I-19. We passed the exit for California Gulch and, as far as we knew, our only opportunity to find Five-striped Sparrow. Linda was more intrigued about this rare bird than I allowed my listing fever to entertain. Besides, time was a-wasting, notwithstanding the concern that our vehicle might not take the punishing road up the remote canyon. Maybe another time. Perhaps we should rent an SUV just for the sparrow. Yeah, that's it, but, in reality, there was no time for California Gulch. We drove on, passed Tumacacori National Historical Park, the preserved 300-year-old mission, and sped by Tubac, once the sight of a 1691 Jesuit stomping ground and now a community of artists.

Exit 48 took us from the busy interstate to Amado Roadside Rest Area to look for Rufous-winged Sparrows. We found what appeared to be the correct site and drove the dirt tracks north of an inn on the east side of the interstate. The heat from the lateness of the day and the season and being about 1,500 feet lower than Sierra Vista was surprisingly uncomfortable. Although the temperature was only in the mid-eighties, the lack of wind and being inside the Birdmobile turned greenhouse was not a good recipe. Determined, we rolled down the windows and cranked up the CD playing a Rufous-winged Sparrow going for the gold, a mate, and territory to defend. A couple of probable sparrows flew from one grassy knoll to another but did not stop long enough to respond to the recording or for us to see more than just a little brown bird. A few 20-plus-foot trees were full of Wilson's Warblers. There was a handful of Yellow Warblers and a lone Black-headed Grosbeak. A car rolled by during one sparrow calling exercise. The driver slowed down, and a young woman leaned out her window saying disappointedly that that was their favorite place to neck. Linda and I appreciated the dilemma and moved to a different site. As for the sparrow, if it was there, it remained hidden and speechless. We persisted in the heat until we got the hell out of Amado, with windows up and air-conditioner at full tilt boogie. In 1963, several kinds of cars, including the VW, had a small window just forward of the main door window. The small window could be pivoted at an angle to direct air at the driver. The right side of the car had a similar setup. All that was necessary to be naturally cool was to drive fast.

Today we drove fast, heading up Elephant Head and Mount Hopkins Road to Montosa Canyon on the west side of the Santa Rita Mountains. The climb, gradual at first, took us through low growing scrub of the Sonoran Desert. The silvery domes that house four of the telescopes of Smithsonian's Fred Lawrence Whipple Observatory beamed skyward from the top of 8,585-foot Mount Hopkins. Named for Gilbert Hopkins, a mining engineer, it was the mountain where he and his boss William Wrightson of 9,453-foot Wrightson Peak died in 1865. They were surveying a disputed mining claim, and Apaches, probably fed up with so much trespassing, killed them. About 100 years later, the Apache vanished into the Southwestern hinterlands, and Smithsonian Institute built the observatory. My mixed view of the region held appreciation for the spirit of those natives who came before us, their losses, a feeling of pride when I posed for Linda in front of Smithsonian's familiar sunburst logo on the visitor center's sign, and tingling anticipation of birding in Montosa Canyon.

A dry wash crossed the road not far beyond the visitor center. The road widened a few feet beyond where we parked. The prolonged high temperature and the prospect of the sun helped Linda decide to wait in the shade of the car. A breeze offered cooling relief. As I exited the Birdmobile, I said I would be right back, and walked the steeply inclined road to the wash. Two birds in bushes at the road edge stopped to investigate the noisy sound of rocks crunching under my boots, or maybe they just stopped to munch a gnat. In two minutes from leaving Linda, I had my first Black-capped Gnatcatchers. That is more like it!

Before mounting the interstate again, we stopped to check for vacancies at Madera Canyon in the Santa Rita Mountains. We had thought of staying there about a month before we left Oregon. Because sources suggested making reservations a year in advance, and because it was difficult to know our precise location every day, we had not tried for a night in Madera Canyon earlier. We tried today, but nothing was available tonight but tomorrow night was clear. It would cost more than our usual motel fares, but we assured ourselves it would be our treat. We could wake to the sounds of birds, not diesels.

Back on I-19, we traveled north to Green Valley, a planned retirement community where almost everyone is white and over 65 years of age. Founded in 1953, Green Valley is west of the usually dry Santa Cruz River and offers stupendous views of the lofty Santa Rita Mountains. About 500 people lived in Green Valley in 1964. Today, the population is over 20,000, most of whom are retirees. Linda and I made a quick foray in the local grocery store, which was akin to being on the movie set of *Cocoon*. One of a few motels in town was not too costly or too cheap. It was just right, quiet, landscaped with more plants than most sterile lodging sites, and it had a pool and Jacuzzi for our overly birded bodies. However, I am getting ahead of myself.

Before checking in and enjoying the cool water of a swimming pool we had to park our vehicle. Pulling into the only available parking slot was not possible because a female Gambel's Quail was sittings on the tarmac to the right of the front tire of a car in the adjacent parking slot. Our left front tire rolled near the quail, but she did not budge. I leaned out the window, which is all her little quail nerves could tolerate. She instantly sat upright. At that very moment, tiny downy juvenile quail exploded from underneath the female. Each one was barely the diameter of a half-dollar. They ran in every direction. I audibly gasped, something I am not prone to do except during moments of great surprise and certain non-avian pleasures. Seconds ticked as a male joined the female. The parents herded a dozen chicks along a six-inch curb to another curb about 15 feet to our right. The female stood at the top of the curb making almost inaudible noises as the chicks attempted to jump up to reach their parent. They were too short. The watchful male moved the downy balls with legs a few feet to the right where they could achieve high ground before sundown. We sat mesmerized, hardly breathing. As for the swimming pool, a huge but polite party was thriving on the concrete shore. Most of the liquid that the older revelers were enjoying came in a glass. Our deeply tanned arms and faces contrasted to the remainder of bared skin, especially my reflectively lily-white legs. We did not care. We had the heated Jacuzzi and crisp pool to our young selves. I gasped.

4 May 2005

Linda and I stepped from a cool air-conditioned motel to a warmer outside temperature, one that had dropped during the desert night, but a temperature already beginning the climb that would rise to discomfort. We drove just east of I-19 to Continental, a tiny settlement at 2,864 feet in elevation, and motored up White House Canyon Road for about four miles before turning southward on Madera Canyon Road for another four miles. On the way up, we drove past Florida and McCleary Washes. Our reserved Madera Kubo cabin at 4,800 feet in elevation nestled below healthy riparian cottonwoods and sycamores towering over Madera Creek. An 1800s lumber mill once stood near the big rock at the entrance to our blue lodging. The air was cool and clean, and the only sound was the faint gurgling creek and birds. For a place in a range named for the saint of hopelessness, the Santa Rita Mountains was home to a superb canyon.

The little blue house, Madera Canyon, Santa Rita Mountains, Arizona.

After 30 minutes of unpacking, Linda and I began to realize why and how lucky we were. Standing at the entrance to the driveway were two birders looking toward our little blue cabin and a chance encounter with a rare tanager. From our vantage, we saw a brilliant male bird clad in colors somewhere in the rainbow between orange and red, a splash of yellow and black accenting just the right places. It landed in a tree not more than 25 feet before our astonished eyes. The male's yellowish partner promptly joined it. The birds were 100 percent purebred, card-carrying Flame-colored Tanagers. The male was particularly interested in a halved orange impaled on the tree and the female seemed especially interested in the male. A red and green male Elegant Trogon perched several feet above, silently watching the scene below. This was too easy.

Linda and I unwillingly resumed setting up house for the next two nights. That was not difficult in the well-appointed one-bedroom cabin, replete with a large living room, full kitchen, bathroom, even a TV that we were not going to switch on, and suitable space between neighboring cabins. What a wonderful place to live.

We abandoned homemaking chores as soon as possible. By now three different people had posted themselves at the driveway to view the tanagers. We felt guilty, almost, that the tanagers and a trogon were in our yard. A few feet from the cabin door was close enough to see that two of the group of people were the Parkers. This was our third unplanned meeting. We invited them for a closer look before walking with them to their vehicle at the nearby Madera Amphitheater parking lot. Last night, they lodged at the same Green Valley motel where Linda and I had earlier stayed. It is a large establishment, and the Parkers might have noticed us if we had joined the other motel guests splashing and yelling from our evening swim. Perhaps we were too sedate. Today, the Parkers were headed back to the Huachuca Mountains before returning to their California home. Linda and I doubted we would see them again, at least this year, and said goodbye. Before the day was over, several other birders stood vigil at the edge of the driveway. Flame-colored Tanagers were found in Madera Canyon in the mid-1990s. In 1963, should the tanagers or other such fantastic species have been there, I would be standing at the edge of the driveway.

A trail from the amphitheater parking lot meanders on the other side of the creek. We followed it downstream, locating three more calling trogons, Dusky-capped Flycatchers, and a couple of unfamiliar sounding White-breasted Nuthatches. Although not an expert in identifying bird sounds, being interested in composing and classical music had helped tune my ears, and the nuthatches did not sound like White-breasted Nuthatches from southwestern Oregon. Linda agreed. Of course, the difference in vocalizations were breaking ornithological news. The seventh edition of the AOU check-list stated that further study of the vocal and other differences of the Pacific coast, interior, and eastern populations are needed to sort out the species limits of what we call White-breasted Nuthatch. Are these populations currently recognized as three separate subspecies, distinct species?

Should birders pay more attention to detail and maintain better notes? Only the last question is answerable, and that is by a firm yes. As for Linda and me, we could prove, at least to ourselves, that we had noticed differences in the morphology and especially the vocalizations of eastern, Pacific Northwest, and now, southwestern nuthatches. No, I did not own an archive of photographs and audio recordings, but I was confident to add three different types of nuthatches to my escrow list. Would we someday add more species of nuthatches to our ABA life lists?

A few rivulets beyond, we crossed the creek and entered the backside of Santa Rita Lodge. The hummingbird feeders were under the guard of patrolling Black-chinned and fewer Rivoli's Hummingbirds. The strange-sounding nuthatches fussed in the shade of oaks. Even at our elevation, the temperature angled upward, and birds were becoming quiet. It was time for a siesta when we climbed the paved road back to the cabin. Four birders were glassing and photographing the obliging Flame-colored Tanagers that displayed from our temporary yard.

After the siesta and a home-cooked dinner, we waited for darkness. About 30 minutes after sunset, we drove the short distance to Santa Rita Lodge, where, at around 10 o'clock, so a birder in Texas had told us, we would be treated to an Elf Owl. The birds were likely descendants of the ones Peterson and Fisher described in *Wild America*. We parked and found a good seat. Finally, when we could see only darkness, a battery of floodlights exploded white rays on a nearby utility pole. The waiting humans were ready for the sudden Edison event. A tiny owl emerging from the woodpecker hole blinked its yellow eyes and stared into the light. The blinding white light made me wonder if the owl thought it was dead. What it might have actually thought was, Great, the light will attract a meal of unsuspecting moths, but will it be possible to see them in this brightness. On the other hand, the bright light was appreciated by an audience of interested bystanders and a local television crew setting up even more banks of lights and a couple of cameras for a photoshoot of the owl. The owl, accustomed to noisy humans, perched in the cusp of the entrance hole, occasionally chattered, and made a foray after what appeared to be a moth. The bill snapped its prey as did cameras, and the owl returned to its vigil from the hole.

Meanwhile, Linda had stationed herself about 20 feet from a different utility pole and was joined by another birder. Under far less candlepower, an Elf Owl emerged in the shadow and beams of a couple of 5-cell flashlights. The diminutive round head rotated first at its paparazzi of two, and then it fixed its gaze toward the dazzling scene near the spotlights. I joined Linda before the second owl disappeared where we congratulated each other without the aid of powerfully bright television lights. We crunched the gravel under our boots as we slowly crept to the first owl. The TV photographers, who had been standing on the roof of a cabin, eventually decided to call it quits. The owls, once their night vision returned, could go back to chortling and foraging for insects.

After the thrilling Elf Owl show, we jumped in the Birdmobile, headed down the canyon to Proctor Road, and parked in the pitch black. In minutes, we heard an Elf Owl calling, but could not locate it from the car. Neither of us was keen on walking since rattlesnakes might be around, and besides, we were satisfied with the two owls we had earlier observed. After an hour of listening and patrolling the road, we rounded up our enthusiasm and went home. The cool night and owling adventure whetted our appetites, so we raided our refrigerator for a snack while a ring-tailed cat boldly raided the hummingbird feeder on the back porch. Except for the lack of thumbs, this mammal was an expert at drinking the sugar water meant for hummingbirds. The fantastic night added a new life mammal for me. Linda had enjoyed them in earlier times, but I was, except for a week documenting 1980s off-road vehicle damage in the Mojave Desert, basically a southwestern virgin. By now, I was delightfully satisfied. Two Elf Owls were seen, and another heard! Linda and I were glowing.

5 May 2005

The alarm did not go off. With a preemptive motion, I turned it off in a semi-awake slumber and silently pulled on my shaken jeans. Even though I was just a southwestern novice, Linda earlier suggested I could help avoid pesky scorpions and spiders by the practice of a good morning jean shake. No potentially ambushing critters was a good way to start the day. Thoughts of owls, including a familiar Western Screech-Owl and a Whip-poor-will, heard last night rolled into the back of my brain while I concentrated on breakfast and packing a lunch. Not unlike the 1960s parts of the journey, I was always hungry. In fact, a doctor more or less ordered me to always have food with me. What an agreeable idea. With adequate provisions, including the traditional peanut butter sandwich and plenty of water, I slipped out the door. Linda decided to soak in the immediate surrounding tanagers and hummingbirds at a more civilized hour.

My goal was the hot climes below the canyon at Florida Wash. As most birders and those fluent in Spanish know, the word Florida is pronounced as Flow-REE-dah. It means full of flowers. Perhaps the wash was full of flowers when it was named, but on this day in May, the weather and roaming cattle did not suggest flowers. A Black-throated Sparrow was drinking from a small black rubber hose that dribbled water near the bank of the bone-dry creek bed. No flowers. I walked down a barbed wire fence to a stile, crossed, and meandered past mesquite and over newly passed and weathered cow patties to the wash. Song did not fill the cool morning air. Occasionally, a Bewick's Wren or Bell's Vireo called, but my targeted Rufous-winged and Botteri's sparrow were silent.

Black-throated Sparrows kept jumping into view, tantalizing me to alertness. A migrant Lincoln's Sparrow foraging at the top of the vertical bank surprised me, but the Black-throats were almost annoying. By now, so many of those sparrows had fooled me. Each one could be the target bird, but each one was not. Black-throated Sparrows had become the nemesis species du jour by repeatedly demanding attention while I was trying to find a different species. Even big red Northern Cardinals were nemesis species du jour on several dates along the coast of Texas. Cardinals were absent in Florida Wash, but there were a few Bewick's Wrens to remind me that they had once been nemesis species. By now, the sun warmed the wash and the cow patties that had not yet succumbed to complete biodegradation. A new nemesis species, the Full of Flowers Cow Patty Fly (FFCPF), was buzzing around. There was more than one FFCPF, and each step brought more to enter my air space. I returned to the stile in time to greet four older birders, who had found Rufous-winged Sparrows near Continental.

Across the road and down Florida Wash seemed a promising option. Although it was hotter now, the pesky flies were absent, as was the evidence from cattle. A few yards down the wash took me to a dirt road and the surprise of seeing a border patrol vehicle. The vehicle stopped. Eventually, I was within earshot when a patrol officer asked if I left the gate open. I replied that I was walking down the wash from the paved road and that I did not know anything about a gate. That seemed to be a satisfactory answer as the green and white vehicle roared out of sight. While recovering from yet another Black-throated Sparrow at the edge of the dirt track, I was interrupted by a red pickup grinding to a dusty stop. The driver and two passengers stared for a moment before one of them asked if I would close the gate on my way out. I told them I had just walked down the wash from the main road and did not have knowledge of a gate. Maybe I needed a T-shirt or a cardboard placard stating that I have no knowledge of a gate, which I did not leave open. At least my verbal answer seemed all right, and the pickup left, and at last, I was alone. Ten minutes passed as I sat on a rock munching on a peanut butter and orange marmalade sandwich. Not the eleventh hour, but at the eleventh minute of my recess, I heard the song Linda and I played over and over at the Amado roadside area. The Rufous-winged Sparrow sang long enough to trace it to its perch.

Slightly a mile up from Florida Wash was McCleary Wash. The sight and sound of Verdins filled the slopes along the trail to the overlook of the deep wash. Tall red blooming ocotillos waved in the hot wind gusts blowing down from Madera Canyon. A brief trek up the trail from the Proctor Road parking did not reveal any Montezuma Quail or Varied Bunting. It did reveal that Linda and I parked last night near utility poles that might have been in use by the Elf Owl we heard.

Back home, that is, back to Linda at Madera Kubo, I was greeted by her, Flame-colored Tanagers now visiting the feeder hanging at our back porch, and a Townsend's Warbler on its way to Oregon or possibly all the way to Alaska. We left this haven for a hike up Hopkins Fork, one of several trails accessed at the upper end of Madera Canyon Road. Our targeted bird was a chance meeting with a Sulphur-bellied Flycatcher. Several birders coming down the steep trail asked if we had seen any trogons. Most of them seemed surprised to learn that we found them easy to see near the inn. Of course, we asked about the flycatcher. No one had seen them. At around 6,500 feet, I saw only the flash of a rufous tail of a bird high above the trail. We never relocated or heard the bird. With our remaining daylight, we drove down Madera Canyon to Florida Wash to listen for an evening songfest of Botteri's Sparrows. Again, we were met with silence. Back to the little blue cottage, and after dinner, we sat on the back porch. A Western Screech-Owl called over the quiet murmur of the rocky creek. Our birding night ended hearing a Whiskered Screech-Owl and an oddly sounding Whip-poor-will.

6 May 2005

Packing the trusty Birdmobile after two glorious nights in Madera Canyon went at dawdling speed. We did not want to leave, and the calls of the male Flame-colored Tanager accentuated our regret. A Rivoli's Hummingbird flew within three feet of my face as I carried our ice chest to the car. Broad-billed Hummingbirds were at the back porch feeder, and a Dusky-capped Flycatcher snapped an insect from the shady canyon. Linda wrote in the visitors' log of the cabin how much we enjoyed the tanagers, other birds, and our appreciation of the comforts of the accommodations. We would have to come back someday.

A quick stop at the Santa Rita Lodge feeders revealed the usual suspects. Linda and I knew we were saying goodbye to witnessing a couple of missing species of hummingbirds, but we could not wait for them. Zipping passed Florida Wash and on to Continental, we bade adieu for our chances to see Botteri's Sparrow. Filling the gas tank at the brink of the interstate, we glanced back with fondness and looked forward to a hard drive to California.

Our itinerary had included the Arizona-Sonora Desert Museum and Kitt Peak, both places that Linda wanted to revisit, but we agreed to push onward. My 1963 itinerary included Organ Pipes National Monument, but the monument and its birds will have to wait some other year. Going west, we were on our last miles of Arizona highways.

∾

The Santa Rita Mountains and Madera Canyon was a favorite time while in Arizona. Later, in 2009, I revisited the mountains and the canyon, this time in July and this time when Sulphur-bellied Flycatchers were present. My first Sulphur-bellied Flycatchers were foraging in trees above the same blue cottage that Linda and I so enjoyed in 2005. Down Madera Canyon, Florida Wash to be exact, were Botteri's Sparrows, a Plain-capped Starthroat, and wren-like Rufous-capped Warblers. In 2015, Linda and I spent the winter in the Southwest, and much of it at Bog Springs not far from the blue cottage, and hiked up and down the mountain trails. Montezuma Quail, with young, strolled within feet from our parked RV. It is another story.

Madera Kubo B and B, where we stayed, cost $100 per night in 2005. Demand and inflation garner a nightly stay in 2021 to $160. I am not sure of the age of the fine cabins, but they are old enough for web-based reviewers to use the words "quaint" and "rustic." The Santa Rita Lodge, just downstream, was built in 1922. The B and B, the lodge, Bog Springs Campground, 9,453-foot Mount Wrightson, the washes, and much more of southeastern Arizona are under the purview of the Coronado National Forest.

The Paton's Hummingbird Haven at the edge of Patagonia has changed its name since 2005. At that time, proprietor Marion Paton attracted a wide array of birds for a cross-section of birders. She passed in 2009. The hummingbird mecca is now known as the Paton Center for Hummingbirds. By any name, the feeders did not exist during my proposed trip in the 1960s.

Name changes are not limited to localities. The wren-like warbler I mentioned not seeing in 2005 but finding in 2009 and 2015 in Florida Wash is now known as Rufous-capped Warbler. Wait. The Arizona birds are taxonomically a different species than what ornithologists once called Rufous-capped Warblers in Panama. What is going on is that the keepers of the North American checklist now treat the warblers as two species. However, even though there are two species, the keeper people decided to use the name Rufous-capped for one of the species even though the taxonomic split requires a different scientific binomial or specific name. Yes, this is confusing, and I am trying to hold my reins in on something that should not be confusing. As a taxonomist and otherwise mostly normal person, it is beyond me that the keepers of the checklist did not provide a new English name for the new entity. Of course, the warbler problem is not as serious as splitting birds formerly known as Winter Wrens into Pacific Wren and, you guessed it, Winter Wren. Put another way, if "C" is subdivided into two units, neither unit can be called "C." What is left is units "A" and "B." However, the keepers of the list really leave us with a quote from the movie *Cool Hand Luke*, which is, "Whut we have hea is a failya to communicate." Oh, that odd-sounding Whip-poor-will Linda and I heard in Madera Canyon is a different species. Fortunately, when the checklist people made the split official, they rightfully changed the name of the species of eastern North America as Eastern Whip-poor-will and the southwestern species as Mexican Whip-poor-will.

Madera Canyon and the Santa Rita Mountains were our favorite locations in Arizona, not just for the birds but for the panorama, the people lucky to live there, the clean air, and more reasons beyond description. We missed the region the moment we drove away. Later, that same year, we were especially sad and worried about a wildfire that threatened to burn our paradise. There were closures, evacuations, and uncertainty. Linda and I held our breath while monitoring the dire situation from our home perch in Oregon. On 7 July, the fire was 100 percent contained. Determined as caused by lightning striking Florida Peak, the wildfire burned 23,183 acres. Fortunately, about 80 percent of the area burned was deemed by the Forest Service as being low severity, meaning most plants survived to live another day. The fire never reached down into the canyon. What a relief. Visits to the canyon and surrounding mountain trails in 2009 and 2015 revealed good health, with plenty of birds everywhere.

Perhaps more famous than Madera Canyon is Patagonia Lake State Park. Linda and I were aware of the famous Nutting's Flycatcher seen there by fortunate birders in 1997. Our 2005 itinerary included the park. At that time, statements or even rumors of the rare bird would have drawn us there beyond our brief visit. However, Nutting's Flycatchers were then south of the border. By 2015, Linda and I had read *The Big Year* and watched the 2011 movie of the same name that depicted the excitement of finding the flycatcher.[1] Although it was winter in 2015, we did visit the state park and

---

1. Mark Obmascik. *The Big Year: A Tale of Man, Nature, and Fowl Obsession*. (New York: Simon and Schuster, 2004).

walked the trails. Sometimes, there is a smidgen of pleasure being at a location where a rare bird once occurred. Sometimes.

Chapter 28

Oh, Those California Birds

THE DRIVE TO CALIFORNIA was difficult. On the way were saguaro, sand, and birds out there, beyond the pavement of our road, birds that we missed at previous localities. It was hard knowing we were so close to a few species that might be not that far away but were too far for the time allotted for us to be elsewhere, such as somewhere we might find new and different target species in California. A LeConte's Thrasher might be skulking in the desert bushes, perhaps a Black-chinned Sparrow on a faraway hillside, or maybe a . . . No, we told ourselves. It was time to stop lamenting about what we might have seen in Arizona, start dreaming about the great birds to see in California, and, for the benefit of our immediate future, watch the road. We were on I-8, the interstate that funnels gas and diesel-powered engines ferrying people and cargo back and forth from Arizona and beyond to San Diego, California.

Yuma was our last locality in Arizona. My previous remembrance of being in Yuma was while still licking my wounds of disappointment from prematurely ending my big birding tour of the country. It was late March 1963 when arriving on a Greyhound bus for a rest stop, and it was exceedingly hot that day as I stepped into the oven-baked air. I was wearing a western-style shirt, brand new cowboy boots, and a straw western hat that my favorite uncle gave me. Who knew that the sunburst design on my boots was like the logo of my future alma mater, the logo adopted by the Smithsonian Institution? In the 1960s trip, I had traveled hatless, mostly laced-up boots, jeans, and T-shirts. I had suffered a bad case of self-pity when I knew the trip was over, and, feeling sorry for myself and with little thought, I decided to change my appearance. Pretty silly, but it seemed to work. The comfortable boots, sans several new heels and half-soles over the years, got me through college and beyond. They now reside in the back of my closet but receive a dusting and polishing now and then. As luck would have it, during the bus trip back to Oregon while wearing my boots, my trip list grew with window sightings of Prairie Falcon and Yellow-billed Magpie.

Another recollection of Yuma was years later when collaborating with my friend and mentor Richard Banks on the taxonomy of Clapper Rails. I spent hours meticulously preparing specimens collected from the brackish marshes along the Colorado River. I was relearning how to prepare study skins, and Roxie Laybourne was determined to teach me her way. Joining what she called her skinning class was a learning experience and badge of courage. When I, or any of the students, made mistakes, she would frequently and loudly announce the error, snatch up someone's unfinished specimen, and show everyone how it should look. Despite everything, everyone loved her for her decades of teaching and friendship.

The lower Colorado and parts of the Imperial Valley had fostered a distinct subspecies Clapper Rail known since 1923 as *Rallus longirostris yumanensis*, but the region has rates of extinction and endangerment of wildlife that is higher than anywhere on the continent. It seems little to nothing will halt habitat degradation of the lower Colorado. There is certainly considerable talk about the subject, but it was much cheaper to determine the taxonomic status of the rails, which was to have a few ornithologists decide if the birds recognized under the name *yumanensis* deserve a subspecies name. That is, are the rails nomenclaturally unique? Science was required to prove, again, that the subspecies should be recognized under the name *yumanensis*. It is tough being a water bird in a region warring over the politics of water let alone going through an ornithological identity crisis.

Linda and I did not stop to look for rails by any name and traveled west on the interstate through the southern end of the Imperial Sand Dunes Bureau of Land Management Recreation and Wilderness Area. It took a while to realize that it was hard to read nine words, not counting the "of" and "and" on the sign on the road when traveling 80 miles per hour. Too many words, to paraphrase a critique of Mozart's music having too many notes. The mountains of sand, also known as the Algodones Dunes, sometimes rise as high as 300 feet, average five miles wide, and extend 40 miles along the eastern edge of the Imperial Valley. Critics will wonder why the dunes "sometimes" rise as high as 300 feet. That is because dunes shift, ebb and flow as the sand is blown by the wind and spun into the area to be reshaped by recreationists. Yes, the BLM permits off-road vehicle drivers to play in a large part of the giant 118,000-acre sandbox. A lawsuit produced the closure of 48,000 acres of the vast dunes to protect an endangered plant, a species of locoweed. I wondered how many plants and animals were ground to smithereens after my colleagues and I helped study damage of off-road vehicles in the Mojave decades ago.

Strong blasts of wind blew the sand and us from side to side, as we pretended to be motoring across the Sahara. In several more westward miles, we slumped into El Centro for a welcome respite.

7 May 2005

Deep, 12-hour, and restful sleep readied us for a big day. We had lots of ground to cover before San Diego. Leaving our El Centro motel, we traveled east, picked up Highway 111, drove north to Calipatria, and west out of town. At the corner of Sperry and Eddins Roads, just as Guy McCaskie told me, we found Ruddy Ground-Doves. I had earlier bumped into Guy a couple of times at meetings as I recall. He is the go-to person for things of the Salton Sea. Guy was one of three who authored the definitive treatment of the bird of the Salton Sea.[1]

We hurried back to Calipatria, partly to beat the clock and rising temperature and partly to find a restroom. Water is scarce in Calipatria and finding a used coffee department was becoming desperate. A woman in a laundromat told Linda, in broken English, that she was welcome at her house. The kindness of strangers is often surprising. Declining the offer, we located a crowded store where relief was in sight. That is, it was possible to find privacy behind a closed restroom door. Where is a bush when you need one? Certainly not near the Salton Sea.

Sonny Bono Salton Sea NWR headquarters was closed. Our wished species there were Clark's and Western grebes. During the sixties trip I saw plenty of *Aechmophorus* grebes, then under the singular name, Western Grebe. Because I could not be certain which species I saw during my 1962 journey across North America, I needed to see these birds again. We looked toward the lake, but if there was a grebe out there, I could not say. The water seemed miles away.

In 1963, I would have visited Salton Sea NWR. Sonny Bono's name was added to the name of the refuge in 1998, in recognition of his efforts to save the Salton Sea. The lake, accidentally began in 1905, has no outlet, and by 1960, salinity was increasing. I would have taken a swim in 1963 and bobbed like a cork. I survived a dunking in polluted Lake Erie, but now, in the twenty-first century, I would hesitate even wading in the Salton Sea. I imagined the sea crawling with invisible bacteria courting with the original

---

1. Michael Patten et al. *Birds of the Salton Sea: Status, Biogeography, and Ecology.* (University of California Press, 2003).

primordial soup that eventually spawned us all. The salinity of the aptly named Salton Sea is now 25 percent greater than that of the Pacific and increasing. The sea is still less salty than the Great Salt Lake. Soon it will be possible to walk on the troubled water. The shallow Salton Sea, about 228 feet below sea level, receives water drained from farms and hydrated cow patties beyond my taste. Perhaps there is a better word than "taste." The 500,000-acre watershed has its ups and downs and in 1996 at least 13,400 fish-eating birds died from avian botulism. This is a continuing problem. Low water levels, climate change, and invasive species help the deadly bacterium. Presently there are plans to, and I quote, "restore" the lake. Meanwhile, thousands of people visit the stinky lake for boating, fishing, water-skiing, and, of course, birding.

The Sonny Bono Salton Sea NWR was established in 1930 and offers prime birding localities. The refuge is ridiculously tiny compared to the sea. Sources provide differing values for the number of miles of shoreline of the entire Salton Sea, probably because the sea is shrinking. One common value is 110 miles of shoreline. Currently the sea occupies 245,000 acres while the fragmented refuge occupies 37,900 acres, including three regions on the southern and southeastern shoreline and a larger area of sea.

Linda and I were still looking for grebes and banking on a slim chance to find a disoriented Yellow-footed Gull or Blue-footed Booby. Our timing could not have been more imperfect; we were too early for most of our target species. We did find a few species new to our travels: sentinel Burrowing Owls stood along weedy edges of fields, and a handful of Gull-billed Terns were among several louder Caspian Terns. Not willing to give up on the grebes, we drove to the road's end at Obsidian Cove. Barren, hot, and almost unearthly, Obsidian Cove was a place to melt away sunscreen. The one positive aspect of the visit was when we drove back to the main road. Halfway there, we met a car. Our respective windows powered down enough for me to recognize that the driver was Guy McCaskie. A few months earlier, when we talked on the phone, he said to call when we were in the region of the Salton Sea. However, no phoning was necessary today at the edge of the salty water, and no unusual birds were reported by the sage and pioneer of modern California birding. We thanked him for the doves near Calipatria and asked about grebes. He saw them in a pond, but it was too far east for our schedule.

Linda and I were getting hotter by the minute, said goodbye to Guy, and negotiated our way south, then west, to Poe Road at the lonely south end of Salton Sea. A section of the refuge is west of the road. This southern section was where we decided to eat lunch, and it was where, for the first time today, we were rewarded by 100 percent of the infamous foul odor of the lake. Linda took it quite well. Lunch was okay, despite the smell. Birding was not good, but we tried to get closer to a flock of Western Sandpipers foraging in the simmering distance. Maybe other shorebirds were out there. Somehow, we managed to get too far into shorebird territory and sunk a couple of inches into a gray and stinking mud that only a dog would love to roll in. Luckily, we were not stuck. The sun quickly baked the gray ooze to a crust that we scraped off our boots. A nearby Horned Lark erupted into song as we pulled away from our last attempt to bird the Salton Sea.

During our whistle stops in the Salton Sea region, we checked off a paltry 32 species out of 384. A refuge checklist I would have used in 1963 included only 239 species. My arrival would have also been in May. If I had then seen an *Aechmophorus* grebe, it would have been counted as a Western Grebe. Finding the two species of these grebes now would have to wait until we reached the Pacific, and that was very soon.

To reach the Pacific Ocean, we needed to traverse most of the southern breath of California. Anza-Borrego State Park on the way offered a chance to see a LeConte's Thrasher. The park, its 600,000 acres making it larger than several national parks, was daunting, beautiful, and windy. Our attempts to find our target species at three separate places came up thrasherless. About 30 minutes of searching for Lawrence's Goldfinches at Tamarisk Grove was fruitless. We headed west, leaving Yaqui Pass Road, straddled California 78, crossed Lizard Wash and Plum Canyon, and onward through beautiful green mountains and misty rain to Julian, a small remnant of a mining town. Julian, our destination for the night, sits at about 4,200 feet in elevation and 50 miles from San Diego.

We steered to our destination by first pointing south, traversing part of the Cedar Fire, the largest in the history of California. Fires generally are named for geographic point of origin; in this case, the inferno began near Cedar Creek Falls in October 2003. Before the fire was out, 280,278 acres burned, and 2,820 buildings, including homes, were destroyed. Remarkably, a hunter, who claimed to have started the fire because he was lost, faces only 10 years in prison and a $500,000 fine for a blaze costing $400 million in damages and 15 lives. In silence, we continued south through the funeral of blackened snags, gutted canyons, and parks, skeletal buildings, and dream homes turned to black charcoal and death-gray ash. The western shore of Cuyamaca Lake lay in cold heavy moisture hovering between fog and clouds. Wildflowers filled the bare ground with yellows and reds among the emerging green grass as in memoriam to nearby Cuyamaca, a town that disappeared in the fire. It would take decades before the landscape would look anything but burned to hell. Most everything, including the trees, would remain but a memory.

OH, THOSE CALIFORNIA BIRDS

Merging on I-8 was almost a welcome scene. We stopped for gas at Alpine, a hamlet of around 14,000 and surrounded by the burned Cleveland National Forest. The proprietor at the gas station related his fear when the fire threatened to burn the city. Not far beyond lay the metropolis of San Diego. I had not been there since 1967. Not wanting to be an officer, I first spent an inglorious time at boot camp and later attended a school to learn navigation. Typically, and contrary to any promises, I did not see the world. My navigation skills did come to use for commuting in the inner sanctum of the Pentagon. In 1967, I did manage weekend birding in San Diego region once I completed my boot camp sentence. Birding near the end of the commuter bus line for part of the city routes brought me my first California Thrasher and Black-chinned Hummingbird. California Gnatcatcher was a subspecies of Blue-gray Gnatcatcher then and thus was not on my radar. Tomorrow California Gnatcatchers will be a trophy species.

Linda and Ralph, happy in San Diego.

It was late, but our reservation for a motel held our room at the south end of San Diego. Our trip list stood at only 337. We had about a week of West Coast birding to drive up our total. Tomorrow will be our first full day driving in legendary Southern California traffic. Thus far, it was beginning to measure up to expectations of dread.

8 May 2005

Phil Unitt had given me detailed instructions for finding Elegant Terns and California Gnatcatchers. Phil had also provided me superb editorial advice on papers I wrote for *Western Birds*, the journal he edits for the Western Field Ornithologists. We once authored separate articles published a few years apart, what we science folk call papers, on Willow Flycatchers. I recognized a subspecies he did not but that never frayed our relationship. Such is science and scientist, most of the time. Once I provided data showing why a subspecies that Allan Phillips named was not recognizable. In his later works, he followed my taxonomy, even proposed the name *browningi* for a subspecies of vireo, and we remained friends to the end. Secretary of Smithsonian Dillon Ripley once made a mistake in naming a southeastern Asian kingfisher. While curating the collection of specimens in the kingfisher family, I discovered the error and informed Mr. Ripley. He corrected the oversight and, to my surprise, named a subspecies of kingfisher *browningi*. However, there may be genuine and public differences among ornithologists and birders. Two that come to mind concern investigative methods in the Canadian Archipelago on Thayer's and other gulls and controversies surrounding recent Ivory-billed Woodpecker observations. Most of the time, we taxonomists get along famously or at least attempt to bury any exceptionally rare hatchets.

Not far down the road from our motel, Phil Unitt emailed, we would see Elegant Terns. Not unlike my fantasy of Spotted Owls dripping from the trees in Scheelite Canyon, I had envisioned a chaotic swirling jumble of Elegant Terns churning the overhead sky. Instead, after driving down a residential street, we parked, looked north toward the city, and saw nothing. Minutes ticked as Mother's Day revelers walked, cycled, and skateboarded along the trail between houses and marsh at the south end of South San Diego Bay. As a couple with children chortled by, I heard a raspy sound scratching the sky. A Caspian Tern raced in and out of view, but it was followed by a smaller and gentler call of our first Elegant Tern. The endangered Elegant Terns nest on protected dikes in the bay and breed only at four other sites in Southern California and northwestern Mexico. According to the Audubon Society, most of the population, 90 percent to 97 percent, breed on Isla Mira, Mexico. The terns there are unprotected from egg harvesters, guano mining, and other disruptive human activities. We were glad that the Elegant Terns we saw today had a chance of mothering their chicks.

Before leaving our vantage point, we found a Savannah Sparrow. Of course, we had seen Savannah Sparrows during the journey, but the sparrow in front of us looked different. It was not a typical Savannah Sparrow. It had a large bill, plain unmarked back, and was late for a very important date, the time it should be breeding in northwestern Mexico. The sparrow, 20 feet away, was either a distinct subspecies or a species. Missing was the familiarly thin *sip* or *seep* call of typical Savannah Sparrows. What we heard sounded like *zink*, ironically as if calling out the last name of Bob Zink, who with three other investigators presented mitochondrial DNA evidence showing the bird to be genetically distinct from other Savannah Sparrows. That was in 1991. If specifically distinct from other relatives, the bird would probably be known as Large-billed Sparrow, but today the jury or the committee is still out.

We left the Elegant Terns, stilts, a singing Marsh Wren, and the odd Savannah Sparrow before driving along the Silver Strand, sandy land between the bay and the Pacific Ocean. Weekenders were everywhere and we lamented that our itinerary did not consider crowds of people during weekends and holidays. We kept going and soon crossed the almost two-mile-long Coronado Bay Bridge. I liked bridges in the 1960s and like them today. However, in the twenty-first century, my tolerance for heights was not forgiving. This bridge, built in 1969, had guardrails only 34 inches high, which was low enough to see water 200 feet below. My palms were sweaty. What happened between the virtual fearlessness where I experienced literal, not literary, cliffhangers? Hopefully, a bird would not fly by during the crossing. If one did, I would have to look, or would I?

At last, across the frightful bridge, we followed directions in our birding guide to the San Diego River and Shelter Island near the entrance of the bay. People far outnumbered any birds we saw, and parking was almost impossible. Nonetheless, we quickly picked up Western, California, and Heerman's gulls. Going south to Point Loma seemed pointless. What right-minded shorebird would be sharing the sand with so many humans?

Hoping for a Pacific pelagic.

Linda and I circled back to northbound I-5 and exited at La Jolla. I had birded the area during my Navy days, but for fear of theft from my fellow bunkmates, my birding was without the benefit of optics. Today, I was well-armed with a scope and binoculars, but the ocean sky was empty, and the beaches clear of birds. Farther up the beach, we witnessed hundreds of hang gliders jumping from the cliff and sailing up and down the ocean shore. We expected to see a mid-air collision. I scoped the horizon from the cliff-top for an avian glimmer, but the view was interrupted by colorful gliders passing by. The wide flat beach below was heaving with unleashed dogs, bikinis, bare feet, and surfboarders coming and going with the cool waves. A disheveled man stomped from a pickup camper at the cliff-top parking lot, ranted and cursed at the noisy throng of people and cars milling over his domain. Only yards away, a dark California Thrasher popped up, possibly to check out the racket. The thrasher, gulls, and other birds must have noticed the human activity. Were they dismayed by the loss of peace that was replaced by clamoring humans and dogs, some of them flying on hang gliders, or is that a question verging on an anthropomorphic scale, or might it be simply equated as fear? Was that fear too great to forage, to mark territory with song, a fear to not breed, abandon a nest full of hungry juveniles? When we were about to leave, eight to ten Black Swifts flew south along the cliff. In an instant, the swifts disappeared, the man continued to gesture at the inflow of vehicles, and Linda and I departed.

California Gnatcatchers were a target species at San Elijo Lagoon Ecological Reserve, a California Department of Fish and Game sanctuary of 885 acres protecting fresh and salt marshes, riparian and coastal scrub, and open water. More than 90 percent of coastal wetlands in California have been destroyed since 1850. Destruction of wetlands and other habitats greatly accelerated in the 1970s and 1980s when the California population grew twice as fast as that of the rest of the country. San Diego has gone from the round figure of 573,000 people in 1960 to 1,223,000 in 2000. Not far to the north, Los Angeles proper grew by only a million in the same period. Only a million? The LA metropolitan area, hundreds of square miles, is now occupied by over 12 million humans. Add up the outdoor cats and unleashed dogs, and there is little room for birds.

We were grateful that the San Elijo Lagoon is protected from urban blight and hopeful that we would find California Gnatcatchers. We hiked from a parking area adjacent to expensive-looking houses down into the reserve. The trail descended a steep hillside to the gentler slopes of the west basin of the lagoon. The habitat looked perfect for California Gnatcatchers, and a uniformed warden walking back up the trail told us she had heard them today. We hiked, listened, hiked, and searched to no avail. Our San Elijo list included our first Wrentit for the trip, but no gnatcatchers yet. Bushtits kept us alert to the point of being annoying. They became the nemesis species on this hunt. A small flock of Scaly-breasted Munia, a cage bird escapee, stopped in some local brush long enough for identification.

Our last-minute chance to find California Gnatcatchers came from what the warden told us as she was walking away. "They're near the office across the lagoon." Getting across the lagoon meant getting back on I-5. We did the quarter-mile to the next exit in record time. In 15 minutes, the office gate would be locked. The path near the office split. Linda struck out to the right; I took the lower trail around a set of bushes. Linda, in classic fashion, spotted the quarry, or at least I thought so by her anxious if not demanding come-hither gestures. A small, dark gnatcatcher flicked its wings, and, in a split second, it was out of sight. Linda and I continued searching, and I soon was afforded a full California Gnatcatcher vista.

Onward and northward, we were pushed forward by the evening traffic toward the enormity of the Los Angeles sprawl. We left the madding crowd, ignoble or not, for a peaceful night in Temecula. Our modern motel was within earshot of the interstate that throbbed for hours as if a giant artery with vehicular-sized cells ground down a cholesterol choked tube.

9 May 2005

We waited for the Monday morning rush hour vehicles to flush from the scene before embarking on our ride to La Cañada Flintridge north of Los Angeles. Unfortunately, getting there meant taking three different interstates, hundreds of exits not to take, thousands of drivers to avoid, and millions of frazzled nerves to keep in check. I could hear Johnny Carson giving directions to the fork in the road. Linda warned, "We better not be going to downtown LA!" I could not agree more. If there was a bird along the way, we did not dare to see it. Miraculously, we kept up with the 70 to 80 mile per hour flow and turned north on California Highway 2 to the San Gabriel Mountains.

The first time I saw the lofty San Gabriel Mountains was in 1953 at age seven when I barely knew the difference between a sparrow and a dove, but the mountains had a power about them even then. I saw them again in the late 1960s during my Navy daze; I bused up from San Diego to see Everett Dirksen in the Rose Parade. Of course, I saw the San Gabriel Mountains on the weekly episodes of *LA Law*, but I did not see the range today.

When it might have been possible, I did not dare today to risk a glance at the mountains shrouded in clouds. Soon, we were in them, driving up the winding two-lane path in visibility less than perfect. A dump truck was blocking the road just north of La Cañada Flintridge. The driver sat motionlessly. I got out, fearing that the road was closed, but hoping that the problem was a momentary delay. I was told it would be a few minutes and returned to the car to wait. A fine mist had begun to drift down with the cool mountain air. Finally, the trucker motioned us around his vehicle, and in less than a mile, we had ascended from the inferno into alpine air and green trees.

Leaving the main road, we turned down a steep paved lane to Switzer Picnic Area at 3,300 feet in an oak, alder, and sycamore canyon, where the mist evolved to cold and steady rain. Our first Oak Titmouse for the trip called over the water falling from the sky and down the narrow rocky creek. Of course, the Oak Titmouse of today was the Plain Titmouse of the 1960s. Regardless of its taxonomy, and do not get me started, that is a species I should have found in 1962 but I was then too anxiously in a hurry to go east. In today's mountain mist, Dark-eyed Juncos pecked at something on the only dry ground under the umbrella of a leafy sycamore. Hiking the trail from Red Box Station might have helped fill in a gap or two, but the fog, cold drizzle, and time, really our greatest nemesis, imposed us to move on. We passed Charlton Flats and slowly meandered to Chilao Visitors Center. At 5,200 feet, the air was cool, and it had stopped raining. The center was closed. We had the place to ourselves, ate lunch, and searched the area for birds. Red Crossbills, possibly 10, paraded from one tree to another. We had read that White-headed Woodpeckers were easy to find at the centers' feeders, but the feeders were picked clean. An *Empidonax* flycatcher stopped on its way into the fog long enough for a glimpse but not long enough to sing.

We could have driven up the mountain highway to the snow, but the dark weather persuaded us to start our return toward Los Angeles. A stop at Charlton Flat Picnic Area held promise, but when we pulled into the deserted parking lot a thick bank of fog began to cloak the area. A loud and hard tapping broke the silence. We followed the sound into the fog-shrouded branches of a conifer a mere 20 feet above our peering eyes. Visibility at first revealed only size. Color and pattern were impossible to discern until a weak breeze swirled the translucent fog to reveal a White-headed Woodpecker. Then, ever so quiet tapping on a different limb drew our attention to a different woodpecker. By straining, wiping, and re-wiping the condensation from our binoculars, we could see the second bird was a White-headed Woodpecker and that the two were male and female. Linda and I strolled around the picnic area, enjoying the solitude. Our time in the San Gabriel Mountains was almost devoid of people. We noticed only six cars and four rangers during our journey in the San Gabriel Mountains. On our descent, the cool, quiet, and clean air became less and less foggy, the tires once singing on the wet pavement sounded dry again, and an acceleration lane took us back to millions of people careening down the multitude of highways.

Ventura was just ahead, but we had entered dreaded rush-hour traffic. I called up all my best rush-hour moves I had learned repeatedly during the days treading the pavement from the museum in Washington, DC, to home in Arlington, Virginia. A gull, a starling, and a crow drifted in and out of my peripheral vision as I kept vigil on bumpers, signal lights and lack thereof, road signs, and the exit lane to Ventura and US 101, the highway of the Pacific coast from Southern California to northern Washington. Time before sunset allowed us to locate where tomorrow's adventure will begin and a restful motel for our night.

10 May 2005

After an early microwaved breakfast, we headed south of the harbor and Island Packers for transport to Santa Cruz Island. We accidentally passed the entrance to the harbor and had to back-track and were worried about being late. Luckily, there was ample time before joining the crowd on the 60-plus-foot catamaran that would ferry us to the largest of the five main islands in the 249,353-acre Channel Islands National Park. The park, first administered as a national monument in 1938 and as a national park in 1980, did not include Santa Cruz Island, which was then privately owned from 1839 to 1985.

There were four groups of people on the 20-mile journey to Santa Cruz Island. First was a cheerful group of the crew working to keep everyone happy and safe. The second group was a small gathering of women docents working for The Nature Conservancy, who would be spending the night on the island. The third group was a larger group of a mix of excited women and men tourists from Poland. The fourth group was Linda and I, the only birders on the trip. Although the crew was not laden with binoculars and field guides, Linda and I were glad they were bird savvy. Dave, one of the crew, called out the few seabirds as we came to them once we were over deeper water. Sooty and Pink-footed shearwaters glided low over the waves on stiff narrow wings, occasionally dipping into the water and drifting away at our approach. Dave identified a tight flock of Red-necked Phalaropes rocketing north. Later, another flock was close enough for me to identify individual birds. Alcids splashed from the surface and, with stubby wings, whirred away. Dave called them out, but I was not comfortable about names until the second group we encountered. Cassin's Auklets were familiar birds, a species seen in the mid-1960s when Bill English, a classmate, and I surveyed birds breeding on coastal islands of Oregon. The white-throated Scripp's Murrelet was a life bird.

Whitecaps and the boat bouncing and pounding the water also punctuated the brisk ride across the channel. Linda and I were determined to stay out on the deck and stood sideways, with one foot well ahead of the other on the port side adjacent to the wheelhouse. The up and down motion required one hand on the rail, and the birds required one hand on the binoculars. The method of not going sailing into the air or hitting the deck was similar to riding a bucking horse while wearing binoculars. About every fourth or fifth trough and wave were large enough to smack the bottom of the boat loudly and then send water over the bow. Most of the time, the shelter from the wheelhouse prevented the cold water from drenching our enthusiasm.

Santa Cruz Island is 24 miles long and about six miles wide, or, as the Park Service equates, it is nearly three times larger than Manhattan. The Nature Conservancy owns 46,000 acres; the Park Service administers the remainder of the 60,645-acre island. Although we were on the island to see the Island Scrub-Jay, we kept our eye out for any of the four endemic mammals. The island has 1,000 species of plants, with varying habitats from sea level to its 2,400-foot summit. There is geologic and archaeologic wealth ranging from igneous and sedimentary rocks and evidence of natives dating from 10,000 years ago. Adobe ranch houses date from the 1900s. Early privatization, mainly involving sheep, cattle, and wine left the island with introduced plants, feral pigs, and sheep. The pigs rooted up and ate almost anything, thus reducing foliage cover for native animals, including the tiny domestic cat-sized fox. The pigs attracted Golden Eagles that now forage on the pigs and the foxes. There are ongoing efforts to root out and eradicate the pigs.

The first stop on Santa Cruz Island was at Scorpion Cove in the eastern part of the national park. The Polish contingent went ashore at the cove. The rest of us cruised about eight miles west to Prisoners' Cove at the boundary between the park and Nature Conservancy properties. While the crew unloaded the docents' overnight luggage and huge ice chests, Linda and I walked to the end of the dock. We were soon joined by Katey, a crew member, who gave us directions to the trail to Pelican Bay. She informed us that jays were seen from the trail. However, we did not need to go farther than a few yards from the dock. Before we could walk past the restrooms, we saw the birds. The Island Scrub-Jay, a large and deep blue counterpart to the California Scrub-Jay on the mainland, were tame beautiful beggars. The voice of Island Scrub-Jay is hoarse. We found more jays in a wooded canyon about halfway to Pelican Bay, but these birds were more secretive. We looked for other species with breeding ranges confined to the islands of southwestern California including a subspecies of Horned Lark appropriately carrying the trinomial or subspecific name *insularis* and a subspecies of Loggerhead Shrike, Rufous-crowned, and Song sparrows. Even a subspecies of California Quail unique to the Channel Islands was introduced to Santa Cruz. Three subspecies of Bewick's Wrens breed on the southwestern islands, possibly including one on Santa Cruz Island. Of the other subspecies of the wren, one is now extinct, and the other, along with the Santa Cruz subspecies, may be recognizable. That is, in a study by Amadeo Rea published in Allan Phillips's volume one of *Known Birds* in 1986, the specimens of the two subspecies appeared like a mainland subspecies. Although Orange-crowned Warbler, Spotted Towhee, and House Finch are represented by subspecies breeding in the Channel Islands, the subspecies of the three species breeding on Santa Cruz Island also breed on the mainland.

The Island Scrub-Jay is presently the only species with a breeding range limited exclusively to the southwestern California Islands, where it is found only on Santa Cruz Island. Birds entering our field notes during our hike to Pelican Bay as Pacific-slope Flycatcher may be the next island species. It differs genetically and I thought it sounded different from the mainland birds. Those birds are among many that made my taxonomic senses tingle. Can we add Channel Islands Flycatcher? Maybe another day.

We hiked toward Pelican Bay until it seemed there would not be enough time to be at the pier for the trip back to Ventura Harbor. A hummingbird was buzzing in and out of our minds. Following Katey's suggestion that Allen's Hummingbirds should be near the trailhead, we found a few struggling agaves and waited. Leaning up against a fence in the shade of a eucalyptus made a comfortable hide. By the time the docents started to come down the steep trail, a hummingbird darted around the dried flowers of the agave. It steered to and fro with a rufous tail, flashed a brilliant orange-red throat, and identified itself with its shining green back. Trip hummingbird number 13 was also trip species number 374.

Back at the pier, we waited as the Park Service staff unloaded more equipment from the boat. That gave us time to get our notes written and have a much-needed water, peanut butter, and cheese snack. Linda and I waved goodbye to the docents and boarded as the sole passengers of the cruise until we picked up the Polish tour group at Scorpion Cove. They boarded quietly, looking tired and ready to depart. Linda and I probably also looked tired but were not so anxious to return to the mainland.

We were anticipating what might be our next species of bird. The question was answered by a pair of Surf Scoters, number 375, that swam a few yards from the shore. A tailwind reduced our travel time back to the mainland. On the return, Linda and I stood on the deck in the blustery wind of the afternoon sun. We hoped for a new species. Hanging on was not difficult during the smoother ride east, which allowed a few jerky looks at more Scripp's Auklets and shearwaters. During the slowed approach as we entered the harbor, I spotted a few Surfbirds foraging. They were number 376.

Linda and I waited for the boat to dock and admired each other's wind and sunburned faces. We smiled, thanked the crew, and climbed up the pier to our waiting vehicle. The western sun was behind Santa Cruz Island. As with most places we had been, we missed being there the minute we left.

Birding often brings surprises. The surprise at the Salton Sea was our chance meeting with venerable Guy McCaskie coming in second to the sea itself. He continues to conduct weekly field trips to the Salton Sea. Each visit includes the number of individuals of every species he finds. He has amassed almost 15 years of such data, which clearly documents the rapid crash of habitat and bird populations. I have little personal experience with the birds of the Salton Sea, but anecdotally, there seemed to be fewer birds seen during a 2009 visit and even fewer in 2015. Efforts to save valuable habitat is mired with the politics of what exactly needs to happen and money to implement changes. Additionally, chronic drought and climate change are severe impediments to any progress toward saving the region. Should the sea dry up, it will not blow away, but what is left will be a dehydrated toxic mixture enough to endanger human populations dotted in the region.

Among the waterbirds that will lose their Salton Sea habitat will be rails. Presently, one of the best places to see what we once dubbed a unique subspecies of Clapper Rail is the southern end of the Salton. The split rails now include the east coastal species still called Clapper Rail and the new western species, Ridgway's Rail. Linda and I checked off both species in our year-long journey in 2015.

A surprise in San Diego was what appeared to be a Large-billed Savannah Sparrow, a bird I had seen back in the late 1960s while serving in the Navy. By then, I had looked into the subspecies of Savannah Sparrows but not nearly enough to contemplate a serious taxonomic study. The surprise sparrow that May day should not have been there. Philip Unitt emailed me later that nonbreeding Large-bills occur in San Diego from 8 August to 10 March. Our bird obviously had not read the book. Unfortunately, taking a picture for proof was not possible, and no one was around to confirm our unusual sighting. Could the bird have been a subspecies other than the large-billed bird? During my museum days, I was always reluctant to believe sight records of subspecies. However, *rostratus*, the scientific name of the large-billed birds, differs sufficiently from the other subspecies to permit relatively easy field identifications. Nonetheless, studying thousands of specimens of different species has taught me that individual variation may make some field identifications impossible.

Years ago, at the museum, John du Pont, who at the time was a bird enthusiast, and I laughed at the suggestion of sorting out the taxonomy of the subspecies of Savannah Sparrows. Neither one of us wanted to wrestle with such a task. The question remains, Did Linda and I see an unseasonable Large-billed Savannah Sparrow or an extreme version of a different subspecies? The sparrow certainly resembled birds I witnessed during the 1967 Navy winter in San Diego. There are a few of us bird people who believe there is more than one species of Savannah Sparrow. For now, the large-billed bird is on the escrow list of birds that could be added to the life list of species. Why wait? Well, I follow the AOS Check-list Committee's presently conservative treatment of North American birds. Perhaps someone will publish a paper someday that will offer information to convince the committee to recognize more than one species within the Savannah Sparrow complex. It will not be me, but I cheer the person who might do the deed.

Those introduced Scaly-breasted Munia that barely got our attention while searching for California Gnatcatchers were regarded as an established species and officially became countable birds in 2013. Though there are several species of introduced birds in southwestern California, we did not try to find any of them. Some have become established breeding birds but qualifying under the criteria for an introduced species to be deemed as established is a long process. The ABA accepts local and state bird committee decisions on establishment, and California's reputation for accepting information that might lead to a consideration of establishment appears to favor listing natural occurring avifauna versus established non-native species. For example, the lack of accepting the growing Bakersfield population of Rose-ringed Parakeet illustrates the reluctance of Californians to recognize that some introduced species sometimes become part of the ecology of local avifauna. Like it or not, it appears the Bakersfield parakeets will eventually be regarded as established there.

Sure, introduced species of birds may not be as desirable as seeing a Carolina Parakeet, a species dead at least partly at the hand of man, but most ecological disasters are not caused by introduced birds. Some disruptions of ecology are human induced while fewer are naturally caused. The worst ecological disasters in California are wildfires, which usually are the result of human behavior and lightning. Wildfires are not limited to the southern part of the state or to Yellowstone NP as discussed thousands of miles ago. Essentially all the West, from the Rocky Mountains to the Pacific shore, is suffering from a chronic drought and increasing temperatures. In California alone, millions of acres of forests burned in 2020. By millions, the statistic is four million acres! Think of that in square miles, which is 6,250 square miles. Place each square mile in a single line, one square mile next to another, and you have, surprise, a space from one end to the other of 6,250 miles. How much time would be consumed when driving such a length? Of course, that would depend on speed, but let us say 60 miles per hour. Okay, by now it should be obvious we are talking a vast amount of time, a huge area of space, and a colossal area burned to ash, destroyed, gone. Sadly, 84 percent of wildfires are started by humans. We are our own worst enemy.

Chapter 29

The Last Bird

11–12 May 2005

Departing Ventura was the beginning of leaving Southern California. Linda and I were glad to be putting a large chunk of the throbbing stream of traffic behind and were looking forward to going north to find new species. A former and unnamed ornithologist once proved that the farther north you go, the fewer southern birds you see. Of course, there was more to his monograph than the simplistic idea of more northern birds occur more north than south, or was there? How much of the monograph was understood? By "understood," I mean the ideas within the text were not easily accessible. An editor friend told me he had trouble determining the relationships of adjacent sentences and paragraphs. Another person found some ideas in the monograph did not always agree with established knowledge base.[1] Aside from the difficulty of reading the monograph, the ridiculousness of the premise about fewer southern birds the further one goes north is both funny and not so much. Since it was printed in a serious publication it is not a joke and is embarrassing to scientists. The author was not later promoted to a higher pay grade even though his biological theory, a fact a fifth grader would know, is repeatedly proven.

Linda and I drove north to look for northern birds, traveling up part of the 1,540-mile-long coastal US Highway 101. We were on the southern section, the old Camino del Real. That reminded me of my hero, David Douglas, finder of Mountain Quail and other new kinds of wildlife, who

---

1. Review of the subject monograph appears in *Wilson Bulletin* 89.3 (1977) 499–501.

had sailed out of the Pacific Northwest in the early nineteenth century to visit coastal California. Douglas was steering our thoughts of Oregon and home. The birding circle was almost complete, but first, Linda and I had more birds to find. We stopped at a pull-out along the busy highway to check out something bouncing on the surf. Linda put the scope on it and announced "Clark's Grebe" with a smile. Though the sea was calmer than yesterday's whitecaps, other *Aechmophorus* grebes were too far to discern Western from Clark's species. We next stopped at Goleta Beach County Park. It was unpredictably full of sunbathers, a few hardy swimmers, strollers, and little parking room. It was Wednesday. Perhaps the onslaught was from people not wishing to pay the high entrance fees of California's state parks compared to the free county parks.

We returned to northbound US 101. The goal was Nojoqui Falls County Park, which would be our first opportunity for finding Chestnut-backed Chickadee, a northern species to support the north/south biological theory. Yes, I should have found the species in the 1960s. Getting to the park required us to detour through Solvang since the bridge via the shorter and more direct route had washed out a couple of weeks earlier. A stop in Solvang, the self-proclaimed Danish capital of America, revealed a town full of Old World nineteenth-century-architecture. The thatched roofs lacked storks sitting on them, but there were starlings and House Sparrows to make any European feel at home. I checked in at the information center about the location of the falls. A kindly octogenarian provided explicit directions to the park. She also politely but sternly warned me not to climb the rocks at the falls. "My grandson was climbing and became trapped. The police had to use ropes to get him down." I assured her I would stay on the designated trails. Linda and I had no desire to get involved with police and questionable ropes. Besides, our waning energy would not permit climbing rock walls even if we wanted to.

The road south of Solvang to Nojoqui Falls was narrow, nearly deserted, and quiet. It was the opposite of the wide, traffic-choked, and noisy pikes we had been traveling since the short respite in the San Gabriel Mountains just outside Los Angeles. Rolling grass covered the fields, and smatterings of tall deciduous trees decorated the route. Seconds after turning into the park, I heard a call note that could have come only from a pied woodpecker. Perhaps it was a Hairy, but it did not sound exactly like that species. Linda and I hunted the dark oaks and mottle-barked sycamores to no avail. Pacific-slope Flycatchers, Bullock's Orioles, and American Robins kept us alert to the possibility of the wanted Nuttall's Woodpecker. We strolled to the falls and back without any avian individual imitating a Nuttall's Woodpecker or any other species to collect for our trip list.

While returning to Solvang, we encountered three Yellow-billed Magpies, a new trip species. Not having seen these birds in a few years, I was struck by how much smaller they are from the black-billed species. Two and a half inches might not seem much but, to a person using dial calipers for decades to measure specimens, 60 plus millimeters is, well, sizable.

Accelerating back on US 101, I announced, "Here goes Beetle-baum" or was it "Beetle-balm." However spelled, Beetle-baum was a horse in a race announced by band leader Spike Jones. The announcement was set to Rossini's *William Tell Overture*. The running "joke" was that each time entering a freeway seemed like entering a race. I suppose an apology is in order here, but we thought the announcement was funny. Anyway, we dashed northward to reach our motel in San Luis Obispo. Linda and I were tired of the traffic and needed a rest before entering the last hurdle of the trip. We spent the next day supplying our food reserve and catching up on our notes.

13 May 2005

Up early. Several trees, including a large and handsome sycamore, formed a boundary on one side of our motel. While carrying a couple of bags to the car, I heard a pied woodpecker. It did not sound like a Hairy or Downy. A bird flew. It was large enough to be a Nuttall's Woodpecker. Tantalized, I walked down to the tree. The only sound was a Western Kingbird cavorting near the treetop. The woodpecker was gone.

It seems ironic that we were to miss Nuttall's Woodpecker. I had not seen one in 30 years, although the species had been the primary subject on a 1994 paper that I co-authored with a former college professor. We reported a specimen from Oregon. Nuttall's Woodpecker was also a species chronicled in my study on generic relationships of all species of pied woodpeckers. I know it well from its plumage to its skeleton but not well enough to identify those fleeing suspects that might have been Nuttall's. It would be nice to see a live one again.

We planned to drive to Redding today, a seven-hour drive, without stops. Our ride inland took us across semiarid hill country, a rolling landscape barren of trees and brush. Occasional bovines dotted the slopes, and less occasionally, a lone ranch house marked the scene. Farther inland, the road climbed the northern slopes of the Temblor Range. It is a small range of the Coastal Mountains bounded on the west by the Carrizo Plain, apparently a productive place to see Sage Sparrows, and the San Andreas Rift Zone, a place to lose your balance and worse. We missed Sage Sparrows, and we were happy that an earthquake had not been scheduled. Westward, we crossed the Kettleman Hills, which are paleontologically important for fossil-bearing sites, especially invertebrates, and for having concentrations of the fungi *Coccidioides immitis* that can cause Valley fever. It is a potentially fatal disease frequently affecting the lungs. Farmers, construction workers, and others digging in the dirt are more apt to get Valley fever, a disease found from Arizona to California. Unscathed and finally descending into the San Joaquin Valley, we arrived at the I-5 freeway and thus we came full circle with our route southward to Bakersfield in late March. We had held our breath as we eased down the slope of the hills, and held it again, several times, as we passed mammoth cattle feedlots, the bovines practically stacked on top of each other, a few playing cow of the mountain on tall mounds of their own feces. Dead cattle walking. Our next stop would not be for a hamburger.

    Travel on I-5 equated to speeding up and watching the gas mileage going down. The number of bugs hitting the windshield went up while my enthusiasm for driving diminished. The highway took us quickly beyond the capital and up the Sacramento River, the northern part of the great Central Valley. It was good that we found Yellow-billed Magpies near Nojoqui Falls County Park a couple of days ago. Interstate speed limits, widths, and nearly sterile highway right of ways are not attractive to roadside birds.

14 May 2005

Early morning revelry by our Redding motel neighbors woke us before we were ready. The nearby motel guests were loud enough for us to learn from our closed door that this was the prelude to a large family reunion. What we needed was a reunion with coffee and breakfast for a rendezvous with Sooty and perhaps Ruffed grouse in a canyon known as French Gulch. The drive to the mountains northwest of Redding soon revealed that finding grouse would be difficult because a wildfire burned 13,005 acres of the canyon last August. The fire, officially called the French Fire, was one of many such fires during last fall. I overlooked, during planning, that the fire destroyed much of French Gulch. We drove in silence, disappointed and shaken. Fire is unforgiving. Amid the acrid smell of burnt and lifeless pines and firs were spring wildflowers covering the treeless mountains and flat black ground with reflective yellows and deep violets. The blossoms were the beginning of plants reclaiming the scorched earth. It would be decades or more before the region returned to suitable Sooty Grouse habitat. There are such regions in southern Oregon, places that burned when I was a pre-birder, before 1957, and since. Recovery is a slow process.

Unfortunately, burned regions do not always return to forests. That is because water tables are often lowered when former forests no longer protect the slopes from evaporation and erosion, there is a lack of replanting, and invading brush not needing as much water as trees prevents the growth of trees. After 50 years, a plethora of such formerly burned forests are eroded brush-covered slopes. Such habitats are subject to furious fires and may function as fuses that ignite forests. Parts of the infamous Tillamook Burn, the collective name for four major fires in northwestern Oregon, have never fully recovered. The first two fires, in 1933 and 1939, were the result of logging operations and the third from a cigarette. Sources disagree whether the fourth fire was in 1951 or 1952, and do not reveal its cause. The legendary burn destroyed 360,882 acres, or 563 square miles, or almost half the size of Rhode Island. The time needed for the destroyed forest, some of it with its once 400-year-old trees, to return to its former glory is incomprehensible. Of course, that is assuming the region is no longer the victim of logging or repeated fires, which is an unlikely scenario.

Below the barren charcoal mountain slopes, birds crowded into surviving riparian trees along the creek and tributary ravines of the French Gulch. Linda and I searched for MacGillivray's Warbler but found only Yellow, Wilson's, and Orange-crowned warblers. The calls of Mountain Quail echoed down the slopes. We drove upward on an eroded dirt track, finding active mining claims along the creek and a large mining operation perched on a steep slope on our way to the summit. The mining claims attested to the fact that there is "gold in them thar hills." Searching for gold started in 1849, the year French Gulch, the town, sprung up to become one of California's major gold-producing regions. Gold was worth about $36 an ounce back when I was heading east for my first Kirtland's Warbler in 1962. The average rate in 2005 approached $450 an ounce. Between the early 1960s to 2005, the price of gold per ounce has varied from approximately $2,000 and downward, but its value is often enough for modern mining operations to put the bite on natural habitat. Gold mining is a destructive process, and it has left its mark across much of the country. From our brief look, the activity of modern machinery and the coming and going of miners might, at the very least, scare off a grouse or two.

Working gold mining operation.

Mining activity for this weekend seemed shut down, but a low hum exhaled from the otherwise quiet mountain. Continuing our drive farther up the mountain, we discovered busy weekend workers above the fire damage. At the same time, as we began seeing large trees in a dense forest, and just as our hopes for Sooty Grouse increased, the noise of tree cutting and road-building rolled down the narrowing road. We gave up and turned around.

Later and east of Redding, we sped by the northwest entrance of Lassen Volcanic National Park, where much of the roads remained choked with mounds of snow. Our goal was Hat Creek, a Forest Service area not far to the north. Black-backed Woodpeckers had been found there, but not recently and not by us today. The tall pines stood as if welcoming any woodpecker, but the forest was mostly silent. Time was pushing us onward to the 910-acre McArthur-Burney Falls Memorial Park. The falls is a 129-foot drop that plummets over volcanic basalt into a cool misty chasm. I had last been to the falls in 1961 to visit Lassen, which was a test run for my car and myself before embarking on the birding trip east in 1962. Now, more people clogged the entrance way than during my visit 43 years ago. When Linda and I entered the McArthur-Burney Park, I mentioned to the ranger that I had not been to the falls in decades; he said with a sly grin that the only thing that had changed was the location of the restrooms.

Burney Falls, California, without Black Swifts.

Linda and I hiked to the base of the falls while searching for nesting Black Swifts, traditionally a sure thing at Burney Falls. There was not a swift to see or hear. Our only other opportunity for the swifts was Mill Creek Falls in southern Oregon. I had hurriedly birded that falls on 2 June 1962, the initiation day of the trip. There were no Black Swifts that day, and the swifts were unknown at Mill Creek Falls until 2004 when the species was suspected to be nesting. Fortunately, we had seen migrant Black Swifts along the cliffs near La Jolla.

As Linda and I motored toward McCloud, we passed the massive southern slopes of Mount Shasta, a 14,162-foot white mountain of snow and glaciers rivaling Mount Rainier in Washington in size. It also challenged Rainier by its imposing beauty. Mount Shasta should have been a national park. Fond memories of skiing Mount Shasta's lower slopes during high school days interrupted thoughts about warblers. Also recalled was the year 1964 when I climbed to the summit of Mount Shasta. No binoculars weighed down my oxygen-hungry lungs. I was too busy breathing and watching my step on the way up and practicing extra care when my party had zero visibility for what seemed like an interminable time while descending. Coming back to reality, a sign a few miles up Pilgrim Creek Road, a route on the east slope of Mount Shasta, read "Road Closed." The road was still covered with snow, which meant another chance to find Black-backed Woodpeckers was gone.

McCloud, a hamlet due south of Mount Shasta, was our next destination. We had not been there for decades. In 1961, when I passed through, McCloud was a privatized company town geared to logging and lumber. Now, no longer privatized, the town of 1,343 people, about a thousand less than in the 1960s, caters to tourism. Our tourist interests were south of town, along mountain meadows and streamside willows to look for none other than Willow Flycatchers, MacGillivray's Warblers, and a few others. We heard MacGillivray's singing. Our luck continued as we ticked off Green-tailed Towhee and Hammond's Flycatcher, a species missed on the earlier part of the trip. We found Chestnut-backed Chickadees, another new bird missed in the sixties, near the canopy just off a Forest Service road. We flushed a Fox Sparrow just before piling back in the Birdmobile.

It was late. We were tired and running out of money. We could spend a night in Shasta City and tomorrow morning drive up the old ski bowl where I once skied, and the start of the way to the summit of Mount Shasta. Possibly we would now find Sooty Grouse, Williamson's Sapsucker, and Gray-crowned Rosy-Finch or, maybe we would not. We decided that we would pass and not make the journey. It was time to go home.

Linda drove the last 100 or so miles home. I caught up on my notes, enjoyed the scenery, the green slopes. Northern California awarded fleeting observations of birds long enough to identify an immature Bald Eagle north of Yreka, an unmistakable Black-billed Magpie near the small town of Hornbrook, and a clear view of a Peregrine Falcon on the north slope of the Siskiyou Mountains in Oregon. These were familiar but new trip birds at familiar places. Home was near. Our final seconds of driving this year came full circle. We arrived home in Jacksonville, the historical city visited by Charles Bendire, past resident and early explorer of Fort Klamath and Malheur. Perhaps the slower mode of travel by Bendire would have increased our chances of seeing more birds, but we will never know.

15 May 2005

Today we slept and slept and slept. We rested between slumber and the enjoyment of our familiarly comfortable bed. As near exhaustion slipped away, I began mentally plotting how to find a few of the species we had missed. According to our self-imposed rules for the trip, we could include species we might find before 2 June, which would complete a year of birding, albeit interrupted time. There was a promising chance to find a couple of northern breeding birds, including and perhaps a lingering Golden-crowned Sparrow. Then, the welcome sound of rain pattering on the roof dampened my thoughts. I fell back to sleep.

16 May 2005

In 1962, I was so anxious to travel east that I ignored the local birds. Consequently, I had missed several western Oregon species, and today was an opportunity to find them. Armed with a list of eight species that I thought would be easy to find, I set out to skim the better local birding sites. Before I left the house, before I ate breakfast, before I did anything, I heard the unmistakable pecking of a sapsucker from the bathroom window. I hurried downstairs as fast as the early morning would allow, and from the back door, saw a Red-breasted Sapsucker foraging on a creek-side cottonwood. That was easy. Of course, why was the species missed in the early 1960s?

I drove to one of the local state-owned wetlands, heard a lingering Golden-crowned Sparrow that gave a clean sweep of all the *Zonotrichia* sparrows. White-tailed Kites and Ring-necked Pheasants were expected, but only the kites were forthcoming. White-tailed Kites were nesting at my high school friend's ranch where I had once worked for his late father to save money for the 1960s trip. White-tailed Kites were rare in southern Oregon then. I was happy that they were more common today. A rush to the local sewage treatment rendered a handful of Wilson's Phalaropes, a new species. A couple dozen foraging Red-necked Phalaropes there were less fleeting than those on the trip to Santa Cruz Island. Later, I birded in the Lost Creek Reservoir region where a Brown Creeper quietly minced up a Douglas fir. It was the first one seen this year, but not a new species for the trip list. By the end of the day, I had ticked off a dozen new species for the trip list.

17 May 2005

An early start was not necessary today for a chance to add a new species within about an hour of driving. Sleeping late into the morning was okay since an appointment with Steve Godwin, a biologist working out of the Medford, Oregon, BLM office, was not until 1 p.m. He told us back in February he could deliver a Great Gray Owl, and yesterday he suggested meeting in the early afternoon. Great Gray Owl! The species was almost common around Fort Klamath, Oregon, in 1962, but not the day I visited there or any earlier times when I was a fledgling birder. Great Gray Owls eluded me everywhere I looked. Even though I had been within the owl's range during the 1960s, I did not find one. The owl was not a species on my life list. Great Gray Owls were avoiding me.

Back in the days at the Division of Birds, I had read R. W. Nero and R. Taylor's *The Great Gray Owl, Phantom of the Northern Forest*, a 1980 book published by Smithsonian Institution Press. Phantom was a good choice to describe the elusive owl, a species I wondered if I would ever witness. How could the largest of North American owls, with its four-foot wing-span, be so difficult to locate? Part of the answer is being in the right place and the right time, but that is important for finding any species, just as getting in, or avoiding, an auto accident and finding a clean service station restroom. Great Gray Owls are also hard to find. The phantom owls breed in dense forests where they often sit motionless for lengthy periods, and their vocalizations are generally infrequent and usually are not loud.

When I once announced to Linda that we had yet to see a Golden Eagle, she replied that "probably more than one had seen us." How true, and more than likely a gray oval face and yellow eyes had pointed downward as I searched over the years for the phantom Great Gray Owl. Today would be different. Unfortunately, my sage and best friend was busy reorganizing after our travel, so I went alone.

Slightly after noon, I topped the Green Springs Summit in the Cascade Mountains of Oregon. The road, another Route 66, is a state highway and was the principal link across the Cascades in southern Oregon during my growing-up years. Just as then, the highway is a narrow two-lane route carved on the slopes, with abrupt and dizzying heights frequently without the psychologically appealing guardrails. Part of Highway 66 was the same or parallel route as the Applegate Trail of 1846 and later the Southern

Oregon Trail, an alternative to the then-dangerous Oregon Trail along the Columbia River.

The summit is just north of the new 114,000-acre Cascade-Siskiyou National Monument founded in 2000. Steve Godwin was waiting in his vehicle at the 4,618-foot Green Springs summit. We were at the northern boundary of the monument. Steve told me a volunteer working on the Pacific Crest Trail (PCT) discovered a nesting pair of Great Gray Owls. The discovery was last week, and the birds should still be there. It was just up a lightly graveled road from the summit, a left turn on a dirt road, and then a short jaunt on the PCT. We jumped in our respective vehicles and sloshed up the wet dirt road to a gate where we parked, and we then hiked for about 15 minutes. Getting there took us along a solid dirt road full of potholes drowning from a prolonged period of spring rain and in view of wet roadsides dripping with a multitude of colors of wildflowers. Snow Queens, the flower Linda and I chose for our February wedding too few years ago, should not be blooming among the trilliums and fawn lilies, but they were. The cool and wet May and the warm and dry February and March had turned the season upside down. Like the road, the PCT was muddy, so wet in places small streams formed. Each side of the PCT was graced with deep purple larkspurs, bright yellow buttercups, and more, all with a bright green of new spring grasses. Hiking any part of the 2,650-mile PCT was always rewarding if it was only to see what was around the next bend. Linda and I had last crossed the trail near the Siskiyou Summit four days earlier. We were so tired we did not notice. Earlier, we crossed the PCT at McArthur-Burney Falls State Park, California, where we searched for Black Swifts. We were near the trail in the San Gabriel Mountains and crossed it several miles east of San Diego, or not all that far from the Mexican border where the trail begins its way to Canada. The PCT was designated a National Trails System by Congress in 1968 but was not dedicated formally until 1993. What took so long? Perhaps they were waiting for someone to discover Great Gray Owls nesting along the trail. Today, the trail would take me to one of the greatest and most elusive of North American owls. I hoped.

Steve led the way on the single-file trail, and we soon arrived at the owl nesting site where two juveniles, one about half the size of its sibling, were attended by two intent adults. The nest tree, a tree broken about 25 feet up, was empty. A young Great Gray Owl sat six feet away, and perched on top of a similar though shorter broken snag sat a smaller Great Gray Owl. It sat erect and alert. We left the trail, climbed the slope, and circled above the juvenile, then looked down toward the nest tree. It was just a broken top with a slight hollow and hardly big enough for a 27-inch owl. The larger juvenile crouched into the hollow of its broken snag was hiding in plain sight. A few minutes later, Steve asked, "Did you hear that?" I admitted just barely and did not know what I was hearing. I heard the sound again. It was a soft and hardly audible *whoooo*, a sound that was the owl world equivalent to Seinfeld's quiet-talker. The female owl uttered the call while it sat on a dead limb located about a foot from the trunk of a Douglas fir. The gorgeous gray bird stared with big yellow eyes, then her round head seemed to float on her torso as it turned from side to side. Was the bird listening for prey or locating her mate? Mostly, she watched us watching her. The stern softness of her intently curious gaze penetrated the surrounding air and merged with the spirit of the forest. The phantom, the elusive Great Gray Owl, was real. Before leaving the grand sentinel, Steve attempted to mimic the soft call of the now silent female. His rendition was louder and rougher than the docile-sounding owl. Nonetheless, the female immediately responded with a similar but quieter *whoooo*.

A juvenile Great Gray Owl almost disappears into the forest.

During the drive down from the summit, I spotted an adult Golden Eagle. It probably spotted me first, just as had so many species, most, I hoped I saw, but some, I am certain were not detected. The eagle today received only my quick glance since I was driving and did not want to go careening over the scary edge of the narrow highway.

THE LAST BIRD

18 May 2005

Linda and I left Jacksonville and were on the PCT in mid-afternoon, aware that the dark clouds above could bring down dangerous lightning or a deluge of rain at any moment. Rain last night made the trail softer and more slippery than yesterday. The spring rains had choked the streams and filled the southern Oregon reservoirs, which was a far cry from late March fraught with predictions of a drought. We worried that the heavy and chilly rain would be hard on the juvenile owls.

Near the nesting site, we heard a screeching sound, a sound identical to a calling juvenile heard yesterday. The same juvenile in the same tree eyed us alertly as we approached. Unlike yesterday, it was standing more erect and watchful. Linda photographed the juvenile and we watched and listened for an adult. Nothing. We took turns attempting to replicate the female call; Linda's higher voice came closer to my recollection of the female yesterday. However, nothing appeared. We decided to continue north on the trail, partly to give the owls space and time and partly to see what was around the next bend. The clouds darkened. We returned to the nesting site and discovered another overlooked juvenile, which was also at the top of a broken snag. It was twice the size of the first sibling, and even more alert, almost angry looking, as it aimed its round face at us. We walked on up the trail past the first and diminutive juvenile, made more pitiful attempts to lure the birds, and noticed the thickening clouds scudding above the treetops. That is when an adult flew down the slope and landed in a fir about 75 feet from us. At first, it appeared to be examining us, and then it seemed to ignore us. I squeaked a few times so that it would look directly into Linda's ready camera, then, not wishing to disturb the phantom, we trekked back to the waiting Birdmobile. We were grateful that the rain did not fall until after we were snug inside. During the last weeks, we had kept ahead of or behind bad weather; found adventure, mosquitoes, and chiggers; completed a decades-old birding trip; and shared trip species number 418. At last, a Great Gray Owl.

19 May to 1 June 2005

With 14 days remaining to complete a year's worth of birding, the choice of what species might be added to our trip list and where might we find those missing species was not easy to determine. It would be possible to travel a considerable distance during the last days of the trip, but we had to be practical. We had already traveled thousands of miles and spent thousands of dollars. Therefore, searching within Oregon seemed a promising idea. You know, bird the localities you know best. So, what species could we add to our trip list? Travel to the coast or interior sounded remotely promising, but not by much. We tried. Day trips from home allowed avoiding the cost of a motel, but the short distances did not allow detecting a new trip species. Of course, a few of those pesky species were within reach, but we just could not find them. Where is a Williamson's Sapsucker when you need one? We needed one. Even very locally, that is, inside our home county line, might reward us a Sooty Grouse, but we found nothing. How could we complain? Just across the county line loomed Crater Lake NP and the possibility of Gray-crowned Rosy-Finch, and on the way to the park, we might chance upon one of the three-toed woodpeckers. However, we were striking out. We ultimately decided to be satisfied with what we had and keep the other species for dreams of another day.

∼

The trip circumnavigating the contiguous US began with a few of the usual suspects and ended with a species I thought I would never see. Thousands of miles and decades had delivered the owl of owls, the Great Gray Owl. As some consider the fickleness of fate, the target of my long search was hardly more than an hour from home. Great Gray Owls are good birds to end any birding trip, but overall, how did the journey fare in its makeup? Species such as Red-necked Stint and Zenaida Dove were probably the two best species of the trip.

Circumstances that produced the 1960s list and the 2005 list are different. Whatever one might call the interrupted trip, the fragmented year, it cannot be a big year in the traditional sense. One winter was included in that 1960s journey. That is a handicap in picking up accidentals potentially available to parts of two winters that occur during a traditional calendar big year. Maybe I am wrong about that. However, from years of birding my local southwestern Oregon patch, I find the best season for rarities, other than migrations time, is during and around winter.

Now, for those paying attention, some may wonder, was I shooting for a big list or not? My answer must be a yes and a no. Sure, I kept track of the number of species I witnessed. By my count, I detected 384 birds from June 1962 through March 1963 and 418 species from April and May in 2005. Of course, the two lists have many of the same species, but expectedly, many species are also unique to the other list. The total number of species in the two lists is 553 birds. A couple of pelagics, one on the Atlantic and one on the Pacific, would have added several species, including shearwaters, storm-petrels, and alcids. A handful of species would have been added to the list by a trip to the Dry Tortugas.

How did the combined lists from the early 1960s and the 2005 jaunt compare with Peterson and Fisher and others? There is no comparison since Peterson and Fisher's total included birds found in Alaska. That is also true for Stuart Keith's 594 species, Harold Axtell, and his wife Rachael's slightly over 600 species in 1970, and Ted Parker's 626 species the next year. Others, including Kenn Kaufman and Pete Dunne, have birded the US, including Alaska, and lived to write about it. They saw more species than I did.

But, yes, I was counting in the sixties. Yes, Linda and I were counting in 2005. Some travelers keep track of state license plates, the number of national parks visited, the number of birds seen. It seems so natural. But, no, there was no competition with anyone, excluding ourselves, for a high total of species. Having shallow pockets did not help add species. Birders desiring a big list for their big year need deep pockets. Money allows travel where the birds are or where they ought to occur and also to tick the waifs, the accidentals, the individual species that took a wrong turn and ended up out of their normal range. Money and effort are also required since there are fewer individual birds to see compared to only a few decades ago. Thus, it is sometimes harder to detect those fewer remaining birds. On the other hand, increases in the number of birders and improved communication for finding birds possibly gives the illusion that birds are easy to find and therefore their numbers are not in plight. Five Brown-toasted Scrub-Sparrows might be difficult to locate by a single birder, but easier by five birders. In short order and after the target birds are exposed to biochemicals and habitat loss, we are left with two living Brown-toasted Scrub-Sparrows. As the species decrease in number, the number of birders increases. Now 500 birders are looking for a single bird. The bird is found, the sighting is reported on the internet, and the Brown-toasted Scrub-Sparrow becomes easy to find. Some Oregon species, including Barn Swallows and Bullock's Orioles, are so easy to locate that most people do not believe the species have decreased. Unfortunately, not everyone realizes the plight of birds and the environment, though they should. If they had, we would be doing more to save the birds and ourselves. All those freeways, housing projects, airports, shopping centers, cattle lots, soy, corn, and other human products and by-products have an impact on birds.

The average citizen does not often notice loss of habitat until it is gone. Habitat loss equates to the loss of insects, loss of water, and loss of wildlife. Loss of birds is especially noticeable for those looking. Someone recently asked me if there are fewer individual birds today. After gulping to the realization that the passing of many moons was revealing my age, I said yes. Locally, in southwestern Oregon and elsewhere, migrating shorebirds lost a place to rest and refuel, several montane birds are hard to find, and the remaining forests are worrisomely becoming silent. It is not just my senior ears. The last colony of Burrowing Owls disappeared under a new school and residential houses while the fields full of Western Meadowlarks and Ring-necked Pheasants became commercial property for parking lots, residential plots, and fast-food establishments. The Western Kingbirds that nested nearby on a power pole transformer cannot live with the increased car traffic flowing below. These anecdotal observations are not nearly as disastrous as the facts. Breeding Bird Surveys in Oregon revealed Neotropical migrants decreased by 36 percent from 1968 to 2002. Some species have fared much worse. In 30 years, Rufous Hummingbird populations dropped by 50 percent. Breeding populations of Olive-sided Flycatchers in Oregon have declined about 5 percent per year in 30 years. Western Meadowlarks, the state bird of Oregon and five other states, have been losing the habitat battle. Most other grassland species in North America are rapidly decreasing. Shorebird populations are decimated on at least two fronts: lack of wetlands during migration and climate change causing rapid warming of the Arctic nesting grounds. There are so many other similar examples.

As one rapidly approaching the title of octogenarian and being a student of birds most of those years, I feel I have earned the right to impose a few anecdotal sentences, statements really that hopefully will make a point. What I heard as a young man from elderly naturalists and what I hold as truth today is that there are fewer birds today than there were decades ago. The disappearance of species occurred so slowly that people did not notice. Depletion of bird populations has been happening for centuries, but Peterson and Fisher made their epic trip at a time when the rapidity and the level of habitat destruction accelerated with a vengeance. Populations of birds continue declining as habitat loss and fragmentation persists, with too many instances of disappearing birds to fit in most books. For example, Ruddy Turnstones have plummeted in numbers by 80 percent since 1974. That is four-fifths of a species! There are lots more dreadful examples. It is a pattern. Even the Dark-eyed Junco, the endearing snowbird to even nonbirders, is declining.

As watchful individuals have pointed out, there have been a plethora of governmental policies and laws to protect birds. Many policies and laws have been set in stone since Peterson and Fisher's *Wild America*. Sure, there may be more land protected from commerce, but the burgeoning human population and lack of financial support for enforcement is a necessary and often missing ingredient of policy and law. Funding is not the only missing link between policy and implementation. An example is the debilitation of the Rare and Endangered Species Act established in 1972. The act has become, in too many instances, a political football and subjected to the human economy rather than the organisms to be protected. One does not need to look hard to learn about the controversies of the Rare and Endangered Species Act and players who would delight in the act's demise.[2]

Laws and policies require public and political support, but it appears that the general populace, especially those with money, have more authority to regulate our environment and ultimately the birds we might be lucky to protect. Another way of stating the preceding is money talks. If power wants a swamp, marshland, or forests to go away, to become a parking lot, the habitat will go away. Money usually wins. Even in my birding patch, agencies must direct steps toward water conservation in the Klamath Basin in the battle for wildlife versus ranching and farming. Closer to home, wetlands have been paved over or victims from the scourge of off-road vehicles. We cannot be lulled into the false notion that most North American birds are doing well. They are not.

Habitat loss is never-ending. The reasons are numerous though everything boils down to the enormous number of people abusing the environment and ultimately endangering the planet. According to the census data, 152 million people occupied the US in 1950. By 1960 the number was 181 million. In 1970 the human population jumped to 205 million, a few people below an estimated 211.9 million when Kenn Kaufman was birding the country in 1973. Give or take way too many people, the US population rose to 282 million in 2000 and jumped to an estimated 295 million in 2005. Compared to the human population during Peterson and Fisher's time, I experienced 30 million more people competing for space in the early 1960s. That is slightly more than the current population of Texas. By 2005, the population increased by 114 million. That is about the same as the combined current populations of California, Texas, Florida, and New York. Imagine! It is frightening, especially if everyone continues to use and or abuse what we have left. The last census pegged us at 331 million and predicts 359.4 million people in the US by 2030. Even without COVID-19 and global climate change, I wonder how the wild of America will survive. How many birds will be left?

That an abundance of species of birds are now in peril reinforces the personal importance of birding, whether it is a long odyssey or not. Was my

---

2. Dan Spinelli. "This Is Why Lawmakers Want to Gut the Endangered Species Act." *Mother Jones*, Jul 25, 2018.

Maya L. Kapoor. "For Endangered Species, Politics Replaces Science." *High Country News*, Jan 4, 2018.

early 1960s journey worth it? Absolutely. Besides the incalculable pleasure of birding, I began to learn that birds were more than a checkmark for a list. Was completing the trip, even after 42 years, worth it? Yes, even more than in the 1960s, since I had learned to appreciate birds and the environment with a better base than my wet-behind-the-ears youth.

From a practical standpoint, the last eight weeks in 2005 were far more costly than the first ten months in the early 1960s. Those last two months were as carefully budgeted as the first ten, though I wonder, what is the cost to see a new species? Does it cost more to see more species of birds in 2005 than in the early 1960s? Of course, it does, but perhaps a better question might be, is it easier or more difficult to see the same species in the 1960s compared to 2005? What would be the answer comparing the early 1960s with today (2023)? Aside from birder economics 101 issues such as life bird inflation, my diet and sleeping quarters in 2005 were much improved. That was partly because advancing age demanded more creature comfort than the younger version of myself. Also, what most people, regardless of age, regard as tolerable 50 years ago is not considered acceptable today. The average creature comfort index (CCI) today is higher than that of David Douglas, Charles Bendire, and John James Audubon and has gradually climbed to bird meeting and guided tours often putting up participants in five-star accommodations. Do not expect finding someone wearing jeans and a T-shirt. That just will not do. We now believe we need to strut different plumage that sports a plethora of pockets and zippers. Prism style binoculars are out, cameras and tripods taking up the space of a person are in, and the list goes on and on.

Another issue about birding is related to carbon footprints. Traveling in 1962 and 1963 required burning fossil fuels. As for me, I was out of doors a good part of the time, which meant fuel for air conditioning or heat was not consumed. In 2005, my vehicle was also gas powered and got less miles per gallon than my old VW. Motels and cooling air conditioning enlarged the carbon footprint. Okay, now add other modes of travel, and think of the jet fuel of a big year birder. Travel is a good teacher, but at what cost? How does a carbon footprint compare with the experience of seeing a particular bird? Is birding, especially beyond one's backyard, ecologically selfish? Perhaps, but appreciation of birds can and often leads to conservation of birds. Does that offset our carbon footprint?

Thanks to the people during the 1960s, my youthful Danny McSkunk brain gradually aimed me toward a career in birds. By 2005, I had morphed into a slightly different animal. So had other birders, who are no longer ridiculed and now accepted for their binocular pointing (up to a point, but that is another story). There may be around 45 million birders, with at least

16 million leaving home to chase birds. Besides the sheer fun of it, I have learned a little about avian taxonomy, but do not get me started.

So, the interrupted trip was completed. Linda and I, though worn, weathered, unfashionably dressed in jeans, had learned a thing or two. We rested and dreamed of being around a new corner and seeing new birds. Mostly, we were happy to complete the long interrupted trip that was a heck of a lot of fun.

www.ingramcontent.com/pod-product-compliance
Lightning Source LLC
Chambersburg PA
CBHW071221230426
43668CB00011B/1261